Global Democracy and Sustainable Jurisprudence

Global Democracy and Sustainable Jurisprudence: Deliberative Environmental Law

Walter F. Baber and Robert V. Bartlett

The MIT Press
Cambridge, Massachusetts
London, England

For information about special quantity discounts, please email special_sales @mitpress.mit.edu.

This book was set in Sabon by Binghamton Valley Composition. Printed and bound in the United States of America.

Library of Congress Cataloging-in-Publication Data

Baber, Walter F., 1953–
Global democracy and sustainable jurisprudence : deliberative environmental law / Walter F. Baber and Robert V. Bartlett.
    p. cm.
Includes bibliographical references and index.
ISBN 978-0-262-01302-4 (hardcover : alk. paper)—ISBN 978-0-262-51291-6 (pbk. : alk. paper) 1. Environmental law, International. 2. Environmental policy. I. Bartlett, Robert V. II. Title.
K3585.B33 2009
344.04'6—dc22   2008044233

10 9 8 7 6 5 4 3 2 1

To
Evalena Baber
and
Catherine Bartlett

Contents

A Preface to Global Democratic Anarchism

In *Democracy in America*, Alexis de Tocqueville frequently mentions a singular advantage that the democrats of the New World enjoyed over those of the Old. Americans had no monarchic past to slough off on their way to democracy. This advantage manifested itself in the structural looseness of American institutions and in the absence of any large entrenched elite that might resist the idea of popular sovereignty. Thus it was possible for Americans to "have arrived at democracy without suffering through democratic revolutions, and to be born equal instead of becoming equal" (S. Wolin 2001, 119–127). The advantage enjoyed by Americans was more than tactical. Having avoided the social traumas that Old World wars of revolution involved, Americans never found it necessary to overcome the implacable hatreds among different classes that slowed the development of democracy in Europe. To put it succinctly, America's democratic revolution didn't cost very many Americans very much.

As we witness the emergence of what Jürgen Habermas characterizes as a postnational constellation, one might be forgiven for wondering if the advantage has shifted away from Americans (Habermas 2001b). Having become, by so many measures, the world's privileged class, will Americans yield gracefully to a movement toward democratization at the global level? Might it not be that citizens of the Old World, who suffered so grievously at the hands of nationalists during the last century, will prove far more open to new forms of transnationalism that empower individuals and groups at the expense of sovereign states? In an era when the democratic impulse begins to erode both national boundaries and structures of arbitrary authority within human institutions, are the citizens of the world's last "superpower" destined to be the rearguard of the old world order? We have written this book for a global audience, but early in the twenty-first century its arguments and proposals may fall on less receptive ears in the United States than elsewhere.

In 2005, we published a book entitled *Deliberative Environmental Politics*. Our limited objective in that volume was twofold. First, we wanted to describe what we took to be areas of conceptual consistency between deliberative democracy and the imperatives of environmental protection. Second, we wished to identify institutional innovations and political trends that at least suggested that the areas of conceptual consistency we had described were not sterile ground.

In this volume our objective is similarly limited. It is to indicate that theories of political deliberation offer useful insights into the "democratic deficit" in international law. Our discussion of international institutions and procedures is not intended to be comprehensive. It is intended only to suggest that there are approaches to the problem of global environmental protection that require nothing more than a new conceptual orientation and a renewed sense of the possibilities of cosmopolitanism. Here, as in our earlier work, we focus on the environment because it provides the most nearly universal human interest that can be described with any level of precision.

We also advance a proposal for institutional innovation not because we conceive of it as the only (or even, necessarily, the best) approach to the problem of developing transnational environmental consensus, but rather because it is necessary to start somewhere. We have made no claims, and have none to make, about the content of the decisions people would reach on environmental matters—we do not claim that juristic democracy would resolve all or part of the environmental problematique or even that any choices made will necessarily be better choices environmentally. As in every realm of human endeavor, bad choices *can* be made by the most democratic of processes, although there are good reasons—and evidence—to suggest this will happen less often and the bad choices will be less bad than when made by nondemocratic processes. Moreover, we assume that the capacity of any polity to recover from what turn out to be environmentally substantive mistakes will be enhanced if decisions are made in processes that create social capital rather than spend it. We only assert that environmental norms with genuinely democratic lineage, if they could be developed, would be well worth having.

Our argument in the book proceeds as follows. After exploring the necessary characteristics of a meaningful global jurisprudence, a jurisprudence that would underpin truly effective international environmental law, we back up and reconsider the possible theoretical foundations for that jurisprudence in realism, pragmatism, and deliberative democracy. Building on this analysis, we suggest a conceptual framework for international politics and law that offers the prospect of workable, democratic, and environment-friendly rule-governed behavior within a system of global politics that is likely to remain (and perhaps ought to remain) anarchic in important respects. Specifically, we suggest the development of a global environmental jurisprudence based on democratically generated norms. We propose a concrete process for identifying and generating global environmental norms for translation into international law—law that, unlike all current international law, can be universally recognized as both fact and norm because of its inherent democratic legitimacy.

Acknowledgments

We thank the three anonymous reviewers for the MIT Press whose many suggestions and recommendations led to numerous improvements in the manuscript. Particular thanks to MIT Press Senior Acquisitions Editor Clay Morgan.

Baber thanks the College of Health and Human Services at California State University, Long Beach, for a sabbatical leave in fall 2008. He particularly thanks Dean Ron Vogel for ongoing professional and personal support. He acknowledges the encouragement and assistance provided by his colleagues in the Graduate Center for Public Policy and the Environmental Science and Policy Program.

Bartlett thanks the University of Vermont College of Arts and Sciences and Dean Eleanor Miller for a research leave that greatly speeded completion of this book. He thanks the Fulbright Distinguished Chairs Program for making possible a very productive stay at the Politecnico di Torino in Turin, Italy. He also thanks colleagues at Waikato University, Purdue University, and the University of Vermont who read early drafts of a couple of chapters and offered suggestions for clarification.

Once again, our deepest gratitude is owed to Carolyn and Sally—pragmatists, realists, and deliberators extraordinaire—who support us in exploring our ideas and encourage us to go where those ideas lead, and whose continuing company makes the journey sustainable.

1

Toward an International Environmental Jurisprudence: Problems and Prospects

It has become commonplace in the environmental community to hear people wonder whether now, at the dawn of the twenty-first century, humankind will finally develop the intelligence necessary to ensure our survival as a species (Caldwell 1998, 5). As compelling a question as this often seems, it misses the most essential point in a variety of ways. First, the twenty-first century, like the centuries that preceded it, is an entirely human construct of no ecological significance. Now is no more opportune a moment than any other for the development of a new relationship between humans and their environment. Second, the survival of humankind as a species is no more important ecologically than the turning of a calendar page. Third, it is far from clear that the essential challenge to human survival is a shortage of intelligence. From the perspective of evolutionary biology, it may be that humankind is already too smart for its own good. Indeed, the noted biologist Ernst Mayr has argued that, judging by the empirical record regarding species success, it is clearly better to be stupid than to be smart (Chomsky 2005, 1). Our ability to use what we know should be more central to our concerns.

So how might the environmentalist's question be appropriately rephrased? Assuming that our focus will continue to be human survival, regardless of nature's indifference to that issue, we might pose the following question. What changes in our collective behavior are required if the biological preconditions of our continued existence are to be satisfied and how are those changes to be brought about? This formulation of the problem has several distinct advantages.

First, an emphasis on behavior allows us to focus our attention on human agency. Our actions, for better or worse, are willed events. They are subject to our control to an extent that other environmental variables often are not. Placing our own actions at the center of our environmentalism puts humankind's fate in our own hands (to the greatest degree that is possible). In addition, a focus on willed action has the salutary effect of preempting excuses for environmentally unsustainable behavior as the unavoidable consequence of impersonal systems such as nations and markets (Hiskes 1998). In other words, it allows us to hold one another responsible for environmental protection.

Second, attending to the biological preconditions of human survival, as broad a topic as that is, will lend our environmentalism a measure of focus and a sense of urgency that other approaches often lack. Perfectly valid concerns for issues like animal rights and ecological amenities such as pristine wilderness have shown only a limited capacity to seize the imagination of the general populace, even in the wealthiest and most literate countries where appeals on their behalf might have been expected to resonate. If protection of the environment in the developing world is any part of our agenda, our emphasis must move even more strongly to those matters that impinge directly on the health and welfare of humankind as a whole (Porter, Brown, and Chasek 2000, esp. chap. 5).

Finally, concentrating on the methods by which the environmentally necessary changes in human behavior can be brought about will help to prevent what is necessarily a conceptual enterprise from becoming entirely detached from reality. Our concern for a theoretically sound understanding of the ethical issues we confront and the ecological challenges that we face cannot so preoccupy us that we neglect the question of the institutions and resources that are necessary to implement any decisions we are able to formulate. Effective knowledge of what our survival requires and the will to use that knowledge must still be supported by political power in some form (O. Young 1994).

Our task, then, is immodest in the extreme. It is to outline an approach to collective will formation, the development of applied policy expertise, and the creation of institutions and the marshalling of political resources that can be appropriate to the protection of the environment on a global scale. This approach must constitute an international environmental jurisprudence, not only an explanation of what the law of the global environment should be, but also a theoretical construct to aid in its interpretation and implementation.

Will Formation—Policy Prerequisites

It is necessary to address a threshold question, the answer to which will guide our subsequent analysis. Is it even possible to construct an environmental jurisprudence at the global level? No one doubts that treaties can be negotiated between nations to advance the cause of environmental protection. But is it really possible that an international environmental consensus, amounting to a collective determination to follow a shared course for reasons held in common, can emerge from our disjointed and competitive system of global governance?

One view of international law, perhaps the dominant view, is that it can never really be law in the proper sense. The "law obtaining between nations is not positive law" because "every positive law . . . is set by a sovereign person, or sovereign body of persons" (Austin [1832] 2000, 201, 193). Any effort to conceptualize an international polity must, therefore, recognize that "the universal society formed by mankind, is the aggregate good of the particular societies into which mankind is divided; just as the happiness of any of those societies is the aggregate happiness of its single or individual members" (294). This perspective on international law provides a foundation for the "realist" analysis of international affairs generally, which emphasizes that the only significant actors on the world stage are nations, which pursue their own interests always and in all things (Morganthau 1978).

The fundamental insights captured by the realist viewpoint are appealing because they explain a great deal of what we think we know about international politics generally and international environmental affairs in particular. It makes sense of the fact that, whereas it is often considered a moral duty to be informed about world events, one is not normally expected to do much about them (Belshaw 2001). Moreover, the inherent limits of democratic discourse seem to argue against its use at the international level. A shared sense of community obligation, absent beyond the boundaries of the state, is often thought to be necessary to overcome the presumption that mere political argument by one actor cannot change the preferences of another actor (Austin-Smith 1992). The resulting conclusion, that all speech acts in international politics are merely strategic, leads one to doubt that any shared will at the global level is possible. It may also explain why "democracy has achieved real gains within states, but very meager ones in the wider sphere, both in terms of relations between states and on global issues" (Archibugi 2003, 5).

With respect to global environmental affairs in particular, there are additional reasons to doubt the possibility of international consensus. First, early nation-states lived within boundaries that usually conformed to some set of natural criteria. This allowed for a genuine, if sometimes fluid and indistinct, sense of a home region that provided the basis for an ecological knowledge and community solidarity that was facilitative of collective action (Snyder 1998). The expanded boundaries of modern nation-states, and emerging regional communities like the European Union, undermine the existence of that shared sense of place. In its absence, the citizens of existing nations find it hard to build a domestic consensus on the environment, let alone participate in an international environmental concord. This difficulty is reflected in the problems confronted by the European Union in implementing its developing environmental policies (Demmke 2004). The trend toward globalization has, in many ways, made matters worse. National governments have been forced into "a zero-sum game where necessary economic objectives can be reached only at the expense of social and political objectives" (Habermas 2001b, 51). Among the most troublesome manifestations of this global game, also evident within nation-states lacking strong central authority, are the tendency to discount excessively future environmental damage (Cumberland 1979) and the temptation to export environmental problems resulting from patterns of economic trade (Gormley 1987).

Taking all of these matters into account, why would anyone be optimistic about the prospects for a global consensus on environmental protection? One reason might be that optimism at the global level is the only realistic alternative to a universal and thoroughly depressing pessimism. Yet beyond this general preference for hope over despair, environmental problems provide an obvious example of issues that rightly belong to the global community because the level of "interconnectedness and interdependence" involved makes those problems impossible for national or regional authorities to resolve alone (Held 1995, 235). As far back as John Stuart Mill there has existed a concept of joint ownership of natural resources from which specific rights can legitimately be inferred (Nathan 2002). There is a growing realization that states are interdependent, sharing common interests that lead them to cooperate, and that cooperation is self-reinforcing because cooperative institutions come to be valued in themselves over time (Keohane and Nye 1977; Miles et al. 2002).

So, in an age of globalization, political, moral, and cultural boundaries are all unstable. Both genetic and human diversity are at risk (Curtin 1999).

Humankind is irreducibly heterogeneous and is destined to remain so. But collective identities from the local to the global are made, not found. They have the potential to unify the heterogeneous in a common political life in which all participate on equal terms while they remain "others to one another" (Habermas 2001b, 19). In the final analysis, the fundamental issue is "whether we can foster democratic, or at least relatively noncoercive, discourse about global change" (Curtin 1999, 17). The development of such a discourse is essential if we are to develop the extended political alliances that will allow democracy to "catch up with the forces of a globalized economy" (Habermas 2001b, 53).

Clearly, globalization and the environmental challenges it presents suggest the need for a form of ecological thinking that transcends narrowly nationalistic frames of reference (Lahsen 2004). Optimism about this project is justified by the fact that nations do not have intrinsic and unalterable characters but are, rather, imagined communities that rely on a variety of symbolic elements, historical narratives, customs, and institutional structures to create and reinforce a sense of shared identity (Anderson 1983). Environmental sustainability is largely a concept of community, or common purpose (Bryner 2004). To build a consensus in support of sustainability is a necessarily democratic and participatory exercise for at least two reasons. First, developing a consensus for sustainability requires a breaking down of the polarized and polarizing languages that reflect entrenched political ideologies. This kind of consensus building is essential for the development of community-based solutions to issues of sustainability that can survive outside the carefully constructed confines of environmental interest groups (Plevin 1997) and can penetrate the well-defended bastions of business and government. So, for entirely practical reasons at least, any global environmental initiative must be democratic and broadly participatory.

Second, environmental values and democracy are bound together at the level of principle (Eckersley 1996). To understand why this is so, we must only recognize that politics is increasingly organized around risk allocation. The targets of risk are so numerous, and so capable of political mobilization, that they undermine the legitimacy of the socioeconomic power structure. The resulting crisis of legitimacy can only be addressed by public participation in the allocation and amelioration of risk (U. Beck 1992). In this way, the challenge of global sustainability demonstrates that the crises of ecology and democratic legitimacy are inextricably linked. A discursive form of democracy is better placed than alternate political models to foster a fruitful engagement between humans and their environment (Dryzek 2000) because only it can give voice to the otherwise silent revolution of postmaterialist values that environmentalism represents (Ingehart 1977). Thus, arbitrary or authoritarian approaches to protection of the environment have to be dismissed as unacceptable in principle, even if they were not destined to fail (which, of course, they are).

From Willing to Knowing: Is Smarter Better after All?

Having argued that a global consensus in support of environmental sustainability is possible (provided that it is democratic), the next logical step is to suggest what content that consensus will have to encompass. Some of the challenges that we face are clear. Whereas the character of global environmental problems suggests the need for a form of ecological thinking that transcends narrowly nationalistic frames of reference, universalizing discourses must be approached with caution. They can distract us from the need to confront concrete and local inequities and can mask the interests of those who (often claiming to support "sustainability") advocate measures that generate those inequities. The emergence of a global epistemic community is undoubtedly essential for environmental protection. But experience suggests that it will be a complex domain characterized by both transnational networks tending toward cognitive convergence as well as persistent lines of division that will render any global environmental consensus precarious and unstable (Lahsen 2004).

It has long been recognized as something of a paradox that environmentalism both blames modern science for environmental degradation and looks to it for support and solutions (Yearly 1992). In fact, an environmental crisis cannot even be perceived as such without a great deal of scientific information and technological sophistication (Caldwell 1990). Given the limits of the sciences, the dependence of environmentalism on them means that there will always be a degree of uncertainty about the true nature and severity of environmental problems (Kirkman 2002). This uncertainty will be exacerbated by certain tensions that are inherent in the interrelationship of science, environmentalism, and democracy.

A fundamental element of modernity is its empiricism. At its most basic, this article of the modern faith is captured by John Locke's assertion in *An Essay Concerning Human Understanding* that "all the materials of reason and knowledge" derive from experience (Locke [1689] 1952,

121–122). Yet the amount of knowledge that we can justify from evidence directly available to us can never be very large. The overwhelming proportion of our factual beliefs will, necessarily, be held at secondhand through trusting others (Polanyi 1958), others whom we often refer to as experts. It is hardly irrational to recognize an expert's authority by taking his or her reasoning as a proxy for our own when we have grounds to suppose that he or she knows more than we do and that, if we had access to that knowledge, we would draw the same conclusions (R. Friedman 1973). The advantages of a respect for the authority of science-based expertise are numerous. We stand to gain the accuracy of judgment and depth of ecological understanding that is provided by the specialized training and quality-control mechanisms of modern scientific disciplines (MacRae and Wittington 1997). Moreover, the habits of thought encompassed and encouraged by modern environmental science carry benefits not specific to the environmental arena. The development of an ecological consciousness, grounded in the environmental sciences, can promote more enlightened and progressive policy choices generally by highlighting the actual and potential relationships between the interdependencies in nature and those in the social realm (Valadez 2001). There are many, however, who argue that science is at best a mixed blessing.

All of science is, at least in part, a matter of observation. What we choose to observe in any situation is a function of our background theories and assumptions. It can hardly be otherwise (N. Hanson 1958). Our ability to deal with knowledge is hugely exceeded by the potential knowledge contained in our environment. To cope with this diversity, our perception, memory, and thought processes long ago came to be governed by strategies for protecting our limited capacities from the confusion of overloading (Bruner 1962). Even science, therefore, is irreducibly personal. When it takes the form of expert judgment, it constitutes a form of tacit knowledge that people know for reasons beyond those that they can clearly enunciate (Stone 2002). The situation is further complicated by the fact that most policy problems, including those related to the environment, transcend the domain of any one discipline (MacRae and Wittington 1997). They arise within the context of a civil society in which everyone, no matter how accomplished, is a layman in the face of the expertise possessed by others (Habermas 2001c).

For all of these reasons, the supposed objectivity of science and its claims to expertise may not take us very far. What we think of as facts, assertions intended as true representations about the state of the world, are produced by complex social processes. They come not from direct observation, but from social knowledge that is an accumulation and presentation of observations and beliefs that are structured by both our shared as well as our personal experiences (Stone 2002). This opens science-based environmental expertise to a variety of criticisms. As an example, it is alleged that science is closed to the oppressed and disadvantaged (Jennings and Jennings 1993). This is a criticism that, to the extent it is true, is even more troubling at the international level than it is within nation-states. Others suggest that normative commitments, like the balance of nature (nature in balance) vision, have distorted model building in environmental science (Shrader-Frechette and McCoy 1994). Still others complain that scientific detachment from the realm of human values and ethical principles allows even those whose careers involve the study of nature to participate in its devaluation (Gismondi and Richardson 1994). No wonder that many people, citizens and scientists alike, resist even the most apparently objective and factual knowledge because of its source, its implications, or the challenge it presents to their own tacit knowledge (Stone 2002).

Beyond these general limitations to the reach of science, the search for knowledge about the relationship between humans and their environment confronts a special challenge. Since at least the time of Kant, it has been recognized by cognitive scientists that understanding even so basic a cognitive function as perception requires us to focus on the environment rather than on what goes on within the human organism (Ben-Zeev 1984). Social theorists, in their more lyrical mode, agree that "the very ground and horizon of all our knowing" is the earth itself (Abram 1996, 217). The environment cannot be understood merely as surroundings, no matter how static one's analytical perspective. It is, rather, a dynamic relationship (Caldwell 1971, 5). Neither environments nor organisms are independent entities, captured by a biology that views one as a source of demands for adaptation and the other as a survival calculus at work (Lewontin 1992). In the case of humans, the relationship between the knower and the known is more complex still.

Physical environments play a constitutive role in the most basic activities of the mind. Vision, for example, is an activity rather than a passive response to stimulus. What humans see is a function of what they look at, what they look for, and what they notice (Gibson 1979). There is a connection between cognition and the landscape within which, from our earliest experiences, we are able to think about ourselves and structure our relationships with others (Cobb 1977). So the physical environment is not simply a site in which knowing occurs. It is, rather, a highly specific and normatively significant place that continually presents alternative possibilities for active knowing (Casey 1997). Thus the ecological forms of thought we are called upon to develop are patterns of understanding in which human cognition interacts with an environment rich in the information resources that are vital for organizing our individual and collective existence (Hutchins 1995).

This relationship between knowledge and place might be regarded, for good or ill, as a limitation on the reach of science. But need it be? A general suspicion of science, coupled with the inherent uncertainty of its results, can make the gulf separating scientists and grassroots environmentalists difficult to bridge (Foreman 2002). Moreover, information regarding long-term environmental hazards and necessary hazard adjustments are comprehended by residents of an area at risk only to the degree that they are communicated in language that is familiar to them (Lindell and Perry 2004). Is it too much to expect that scientists will adapt their messages to suit their audiences and that citizens be asked to meet them halfway? In a democratic and multicultural environment, scientists must recognize this necessity (Habermas 2001b). It makes little sense for indigenous populations to claim that coming to terms with what science can tell us is damaging to their cultural institutions. After all, a society becomes ecologically irrational when its forms of epistemic authority and institutional practices threaten the ecosystemic relations on which it relies (R. Bartlett 1986, 2005; Dryzek 1987). When a society fails to preserve the life-support systems on which its members depend, the preconditions of the society's continued existence (and that of its cultural and social institutions) are compromised (Dryzek 1983).

In light of these considerations, the local specificity of knowledge can be regarded as positive rather than limiting, especially given the enormously heterogeneous character of both the natural environment and human society. Important categories of "localness" may include culturally distinctive interests, ways of organizing knowledge production, and discursive traditions (Harding 1998). Yet the essential character of scientific understanding is not surrendered simply by recognizing that knowledge is not a transcendental phenomenon, but, rather, a local commodity designed to satisfy local needs and solve local problems (Feyerabend 1987). Environmental science and politics should be seen as coproduced, or as mutually reinforcing at every step. Politics are not merely stimulated by scientific findings but are prevalent in the shaping and dissemination of environmental science (Forsyth 2003).

Just as the production of a critical political ecology requires adaptation in the scientific community, science has significant transformative potential for politics. There is little doubt that the move to exclude metaphysical perspectives and forms of discourse from discussions of ethics and politics in this century has been inspired by the success of the natural sciences (Williams 1999). The consequences of this have been positive for both democracy and environmental protection (Baber and Bartlett 2005). Realizing that science and politics are coproduced carries with it the power to reveal the covert uses of science for political objectives. It also allows for the devolution of environmental scientific governance within diverse social groupings in pursuit of democratically determined solutions at the local level (Forsyth 2003). This can promote the more effective use of scientific knowledge by creating "ecologies of knowledge"—dense, cross-hatched relationships of practice and process that retain environmental knowledge through use rather than allowing it to dissipate through suspicion or indifference (Brown and Duguid 2002).

Having suggested that there is a particular form of ecological science that is appropriate as a foundation for an international consensus in support of environmental protection, it remains to suggest what institutional forms that consensus might take and by what means they might be developed. One of our initial premises is that any global environmental consensus will have to be democratic. But what, precisely, does democratic mean in this context? Indeed, what can it mean?

From Thinking Locally to Acting Globally

As a general matter, it is widely believed that international politics suffers from a "democracy deficit" (Wallace 2001). This deficit is a consequence of the fact that the decisions made within international institutions are driven by democratic concerns only to the extent that domestic foreign policy in the various nations is the result of democratic politics. International democracy, so it might be argued, will never be more than a theoretical possibility in the absence of a sovereign and democratically elected legislature at the global level (Slaughter 2004). Recent explorations of the idea of deliberative democracy, however, hold out a different hope. Deliberative democracy is particularly well suited to the task of environmental protection (Baber and Bartlett 2005; Meadowcraft 2004). Deliberative democracy, operating at the boundary between the state and civil society, is a political practice that can generate broader public support for more ecologically sound policies while enhancing the institutional capacities of public agencies (Meadowcraft 2004). As we have seen, the challenges of popular participation, environmental knowledge building, and institutional adequacy are even more acute at the international level than they are within states. To see how deliberative democracy might help us confront these challenges, a more complete understanding of the concept is necessary.

Deliberative democracy is a concept that defies easy definition. The deliberative democracy movement has been spawned by a growing realization that contemporary liberalism has lost something of its democratic character. Modern democracies, confronted by cultural pluralism, social complexity, vast inequities of wealth and influence, and ideological biases that discourage fundamental change, have allowed their political institutions to degenerate into arenas for strategic gamesmanship in which there is little possibility for genuine deliberation (Bohman 1996, 18–24). True democracy is impossible where citizens are mere competitors with no commitments beyond their own narrow self-interests. How to move beyond mere interest is a matter of considerable debate. Elsewhere (Baber and Bartlett 2005) we have described three distinct approaches to deliberative democracy—public reason, ideal discourse, and full liberalism. Our ultimate objective in this book is to suggest how deliberative democracy might inform our thinking about the international "democracy deficit" in general and the challenge of developing an international environmental jurisprudence in particular.

Public reason is an approach to deliberative democracy advanced most prominently by John Rawls (1993, 1999a, 1999b, 2001). Rawls ventured beyond fundamental rights and goals of distributive justice by using only the Kantian pursuit of universalizable principles and the perspective of the least favored (I. Shapiro 2001). The intuition at work is that if persons would agree to a policy principle when they might be the ones most adversely affected by it, they should agree to it in every other circumstance as well (applying the transivity principle of rationality). For Rawls, "public reason is the reason of equal citizens who, as a collective body, exercise final political and coercive power over one another in enacting laws and in amending their constitution" (Rawls 1993, 214). Deliberation is a search for binding precommitments to political values that are fundamentally important but limited in scope.(Bartlett and Baber 2005). In this form of deliberation, one reasons from the little one knows in the "original position" (wherein all information about one's personal situation is hidden by a veil of ignorance) in pursuit of unanimity based on reasons with which anyone similarly situated would freely agree. In this mode of deliberation, individual interests are neither compromised nor reconciled. They are eliminated as reasons that can justly be offered in defense of one's positions (36–38).

The conception of individual citizens advanced by Rawls's theory of public reason is the most difficult approach of the three we will deal with because it diverges the most dramatically from our everyday experience. Rawls's well-ordered society is populated by people who are "equal . . . autonomous . . . reasonable" and possessed of the "capacity for social co-operation" (Rawls 1993, 306). Furthermore, they view society as "a fair system of cooperation over time, from one generation to the next" (15). Also, they aspire to be both rational in a technical sense and reasonable in a broader political sense. This is because "merely reasonable agents would have no ends of their own they would want to advance through fair cooper-ation; merely rational agents lack a sense of justice and fail to recognize the independent validity of the claims of others" (52). Because they share these characteristics, the citizens of a well-ordered society would readily commit themselves to abide by the principles of justice flowing from a discourse in which they (or their representatives) were guided by the regulative concept of the veil of ignorance. This concept requires decision makers to ignore vir-tually all information about their positions in society, their individual inter-ests, and even which generation they represent (Rawls 1999c).

The approach taken by Rawls has both advantages and difficulties. Some critics of deliberative democracy have complained that deliberation of this sort has a sedative effect that curbs the behavior (and thus the in-fluence) of the historically disadvantaged. They also argue that some cit-izens are better at articulating their arguments than others, so much so that well-educated white males are destined to prevail in the deliberative environment (Sanders 1997). The Rawlsian approach, however, sedates all participants with the same dosage of the same drug. Although Rawls ac-knowledges that we all have a right to products of our own abilities, they can justly provide us only what we become entitled to "by taking part in a fair social process" (Rawls 1993, 284). Presumably, fine debating skills, whether innate or acquired, are covered by that injunction.

Others have suggested that Rawls's conception of public reason is too narrow because it is based upon the assumption that people's preferences are determined prior to political interaction and do not change as a result of such interaction (Offe 1997). But this is true only to the extent that Rawls's theory embodies an attempt to justify collective decisions by appealing to reasons that can be adopted by people simply by virtue of their common citizenship and the shared interests implied by that common status (Evans 1999). Indeed, the greatest problem with Rawls's approach to public reason may be that, rather than counting too little on change, it counts on change far more than is reasonable. Deliberative democracy of the kind he advocates requires a radical equality of access for individuals, groups, and interests that have been historically excluded from decision making (Rawls 1999a, 580–581) If actually achieved, such a circumstance would unsettle, if not subvert, existing understandings about the dimensions and boundaries of political conflict (Knight and Johnson 1994, 289).

A second form of deliberative democracy, ideal discourse, is most closely associated with the work of Jürgen Habermas. In this view, deliberative democracy relies on a shared political culture and is rooted less in government institutions than in civic society. For Habermas, deliberation is a process of testing the competing validity claims put forward by citizens in search of a general consensus based upon reasons that are shared, not merely public. In ideal discourse, individual interests are the source of these competing validity claims. But those interests are not regarded as givens, the fundamental stuff of politics. Interests must be open to change because citizens engaged in ideal discourse are committed to search for a genuine meeting of the minds, rather than the modus vivendi that less demanding approaches, such as full liberalism (discussed next), might allow (Baber and Bartlett 2005, 35–36).

The view of citizens in the ideal discourse situation adopted by Habermas shares much with that of Rawls, but differs in some important ways. Habermas speaks of personally autonomous participants in deliberative discourse who are "free and equal," each of whom is "required to take the perspective of everyone else," and who thus project themselves "into the understandings of self and the world of all others" (Habermas 1995, 117). They do not, however, adopt this attitude out of any commitment to abstract principles of justice produced in a reflective equilibrium free of ideology and interest. These citizens are committed to advancing their normative validity claims in forms that can be treated like truth claims; that is, in forms that can be subjected to empirical evaluation (Habermas 1990). There is no mechanism of impartiality at work. Indeed, Habermas (1995) criticizes Rawls for his willingness to purchase the neutrality of his conception of justice at the cost of forsaking its cognitive validity claim. It is as if Habermas is invoking the second clause of Rawls's own maxim that "justice is the first virtue of social institutions just as truth is of systems of thought" (Rawls 1999c, 3).

The reasonableness Habermas seeks is born of a social and cultural commitment to an inclusive and rational discourse (Habermas 1995) based upon "the justified supposition of a 'legitimate order' " (Habermas 1996, 68). It is true that the processes of internalization that structure the normative foundations of the values espoused by citizens are not free of repressive and reactionary tendencies (Habermas 1996). It is also true that those who constitute the politically interested and informed class of the public may be disinclined to seriously submit their view to discussion (Habermas 1998d). Ultimately, however, the consciousness of their own autonomy gives rise to an "authority of conscience" that becomes an integral part of the politically informed and active citizen's motivational foundation (Habermas 1996, 67). This commitment to intellectual honesty would seem to be an essential element of the ideal discourse situation, conceived of as a rational and noncoercive discourse designed to test empirically the truth-value of competing normative claims.

Finally, full liberalism is a widely shared perspective exemplified most clearly by the ideas of James Bohman, Amy Gutmann, and Dennis Thompson. Their work can be viewed as an attempt to reconcile the divergent approaches of Rawls and Habermas in ways that make deliberative democracy more feasible in a complex and normatively fragmented society. Bohman describes a politics characterized by equality of both access and influence, good-faith bargaining, and plurality rule accompanied by continuing minority acceptance of the fairness of the process. Thus, in full liberalism one's individual interests are the primary source of individual preferences and motivation. But the reasons a citizen offers to others in support of his or her policy positions must transcend personal interests, at least to some extent. They must be public reasons, but only in the limited sense that their acceptability is not dependent on membership in some particular social group (Baber and Bartlett 2005, 34–35).

The theory of full liberalism is, in many ways, less demanding than either public reason or ideal discourse (Baber 2004). For example, Bohman assumes that citizens in a democracy are unavoidably divided by deep-seated normative differences he describes as cultural pluralism (Bohman 1994). He also doubts the possibility that any form of public reason or any view of the common good can ever command a consensus in communities as complex as the modern democracies. In Bohman's view, "community biases" and the exclusion of many from "effective political participation" are unavoidable, at least to some extent (Bohman 1996, 238). Finally, Bohman argues that knowledge and information are always scarce resources in a complex society, and that neither innate capacities nor acquired knowledge can ever be evenly or widely distributed. Consequently, citizens in pluralistic democracies will inevitably "surrender their autonomy to experts, delegates, and other forms of the division of labor" (168).

This does not suggest that deliberative democrats should surrender to the injustices currently observable in democratic life. Bohman supports an equalization of deliberative resources and capacities as far as that is possible, as do other deliberative democrats (Cohen 1997; Gutmann and Thompson 1996). But as Dryzek has pointed out, some degree of inequality may not only be unavoidable, it also may actually serve as grist for the deliberative contest (Dryzek 2000, 172–173). The point of providing support to the disadvantaged in the context of public deliberation is not to equalize their position with "the other interest groups jostling for influence" but, rather, to ensure that they can make "effective use of their political liberties" (Gutmann and Thompson 1996, 305, 277). Strict equality is neither necessary nor desirable from the point of view of maintaining the critical edge brought to deliberation by the disadvantaged. After all, it is not as if deliberation under full liberalism is a search for one correct solution.

Having rejected the notion of a singular form of public reason, it is not surprising that theorists of full liberalism should find themselves in the company of the majority of representative democrats who, from Burke's time, have regarded political questions as inevitably controversial ones without a right answer (Pitkin 1967). The objects of deliberation, in their view, are the interests of specific persons who have a right to help define them. Politics is recognizably democratic when it gives them that right. These deliberative democrats do not try to specify a single form of citizenship. They search for "models of representation that support the give-and-take of serious and sustained moral argument within legislative bodies, between legislators and citizens, and among citizens themselves" (Gutmann and Thompson 1996, 131). In this way, deliberative democracy is not so much a search for ethically or empirically defensible solutions as it is a process of personal development for citizens. John Dryzek has argued that, in the face of ideologies and structural forces that perpetuate distorted views of the political world, we should seek the competence of citizens themselves to recognize and oppose such forces, which "can be promoted through participation in authentically democratic politics" (Dryzek 2000, 21). Thus, one might say that the most important product of deliberative democracy is neither just principles nor rational policies but, rather, the critical capacities of the citizens themselves. It might further be argued that this objective is the most important one that collective-will formation can pursue. After all, to the extent that permanent solutions to the ecological crisis require significant changes of collective consciousness, preserving our species and its environment may be possible only through such a process of social evolution.

Full liberalism's most important contribution to our concerns in this book arises from Bohman's notion of a plural form of public reason and the advocacy, by Gutmann and Thompson, of give-and-take in representative institutions. Both of these ideas touch upon one of the most serious criticisms that has been leveled at theorists of deliberative democracy, namely, that both Habermas and Rawls have made a mistake by insisting that citizens converge on the same reasons for a decision rather than agreeing on a course of action each for his or her own reasons. This convergence, it has been suggested, can be no more than an ideal of democratic citizenship rather than an actual requirement of public reason (Bohman 1996). Worse yet, according to these critics, this preoccupation with convergence has led Habermas to the strong principle of unanimity that will ultimately render his theories impractical in a world characterized by social complexity and moral pluralism (Bohman 1994). In fact, Dryzek has concluded that Habermas "long ago realized the practical difficulties that precluded the realization of consensus in practice" (Dryzek 2000, 72). Habermas may, however, have actually done something rather more subtle.

In his recent work, Habermas (1996) maintains a strong emphasis on reasoned consensus while showing a willingness to discuss majority rule in certain circumstances. Some have concluded that he has abandoned his earlier commitment to unanimity in the face of moral complexity and now regards consensus as merely a "regulative ideal" (Gaus 1997). On this view, consensus is merely "a model for real world discourse in concrete, historical conditions" (Postema 1995, 359).

Habermas, however, describes a form of majority rule that suggests a certain practical priority for consensus (Habermas 1997b). Consensus and majority rule are compatible, in his view, "only if the latter has an internal relation to the search for truth." Public reason must "mediate between reason and will, between the opinion-formation of all and the majoritarian will-formation of the representatives" (Habermas 1997b). A decision arrived at in the political realm through majority rule is legitimate only if "its content is regarded as the rationally motivated but fallible result of an attempt to determine what is right through a discussion that has been brought to a *provisional* close under the pressure to decide" (47; emphasis in the original). Habermas is careful to indicate that such a decision does not require the minority to concede that it is in error or to give up its aims. It requires only that they forgo the implementation of their view until they better establish their reasons and gain the necessary support (47). Ideally, then, a vote is only "the concluding act of a continuous controversy" carried out publicly between argument and counterargument (Habermas 1998d, 212). If the idea of a concluding act seems to fit poorly with the concept of a continuous controversy, we can better understand why many have found Habermas to be elusive on this subject.

What are the practical implications of this view of majoritarianism? First, it should be apparent that accepting something less than consensus is justified only where the pressure to decide precludes further deliberation. In some circumstances, action must be taken if an opportunity is not to be lost. In other cases an institutional imperative may require that something be done in a circumstance where the perfect may have become the enemy of the good. Often the prospect of immediate and irreparable harm to the environment or to human interests justifies action in the face of what may be significant uncertainty about the facts. Other principles of immediacy are certainly conceivable. But the concepts of lost opportunity, institutional imperative, and imminent harm are clearly major categories of the pressure to decide.

A second implication of this view is that public reason must be the tool used to determine when the pressure to decide is sufficient to justify majority rule. In this way, the political process of majoritarian will formation is disciplined by the social process of the opinion formation of all. In effect, the minority maintains a veto on collective action but chooses not to exercise it immediately in the expectation that the discourse will continue and any intermediate action will be regarded as a provisional decision based upon only a weak consensus that prompt action is required. So majority rule will always be available, but it will be legitimate only where members of the minority are satisfied that the discourse will continue and they will not ultimately be required to yield to the force of numbers.

Finally, where lost opportunities and immediate harms are major concerns, and where many (if not most) decisions will be regarded as legitimate only if they are provisional, there must be a strong bias against any action (or inaction) with irreversible consequences. Providing protection for an endangered species is a positive manifestation of this negative bias. The species can be de-listed, should further research warrant. But an old growth forest that is logged, or a wetland that is paved over, is a permanent loss that later regrets cannot recover. These are actions that a majority could not justify as provisional decisions. So, if our description of Habermas's theory is sound, neither he nor other deliberative democrats who accept his reasoning should ever tolerate such decisions absent a genuine consensus among all those choosing to debate the issues in the ideal discourse situation.

From Municipal to Cosmopolitan Environmental Law

At this point in our discussion, are there any tentative conclusions that could guide us in conceptualizing an international environmental jurisprudence? In our view, three general remarks are in order. First, for environmental law to attain global reach humankind must invent a mechanism that allows for the formation of a collective will in the absence of sovereignty as it is conventionally understood. If environmentalism represents an intersection of science and reason, one would never expect it to exist solely within the narrow confines of government (Ehrlich and Ehrlich 1996). Why, then, would we assume that environmentalism can be held captive by so limited an institution as the sovereign state (Dryzek et al. 2003; Dryzek 2005; Dryzek and Schlosberg 2005)? Benvenisti and others have discussed the idea of formally empowering substate units of government to enter into international agreements (Benvenisti 2000). The potential of non-state-centric environmental governance has been explored by Wapner (1996) and others. How much further a step would it be to empower citizens to engage one another on the international stage in deliberation regarding the survival of the species? After all, "just as there are issues of scale inherent in any environmental issue, so citizenship is an issue of scale. Each begins, although neither ends, at a local level with local knowledge" (Curtin 1999, 179).

Second, this insight provides the foundation for our general observation that international environmental jurisprudence must be grounded in a knowledge base that is local and concrete. Environmentalism has long been understood to be dependent on the insights of scientific disciplines that advance universal propositions based upon empirical research. As we have argued, it could hardly be otherwise. But the political ecology upon which international environmental law must be founded must adopt a "critical attitude" toward supposedly neutral explanations of ecological reality (Forsyth 2003, 267). Environmental problems are not merely particular manifestations of general principles. They always arise in a human context, and dealing with them effectively requires a wisdom of place, an understanding of the role that the environment plays in the cultural experiences of resident populations (Basso and Felds 1996). International environmental agreements benefit from strong support in civil society from coalitions of interest and ideology that unite private and public actors (Zartman 2001). The positive relationship between international environmental agreements and civic environmentalism runs in the opposite direction as well. International agreements give rise to support groups throughout member nations (transnational coalitions, grass-roots organizations, and monitor and watch groups), which are crucial to building and sustaining the information base and political resources necessary for implementation of the agreements themselves (Deng and Zartman 2002).

Third, just as the knowledge base of international environmental law must be "democratized," so must be the political processes that produce it. International environmental agreements are sustained as meaningful regulatory processes over time by constant give-and-take over changing conceptions of consensual knowledge (Sjöstedt 2003). The importance of consensus in this regard can be traced to the fact that international environmental agreements are largely self-enforcing by their very nature. There are often political costs for noncompliance that pose significant trade-offs for negotiation purposes. But there are rarely significant inducements to comply or sanctions for noncompliance (Barrett 1998). It is in this context that the debate among deliberative democrats over the place of consensus in popular government finds its natural home. Consensus in collective decision making at the national or subnational level may be a regulative norm or a mere aspiration. But when one steps on the international stage, consensus becomes a practical necessity.

So what we seek, then, is nothing less than collective choice without sovereignty, reliable knowledge without abstraction, and effective implementation without coercion. Reasons for rejecting this agenda abound. Only the necessities of human survival can be offered in its defense. But pessimism at the outset is unwarranted in light of the fact that popular government appears to be succeeding at the level of the nation-state. After all, effective environmental law at the international level only requires us to perform the same basic functions that domestic governments perform—the legislative, administrative, and adjudicatory functions (Sands and Peel 2005). We must remember that whether the international institutions and process that eventually develop to satisfy these functional requirements resemble their municipal counterparts is less important than that they be fully democratic and ecologically sustainable.

In later chapters, we offer a specific proposal for global collective will formation, such that general commitments to abstract principles of environmental protection can be developed into more concrete and specific obligations that would allow organizations and individuals to assert and answer claims in coherent ways. A deliberatively democratic approach suggests both a jurisdictional and a jurisprudential rationale for the resolution of environmental disputes by international tribunals, namely, by reference to a juristically democratic kind of transnational common law. Specifically, we imagine certain institutions—innumerable citizen-constituted policy juries that deliberate hypothetical cases, at least one global codifying agency, and a resulting cosmopolitan and transnational common law—that can provide for "scaling up" deliberative democracy to the global level, by offering processes that can integrate local knowledge and contextual ecological science in ongoing global democratic will formation. Imperatives of the current world order of states and global capitalism pose challenges, but success would not be contingent on these being abolished or ignored or wished away.

Our intent is to advance a proposal that is entirely realistic and pragmatic, in the hardest-headed senses of those words. But both of those words come with philosophical and ideological baggage that immediately entangles, potentially introducing a level of complexity and confusion into the understanding of terms that most ordinary people use in relatively unproblematic ways. Essential to our argument that follows is a functional analysis of the requirements of international law and of the necessity of freeing ourselves from the constraints imposed by assumptions about how those requirements should be met. Essential as well is an analysis of the merits of a foundation in philosophical pragmatism for both deliberative democratic theory and international relations theory and the necessity of freeing ourselves from the constraints imposed by assumptions about the pluralist and statist context of international politics. These are the tasks of the next three chapters, before we turn explicitly to an exploration of how we might cultivate a transnational common law.

2

Political Realism: How Realist, How Realistic?

Realism, as the term is used in political science and international relations (IR), is seldom examined in the context of the broad sweep of the way it has been used in scholarly work generally. IR realism shares some of the theoretical premises of realism in the arts, law, and philosophy. But unlike these other intellectual endeavors, IR realism is only partly a theoretical perspective. The term *realism* was adopted in IR because it had (and has) political appeal beyond the realm of theories and scholarship. Realist theorists and ideologues gain an advantage over intellectual and political opponents by defining them into an untenable position.[1]

To self-define a perspective as realism is to declare that perspective to be dealing with the *real* and to characterize its proponents as *realistic* and *realists*. Thus when a perspective such as IR realism does battle in "real world" political conflicts of ideas and ideologies, it does so after it has preemptively occupied all the linguistic high ground. When, to be understood, even its putative political opponents must refer to it as realism, they implicitly acknowledge that all other perspectives must therefore be unrealistic and dealing with the unreal, or at least less realistic and less real. In the face of this linguistic hegemony, any possible new order, however sweeping or modest, must embrace the realism terminology of the old.

There is much that is problematic in the traditional perspectives of IR realism, but, perhaps a bit like democracy, the alternatives are even more flawed. At least in realism there is an often-unacknowledged core of philosophical pragmatism that offers a foundation for development of any workable jurisprudence for international environmental law. Thus, for reasons both substantive (real) and strategic (realistic), any workable system of international environmental jurisprudence probably must build upon a perspective of realism, albeit a less constraining and more humble realism than that offered by traditional IR realism.

Excavating this foundation requires, first, identifying how IR realism has departed from the way scholars in philosophy, the arts, and law have conceived of realism and, second, distinguishing what is common and worthwhile in all these endeavors. Upon that exposed rock, a more modest realism can be erected to serve as a useful guide to building international environmental law and policy.

Political Realism

There are many kinds of realism, including philosophical realism, aesthetic realism, mathematical realism, logical realism, and linguistic realism, to name but a few. Many forms are attendant to the formal sciences and could be subsumed as subtypes of philosophical realism. This level of detail, however, is unnecessary to our present purpose. It suffices to observe that the various forms of philosophical realism share a commitment to the reality of abstract objects, objects that necessarily have no spatial or temporal location.[2] This view is "the core conception of an abstract object in realist thought from Plato to Gödel" and it constitutes the most compact definition "that fits the usage of both realists and their critics" (Katz 1998, 1). Adding additional defining elements (e.g., that abstract objects are causally inert or mind-independent) is generally redundant because the original definition implies those other properties.

Aesthetic realism might be perceived as a phenomenon entirely distinct from such arid philosophizing. But that distinction is not as clear as one might imagine.[3] To take an admittedly simplistic example, realism has always been considered to be at least one way to deal with the problem of illusory perceptions. For instance, a round, green table can appear to be an oval from a certain angle or appear to be blue in a certain light. The realist, however, can be certain of the table's true nature because he knows that it possesses the qualities of roundness and greenness and that those qualities are real and determinate even if they are abstract. Moreover, the realist is in the happy position of being able to definitively evaluate his own perceptions, as well as those of others, because he is in touch with the facts as they really are, roundness and greenness being no less factual than extension and mass. This opportunity to get beyond mere perception was very appealing in the Victorian era, when there was an eagerness to shake off the timidities and romanticism of transcendentalism. It was, according to Henry James (1879), an age with a taste for realism. If transcendental idealism was illusory (a blue oval table), the writers, artists,

and scientists of the late nineteenth century would apply the disillusion-
ment that was called for and lead, in the bargain, toward new levels of
social progress that only a hardnosed critique of the status quo could produce. It was during this period that a realistic outlook came to pervade
every aspect of intellectual and artistic life (Shi 1995).

In this cultural context it should not be surprising that those whose
primary interests were political should look for ways to get in on the realist revolution. The romanticism surrounding the founding of the American republic, for example, had long since worn thin, particularly after it
was exposed to the trauma of the Civil War. But by the early decades of
the twentieth century, the search for social facts had begun to express itself, on both sides of the Atlantic, in the development of a philosophy in
the social sciences that would ultimately prove hostile to the realist projects. Positivism distinguished itself from theological or metaphysical conceptions of the world by laying claim to positive knowledge of human
affairs. Represented by Rudolf Carnap, Carl Hempel, and Ernst Nagel in
the United States and Karl Popper in Great Britain, this approach emphasized the continuity of all science, including the social sciences and
history. A central element of their thinking has been referred to as the
law-explanation orthodoxy (Outhwaite 1987). At its simplest, this is the
view that all science is the search for explanations that take the form of
general laws. This view is grounded in Hume's theory of causation "according to which all we can ever observe is the 'constant conjunction' of
events" and that this is "all we need to know for empirical science to be
possible" (7).

This new logical positivism, however, presented both an opportunity
and a challenge to realism. The obvious opportunity was to focus one's
attention on perceived objects and events and to build, on that observa-
tional base, a superstructure of universals that a realist might choose to
regard as more real than the underlying experiences. Our perception of
social facts is, after all, subject to the inaccuracy of observation or the
imprecision of operationalization for which the social sciences are noto-
rious. The logical positivists, however, help us avoid any inferiority complex by reassuring us that we actually are inferior. They very kindly let
us off the hook by dismissing questions about the true nature of social
forms—reducing them to the status of mere definitional matters. But notice the bitter that accompanies this particular sweet. Ontological questions, questions about what exists, have thus been resolved into either
formal postulates of a theory or meaningless metaphysics. What room

remains, then, for the realists' actually existing universals? Or, indeed, for the values associated with social progress and political reformism?

Political realism, if it is have any vitality at all, clearly must not acquiesce in this trivialization of ontology. But how should it be answered? To begin to understand how political realism has approached the problem, we begin with a classical formulation. According to Brian Leiter, classical realism is a reconstruction of a long-neglected perspective on questions of moral, political, and legal theory (Leiter 2001a). Classical realists accept three basic doctrines. First, they subscribe to a *naturalism* that holds "there are certain (largely) incorrigible and generally unattractive facts about human beings and human nature." Second, they hold to a *pragmatism* that assumes "only theories which make a difference to practice are worth the effort." Third, they adopt a *quietism* based on the view that any normative theorizing that fails to respect the limits imposed by the facts of human nature is "idle and pointless" and that it is better to keep quiet than "to theorize in ways that make no difference" (245). Before discussing how classical realism manifests itself in the more particular forms of legal realism and realism in international relations theory, let us examine these three conceptual elements more closely.

What does it mean to say that human nature is an incorrigible and unattractive fact? To begin, if we mean by incorrigible that human nature is not subject to change, then we have said very little. Ignoring the possibility of intentional genetic manipulation, which we should not ignore (Habermas 2003a), if we take the point seriously it tells us nothing. Even over the course of geologic time, no species transcends the limits of its genetic potentiality. If we reduce that potentiality to a sufficiently definitive present state such that the label "human nature" makes sense, pointing out that it is constant adds nothing to our understanding of it. If by incorrigible, however, we simply mean that human nature is not subject to control, then the argument is not only refuted by our every social experience but it is also inconsistent with the very idea of having the kinds of theoretical arguments that realists wish to have. If humans are literally beyond any control, then the ideas of law, politics, and social science are of no practical (one might say pragmatic) utility and to even discuss them is a waste of time.

If we argue for an intermediate position that human nature can be controlled but never corrected, then the appropriate response is both "so what" and "how do you know"? From a pragmatic point of view, it is quite enough to govern people's behavior and leave their underlying per-

sonae unaffected. That we have knowledge of both those underlying per-
sonae and the abstract model of which they are representations can be
assumed (as classical realists do) but not proven (as both pragmatists and
logical empiricists would require). Finally, and incongruously, the judgment that human nature is an unattractive fact assumes both its incorri-
gibility and our ability to imagine it otherwise. From what vantage point
could something that is immutable be regarded as unattractive? It is difficult to see how we would even begin to make sense of such an idea,
much less couch it in theoretical terms that would make it anything other
than the kind of useless theorizing that classical realists claim they wish
to avoid.

Passing over the element of pragmatism, to which we shall ultimately
return, the realist's commitment to quietism is worthy of closer but not
lengthy examination. Recall that the idea behind quietism is that any normative theorizing that is inconsistent with human nature (in all its incorrigible and unattractive glory) is "idle and pointless" (Leiter 2001a, 245).
It is therefore better to keep quiet about normative matters than to engage
in theorizing that makes no difference. But if human nature is truly incorrigible, then how could we ever assess it in normative terms? If we are
trapped by our nature, then our actions are not appropriate subjects for
normative theorizing at all. What humans do is just what humans do, and
there is nothing more worthwhile to say about it normatively, any more
than it makes sense to condemn a cat for eating meat or a cow for walking on four legs. That, in fact, is what at least one classical realist has concluded. Leiter has argued that, "given what human beings are really like,
one should not expect moral claims or normative theory to have much
impact upon them: either people are such that they won't answer to moral
demands, or they are such that moral theory will not affect them" (248).
Theorizing, then, should be "essentially descriptive and explanatory,
rather than normative" (248). But even this limited kind of theorizing is
problematic. A descriptive theory, to be a theory at all, must do something more than describe. Ultimately, the only explanation that a realist
could add regarding any instance of human behavior is that it is consistent with human nature. Reduced to its logical form, the explanation for
any human action a in response to circumstance c, is that when confronted
with circumstances such as c, human beings manifest such behaviors as a.
No amount of regression through the causal chain will ever produce any
different, or more informative, result. That being the case, quietism is an
entirely appropriate attitude to adopt. When asked why George Bush

invaded Iraq, the clear-thinking realist will simply shrug his shoulders and smile a knowing smile. But is that what real realists do?

The volume of the literature in legal realism and in the realist school of international relations suggests very strongly that the quietism of classical realism has not translated well into practice. Having made so encompassing an assertion as that moral theorizing "furnishes no motive, and creates no motivation" and that "motive and motivation have to come from outside morality" (Posner 1999, 7), one might expect an author to fall silent. Silence would be especially appropriate if the author has also attributed all human behavior to a single and invariable force such as self-interest. If both of those things are true, there is literally nothing more to be said, except perhaps that all human interactions are greater or lesser forms of direct or indirect coercion. That, in fact, is one interpretation of much else that realists have had to say. But here we are getting ahead of ourselves. At this point it is necessary to divert from our main line of questioning and explore the manifestations of realism in law and international relations. We will then be prepared to return to the pragmatist element of realism, discussion of which we have postponed.

Legal Realism

The impression one gains of legal realism depends to a significant degree upon which of its advocates one reads. Some take a flat, descriptive approach to their topic while others display a level of rhetorical flourish not usually associated with the work of lawyers. At its most basic, legal realism is no more than a rejection of the formalism and conservatism that dominated legal philosophy in the nineteenth century. It can trace its origins back to Oliver Wendell Holmes Jr.'s claim that "the life of the law has not been logic: it has been experience" (Holmes [1881] 1991, 1). On that same page, Holmes added that "law embodies the story of a nation's development through many centuries, and it cannot be dealt with as if it contained only the axioms and corollaries of a book of mathematics." This argument, radical for its time, inspired a group of American legal scholars led by K. N. Llewellyn (1962) and Jerome Frank (1963), among others, to reject the notion that the law was a complete and autonomous system of socially neutral rules and principles that judges merely applied to cases as they presented themselves. In the hands of these legal realists, the law no longer presented questions of logical consistency but, rather, of socially desirable outcomes.

A less modest and moderate form of legal realism emphasizes the intuitive sense of justice brought to cases by judges. For instance, Frank quoted Judge Chancellor Kent who described his approach to cases in the following way. First, said Kent, he made himself "master of the facts" and "I saw where justice lay." Then, "when I sat down to search the authorities," Kent said, "I almost always found principles to suit my view of the case" (Frank 1963, 104). This emphasis on the intuitive sense of justice possessed by judges led to the exciting, if unfortunate, rhetoric of the early realist movement, which claimed that there was actually no such thing as law, that law is merely a set of predictions about what judges will do, or that law is simply a matter of what the judge had for breakfast (Dworkin 1986). We should, however, eschew these more inflammatory statements of the realist view in favor of the most plausible one that can be found, so that if we eventually decide against realism we will not have merely succeeded in demolishing a straw man.

We take the work of Brian Leiter to be the strongest contemporary statement of legal realism. The core claim of legal realism, in Leiter's view, is that judges respond primarily to the stimulus of the facts of a case rather than to the rational demands of a system of legal rules (Leiter 1997, 277). This does not require us to conclude that law doesn't exist because, as every attorney knows, what counts as a fact in any case is a function not only of the actual historical events and the predisposition of judges but also of the operation of "secondary" rules (or rules of adjudication) that focus the attention of judges on one set of events rather than another (Hart 1994). Even if we wished to deny the existence or importance of primary laws (rules of legal obligation), we would have to concede that adjudication is rule-governed behavior, and that at least in the minimal sense it is what contemporary linguistic philosophers would describe as a language game. Without at least that sense of legal order, there would quite literally be nothing we could say about the actions of judges. We would be unable to designate some actions as adjudication and exclude other actions from that category. Even an inquiry into the morning eating habits of judges would be pointless because we would lack the linguistic and conceptual tools necessary to discuss the adjudicatory significance of eggs and oatmeal.

A few additional points are necessary. First, Leiter's understanding of realism sets that doctrine against the sort of formalism that views judges as automatons, acting out the inescapable consequences of a deterministic system of normative law. Second, Leiter's core claim is intentionally behaviorist in character. It directs our attention away from internal mental states, beliefs, and desires, focusing instead on the role of facts in triggering adjudicatory responses (Leiter 1997, 277–279). Leiter's realism differs from what he characterizes as the received view, which consists of the idea that judges exercise unfettered discretion to reach results based on their personal tastes and values and that they use legal rules and reason only as post-hoc rationalizations of their actions. Our ability to predict with fair accuracy what judges will do belies the idea that their actions are truly unfettered. Our ability to discern patterns in the actions of judges as a group suggests that whatever forces constrain their behavior, they are of sufficient generality and commonality that they are potentially accessible to systematic inquiry. Indeed, something like Leiter's twin theses of determinism and generality would seem to be essential if legal realism is to exist as a tradition of inquiry with any content whatsoever.

Leiter has conceded, however, that legal realism has suffered telling criticism (Leiter 2001b)—in particular, H. L. A. Hart's critique of realism as a form of rule skepticism (Hart 1994). By demolishing the predictive theory of law (that law is merely a prediction about what a court will do), Hart is widely perceived to have cut the legs from under realists who deny that legal rules bind the decisions of judges in any important way. The form that rule skepticism takes is, however, subject to some variation. Hart first describes it as a claim that "talk of rules is a myth, cloaking the truth that law consists simply of the decisions of courts and the prediction of them" (138). This view Leiter usefully characterizes as conceptual rule skepticism, because it has to do with our understanding of what the very concept of law means (Leiter 2001b). Hart also discusses another sort of skepticism, one that offers a theory about "the function of legal rules in judicial decisions" (Hart 1994, 138), which Leiter characterizes as empirical rule skepticism. Empirical rule skepticism is, generally speaking, the view that legal rules have no inherent meaning or significance. They are only generalizations about what courts do when confronted with particular sets of circumstances. Leiter claims that "Hart never offers any argument against empirical rule skepticism" (Leiter 2001b). Hart does, however, use language that might lead one to a different conclusion.

In discussing the sources of support for empirical rule skepticism, Hart first claims that the skeptic is "sometimes a disappointed absolutist" who has discovered that legal rules are "not all they would be in a formalist's heaven." He suggests that some people adopt this view not because legal rules are literally meaningless, but because they want legal rules to be moral and ethical absolutes (elements of the real world that entirely determine judicial actions for moral rather than prudential reasons) and when these rules fall short of that, they conclude that they mean nothing at all. Hart adds that "it does not follow from the fact that such rules have exceptions incapable of exhaustive statement, that in every situation we are left to our own discretion" (Hart 1994, 139). He also attributes empirical rule skepticism to realists having confused the question of whether an action manifests acceptance of the binding character of a rule with the psychological question of what thought processes led a person to that acceptance. The fact that a psychological process is sometimes intuitive does not render it inexplicable.

Moreover, in Hart's view the most important factor in showing that our intuitive actions involve obeying rules is "that *if* our behavior is challenged we are disposed to justify it by reference to the rule." Hart adds that "the genuineness of our acceptance of the rule may be manifested not only in our past and subsequent general acknowledgements of it and conformity to it, but in our criticism of our own and others' deviation from it" (Hart 1994, 140). It would make no sense to claim that an action was unjustified simply because it went unquestioned. Nor would it be sensible to argue that the justification a person offered of their action could be written off simply because they might be lying. "Tests for whether a person has merely pretended ex post facto that he acted on a rule are, like all empirical tests, inherently fallible but they are not inveterately so" (140). Some further empirical premise would be required to justify that conclusion. In response, it appears that political realism can offer only the assumption that human nature is incorrigible and unfortunate. But this would seem to be too heavily freighted with normative content (dare one call it a violation of the quietist moratorium on moral theorizing?) to function well as an empirical premise of the sort required.

Realism in International Relations

International relations (IR) realism has found expression in variety of ways. In fact, this is probably more true of IR realism than it is of legal realism. Here we will focus on three constituent elements of IR realism; *statism, anarchism,* and *utilitarianism.* (Earlier in this chapter we briefly explored a fourth element, *positivism.*) Each of these elements is characterized not by a single definition, but by a range of meaning arising from its application.

Statism, at the most general level, is the view that international relations consists of the relationships among states. This can be asserted with varying degrees of force. In its most limited form, this can mean merely that states consider themselves to be the ultimate ends of international relations (Schwarzenberger 1951). In response to this, one can only observe that any egoist would make the same argument, and if statism is reduced to official egoism it seems at once less surprising, less interesting, and less important. At the other end of the spectrum, it is argued that state interests provide the spring of all international action (Waltz 1979). This formulation at least suggests that the state is the necessary and sufficient component in any explanation of international events. Between this point and official egoism there is an intermediate form of statism.

The intermediate formulation is that the state is the central, but not the sole, actor on the international stage (Frankel 1996; Keohane 1986). Additional content is provided to this view of statism through various observations and premises that can most accurately be characterized as sociological. There is, first, the idea that humans face one another primarily as members of groups (Schweller 1997). This view can be extended by adding the element of conflict. If social and political relations are inherently conflictual, then approaching these relations as a member of a group can be viewed as an adaptation with significant survival potential (Gilpin 1996). This would seem to be sufficient warrant for statism if we interpret that idea as embodying an assumption that the important unit of social life is the collectivity, and on the international level the most important collective actor is the state because these actors recognize no collectivity above them (Smith 1986).

Anarchism, like statism, has a range of possible meanings. At its simplest and least taxing, as an element of IR realism, it is nothing more than the assumption that states possess military capabilities that allow them to hurt one another if they choose to do so (Mearsheimer 1990, 1994–1995). Beyond this fundamental observation, one might add ideas associated with power. It is hard to dispute the fact that states tend to seek power and to calculate their interests in terms of power (Keohane 1986). No state can ever be certain that another state, even an ally, will not exploit its military weakness (Mearsheimer 1994–1995). The logical conclusion is that power relationships will be the fundamental feature of international affairs (Gilpin 1996). But many, if not most, realists take this line of thinking one step further.

If one adds to the fundamental importance of power in international relations the assumption of an ineradicable tendency toward evil (Smith 1986), an entirely new sense is given to the idea of anarchism. If conflict is an essential rather than contingent feature of international relations, then the realist should resist the temptation of identifying the moral aspirations of any particular nation with any universal moral laws that might be thought to govern the universe (Morganthau 1978). Indeed, if Morgenthau is correct in arguing that politics is governed by objective laws rooted in an essentially evil human nature, then politics is not and cannot be a function of ethics. Necessity and reasons of state will always trump morality, and the power of reason is so weak that humankind is incapable of transcending the international war of all against all (Schweller 1997). When this version of anarchism is appended to virtually any form of statism, utilitarianism becomes nearly unavoidable.

Utilitarianism is, to put it simply, the view that states participate in the international system as utility maximizers—they pursue their material power interests to the virtual exclusion of any other concerns. At the outset, the realist stipulates that the most basic motivation driving state behavior is survival (Mearsheimer 1994–1995). Realists assume that international relations can be understood by the rational analysis of competing state interests defined in terms of the constituent elements of state power (Smith 1986). The necessities involved in the pursuit of state power result from the unregulated competition of states over the resources that support the existence of power. Rational calculation based on an understanding of those resources and the means by which they are converted to competitive advantage allows state actors to plan their course of action and it allows observers of international affairs to predict those actions. Success of these actions is understood as strengthening and preserving the state, and success in those terms is the ultimate test of state policy (Waltz 1979).

If pursuit of power is as ubiquitous and inescapable as realists take it to be (Smith 1986), certain other views would seem to follow. From an analytical perspective, it would seem reasonable to conclude that theory does not lead to practice, but practice leads to theory. At the moral level, politics cannot be a function of ethics. Ethics must follow and serve politics (Carr 1946). All that there is to understand about the use of force in international relations is, therefore, its utility (Frankel 1996). This leads to the chilling conclusion that law and morality can never rise above the level of apologetics and that any action thought by a state to be necessary for its self-preservation is justified (Schwarzenberger 1951).

Few of realism's adherents are still willing to go so far. Most would readily concede that if the postwar tendency toward naïve idealism justified the cold shower of realism, it is now equally important to cool the overheated rhetoric of an unrestrained cynicism (Schwarzenberger 1951). A reflection of this moderation has been the move away from the "classical" realism of Morgenthau in the direction of the structuralist perspective of "neorealism" (Waltz 1979). Rather than seeing power as an end in itself, some neorealists "see power as a possibly useful means, with states running risks if they have either too little or too much of it" (Waltz 2008, 79). Other neorealists still see states relentlessly seeking power, not for its own sake but because the international system creates powerful incentives to do so "by taking advantage of those situations when the benefits outweigh the costs" (Mearsheimer 2001, 21). Perhaps the most significant implication of this trend is a reduced reliance on (or abandonment of) the concept of an incorrigible and negative human nature in favor of a perspective that locates the source of aggressiveness in the structure of the international system (Herz 1976). Neorealists have recognized that it is unhelpful for their analytical perspective to be viewed as an immoral doctrine that can be used to excuse the worst forms of violence humankind has so far devised (Gilpin 1986).

So where does this leave our critique of political realism? At a minimum, it raises a significant doubt about the usefulness of realism's core assumption regarding human nature. Moreover, it leaves us still in need of some perspective on the role played by pragmatism in the superstructure of political realism.

Pragmatism and the Nature of Humankind

If the realists in international relations have abandoned their commitment to the idea of an incorrigible and negative human nature, perhaps their reasons go beyond the obvious problems with their public image. The concept of human nature is exactly the kind of abstract object the reality of which realists wish to not affirm. It is, in their view, an atemporal, non-natural object comparable to the objects of mathematical knowledge (Katz 1998). A nominalist might well reply that "human nature" is merely a label for an indeterminate set of characteristics that we have observed in human behavior. So here we have again the very nearly eternal dispute among philosophers about what actually exists. Should our attitude about the abstract concept of human nature be "realist" or should it be "realistic"? We hasten to add, however, that this is not a dispute that we actually need to resolve, particularly if we, like IR realists, fancy ourselves to be pragmatists.

Returning to Leiter's formulation of political realism (which he characterized as "classical realism"), recall that he included pragmatism among realism's essential elements. Here we find pragmatism taken to be the view that "only theories which make a difference to practice are worth the effort: the effect or 'practical pay-off' is the relevant measure of value in theoretical matters" (Leiter 2001a, 245). The ability of neorealists in international relations to give up the abstract concept of human nature for a more theoretically useful and politically palatable focus on the influence of institutions betrays exactly this kind of pragmatism. Were he able to offer an opinion, we suggest that John Dewey would congratulate them for outgrowing a philosophical dispute we were never destined to resolve. The ontological status of international institutions is, of course, another matter for a future debate. But a consistently pragmatic approach would be fully able to shift our attention again if the structural focus of neorealism becomes cumbersome or simply outlives its usefulness.

The demise of human nature as an immutable object of our social terrain also offers a new perspective on the third element of realism identified by Leiter. Quietism, he suggested, was the only reasonable approach to theorizing that failed to respect what he took to be the incorrigible facts about human nature (Leiter 2001a). But if, as card-carrying pragmatists, we abandon the idea of immutable and determinative human nature, what do we have to be quiet about? Are we not free to "moralize" human nature as Habermas (2003a) has urged us to do?

Technological change in the fields of production and exchange, communication, and transportation, as well as our military and medical capabilities, have all required changes in normative regulation in support of the resulting social transformations. By enlarging the scope of human choice, science and technology have formed an evident alliance with the fundamental credo of political liberalism—that all citizens are entitled to an equal opportunity for autonomous direction of their own lives. These technical advances also create the social space in which we can achieve an ethical self-understanding of the species, allowing us to recognize others as autonomous persons who are the authors of their own life histories. Technological control of human nature (through genetic manipulation, behavior modification, and other techniques) is only the most recent man-ifestation of our persistent tendency to extend the range of our control over our natural environment (Habermas 2003a).

If our future is to be largely about continuously remaking our own na-ture, then "quietism" on the subject is singularly inappropriate. Moreover, the "naturalism" of classical realism has become a wholly inappropriate attitude, not because it is suddenly wrong but simply because it is no longer useful.

So the last man standing on political realism's team is pragmatism. The rest of realism turns out to be a set of questions that were never answer-able or useful. In the best pragmatist tradition, realism must outgrow them. If, however, pragmatism is to be our guide to a more human fu-ture, can it offer us a form of politics that is both robustly democratic and scalable? That is, can we deploy pragmatic realism on a global scale? To answer these questions, or even begin the process of answering them, it will be necessary to excavate the foundations of pragmatism in much the same way we have realism.

3

"Dewey Defeats Truman": Pragmatism versus Pluralism in Deliberative Democracy

Around 1990 the theory of democracy took a definite deliberative turn. Prior to that turn, the democratic ideal was seen mainly in terms of aggregation of preferences or interests into collective decisions through devices such as voting and representation. Under deliberative democracy, the essence of democratic legitimacy should be sought instead in the ability of all individuals subject to a collective decision to engage in authentic deliberation about that decision.
—John S. Dryzek, *Deliberative Democracy and Beyond*

The emergent theory of deliberative democracy holds many attractions for those who have grown frustrated with the limitations of interest-group liberalism. In the world imagined by deliberative theorists, the mechanisms and institutions of interest aggregation (voting, parties, interest groups) are to be supplemented by processes that allow for "genuinely thoughtful and discursive public participation in decision making." These new direct approaches to democracy, it is hoped, will lead to policies "more just and rational" than those produced by existing representative practices (Baber and Bartlett 2005, 3). But, as with democrats generally, deliberative democrats have often blunted their swords though disagreements among themselves.

Elsewhere we have cataloged many of the points of disagreement among deliberative democrats (Baber and Bartlett 2005). In doing so, we identified five conceptual dimensions that can be used to understand the issues at stake. These dimensions include

1. the prerequisites for successful political deliberation,
2. the style of reasoning appropriate to political deliberation,
3. the role of self-interest in political deliberation,
4. the role of experts in political deliberation, and, finally,
5. the standard of success for political deliberation.

Using this analytical scheme, we described three general models of deliberative democracy. These we have characterized as *full liberalism*, *ideal discourse*, and *public reason*.

In comparing these three models, one noteworthy observation is that deliberative democrats take different approaches to dealing with the underlying reality of political pluralism. As one might imagine, all deliberative democrats accept, indeed celebrate, the fact that modern democratic societies are highly pluralistic. But after the cheering dies away, the celebrants are left with a hangover in the form of a nagging doubt about how much pluralism a coherent political system actually can tolerate. To borrow a phrase from Habermas, pluralism presents the challenge of developing a pragmatics of social interaction that is appropriate to deliberative democracy (Habermas 2001c). The task is to specify a form of "communicative competence" (75) within which participants in deliberative discourse can put forward their claims and assess the claims of others. For Habermas, this competency is achieved when "the democratic procedure is institutionalized in discourses and bargaining processes by employing forms of communication that promise that all outcomes reached in conformity with the procedure are reasonable" (Habermas 1996, 304). According to Habermas, no one has worked out this view more energetically than John Dewey (304).

It is ironic that the deliberative democrat who has had the most to say about pragmatism generally, and about John Dewey in particular, is the German, Jürgen Habermas. Whereas John Rawls mentions Dewey only in two footnotes in *A Theory of Justice*, Habermas refers to Dewey repeatedly in at least eight of his major works. It might be that pragmatism is so much a part of the life-world of American philosophers that they hardly notice its influence anymore. But whatever the reason, the influence of pragmatism may well be the greatest underacknowledged debt owed by deliberative democrats. It may also be that a satisfactory resolution of the quandary of pluralism will continue to elude deliberative democrats until that debt is honored. We think it entirely likely that unless deliberative democrats, like IR realists, take more seriously their roots in pragmatism, a triumph of their ideas in the political world of policy and problem solving will elude them as well.

In pursuit of a more satisfactory understanding of the relationship of pragmatism to political realism, and a better account of the relationship between pragmatism and deliberative democracy, we will apply to the pragmatist approach to politics the same five-part analytical framework we used in our previous research. We will take John Dewey as our representative pragmatist because, as is well known, he had far more to say about politics than Charles Peirce or William James or Oliver Wendell Holmes Jr. We will then suggest how this pragmatist model can advance the deliberative agenda—reconciling differences among its advocates here, extending its reach there. But as a preliminary step, it will be useful to also apply our analytical framework to the practice of aggregative democracy, against which both Dewey's pragmatism and contemporary deliberative democracy can be seen as reactions. And as our avatar of aggregative democracy we take the foremost analyst of interest-group liberalism, David Truman.[4]

The Conceptual Structure of Aggregative Democracy

To take a single scholar as representative of so vast a literature as that associated with the idea that politics is about the aggregation of interests is, of course, unfair both to the chosen representative and to those others who are overlooked. There is, however, a practical reason for doing so. One of the recurring issues in the deliberative democratic literature is how to take account of pluralism, both as a social fact and as an organizing principle of politics and government. For example, various accounts of social pluralism have played an important role in the choices of deliberative theorists among the basic decision-threshold requirements of plurality rule, general consensus, and unanimity (Baber and Bartlett 2005). Yet in the form of interest-group liberalism, pluralism provides deliberative democrats a target for their criticisms of both the quality of political life and the performance of governing institutions. Thus the leading advocate of what he calls "strong democracy," Benjamin Barber has identified the interest-group scholarship of David Truman as the "modern locus classicus" for the pluralist model (Barber 2004, 144).

In applying our analytical framework to Truman's interest-group liberal theory of politics, certain allowances need to be made. For example, we have characterized our first point of comparison as the "prerequisites of successful political deliberation." Clearly, use of the term *deliberation* to describe the objective of politics is inconsistent with Truman's basic approach. We will, therefore, allow ourselves to describe the conceptual elements that constitute our framework in more general terms in this section than we have elsewhere.

Prerequisites for Successful Politics

For Truman, anyone active in politics is striving for power, either as a means in serving some other ends or for the satisfactions associated with the possession of power itself. The key prerequisite to success in this effort is the "development and improvement" of access to the "key points of decision" in government. These factors are the common denominators of the tactics of all interest groups (Truman 1951, 264). In order for this contest to proceed in an orderly way, any polity requires a set of "rules of the game" that are associated with some "minimal recognition" of the claims of other groups (524). That recognition results from the existence of others who are affected by one's actions and who are aware of those consequences. This awareness is "the basic attitude or opinion" necessary for the existence of an interest group (218). The existence of such a widespread "censoring and restraining" force might be taken as evidence of some "harmony in the body politic" (516). That assumption, however, would be unwarranted. In fact, without the multiple and conflicting memberships in actual and potential groups that characterize modern societies, "it is literally impossible to account for the existence of a viable polity such as that in the United States or develop a clear conception of the political process" (514). With reliable rules of engagement and a wide diversity of interest groups with which individuals can affiliate, neither shared cultural commitments nor equality of political resources are required for a successful political process to be sustained.

Appropriate Style of Reasoning

Is "reasoning" even an issue in interest-group politics? In a way, it is. In the practice of interest-group politics, manipulating the attitudes and opinions of others is the fundamental form of human interaction. Indeed, shared attitudes and opinions are the foundations upon which interest groups are built (Truman 1951, 33–34). The major ways political actors can manipulate the attitudes and opinions of others are through the use of economic power and propaganda. Economic power can be converted into political power only at a significant discount (258) and it is occasionally found to be illegal. So as a general matter, the preferred approach is propaganda. But political advantages in the area of propaganda are unstable for a variety of reasons (261). Understood as an attempt to control the behavior of others "by the manipulation of words and word substitutes," propaganda is inherently problematic. For example, the line between education and propaganda often seems entirely arbitrary. On the one hand, in

Truman's view, "to promote a favorable attitude toward individualism would be education in the United States, but propaganda in the Soviet Union." On the other hand, "to train people in the principles of aerodynamics would be education in both places." And lest some moral commitment to science should be assumed, the characteristic of aerodynamics that is important here is that it is "accepted by the society under examination" (223). In fact, "as a social process . . . propaganda is no more a matter of morals than is the process of buying and selling" (222). The reasoning involved in interest-group politics is, therefore, entirely strategic in character.

The Role of Self-Interest
In Truman's view, human behaviors and experiences "cannot even be described, much less accounted for, in isolation" (Truman 1951, 17). Human interests are, therefore, inescapably a group phenomenon. Moreover, no individual is "wholly absorbed" in any one group to which he belongs. Only a fraction of his attitudes are expressed through any one such affiliation (157). Accordingly, those involved in political activity pursue a diversity of interests, both personal and group (335). Interests, therefore, serve a variety of important roles in the political process. They form the basic motivations that bring people into the political process (47–52). They generate the shared attitudes and opinions that form the basis for group affiliations (16–23). And they create a network of cross-cutting and countervailing affiliations that give rise to the rules of the game (348–350). Self-interest, therefore, is the very essence of politics for the interest-group pluralist and it is a group phenomenon by its very nature.

The Political Role of Experts
For Truman, the role of the expert in politics is twofold. First, the very nature of contemporary political issues lends a special importance to the policy inputs originating in the scientific community. "The development of atomic power, the increasing recognition of the importance of basic research in all the sciences, and the increased importance of military considerations in American politics, to mention only a few changes, have combined to give organized scientists a greatly augmented political role" (Truman 1951, 64). This is not merely to say that expertise provides important bargaining chips for interest groups to whatever extent science lends empirical support to their respective arguments. Truman goes on to characterize the scientist as the "functional descendant" of the ancient

shaman. The activities of both shamans and scientists "consist of techniques for adjustment to the environment fully as much as do those of the farmer, the weaver, and the bricklayer." All of these occupations deploy skills that are "parts of different group patterns and their resulting attitudes and behavioral norms" that identify them as interest groups in themselves (26).

The Standard of Political Success

Interest-group politics does not have to produce grand syntheses. According to Truman, in developing a group interpretation of politics "we do not need to account for a totally inclusive interest, because one does not exist" (Truman 1951, 51). The great task of politics is what it always has been. It is to maintain the conditions under which a multiplicity of organized interests can pursue their objectives without undermining the viability of the governmental system (524). This is made easier by the fact that "violation of the rules of the game normally will weaken a group's cohesion, reduce its status in the community, and expose it to the claims of other groups" (513). There is no necessity to actually adjudicate the validity of competing group claims. Each can realize the benefits that their guile and resources provide. No particular level of agreement, among either groups or individuals, is required. It is necessary only that the contestants continue to play. And the game as a whole is intended only to produce a "dynamic stability" permitting an ongoing process of gradual adaptation that will avoid "domestic or international disasters" of such severity that they completely discredit the system (535).

Pragmatism as Democratic Theory

John Dewey has been described as a "halfway modernist" who "sensing the implications of modernism did everything possible to avoid its conclusions" (Diggins 1994, 5). Taken as a reaction to the modern world, modernism can be viewed as the consciousness of what we presume to have once had but now have lost. "Knowledge without truth, power without authority, society without spirit, self without identity, politics without virtue, existence without purpose, history without meaning" (8); these were the felt absences of Dewey's time. They are gaps between nature and spirit that philosophy has tried to bridge since before Plato, but that Dewey was convinced had no practical bearing in daily life. Problems such as these are ultimately abandoned precisely because they are not important to human concerns. "We do not solve them, we get over them" (Dewey 1973b, 41).

For Dewey, it is of special importance to the development of a decent form of politics that we get over problems of this sort. In his view, the harsh conditions of the predemocratic and prescientific world stemmed from two philosophical premises that lay behind the dualisms posed by modernism. These premises are that "the object of knowledge is some form of ultimate Being which is antecedent to reflective inquiry and independent of it" and that "this antecedent Being has among its defining characteristics those properties which alone have authority over the formation of our judgments of values" (Dewey 1929b, 69). Dewey's conception of truth serves as a refutation of these two premises—premises that unless overcome would prevent us from realizing his vision of a unique individualism with a distinctive moral element. In contrast to Truman and others who obsess about pluralism, Dewey's primary commitment is to the integrity and inherent value of the *individual*. He would not count as a bargain any politics that does violence to the integrity and inherent value of the individual even if it comes wrapped in democratic clothing (which is all elections and universal suffrage necessarily are). Creating relatively open public institutions and securing the vote for all adults, admirable as these accomplishments are, will not serve our needs fully because, alone, they do not promote an individualism that expresses equality and freedom "not merely externally and politically but through personal participation in the development of a shared culture" (Dewey 1929a, 119). This fundamental concern is the backdrop against which Dewey's approach to our five points of comparison can best be understood.

The Prerequisites of Successful Deliberation

The challenges to achieving a successful democracy are, in Dewey's view, "not solved, hardly more than externally touched, by the establishment of universal suffrage and representative government" (Dewey [1935] 2000, 39). These are certainly important preconditions for democracy, but they are far from sufficient. Popular government may have been successful in creating a form of democratic public spirit, but its "success in informing that spirit" has not so far been great (Dewey [1927] 1954, 207). Any liberalism that "intends to be a vital force" has as its primary work "first of all education, in the broadest sense of that term" (Dewey [1935] 2000, 63). The challenge to democracy then becomes extending that form of organization "to all the areas and ways of living, in which the powers of individuals shall not be merely released from mechanical external constraint but shall be fed, sustained and directed" (40). To say that the first object of a renascent liberalism is education is to indicate that its task is to "aid in producing the habits of mind and character, the intellectual and moral patterns, that are somewhere near even with the actual movements of events" (65–66). This task has dimensions that are individual, social, and institutional.

The individualism inherent in the American approach to democracy has often been viewed as problematic. From the concerns of *The Federalist* papers through those of the public choice theorist, an excessive preoccupation with the individual has been taken to be a practical obstacle to effective government (H. Richardson 2002). Dewey, on the other hand, is unprepared to sacrifice anything of the individual to the collective. He goes so far as to suggest that the choice we are offered between individual and collective interests is a false one. After all, Dewey reminds us, "all valuable as well as new ideas begin with minorities, perhaps a minority of one" (Dewey [1927] 1954, 208). Beyond the level of the individual, liberalism has to "assume the responsibility for making it clear that intelligence is a social asset . . . clothed with a function as public as its origin" in concrete social cooperation (Dewey [1935] 2000, 70). The importance of this task goes beyond merely laying claim to the advantages that cooperative inquiry offers. It provides an important form of protection for freedom of inquiry itself. "As long as freedom of thought and speech is claimed merely as individual right, it will give way, as do other merely personal claims, when it is, or is successfully represented to be, in opposition to the general welfare" (69). Just as our collective success is dependent upon our success as individuals, individuals cannot succeed in isolation. The power of thought "frees us from servile subjection to instinct, appetite, and routine, it also brings with it the occasion and possibility of error and mistake" (Dewey [1910] 1997, 19). All the fear and lack of confidence that gather about our own thoughts, "cluster also about the thought of the actions in which we are partners" (Dewey 1929b, 6). Resolution of these doubts is, obviously, a collective endeavor, requiring a particular form of reasoning.

The Style of Reasoning Appropriate to Deliberation

To learn to be fully human, in Dewey's view, is to "develop through the give-and-take of communication an effective sense of being an individually distinctive member of a community; one who understands and appreciates its beliefs, desires and methods, and who contributes to a further conversion of organic powers into human resources and values" (Dewey [1927] 1954, 154). The advent of modern democracy has made this process "primarily and essentially an intellectual problem, in a degree to which the political affairs of prior ages offer no parallel" (154). The pressing need of democracy is the "improvement of the methods and conditions of debate, discussion and persuasion . . . freeing and perfecting the processes of inquiry and of dissemination" of the conclusions reached (208). This can be accomplished by applying "the method of discrimination, of test by verifiable consequences . . . in all the matters, of large and of detailed scope, that arise for judgment" (Dewey [1935] 2000, 40).[5]

Dewey focuses on the collaborative and participatory character of science more than on the particulars of its methodology. What is important is that "we shall discriminate between beliefs that rest upon tested evidence and those that do not, and shall be accordingly on our guard as to the kind and degree of assent yielded" (Dewey [1910] 1997, 27). What is required is "approximation to use of scientific method in investigation and of the engineering mind" in our collective "invention and projection of far-reaching social plans" (Dewey [1935] 2000, 75). It is not necessary for Dewey that "the many should have the knowledge and skill to carry on the needed investigation" but, rather, that they "have the ability to judge of the bearing of the knowledge supplied by others upon common concerns" (Dewey [1927] 1954, 209). The role of the public, is, therefore, to yield its assent to the conclusions that have been drawn by communities of scholars consistent (in the general view) with the cannons of their respective disciplines. Given the proper education, Dewey thought all citizens capable of becoming democratic experimentalists "who would see to it that the method depended upon by all in some degree in every democratic community be followed through to completion" (Dewey [1935] 2000, 81).

The Role of Self-Interest in Deliberation

To understand how so well-educated and widely experienced a person as Dewey could be so optimistic about democracy, it is essential to appreciate his views about self-interest, expertise, and the relationship between the two. According to Dewey, "majority rule, just as majority rule, is as foolish as its critics charge it with being. But it never is merely majority rule" (Dewey [1927] 1954, 207). The driving force behind our collective activities is, of course, personal. But in that there is reason for neither shame nor pessimism. The problem bears the seeds of its solution. After all, it is the interactive effects of people pursuing their self-interests that create the public. It is the "indirect, extensive, enduring and serious consequences of conjoint and interacting behavior" that calls into existence a "public having a common interest in controlling these consequences" (126). And this public is more than merely social.

All interactions among individuals are social in character. But the public carries with it an inherent problematique, an awareness of the need for co-ordination of activity and reconciliation of difference. In other words, public activity is more than mere interaction. It is a form of problem solving (Dewey [1927] 1954, 12–17). The method of democracy, understood as that of "organized intelligence," is to bring the conflicts among interests into the open where their "special claims can be discussed and judged in the light of more inclusive interests" than are represented by any of them separately (Dewey [1935] 2000, 81). Popular government, therefore, can be understood as a form of collective inquiry. It is "educative as other modes of political regulation are not. It forces a recognition that there are common interests, even though the recognition of what they are is confused; and the need it enforces of discussion and publicity brings about some clarification of what they are" (Dewey [1927] 1954, 207). Self-interest is not, therefore, an evil to be avoided. It provides the motivation, agenda, and raw material for public interaction in a participatory democracy.

The Role of Experts in Deliberation

If it is our objective to develop a fully participatory democracy, its citizens in constant pursuit of a consensus regarding those beliefs warranted by the facts, what role should we imagine for scientists and other technical experts? For many democrats, deliberative and otherwise, the very topic of the expert's role in political decision making creates unease (often bordering on queasiness). In the modern age, they sense that "rule by experts," lurks around every corner. They may, in fact, be correct. One does not have to lose sleep over the military-industrial complex to worry that we may trade away too much of our democracy for the effectiveness that experts offer. Dewey shared these concerns. "No government by experts," he argued, "can be anything but an oligarchy managed in the interests of the few." The masses must always have "the chance to inform the experts as to their needs" (Dewey [1927] 1954, 208). This is more than a gesture in the democratic direction; it is an epistemic necessity.

Any class of experts, regardless of their disciplinary foundation, inevitably becomes so "removed from common interests as to become a class with private interests and private knowledge, which in social matters is no knowledge at all" (Dewey [1927] 1954, 207). Expertise is most readily attained in "specialized technical matters, matters of administration and execution which postulate that general policies are already satisfactorily framed." In light of the fact that experts become a specialized class, "shut off from knowledge of the needs they are supposed to serve" (206), their role at the macrolevel of policy cannot be great. In a participatory democracy, "expertness is not shown in framing and executing policy, but in discovering and making known the facts upon which the former depend" (208). The challenge for experts is "no longer merely technological applications for increase of material productivity, but imbuing the minds of individuals with a spirit of reasonableness, fostered by social organization and contributing to its development" (Dewey [1935] 2000, 39). It is not, therefore, an act of anti-intellectualism for citizens to question or even reject the input of experts. It is not necessary that the many should have the knowledge and skill to carry out the necessary inquiries. It is sufficient that they have "the ability to judge of the bearing of the knowledge supplied by others upon common concerns" (Dewey [1927] 1954, 209).

The Standard of Success for Deliberation

For what might advocates of deliberative democracy reasonably hope? Is democracy nothing more than an expedient, a rationalization for the strong to assert themselves? Or does nature itself, as it is uncovered and understood by our best methods of inquiry, sustain and support our aspirations for something more? For Dewey, democracy is "a wider and fuller idea than can be exemplified in the state even at its best" (Dewey [1927] 1954, 143). From the standpoint of the individual, democracy consists in having a "responsible share according to capacity in forming and directing the activities of the groups to which one belongs and in participating according to need in the values which the groups sustain." From the standpoint of interest groups, democracy involves the liberation of the potentialities of members of the group "in harmony with the interests and goods which are common" (147). So democracy is about empowerment of citizens both as individuals and as members of the myriad groups in which they affiliate. The free give-and-take that democratic politics offers is valued because of the "fullness of integrated personality" that it promises (148). Moreover, when viewed as an expression of social intelligence, democracy addresses our need to unite "earlier ideas of freedom with an insistent demand for social organization" and to achieve a "constructive synthesis in the realm of thought and social institutions" (Dewey [1935] 2000, 39).

But what threshold should we require ourselves to reach? Is it sufficient, as the interest-group liberal might argue, to achieve a stable governing coalition that perpetuates the social and economic system? Or should we join with the most demanding of the deliberative democrats and hold out for unanimity based upon what we regard as correct reasons? The appropriate objective of democracy at the level of the individual is, for Dewey, relatively easy to describe. It is to "develop through the give-and-take of communication an effective sense of being an individually distinctive member of a community; one who understands and appreciates its beliefs, desires and methods, and who contributes to a further conversion of organic powers into human resources and values" (Dewey [1927] 1954, 154). But what hurdle must the polity clear for its decisions to deserve the label "democratic"? The only answer that can reasonably be formulated is likely to leave many unsatisfied.

For Dewey, democracy is a search for consensus but "consensus demands communication" (Dewey [1916] 1944, 5). Whenever our participatory processes fall short of achieving the necessary level of consensus, there is no alternative but to hold to our method and to continue our inquiry. It is in this sense that Dewey famously observed that "the cure for the ailments of democracy is more democracy" (Dewey [1944] 1916, 146). Persistence in the methods of participatory democracy is justified by the fact that it is simple defeatism to "assume in advance of actual trial" that such methods are incapable of "either further development or of constructive social application" (Dewey [1935] 2000, 86). Simple majority rule is, of course, an important improvement on the various oligarchies of the past. But to satisfy ourselves with that is to make "the better . . . the enemy of the still better" (73). The further improvements in democratic inquiry that Dewey envisions are both institutional and individual.

Concluding that the existing level of social intelligence is insufficient to our common tasks is unreasonable until "secrecy, prejudice, bias, misrepresentation, and propaganda as well as sheer ignorance are replaced by inquiry and publicity" (Dewey [1927] 1954, 209). This obviously requires both ongoing reform of the processes of democratic inquiry and continued education of the public for political participation. As long as the communication processes of democratic inquiry continue, "all natural events are subject to reconsideration and revision; they are readapted to meet the requirements of conversation, whether it be public discourse or that preliminary discourse termed thinking" (Dewey [1929] 1958, 132). It is unwarranted ever to admit that we have failed to achieve understanding as long as this kind of communication can be sustained. Moreover, education of citizens for democratic inquiry is never complete. The "unregenerate element" in humanity persists. It shows itself whenever the methods of coercion replace the "method of communication and enlightenment." It manifests itself "more subtly, pervasively and effectually" when the "knowledge and instrumentalities of skill which are the produce of communal life" are employed in the service of interests "which have not themselves been modified by reference to a shared interest" (Dewey [1927] 1954, 154–155). So there is no threshold for success in deliberation because the deliberative project is never finished: a commitment to its process is its product. And, as with democracy, the cure for what ails deliberation is more deliberation.

The Pragmatic Value of Pragmatism

What lessons of practical value might a deliberative democrat draw from subjecting pragmatism to this exercise in philosophical taxonomy? The benefits of exploring the rich relationships between pragmatism and deliberative democracy are limited only by the energy and imagination of democratic theorists. But we would be remiss if we did not at least indicate what we take to be some particularly fruitful lines of continued investigation. These we associate with the ideas of truth, consensus, and scalability.

Truth
The contemporary pragmatist Richard Rorty (1995) poses the question, is truth a goal of inquiry? Rorty admits to having swung back and forth between "trying to reduce truth to justification and propounding some form of minimalism about truth." The *reductionist* view would deny that asserting something to be true is a rather unimpressive claim. It is merely to say that a proposition can legitimately be asserted as the result of some identifiable process of inquiry (Rorty 1995, 282). The *minimalist*, on the other hand, might account for our use of the term *truth* as follows. All of our propositional utterances share a "fundamentally rational pattern" that all rational creatures must share. This rational pattern makes "the same pattern as truth makes, and the same pattern that meaning makes. You cannot have language without rationality, nor either without truth"

(284). So in the minimalist view, all one claims when one characterizes an assertion as true is that it comports with the manner in which the terms comprising it are properly used.

We assume, with Rorty, that nearly a century of analytic philosophy has moved us beyond the idea that there is a mind-independent truth, the measure of which is the correspondence of our ideas to an unmediated external reality. So which of these pragmatic theories of truth is now to be preferred? The reductionist view would be consistent with Peirce's view that reasoned inquiry had little to say about morality, politics, and "all that relates to the conduct of life" (Peirce [1898] 1997, 29). For Peirce, truth was that opinion "which is fated to be ultimately agreed to by all who investigate" it and "the object represented in this opinion is the real" (45). This theory of truth limits our use of that concept to an ideal situation in which all investigators are members of an epistemic community, the archetype of which is modern empirical science. Dewey referred specifically to this formulation as "the best definition of truth from the logical standpoint which is known to me" (Dewey 1938, 345). Yet Dewey had more to say about truth.

Without ever adopting William James's language about truth having a cash value, Dewey showed far more interest than did Peirce in truth as a lived experience. Dewey illustrates his approach to truth in a discussion of knowledge as intention. Choosing an example that hardly seems coincidental, he says that knowledge of hunting dogs is essential for one who intends to hunt with hounds. But there is a difference between "knowledge of the dog, *qua* knowledge," and the use of that knowledge in the "fulfillment experience" of the hunt. For Dewey, "the hunt is a *realization* of knowledge; it alone . . . verifies, validates, knowledge or supplies tests of truth" and "makes faith good in works" (Dewey 1973a, 180). What faith does our "hunt" redeem? The confidence in our knowledge of hounds, perhaps. But more important, the hunt itself is a form of redemption. The hunt can be seen as an expression of faith that there exists something out there for us capture. "The fulfilling experience is not knowledge itself" (181). The tests of truth or falsity present themselves as significant facts "only in situations in which specific meanings and their already experienced fulfillments . . . are intentionally compared and contrasted with reference to the question of the worth, as to reliability of meaning, of the given meaning or class of meanings" (185).

Rorty would recognize Dewey's emphasis on truth as a function of meaning. It speaks of the minimalist position in which Rorty eventually finds himself. But it does not reduce our inquiry (our hunt) to a nominalist exercise in parsing language. Neither is the search for truth a solitary enterprise. After all, one unsuccessful day of hunting tells us very little. We do not need to question our knowledge of dogs or our choice of hunting grounds merely because we caught nothing today. But if our entire hunting party is frustrated day after day, we must consider the faith we have taken to the field. A consultation among the hunters is in order. The same logic applies to our hunt for solutions to problems confronting our democracy. It is not necessary that each of us should have all the "knowledge and skill to carry on the needed investigations" but, rather, that we have "the ability to judge of the bearing of the knowledge supplied by others upon common concerns" (Dewey [1927] 1954, 209). As with any hunt, a consensus among the members of the party is more likely to be correct than any individual's intuition. This certainly places us at a great remove from the aggregative democrat's struggle for minimum winning coalitions among interests defined entirely in terms of the self. But how seriously must we take this notion of consensus?

Consensus
Elsewhere we have noted that deliberative democrats take a variety of positions on the question of how nearly we must approach unanimity for collective decisions to be legitimate. Theorists we have characterized as advocates of "full liberalism" would require plurality rule with an acceptance on the part of the minority of the fairness of the underlying decision process, as evidenced by their acquiescence in the result and their willingness to continue in deliberation. Habermas is more demanding. He requires that deliberations produce a wider general consensus based upon reasons that are shared among those participating in an ideal discourse situation (where participants yield only to the force of the better argument). Yet Habermas does not go so far as Rawls, who insists on unanimity based upon reasons that are not only shared but also right, in that they satisfy the condition of being fully public and comport with our shared principles of justice. But both Habermas and Rawls go beyond the point of full liberalism, agreeing that something approaching unanimity based upon something beyond private interest is necessary for decisions to be both democratic and legitimate (Baber and Bartlett 2005, 29–58).

What might pragmatism do to help us bridge, or at least better understand, this disagreement among deliberative democrats? Recall that both

Peirce and Dewey take as their model for reasoned inquiry the practices of modern science. They view truth (or its nearest approximation to which we can reasonably aspire) to be the product of collaborative investigation. They appear to differ, however, on how large a community of minds can be involved in that inquiry. Whereas Peirce is far from sanguine about the intellectual potential of average citizens, Dewey regards training in both the substance and methods of science and the procedures of democratic politics to be essential for everyone. For Dewey, any education that failed to include such training would also fail to "acknowledge the full intellectual and social meaning of a vocation." For democracy to flourish, every citizen requires an education that includes "instruction in the historic background of present conditions; training in science to give intelligence and initiative in dealing with material and agencies of production; and study of economics, civics, and politics, to bring the future worker in touch with the problems of the day and the various methods proposed for its improvement" (Dewey [1916] 1944, 318). More important still, vocational education would provide citizens the "power of readaptation to changing conditions so that future workers would not become blindly subject to a fate imposed upon them" (319).

Dewey's emphasis on the intimate and essential relationship between democracy and education is evidence of his belief that full participation in every aspect of our collective existence is the birthright of every individual. It is also evidence of the extent to which Dewey regards democracy as a face-to-face proposition. American democracy, Dewey observes, was "developed out of genuine community life . . . the township or some not much larger area was the political unit, the town meeting the political medium, and roads, schools, the peace of the community were the political objectives" (Dewey [1927] 1954, 111). Political life in this style is the form of democracy that Dewey believed was educative. Through such give-and-take, we learn to be fully human by developing "an effective sense of being an individually distinctive member of a community" (154). This view runs counter to a tendency among deliberative democrats to move away from the small-group techniques associated with deliberative polling and various forms of participatory local planning. These face-to-face procedures are often regarded as limited in the range of their application, a complaint to which we shall return. More troubling, however, is the allegation that the immediacy of this form of deliberation places at a disadvantage those who have been isolated historically and are, as a result, less able to assert themselves in heterogeneous groups.

This last criticism, pressed most insistently by those known collectively as *difference democrats*, might actually be said to prove Dewey's point. If in any political community there are minorities of the population who have historically been disenfranchised, it is likely that the method of their oppression has been exclusion from the processes of "converting organic powers into human resources and values" (Dewey [1927] 1954, 154), which are the very business of the political community. If our communities are ever to be guided by a "genuinely shared interest in the consequences of interdependent activities" (155), the politics of those communities must be fully participatory and the decisions they reach consensual. This insight helps us make sense of Habermas's declaration that "truth is public" (Habermas 1971, 100). It is not only the interest of the minority that is at stake. So too is the accuracy of the process of inquiry itself, which depends upon the effective participation of the entire community. It makes no more sense to exclude or excuse members of minority groups from the discursive rigors of deliberative democracy than it would to leave them out of the jury process or alter its essential character for the sake of their comfort. That truth that results from the involvement of all serves the legitimate and genuine interests of all.

To return to the problems of applying face-to-face methods of deliberation beyond the level of the local community, this is a challenge to which Dewey was fully attentive. Dewey, it is true, claimed that "democracy begins at home, and its home is the neighborly community" which must always remain "a matter of face-to-face intercourse" (Dewey [1927] 1954, 213, 211). But he was fully aware that democrats would accomplish little if their insights proved worthless when one traveled from one town (or state, or nation) to another. Happily enough, however, there is a silver lining to the cloud of scalability. Since the foundation of genuine democracy is in the local community, there is no difference in principle between transferring our democratic insights to the national level and deploying them internationally. Neither task is easy. But our success in achieving the former, whatever its extent, should give us grounds for hope about the latter.

Scalability

If, when we think of deliberative democracy, we think only about planning cells in Germany, policy juries in Britain, or watershed partnerships in the U.S. Pacific Northwest, we will have trouble imagining how international politics can ever be genuinely democratic. It is quite true that the deliberative mechanisms and approaches with which we are most familiar have been developed primarily at the local level. Dewey would tell us, of course, that this is neither surprising nor is it grounds for pessimism. He, too, recognized that "for the world's peace it is necessary that we understand the peoples of foreign lands." He went on to wonder, however, how well we truly understand those next door to us. The chances of our regard for distant peoples being effective seemed remote to Dewey where there is no close community experience "to bring with it insight and understanding of neighbors" (Dewey [1927] 1954, 213).

Our eventual success in globalizing deliberative democracy depends at least as much on our expectations as it does our choice of deliberative mechanisms. To expect that the global community will approach atmospheric warming in the same intensely participatory way as loggers and environmentalists might collaborate to manage the resources of a single river basin is obviously unreasonable.[6] But the collaboration of interested parties in resolving specific political disputes is neither the only nor necessarily the best model for deliberative democracy. Indeed, many theorists have begun to wonder whether the disinterestedness of the policy jury might not be preferable to negotiations among stakeholders. If this question is posed at the national and international level, interesting possibilities are opened.

As an example, deliberative polling in the United States and policy juries in Europe have tended to ask participants to formulate broad-ranging positions on specific policy questions. An example is By the People, a citizen deliberation project of local organizations, PBS stations, community colleges, and MacNeil/Lehrer Productions, staged around the United States to discuss such issues as health care, education, and the future of the Social Security program (By the People 2005). Participants in jury-sized groups read preliminary material, listen to expert presentations, and discuss various policy alternatives with one another. There is no particular attempt to get participants to reconcile, or even to recognize, the underlying normative differences that lead to their divergent preferences. The choice among general policy alternatives is more important than any consensus on values that might (or might not) support that outcome.

Imagine, however, a situation in which deliberative juries were presented with a hypothetical (but concrete) dispute and were then asked to produce a decision for one of the parties to that dispute. The jury would be required only to produce a concise general statement in support of their ruling, in much the same way that an administrative law judge explains his or her regulatory decision. One such ruling would be an interesting, perhaps fascinating, curiosity. A hundred decisions of this sort would constitute a useful database on the normative issue captured by the hypothetical. Add a few hundred more decisions, spread across many communities, and you would have the raw material necessary for an analytical exercise such as the restatements produced by the American Law Institute that capture and organize the normative consensus we generally refer to as the common law.

If analytical work of this sort were done, and done well, there would be nothing to prevent administrative law judges from looking to the results as persuasive authority in their rulings (both adjudicatory and rule making) on actual policy questions. The implementation of those rulings by policy experts in government would then be guided, for the first time, by normative premises of a distinctly democratic pedigree. Here we have a model for integrating popular wisdom of direct and participatory politics with the analytical capacities of epistemic communities in a way that Dewey might well recognize as a next step in the evolution of democracy.

Dewey or Don't We?

Notice that the model we have described can be implemented at any level of government, from the local to the global. At the national level, this approach answers to the general description of "decentered democracy" provided by James Bohman. In his view, modern democracies are becoming decentered along two different dimensions, "at the microdimension of the sort of processes that constitute decision making and at the macrodimension of the scale of interlocking levels of governance from cities to regions, to global society" (Bohman 2004b, 39; 2004a). At the international level, this form of democracy is consistent with Anne-Marie Slaughter's concept of the disaggregated state system. In this account, the world increasingly consists of governments "with all the basic institutions that perform the basic functions of government—legislation, adjudication, implementation—interacting both with each other domestically and also with their foreign and supranational counterparts" (Slaughter 2004, 5). As both Bohman and Slaughter have pointed out, one of the essential facts about globalization is that it reduces the practical value of state sovereignty in myriad ways. This can either undermine our control over the forces of production and distribution, as many fear it will, or it can enhance our ability to choose our own fate, as Dewey hoped one day we would. At the very least, distinguishing these two alternate futures gives us a finer appreciation of all that is at stake in our choice between a democracy that is merely aggregative and one that is genuinely deliberative.

At this point, however, one might reasonably ask how important it is for us to choose between a future politics of aggregation and one of deliberation. Could we not continue indefinitely with the "better than average" results that interest-group liberalism provides? Is there no risk with the direction that pragmatism and deliberative democracy propose that we take? To answer these questions, and relate them more clearly to the problems of international norm building, it will be helpful to summarize the argument we have made to this point.

The pragmatist foundations of deliberative democracy rest upon three basic insights. First, both Dewey and contemporary deliberative theorists have recognized that a certain level of agnosticism is helpful in human affairs. Whether they opt for Rawls's veil of ignorance, the restrictions of Habermas's ideal speech situation, or some variation of these, deliberative democrats would agree that the idea of truth as something one brings to a conversation makes less sense than the idea of truth as something that results from conversation. Where Dewey advanced what he referred to as a "coherence" theory of truth and Habermas prefers the term *consensus*, they would have agreed that truth is not the correspondence of our thinking to some external absolute. Rather, we can most intelligently regard as true those ideas that cohere in a system of ideas that achieves our intentions. This approach to the subject places in philosophical context the commitment to intellectual growth and an experiential style of reasoning that we have discussed here.

Second, both pragmatism and deliberative democracy share a common view of language and its use. For Dewey, our use of language, our ascription of meaning to utterances, was an instrumental issue. He argued that "to find out what facts, just as they stand, mean, is the object of all discovery; to find out what facts will carry out, substantiate, support a given meaning, is the object of all testing (Dewey [1910] 1997, 116). Carrying the insight further, Habermas has suggested that our use of language evidences a number of different intentions. Although it is true that we often use language in an attempt to represent reality to one another, language is a product of that intention, not a feature of reality. We also use language to establish and assess the legitimacy of interpersonal relations as well as to disclose to others the elements of our own subjectivity

(Habermas 1979). This instrumental view of language, which Rorty has characterized as antirepresentationalism, leads to an understanding of inquiry that emphasizes a continual process of "recontextualization" rather than an ever-closer approximation to reality (Rorty 1991). This attitude is most clearly evident in the pragmatist intention toward the development of ever more inclusive concepts of our shared interests and an approach to discourse that makes use of, but does not defer to, assertions of expert knowledge.

Finally, pragmatism and deliberative democracy share a common view of law and its purposes. Dewey observed that the laws of the state are "misconceived when they are viewed as commands (Dewey [1927] 1954, 53). Law, he argued, is the result not of sovereign authorship but of "widely distributed consequences, which, when they are perceived, create a common interest and the need of special agencies to care for it" (54). As Holmes warned, law is not a formal system of logic but, rather, an organic product of our shared experiences (Holmes [1881] 1991). This formulation is suggestive of Habermas's (1996) later description of law as having the character of both a fact (consisting in the institutions of its interpretation and enforcement) and a norm (deriving from a commitment to the shared interest that gave rise to it). This approach encourages us to accept, indeed embrace, the "large arbitrary and contingent element" in law as well as law's "plausible identification with reason" as a limit to those troubling elements (Dewey [1927] 1954, 55). This perspective lends a clearer sense to the pragmatist view that the measure of success in all of our deliberative inquiries is a continuing tendency toward higher levels of consensus.

These three philosophical elements (a coherence theory of truth, an antirepresentationalist view of language, and an antiformalist approach to law) are the philosophical bedrock of both pragmatism and deliberative democracy. But Dewey's liberal reformism and prophecies of social progress are not the only possible products of these philosophical positions. As Rorty has pointed out, Martin Heidegger came out of the same starting blocks, turned right instead of left, and dreamt far different dreams than those of Dewey and the deliberative democrats (Rorty 1999). The problem with pragmatism's starting points is that they appear to offer no syllogism, no process of argument, which takes us inevitably away from totalitarianism and toward reform liberalism. Pragmatists appear to be divided on what we should do about this. Some, like Peirce and Rorty, seem to conclude that pragmatism as a philosophy is a useful theory of truth and inquiry, but can ultimately tell us little about moral and political issues. Others, like Dewey and Hilary Putnam, argue that pragmatism can (and must) guide us in our ethical commitments (H. Putnam 2004). Their imperative tone can, we believe, be traced to a concern that Richard Wolin described as the "intellectual romance with fascism" (R. Wolin 2004).

The victory of fascism over socialism throughout much of fin-de-siècle Europe is difficult to understand if it is regarded only as a matter of brute force, although it certainly was that in part. By the time Hitler stormed onto the world stage, the people of Europe had been subjected to a parade of economic dislocations and political debacles that left them groping for an escape from the social decadence and institutional decay they perceived, which were then compounded by the trauma of World War I. What they lacked, it has been argued, was a language that gave the term *good* a use more rigorous than it got in the phrase "good taste"—a language in which questioning the decisions of their political leaders was no longer a meaningless exercise (Janik and Toulmin 1973). This insight suggests that it would be unfair to attribute the rise of fascism solely to a lack of moral character and sloppy thinking on the part of average Europeans. The leadership of the left also shares some of the responsibility as a consequence of its inability to enunciate a sufficiently persuasive counterargument. Where socialism offered the abstractions of internationalism and class consciousness, *national* socialism offered the far more concrete and familiar solidarity of state and ethnic affiliation. Moreover, where socialists actually took control of governmental institutions, their willingness to play the game of parliamentary politics betrayed them to radicals of both the right and the left as false prophets of revolution (R. Wolin 2004).

What does all of this tell us about our current situation and the prospects for developing an international jurisprudence that would be both democratic in character and effective in use? One might argue that, as a century ago, we face our own fin-de-siècle. Starting with Vietnam and continuing through Watergate to the debacle in Iraq, we have witnessed what seems to be the unraveling of what had been a reasonably democratic and competent collection of governmental institutions. Add to that the mounting economic pressures resulting from globalization and the immense gulf between today's super-rich and the average citizen, and you create the conditions for a level of social and political disquiet that pollsters routinely measure and report. Then comes the terrorist. Although no one would argue that the events of September 11, 2001, were as traumatic for America as World War I was for Europe, the timing was equally unfortunate. Is it any wonder, then, that Americans seem to want to relate to the rest of the world primarily in military terms, and the politics of ethnocentrism and xenophobia are on the rise? Where in all of this is there room for an approach to political will formation that does more than merely aggregate interests and divvy up the spoils?

Pragmatism's answer to these questions is a politics that is decentralized and experimental. It asks of citizens that they confront problems with universal implications, but not that they do so in ways that are abstract or deprive them of the context within which their languages have meaning. It allows for a form of discourse that includes both rigorous argument and the kind of inspirational storytelling that may take us beyond where argument alone can reach (Rorty 1989). Pragmatism offers an approach to politics within which it would be no less remarkable that nation-states tolerated meaningful forms of international government than that they provided for effective institutions of provincial and local government. If politics is "recontextualized" (to borrow Rorty's term) as problem solving rather than competition, the way is open for a democratic experimentalism that will provide us with both the rigorous arguments we need to test each other's policy preferences and the stories we need to tell each other in order to keep the world turning left instead of right.

In short, what pragmatism offers on the global level is the possibility of a grounded, bottom-up approach to international law, policy, and politics: an experimental perspective that gets beyond setting up questions based on false dichotomies such as liberalism (idealism) versus realism, questions of the type that Dewey suggests we outgrow rather than try to answer. The potential of any such pragmatic realism will, however, require us to confront, rather than merely assume away, some deeply held mental constructs about nation-states, democratic institutions, and law. We turn to the first of these next.

4

International Environmental Jurisprudence: Conceptual Elements and Options

A conceptual inquiry into any subject is necessarily a battle with and about words and the ways in which they have been used. This is certainly true of our present endeavor. Our premise is that in the field of international law our understanding of the world around us and our options for living within that world have been limited by our own language and the mental constructs that our language is used to represent. This is more than a matter of quibbling over words (though it may sometimes seem to be that as well). There are mental constructs, valid and useful within certain parameters, that have been distorted in ways that prevent us from gaining a clear understanding of both the challenges and opportunities of globalization. So our project is similar to, though far less expansive than, the task undertaken by John Locke in his *Essay Concerning Human Understanding* (Locke [1689] 1952). Locke characterized himself in that volume as an "under labourer" who was content in "clearing the ground a little, and removing some of the rubbish that lies in the way to knowledge" (89).

Perhaps the most important thing for any underlaborer to do is to accurately identify the underbrush that should be removed. The conceptual obstacles to a more useful (and hopeful) understanding of international law that primarily concern us are four of the constituent elements of the realist school of international relations that we identified in chapter 2:

Statism—the idea that nation-states are the only significant actors on the world stage.
Anarchism—the notion that there is and can be no over-arching normative order in international affairs.
Utilitarianism—the view that nation-states always, and to the exclusion of all else, pursue their own material interests.

Positivism—the assumption that law is the authoritative pronouncement of governmental institutions backed up by the use or threat of coercive force.

These general concepts pose at least three important problems. First, they discourage the growth of a fuller transboundary understanding of the problems that confront humankind. As an example, state court judges in the United States automatically canvass the case law of sister states for solutions to the adjudicatory challenges they confront, but they ignore even so close a geographic and cultural neighbor as Canada (Abrahamson and Fischer 1997).

Second, when combined with the emergence of global challenges to human survival and the growing insistence that governments be responsible to those for whom they act, the conceptual straitjacket of realism imposes on us what Anne-Marie Slaughter has characterized as the "trilemma" of global governance (Slaughter 2004, 10). We are confronted with the need for effective rules of global governance, enforced by government actors who do not possess the power of centralized government, held accountable by democratic political institutions that do not exist.

Third, the conceptual framework of realism disempowers ordinary people by radically distancing them from the reality of international politics. It is often considered a social duty, or even a moral duty, to be informed about world events, in spite of the fact that no one is expected to do anything about them. This apparent contradiction can be traced to the fact that our knowledge of the world is typically superficial and emotionally charged, due to the manner of its presentation (Belshaw 2001). International events are presented by a mass media that treats us to an endless parade of horrible images set just beyond our reach and produced by the selfish, lawless, and uncontrollable behavior of others.

In this chapter, we pursue three objectives. First, we will subject the first of these four conceptual elements, statism, to a fundamental reevaluation. We will assess its validity as a description of reality, as a predication about future states of affairs, and as a prescription about how matters should be. Second, we will subject statism to a critique from the dual perspectives of the deliberative democratic theorist and the environmentalist. These are perspectives on domestic and international politics that, we have argued elsewhere, are essentially complementary (Baber and Bartlett 2005). Our commentaries on the merits of anarchism, utilitarianism, and positivm will be presented incidentally, inasmuch as these elements are all to some degree implicit in statism and consequently any separate systematic attention to them would be largely redundant of a critique of statism. Third, we will end this chapter by proposing an alternate agenda for international law, particularly in the area of environmental protection. This will not be a set of procedural or institutional reform proposals. Rather, we hope to achieve the more limited goal of spelling out the search criteria that should be used in finding international arrangements that will more effectively and legitimately govern the behavior of humans (both individually and in national collectives) and their relationship to the natural environment.

One Concept, Three Problems

The view that nation-states are the only actors of consequence on the international stage is most closely associated with the realist analysis of Hans J. Morgenthau. This is, in some ways, ironic because Morgenthau regarded the struggle for power among nations as an accident of history rather than an essential element of human nature (Morganthau 1978). It resulted from a conjunction of obsolescent institutions and selfish individuals and groups that could, he believed, be overcome through rational political reform (Morganthau 1946, 1951). Nevertheless, many later writers seemed to take it for granted that nation-states are the only appropriate focus for our study of international relations and that they are both the only source and proper object of international law (McCaffrey et al. 1998).

In turning Morgenthau's observation about the significance of nation-states into an intellectual article of faith, three steps were required. First, it was necessary to ignore or discount examples of significant impacts on international decision making produced by non-state actors. This step established the descriptive hegemony of statism in international relations. Second, it was essential to develop a theoretical construct within which states were the only significant actors and it was not reasonable to expect other actors to emerge. In other words, for statism to hold sway, it had to be strongly predictive of future patterns of influence. Finally, for statism to prevail it was important that students of international relations regard the preeminence of the state actor as actually desirable from a normative point of view. Although widely accepted, often unthinkingly, at each of these levels of necessity the unique role of the nation-state has recently been challenged in significant ways.

The Descriptive Problem

As a description of reality, statism has much to recommend it. Even those writers who are essentially cosmopolitan in orientation pay homage to the state. Daniele Archibugi has argued that the nation-state is the most successful social structure in human history, offering the hope that the benefits of full democracy may one day be realized for all humankind (Archibugi 2003). David Chandler (2003) asserts that international law derives its legitimacy only from the voluntary assent of nation-states. The international regimes and institutions that might be cited as actors of importance along with nation-states are important "not because they constitute centralized quasi-governments, but because they can facilitate agreements, and decentralized enforcement of agreements, among governments" (Keohane 2005, 244). Even the strongest advocates of international environmental regimes are compelled to admit that they are self-enforcing by nature, involving some tradeoffs in the process of their negotiation, but having no significant sanctions or inducements to comply (Barrett 1998). As strong a case for the nation-state as this all may be, however, there are significant reasons to doubt that the international arena is populated by no other entities of significance.

States are neither omniscient nor omnipotent. The small-scale nations of the past generally lived within territorial boundaries that conformed to a set of natural variables. The older human experience of a fluid and indistinct but genuine home region was gradually replaced by the arbitrary and often violently imposed boundaries of the states that we know today. In this process of consolidation, there were significant losses in our knowledge of the environment that sustains us and the nature of the social relations upon which we depend (Snyder 1998). The process of social consolidation has not stopped there. National governments are now losing their ability to formulate and implement policy within territorial boundaries that have been rendered increasingly porous by globalization, immigration, and the information revolution (Reinecke 1998). In short, there is reason to doubt whether contemporary nation-states understand their situation or control their future as they once did.

Moreover, it may not make as much sense as it once did to regard states as unitary entities. For example, heads of state play a two-level game in which they manipulate international policy to enhance their strength domestically and take advantage of domestic politics to strengthen their position in international negotiation (R. Putnam 1988). A game-theoretic analysis of the behavior of policy entrepreneurs describes their use of international regimes to overcome resistant forces in their own legislature (Reinhardt 2003). For example, President Bill Clinton was able to blunt congressional opposition to U.S. participation in armed humanitarian intervention. His commitment to participation in international organizations increased the costs to the United States of backing down, forcing a Congress that was unwilling to accept the responsibility for undermining presidential initiative to limit itself to symbolic action (Schultz 2003). In developing nations, policy initiators use international organizations as a means of consolidating domestic reform. By empowering domestic private capital interests through participation in liberal international regimes (Keohane 2005), by raising the costs of backtracking, and by compensating elites that are out of power, they reduce the temptation to seize power by extraconstitutional means (Pevenhouse 2003). These observations suggest that our understanding of the state is in need of adjustment. The idea of sovereignty can increasingly be seen as "relational rather than insular, in the sense that it describes the capacity to engage rather than a right to resist" (Slaughter 2004, 268). So, although it would not be correct to say that the state is disappearing, it might well be accurate to say that the state is "disaggregating" (31). Taking this view suggests that heads of state, ministers, legislators, and judges play dual roles as domestic officers and as participants in transgovernmental networks that are challenging the primacy of states on the global stage.

The Predictive Problem

The idea that states may be in the process of disaggregating leads us to a discussion of the second aspect of statism, its value as a predictive construct. There are a number of reasons to doubt that nation-states will continue to dominate the global arena to the extent that they have in the past. Beyond the fact of disaggregation mentioned above, there is a clear trend in the direction of state disintegration. By this we mean the growing importance of substate units of government that are finding their way into transnational agreements. An example is the Alpine-Adria Working Group, which is an organization of sixteen subnational members from five European states that has been established to foster cooperation on cultural, environmental, and commercial matters that transcend state borders (Arend 1999). Another development that undermines the hegemony of the state as a political form is the process of regional integration. The most prominent (though not the only) example of regional integration is the European Union. Western European political organization no longer fits into the traditional state format of territorial sovereignty and exclusivity. The member states of the EU are no longer fully sovereign in the classical sense, but neither has the EU itself become a sovereign state (Waever 1997).

There is a second group of factors that challenge the preeminence of the state, those from outside the governmental sphere. First, the development of advanced communication technology associated with the more general process of globalization is breaking down the boundaries of national consciousness upon which states have traditionally been built by allowing individuals to develop a more global sense of identity (Bohman 2004a). Second, there has been a marked growth in the number of transnational organizations that exercise a parallel authority along side states in matters of technological innovation, economic management, and labor relations. This arena is populated by both transnational corporations (Strange 1996) and emerging global social movements that seek to challenge corporate interests on the world stage (O'Brien et al. 2000). Finally, and most ominously, challenges have arisen to the role of the states as the only actors on the global stage that employ coercive force. Terrorist organizations, long a plague to individual states, have globalized along with economic institutions (Held 2003).

The Prescriptive Problem

Having suggested that statism is not particularly successful as either a description of reality or as a prediction about our emerging future, it remains only to be decided whether these failings are something we should regret and try to repair. Put somewhat differently, should states remain (or once again become) the preeminent actors on the world stage? Arguments in favor of the hegemony of the state seem to fall into two general categories. First, it is argued that the state is a uniquely legitimate form of organization. This point of view is sometimes further refined to suggest that states are, at least potentially, the form of political organization in which genuine democracy stands the greatest chance of success. The sine qua non of legitimacy in the modern age is democracy, whatever that is taken to mean. Second, it is often argued that there is something particularly effective about the modern nation-state. Coming in various forms and flavors, the argument for effectiveness generally amounts to a suggestion that (communitarian and cosmopolitan theories aside) units of government either smaller or larger than the nation-state simply do not work very well as a matter of fact. Even after setting aside the questions of legitimacy and effectiveness as they apply to subnational governments, an exhaustive evaluation of these two arguments is obviously beyond the scope of this book. It is possible, however, to suggest in general terms why each argument should be regarded as suspect when used as a critique of transnational institutions of governance.

Mancur Olson observed that small groups are better suited to overcome the problems of collective action than are large ones because the benefits they realize from providing collective goods are more likely to exceed the costs and because social pressure and incentives can be used to encourage compliance rather than coercion (Olson 1965). Robert Keohane has applied the same logic to the international arena (Keohane 2005). He argues that if there were a very large number of equally small actors in world politics, the general desirability of reducing collective uncertainty through the formation of international agreements would not lead to the creation of those agreements. But the fact that the number of key actors in the international political economy of the advanced industrialized countries is small gives each state incentives to make and keep commitments so that others "may be persuaded to do so" (258). Keohane is quick to add that a single world state is not a desirable alternative because it would lead not to cooperation but coercion. In fact, "the prospect of discord creates incentives for cooperation" (215). Therefore, the legitimacy of the international system, conceived as a free association of sovereign states, resides in the fact that the only binding obligations it involves are those into which the parties freely enter.

A variation on this theme is that global government of any sort would face an unavoidable "democratic deficit." This deficit has been traced to the fact that the legislative function of government is underdeveloped at the international level (Wallace 2001). The democratic deficit is also attributed to the simple truth that as one ascends from the local to the global the voice of the people "province by province, country by country, region by region is much softer and less likely to be heard" than the voices of regulators, judges, ministers, and heads of state (Slaughter 2004, 104). Little wonder, then, that democracy is reputed to have achieved "real gains within states, but very meager ones in the wider sphere," both in terms of relations between states and the resolution of global issues in ways that respond to global public opinion (Archibugi 2003, 5). It is also clear why John Austin argued that while the happiness of a society is the aggregate happiness of its individual members, "the good of universal society formed by mankind is the aggregate good of the *particular societies* into which mankind is divided" (Austin [1832] 2000, 294; emphasis added).

The argument for state supremacy based on the effectiveness of states proceeds in a rather less grand fashion. It begins with the simple observation that a continuing respect for state sovereignty is likely to keep enforcement powers in the hands of those officials who have the coercive power necessary to ensure compliance with whatever standards of behavior are agreed to (Slaughter 2004). With respect to environmental enforcement in particular, this might be a positive rather than a limiting factor because the heterogeneous character of nature places a premium on local knowledge (Harding 1998). More generally, in a global culture of democratic experimentalism, states can ensure efficiency as well as compliance with international standards by borrowing emerging "best practices" from other international actors. In fact, such an infrastructure of decentralized learning can lead to the discovery of unanticipated goals and the means for attaining them (Dorf and Sabel 1998).

An example of how this decentralized learning can evolve is provided by the history of executive agreements negotiated between Presidents of the United States and Presidents of the European Union Commission. These agreements have generally led to ad hoc meetings between lower-level officials as well as among business, environmental, and consumer groups. These contacts have often resulted in the creation of working groups and other fluid arrangements designed to address common problems identified in the process of implementing the broader executive agreements. Although many of these informal networks were already emerging for functional reasons, the added impetus of executive agreements accelerated their development and enhanced their legitimacy (Pollack and Shaffer 2001). Observations of this sort can be offered to illustrate the continued vitality of the state as the central element of international relations. They also, however, open the door to a telling normative critique of statism as an organizing concept in international relations theory.

International networks of government officials and the nongovernmental organizations with which they interact are undoubtedly highly functional arrangements. They can "promote convergence of national law, regulations and institutions in ways that facilitate the movement of people, goods and money" in an increasingly free global economy. They have the potential to assure a "high and increasingly uniform level of protection of legal rights." And they can generate a "cross-fertilization of ideas and approaches to common governance problems" that may help improve the domestic performance of the participating countries (Slaughter 2004, 213). A chronic lack of legitimacy, however, plagues direct international contacts at the substate level among national officials and administrators. These transgovernmental networks of government officials are part of a general shift "from government to governance" (Picciotto 1996–1997, 1039), involving the delegation or transfer of public functions to particularized bodies operating on the basis of professional or scientific expertise rather than democratic accountability. This problem of legitimacy is exacerbated by the fact that there are "tremendous asymmetries built into our current world order" (Slaughter 2004) that systematically disadvantage both peoples and issues that are disfavored by wealth, geography, and other variables unrelated to the merits of their claims. Keohane has summarized the problem trenchantly by observing that international regimes are plagued by moral deficiencies that "reflect the inequities inherent in the political and social systems of advanced industrialized countries" (Keohane 2005, 252), which are, of course, the dominant architects of those regimes. If the international agreements crafted by nation-states do no more than imprint their domestic injustices and irrationalities on the global landscape, why should we regard that as either legitimate or effective? Why should we assume that there are no alternatives?

A Deliberative Alternative?

One of the most hopeful developments in recent political theory, both for the fulfillment of the promise of democracy and for the prospects of environmental protection is the turn toward the idea of public deliberation. Given the conceptual difficulties with the assumption of state supremacy that we have discussed, it could prove worthwhile to explore deliberative democracy's potential to "repopulate" the international stage with actors other than (or, in addition to) states. Before that exploration can begin, however, it will be necessary to examine theories of deliberative democracy a bit further and to suggest how a discourse that has concerned itself almost exclusively with the domestic politics of Western democracies might be deployed globally.

In order to suggest what the deliberative democracy movement might have to contribute to international relations generally, and to the development of international environmental law in particular, it is necessary to provide some sense of how public deliberation differs from other forms of political life. To that end, it is useful to begin with two essential questions:

1. What is required for successful public deliberation?
2. What is the objective of public deliberation?

We focus our discussion of these issues on the three responses in the deliberative democracy literature that we introduced in chapter 1: public reason as advocated by John Rawls, the ideal discourse theory of Jürgen Habermas, and full liberalism as advanced by James Bohman and others.

Public Reason

Rawls's central concern is that basic political institutions be just. His classical formulation of the two principles of justice is, by now, well known to most social theorists. Justice requires, first, that "each person is to have an equal right to the most extensive basic liberty compatible with a similar liberty for others," and, second, that "social and economic inequalities are to be arranged so that they are both (a) reasonably expected to be to everyone's advantage and (b) attached to positions and offices open to all" (Rawls 1971, 60). These are the principles, according to Rawls, that reasonable persons in the original position would always agree to. Their decision is legitimate because it is reasonable, the result of a general and wide reflective equilibrium.

Rawls specifically denies that the justification of his principles is based in any way upon systems of opinion or belief. They are no more subject, he claims, to such preferences than are the axioms, principles, and rules of inference of mathematics or logic (Rawls 1995, 141–142, 144). In offering this justification, no appeal is made to any source of authority beyond generally accepted forms of reasoning found in common sense and the settled methods and conclusions of science. As for the preferences and values of specific persons, Rawls assumes only that people subscribe to reasonable comprehensive doctrines and that there is a possibility of their forming an overlapping consensus among those doctrines. A doctrine is fully comprehensive when it "covers all recognized values and virtues within one rather precisely articulated scheme of thought; whereas a doctrine is only partially comprehensive when it comprises certain (but not all) nonpolitical values and virtues and is rather loosely articulated" (Rawls 1993, 175, 224). The existence of such doctrines is regarded as a fact about the political and cultural nature of a pluralist democratic society. Rawls further assumes that these doctrines can be used like any other facts, that reference can be made to them and assumptions can be made about them without relying on the religious, metaphysical, or moral content (Rawls 1995, 144).

Ideal Discourse

For Jürgen Habermas, public discourses succeed only under conditions of broad and active participation. "This in turn requires a background political culture that is egalitarian, divested of all educational privileges, and thoroughly intellectual" in its orientation to public deliberation (Habermas 1996, 490). Habermas makes it clear that democratic citizenship need not be rooted in the national identity of a people. But he does insist that democracy requires that "every citizen be socialized into a common political culture" (500). But what does this suggest about the social requirements of public discourse?

Habermas argues "that constitutionally protected institutions of freedom are worth only what a population accustomed to political freedom and settled in the 'we' perspective of active self-determination makes of them" (Habermas 1996, 499). But what form of deliberation does this model suggest? For Habermas, a public agreement counts as rational, that is, as an expression of a general intent, if it could only have come to pass under the ideal conditions that alone create legitimacy. Democratic society can best be envisioned as a self-controlled learning process. Any deliberative arrangements must support the presumption that the basic institutions of society and its basic political decisions would meet "the unforced agreement of all of those involved, if they could participate, as free and equal, in discursive will-formation" (Habermas 1979, 186). For Habermas, the object of deliberation is legitimation. The general problem of legitimation results from the fact that traditional world views have lost their power and validity (as public religion, customary ritual, justifying metaphysic, and unquestionable tradition). They have reshaped themselves into subjective systems of belief that serve to ensure the cogency of a capitalist and bureaucratic culture. The promise of that culture is that the exchange relationships that have come to dominate society will be legitimate because of the presumed equivalence of position occupied by parties to transactions. Thus in principle the political domination of a market economy can be legitimated "from below," rather than from above, through institutions of traditional culture (Habermas 1970, 96–99).

To the extent markets have become politicized, however, the requirement for direct legitimation of social relations, which existed in precapitalist societies, reappears in the modern era (Habermas 1970, 102). Loss of the independent power of capitalism to legitimate social relations has created a problem of circularity (Habermas 1979). States justify their actions through presumptions and procedures—namely, all of the presumptions and procedures that constitute interest-group liberalism—that are not themselves based on any normative order because capitalist-instrumental rationality allows for none. These presumptions and procedures exist to satisfy the demands of the legitimation crisis and are accepted, not because they make sense morally or ethically, but because they serve that social function. In this sense, they are reflective (self-validating to the extent that validation is considered relevant by the established order). "The procedures and presuppositions of justification are themselves now the legitimating grounds on which the validity of legitimation is based" (185). To rationalize this apparently irrational situation is the central challenge to modern legal theory.

In Habermas's view, procedural law must be enlisted to build a legitimation filter into the decision processes of state bureaucracies that are oriented as much as ever toward efficiency. A legal norm has validity whenever the state guarantees two things at once. First, the state must ensure compliance among the population at large, compelled by coercive force if necessary. Second, the state must guarantee the institutional preconditions for the legitimate development of the norm itself, so that it is always at least possible for the citizens to comply out of respect for the law instead of fear of coercion (Habermas 1996, 38–39).

The procedures for the production of law form the only possible source of legitimacy that is not anchored in a metaphysical worldview. Procedures of democratic discourse make it possible for issues and arguments, information and reasons, to flow freely. They secure "a discursive character for political will-formation" and, thereby, ground the "assumption that results issuing from proper procedure are more or less reasonable" (Habermas 1996, 448). From this perspective, Habermas foresees that constitutional democracy will become "at once the outcome and the accelerating catalyst of a rationalization of the lifeworld reaching far beyond the political. The sole substantial aim of the project is the gradual improvement of institutionalized procedures of rational collective will-formation," procedures that do not prejudge participants or their goals (489). By rationalizing the power of markets and bureaucracies and creating the possibility that legal commands may be regarded as both social facts and legitimate norms, public discourse allows modern societies to be integrated not only through instrumental rationality but also by shared values and mutual understandings (39).

Full Liberalism

According to James Bohman, democratic deliberation is constrained by the facts of cultural pluralism, large inequities of wealth and influence, social complexity, and community-wide biases and ideologies that discourage change (Bohman 1996, 20). A fully developed system of constitutional rights is a necessary condition for successful deliberation in that it prevents the worst abuses of bias and inequity. But the political institutions created by a system of rights can become less a forum for deliberation than an arena for strategic gamesmanship. In Bohman's view, rights make deliberation possible, in part by placing limits on it. But these rights tell us nothing about what deliberation is or about how it is best conducted under the existing conditions and constraints (23–24). Bohman outlines a set of conditions under which public discourse might be expected to succeed.

Bohman's core assumption is that "a people cannot be sovereign unless they are able to deliberate together successfully and unless they have something to say about the conditions under which they deliberate" (Bohman 1996, 198). The discursive structures of deliberation, whatever specific form they take, must discourage irrational and untenable (nonpublic) arguments. It is also essential that discursive procedures be broadly inclusive, allowing for the creation of neither persistent majorities nor permanently disenfranchised minorities. To assure that the losers in any given public deliberation will continue to participate, discursive procedures must allow for ongoing revisions that take up compatible features of defeated positions or improve their chances of being heard (100).

In full liberalism, successful public discourse produces "a shared intention that is acceptable to a plurality of the agents who participate in the activity of forming it." To this Bohman adds the notion that the success of deliberation should be "measured reconstructively," that is, in light of the observed development of democratic institutions, rather than by some a priori standard of justification. These arguments, in turn, suggest the basic requirements for the legitimacy of collective decisions resulting from public deliberation. To be legitimate, decisions must result from fair and open decision-making processes in which all public reasons are given equal respect. Decisions must reflect the views of the majority, but the deliberative process must give the minority reason to continue to cooperate in deliberation rather than merely comply with the majority will (Bohman 1996, 56, 187, 241). This can suggest that the majority is a shifting coalition of interests in which every individual is included with sufficient frequency that none feels permanently disenfranchised. Or it can imply that a permanent minority is treated by the majority with consideration sufficient to retain its commitment to the ongoing deliberation in spite of its minority status. As a practical matter, successful public deliberation will always be sustained by both of these conditions (representing pluralism and individual rights, respectively).

What do comparisons of the work of these three theorists suggest concerning the nature of public deliberation? Each of these approaches was developed from the perspective of Western domestic political experience. What Bohman requires for public discourse might be described as interest-group pluralism at its best. Citizens are entitled to use public discourse to pursue their own ends and are entitled to expect that other citizens will hold no more influence over collective processes than they themselves enjoy. Habermas would undoubtedly view this as necessary but insufficient. In his view, a shared political culture is necessary for successful public discourse. This does not have to rise to the level of a national identity. But there must be a shared commitment to the use of public reasons (reasons not derived from particular ethical or religious perspectives) in defense of positions adopted in the arena of public discourse and a commitment to testing the truth claims of competing world views. For his part, Rawls requires that fundamental decisions arise from an initial position that is purged of ethical and religious suppositions as well as any specific information about the situation of individuals in the collective arrangement being constructed. Bohman, Habermas, and Rawls, therefore, present three fundamentally different visions of what is required for successful public discourse. But what, if anything, can these theories of deliberation tell us about politics at the international level? More particularly, can they provide any insight regarding statism? Is it possible to escape the assumption that only states populate the global stage? Is it an assumption that we should even be trying to escape?

International Deliberation and the State

These three major theorists of deliberation have each had a good deal to say on the subject of international affairs. Yet none of the three provides us a direct critique of statism.

Rawls
John Rawls provided the most complete discussion of his views on international affairs in his book, *The Law of Peoples* (1999a), but he never

advanced a general theory of international relations, much less a plan for global government. *The Law of Peoples* is, rather, a conceptual exploration of what might be called the foreign policy of liberal democracy. A central premise of Rawls's approach is that the citizens of democratic countries should relate to one another as "peoples" rather than as individuals. This would seem, at first, to actually reinforce the assumption of state preeminence in international affairs. But that is not necessarily so.

Rawls is careful to point out the difference between a people and a state. Starting from his "political conception" of society, Rawls "describes both citizens and peoples by political conceptions that specify their nature." A liberal people are characterized by "a reasonably just constitutional government that serves their fundamental interests." Moreover, the citizens who comprise a people are united by "common sympathies" and a "moral nature" that they express through the state that serves them (Rawls 1999b, 23). Liberal peoples "limit their basic interests as required by the reasonable," whereas the interests of states do not allow them to be "stable for the right reasons" (29). The state is merely an instrumentality of governance, not capable of acting from any commitment to a conception of what justice requires.

It is not entirely clear why Rawls never extended his theories about the role of and relationship between citizens in a just society to develop a theory of citizenship in a global state.[7] He views his principles of justice as the results of an analytical process that logically extends from "local justice (applying to institutions and associations)" through "domestic justice (applying to the basic structures of society)" to "global justice (applying to international law)" (Rawls 2001, 11). So, then, why not allow deliberation among citizens on the international level in pursuit of international justice and a government to sustain it? Perhaps his most direct answer to that question is that a world government would "either be a global despotism or else would rule over a fragile empire torn by frequent civil strife as various regions and peoples tried to gain their political freedom and autonomy" (Rawls 1999b, 36). This, of course, is the argument advanced by Immanuel Kant in *Perpetual Peace* that has shaped the thinking of political scholars for more than two centuries (Kant [1795] 1939). But it is precisely this assumption that we are interested in evaluating. Is there no global institution of government that individuals, relating to each other as citizens of the world, might aspire to establish?

The reception accorded *The Law of Peoples* has been generally critical (Reidy 2004), but not for its failure to answer our question. A number of critics allege that Rawls's approach is insufficient to secure results that any reasonable person would support. Allen Buchanan contends that Rawls's approach cannot provide guidance for two of the most important topics a moral theory of international law must address: global distributive justice and interstate conflict (Buchanan 2000). According to Brian Shaw, Rawls fails to provide any compelling moral reason why liberal and other decent peoples would wrongly suffer a diminution of their political autonomy if they were obliged to alleviate the worst consequences of burdened peoples' disadvantages (Shaw 2005). These and other questions of distributive justice have led both Charles Beitz and Thomas Pogge to advance more egalitarian principles that apply Rawls's difference principle to the relations between peoples (Pogge 1994; Beitz 1979).

Others have focused on what they regard as an inability of Rawls's approach to deal appropriately with specific issues of justice. Anton A. van Niekerk argues that the law of peoples deals inadequately with the fundamental interest in human health and should be extended to require that catastrophic events, like the AIDS pandemic, be dealt with according to rules of international justice that require redistributions from unaffected peoples to those most disadvantaged (van Niekerk 2004). Andrew Kuper and Chris Naticchia contend that Rawls deals inadequately with human rights issues. Naticchia argues that Rawls's approach is conceptually flawed because he makes the protection of human rights a precondition for the deliberative process, the outcome of which is supposed to justify their protection (Naticchia 1998). Kuper maintains that there can be no secure minimal human rights without a right to democracy, and that as long as securing democratic rights remains a national issue—rather than a global obligation—the development of international democracy remains stunted and human rights are removed from global view (Kuper 2000).

A final group of criticisms have to do with the reasoning that Rawls has employed, rather than the results he has produced. Farid Abdel-Nour argues that Rawls's claim that both liberal democratic and decent hierarchical societies would accept the law of peoples is unfounded (Abdel-Nour 1999). Abdel-Nour contends that a hierarchical society would be willing to accept Rawls's reasoning only if its advocates (liberal democrats) were willing to intervene in that society's ethical and philosophical debates and forge the necessary overlapping consensus among competing doctrines. Shaw suggests that in order to achieve anything like distributive justice across a range of countries and cultures, some comprehensive doctrine (probably one sustaining the importance of individuals' rights) is likely to be necessary (Shaw 2005). If this is so, it may be due to another alleged flaw in Rawls's reasoning, namely, the failure to recognize that there is a basic global structure that sustains inequity and that the populations of states are not peoples in the sense that Rawls uses the term (Buchanan 2000).

Nowhere in this bill of indictment appears the allegation that Rawls should have provided for direct deliberation among citizens on the global stage. The closest we find is an unflattering comparison, drawn by Beitz, between the law of peoples and cosmopolitan approaches that are committed to justifying and assessing social arrangements by their consequences for individuals (Beitz 2000). But even in this instance, the critic is only proposing different criteria of evaluation, not a genuinely participatory form of international democracy. Of course, Rawls's defenders are concerned to show that his focus on peoples as opposed to states is reasonable (Reidy 2004). This obviously offers little help in deciding whether Rawlsian deliberation might be transplanted from the domestic to the international level without relying entirely upon states to represent citizens.

Habermas

Jürgen Habermas's approach to international affairs is more wide-ranging and less easily summarized than is that of John Rawls. Habermas begins with the observation that national governments, whatever shape their internal profiles assume, are increasingly entangled in transnational policy networks. For this reason, nation-states are becoming ever more dependent on "asymmetrically negotiated" (Habermas 1998a, 11; 1998b, 11) arrangements designed to improve the flow of goods, capital, people, and information across national borders that are rendered increasingly irrelevant to the lives of their citizens. As a consequence, the individual's sense of identification with what might be called a national identity becomes ever more attenuated. This, in turn, threatens what has been the singular achievement of the modern nation-state—the creation and maintenance of "a new mode of legitimation based on a new, more abstract form of social integration" (Habermas 1998b, 111). The growing inability of states to cushion their citizens from the more inegalitarian consequences of globalization, together with this delegitimization of national identification, destabilizes national politics and gives new life to older forms of social integration arising from tribal and metaphysical traditions.

This rather dire picture is brightened, somewhat, by recalling what it is that nations have done well and how those successes might form the basis for improvements in the international situation. Nations are widely recognized to be the arena in which democracy was finally able to assert itself to the fullest. Far from dissenting, Habermas goes further. He observes that "the idea that societies are capable of democratic self-control and self-realization has until now been credibly realized only in the context of the nation-state" (Habermas 2001b, 61). He further suggests that the spread of liberal democracy domestically promotes the development of domestic public spheres that eventually extend their influence across borders (Habermas 1997a) and that "the artificial conditions in which national consciousness arose argue against the defeatist assumption that a form of civil solidarity among strangers can only be generated within the confines of the nation" (Habermas 2001b, 102). Reproducing the egalitarian institutions characteristic of liberal democracies is conceivable at the global level if we can "outline new transnational procedures and institutions that reflect political opinion, and that suggest how compromise between obviously conflicting interests could reasonably be achieved within the existing global political order" (Habermas 1998a, 240). Like Rawls, Habermas rejects the project of global government, but not the development of a global domestic policy. He envisions a cosmopolitan project carried out "from a perspective that aims at harmonization instead of synchronization, without granting a false, long-term legitimacy to the temporary multiplicity of ecological and social standards" that result (Habermas 2003b, 99). The long-term objective that lends legitimacy to the process will be a "steady overcoming of social divisions and stratification within global society," which also protects the "cultural distinctiveness" that provides meaning in the lives of citizens (99).

Lest his views be thought utopian, Habermas provides the hopeful example of the European Union, a subject to which he returns regularly. The European experience is, for Habermas, the best evidence that we can eventually "develop the present loosely woven net of transnational regimes and then use it to enable a global domestic politics to emerge in the absence of a global government" (Habermas 1999, 59). In his view, the member nations of the EU have a clear incentive to form a stronger union in order to "seek a certain re-regulation of the global economy, to counterbalance its undesired economic, social and cultural consequences" (Habermas 2001a, 12).

To achieve this end, Habermas identifies three important steps. First, the creation of an identifiable European civic society is essential. A hopeful sign in this regard is the strength of the transnational movement for human rights. This development is crucial because, where the civic solidarity of a nation-state is rooted in particular collective identities, "cosmopolitan solidarity has to support itself on the moral universalism of human rights" and the egalitarian democracy it suggests (Habermas 2001b, 108). The second requirement of a stronger European Union is the buildup of a politically oriented European public. This involves the self-awareness of a society that is "capable of learning and of consciously shaping itself through its political will," a project that the recent European experience suggests is "still viable even after the demise of a world of nation-states" (Habermas 1998b, 124). Finally, the creation of a more unified Europe will require the development of a distinctively European political culture (Habermas 2002b). This will require the creation of a "constitutional patriotism" grounded in culturally distinct interpretation of republican principles that "can take the place originally occupied by nationalism" (Habermas 1998b, 118). These developments are, in Habermas's view, already underway. They will lead, in his view, to a Europe that is "able to act on the basis of an integrated multilevel policy" on behalf of European citizens who have learned "to mutually recognize one another as members of a common political existence beyond existing national borders" (Habermas 2001b, 99).

Bohman

In formulating his approach to international politics, James Bohman navigates the waters that lie between the work of Habermas and Rawls. Bohman shows the greatest affinity for the work of Habermas, which he takes to show a greater awareness of and concern for the implications of social complexity on the development of democratic norms (Bohman 1994). Rawls, on the other hand, is criticized by Bohman for an inadequate response to problems generated by irreconcilable values grounded in deep cultural conflict (Bohman 1995). In particular, Bohman argues that recent debates about the public or nonpublic character of religiously grounded reasons for policy preferences provide a test case of the Rawlsian view of public reason. They suggest that liberal democratic theorists are intolerant in this area and fail to live up to the democratic obligation to provide justifications to all members of the deliberative community. Accommodations to religious minorities must be built into the reflective equilibrium if the democratic ideal is to be achieved through public deliberations (Bohman 2003).

It is critically important to Bohman that our view of what counts as a "public" reason for policy positions should take adequate account of the existence of cultural pluralism (Bohman 1999a). His is an avowedly "non-ideal" theory of cosmopolitan democracy (Bohman 1999c) in that he views our public deliberations as culturally specific and embedded in a particular social milieu. This is important for both cognitive and normative reasons.

For Bohman, democracy can be seen as a form of inquiry incorporating a cognitive division of labor. Citizens both advance their own understandings of public issues and participate in the creation of norms governing the cooperation between expert agents and lay principals (Bohman 1999b). Thus the development of the social sciences has a fundamentally practical and political character. The creation of a thoroughgoing pluralism strengthens, rather than weakens, both the social scientific and political aims of this critical social science (Bohman 1999d). Beyond this cognitive significance, the development of deliberative procedures has a profoundly ethical dimension. Human freedom and social development are, for Bohman, a matter of advancements in the human powers of action, particularly the power to create and interpret norms (Bohman 2005). Without reason-responsive institutions, citizens are able to influence political decisions only indirectly by means of public actions that are purely strategic rather than aimed at consensus building. This places a severe limitation on the range and quality of citizen involvement in transnational civil society as it is represented by the activities of human rights and environmental NGOs and other citizen-based organizations (Bohman 2001). To cross the threshold of strategic action and create a genuinely democratic international public sphere, a number of developments will be required.

First, it will be necessary to create a forum in which "speakers may express their views to others who in turn respond to them and raise their own opinions and concerns" (Bohman 2004a, 133). The fundamental impetus for more democracy in the international arena lies in "a vigorous civil society containing oppositional public spheres," in which both individual and corporate actors "organize against the state or appeal to it when making violations of agreements public" (Bohman 1999c, 506–507).

Second, there must be a "manifest commitment to freedom and equality" in the communicative interaction within this forum. A republican understanding of world citizenship, emphasizing freedom from subordination, is the best and most feasible cosmopolitan ideal of freedom under current circumstances (Bohman 2001). Moreover, cosmopolitanism ought to seek democracy (not merely its functional equivalent) by promoting "the conditions of equal access" to the institutionalization of citizens' interests. The object is to create "opportunities and access to political influence and an environment for decision-making in which effective social freedom is widely distributed in international society" (Bohman 1999c, 512–513).

Finally, communication in the international public sphere must address an indefinite audience (Bohman 2004a, 133–134). Communicative public interaction is fully public if it is directed at an indefinite audience and offered with some expectation of a response, especially with regard to matters of interpretability and justifiability (135). Moreover, international communicative action must aspire to a "higher order" of publicity. This involves not just the expectation of a response, but also expectations about the nature of "responsiveness and accountability to others" as well as the characteristics of a "socially structured setting" that minimizes communicative inequality. This order of publicity produces international "talk about talk" that involves deliberations about "the norms of publicity and the normative contours of the social space that is opened up by communicative interaction" (136). This is essential for the long-term prospects of an international deliberative democracy because eliminating asymmetries of communicative capacity allows the uncertainties and instabilities of democracy to be "reduced over time by repeated interactions" that are "typical among free and equal citizens" in a unified polity (Bohman 1999c, 503).

Deriving Some Principles

It remains only to suggest the general principles that deliberative democracy offers us in a search for more effective and more democratic international institutions for environmental protection. We will attempt to state these principles at a level of abstraction that will allow for their imaginative interpretation in the search for political alternatives that we wish to encourage. We do so in the hope that John Dryzek's view that "democracy and democratization may be sought across states as well as in states and against states" (Dryzek 1996, 150) will not prove to be overly optimistic.

Based on the theories advanced by John Rawls, we have described a foreign policy that might be appropriate to a liberal democratic state. Such a state affirms the fundamental importance of personal autonomy, equality of opportunity, and a level of distributive justice that assures each individual a decent existence and the full value of his or her basic rights. It encourages a form of public reasoning in which autonomous individuals reason together under conditions of impartiality that are created by a veil of ignorance that deprives them of all but the most basic information about their shared existence. Elsewhere we have advanced the hypothesis that this political procedure might be employed to produce a form of "ethical precommitment." This we take to be the normative foundation for environmental policies like the Endangered Species Act, which establishes a set of abstract criteria that mandate specific actions under concrete circumstances (Bartlett and Baber 2005).

Our discussion of the work of Habermas reveals a form of deliberative discourse in which interested parties measure validity claims advanced under circumstances of discursive equality in which the force of the better argument is dispositive and decision by consensus is the stated objective. This ideal discourse theory provides the foundation for a theory of jurisprudence in which the possession and use of political power is legitimated by the self-imposition of laws that citizens can both comply with as facts and respect as norms. As an example of the environmental application of this theoretical approach, one might offer the tradition of environmental impact assessment (Baber and Bartlett 2005). At its most general level, environmental impact assessment is a process of public discourse in which a wide array of policy actors may participate in the evaluation of knowledge claims about the probable consequences of ecologically significant decisions. Government officials are accountable to a legal standard requiring that their decisions meet both procedural and substantive requirements that are also legitimate subjects of discussion and compromise. Moreover, opportunities for appeal to judicial review often operate to impose a de facto requirement for decision by consensus (or near consensus) by imposing high decision costs in the presence of significant dissent.

Finally, the deliberative democracy of Bohman does not require public reasoning in the tradition of Rawls. Nor does it insist that citizens necessarily share a common political culture in the sense that Habermas has discussed. Rather, Bohman envisions a discourse characterized by equality of both access and influence that emphasizes good-faith bargaining rather than a true convergence of underlying opinions. He adopts this more modest theory of deliberation in order to avoid what he regards as insensitivity to cultural diversity and the deep disagreements that it can produce. His emphasis is on a discursive process that respects the values and insights of local culture while allowing for the development of new global awareness.

This approach offers a theoretical context for what otherwise might be characterized as little more than ecological consciousness-raising (Baber 2004). Bohman's commitment to communicative equality offers at least one answer to the problem described as the tendency of international deliberation to dissolve into violence without the restraining structure of the nation-state (Mitzen 2005). Mitzen raises the entirely legitimate concern that the anarchic environment of international relations lacks the "shared normative context" that provides "decision makers the motivation for self-restraint and citizens the motivation to participate rather than withdraw or rebel" (403). The response offered by Bohman is that in the absence of asymmetries of communicative capacity, a "relatively unrestricted communication" would lead citizens to the "reasonable expectation of influencing decisions in their favor" as well as the knowledge of when their proposals would be likely to succeed (Bohman 1999c). In this way, the uncertainties and instabilities of deliberative democracy are reduced over time as a consciousness of shared interests evolves.

It might be added at this point that few interests are more obvious and intuitively shared than the need for a sustainable environment. What options might emerge in a search for, or design of, effective institutional arrangements for environmental protection that derive from these principles? What should be part of an agenda for global jurisprudential development?

5

International Environmental Law
and Jurisprudence: Institutionalizing
Rule-Governed Behavior

In previous chapters we critiqued the conceptual foundations of international environmental law from the perspective of the deliberative democrat. We argued that environmental protection has been held hostage to certain assumptions about the nature of international law that are, at a minimum, suspect. These assumptions include the view that international law can exist only in the form of explicit and positive agreements between states, that the global arena is characterized by normative anarchy,[8] and that the behavior of states in that arena is invariably materialistic and utilitarian. We have further indicated that each of these assumptions has a descriptive, predictive, and prescriptive character. Each purports to describe accurately the current state of affairs, asserts that matters cannot be otherwise, and alleges that alternatives are not merely unavailable but undesirable as well. In critiquing these assumptions, we have associated them with the view of international affairs generally referred to as realism.

We have dissented from this realist perspective, but we have done so without explicitly adopting the idealist alternative. We have declined to embrace that label for two reasons. Self-labeling is inherently presumptuous. But more important, we are even less sanguine about idealism's underlying assumptions. It is far from clear that humans will or can rise above their self-interests, eschew strategic and coercive behavior, and pursue normative commitments to the well-being of the species in ways that may require putting aside some of the pleasures of personal autonomy. We argue only that this more optimistic collection of assumptions about the potential of international politics should not be dismissed out of hand, especially by democratic theorists who hold similarly high hopes about domestic political life. If, however, we are to assess the real potential for an approach to international law that is both more democratic and more ecologically sustainable, we must begin with some basic appraisals of our experiences to date with environmental protection at the global level.

Charlotte Ku and Paul Diehl (1998) argue that international law has a dual character. It is, in the first instance, an operating system. On the one hand, it provides "the framework for establishing rules and norms, outlines the parameters of interaction, and provides the procedures and forums for resolving disputes" among the nations that participate in its interactions (6). On the other hand, international law is also a normative system that "provides direction for international relations by identifying the substantive values and goals" that may appropriately be pursued by members of the global community (7). Ku and Diehl's analysis tracks quite closely the jurisprudence of deliberative democracy as espoused by Habermas. In his view, law has the dual character of fact and norm (Habermas 1996). To be legitimate, law must assert itself in the world as an empirical fact. An imperative that does not actually govern behavior may qualify as exhortation, but it cannot reasonably be called a law. It must also be possible, at least in principle, for the addressees of law to regard its requirements as possessing the quality of a norm to which they can be committed. Otherwise, the putative law is nothing more than coercive power thinly disguised. So Habermas might be expected to agree with Ku and Diehl that international law must function acceptably well and must be able to at least claim to have produced normatively desirable outcomes.

At this point, however, our project runs the risk of being misunderstood. Focusing our discussion of international law on the functional requirements imposed by its role in institutionalizing rule-governed behavior among states might identify this as an exercise in structuralist social anthropology or sociological systems theory. Habermas characterizes these models of society as "subjectless rule systems" (Habermas 2001c, 16). They conceive of society as a structure of either symbolic forms or channels of information flow produced by underlying systems of rules that are impersonal and anonymous. Neither approach is suited for giving an account of how structures of intersubjectively binding meanings (including norms) are generated. That task requires resort to the analysis of communicative action (Habermas 1987). Here we are concerned with the generation of intersubjective situations of speaking and acting together—that is, with "the form of the intersubjectivity of possible understanding" (Habermas 2001c, 17). In adopting this approach, we ultimately concern ourselves with explaining both the generation of shared meanings and their institutionalization in purposeful action. If the substantive content of international environmental law cannot be rendered sensible at this level, then the idealist vision of international affairs is cast into doubt.

In the remainder of this chapter, we discuss examples of how rule-governed behavior has emerged from the supposedly chaotic maelstrom of state activity and whether that behavior rises to the level of communicative action in pursuit of environmental protection. In order to maintain focus and to ground our discussion in the reality of existing international organizations, we identify these behaviors by reference to their sources in judicial, executive, and legislative institutions. In doing so, we hope to create an agenda for further action and research designed to enhance the existing democratic tendencies in international politics and extend their potential reach into new areas of collective will formation.

A cautionary note: we assume that readers have a basic understanding of the depth and scope of the common law tradition, enough to appreciate that common law is not a vast collection of dusty precedents but, rather, the living and breathing heart of modern adjudication and legislation in the English-speaking world. Common law is not merely law operating in the spaces between statutes; indeed, virtually all of the statutory law produced in the last two centuries in the United States can be seen as just common law doctrine working itself out in the form of first-order generalizations.[9]

Adjudication and the "Common Law" of the Environment

It may at first seem incongruous to speak of an international common law. After all, in *Southern Pacific v. Jensen* the great expositor of common law, Justice Oliver Wendell Holmes Jr. chided certain of his fellow jurists for forgetting that the common law is not a "brooding omnipresence in the sky" but rather the "articulate voice of some sovereign or quasi-sovereign that can be identified" (*Southern Pacific Co. v. Jensen* 1917, 207). This might be taken to mean that no international common law is possible, in that no sovereign institution exists at the global level. But in a letter to Harold Laski, Holmes limited the scope of his own observation by saying that for a judge to try to impose his own abstract understanding of the common law on the state is "like shaking one's fist at the sky, when the sky furnishes the energy that enables one to raise the fist" (Posner 1992, 235). The problem is not philosophical, but practical.

The judges of a state cannot forget that they derive their authority from the state, even if the content of the law comes from elsewhere. As Holmes argued in *The Western Maid* case, when an issue is said to be governed by foreign law, that is only a short way of saying that the sovereign has taken up a rule suggested from without and made it part of its own structure of rules (*The Western Maid* 1922).

How, then, are we to make sense of the idea of an international environmental common law? Perhaps we can clarify the matter by examining the case that is most widely referred to as an example of that law. *The Trail Smelter Arbitration* case (*United States v. Canada* 1938; *United States v. Canada* 1941) involved a controversy between two governments over damage that had occurred and was occurring in the territory of one that was alleged to be the consequence of behavior of an actor situated in the territory of the other. The Consolidated Mining and Smelting Company of Canada, Ltd. operated a zinc and lead smelter at Trail, British Columbia, on the Columbia River just north of the international border. The smelter emitted sulfur dioxide that was carried by the prevailing winds down the river valley into the state of Washington, where it damaged farms and timberlands. The law of the time in British Columbia held that actions for damages to foreign property were local actions that had to be brought in the state where the property was located. Yet the residents of Washington had no local recourse because their state had no "long arm" statute that would have allowed it to assert jurisdiction over a foreign party.

The Canadian and American governments referred the issue to the International Joint Commission (IJC), established by them in 1901 under the Boundary Waters Treaty, requesting that the IJC investigate the matter and issue a report. The unacceptability of that report to the United States led to the negotiation of a convention between the two countries establishing a tribunal that would arbitrate the case. The particulars of the tribunal's judgment are of limited interest in the present discussion. More important is the analytical approach taken by the tribunal and the general reasoning offered in support of its decision.

The tribunal's essential holding is clear. The principle of state sovereignty cannot be understood to include the right of one state to use or permit the use of its territory in such a manner as to cause injury in or to the territory of another. When there is clear and convincing evidence that damage of this sort has been caused, compensation can be awarded and a preventative system of regulation imposed. Despite the lack of any general jurisdiction or any means of enforcing its edict, the tribunal confronted the issues of the case in a direct and determined manner. Perhaps its members were emboldened by the fact that the tribunal had little to lose. At worst, its ruling might have been ignored. But a close reading of its decision hints at more.

The tribunal argued that "as between the two countries involved, each has an equal interest that if a nuisance is proved, the indemnity to damaged parties for proven damage shall be just and adequate and each has also an equal interest that unproven or unwarranted claims shall not be allowed" (*United States v. Canada* 1941, 685). The opinion also noted that in the creating the tribunal, each country had acknowledged the desirability and necessity of a permanent settlement of the dispute. Language such as this might easily be written off as either dicta or diplomatic doublespeak. But if taken seriously, these phrases are rich with meaning. They suggest that the interests of the countries involved are separate from and more encompassing than those of the Canadian industrialists and the American loggers. Furthermore, the focus on proof of damages and the need for finality of judgment evidences a primary concern for a continuing and orderly relationship that transcends the issues at hand. The assertion that the interests of the countries are complementary (indeed, symmetrical) implies an equality of status that refutes the realist notion that power is the defining quality and final arbiter of international relations and that wider norms yield to immediate interests in all circumstances.

Of even greater importance is the tribunal's reference to the common law doctrines upon which it relied in reaching its conclusion. The tribunal stated that the decisions of the Supreme Court of the United States which are the basis of these conclusions are "decisions in equity" and that the obligations of the Dominion of Canada under its decision exist "apart from the Convention" that established the tribunal (*United States v. Canada* 1941, 691). The reference to the Supreme Court's use of equity is more than a courtesy, more even than a suggestion, that the United States should consider itself bound by its own words to the tribunal's ruling. It is the invocation of a uniquely Anglo-American approach to remedies that evolved as an alternative to the sometimes harsh rules of common law. The term *equity* denotes a spirit and a habit of fairness, justness, and right dealing that regulates the affairs of men (*Gilles v. Department of Human Resources Development* 1974). As a body of jurisprudence, equity differs from the common law in its origin, theory, and methods.[10] But in the United States, procedurally, equity and the rights and remedies of the common law are administered in the same courts at both the federal and state levels. The objective of this combination is to render the law more complete and its operation more just by affording relief where a court of common law would be incompetent to give it and no statutory remedy exists. Without involving itself in the complications attendant to a natural law analysis, the tribunal was able to invoke a form of jurisprudence that can seek an outcome that would strike the ordinary conscience and sense of justice as being right, fair, and equitable in advance of the question of whether the more technical jurisprudence of a court would so regard it. This broader analysis of the problem makes sense of the tribunal's assertion that the obligations of the Dominion of Canada arise from a source beyond the convention that provided for the tribunal itself.

By grounding its opinion in the use of equitable principles by the United States Supreme Court, the Trail Smelter tribunal invoked a tradition of jurisprudence that has traditionally been marked by a commitment to "practical flexibility" in the shaping of remedies (Kluger 1976, 715). It has been argued that the tribunal overstated the scope of state responsibility in describing Canada's obligations because of the Dominion's "voluntary acceptance of responsibility" for the damages and the implied agreement to abide by the tribunal's ruling (Bleicher 1972, 22). In fact, the Canadian government yoked itself to the smelter's owner in order to eliminate any doubt that an order from the tribunal would be carried out (Read 1963, 229). But this merely reflected a commitment to resolution of the dispute that was mirrored by the U.S. government, which held open the possibility that the tribunal would allow some level of ongoing pollution from the smelter. The American representatives were not prepared to press the claims of their citizens to the point of complete cessation of damage because a principle of that sort "would also have brought Detroit, Buffalo and Niagara Falls to an untimely end" (224–225). This perspective on the matter suggests that equitable analysis of international environmental disputes has the potential to serve (as it does domestically) as a "principle of interpretation" in disputes among states that elevates the norms of reasonableness and distributive justice while allowing for a greater degree of "judicial discretion" than is commonly appreciated (Arend 1999, 51).

International "Administrative Law" and the Environment

Discussions of the executive function at any level of government seem almost inevitably to degenerate into an argument between advocates of the parliamentary and presidential systems. This is particularly unfortunate when it occurs at the level of international politics because there the best answer may be "neither one, but thanks anyway."

The contemporary political experience of Africa and Asia is a testament to the danger of uprooting the European institution of parliament and depositing it indiscriminately in more heterogeneous and less stable societies. The executive function in a parliamentary system is necessarily less than wholly visible and a captive of the legislative process (Rockman 2000). As a result, the performance of the "plural" executive in parliamentary systems tends to reflect the divisions (and diversions) involved in maintaining a legislative majority. This has proved unfortunate in countries that were being held together through their postcolonial periods largely by wishful thinking. On the other hand, even a casual familiarity with the varieties of despotism practiced in Latin America suggests that the most dangerous American export is not weapons or genetically engineered food, but rather the presidential system of government.

Happily, another approach to the executive function is available. Anne-Marie Slaughter has argued that the executive function in foreign affairs is becoming "increasingly complex and differentiated" and has come to include "a variety of actors networking with their counterparts for different reasons" (Slaughter 2004, 38). Heads of state continue to play a two-level game in which they manipulate international policy to enhance their strength domestically and simultaneously exploit domestic politics to strengthen their positions in international negotiation (R. Putnam 1988). Beneath this level of grand diplomacy, and below the fold in the morning paper, regulators from nations all over the world are assembling the elements of a "disaggregated state." This structure consists of myriad specialized networks of subject-area specialists pursuing policy initiatives driven more by professional expertise than by national interest. The evolution of these policy networks has led Slaughter to argue that regulators have become the "new diplomats," threatening to eclipse both national legislatures and heads of state in importance (Slaughter 2004, 36–64). Many examples of this dynamic at work could be offered. We will discuss just a few.

Experts
In 1985, the World Commission on Environmental and Development (the Brundtland Commission) established the Experts Group on Environmental Law. The Experts Group was charged with preparing a report for the Brundtland Commission on legal principles for environmental protection and sustainable development as well as proposals for accelerating the development of international environmental law. The thirteen-member group was chaired by Robert Munro of Canada and included lawyers from ten countries. Certain of the provisions of the group's final report can be regarded as reflections of existing law (World Commission on Environment and Development 1987). Others, however, appear to break new ground and amount to suggestions for the progressive development of international environmental law.

As an example, article 10 of the Final Report of the Experts Group declares that "States shall . . . prevent or abate any transboundary environmental interference or a significant risk thereof which causes harm—i.e. harm which is not minor or insignificant" (World Commission on Environment and Development 1987, 75). In its commentary, the Experts Group cites the arbitration decision of the Trail Smelter tribunal. But can the tribunal's declaration, that no state has the right to use its territory in such a manner as to cause injury in or to another state, really be generalized in this manner? Doesn't the persistence of problems like the spread of both airborne and waterborne pollution along multinational waterways suggest that states have not really accepted such a general legal obligation? What are we to make of the group's claim that states are obligated to prevent risk? Would one state have a justiciable claim against another if a risk were created but no actual harm was caused? What threshold should be set for a finding of substantial harm? If mere risk is a sufficient cause of action, why do we even need a threshold?

Entrepreneurs
The Experts Group of the Brundtland Commission is just one example of an ad hoc intergovernmental organization (IGO) that has produced regulatory policies that, at least in form, present themselves to the world community as environmental law. Other IGOs enjoy a more permanent status and, consequently, exercise a wider reach in addressing international environmental problems. The leading example is, of course, the United Nations Environmental Programme (UNEP).

Established by the UN General Assembly in 1972, UNEP is an agency of small size and modest mission (Soroos 2005). Yet it has become one of the most entrepreneurial organizations within the United Nations framework and, in some ways, one of the most effective (Downie 1995). Originally created as a quasi-autonomous collection of several different organs, it has stimulated considerable research, promoted the collection and coordination of environmental information, created publications and educational programs, and sponsored numerous negotiations that have led to the establishment of other environmental organizations and the adoption of interstate agreements for environmental protection (McCaffrey et al. 1998).

In 1974 UNEP launched its Regional Seas Programme. Originally involving the conflict-prone states of the Mediterranean Sea, the program produced the Mediterranean Blue Plan for the control of both vessel-based and land-based ocean pollution (Haas 1990). This plan has become the prototype for similar projects that address the environmental problems of the Persian Gulf, the West and Central African Seas, the South Pacific, and the East Asian seas, which now collectively involve more than one hundred and forty coastal states (Soroos 2005). It has also given rise to the 1985 Montreal Guidelines on the protection of the marine environment against pollution.

The Montreal Guidelines are nonbonding in the sense that treaties are binding on the parties to them, except to the extent that the guidelines may represent customary international law. They are, however, quite far-reaching and ambitious. They impose a general obligation upon states to prevent, reduce, and control pollution of the marine environment. They specifically require states to ensure that land-based sources of pollution within their territories do not pollute the marine environment beyond their jurisdiction and to refrain from transferring environmental hazards from one area to another or transforming one type of pollution into another (McCaffrey et al. 1998). These obligatory assertions raise a number of obvious questions. In the absence of international agreements to support them, in what sense are they obligatory? How widely respected would they have to be to be considered a source of customary law? And, of course, whose answers to these questions (and others like them) are likely to be determinative of real-world outcomes?

Financiers

There is a third group of international regulators who have played an important role in protecting the environment. Surprisingly enough, these are the trade and finance specialists who are normally associated with the commercial and industrial activities that pose the greatest threats to the global ecological balance. No mention was made of the environment in the original General Agreement on Tariffs and Trade, and for many years the connection between trade and the environment was generally overlooked (Esty 2005). That situation began to change as the environmental movement gained ground worldwide and, by the time of the Earth Summit in 1992, the linkages between economic development and environmental protection were clearly front and center (Gardner 1992). The World Trade Organization has responded by moving away from its strict opposition to the use of trade sanctions to impose and enforce environmental obligations (Wofford 2000). Similarly, the World Bank has done much to facilitate international economic development, but it has been severely criticized for its apparent indifference to the ecological problems caused by some of the projects it has financed (Le Prestre 1995; Kurian 1995; Caufield 1996; Kurian 2000). Yet, by 2002, projects with environmental and natural resource management objectives and components accounted for 14 percent of the World Bank's total loan portfolio (Soroos 2005). Given the hegemonic character of the free trade and private capital assumptions abroad in the world today, a closer look at these changes in the environmental role of international trade organizations and the World Bank is undoubtedly worthwhile.

The concern among environmentalists over free trade can be summed up in only a few words. The worry is that increased trade will promote economic growth without environmental safeguards, resulting in increased pollution and consumption of natural resources as well as the loss of regulatory sovereignty needed to combat these problems (Esty 2005). Conversely, however, it has been persuasively argued that economic development can contribute to the advancement of human freedom and empowerment in ways that have significant environmental benefits (Sen 2001). This tension is reflected vividly in the fundamental ambivalence with which environmentalists approach the issue of the harmonization of regulatory law.

One view of harmonization focuses on its character as an effort by industry to replace the variety of product standards and other regulatory policies that have been adopted by the nations of the world with one "uniform set of global standards" (Slaughter 2004, 221). On the one hand, many fear this particular form of globalization will promote an international "race toward the bottom" that will only accelerate as increasing economic interdependence reduces the regulatory latitude of every national government (Esty 2005, 151). On the other hand, trade officials and environmental regulators have developed a framework of "fragmented coordination" that has allowed them to implement the Basel, Rotterdam, and Stockholm Conventions in a way that has provided "three sets of largely compatible principles, norms, rules, and procedures" that regulate different substances and stages in the life cycles of hazardous chemicals (Downie, Krueger, and Selin 2005, 141). Cooperation among regulators at this level eventually led to the adoption of the UN Globally Harmonized System of Classification and Labeling of Chemicals, which has contributed to improvements in the safe handling of chemicals worldwide.

An example of environmental entrepreneurship at the World Bank is its leading role in the establishment of the Global Environment Facility (GEF). The GEF is intended to provide funds to developing countries in support of environmental projects that have global benefits. This support has been targeted at ozone protection, limiting greenhouse gas emissions, preserving biodiversity, and protecting marine water quality (Soroos 2005). The United Nations Development Programme and the UNEP are junior partners to the World Bank in operating GEF, providing technical and scientific coordination and oversight. The GEF got off to something of a rocky start in 1991, encountering criticism from certain nongovernmental organizations for making project grants before clear criteria had been established (Jordan 1994). Many developing countries resented the GEF's focus on the global commons, which they believed blinded the organization to a broader range of projects that might have supported sustainable development at the national level. Due at least in part to these criticisms, the GEF underwent a major restructuring after the 1992 Earth Summit. The organization is now comprised of an assembly in which all member countries are represented and a governing council of thirty-two members, sixteen of whom represent developing countries. When consensual decisions cannot be reached, decisions require both a majority of member states and a majority of the votes of countries that make at least 60 percent of the GEF's total contributions. With this new structure in place, in a decade the GEF distributed $4.5 billion to 140 countries in support of 1,300 projects. Thus, in spite of its ad hoc origins and early miscues, the GEF has become a key player in the sustainable development movement around the world (Bryner 2004).

Both the World Bank's role in establishing the GEF and the emergence of environmentalism as a focus of international trade policy have significant potential to enhance environmental protection, though no guarantees are yet justified. The problem with the rule structures developed by these policy entrepreneurs is not (necessarily) that they are ineffective. It is, rather, that they are insufficiently democratic. Both regulatory harmonization and international finance take place within global issue networks of individuals, groups, and organizations (both governmental and nongovernmental) held accountable for their actions in only the loosest manner. This emerging pattern of governance without government (M. Shapiro 2001) is profoundly troubling when it is played out against a backdrop of dictatorships, pseudo-democracies, and emerging democracies with representative institutions that are less than fully developed to begin with. Moreover, the introduction of international imperatives and obligations into domestic judicial processes raises a different problem of representation. A fundamental principle of the rule of law is that judges hand down decisions that are consistent with the controlling precedents in the jurisdiction where they serve. Much as we may want our domestic jurisprudence to be enriched by experiences and perspectives developed globally, how do we integrate those sources of wisdom, and the analytical techniques their use requires, into the theories that have heretofore legitimated the use of coercive power by the judiciary (Fried 2000)? This problem of legitimacy further highlights the problem of international law's democratic deficit (Wallace 2001).

The Search for Global Environmental Law

To whatever extent international law suffers from a democratic deficit, no single explanation can entirely account for the problem. Some of the blame might be laid at the doors of the world's legislators. It is probably true that in the global cacophony "the voice of the people . . . is much softer and less likely to be heard than the voice of the regulators, the judges, the ministers and heads of state" (Slaughter 2004, 104). All the more regrettable, then, that legislators have been so much slower to establish networks among themselves than officials in the other branches of government. That this should be so is hardly surprising. Legislators normally represent either regional or ideological subdivisions within their nations rather than represent the nation as a whole. They tend to be generalists, without the all-consuming interest in issue-specific matters that tend to animate transgovernmental networks of regulators and jurists. The relatively high turnover rate among legislators discourages the long-term investment required to build relationships with their foreign counterparts. All of these facts mitigate against transgovernmental cooperation among legislators (Slaughter 2004, chap. 3). This is reflected in the process by which international environmental regimes are formed. A brief examination of one such regime will illustrate the point, as well as indicate the problems associated with executive dominance of environmental regime formation.

The Montreal Protocol is part of a global ozone regime that seeks to protect the Earth's stratospheric ozone layer. That regime is a set of "integrated principles, norms, rules, and procedures (Downie 2005, 65) that nation-states have created through a negotiating process that began with the Vienna Convention of 1985 and extended through the Beijing Amendment and Adjustment of 1999 (with stops in London and Copenhagen). A number of constituent institutions are crucial to the operation of the protocol. The annual Meeting of the Parties is a gathering of all of the protocol signatories where amendments and adjustments can be negotiated. The Open-Ended Working Group is a panel of policy experts that provides the scientific and technical support needed by the parties. The Multilateral Fund supports the efforts of developing countries to reduce their use of ozone depleting chemicals. The Implementation Committee provides a forum for the discussion of routine administrative issues and the Ozone Secretariat provides administrative support for the other agencies and groups, except the Multilateral Fund, which has its own secretariat (Benedick 1998). A number of other agencies are also critical to the implementation of the protocol. These include the World Bank, the United Nations Development Programme, the United Nations Environmental Programme, and the United Nations Industrial Development Organization (Parson 2003).

The ozone regime imposes significant and binding obligations on its signatories. The most important of these establish "specific targets and timetables" for the parties to "reduce and eventually eliminate the production and use of ozone depleting substances," create reporting requirements, provide for compliance assistance to developing countries, and provide for treaty implementation (Downie 2005, 66–67). Beginning in 1987 and continuing for the first fifteen years of its existence, the evolution of the ozone regime has involved a post-negotiation process that has focused on regime building and adjustment and regime governance issues (Wettestad 2002; Parson 2003). The major actors were the scientific community, which continued to increase its understanding of the mechanics of ozone depletion, and the national governments of the industrialized nations that had to ratify the protocol itself. UNEP was also intimately involved in moving the protocol process along and ensuring that ozone depletion remained on the international agenda (Downie 1995; Chasek 2003; Parson 2003). More recently, the focus of the regime process has shifted to matters of implementation and compliance, particularly in the areas of financial assistance and capacity-building strategies in aid of developing nations (Mainhardt 2002).

A number of observations are possible regarding the development of the Montreal Protocol. First, among the influences that have contributed to the effectiveness of the ozone regime several arise from the entrepreneurial activity of network participants. Of special importance in this regard were the focusing of public attention on skin cancer risks and the development and promotion of technological substitutes for ozone-depleting chemicals (Parson 2003; Wettestad 2002). These achievements were produced over a prolonged timeframe by a coalition of national regulatory officials and representatives of international nongovernmental organizations. Second, the adoption of an international agreement on ozone protection was really just the beginning of a long and slow process involving successively lower levels of governance that was necessary to convert that agreement into sustainable solutions on the ground (Vogler and Jordan 2003). Regulatory specialists from around the world spent hundreds of thousands of hours over nearly two decades in post-negotiation efforts to give substance to the commitments their nations had adopted. Third, at both the negotiation and post-negotiation stages, the national legislatures were virtual bystanders. Although some analysts insist that legislators at the national level have at least the capacity to reign in their executive branches (Slaughter 2004), the fact remains that negotiating international agreements is largely the province of the executive branch. Given the span of time across which such negotiations generally take place, it is the career executives rather than the elected or politically appointed officials who play the greatest role. They are the key players in the "epistemic communities" that form the vital core of transgovernmental issue networks (Haas 1992).

If the preceding analysis is correct, then international law is produced by virtually autonomous policy entrepreneurs rather than by citizens. The law itself only gains clear meaning and effect after extensive development by unelected regulators. This process occurs at a level of specialization and over so prolonged a period of time that elected officials cannot reasonably hope to control it. A similar incapacity of domestic legislatures has led Theodore Lowi to argue that contemporary liberalism has squandered democracy's hard won prize of political legitimacy (Lowi 1979). It is a conception of law that is certainly inconsistent with deliberative democrats' focus on citizen participation and decision by consensus (Habermas 1996). So it may simply be the case that the idea of international democracy is no more practical than its domestic variant. But given the apparent success of the Montreal Protocol, why should environmentalists care?

Our answer to this question is relatively simple. The Montreal Protocol has been relatively effective, but its effectiveness is notable for being exceptional.[11] Like all development to date in international environmental law, its legitimacy is questionable. The Montreal Protocol demonstrates only that policy effectiveness is possible in the absence of legitimacy, not that it is likely. International environmental law must be both effective and legitimate if it is to be durable. Far from being at war with one another, democracy and environmentalism are complementary at their most basic level. Globalization may well present us with the prospect of adjudication without jurisdiction, regulation without authority, and law without legislation. But that should only encourage us to look for new forms of democracy that can allow citizens to engage in direct deliberations that produce normative commitments grounded in a global civil society and then aggregate those commitments through processes of collective will formation. The objective should be to generate rule-governed behavior through laws that are recognized as both intersubjectively meaningful facts and as expressions of value in a shared political culture.

6

Adjudication among Peoples: A Deliberative
Democratic Approach

In this chapter we offer an immanent critique of international environmental jurisprudence. By this characterization, we intend to distinguish
our approach from that of scholars who have discussed international law
from an endogenous perspective, an outstanding recent example of
which is the work of Jack Goldsmith and Eric Posner. They reject the
view that international law is a "check on state interests, causing the state
to behave in a way contrary to its interests" (Goldsmith and Posner 2005,
13). Their view of international law holds it to be the product of rational
choices made by nation-states rather than an independent force shaping
those choices. The choices of states determine the requirements of international law, not the other way around.

Our purpose is not to quarrel with this modernized version of realist
international theory. Indeed, as descriptions of what is, such endogenous
approaches have much to recommend them. We argue, however, that the
rational choice view of international law assumes that what the law is today is all that it ever can be. It is unlikely that we can evaluate this assumption from within the rational-choice frame of reference. To decide
whether state preferences are fixed, we must determine whether there is
anything intrinsic or essential about international law that prevents it from
modifying the interests of states or independently restraining their pursuit
of them. In short, we must discover whether international law has (at least
potentially) an independent source of legitimacy. It is our argument that a
possible source of legitimacy for international law can be found in the literature on deliberative democracy, particularly in the jurisprudence of
Habermas.

Habermas has argued that the legitimacy of law depends upon the
ability of those to whom it is addressed to regard it as both a fact and a
norm (Habermas 1996). By this he means that citizens must see that law

establishes behavioral requirements that are backed up by appropriate and effective mechanisms of enforcement and that those requirements reflect a value or set of values that have been freely subscribed to in an act of collective will formation. Moreover, for any law to be democratic, two further conditions must be satisfied. First, the mechanisms of enforcement must be constrained by procedural guarantees of the kind that we generally associate with the ideas of equal protection and due process. Second, the act of will formation that produced the law must be broadly participatory and free of any coercion other than the force of the better argument. This much is well understood by students of contemporary democratic theory and these basic ideas form the underlying consensus in support of deliberative democracy that emerged from the rich debate between Habermas and John Rawls (Habermas 1995; Rawls 1995). Deploying this theory of legitimacy in the area of international environmental law is the objective of the remainder this chapter.

As a first step, we must explore the implications of deliberative democratic theory for the practice of environmental politics at the levels of the nation-state or substate. This we have done at considerable length elsewhere (Baber and Bartlett 2005). Here we limit ourselves to recounting the general contours of environmental democracy at the levels of the state or substate. This preliminary step is necessary in order that we may identify the problems that can be anticipated in any attempt to apply deliberative democratic theory to the question of international environmental law. At the national level, a deliberative environmental politics is grounded on the fundamental assumption that no regime of environmental protection can achieve the long-run, overall goal of ecological sustainability if it does not also satisfy the basic requirements of democratic legitimacy. Indeed, democracy is a constitutive element of ecological rationality. It suggests that a consensus criteria for decision making is essential both as a regulative norm of democracy and as a practical foundation for overcoming the network of mutual vetoes that has come to characterize the relationship in which stakeholders in environmental politics find themselves. It also leads to the conclusion that this consensus must be achieved among those who are most closely affected by the ecological issues at hand under circumstances of deliberative equality sufficient to assure the resulting agreement results from persuasion rather than coercion.

This account of environmental democracy at the levels of the nation-state or substate poses a number of challenges for adapting the conceptual demands of deliberative democracy to the circumstances of collective will formation at the international level. At the outset it is worth noting that not all of the news is bad. Deliberative democracy's commitment to decision making by consensus would seem to fit well in a decision framework that contains the idea of sovereignty as a central (some might say defining) characteristic of the parties involved. But as ancient mariners would say, beyond this point there be monsters. The truly monstrous nature of the seas that lie ahead can be appreciated if we take note of three general problems.

First, international environmental politics is plagued by a democratic deficit. To the extent that international environmental decisions contain any democratic content, it is a happy coincidence that can be traced to the existence of democratic processes within the countries that are parties to those agreements. In this sense, international democracy (to the extent that there is any) is always derivative rather than direct and participatory. This is troubling as a general matter, but it is especially problematic in the area of environmental decision making if one accepts the premise that democracy is a constitutive element of ecological sustainability. To the extent that premise is true, it might seem that protecting environmental values at the international level is a game that is lost before it is even begun.

Second, international environmental agreements (like other international accords) are not self-executing. The interpretation and enforcement of the provisions they contain cannot be delegated to an executive or regulatory agency as we would do at the domestic level. From Habermas's perspective, this problem casts doubt on the "facticity" of international environmental law. Without the ability effectively to alter the behavior of the parties to whom it is addressed, it is arguable that international law generally does not deserve to be called law at all. This is more than the semantic quibble that it is sometimes taken to be. It draws attention to the fact that the parties to international environmental agreements are states, but the actors to whom behavioral requirements contained in those agreements are generally addressed are private corporations and individuals. Taking this into account, one might go so far as to argue that the incapacity of environmental law to impose its requirements on legal individuals is just as well because that law is not the result of any unforced agreement among those individuals in the first instance.

Third, there would appear to be no way to resolve in any authoritative manner the disputes that arise under international environmental agreements. Even if their meaning could be specified with greater precision and concreteness, and even if enforcement mechanisms were readily available, international tribunals seem to lack both the jurisdiction and the jurisprudence that would be necessary to adjudicate the claims and counterclaims certain to arise. In negotiating the terrain between facts and norms, this problem can be seen as both cause and effect. It is a further contributor to the inability of international environmental law to pose a social fact to those actors whose behavior it seeks to modify. It is a result of the incapacity of international negotiations to incorporate normative commitments that are genuinely representative of the values held by those whom the resulting agreements address. To borrow an idea from the law of contract, international environmental agreements fail to achieve meetings of the minds. They provide international tribunals with no ground upon which to erect the structure of a decision and no rationale for determining its content.

A full analysis of these three problems and a discussion of possible solutions are clearly beyond the scope of this book. Here we limit ourselves to discussing in more detail the problem of the alleged democratic deficit in international environmental law and suggesting a deliberative approach to collective will formation and the development of regulatory mechanisms that might bring a more direct and participatory form of democracy to bear on the creation of international law in this critical policy arena.

Viewed as acts of legislation, international environmental agreements, and international agreements in general, leave much to be desired. Most of these shortcomings fall into one of two broad categories, corresponding generally to Habermas's distinction between law as fact and law as norm. First, international environmental agreements are ineffective for a variety of reasons. Second, international environmental agreements do not capture any normative consensus among the organizations and individuals whose behavior those agreements seek to regulate. These two general problems are obviously interrelated. But it will be useful for analytical purposes to discuss them separately before suggesting a means of ameliorating their consequences.

Effectiveness

Lynton Caldwell has identified three fundamental questions that will inevitably arise with respect to the effectiveness of any international environmental agreement (Caldwell 1991). First, we will want to know whether the coverage is adequate. Are all of the necessary parties and all of the essential issues included? Second, are the provisions of the agreement compatible with the corresponding elements of the domestic law of the signatories? Third, are the provisions structured in such a way as to produce a sufficient level of compliance on the part of the parties to the agreement?

Coverage

The problem of inadequate coverage in international environmental agreements can be traced to several underlying causes. For one thing, the general structure of environmental issues tends to make adequate coverage difficult to achieve. The ecological axiom that all things are ultimately interrelated is hardly compatible with the categorizing logic of Western-style law (Caldwell 1991). Moreover, even in countries where environmental awareness and commitment are relatively high, there is a growing problem of "green fatigue." The inability of international law to stop various forms of environmental degradation has undermined the ability of domestic leadership to translate general support for environmental protection into a mandate for stringent multilateral environmental accords (VanDeveer 2003). The ultimate success of international environmental agreements is heavily dependant on the ability of domestic leadership to generate popular political support for them (Hierlmeier 2002).

The difficulty in creating political support for environmental accords can be traced to more than simple fatigue or a sense of futility. The inherent elitism of the international political process certainly discourages citizen participation. As an example, success in controlling the use of ozone-depleting chemicals proved to be elusive until a leading role was assumed by the largest chemical companies whose behavior was at the root of the problem (Falkner 2005). Their economic and technological power gave a few enormous corporations the edge over other actors (including other corporations) in shaping the regulatory discourse that unfolded as development and implementation of the ozone regime got underway. The observation that the power of these corporations was moderated only by the agency of states and international organizations in no way changes the fact that the process was one of elite bargaining rather than popular will formation. Although we may feel some satisfaction with the outcome, it is simply not possible to argue that the process was democratic in any meaningful sense.

A final obstacle to adequate coverage in international environmental agreements is the tenacity of the idea of state sovereignty as the primary organizing principle in international law. The nation-state, as natural and inevitable as it may seem to us today, is a relatively recent and historically contingent development (Brooks 2005). Moreover, there are a number of reasons to believe that nations as a form of organization are not well adapted to the challenges of environmental protection in the age of globalization. Despite the large number of multilateral environmental agreements that have been negotiated and the high rate of compliance with their requirements, many assessments suggest that the state of the global environment continues to deteriorate (Crossen 2004). One reason for this pattern is that asymmetries between interest groups in the cost of lobbying are greater at the national level than they are globally. This results in a disadvantage for environmentalists in national capitals (Johal and Ulph 2002). Moreover, the globalizing forces of scientific advancement, mass communication, economic integration, population growth, and mobility are all conspiring to create pressure for universalizing basic ecological responsibilities irrespective of national boundaries (Caldwell 1999). It is becoming increasingly clear that, even from the domestic perspective, the populations of many failed or failing states would benefit from living under the norms of a non-state international society instead of the dysfunctional regimes within their own countries (Brooks 2005).

All of these problems contribute to a pattern in which multilateral environmental agreements fail to protect the environment, not primarily because their signatories fail to comply, but because the terms of the agreement contained weak obligations to begin with (Crossen 2004). The states that negotiate these agreements are so preoccupied with protecting their sovereign rights they overlook the fact that the soundest basis for protection of the environment is the affirmation of responsibilities (Caldwell 1991). This is the reason that assumptions regarding the autonomy of national law and sovereignty are beginning to change in fact even though traditional doctrines persist in political and judicial rhetoric (Caldwell 1999).

Compatibility

Given what has been said regarding the status of the nation-state, one might argue that the issue of whether or not international environmental regimes are compatible with domestic law is not particularly important. This argument would be persuasive only if sufficient resources to implement international agreements existed at the supranational level. At the present time, and for the foreseeable future, this simply is not the case. As outmoded as institutions of national government may have become, the global system is still fundamentally anarchic in the sense that it lacks an authoritative government that can enact and enforce rules of behavior (Keohane 2005). Moreover, the complexities of ecological preservation require the use of policy networks comprised of actors who represent both national and supranational interests in an environment characterized by disaggregated government (Slaughter 2004). For both of these reasons, the compatibility of national and international environmental law will continue to be of concern.

The problem of reconciling international and domestic law arises in part from the fact that their modes of origin, administration, and enforcement are distinctly different. International law developed as the law of relations among states during the consolidation of modern nations as the primary institutions for governing the behavior of individuals and organizations (Caldwell 1991). This renders the very idea of environmental law among nations problematic. The direct object of environmental regulation is not wildlife, water quality, erosion, deforestation, or even global climate change. The object of environmental regulation is people, the only entities whose behavior has direct ecological consequences and the only actors over whom law has any real bearing (Caldwell 1999). To this extent, law among nations is rarely of direct environmental significance. What matters is what national governments are willing to do with respect to the regulation of their citizens in pursuit of environmental protection.

Our understanding of these matters is often obscured as a consequence of the fact that both domestic and international regulatory structures are too often simplistically characterized as mere compromises among stakeholders when they are, in fact, far more complex efforts to develop hegemonic formations of governance in specific markets or policy arenas (Andree 2005). Moreover, governments, international organizations, and nongovernmental groups typically focus on particular issues and developments with little regard to their broader contexts and implications. This ignores the fact that, through a significantly anthropogenic and additive process, specific decisions cumulate to change the environment as a whole (Caldwell 1999). As an example, global coordination of environmental protection is threatened by strategic policy competition among states in search of investment capital, which threatens to weaken environmental commitments (Johal and Ulph 2002). This has led to the development of the idea of "common but differentiated responsibility," which yields ground on environmental standards in the face of a dubious argument that uniform and binding requirements would necessarily cripple the economies of developing nations (Weisslitz 2002). Thus, in order to incorporate the necessary parties and issues in any given international environmental accord, there is often a strong pressure to establish differential levels of obligation that ultimately undermine the legitimacy of the accord itself and further erode the global commitment to stringent standards of ecological behavior—the precise difficulty faced by the Framework Convention on Climate Change and its Kyoto Protocol.

Compliance

The signatories to any multilateral environmental agreement will fail to comply with its provisions (when they fail) for one of two reasons. Some could comply but will not and others would comply but cannot (Caldwell 1991). These circumstances present two distinct compliance challenges. In the case of willful noncompliance, both the systemic failings of international law and the inadequacy of its underlying political consensus are evident. In the early 1990s, it was possible to argue that although international law had failed to adequately address global environmental issues, some progress was being made (Brunnee 1993). More recently, however, it has been observed that the field of international environmental law has gone rather quickly from maturation to an infirm old age. International environmental problems have become more daunting, but the law has not responded to these problems with any growth in vigor (Driesen 2003). A number of factors are involved in this failure.

First, the general structure and formal characteristics of international norms of behavior are often problematic. For example, it is often difficult to state these norms with sufficient precision. Decision makers encounter different types of challenges using scientific information to judge the health and environmental risks involved in various types of disputes or decision scenarios. Where substantive standards of risk must be established, decision makers will face questions of how much emphasis to place on scientific assessments and how much on nonscientific (i.e., political) factors in assessing risk (Raustiala et al. 2004). Second, traditional international law based entirely upon interstate relations is incapable of addressing emerging global and cross-border issues. International justice based on state interest, state sovereignty, state equality and state responsibility is largely irrelevant in resolving transboundary environmental problems such as global warming. Addressing such issues requires that different rights and duties be assigned to different countries with different levels of economic and technological development. Further, it requires that we take into account not only interstate and interpersonal justice, but also intergenerational justice (Yokota 1999). Finally, international norms are often easy enough to identify but they are difficult to elevate to the level of enforceable law. As an example, the general idea of sustainable development is a well-understood principle that could be a very effective legal concept. It falls short of being a principle of customary international law, however, even though it enjoys significant support in international legal instruments and is endorsed by a wide variety of international actors (Marong 2003). These problems help explain both a pattern of multilateral environmental agreements that achieve high levels of compliance because they require only shallow levels of cooperation (Crossen 2004) and a situation in which a norm of international behavior like the precautionary principle fails to develop into an effective system of prevention and remediation of international harms in the way that America's system of tort law evolved (Garrett 2005).

A different set of problems emerges when we turn our attention to nations that would comply with international environmental norms if they were able. Many Third World states can make compelling arguments that if they were held to the same environmental standards as First World nations, their economic development would be severely curtailed. They further argue, therefore, that to impose uniform environmental standards would work a serious injustice upon sectors of the world's population that are least able to assert themselves in international political debates (Weisslitz 2002). Moreover, some states appear to be entirely failed enterprises. Some nations are so dysfunctional in so many ways that we cannot expect them to even attempt to meet international environmental standards. They are often characterized by minimal domestic environmental requirements or systems that are adequate at a formal level but underfunded to such a degree that the black-letter law on their books is simply irrelevant. The state-centric approach of our existing international legal system is to "restore" these failed states to a more successful level of performance. But many of these states never were successful and are unlikely ever to be (within decades, anyway). To continue to focus on the state in these circumstances is a misguided approach that is likely to do as much harm as good (Brooks 2005). In the case of these nations, common but differentiated responsibility is destined to fail as an equitable principle of law.

Substituting differential contribution norms for differential compliance norms as some have suggested (Weisslitz 2002) would merely result in the transfer of financial resources to failed states with predictable results. But the long-term non-state alternatives that might be appropriate would require international institutions much stronger, in terms of both political and analytical resources, than those that currently exist (Bodansky 1999). Of these resources, the political are arguably the most important.

Institutional change is, ultimately, dependent on political will and can be sustained only with popular political support (Hierlmeier 2002). Any system of transnational environmental enforcement would require nations to concede a right of international inspection, a right of performance audit and public reporting, and a common interpretive, meditative, and adjudicatory authority. In the final analysis, it would seem to be necessary for nations to subscribe to some institution capable of applying sanctions as a last resort (Caldwell 1991). The largest stumbling block is obviously the issue of coercive sanctions. Standards of national conduct and acceptable methods of mutual coercion, captured in legal principles enforceable as world law, would be necessary attributes of global environmental governance (Caldwell 1999). Mutual coercion would be less necessary, however, if mutual values and goals were more universal. And this brings us to the second major failing of international law, its inability to capture a normative consensus through the practice of global democracy.

Normative Consensus

Law is shaped both by the persistence of custom and the perception of change. Law is inherently conservative. Its continuity and predictability is presumed to protect the stability and survival of the society it serves. But contemporary legal doctrines (at both the national and international level) are being overtaken by unprecedented developments that pose the dilemma of whether serving their conservative function involves adhering to conventional arrangements or adapting to meet new and evolving circumstances (Caldwell 1999). The dilemma is all the more daunting if we add the requirement, derived from deliberative democratic theory, that law should embody a normative consensus that results from the unforced agreement of those whose behavior it seeks to govern. Having turned this corner in our discussion of international environmental law, we are confronted immediately with a problem widely known as the democratic deficit.

The democratic deficit is not unique to international law or to the arena of environmental policy. It has been argued that a democratic deficit is at the heart of America's slide into the anomic form of democracy that most citizens find so unsatisfying (Durant 1995). There also seems to be a democratic deficit afflicting British politics. Thus an effort is underway to imagine a constitutional role for monarchy at the center of a progressive agenda of democratic reform (Harvey 2004). In addition, the discussion of the democratic deficit has expanded to include the deficit of jobs, equality, and justice that suggest a deficit in the democratic system itself in the world's most developed nations (Gindin 1994). Our present concern, however, is limited to the democratic deficit in the relations among nations. Broad as even that subject is, we shall focus on the problem of a democratic deficit as it manifests itself in the most fully developed example of international cooperation available to us—the European Union.

Political scientists generally agree that the European Union is undemocratic, but they do not agree about how undemocratic it is or even about how serious a criticism the democratic deficit charge really is (Neundeither 1994). Part of the difficulty is that we lack a generally accepted method for assessing democracy in a political system such that there would be agreement on what would constitute adequately democratic institutions (Lord 2001). As a more general matter, there is considerable evidence that perceptions of EU democracy vary with perceptions of the economic costs and benefits of membership (Karp, Banducci, and Bowler 2003), suggesting that among mere mortals the normative value assigned to democracy will depend to some extent on its relative costs.

There is also disagreement about the source of the democratic deficit. One view is that the essence of the problem is that Europeans lack a party system that offers a meaningful choice to voters with respect to pan-European issues and that this failing is reflected in the unrepresentative qualities of the European Parliament (Andeweg 1995). The diagnosis would lead one to advocate the creation of genuine pan-European elections and parties. This, in turn, would require that the EU be transformed into a classic parliamentary system with a parliament vested with genuine legislative power and control of the executive selection process (Hix 1998). Others have argued, however, that it is simplistic to suggest that the democratic deficit can be solved simply by the direct election of a meaningful European Parliament. The issue is more complex and multifaceted. Democratic legitimacy in the EU is contested and divided between the supranational and national levels of government. It is conditional and evolutionary. It is expressed through the dispute over the balance of power among the key supranational decision-making institutions and the argument over decision-making efficiency, transparency, and accountability (J. Lodge 1995). As for the unrepresentative qualities of the existing European Parliament, there is an argument to be made that the EU is already a highly open and accessible system that is actually burdened with a high level of interest representation (Greenwood 2002). According to this view, the EU suffers more from a democratic overload than a democratic deficit.

This ambiguity about the sources of and solutions for the democratic deficit lead to further questions about the scope of the deficit. For instance, we might legitimately question whether introduction of a common currency puts a negative entry into the democratic ledger, quite apart from any advantage it may confer in the area of economic growth (Martin and Ross 1999). And the development of immigration policies in the EU seems to emphasize tighter control of the numbers of immigrants and asylum seekers rather than the development of measures to combat racism and xenophobia. The consequence of this approach may have been an aggravation of both institutional and participatory aspects of the democratic deficit (Geddes 1995). But notice, these two observations, when taken together, could be viewed as evidence that the EU is damned if it does and damned if it doesn't. On the one hand, the complaint that a common currency is undemocratic would appear to rest on the idea that, at least in the area of monetary policy, too high a level of centralization has been reached. On the other hand, criticism of the immigration policies of EU members would seem to involve a claim that the Union fails to exert sufficient pressure toward uniformity in this policy arena.

In light of all this, it is little wonder that there is a lack of consensus about the EU's lack of consensus. Some argue that the democratic deficit is designed right into the EU's basic structure. The process of European integration, so the story goes, was marked from the beginning by a form of technocratic elitism that made a backlash against the Maastricht Treaty virtually inevitable. According to this view, the EU needs to achieve the same executive-legislative model found among existing European states (Featherstone 1994). A contrasting view is that concern about the democratic deficit in the EU is misplaced. Judged against existing industrial democracies, rather than against an ideal plebiscitary or parliamentary democracy, the EU can be regarded as entirely legitimate. Its institutions are tightly constrained by constitutional checks and balances, narrow mandates, fiscal limits, supermajoritarian and concurrent voting requirements, and a system of separation of powers (Moravcsik 2002). If comparing the EU favorably to existing democracies is regarded as damning with faint praise, additional reassurance is available in the form of an argument that democratic legitimacy for the EU actually becomes problematic only if it is seen as a future nation-state. If instead the EU is regarded as a regional state with shared sovereignty, variable boundaries, a composite identity, a compound form of governance, and a fragmented democracy, the problem of a democratic deficit diminishes considerably (Schmidt 2004).

This more affirmative view of the European Union allows us to imagine further improvements in the democratic quality of international law. The recent history of EU political development is characterized by a heightened concern for inclusiveness and transparency in institution building (Fossum and Menendez 2005). For years, academicians and political actors have advocated new modes of governance in the EU. Many have limited their proposals to mechanisms that are mere extensions of existing participatory practices, restricted to so-called stakeholders and underpinned by the same elitist and functionalist philosophy that has animated the EU from its inception (Magnette 2003). This approach might be justified if we accepted the argument that the European public space is unavoidably dominated by an instrumental form of rationality that makes any form of democracy other than interest-group liberalism impractical (Meadowcroft 2002). Indeed, reproducing interest-group liberalism at the regional level would be a historic accomplishment if nothing more was ever achieved. It is doubtful, however, that European publics will be satisfied with that in the long run. This conclusion seems all the more likely when we consider that other regional agreements, far less ambitious than those constituting the EU, have been forced by public opinion to include features allowing for direct citizen participation. As an example, the North American Free Trade Agreement carried with it a side agreement officially entitled the North American Agreement on Environmental Cooperation (NAAEC). This agreement established the Commission for Environmental Cooperation, which has developed an innovative citizen submission process that provides a promising template for future multilateral environmental agreements (Markell 2000; DiMento 2003, 119–127). The continuing demands for a larger role for citizens in the international system following protests at the World Trade Organization meeting in Seattle in 1999 suggest that the pressure for greater public participation in global policymaking is unlikely to subside (Strauss, Falk, and Franck 2001).

It is against this backdrop that current efforts to further democratize the EU must be understood. Efforts to adapt forms of representative democracy familiar from the domestic experience for use by the EU are destined to confront two fundamental challenges: the relatively stronger emphasis on executive government at the regional level and the multilevel character of the polity itself (Crum 2005). The relative weakness of the European Parliament is a major reason why democratic legitimacy in the EU has conventionally been discussed as a problem of direct election of legislators at the regional level (J. Lodge 1995). But since a European demos does not currently exist, and does not appear to be in the offing, the introduction of elements of direct democracy would seem a more promising approach (Feld 2005). Opportunities for direct participation are important both as a source of democratic legitimacy and as a matter of political acceptability (Giorgi and Pohoryles 2005). The disaggregated character of the European polity suggests that a conception of civil society based on contestation and communication within and across multiple public spheres is not only good for ecological democracy but also more consistent with imaginable political scenarios (Hunold 2005).

By way of summary, the next iteration of international environmental law will have to satisfy a dual imperative that is conceptually consistent with the jurisprudential theories of Habermas (1995). As social fact, international environmental law will have to achieve coverage of all the essential parties and issues. It will have to demonstrate its compatibility with existing environmental regimes at the national level. And it will have to present nations with political imperatives that encourage a significant level of compliance with international obligations. As an expression of international norms, environmental law will have to capture an international consensus regarding the obligations of those individuals to whom the law is addressed. That level of consensus can only be produced by methods of collective will formation that are both open and participatory and that generate the uncoerced agreement of at least a representative sample of the population to be governed.

Deliberative Democracy and International Environmental Law

Deliberative democrats have not always paid enough attention to matters of practice. For anyone who has followed the development of the field, this observation will seem entirely unremarkable. An excuse that might be offered for this shortcoming is that political practice is derivative of preexisting communities. In other words, the contours of our political practice are so dependent on antecedent social constraints that it is pointless to include them in our efforts to theorize democracy. This defense is of little use, however, in excusing us from discussing the practical issues involved in globalizing environmental democracy. The social and economic variables that determine political practice at the national level vary so widely at the global level, and the bonds of community at that level are so weak, that every institutional possibility would seem to be on the table. Moreover, we find ourselves in a time of rapid social and political change, when constitutional issues are in play in virtually every nation. In these circumstances it can be argued persuasively that communities do not predate politics but, rather, that politics leads to the formation of new communities (Hajer and Wagenaar 2003).

It is incumbent on deliberative democrats, therefore, at least to suggest institutional designs and political processes that might capture some of the theoretical ether that they have generated. Few of these theorists have been as active in this practical endeavor as James Fishkin. Fishkin's experiments with a procedure that he refers to as deliberative polling constitute one of the most creative approaches to deliberative politics. Deliberative polling assembles a stratified random sample of citizens to discuss the policy positions of competing candidates or parties (Fishkin 1995). This group of citizens is brought together, at the investigator's expense, to participate in a weekend of small-group discussions and larger plenary sessions that allow them to assimilate extensive and well-balanced information about their subject, exchange competing points of view, and come to considered judgments that represent a consensus of the group. In other words, deliberative polling is a procedure that explores what public opinion would be like if the public were motivated to behave more like deliberative democrats (Ackerman and Fishkin 2003).

Citizen juries, as Fishkin's small-group discussions are sometimes called, engage in a very particular form of reasoning. As with juries in civil and criminal courts, they work to arrive at deliberative judgments through a collective, interactive discourse. This process is easily distinguished from the kind of systematic, principled reasoning that is typical of traditional moral philosophy. It is an effort to find workable definitions of a problem that yield solutions that can command the unforced assent of the deliberators. These concrete situations are characterized by what Hilary Putnam has called the "interpenetration" of fact, value, and theory, an interdependence of elements that often cannot be distinguished even notionally (H. Putnam 1995). Experience with citizen juries in the United States, Great Britain, and Australia suggests that the approach enjoys a number of significant advantages over other policy processes.

First, although allowing for a significant level of direct democratic participation on the part of average citizens, service on a citizen jury is no more intrusive than ordinary jury duty and far more educative than are ordinary political campaigns (Gutmann and Thompson 2004). Second, citizen juries tend to produce consensus rather than polarization (Fishkin and Luskin 1999). This can be traced to the fact that citizen juries do not begin their deliberations with votes but, rather, with discussion. Moreover, the plenary groups within which citizen juries operate are large enough to contain representative samples of public opinion and are led by moderators who ensure that all perspectives receive a fair hearing. Experts are available to clarify questions of fact, and all participants receive extensive information on the subject in advance (Gutmann and Thompson 2004). Third, unlike mechanisms of political representation that are closely identified with the particular experiences of national populations, the citizen jury is a broadly deployable approach that will resonate in the widest variety of cultures. (The use of the term *jury* is solely to fix the concept in the Western mind. Deliberative polling is another way to describe the process. How it is presented to participants or sponsors can be tailored in ways that are culturally specific without any loss of conceptual clarity of practical value.) In fact, the use of citizen juries is one of the few techniques that allow us to imagine a form of world assembly in which citizens could deliberate as members of the whole order of humans rather than as representatives of particular nation-states (Laslett 2003). Finally, the deliberative form of rationality that citizen juries promote is more than just talk. It is an accomplishment in itself, forged by the direct efforts of citizens to deal with concrete, ambiguous, tenacious, practical problems (Fischer and Forester 1993). In short, the judgments of citizen juries transcend the forms of interest aggregation that are typical of interest-group liberalism. For this reason, the deliberative process exemplified by citizen juries has come to be regarded as an especially appropriate response to the environmental problematique, in the face of which existing political institutions (both domestic and international) are obsolescent (Laslett 2003).

on the basis of tens of thousands of practical judgments, which promises we should be held to and which we should not. The vast majority of those rulings were arrived at by judges rather than juries. But the work of citizen juries suggests that the effectiveness of judges can be approximated by the rest of us if we are provided with sufficient information and an adequately structured decision environment. What, after all, are our rules of civil and criminal procedure if they are not systems that provide judicial decision makers with appropriate information and rules of choice?

It is important to point out, however, that the law of contract is similar to all other areas of common law in that it developed as a series of quite limited responses to particular problems encountered by real parties to actual legal disputes. The work of either judges or juries in resolving those disputes is rarely done with the idea that over the course of centuries a coherent body of general legal propositions will result. The coherence and legitimacy of the common law were hard won, but not by tackling big issues with big ideas. The common law was a bottom-up enterprise, much as empirical science tends to be. It involved repeated "observations" of what our senses (particularly our sense of justice) suggested about a particular set of circumstances. Are we not confronted with a similar challenge when we consider the practical impossibility of grappling with problems of environmental policy in their imponderably complicated entirety? Do we not also encounter, once again, Lowi's argument that to be enforceable law must be legitimate and to be legitimate law must be specific? The common law, after all, tended to be quite specific for centuries before it aspired to become general. So how are we to approach the need to create environmental law at the international level that is grounded in our shared understanding of reality and, yet, comprehensive enough to actually protect the environment?

A possible solution may be found in an idea advanced by Kenneth Davis that he intended to assist administrative law judges in their efforts to deal with the complexities of regulation through rule making. Davis suggested that it would be possible to capture something of the practicality of the common law by using hypothetical cases in administrative rule making. These cases would be designed to pose important, but limited, problems of regulatory policy. They would allow administrative law judges to rule on narrow and well-defined questions. Those rulings, if accumulated properly, would provide the precedents that regulators could rely on in exercising their administrative discretion (Davis 1969). They

But when we come to the matter of using deliberative democratic dures like the citizen jury to address problems of environmental pro at the international level, we face a daunting challenge. It is diffic imagine a more convoluted set of policy issues, more thoroughly enta with concrete economic and political interests, than those involved ir serving the global environment. When one compares this policy arena those in which domestic issues are addressed, it is hard not to be disc aged by its complexities. Even at the national level, the difficulties invo in legislating for a modern industrialized society have created a patter. decision making that entails stating legal obligations at relatively high els of generality and relying upon members of executive and regulat agencies to fill in the details in the exercise of what Kenneth C. Davis l referred to as discretionary justice (Davis 1969). This trend in intere group liberalism has been criticized most trenchantly by Theodore Lov who has called for a "juridical" form of democracy. Lowi's approac would require legislatures to adopt far more concrete and specific rules (behavior that both constrain the exercise of administrative discretion an put citizens on notice as to the particulars of their legal obligations (Low 1979). Lowi's proposal is one response to the growing concern that mod ern regulatory regimes are insufficiently grounded in law and that, as William Pitt the Elder warned in a 1770 speech to the House of Lords, "where laws end, tyranny begins" (J. Bartlett 1968, 426). So the complexities of environmental regulation at the international level are more than practical problems. They pose a challenge to our theoretical account of the legitimacy of international law in the same way that the vagaries of domestic legislation challenge the legitimacy of the democratic nation-state.

Negotiation of international environmental agreements that spell out in detail the legal obligations of the parties has been discussed quite thoroughly in the realist literature. It has produced a body of generally unenforceable law with which the parties comply because it requires little of them that they are not already willing to do. In that respect, international environmental law is less a body of law than it is a collection of contracts. Bringing to this collection of agreements the questions of legitimacy involved in democratic politics would seem to be senseless. But even in the world of contracts, there must be a background of law that is obligatory. In thinking about the law of contract, it has long been recognized that the law "does not enforce every promise which a man may make" (Holmes [1881] 1991). It is the collective genius of generations captured in the tradition of the common law that it allows us to decide, would have an advantage over rule making in that they would be concrete rulings that would neither leave regulated parties wondering what specific obligations they imposed (the "Lowi problem") nor require decision makers to bite off more of the subject than they could chew (the "problem with the Lowi solution").

We suggest that the process of rule making through hypothetical adjudication can be married to the use of citizen juries to create what we call *juristic democracy*. Rather than ask citizen juries to weigh the arguments for competing solutions to big policy problems (like global climate change), it is possible to frame hypothetical disputes that would arise under a variety of regulatory approaches and then ask the world's citizens to apply the same common sense of justice that they already use when serving jury duty at their local town halls. The citizens would enjoy both the educative and expressive advantages associated with direct political participation. If a sufficient number of properly selected juries ruled on the same case across the globe, the international community would be provided with the results of a process of collective will formation unmediated by any elected elite.

It is worth pausing to emphasize several points. The range across which citizen juries can disagree would be limited by the simplicity and artificiality of the posed hypothetical cases. Moreover, the analytical task for these citizens can be focused through hypotheticals in a way that real courts never are able to do. Precedents would be of concern only for the agencies that posed the cases and attempted to restate or codify the normative principles that might emerge from a large number of juries, not for the juries themselves. The disinterestedness of citizens is not dependent on their assumption that no precedent is being created that might one day apply to them. Rather, it results from the fact that people adjudicating a concrete dispute engage in nothing more than first-order abstractions because resolving the case does not require them to do more and, in any event, they have no reason to see themselves in the place of the disputants and rarely do. Citizens would be motivated participants because they would expect that their decision, although only one data point, would directly contribute to the development of norms and laws of potentially major consequence.

It remains to describe the executive functions that would be appropriate to carry out this sort of collective will. How we answer that difficult question will, ultimately, determine whether an international environmental law capable of independently affecting the behavior of nations can be developed. But the fact that doctrines of common law form the foundation of some of the world's most durable democracies should provide us with all the encouragement we need to explore these issues further.

Regulation as Interpretation

The idea of globalizing environmental democracy through the use of a deliberative approach such as the citizen jury would appear to confront existing institutions of international governance with a challenge they are ill equipped to handle. The "executive" branch of international government is, at best, a collection of improvisations and compromises. Despite significant strides in recent years, there is a growing perception that the current international governance system remains weak and ineffective, resulting in a global environmental crisis (Speth 2004). Because there is no world government or sovereign global political authority, international environmental agencies often work at cross purposes and their efforts are frustrated by their reliance upon individual states to carry out their policies (Axelrod, Downie, and Vig 2005). It is not that we lack models for the development of effective international environmental organizations. Several options exist, from the speculative "Global Environmental Organization" that would exist as a wholly new comprehensive regulatory agency, to the proposed "International Environmental Organization" that would consolidate existing regimes in search of greater levels of mutual cooperation, to the suggested "World Environmental Organization" that would promote market strategies and environmental bargaining (Marshall 2002). Failing to adopt any of these approaches, it is always possible to resort to strictly bilateral or regional efforts to manage transboundary environmental problems (Parris 2004).

Neither is it a problem to find international environmental law to implement. One recent study identified more than nine hundred international agreements with some environmental provisions (Weiss 1999). So the adoption of new instruments may ultimately be less important than their effective implementation. After all, any form of international rule making that lacks a concern for the effectiveness of the norms already enacted, as demonstrated by the commitments of states to respect them, is self-defeating (Handl 1994). The challenge is to create international environmental institutions (like those created by the NAFTA environmental side agreements) that are able to coordinate treaty obligations and policy development in pursuit of agreements that synthesize competing interests and increasingly devolve monitoring and management duties to environmental NGOs (Kelly 1997). This must be done in a way that rebuilds the legitimacy of international organizations, which has been undermined by a lack of transparency, accountability, and normative grounding (Nye 2001).

A potentially useful conceptual structure for this effort has been provided by Lynton Caldwell (Caldwell 1999). He has argued that the process of globalizing the human environment has been driven by six particular elements of the more general process of globalization. These elements include

1. the growth of science and its technological applications,
2. the ever widening dissemination of information,
3. increasingly organized public action in international public affairs,
4. the emergence of new international nongovernmental organizations,
5. global economic growth, and
6. global population growth.

These elements of globalization cluster around three general issues. First, the growth of science and the broad dissemination of information suggest that environmental management will become even more knowledge driven than it has been and that the knowledge base involved will be ever more accessible to the world's citizens. Second, the increase in direct public participation in international affairs and the emergence of new international nongovernmental environmental organizations means that the work of environmental management will increasingly be subjected to the pressures of democratic politics. Finally, the facts of global economic and population growth clearly suggest that it will become increasingly important that international policies, across the widest spectrum of particular topics, be developed in ways that are sustainable from an ecological perspective. Thus the challenge to international executives will be to manage knowledge resources in ways that produce policies that are defensible in terms of both their democratic content and their environmental sustainability.

Knowledge

That our focus at this point turns to knowledge production and dissemination is, in some ways, propitious. Not only is our ability to recognize environmental issues dependent on scientific knowledge, but also science has assumed an often decisive role in promoting environmental issues to the level of international significance (Rosenbaum 2002). Moreover, the deployment of knowledge by networks of policy specialists in the global arena is critical to the idea of transgovernmentalism, which offers an answer to the most important challenges facing advanced industrial countries. These include the loss of national regulatory power under conditions of economic globalization, perceptions of a deficit of legitimacy as international institutions step in to fill the regulatory gap, and the difficulties involved in bringing less than fully democratic states into regulatory regimes (Slaughter 1997). The institutions of science and technology link people together through extensive systems of communication and commerce, serving as the basis of authority for a wide range of emergent institutions of global governance (Miller 2004). But a primary focus on science and information is a mixed blessing.

As a general matter, theories of international relations tend to ignore the social processes involved in the production of scientific and technical knowledge, assuming that knowledge production occurs outside the processes of international conflict and cooperation that are central to their analyses (VanDeveer 2004). As a consequence, our view of international environmental law frequently overlooks the facts that value-free science is an illusion, that scientific expertise is unevenly distributed both within and between countries, that the generation of environmental information is insufficiently interdisciplinary, and that economic analysis is often employed prematurely to limit the debate over regulatory alternatives (Zapfel 2002). From nearly any perspective, these blind spots are ultimately self-defeating. They generally result in a shift in focus from dialogue on matters of evidence and principle to an exchange of accusation in which objectivity is the first casualty and stalemate is the final result (Najim 2002).

The institutionalization of scientific research can either reinforce exploitive patterns of the past or introduce greater reciprocity in the interaction between global and local knowledge (Scholtz 2004). Despite the efforts of industry to globalize and standardize expertise, local and global knowledge increasingly depend on each other for their existence. Finding ways to build upon and use this interaction can help advance the cause of environmental protection in significant ways. Local activists can strengthen their ability to participate in international decision making by combining scientific and technical resources with their situated knowledge. Creating new social, political, and cognitive institutions (joint employee-activist teams or citizen inspectors for example) can challenge previously constructed boundaries and put greater pressure on both industry and governmental regulators to engage citizens in environmental protection (Iles 2004). In addition to enhancing the democratic content of international environmental politics, this kind of science-based approach holds the promise of more environmentally sustainable outcomes. International environmental agreements are not self-implementing. As a consequence of the particular dynamics of any negotiating forum, apparently standardized terminology and requirements tend to be locally contingent in practice. Even where such agreements arose from particular local issues, they will require "relocalization" if they are to be effectively applied in specific contexts (Gupta 2004). Moreover, local knowledge has become more than just a basis for competing knowledge claims; it is now a tool for exercising voice in global politics (Miller 2004).

According to some scholarly accounts, globalization is a process (or collection of processes) that simply happens to people, shaping the circumstances in which they live. But attempts by international environmental and developmental institutions to preserve traditional ways of life show that globalization can be a powerful tool for constructing as well as questioning the meaning of the local as well as crafting and negotiating the meaning of the global (Lahsen 2004). Science-based techniques like risk assessment are not tools for making decisions but, rather, for illuminating decisions. Whatever enlightenment risk assessment offers should not be a benefit for the elite few but a means by which public concerns and attitudes may be better integrated into risk-control strategies (Case 1993).

At this point it should be clear that the relationship between global and local knowledge is both promising and problematic from both the democratic and ecological perspective. Even in the presence of relatively unchallenged scientific consensus, local assessments of environmental challenges and obligations will be comprehensible only in light of their surrounding political culture (S. Beck 2004). As an example, environmental management is a prerogative that flows from some system of land tenure. Every system of resource management is, therefore, based upon certain assumptions, frequently unstated, according to which social organization, political authority, and property rights are closely related in culturally significant ways. Thus, cultural diversity is as critical as biological diversity and must be manifested in our methods of relating to the land and its inhabitants (LaDuke 1994). In this context, the challenge to transnational networks of environmental experts is to develop governing institutions that will "relocalize" global knowledge by translating and extrapolating the outputs of global regulatory models into locally relevant information, transmitting this information from sites of production to sites of consumption, and helping recipients interpret and make use of the information in relation to local environmental problems (Miller 2004).

Democracy

The global changes that humankind is now experiencing are being produced, to a very great extent, by what hundreds of millions of individuals are doing. The pace and direction of these changes can be affected only by what hundreds of millions of individuals stop doing or chose to do differently (Cleveland 1993). This realization leads to the conclusion that the concept of national interest, which has long been used to address discussions of foreign policy and international affairs, is not a very useful construct for analyzing global environmental problems. Thus we have seen many international environmental agreements negotiated over the past thirty years in which states have agreed to constrain their operational sovereignty while maintaining formal sovereignty and the rhetoric that supports it (Weiss 1993). This development, however, does not squarely address the problem of creating international environmental law that directly controls the behavior of individuals through mechanisms of democratic self-government.

The most optimistic claim that could probably be made at this point in the history of international environmentalism is that our existing agreements represent important statements concerning emerging global expectations. But candor would require us to add that these expectations have not so far allowed the leaders of the developed nations to recreate even the superficial consensus that linked environment and development at the 1992 Rio Earth Summit (Bryner 1997). In fact, it may be that some of our efforts over the recent decades have been counterproductive in at least one way. Efforts to address environmental problems from the top down, through international and national institutions, have led to a weakening of local environmental institutions and a concomitant decline in the effectiveness of environmental laws and policies in the Third World, for example in efforts to preserve species or maintain forest productivity. This is especially unfortunate because it is at the local level that the institutions for resource ownership and control could be brought together to provide for integrated environmental management of a genuinely democratic nature (B. Richardson 2000; Gupte and Bartlett 2007).

Even among First World publics, the dynamics of direct political action are often difficult. An example of the problem is provided by the fate of the Transatlantic Environmental Dialogue (TAED). The dialogue was an experiment in cooperation among environmental NGOs in Europe and the United States that was intended to set policy priorities for government action. The TAED fell victim to differences in policy-issue agendas (such as a lack of interest in international issues in the United States), the frequently adversarial character of NGOs, and a preference within the NGO community for global rather than regional policy approaches (Lankowski 2004).

If in the face of failures like that of the TAED one were looking for reasons to abandon the idea of countering globalization through greater use of democratic participation, certainly the reasons would not be difficult to find. There is no universally agreed upon definition of globalization, but it clearly embraces vast changes in both economics and culture. Moreover, there is no corresponding global governance mechanism to cope with the multinational and transboundary issues that those changes produce. Intergovernmental organizations of various sorts have been given mandates to deal with certain of those issues, but none has been created with corresponding new powers of governance or organizational structures that would allow them to act decisively on those mandates (Guruswamy 2003).

A determined democrat, however, might counter that this discouraging recitation is merely evidence that democracy has not been given a fair chance. Among its other results, globalization has changed the fora in which nations, organizations, and individuals operate. As a consequence, nongovernmental organizations play an increasingly important role in the international arena, reconfiguring communities across traditional and national boundaries to such an extent that the continuing relevance of states has been called into question (Pagnani 2003). A note of caution, however, is in order. By themselves, social movements and the organizations of civil society they produce may fail to democratize environmental discourses. In fact, they may strengthen preexisting discourses (and their potentially repressive impacts) by reinforcing conventional conceptions of ecology that overlook the underlying complexities of the relationship between nature and human interests. The solution is wider participation in the formation of ecological concepts. This is a practical necessity if temporal and cultural specificity is to be minimized in our pursuit of ecological rationality (Forsyth 2004).

This need for the widest possible participation is the underlying logic of the Aarhus Convention and is widely seen to be a solution to the challenges faced by international environmental NGOs. In order to overcome the numerous obstacles to fundamental change in environmental policy, NGOs must form broad-based coalitions among those affected by environmental hazards. NGOs can accomplish more through networks and alliances with other groups in civil society than through their own efforts at elite bargaining (Dhanapala 2002). In the interpretation and implementation of international environmental law, the important objectives of coherence and predictability will require that decisions be made on the basis of community-accepted norms. What is needed is not a passive dispute resolution body, but rather a mechanism that is able to articulate the aims and objectives of the communities in which it operates (Craik 1998). This is especially true where, as is often the case, local-level institutions for ecological management are informal, based on cultural norms and social conventions rather than the positive enactments of legislatures (Colding and Folke 2000). We must confront the fact that the behavioral rules needed to preserve the environment must be attuned to the conditions of each distinct ecosystem and the human cultures they contain. No general recipe is available, both because of the various types of legal systems involved and because of the varied socioeconomic and environmental conditions presented (Brunnee 1993). Moreover, local knowledge is required to relate ecological concepts to the particulars of specific environments, to place, to history, and to identity. The content of ecological expertise is, therefore, a matter of continual negotiation between universal and particular conceptions of the environment. The mere fact that this pattern is likely to recur globally does not mean that the content of each instantiation can be predetermined in the absence of local input (Lachmund 2004).

As challenging as this "custom-made" approach may be, it offers several distinct advantages if it is seriously undertaken. It is widely accepted that differences between the legal frameworks in force at the national and global levels suggest that different considerations should go into the choices of the instruments of environmental policy. Underlying legal structures do matter. Global environmental regulations must, therefore, be conceived differently from national regulatory schemes (Wiener 1999). But accepting this abstract proposition and acting on it in concrete circumstances are two different things. One example is the relationship between trade and the environment. In the ministries where trade agreements are negotiated, ecology is of limited interest. But in communities around the world, local environmental activists seek to intervene in these negotiations. They understand that there are no environmentally neutral trade issues. They also know that better-quality decisions and a less adversarial relationship between business and environmental groups result from public involvement in trade negotiations. And they are a constant reminder that trade decisions must be viewed as equitable if they are to be politically sustainable (Powell 1995).

Another example of the importance of adapting global policy to local circumstance is presented by the increasing role played by indigenous peoples in international affairs. Around the world, indigenous populations have declared their distinctive identity and existence and the importance of their contributions to the human experience. They have also asserted their right of self-determination and the concomitant rights of political participation. By demanding that international decision makers acknowledge the imposed risks they face, indigenous peoples have mounted a powerful resistance to the global as it is defined by economists, scientists, and policymakers, many of whom are responsible for denying them basic democratic rights in their own countries (Fogel 2004). The importance of this new political force is evident, for example, in the Prior Informed Consent Provision of the Convention on Biological Diversity. The structure of the convention reflects the long-standing tension between local communities and national governments. Its focus on the "fair and equitable sharing" of the benefits of development has produced a complex power struggle between public officials, who see biodiversity as a source of much-needed revenue, and traditional communities, which are the guardians of ancient knowledge of medicinal plants and other biological resources. Requiring the consent of indigenous peoples before development projects are approved is an increasingly important mechanism for ensuring that adequate environmental and social-impact assessment is conducted and that community involvement and self-determination is guaranteed (Firestone 2003).

Sustainability

It remains to describe what a form of environmental policy implementation conceived as interpretation would look like and to suggest how it would make sustainable policy development more likely. Were international environmental norms to be established by thousands of citizen juries across the globe, what would (or could) existing international organizations do to render those norms into effective environmental regulations? Happily enough, we have a model at hand that can help us answer that question.

In 1923, a group of prominent American judges, lawyers, and teachers established the American Law Institute (ALI). The intention of the founders of the ALI was to address what they took to be the two chief defects in American law at that time: its uncertainty and its complexity. Uncertainty in the law, on the one hand, was attributed to a lack of agreement among members of the profession on the fundamental principles of the common law, a lack of precision in the use of legal terms, conflicting and badly drawn statutory provisions, the large volume of reported cases, and the relentless march of novel legal questions. The complexity of the law, on the other hand, was attributed largely to its lack of systematic development and to its numerous variations within the different jurisdictions of the United States. The ALI set as its objective the improvement of law and its administration by promoting the clarification and simplification of the law and its better adaptation to social needs. The ALI uses two major techniques to pursue this objective: restatement and codification.

A *restatement* is the result of a careful survey of the existing state of the common law in a particular field of practice. Its purpose is to tell judges and lawyers what the law is in its current form. Between 1923 and 1944, the ALI developed its "Restatements of the Law" in the areas of agency, conflict of laws, contracts, judgments, property, restitution, security, torts, and trusts. In 1952, the Institute began work on the "Restatement Second," reflecting new analysis employing an expanded list of authorities and adding coverage of areas such as landlord and tenant law and the foreign relations law of the United States. The "Restatement Third" was inaugurated in 1987, adding coverage of unfair competition, the law governing lawyers, and employment law, as well as expanded coverage of topics in the existing areas covered by prior restatements. The singular characteristic of restatements has been their descriptive character. Where significant differences exist among jurisdictions on important points of law, those differences are noted and the restatement report generally limits its editorializing to characterizing one view as the majority position.

A different approach to the progressive improvement of law is the ALI's codification projects. In the most prominent example of this process, the institute has collaborated for over fifty years with the National Conference of Commissioners on Uniform State Laws in developing the Uniform

Commercial Code (UCC). The UCC is a comprehensive code covering most aspects of modern commercial law. It is generally viewed as one of the most important achievements of American law and has been enacted (with some variations) in forty-nine states, the District of Columbia, and the U.S. Virgin Islands. The ALI has pursued other codification projects that have resulted in the development of other model statutes, including the Model Code of Evidence, the Model Penal Code, the Model Code of Pre-Arraignment Procedure, the Model Land Development Code, and a proposed Federal Securities Code. The common characteristic of these documents, which distinguishes them from the restatements, is their prescriptive character. They go beyond describing the law as it is (including its areas of conflict) to propose a unified approach that would comprise, in the institute's view, the legal best practices in a given area of law. In pursuing its codification projects, the ALI has concentrated on areas of the law where uniformity of approach is a substantively desirable goal in itself or where there is a general view that significant reforms are needed. This measure of self-restraint, together with the credibility resulting from the restatement process underlying codification, has served to make the model codes some of the most influential documents in American legal history.

It might be useful at this point to contrast the American Law Institute with its closest global cousin, the International Law Commission (ILC). Established a quarter of a century after the American Law Institute, the ILC is charged by its founding charter with the promotion of the progressive development of international law and its codification. While the distinction is largely one of convenience, the statute distinguishes between progressive development as the preparation of draft conventions on subjects that have not yet been regulated by international law and codification as the more precise formulation and systematization of rules of international law in fields where there already is extensive state practice, precedent, and doctrine. In practice, the commission's work typically involves some elements of both progressive development and codification, with the precise balance depending upon the circumstances in a given area of law. The drafters of the statute conceived of progressive development as a conscious effort to create new rules, the culmination of which would be an international convention. In the case of codification, on the other hand, it was imagined that publication of a report and possible adoption of it by the UN General Assembly was an alternate outcome. The ILC has indicated that the distinction drawn by the statute between progressive development and codification has proven unhelpful in practical terms and it has developed a consolidated procedure and applied that idea to its work in a flexible manner, making adjustments as circumstances demand.

The most obvious point of contrast between the ILC and the ALI is the absence of any correlative at the international level to the process of restatement. Both progressive development and codification as carried on by the commission are forms of advocacy of best practice, as is the codification procedure used by the institute. The ILC was undoubtedly correct in its conclusion that the distinction between development and codification in its statute was not useful. It was based on a distinction between two alternate means by which the proposals of the commission might be adopted, which for our purpose is uninteresting. What occupies our attention is distinguishing between the description of law that goes into a restatement and the proposal of legal reforms that comprise codification.

Relying as it does on the work of thousands of judges and juries, the restatement process serves a legitimation function that may not be entirely unintended. Although the American Law Institute has never (to our knowledge) directly addressed the issue of political legitimacy, others have done so in helpful ways. To cite but one classic example, Alexander Hamilton argued in *The Federalist* #17 that the duty of the states to provide for the "ordinary administration of criminal and civil justice" is the "most powerful, most universal, and most attractive source of popular obedience and attachment" (Hamilton, Madison, and Jay 2005). The intimate involvement of average citizens in this process and the immediacy of its benefits to them were more important, in Hamilton's mind, than any other circumstance in promoting "affection, esteem, and reverence toward the government." *The Federalist* #17, it should be remembered, was an essay put forward in defense of the proposition that the new central government could be allowed the power of "legislation for the individual citizens of America" without the risk of it usurping the legitimate authority of the states.

It is important not to conflate codification and restatement. Restatement is no more than an analytical summary. It does not (necessarily or appropriately) attempt to force a greater degree of coherence or consensus on a body of decisions than the substance of those decisions actually warrants. It is, in that way, descriptive only. Codification attempts to go one step further to suggest how new cases would be decided, based upon what are taken to be the most relevant elements of the "legal database" that the adjudicatory process has accumulated. It is both descriptive and predictive. When that codification is presented as an "ideal code," it also stakes out a normative claim on its own behalf. A juristic democratic process of formulating global environmental norms through the use of citizen juries (as we have described them above) would allow the International Law Commission, for the first time, to pursue restatement activities that would provide a form of democratic legitimacy for its codification efforts independent of any charge from the United Nations or request of member states. With this foundation, progressive development and codification could entail not only pursuit of new international conventions, but also the adoption at the level of the states of model environmental codes that reflect the considered judgment of the world's citizens (in congress disassembled). It could also feed back into environmental practice in the states the collective wisdom of our species as it struggles to master the environmental challenges that manifest themselves everywhere in their various guises. This approach to formulating, interpreting, and implementing ecological norms offers obvious political advantages. It makes it possible to produce rules that are binding (in at least a minimally legal sense) on all nations without unanimous consent in a formal process of negotiation (Palmer 1992). It provides for the creation of an intermediate governing process to supplement states and markets that are neither completely domestic nor fully international and which have been regarded as essential to global environmental governance (Lahsen 2004). These processes will, in turn, allow for the change of policy boundaries and the building of linkages between local, national, and international institutions that any successful environmental regime will require (B. Richardson 2000).

The approach to building and implementing environmental norms that we have been describing also offers advantages in terms of producing more sustainable policy outcomes. For one thing, the effectiveness of compliance-control procedures depends to a significant degree on cooperation and flexibility with regard to response measures. Responses to noncompliance need to be appropriate to the cause, degree, and frequency of noncompliance and they must provide international assistance based upon the assumption that more effective response is a shared objective of all parties. This attitude requires a dialogue within the community of parties rather than conventional approaches to enforcement (Ehrmann 2002; Faure and Lefevere 2005). The added legitimacy provided by a juristic approach to establishing global norms and the implementation strategy it suggests would seem to be the technique most likely to produce such a community dialogue.

A useful example involves the globalization of environmental impact assessment. In the United States, the National Environmental Policy Act (NEPA) requires all federal agencies to prepare environmental impact statements for any action with potential environmental consequences. This requirement, replicated in the American states, has become ubiquitous in development planning in the United States. But virtually every federal agency with domestic NEPA responsibilities has refused to enforce its provisions with respect to its overseas activities (Manheim 1994). This is true despite the fact that a growing global commitment to environmental impact assessment provides an increasingly important safeguard against ecologically irresponsible decisions. While the particulars of this safeguard vary among states (and rightly so), the basic requirements of transparency, public participation, environmental screening, and post-project environmental monitoring are emerging as essential elements of the global environmental impact assessment (EIA) model (Gray 2000). This process has allowed at least one observer to conclude that transboundary environmental impact assessment is emerging as an important global phenomenon not as a function of any international regime but rather as an offshoot of domestic EIA laws (Knox 2002). Developments of this sort have even led the author of NEPA, Lynton Caldwell, to argue that an environmental common law for nations is in fact evolving, albeit without any general recognition of the fact or any dejure modification of the doctrine of national sovereignty (Caldwell 1999).

Against this global backdrop, there is a growing awareness that sustainable resource management requires that people who have traditionally "owned" resources and used them to meet their social and economic needs must enjoy community-based rights of management that give them the incentive to collectively conserve their resources and the political bargaining power to influence the conditions under which interests outside of their communities exploit those resources (B. Richardson 2000). It has even been argued that a global norm of environmental protection has emerged at the expense of international economic law relating to development. This is attributed to the increasing participation of transnational civil society in international environmental lawmaking and the attractiveness of the language of rights and the idea of a right to a healthy environment (Fuentes 2002). If, indeed, the assertion of local rights against global processes has grown so potent, then the time is approaching to close the circle. Local institutions must relate to the global aspects of environmental management by participating in the emerging transnational networks that allow for the generation and exchange of new understandings about environmental management (B. Richardson 2000). It is at this point in the process of developing regulatory practices that the procedure of codification can feed back environmentally rational norms from the global arena into the decision-making activities of local institutions.

Juristic Democracy and International Law: Diversity, Disadvantage, and Deliberation

In the previous chapter, we outlined an approach to collective will formation that we characterized as *juristic democracy*. By way of summary, juristic democracy presents citizen juries with a concrete (but hypothetical) problem of international environmental protection and asks them to come to a unanimous resolution of that problem. Then a substantial number of these deliberative outcomes can be aggregated through a process of restatement into a general description of the considered judgment of a representative sample of the population regarding the question of policy that underlies the adjudicated case. The objective is to use the discursively constrained environment of the jury, and the neutrality resulting from the hypothetical nature of the case, to allow ordinary citizens to contribute to a collective process that strives to achieve what John Rawls calls *reflective equilibrium* (Rawls 2001, 29–32).[12]

In chapter 8 we will further examine the alternatives for implementing an approach like juristic democracy within the context of the existing institutions and processes of international governance. First, however, it is necessary to address the many serious criticisms that have been lodged against the very idea of deliberative democracy. Most of these criticisms allege that deliberative democracy is either not very deliberative or not very democratic. In this chapter we shall detail these complaints, offer a response to them on behalf of deliberative democracy, and refine our model of juristic democracy to more directly address the concerns of deliberation's critics.

Is the Jury Out?

For purposes of theoretical development, it is a fortunate coincidence that our model of deliberative democracy relies on the idea of citizen juries.

The image of "twelve angry men" is deliberative democracy's least appealing face, the one most certain to raise the hackles of deliberation's critics. Deliberation's other guises seem more congenial. The town hall meeting is a comfortable armchair for democratic theorists, particularly in America. Even when a real town convening in a real hall is involved, any less than fully democratic results can be rationalized away. Locals, after all, are assumed to know their own interests and issues better than outside observers. Democracy's discontents are always free to relocate when their concerns occur at the neighborhood level. What the town hall meeting may lack in terms of deliberative purity, it more than makes up in its democratic authenticity (Bryan 2004).

At the other end of democracy's spectrum, the model of the multimember court is often invoked as the paradigmatic case of deliberation. In the abstract, a panel of judges is a defensible model of decision making because the parties are disinterested, similarly skilled and situated, and held in a structure that ensures their relative equality. When actual courts act, they are generally constrained by policies established by the representative institutions of government and their actions are subject to review by higher courts (including, ultimately, the court of public opinion). So we can often accept the seemingly antidemocratic qualities associated with judges (both as individuals and as courts) because they play a limited role in existing political systems.[13] In short, on the one hand, judges can deliberate legitimately and well because we do not ask them to do democracy's heavy lifting. As with the town hall meeting, they enjoy a pass (to a degree) on part of the deliberative democratic promise. Juries, on the other hand, are more problematic. They seem neither as democratic as the town hall meeting nor as calmly and competently deliberative as the panel of judges. But herein lies an opportunity. If the citizen jury (disfavored as it may be) can be acquitted of the charges against it, other models of deliberative democracy should enjoy the benefits of collateral estoppel. That a theoretical and, perhaps, practical opportunity exists in this regard, however, should not blind us to the dilemmas that juries represent.

The American founders thought so highly of the institution of the jury that they made its availability a constitutional right in *both* criminal and civil cases, though the guarantee of a civil jury came in the Bill of Rights as an afterthought and was the subject of some disagreement. Indeed, the absence of an explicit guarantee of a trial by jury in civil cases was one of the concerns raised by anti-federalists about the new Constitution. In *The Federalist* #83, Alexander Hamilton declared that both the advocates and opponents of the U.S. Constitution set a high value on the institution of the jury. He then went on, however, to express doubts about the jury's utility in a class of civil cases including tax collections and prize cases involving the laws and interests of other nations. In these cases, respectively, the costs of jury adjudication would often exceed the amounts at issue and the intricacies of the legal questions involved would present average citizens with too challenging a task. More revealing is the fact that Hamilton also included, in the category of matters inappropriate to the jury system, cases dealing with the law of equity.

According to Hamilton, equity jurisdiction presents a problem for the jury system for two reasons. First, juries do their best work when they are asked to decide questions that are relatively simple, few in number, and covered by generally accepted rules of law. Questions of equity, however, arise from extraordinary problems that involve making exceptions to general rules of law. Hamilton argued that it is unreasonable to ask people who have been drawn away from their usual occupations, and cannot return to them until the matter is decided, to endure the complicated and time-consuming process of resolving the novel and fact-rich problems that a case in equity presents. Even if it were not impractical to ask this of juries, there is no reason to think that juries would bring to the adjudication of extraordinary matters the special advantages that they do to the resolution of problems more characteristic of everyday life.

Second, precisely because a case in equity requires an exception to the general rule, it represents a danger to the general rule. The general rules that govern the outcome of cases in common law courts have become general rules because they are serviceable, though imperfect, resolutions for common problems. Even when they yield manifestly unjust results, we must proceed with a due regard for their average utility (Posner 1981, 101–107). Cases in which we deviate from a general rule must remain extraordinary and be seen as such, if the salutary effects of having general rules are to be preserved. In Hamilton's time, several of the states of the American union accomplished this, in part, by holding to the English tradition of lodging equitable litigation in courts of chancery. These courts were separate from those of legal jurisdiction and, without exception, denied litigants the right to trial by jury. This institutional bifurcation, soon abandoned in America, allowed both for trial by jury in the run of the main cases *and* for deviations from what the law appeared to require where considerations of justice seemed to demand it. With equity and law combined in our contemporary system of courts, however, we are left with the struggle to balance the advantages and disadvantages of the phenomena of jury nullification (Sunstein 1996). This would seem to prove Hamilton's point about keeping equitable issues out of the hands of juries so as to protect the general rule (or rules) of law.

Our discussion of the jury to this point is intended to be more than historical diversion. It serves several important purposes. First, it places the idea of juristic democracy (employing citizen juries) along a deliberative continuum between the most democratic model of deliberative democracy (the town hall meeting) and the most deliberative model of deliberative democracy (the multimember court). Second, it establishes the democratic bona fides of the jury system. In its criminal variant, trial by jury was regarded by the federalists as a "valuable safeguard to liberty" and by the anti-federalists as "the very palladium of free government." In civil matters, the founders were so at pains to reassure critics of the U.S. Constitution that the new plan was no threat to trial by jury that they eventually devised the Seventh and Tenth Amendments to protect the jury in federal and state courts, respectively. Third, the limitations that even so ardent an admirer of the jury system as Alexander Hamilton felt compelled to place on that institution serve as a foundation for the criticisms of the work of juries that we hear today as well as for the doubts that have been expressed about using the jury as a model for deliberative democracy. It is to those criticisms and doubts that we now turn.

Juries on Trial

Criticisms of the work of juries in the real world are, by now, relatively familiar. For one thing, there are at least two ways to evaluate the decisions that juries produce. At its most basic level, the jury verdict provides a single, binary input into the complex and extensive system of adjudicating disputes between parties. The most common form of jury verdict is the general verdict; guilty or not guilty, liable in this amount or not liable. So simple an action can be criticized for providing no grounds upon which to assess its value, discover its error, or reveal its bias (Frank 1949). Yet, the general verdict can also be praised for its ability to introduce compromise into an otherwise uncompromising system and for not forcing juries to say more than they can agree on (Casper 1993). Does a jury do violence to the complexity of the world by reducing it to a verdict, or does it add value to human existence by disposing of a problem in a pragmatic, if imperfect, manner?

Another question, or series of questions, can be raised regarding the composition of juries. In Hamilton's time and before, jurors were selected for their personal knowledge of the circumstances of the case at trial and only propertied males were qualified to serve (Dawson 1960). Even today, the process of assembling jury pools and selecting jurors can produce substantial demographic differences between juries and the population at large (Fukurai, Butler, and Krooth 1993). More may be at stake than merely squandering our best opportunity for nurturing a genuinely representative and participatory institution of government. A lack of jury heterogeneity may actually undermine the jury trial as a technique for accurately resolving problems.

With respect to race, for example, there is significant evidence to suggest it plays a role in determining the outcomes of criminal trials. Some studies have suggested that white jurors produce higher conviction rates for black defendants than for white defendants (Poulson 1990). Other research has failed to produce a consistent pattern of the effect of race on criminal conviction rates (Mazzella and Feingold 1994). Despite this general pattern of mixed results, one particularly troubling regularity has emerged from the research on juries and race. There appears to be a consistent tendency for some juries to acquit defendants where both defendant and victim are black (Kalvern and Zeisel 1966; Myers 1980; Foley and Chamblin 1982). This result, to the extent that it is true, is evidence of something more than unfairness to one party or another in isolated cases. It suggests a systemic indifference to the costs imposed upon society, not to mention the pain inflicted on individuals, resulting from black-on-black crime. It would be hard to imagine a more damning indictment of any system of justice than that it tended to create a legal ghetto in which discrimination and disadvantage were magnified by disinterest.

A similar picture emerges with respect to juries and gender. Much of the research fails to produce evidence of consistent and significant relationships between gender and jury verdicts (Hastie, Penrod, and Pennington 1983). Exceptions, however, emerge in two areas. In the case of both sexual assault (Sealy and Cornish 1973; Bottoms and Goodman 1994) and domestic violence (Pierce and Harris 1993), female jurors are more willing to convict male defendants than are male jurors. As in the case of race, we are left to wonder about the precise mechanisms involved. Are the varied life experiences of men and women (like those of whites and blacks) simply combining in the jury room to produce different and more accurate results than would be the case were the jurors all of the same gender? Or is it a less cognitive, more affective, matter of identification with and sympathy for the victim? In either event, we have empirical evidence to support the theoretical complaint that the jury system is inaccurate and unjust precisely to the extent that it remains unrepresentative.

A third set of questions about the jury system has to do with the normative assumptions we make about jury deliberations. Juries are supposed to be composed of fully independent and equal individuals, all of whom are open to the information provided by the trial itself and to the views of their fellow jurors. Moreover, jurors are supposed to respond only to the force of the better argument, never to coercion or inducement (Kassin and Wrightsman 1988). But how seriously can we take this idealized model? Hollywood has given us the image of a single juror, standing alone, who converts eleven others to his or her point of view through relentless but respectful logic. But if the member of a minority needs to have the performance skills of Henry Fonda to prevail in the jury room, does that not make the jury critics' argument for them?

There is, indeed, research indicating that the power of minorities to influence majorities may be at its lowest ebb in the jury room. Where a group task is purely judgmental (rather than an *intellective* task that has an objectively correct answer), there is evidence to suggest that we rely on socially contingent conceptual structures in ways that might systematically disadvantage those who do not share the perspective of the majority (Kerr 2001). Simply by virtue of their difference, therefore, minorities on juries may face an uphill battle. This might be the case not because the view of the minority is inferior but, rather, because the members of the minority do not share the conceptual framework and habits of interaction that are the dominant patterns of the majority. To the extent that this is true, it undermines the claim that a jury trial is an especially accurate or even a particularly fair method for adjudicating disputes or determining guilt or innocence.

Each of the criticisms of the jury system we have discussed has a parallel in the literature on deliberative democracy. Just as juries in the judicial system have been criticized for reducing complex problems excessively, discriminating against minorities, and privileging particular styles of argumentation, the various approaches to deliberative democracy have been accused of depriving political discourse of its rich detail, ignoring difference and diversity, and compounding the disadvantages against which the powerless already struggle. We turn now to those complaints.

Deliberation in the Dock

The recent ascendance of deliberative democracy in the literature on democratic theory has produced a vociferous response, often (and ironically) from some who have spent years looking for alternatives to interest-group liberalism. At a general level, deliberative democracy, especially in its juristic form, can be criticized for reducing politics to an unnecessarily narrow range of concerns. According to Chantal Mouffe, deliberative democracy is dominated by "an individualistic, universalistic, and rationalistic framework" that renders it unable to grasp the true nature of the challenges facing democratic institutions today (Mouffe 1999, 745). Mouffe focuses her criticism on forms of deliberative democracy that she identifies with the work of Jürgen Habermas. But it is only fair to concede that, by its very nature, the model of juristic democracy we have advanced belongs directly in her crosshairs.

It is probably true that Mouffe's sweeping criticism of deliberative democracy bears more strongly on some deliberative approaches than on others. Perhaps the town hall meeting lies outside her line of fire, allowing as it does a far wider range of arguments and appeals than other deliberative models. And, perhaps, Mouffe would concede that the judicial panel is permissibly narrow in its approach because of its narrow jurisdiction and its justifiable emphasis on deliberative purity over democratic authenticity. But she would not be obliged in any way to make those concessions to juristic democracy, aspiring as it does to bring together a broadly representative group of citizens to engage in an exercise in collective will formation constrained by the substantive boundaries of a specific case and the procedural restrictions of the jury room.

In pursing her critique of deliberative democracy, Mouffe takes as her indicative case the ideal speech situation described by Habermas. This standard for democratic discourse can, she argues, be criticized from a Wittgensteinian perspective. According to Mouffe, Wittgenstein held that for there to be an agreement in opinions there first had to be an agreement on the language used, and this, in turn, required an agreement in forms of life (Mouffe 1999). The "fusion of voices" that rational consensus aspires to is made possible only by a common form of life, not the exercise of reason (749). To this, Mouffe adds the argument that "discourse itself in its fundamental structure is authoritarian since out of the free-floating dispersion of signifiers, it is only through the intervention of a master signifier . . . the signifier of symbolic authority founded only on itself . . . that a consistent field of meaning can emerge" (751). On Mouffe's account, we run several risks by making reason the master signifier of political discourse. One is that we blind ourselves to the place of the passions in the construction of collective political identities. As a result, we fail to see that the main challenge to democracy is not discovering ways to eliminate the passions in order to create a rational consensus, but rather how to mobilize the passions in service of democratic designs (Mouffe 2002). In so doing, we deprive ourselves of the capacity to imagine a global "pluriverse" that would allow us to oppose the hegemonic project of the totalizing forms of globalization with a vision of a multipolar world order (Mouffe 2005).

Without necessarily conceding that the work of Habermas is deliberative democracy's best representative (though we certainly might), let us mount our defense on the ground chosen by Mouffe. Without claiming that Habermas can speak for all deliberative democrats (which he certainly would not), let us allow him to do the talking. We are fortunate in this project that Habermas has taken Wittgenstein seriously, discussing him extensively in at least six of his recent books. Like many other theorists, Habermas relies on Wittgenstein primarily for the concept of language games. According to Habermas, Wittgenstein conceives of a language game as a complex of language and praxis (Habermas 1988). Both he and Wittgenstein regard the intentional contents of language as independent of intentional experiences, having nothing to do at first with "acts of consciousness or inner episodes" (Habermas 2001c, 52).

For Habermas, Wittgenstein's approach constitutes a philosophical turn that is both linguistic and pragmatic. This dual quality of his work is captured in his own words when he defines a language game as "consisting of language and the action into which it is woven" (Wittgenstein 2001, 4). So language is not a tool that we use to pursue a social consensus, rational or otherwise (Habermas 1988). It is, rather, a collection of "symbols and activities" that are "already linked under the reciprocal supervision of an accompanying consensus of all participants" (131). For Habermas (2003) this consensus is linguistic: it is the "world-constituting" quality of language that is able to serve this purpose because the foundational understandings of language are not, in themselves, "capable of being true or false" but rather determine "a priori the standards for the truth and falsity of propositions" (Habermas 2003c, 68–69).

Contrary to Mouffe's suggestion that shared language constitutes an ethics that prejudges all questions, making the distinction between procedure and substance impossible, language games are ontologies (Habermas 2001c). These ontologies ground our use of languages. Our understanding of language is evidenced by our ability to take "communicative action," which is itself "linked to a symbolized expectation of behavior" (Habermas 1988, 131). We then concretize these expectations by creating the language game that is law (Habermas 1996). In this connection, Habermas draws on Wittgenstein's idea of the language game to describe legal rules as "rooted in a practice that, although described externally as a fact, is taken by the participants themselves as self-evidently valid" (202). The rules of language games are normative only in the weakest sense. They are "untouched by any connotations of binding or obligatory practical norms" (Habermas 2003c, 122–123). They bind a subject's will only by channeling intentions in directions that hold out the possibility of justifying one's actions to possible critics and of succeeding in meeting the intersubjective expectations of a community of practitioners. Herein lies the response to Mouffe's second criticism, that discourse itself is authoritarian because it elevates reason to the status of a "master signifier."

If there is, indeed, a master signifier in the practice of discourse ethics as imagined by Habermas, "action" is a better candidate for the job than "reason." We can distinguish action from mere behavior, which is not rule-governed (Habermas 1988). Rule-governed action is "always communicative action, because rules cannot be private rules for one individual but rather must have intersubjective validity for a life form in which at least two subjects participate" (127). So it is inaccurate to say that the ideal speech situation imports some version of rationality that is alien to the lived experiences of discourse participants. The very idea of reasoned discourse can have no substantive meaning outside the structure of intersubjective validity that enables the participants to arrive at a common plan of action. The fact that one language is subject to translation into another is evidence that reason is both "bound up with language" and capable of extension "beyond its languages" (144). It is only this communicative form of reason, as a constituent element of languages generally, that is essential to communicative action.

To go behind reason at this level, as Mouffe attempts to do, is to risk a philosophical regress that is as pointless as it is endless. It is also to depart from the view of Mouffe's own philosophical touchstone, Wittgenstein, who urged that we not attempt to "refine or complete the system of rules for the use of our words in unheard-of ways." For his part, he sought only an understanding "that makes me capable of stopping doing philosophy when I want to . . . that gives philosophy peace, so that it is no longer tormented by questions which bring *itself* into question" (Wittgenstein 2001, 44). In this passage we hear a poignant prelude to Habermas's argument for a form of "communicative reason" that is unconditional without being metaphysical—a sense of reason to which all can subscribe because it is grounded not in any particular form of life, but in our shared capacity for reciprocal understanding (Habermas 2002a).

Diversity's Deliberative Potential

If we take the view that deliberative democracy (as practiced in a policy jury) is an exercise in what Habermas called communicative reason, what roles does that suggest for diversity of race, culture, and gender? Here we discuss what we take to be diversity's three most significant sources of deliberative potential: its tendency to promote language innovation, its utility for testing emergent consensus, and its contribution to political legitimation.

Language Innovation

The role of language in politics, and the potential of language innovation to reorder politics, has two important elements. First, language can be seen as a constituent element in our political ontology. This view suggests a somewhat counterintuitive reason why important political issues are sometimes neglected. It is not so much that we fail to discuss issues because we don't see them but, rather, that we fail to see political issues because we lack any language to describe them. Politics and political phenomena do not simply exist. They are "carved out" through a process of boundary drawing (Gieryn 1995) that partitions reality and assigns labels to the demarcated elements. This work creates a discursive space in which we can intelligibly refer to political categories like the public and the private, the political and the nonpolitical. So our ability to focus our attention on discrete political issues depends crucially on the prior ability to mark out a "political realm" linguistically.

Second, our ability to imagine potential solutions to political problems and to weigh their desirability is also dependent on our linguistic abilities. Language does not so much reflect reality as it structures the way we perceive reality and the choices with which reality confronts us (Fischer and Forester 1993). The manner in which we represent reality, to ourselves and to each other, is necessarily selective. And the way we select which options to consider and which to dismiss reflects assumptions about causality, values, and legitimacy that are built into the very structure of our language. As with so much of the contemporary analytic tradition, the value of this insight is more therapeutic than constructive, disabusing us of what we thought we knew. Just as the "linguistic turn" has undermined our confidence in "the mind" as something about which we could have a philosophical view and "knowledge" as an appropriate object of theorizing (Rorty 1979), so too "politics" loses its valence as a coherent system of thought and is increasingly revealed as a collection of conventional categories that often masks patterns of power and privilege behind a façade of facially neutral terminology. To the extent that these insights have any constructive potential, it consists of their tendency to lead us beyond the boundaries of the language games within which we are comfortable and fluent, in search of policy options that arise from discursive traditions that are not our own.

Consensus Testing

Diversity of race, gender, and ethnicity is conventionally taken to be one of deliberation's most important limiting factors (Bohman 1996). Indeed, it would be difficult to claim that diversity makes it easier to achieve consensus. It can be argued, however, that diversity makes genuine consensus possible. In the first place, an ever-present risk in any form of democracy is that the participation of minorities will, over time, come to be no more than formal. There is, and always has been, reason to be concerned about what has often been called the tyranny of the majority (Guinier 1994). At its most oppressive, the majority generally acts on behalf of a "public" that Lippman characterized as a phantom (Lippman 1925). The contemporary concern with representative democracy is that it fails to give substance to this phantom because it represents only those interests that already enjoy power and privilege in any given society. Whether the result is active hostility to minority interests, or simple indifference to the very existence of minorities, the solution would appear to be the same. Neither hostility nor indifference long survives immersion in the political solvent of difference (Gutmann 2003).

Moreover, there is a growing body of empirical evidence (admittedly anecdotal to some degree) that deliberation among diverse groups of citizens can go beyond merely representing public opinion more accurately. It may also promote the development of new areas of political consensus by allowing citizens to modify and integrate their preexisting preferences into something more closely resembling considered judgments. A series of recent experiments with deliberative polling leads one to conclude that citizens are both willing and able to weigh their own views against those of others and develop "verdicts" that capture a consensus regarding the most appropriate course of action in the circumstances presented to them. During these experiments, it has been observed that participants made significant efforts to prepare for the sessions by reviewing background information on the issues they would be asked to consider. A large percentage of participants actively engaged in the subsequent conversations, during which many took extensive notes and very few behaved in ways that were uncivil. Participants generally indicated a willingness to participate in similar experiments in the future and, most importantly, experimenters were able to measure significant changes in participant attitudes as a result of the deliberative experience (Fishkin 1991, 1995, 1999; Fishkin and Luskin 1999; Leib 2004).

Results such as these lend credence to proposals that have been advanced by some of those who have warned us most strongly about the tyranny of the majority. As an example, it has been argued that persistent problems of political underrepresentation can be addressed by restructuring legislative decision-making processes. Drawing upon research in both jury behavior and small group process, it has been suggested that legislative committee members be held to a consensus standard of decision. Legislators would be forced to actually reconcile majority and minority views in much the same way as compulsory service on civil and criminal juries requires jurors to set aside biases and focus on evidence and court instructions (Guinier 1994). This creative use of gridlock has produced positive results in policy arenas ranging from small-group management (Wysocki 2002) and social services delivery (Fatout and Rose 1995) to environmental mediation (Rydin 2003; van den Belt 2004) and city and regional planning (M. Hanson 2005; Faga 2006). It is hard to believe that a capacity that can be seen at work in so many arenas suddenly vanishes in jury chambers or in a legislative committee room.

Political Legitimation

The potential for juristic approaches to public decisions can be seen most clearly when compared to other suggestions for overcoming the political disadvantages faced by minority groups. Although it is clearly beyond the scope of this chapter to discuss all of the ideas that have been advanced to address the political underrepresentation of minorities and the resulting challenges to regime legitimacy, it is possible to describe the general approaches that have been offered. These fall into two broad categories. First, there are several ways that elections might be manipulated to produce outcomes that are more favorable to minorities. Second, it is possible to leave electoral systems as they are but to exempt minorities (in some way or another) from the powers that those elections confer.

The history of gerrymandering in the United States is one particularly sad example of how elections can be manipulated to the disadvantage of minorities and how difficult it is even for well-intentioned reformers to address the problem. It has never been difficult to design electoral districts in ways that dilute the voting strength of minorities. The difficulty arises when redressing those grievances becomes the issue. Is it better to concentrate minority votes in just a few districts in order to ensure the election of at least some minority officials? Or does this merely "ghettoize" minority voters? Is it preferable to distribute minority voters strategically to create districts that will ultimately be represented by members of the majority who, nevertheless, will provide "virtual" representation to the minority voters without whom they could not be certain of reelection? Lani Guinier has argued persuasively that the entire debate may miss the point for two reasons (Guinier 1994). First, those who advocate both approaches underestimate the extent and tenacity of racial animosity that is unleashed in the privacy of the voting booth. Second, the number of minority representatives in a legislative body is not particularly important if the rules and organization of that body replicate the isolation and powerlessness that afflicts minorities in the society at large. One is tempted to add to this the argument that in modern democracies people are truly free only on election day. Thereafter, they suffer the consequences of having allowed their representatives to steal from them the ultimate responsibility for the values, beliefs, and actions that will characterize their commons. In many important ways, to exercise the franchise is also to renounce it (Barber 2004). This is as true of the majority as it is the minority.

Providing political exemptions (of one sort or another) from the vicissitudes of democratic politics is a second approach to the problem of protecting minorities from tyranny. In the case of deliberative democracy in particular, there have been complaints that a single, homogeneous public sphere dedicated to rational unanimity ignores cultural specificity in favor of social hegemony (Bohman 1994; I. Young 1990). This concern has produced an argument for *deliberative inclusion* (I. Young 1999), which requires not only that all interests, opinions, and perspectives be present in the deliberation but also that disadvantaged groups have a veto power over policies that affect them (I. Young 1989). This demanding version of inclusiveness would be in service of a more general politics of diversity that would resist any attempt to impose universal identities that are rational or neutral on members of minority cultures, as some critics of deliberative democracy have accused it of doing (Mouffe 1996).

The danger inherent in both electoral tinkering and political exemption is that they risk undermining the political legitimacy of the entire political system. To do so would be both unfortunate and unnecessary. It would be unfortunate because a delegitimized government leaves minorities with recourse only to the forces of economic markets and social hierarchies that have disadvantaged them in the past (or to revolution). And it is unnecessary because the political protection being sought can be found in the universal veto imposed by the requirement of consensus decision making suggested by a juristic form of democracy. As we have already suggested, this approach allows institutions of the political realm to "borrow" from the reservoir of legitimacy that the judicial institution of the jury has been accumulating for hundreds of years.

Environmental Justice: An Illustrative Example

It might be helpful at this juncture to provide a concrete illustration of some of the points we have advanced. It has been observed that the environmental justice (EJ) movement has been led precisely by those who are generally underrepresented in mainstream environmentalism. The most active representatives of the EJ community are often women of color who are economically disadvantaged and often motivated (at least in part) by underlying religious convictions (Di Chiro 1998). This pattern suggests that the EJ movement can be a vehicle for bringing together the richly diverse discourses of ecofeminism, environmental racism, socialist-inspired critical ecology, and the more "spiritual" strains of deep ecology into a potent new world view that challenges the individualism and materialism of liberal democracy and establishes the groundwork for a new environmental collectivism.

Before taking to the barricades, however, it might be worthwhile to develop a somewhat longer view of how the disadvantaged (or anyone else for that matter) might best orient themselves to their own interests and to those of other citizens. Part of that view might come from Sheldon Wolin, who provides a useful distinction between an inheritance and a birthright (S. Wolin 1989). In most contemporary legal systems, estates are transferred from one generation to the next in the form of inheritances of essentially fungible resources (commonly money). When an estate is divided among the heirs, its contents become (at least potentially) connected horizontally with all of the other goods for which those contents might be exchanged. A birthright, on the other hand, is transferred whole. The birthright is as much a burden as a bequest. It comes to the recipient still bound vertically to both one's ancestors and one's future offspring, a trust inappropriate by its nature to the logic and language of contract and exchange. It is this quality that lends meaning to the biblical story of Esau, who sold his birthright to Jacob for a bowl of pottage. To appreciate the narrative and to live by its wisdom, it is unnecessary to renounce one's individuality or to forgo material possessions. Indeed, taking both of those values seriously is part of the lesson of Esau.

According to Wolin, the birthright modern humans have sold is the capacity for politicalness—the ability to know and value what it means to participate in and be responsible for the care and improvement of our shared experience. As with any birthright, we are entitled to this upon reaching the age of majority. But we can only enjoy its benefits it by making it our own, by mixing it with our own effort, by sacrificing something for it as Esau refused to do. Here, in this account of seizing one's birthright, we also have a reasonably accurate description of the successes that environmental justice advocates have enjoyed. Theirs have been triumphs of local organizing, of appealing to individuals to deliberate together across the boundaries of their differences (Schlosberg 1998). Had EJ activists pressed their perspective as a comprehensive world view, had they aspired to convince others to abandon individualism or materialism, they would still be waiting for their first victory. EJ activists have succeeded best where they have been able to confront those in power with concrete demands, in face-to-face encounters, using the vocabulary of the majority (in the form of individual rights and interests), under circumstances that encourage (in one way or another) consensus decision making. Of these conditions, consensus is obviously the hardest to satisfy. It is also the most important, particularly to those whose hopes depend on changing existing patterns of political influence. So those at the greatest disadvantage in politics should not fear the juristic model. They should embrace it.

Implementing Global Juristic Democracy in the Real World

To recapitulate: the more significant criticisms of the juristic form of deliberative democracy fall naturally into two broad categories—problems with
juries and problems with deliberation. Jury problems include difficulty
dealing with questions that are novel or complex. These sorts of problems,
critics allege, are more appropriate to trial by judges or panels of judges.
This approach, however, diminishes the democratic quality of deliberation
that we seek to maximize. Critics also allege that jury heterogeneity is a
problem. A lack of jury heterogeneity, it is suggested, casts doubt on both
the fairness of the judicial process and on the likelihood that its results are
accurate. Moreover, critics have cast doubt on the normative assumptions
commonly made about individual jurors—that they are fully independent
and equal individuals who are open to the evidence adduced at trial and to
the opinions of their fellow jurors.

Problems with deliberation are of a different character. Critics assert that
deliberative democracy, particularly in a juristic form, imposes a cramped
and constraining rationalistic framework on political discourse. One result,
it is argued, is an undue reliance on universalistic forms of argument that ignore the unique qualities of particular cases. Another is the encouragement
of a rampant and rapacious form of individualism that denies people a vision of their common humanity. While it is indeed a challenge to understand how deliberative democracy could be both too universal and too
particular, we have not relied on that apparent contradiction to dismiss
complaints about deliberation entirely. Each prong of the criticism must be
taken seriously on its own, and this we have tried to do.

What jury problems and deliberation problems clearly have in common
is a concern for the value of diversity. To address this obviously legitimate
concern, while rebutting the critics of deliberative democracy, has been the
second task of this chapter. We have described diversity's deliberative significance by briefly discussing three of deliberative democracy's key
processes—language innovation, consensus testing, and political legitimation. Drawing on the views of Ludwig Wittgenstein and Jürgen Habermas,
we have conceptualized law as a language game of particular importance.
Law is a language through which diverse social groups communicate their
needs and expectations to one another. Where political processes take on a
"monolingual" character, it is no longer appropriate to assert that they are
either democratic or deliberative. This is made all the clearer when one considers the problems of consensus testing and legitimation. A "monolingual"

law and politics will never know whether any level of consensus it appears to achieve is genuine or merely an artifact of exclusion. And to the extent that consensus is less than genuine, it will fail to provide political legitimation to the course of action it dictates.

In order to illustrate the importance of deliberative diversity, and its compatibility with the evidential and relatively impersonal patterns of discourse involved in juristic democracy, we have provided the example of environmental justice. It is our argument that had environmental justice advocates not perfected a "legalistic" approach to their quest for justice, had they not persuaded others to deliberate across the boundaries of their difference, they would have enjoyed far less success than they have to date. So not only is a juristic approach, one that emphasizes universally accessible decision criteria, compatible with the needs of diverse populations, it is indispensable to it.

It now remains for us to indicate how our model of juristic democracy can be refined so as to take adequate account of the concerns that critics of deliberative democracy have raised. We do this briefly here, and at greater length in the next chapter, by applying the juristic approach to the problem of providing democratic content to international environmental law. In the process, we address three challenges that concern both deliberative democrats and their critics. First, how can we provide institutional mechanisms that will allow members of civil society to develop and refine democratic inputs to existing international environmental law without the use of formal governmental authority? Second, how can processes of formalizing those democratic inputs be cultivated transnationally? Third, how can those who wield governmental authority (particularly those in developed nations) be persuaded to recognize and formalize these emergent principles of law?

Although creating entirely new institutions is a venerable and attractive strategy for changing the world, there already exists a transnational institution that has the capacity to serve as an "access portal" for democratic inputs on the subject of international environmental law, namely, the International Law Commission (ILC), discussed earlier. The ILC finds the raw material for this process in two places. First, there are treaties and conventions that have been negotiated directly among nations. When, as is often the case, the subject matter of these treaties overlap but the rights and obligations established by them differ, there is an opportunity for the ILC to clarify and reconcile matters. Second, the ILC is capable (at least theoretically) of developing international standards from the patterns of interaction between sovereign states that have developed over time into unwritten but recognizable standards that are referred to as "customary law." In principle, therefore, the ILC enjoys a significant opportunity to contribute to the growth of international law.

The commission's effectiveness, however, is constrained by the fact that its agenda is set for it by the UN General Assembly. Moreover, the ILC is subject to the same limitations as courts and their auxiliaries around the world. It can only deal with problems and principles of law as they present themselves in the form of actual cases. At the international level, cases come along at a slower pace than they do in national courts simply because there are fewer courts with less law to enforce and fewer actors to enforce it upon. Finally, the work of the ILC is not especially sensitive to issues of democracy and diversity because the parties in its cases are generally organizations and governments rather than individuals. It is simply assumed, contrary to obvious evidence, that the member nations of the UN adequately represent the diversity of interests present in their respective populations.

All of these problems could be addressed if the ILC were to employ a juristic democracy approach to the development of international environmental norms. Citizen juries could be marshaled to represent the true diversity of the global population (that is, a large number of juries collectively, not each jury individually) and they could deliberate on hypothetical cases designed by the commission itself to squarely address important normative questions in international environmental law. These deliberative processes could be repeated until they generate a genuinely representative sample of considered opinion. An approach of this kind would allow the ILC to become proactive in the area of environmental protection as well as to add much needed democratic content to its resource base.

Were the ILC to actually adopt a procedure of this sort, our second major challenge would immediately arise. How can the results of broadly democratic deliberations over fundamental normative questions regarding global environmental protection be aggregated into formal principles of international governance? The answer will depend, of course, on the level of consensus that an adequately representative collection of deliberative trials produces. Disagreement can occur both within juries and between juries, even from the same locale, that individually have arrived at consensus. In the presence of basic disagreements across national and cultural boundaries, we would at least have a more informed view of the nature of the disagreement. Moreover, disagreement among state representatives would be clarified and legitimated in ways that might ultimately facilitate compromise.

Where global deliberation reveals a significant level of consensus, an agenda for ongoing diplomacy is clearly established. In fact, the democratic character of any such consensus would constitute a fundamental challenge to those views of international relations that proceed from an assumption of anarchy. The suggestion that there may, indeed, be a collection of normative commitments that are transnational (even if not fixed or absolute) would constitute a significant challenge to the *real politic* theories of diplomacy that we discussed in chapter 2. The result, we suggest, would be an altered political dynamic both within and between sovereign states.

Any juristic approach to international law will confront the challenge of political power. Any deliberative democratic approach deployed at the international level will certainly encounter this problem. For one thing, our experience at the national level suggests as much. For another, it is entirely likely that a leveled international playing field would be to the advantage of countries that suffer competitive disadvantages under the current system of nationalistic power politics. Ultimately, our answer to this challenge will be essentially a pragmatic one. It may be true that the advantages of a more democratic and ecologically rational global regime would disproportionately benefit those countries (and those groups within countries) that presently are at a disadvantage in terms of both political power and natural resources. But that does not mean that regional and global powers would not also enjoy advantages over the status quo. Political power is seldom zero sum and rarely blatantly coercive, and becoming even less so. Some political actors can become more powerful without others becoming less powerful. Whether the powerful like it or not, they nevertheless will continue to participate as new channels and processes of exercising power evolve. When the costs of resisting international norms are added to the downside of further environmental degradation, we may discover that even nations that harbor highly competitive and individualistic political cultures can be encouraged toward more responsible global citizenship.

Ultimately, political contests have to become about something other than power. Substituting rationally defensible rules that all can regard as legitimate is what the legal enterprise is all about (Habermas 1996). Legalization is a process characterized by obligation, precision, and delegation, all of which constrain, redirect, and realign power (Goldstein et al. 2001). Moreover, power in all of its conventional forms is of diminishing value, especially as we look at the nature of asymmetrical conflicts and the enhanced roles of small groups. As the world becomes more and more a collection of networks and less a hierarchy of nations, anyone who can martial a plausible public consensus on any question of policy will be well positioned to back recalcitrant state actors into political corners from which there is no escape short of acquiescence.

In the next chapter, our discussion of each of these important challenges—providing for democratic input into the creation of international environmental norms, creating a process for codifying that input, and developing means for encouraging compliance with the resulting codes—will receive more extended attention. Our objective is to describe a plausible scenario for democratizing international law, beginning with the law of the environment.

8

Nature's Regime: Think Locally, Act Globally

A recurring theme in international law is the absence of democratic content in its basic principles and procedures. To the extent that international law captures anything of the political attitudes and preferences of the world's citizens, it does so only in an indirect and coincidental way. Even within the European Union, the world's most highly developed institution of international governance, the existence of a "democratic deficit" is generally acknowledged (Hix 2005). In fact, the relationship between citizens and their representatives on the international stage is so attenuated that the notion that the consent of states to international rules imparts to those rules any normative legitimacy is highly dubious (Buchanan 2003). In light of this, it is commonly argued that because there is no international institution that can legitimately speak for the entire global electorate, the traditional principle of state sovereignty relieves the nations of the world of any moral or ethical obligation to accept a system of global norms (Keohane 2005) even if one were to emerge.

If it is, indeed, the democratic deficit that robs international law of its moral authority and gives states the room they need to evade their international obligations, then the solution must be (at least in part) to provide a direct, participatory element for the world's citizens in the making of international law. This might be accomplished by recreating at the international level the process of doctrinal development observed in the common law of most English-speaking countries. Nearly every American who has been blessed (or cursed) with formal legal training is familiar with Oliver Wendell Holmes Jr.'s aphorism that the life of the law is not logic but, rather, experience. Most could not recite, however, the next sentence of Holmes's *The Common Law*. There Holmes asserts the fundamentally democratic character of the common law. In spite of the fact that it is handed down by judges, the common law reflects "the felt necessities of the time, the prevalent moral and political theories, intuitions of public policy, avowed or unconscious, even the prejudices which judges share with their fellow-men" (Holmes [1881] 1991). The sense of justice that Holmes is describing is the unwritten and yet binding system of obligations that the English common law has developed over the last millennium. [14]

Developing a contemporary international equivalent to the common law would require us, of course, to deviate from the haphazard pattern of development that characterizes historical systems of law if it is to produce useful results over an acceptable frame of time. As we have imagined it, the use of policy juries to adjudicate concrete (but hypothetical) cases of international environmental disputes can provide a substantial collection of decisions that can be aggregated to form a system of legal doctrine in the same way that the resolutions of actual cases were first restated and then later codified.

It is not hard to imagine how the policy specialists working in existing international organizations could develop and administer such an adjudicatory procedure. In the area of environmental protection, the United Nations Environment Programme has the technical capacity to prepare hypothetical cases touching on any of the major issues of the day and the Commission on Sustainable Development could oversee the deliberations in any of the hundred countries where it supports local organizations. Agenda setting would not be controlled by any single body. Other international organizations and nongovernmental organizations could develop hypothetical cases and commission policy juries as well—the more iteration tried on any given normative principle, the firmer the confidence in the result and the better the understanding of its limits of application. The more challenging question is how the resulting decisions could be aggregated into a coherent body of legal doctrine and how that doctrine could be related to the continuing problem of constraining nation-state behavior. To shed some light on those questions is the objective of this chapter. We discuss both the present practice and political potential of the International Law Commission (ILC). We propose direct citizen participation in a transnational process aimed at developing fundamental principles of international obligation for the conservation of environment and nature. We anticipate the criticisms of elitism and insensitivity to cultural diversity commonly directed at deliberative democracy. We conclude by addressing the challenges of bringing the global system of state sovereignty within an emerging framework of international norms that aspires to be more than merely hortatory.

The ILC and Global Environmental Democracy

The International Law Commission consists of thirty-four individual members. They represent each of the world's major regions and serve for staggered terms of five years. They are elected by the UN General Assembly from lists of distinguished jurists and legal scholars submitted by national governments, but they serve in their private capacities rather than as the representatives of their nations of origin. Created in the aftermath of World War II, the ILC is charged with the codification and progressive development of international law. This dual competency relates the commission's work to the two major sources of international law. First, international law has originated in treaties and conventions negotiated directly between nations. Each individual treaty may be clear enough on its face, but the historical accumulation of agreements on related and overlapping legal topics can produce a thicket of confusing, often directly contradictory, rules of state obligation. Second, customary patterns of interaction between sovereign states have evolved over time into recognizable standards that, although unwritten, guide the interpretations of judges and arbitrators as well as the states themselves. The ILC is charged both with distilling systematic treaty law from the multiplicity of existing treaties and with codifying customary principles of international law (Mansfield 2002; Morton 2000).

Scholarship on the ILC can be divided into two general categories. First, there are a number of studies of the commission's organization and operation (Graefrath 1991; Hafner 1996; Morton 2000; Sucharitkul 1990). Some of this research has examined the expansion of the ILC. The commission has grown from a membership of fifteen at its establishment in 1949 to its current size of thirty-four. This growth in membership, and the concomitant growth of the commission's professional staff, has allowed for an increase both in the diversity of the ILC's membership and an expansion of its work. However, this growth has also complicated the task of achieving consensus within the commission, an objective for which few UN organizations strive (Sucharitkul 1990). But beginning in the 1990s, the ability of the commission to resolve matters that had spilled over from the previous decade and to undertake new projects suggests that it has adjusted to its new size and the complexity of its working environment. Turnover in commission membership is also declining, indicating that a greater level of stability and efficiency is in the offing (Morton 2000).

The ILC membership itself is another focus of attention. In principle, at least, members of the commission are independent of their national governments and serve uninstructed based upon their personal expertise in international law. There have been, nevertheless, many members who were foreign ministry personnel in their home countries at the time of their election. This arrangement is obviously a mixed bag. On the one hand, the closer the connection between commission members and their respective governments, the greater the likelihood of self-serving behavior of the sort that has plagued the development of the international criminal court (Best 1997). On the other hand, it is probably the case that some influence over members by their national governments has a salutary effect on the efficacy of commission work, as it is likely that states are more inclined to respect rules they have some role in developing (Morton 2000). Another critique of commission membership is that it possesses little of the expertise required to deal with any but the most general matters of international regulation (Hafner 1996). This critique suggests the need for further increases in both the size and independence of ILC membership, notions that would exacerbate many of the problems discussed so far.

A final area of discussion of the ILC itself has to do with its methods of work. The ILC's program of work is largely determined by a long-term plan that dates back to 1949. The topics included in that plan (state responsibility, jurisdictional immunity, and so forth) were thought to involve primarily the codification of existing rules of customary law that had in common their importance to the maintenance of the continuing system or relations among the sovereign states (Graefrath 1991). The commission's agenda has been supplemented since its initial work plan largely by the addition of topics by the Sixth Committee of the United Nations General Assembly. The work pattern of the ILC is easily described. It proceeds through four stages: issue development, general debate, drafting, and final adoption.

When the ILC takes up an issue, it normally begins by appointing one of its members as a special rapporteur. The rapporteur is responsible for assembling the research necessary to begin formulating the individual elements of eventual articles of a final report. This process includes circulating preliminary drafts for comment by states. In its general debate, the ILC plenary takes up the reports submitted by its special rapporteurs, including comments made by states on questionnaires concerning earlier drafts. At the conclusion of debate, the ILC will normally forward proposed draft articles to a drafting committee, even if there is significant division over the articles among commission members. The drafting committee (normally comprised of fifteen or more members) is the primary forum for negotiation over the content of any eventual report. Its time is used to debate the relevant articles and to develop compromise wording that will reconcile the divergent points of view held by ILC members. The committee produces a report to the ILC plenary, which eventually adopts the final text of the articles that have been developed. This is more than a pro forma matter. Final adoption of articles to be included in the ILC's annual report to the UN General Assembly involves an examination of the commentaries attached to each draft article (Morton 2000).

As one might imagine, every stage in this work process has come in for criticism and has been the subject of proposals for improving the ILC's work. At the very outset, the establishment of the ILC's agenda is problematic in a variety of ways. Early in its history, the commission discovered that maintaining a clear distinction between its dual responsibilities of codification and progressive development of law was virtually impossible. The realization that legal "development" played a role in nearly all of the commission's efforts revealed the inherently political and "legislative" character of its mandate. An instructive illustration is the effort by the United States to narrow the reach of the ILC's codification of the rules of state responsibility by denying standing to complain of a breach of those rules to only those states that are "specially affected" by the breach (Murphy 2001). Much time and effort is necessary to ensure that the ILC is not charged with a task so characterized by political disagreement that its subsequent work on the topic is wasted, inasmuch as the politically neutral expertise that would allow for the creation of a more reasonable issue agenda is present to a much greater degree in the commission than in the Sixth Committee of the UN General Assembly, where the actual responsibility lies (Graefrath 1991).

The work of the ILC's special rapporteurs is also problematic in a variety of ways. For one thing, it is far from clear that the members of the commission possess either the technical expertise or the research support necessary to address any but the most general issues of law. As the global system of politics and economics becomes increasingly complex and integrated, it becomes more doubtful that any collection of international lawyers, however distinguished, can be masters of the technical information generated by that system (Hafner 1996). Moreover, special rapporteurs (like all commission members) are part-time employees. The time available to them to accomplish their tasks is generally quite short. Converting the commission membership to full-time status has been suggested. But such a step would, it is feared, reduce the willingness of international lawyers to fill those positions (appointment to which is for a fixed term of only five years). The ability of rapporteurs to produce quality work is further limited by the availability of resources in their home countries, a problem that obviously has a disproportionate impact on commission members from the developing world (Graefrath 1991). To illustrate this point, consider the recent work of the ILC in the area of ground-water protection. The ILC has a long-standing interest in surface waters, particularly as they often constitute international borders. Surface waters, therefore, have long been a concern for the states that establish the issue agendas of international organizations. Ground water, however, is an integral component of life for a majority of the world's population and has become humankind's most extracted natural resource. To adequately address this emerging issue will require both enormous technical capacity in hydrology and other natural sciences and the careful extrapolation of existing surface water law to the special requirements of groundwater protection (Eckstein 2005). The analytical challenges in both areas would seem to confront developing states with insurmountable obstacles to the effective representation of the interests of their citizens. How ILC rapporteurs are to address this challenge within the limits of their own capacity is far from clear.

The general debate of the ILC can be subjected to a variety of criticisms as well. The sessions are frequently characterized by inadequate preparation and insufficient allotments of debate time. Rapporteur drafts often reach commission members at the beginning, or even in the midst of, debate sessions. As a result, members often limit themselves to "preliminary remarks." In effect, they reserve the right to lodge serious and substantive objections later in the process. The potential for wasted time in the drafting committees is clear. In addition to this, drafting committees conduct their work in circumstances of both information deficit and information overload. Commission staff is so limited as to make it difficult for the ILC to track developments of law at the national level. The research on topics of international law and the social processes with which it is concerned is conducted by so dispersed a network of university, government, and nongovernmental organizations that it is virtually impossible for the ILC to track, let alone use, the torrent of material issuing from those diverse sources (Graefrath 1991). As an example, there has been significant support in the ILC and the Sixth Committee for protecting the interests of developing nations under the evolving rules governing international liability for harms resulting from acts not prohibited by international law. The trend has been to eschew express benefits for developing nations in favor of criteria for assessing damages that tend to reduce the amount of reparations required of developing nations in the event that activities within their boundaries cause transboundary harms. As appealing as this approach may be, it requires a very close analysis of the potentially detrimental effects of those criteria on aggrieved states that may be just as vulnerable as their offending neighbors (Magraw 1986). The inherently contingent quality of this kind of analysis suggests just how politically and ethically sensitive the challenges facing the commission really are.

The overwhelming impression one takes away from a look at the ILC and the challenges it faces is one of growing consensus on the existence of problems and persistent disagreement as to their solutions. Sometimes the disagreement arises from an inability to recognize (or agree upon) the relevant issues of law presented by a particular set of circumstances. The world rarely provides us with clean points of legal decision, stripped of the complexities and vagaries that law professors love using to distract their students from the main issues of a case. On other occasions, the inability (or unwillingness) of states to look past what they perceive to be their own interests leads to behavior that others regard as unreasonable and prevents the adoption of measures that enjoy wide support and promise shared benefits. In still other instances, the issues at hand are clear and parties are both able and willing to look for shared ground. But even under such propitious circumstances, states can fail to reach an accord because of a genuine and well-intentioned difference about how to balance the equities of a given set of circumstances—often resulting from an underlying disagreement about fundamental principles of right.

In the domestic arena, deliberative democratic approaches have addressed each of these challenges. The need to agree on the basic facts of a political or legal question (and, among those facts, to agree on which are the functionally significant ones) is the foundation for what has been called the epistemological justification for participatory democracy (Westbrook 2005). The necessity for moving beyond naked self-interest to levels of political discourse in which political actors offer each other reasons in support of their positions that all can regard as reasonable is often cited as an essential element of any form of government that is genuinely democratic

(Barber 2004). The ability of citizens to agree upon norms of behavior that express their consensus on fundamental matters of mutual recognition and obligation is taken by many to be the defining quality of a politics that is democratic in a fully inclusive and deliberative (rather than merely aggregative) sense (Habermas 1996). So it would appear that deliberative democracy might be good medicine for at least some of what ails the ILC. The remaining concerns are how, more specifically, deliberative democracy might be helpful at the international level and how can states be persuaded to allow themselves to be bypassed by their own citizens on their way to the global commons.

From Policy Juries to International Law

Assuming that the ILC were to initiate a project using citizen juries to search for consensus on basic norms of environmental regulation, what would the commission do with the results? That, of course, would depend on what the results were. It may be that the diversity of cultures and histories among the nations of the world precludes the citizens of those nations from arriving at any shared understanding of what would be fundamentally fair standards of environmental regulation. Or, it may turn out to be the case that when citizens of any country deliberate a well-structured hypothetical case they tend regularly to arrive at a single conclusion. The most likely alternative is that each of these results would be produced across the broad range of environmental issues that might be subjected to such a procedure. So we should think through the consequences of both outcomes.

Where repeated administration of a test case reveals fundamental disagreement, the ILC would at least be able to map the structure of public opinion on the matter in question. This may seem to be a very modest accomplishment. But its potential value can be appreciated if we consider several aspects of the ILC's performance to date. First, empirical evidence suggests that commission members behave as representatives of their national governments, regardless of their formal status as private individuals (Morton 2000). This is sometimes regarded as a failing of the ILC system. If, however, the divergent positions of ILC members were shown to be related to the underlying opinions and values of their countrymen, that democratic legitimation would be well worth demonstrating. To the extent that the popular will were actually shown to be reflected in commissioner behavior, it would require all involved to acknowledge the validity of their opponents' positions and the necessity for genuine compromise (Knight and Johnson 1994, 282, 286).

Second, it has been noted that the legislative processes of the commission, the choice of topic it will take up, and the ordering of its priorities are heavily influenced by the states of the Sixth Committee and the UN General Assembly (Graefrath 1991). In this relationship between the ILC and other UN bodies, the ILC has practically no grounds for asserting a role in establishing its own agenda. If the ILC could provide data indicating that a particular issue was the subject of significant international dissensus, it would be in a stronger position to ward off the assignment of a task that would consume commission resources without offering the prospect that its work would ultimately be accepted.

Finally, it has been argued that the ILC works within a more constricted arena than its formal charge would suggest. Specifically, the commission might be criticized for limiting its activity to "secondary rules," that is, rules concerning the practice of states in implementing the preexisting structure of primary rules of state obligation (Hafner 1996). The premise here is that the age of creating international law is essentially over, there being no substantive disagreements left to resolve. In such a circumstance, codification of existing practice becomes the only legitimate activity for the ILC. Any attempt at progressive development would imply that gaps in substantive international law exist that need to be filled. Finding fundamental transnational disagreement on an important issue of environmental protection would suggest that either a genuine gap of this sort remains or that the nations of the world had foreclosed discussion of that issue prematurely (from a democratic point of view). Where a deliberative democratic experiment both identifies such a gap and isolates its underlying divergence of opinion, progressive development of international law would seem to be more likely.

A different set of considerations is presented by the case in which deliberation across national boundaries reveals a fundamental agreement on some measure of environmental protection that is not currently found in international law. Clearly, an unmet transnational mandate for environmental regulation would present the ILC with an opportunity to add an item to its agenda with reasonable hope that its efforts would ultimately be rewarded by agreement of the states to its recommendation. But it might do even more. Focusing international attention on issues that enjoy broad, cross-national and cross-cultural support could free the ILC from its current conceptual straitjacket. Most scholarly and legal studies in the area of international law have focused exclusively on the supposed absence of any restraining capacity of international law, chiefly its inability to exercise an independent control on the actions of nation-states (Morton 2000). As long as one accepts the assumption that the only source of international law is the self-interested agreement of governing elites (Goldsmith and Posner 2005), this is an entirely reasonable position. This approach reduces international law to an anemic version of contract law. According to this view, states enter into agreements for their own reasons and violation of an agreement is to be expected whenever the advantages outweigh the risk of retaliation and the loss of future advantages that might have resulted from continued cooperation. There is nothing for the ILC to do in this realm of law other than to document the patterns that underlie these contracts and try to reduce (in so far as possible) the confusion that results from the fact that each contract employs slightly different language even when their objectives are fundamentally similar. This sort of task is perfectly consistent with the "positivist" school of thought that dominates scholarly thinking about international law (Morton 2000).

The difficulty with this approach is that it would appear to leave little room for the progressive development component of the ILC's charge. If the commission pursues progressive development only along lines that states have indicated a willingness to accept, then its "development" efforts can be explained in the same positivistic terms that are used to account for the resulting treaties and accords. But this sort of development is hardly "progressive." It reduces the ILC to nothing more than a soliciting agent, placing willing parties in contact with one another and processing their paperwork. If, however, the commission were able to pursue the development of legal rules based upon a normative consensus at the level of participating citizens, new possibilities would arise.

Without relying on the development of a "new paradigm" or a new "world order" (Falk 1989), a transnational consensus on some specific norm of environmental protection would allow the ILC to "restate" international law found in the judgment of citizens rather than in the behavior of states. As the commission continued to develop this international common law (as opposed to customary law) it would become possible to prepare a "restatement" of that law. Built from specific disputes settled by concrete judgments, this form of common law could provide international tribunals (whether permanent or specially created) with raw material for their deliberations that would enjoy the legitimacy conferred by a democratic pedigree. Moreover, the focus on concrete (if hypothetical) international disputes might have one further advantage.

International environmental problems, like their domestic counterparts, usually involve disputes between private parties. The only added element is an international border. It would be fanciful to say that the nation-states involved in such disputes are innocent bystanders pulled unwillingly into the fray. But such fancies are not unknown in the history of law. William Blackstone commented on some of the legal fictions used by the common law to get around dysfunctional precedents handed down from the medieval law of feudal societies. Most interesting for our present purpose is his discussion of the maxim that the king can do no wrong (Blackstone 1979). It might seem that the purpose of this rule is to place the sovereign above the law. The opposite is more nearly true. If one takes the maxim to mean that it is *logically* impossible for the king to commit a wrong, then any evil done in the realm can only be attributed to the king's counselors or retainers. This legal fiction allowed the king's behavior (if not his person) to be subjected to the control of law without producing direct confrontations between the sovereign and the legislature or courts. A similar legal fiction might well evolve in international environmental law if today's "sovereigns" were confronted with adjudications grounded in the judgments of the world's citizens, including those of their own countrymen. Under such circumstances, a sovereign might well stand aside in deference to the considered judgment of the polis against one of his subjects while insisting that his sovereignty remain intact because he was never a party to the dispute.

Global Environmental Democracy in a World of Sovereigns

A favorite tactic of defense attorneys in arguing against a plaintiff's prayer for relief is to argue both that what the plaintiff seeks is impractical (or impossible) and that the plaintiff wouldn't really want what he was asking for if he just knew his own interests better. Among the defenders of state sovereignty, the first prong of this tactic takes the form of argument that the legalization of international politics (in the form of commitments that actually bind sovereign states in the same way that municipal law binds individual citizens) can never be effective. The second element of the defense of sovereignty is that sovereign states protect important democratic values in ways that international regimes cannot and, therefore, democrats should not actually want to develop such regimes. Most critics of international law at least touch upon both of these themes. But to appreciate them, and do them justice, we shall concentrate on arguments for each of these ideas that have been advanced by theorists who concentrate closely on only one.

Goldsmith and Posner offer a forceful claim that international law does not have an independent effect on state behavior (Goldsmith and Posner 2005). They argue that international law is nothing more than a codification of behavior regularities that arise as a result of states maximizing their own interests. This occurs in four ways. First, states often behave in similar ways "simply because each state obtains private advantages from a particular action (which happens to be the same action taken by another state) irrespective of the action of the other" (27). Where this occurs, the states involved may appear to be following a rule, but no such obedience is involved. Second, a state will sometimes find itself subjected to the coercion of another state. The coerced state might appear to be serving the interests of the stronger state, which may even offer a rule in excusing its coercion. But no rule is at work other than the rule of the jungle. Both the coercing state and the coerced state are merely acting rationally "to further their interests based upon the perceived interests and strengths of the other state" (29). Third, states sometimes find themselves in a "bilateral repeated prisoner's dilemma" (42). Under such circumstances, states refrain from cheating one another over a significant period of time, not out of any sense of obligation, but simply because the continuing cooperation that they would forfeit by cheating is worth more than the temporary gain that cheating would yield. Finally, circumstances in which states coordinate their behavior over an extended period of time, each for their own advantage, can be mistaken for the kind of rule-following behavior we normally describe as obedience to law. The claim made by Goldsmith and Posner is that these four patterns of state behavior can account for all instances that others might cite as respect for international law and that they can do so without positing any "exogenous influence" on state behavior resulting from law conceived of as a normative obligation (43).

It is important to be clear about the argument Goldsmith and Posner are making. They do not deny the existence of international law. They merely argue that "international law scholars exaggerate its power and significance" (225). More important to our present purpose, they also aver that they "know of no global democracy approach that spells out how or why states, especially powerful states like the United States (or, for that matter the EU), would submit to a broader form of genuine global governance" (223). Even granting for the sake of argument that Goldsmith and Posner have not overlooked some especially promising approach that would answer their concerns, their quandary may tell us far more about the state of democratic theory than it does the importance of international law. To think of law as nothing more than rules backed by coercive force is a habit of long standing. But there is no reason why the entity that pronounces legal judgments must necessarily be responsible for the enforcement of judgments. Recall that "a number of societies that we would not call stateless, including those of ancient Greece and Rome and Anglo-Saxon England, left prosecution of criminal cases to private individuals" and that in yet other societies all judicial decrees were enforced, if at all, privately (Posner 1995, 313). In fact, all that any form of law enforcement ever does is raise the costs of noncompliance. In governing the behavior of individuals, "coercive law overlays normative expectations with threats of sanctions in such a way that addressees may restrict themselves to the prudential calculation of consequences" (Habermas 1996, 116). Likewise, the "enforcement" mechanisms of international law combine dispute settlement processes with the existence of "countermeasures" (Schachter 1994) that allow aggrieved states to pursue private enforcement under color of official adjudication. So it might be fair to say that if Goldsmith and Posner have erred in any respect it is not in underestimating the robustness of international law but, rather, overestimating the essential differences between international and municipal law (to municipal law's undeserved advantage).

In assessing the argument that friends of democracy around the world would be advocates of state sovereignty if only they saw the question more clearly, we take as our point of departure the work of Jeremy Rabkin (2005). His analysis, unlike that of Goldsmith and Posner, is unabashedly American in perspective. One regrettable consequence is his tendency to generalize about other national cultures in ways that are as unhelpful as they are uncharitable and unfortunate. Nevertheless, Rabkin forcefully presses an argument that no committed democrat can afford to ignore. It is Rabkin's view that the contemporary movement for global governance is a direct threat to the existence of the sovereign state, and moreover, that threat to sovereignty involves an unavoidable threat to democracy. This is the case because democracy is a function of constitutional government and "a world that is equipped to sustain global governance is a world that does not need constitutional government—and probably cannot tolerate it" (38). The obvious and immediate threat is, of course, to democracy of the American sort. Rabkin assumes, perhaps correctly, that the movement for global governance has as its primary target the recalcitrance of the United States. But the long-term threat is, in his view, a threat to every person who values liberty and security. This is because, in the absence of a sovereign to guarantee that law is made and enforced in an orderly manner, the citizen's obligation to obey is forfeit and our remaining choice is between anarchy and arbitrary coercion (with some combination of the two being most likely). In this way, according to Rabkin, international law tends toward lawlessness that is as much a threat to citizens of the developing nations as it is to privileged Americans.

It is difficult to know where to begin discussing Rabkin's views because, in comparison with those of Goldsmith and Posner, his claims are broader and his arguments more strident. It would appear that, like Goldsmith and Posner, Rabkin exaggerates the difference between international and municipal systems of law because he also emphasizes coercion and its legitimacy (as functions of state sovereignty) rather than the more subtle effects of law as a system of behavioral incentives. A useful contrast in this regard is the theory of law in primitive societies advanced by Richard Posner (1983).

Posner's discussion of "primitive" societies and the systems of law they live by is illuminating for our purposes precisely because these systems develop in the absence of a sovereign state or any of the institutions normally associated with them. As an example, Posner describes the legal traditions of the Yurok tribe of California. When a legal claim arose among the Yurok, each of the principals would retain the services of two to four men (neither his relatives nor residents of his village) who would pass back and forth between the litigants collecting evidence and hearing arguments. These private jurors would then render a judgment. A losing party who refused to abide by the judgment was condemned to be the wage slave of the prevailing litigant. Continued refusal to submit rendered the recalcitrant an outlaw who could be killed by anyone without incurring liability for the deed (Posner 1981). Informal institutions of this sort have allowed stateless societies to develop sophisticated systems of property, contract, and family law–even tort law that recognizes the modern doctrine of strict liability.

Even more intriguing is Posner's observations regarding the emergence of criminal law. Stateless societies tend to have well-developed systems of private law but limited or nonexistent criminal law. The development of criminal law, as a system of official violence, replaces (or supplements) pecuniary compensation for personal injuries where there arises a sovereign who comes to view "an act of violence directed at a private citizen to be an offense against him" in his sovereign capacity. Dismissing the notion that protection from harm is part of the bargain between sovereign and subject,[15] Posner's explanation for this development is that the sovereign "owns" an interest in his subjects that is impaired by acts that reduce their productive capacity. This economic interest is not accounted for in the private system of compensation for injury, so the sovereign establishes criminal sanctions that serve as "a method of internalizing this externality" (204). This perspective would explain why the transfer of sovereignty, as when the thirteen states adopted the U.S. Constitution, did not diminish the rights and privileges of Americans generally. The economic interest protected by the coercive power of the sovereign was simply aggregated in a large polity. Moreover, this view suggests that an abrogation of sovereignty at the level of the nation-state is not necessarily a corollary of global governance. If extended to regulate the transboundary relationships between individuals, international law could be considered to be an evolving system of quasi-private law meant to acquit limited and specific rights through mechanisms of collective but private action.

Residua Imperium: Or, "Yes, But What's in It for Us?"

It should be clear by this point that the primary advantages of introducing forms of participatory democracy into international law making would be likely to accrue to states that operate at a political disadvantage under the current system of nationalist power politics. In particular, weaker states that seek to impose a regime of environmental protection on global economic and political powers are likely to enjoy significant public relations advantages from deliberative democratic experiments that lend scope and substance to general public sentiments in favor of environmental protection. These states may even be able to introduce environmental norms that are produced through such processes into proceedings that currently exist to adjudicate disagreements in other areas such as trade and human rights. But this begs the question, why would a powerful state, particularly one that is an environmental recalcitrant, subject itself to such processes, or even tolerate their continuation? It is our argument that even nations with something to lose in a thoroughly democratized global politics have still more to gain. Those potential gains are analytical, political, and, ultimately, environmental.

No discussion of deliberative institutional alternatives could be considered adequate if it omits a comparative or international perspective. To believe that deliberative democracy can be analyzed solely on the basis of domestic experience is simply irrational. How could it be that the comparison of citizen juries in Great Britain and deliberative polling in the United States (Laslett 2003) would fail to yield useful insights? The concept of reciprocity that is central to deliberative democracy knows no logical limit. It "extends to all individuals, not just to citizens of a single society" (Gutmann 1999, 309). Moreover, environmental problems (among many others) depend for their resolution on far more "cross-national deliberation" than can be accomplished within any single set of domestic political institutions (Gutmann and Thompson 2004, 61). This imperative reflects back on the ability of individual states to achieve their domestic environmental objectives. Environmental ends can be assured to a national population only if its government "negotiates and consistently maintains agreements with other governments for the purpose" (Laslett 2003, 217).

Comparative analysis of deliberative democratic experience can serve at least two important goals. First, it can provide a body of analytical comparisons that will aid both theorists and government officials as they try to work out the institutional details of more fully democratic processes. As an example, the state of Oregon established a Health Care Services Commission to set priorities for health care services under Medicaid. Meanwhile, halfway around the world, the British government created the National Institute for Clinical Excellence to provide assessment and treatment guidelines for that country's National Health Service. Both of these bodies sought to incorporate expert and lay opinion into a system of rational priorities for husbanding limited health care resources. They were intended to be deliberative institutions in that they were supposed to provide an "analytical filter" (Gutmann and Thompson 2004, 14) for public opinion that would justify policy outcomes through the imposition of a form of procedural rationality. But the public outcry that resulted in both cases required each group to engage in significant participatory back-filling and ultimately resulted in legislative intervention in both instances. Certainly a careful comparison of these cases would be of interest to public health planners in the future who wish to avoid making the same mistakes thrice.

A second use to which comparative analysis of deliberative institutions can be put is somewhat more theoretical, even normative. A comparison of the Canadian and American experience concludes that institutions for applying the notion of sustainable development are relatively underdeveloped in the United States (John 1994). On the basis of this evaluation, John suggests that the American states follow the example of the Canadian provinces in establishing environmental roundtables to bring together environmentalists, corporations, and government officials to discuss how economic and environmental values might be integrated. Such parallel development might encourage greater transnational environmental cooperation. A pertinent example would be the International Joint Commission, which operates as part of a bi-national and multi-institutional system of regional governance incorporating more than six hundred and fifty stakeholders in the Great Lakes Basin (Rabe 1999).

The South African Truth and Reconciliation Commission represents a form of deliberative institution with even greater normative potential. Unlike a trial court, the commission achieves an "economy of moral disagreement" by eschewing definite binary choices between guilt and innocence in favor of accommodations of conflicting views that fall within the range of "reasonable disagreement" (Gutmann and Thompson 2004, 185). Truth commissions of this sort are not entirely rare. An examination of this form of deliberative institution may provide the model for a normative stance that international environmental monitoring groups might adopt in support of deliberative bodies, like the Green Parliament in the Czech Republic, when they find themselves at odds with their own national governments (Axelrod 2005). It might also lead deliberative democrats in the direction of transferring the insights into democratization at the domestic level to the international arena.

Deliberative democracy's emphasis on justifying collective decisions to the people who must live with the consequences of those choices would seem to argue for extending the requirements of democratic deliberation to the international arena. Yet "most theorists of deliberative democracy apply its principles exclusively to domestic systems of government" (Gutmann and Thompson 2004, 36). This is, to say the least, ironic. While the aggregation of interests across boundaries is hard to conceptualize, "deliberation across boundaries is relatively straightforward" and deliberative theory would seem to be more useful in the international system precisely because it lacks "alternative sources of order" (Dryzek 2000, 116). If we can set aside (for our purposes at least) the fact that the idea of introducing democratic principles abroad can be used to legitimate dubious military adventures (Zolo 1997), there would still seem to be two fundamental reasons to limit deliberative democracy to the national stage.

First, it could be argued that the justification of preferences through public reason demanded by deliberative democracy is owed only to those who share with us the burdens of a common citizenship. Second, the absence of sovereignty at the international level might be thought to deprive deliberative democracy of the background conditions for its success that a stable legal order provides. Gutmann and Thompson (2004) find these objections largely unpersuasive. The differences between domestic and international society are often exaggerated, particularly with respect to the reliability of legal institutions. The argument from shared citizenship, while it may apply to matters such as taxation, is far less convincing with respect to issues such as war, trade, immigration, economic development, and (most especially) the environment. After all, environmental damage can occur virtually anywhere and "environmental liability affects every single citizen of every single state in the world, along with other humans who do not belong to nation-states at all" (Laslett 2003, 217).

Fortunately, there are abundant examples of deliberative democracy's various institutional elements that can be identified on the international environmental stage. Much of the recent progress in international environmental governance (as well as issues like children rights, population control, and social development) has been due to the involvement in collective decision making of nongovernmental organizations (Camilleri, Malhota, and Tehranian 2000). Moreover, this activity has evolved from its earlier reactive form to seize the policy initiative in a number of areas (Snidal and Thompson 2003). For instance, throughout the 1970s the International Whaling Commission was plagued by environmental protesters who would drench its members in faux whale blood at every opportunity. But by 1981, the commission's meeting offered representation to fifty-two nongovernmental organizations ranging from species preservation and animal rights groups to religious organizations and groups representing indigenous peoples. In this more open and democratic environment, the commission agreed to a zero quota for the 1985–1986 season (Birnie 1985). In fact, in this area it is the state actors that are the weak links. Setbacks in whaling regulation after the 1985 moratorium can be attributed to a lack of state follow-through in enforcement and accommodationist backsliding among state members (Vogler 1995).

Our experience with whaling suggests not that deliberative participation in international civil society is futile but, rather, that it must penetrate international governance more deeply to be fully effective. Environmental NGOs now routinely enjoy observer status in international organizations and conferences, sometimes even serving as members of state delegations. Some deploy a level of environmental expertise matched only by the largest and most developed states. Many are able to mobilize consumer boycotts that make them key policy actors (Thomas 1992). This provision of observer status and the increase in NGO participation is one of the most significant trends in international environmental law since the 1970s (Vogler 1995). But environmental interests in international civil society have not been satisfied with this.

By the time of the Earth Summit in 1992, international environmental NGOs had mobilized and coordinated sufficiently to stage a parallel Citizens' Forum that was, in many ways, more promising than the official meeting itself (Susskind 1994). In the absence of central monitoring agencies, much of the international environmental work is likely to fall to NGOs. As an example, the Arctic Treaty System has had to substantially modify its "working rule" of secrecy in response to pressure brought by NGOs. NGO pressure seems to have been the determining factor in changes in the London Convention outlawing the disposal of low-level radioactive waste at sea (Vogler 1995). These experiences have led to the call for a full-fledged advisory and monitoring role for nongovernmental interests in the environmental treaty process (Susskind 1994). A model for civil societies' role in global environmental governance already exists in the EU's European Environmental Bureau, an umbrella organization for over one hundred and forty environmental organizations in both EU countries and neighboring states that monitors the performance of the EU's Environmental Directorate (Axelrod, Vig, and Schuers 2005).

Conclusion

Whatever we may think about the relative merits of (or actual necessity for) some form of international sovereignty, relying on the spontaneous collaboration of individual nation-states seems inadvisable if we wish to move environmental matters in the right direction in the flawed world we now inhabit (Laslett 2003). From the environmental perspective, waiting for the creation of an ideal world order is allowing the perfect to become the enemy of the good. The main hope for democratizing global governance, across a wide range of issues, lies in a partnership between government, industry, and the popular forces of civil society (Camilleri, Malhota, and Tehranian 2000). We concur that institutions of deliberative democracy should be more at home at the international level than liberal aggregative models of democracy precisely because "there are no constitutions worth speaking of in the international system" (Dryzek 2000, 115–116). Dryzek proposes the development of a "network" form of international discursive organization (133), based on exactly the existing institutional models we have been discussing. Whatever particular form they take, we are convinced that deliberative democratic institutions offer an approach to environmental challenges that, if applied internationally, offer an escape from "the trap of nationalism and crystallized community aggressiveness" that seems to both dominate world affairs and threaten the global ecology (Laslett 2003, 220).

We are not postulating how far down that path we can go simply with citizen juries deliberating on hypotheticals. But we are suggesting that we put to the test the notion that, whereas people may not be able to formulate an affirmative statement of what constitutes justice, they are far more likely to be able to recognize the absence of justice and to identify the features of a concrete situation that amount to injustice. At some point, governance institutions must reenter the picture to refine and to solemnize whatever principles seem to enjoy consensus support. This would be true no matter how strong and widespread the consensus was. Regardless of how coherent and complete the results of citizen deliberations are, they give agents of governance genuinely democratic raw material with which to construct positive law. Distilling the collective wisdom contained in the muddied reservoir of public opinion is the best democrats can hope to do.

9

Democracy and the Environment: Fruitful Symbiosis or Uneasy Truce?

Democracy is not a pathway to the stars but only the articles of war under which the race fights an endless battle with itself.
—Bernard DeVoto

At the conclusion of chapter 1, we advanced three preliminary observations about the protection of the global environment. To be effective, international environmental law would have to encourage the formation of transnational collective will in the absence of sovereign authority, incorporate local ecological knowledge, and respect a regulative norm of democratic consensus. We have tried to substantiate those claims theoretically and to suggest how they might be redeemed empirically.

We began (in chapter 2) by discussing some of the conventional views of politics at the global level, views that would lead one to believe that developing a genuinely democratic international environmental jurisprudence is beyond our capacity. These views we found wanting in several important respects.

Next, we substituted for political realism a more hopeful view of international relations grounded in philosophical pragmatism (chapter 3). We contrasted the views of the democratic theorist David Truman with those of deliberative democrats such as Jürgen Habermas and John Rawls. We compared political realism (which we characterized as aggregative democracy) with deliberative democracy along several dimensions. These included the prerequisites for successful politics, the appropriate style of political reasoning, the role of self-interest, the role of scientific experts, and the standards for what outcomes count as political success. Along these dimensions we argued that deliberative democracy is more likely than aggregative democracy to produce results that are both fully democratic *and* protective of environmental resources. This advantage we attributed to the roots in philosophical pragmatism that deliberative democracy enjoys.

Then (in chapters 4 and 5) we began the effort of applying deliberative democratic reasoning to the problems of international law, particularly as they relate to environmental protection. First, we subjected the statist assumptions of conventional international relations theory to a critique from the perspectives of both the deliberative democrat and the environmentalist. In sum, statism was found wanting as a description of reality, as a predictive theory, and as a prescription about how things should be. Next, we suggested a conceptual framework for international politics that offers the hope of producing outcomes that are both more democratic and more environmentally friendly. And we assessed the prospects for a deliberative international politics by examining how rule-governed behavior has actually emerged from the supposedly chaotic maelstrom of state action on the global stage and whether that behavior has ever risen to the level of substantively democratic action in pursuit of environmental protection.

In chapters 6, 7, and 8, we turned our attention more fully to the development of an international environmental jurisprudence and the changes in international institutions that this objective would require. We argued that the differences between domestic and international law have been exaggerated in ways that obscure the need for democratic legitimacy in international jurisprudence. Future iterations of international law will have to play the dual role of both fact and norm. The inadequacies of international law as a fact—its inability to alter state behavior or achieve its stated objectives—are reflections of the democratic deficit at its very core. International law fails as law, not because insufficient coercive force backs it up, but because it fails as a norm that can promote the voluntary compliance upon which all forms of law ultimately rely. Addressing this democratic deficit is possible, we contend, within the boundaries of existing international institutions (both governmental and nongovernmental) if certain techniques employed by deliberative democrats at the domestic level are appropriately adapted for global application, techniques that we have collectively labeled "juristic" democracy.

Juristic democracy draws from the Habermasian approach to deliberative democracy in important ways. A persistent challenge to deliberative democracy is to encourage levels of impartiality sufficient to eliminate personal and ideological bias from processes of collective will formation while conserving "the cultural sources that nurture citizens' solidarity and their normative awareness" (Habermas 2008, 111). A juristic approach to deliberation accomplishes this by posing a hypothetical problem that does not touch deliberating citizens' individual interests and by asking only for the disposition of this concrete problem rather than a general policy statement of abstract principle that would engage their political or ideological commitments. In this way, the "neutrality of state power vis-à-vis different worldviews" is achieved without imposing "the political generalization of secularized worldview" upon citizens as the price of entry into the deliberative arena (113).

Juristic democracy is also Rawlsian in this sense: instead of asking participants to imagine themselves without interests, it asks them to imagine a situation in which they actually have no interests. It asks them only to arrive at a disposition of that situation without necessarily finding a generalized account or justification of that disposition about which they all can agree. It is, in this sense, a Rawlsian overlapping consensus. It yields a principle of justice only insofar as it produces a rule or decision that commands general assent from a broad, representative sample of the deliberating public.

Juristic democracy provides a response to the communitarian complaint that deontological ethics, such as advanced by Rawls, denudes citizens of the group affiliations and resulting elements of selfhood that allow them to respond intelligently (and intelligibly) to questions of policy. Not only does the hypothetical case construct eliminate the role of self interest, it does so without stripping deliberating citizens of their identities. By asking only for a disposition of the concrete case at hand, it dramatically reduces the role of ideology (by not asking respondents to generalize) without asking deliberators to give up their concept of the good.

Finally, a juristic approach to deliberative democracy is also very much in keeping with the work of theorists such as Amy Gutmann, Dennis Thompson, and James Bohman. These second-generation deliberative democrats, whose views we have characterized as "full liberalism," have made valuable efforts to give more concrete form to the foundational theories of Habermas and Rawls. They have tried to reimagine deliberative democracy in ways that make deploying the theory seem more plausible in the face of social complexity and political pluralism. The juristic approach we have described advances that agenda by showing how well-understood techniques such as jury deliberation, restatement of law, and model code construction can be combined to allow average citizens to participate directly in developing fundamental principles of law. This use of "off-the-shelf" techniques for the creation of a new process of collective will formation provides a means for redressing the democratic deficit in international law that is both philosophically defensible and politically practical.

By following the sometimes reflexive logic of these arguments, it is possible to glimpse a fundamentally different international politics immanent in the institutions of the present. However, the reader who has accompanied us this far is entitled to more than the hopeful sense that a more democratic and environmentally rational future is possible. He or she also deserves our best estimate of the lurking dangers in what we propose. For this purpose, we return to where we began—to the notions of encouraging transnational collective will formation, incorporating local ecological knowledge into international environmental regimes, and respecting a regulative norm of democratic consensus.

Transnational Collective Will

The idea of a transnational collective will that is not subject to the mediation of domestic political institutions is both stirring and unsettling. Ever since the advent of the internet, there have been those who have dreamed of a direct, participatory democracy constrained in its size only by the distribution of hardware and in its immediacy only by the speed of light. This fantasy is particularly compelling in America, which has both the experience of the town hall meeting as an element of its political genetics and an abundance of computer hardware (though, perhaps, the speed of our digital democracy generates more heat than light). But it is far from clear that a global plebiscite would be inherently more democratic, or more environmentally friendly, than the aggregative alternatives that currently produce the policy positions adopted by nation-states in international negotiations. This is true for at least two important reasons.

First, direct participatory referenda are subject to biasing by the structure of the propositions presented for consideration. Ever since Kenneth Arrow's demonstration that there is no way to formulate a collective welfare function that does not ultimately produce inconsistent results, policy scientists have had that unpleasantly queasy feeling one gets from having stayed on the merry-go-round too long. In a world where people's first, second, and third choices among ways to solve any given problem of public policy are influenced by their imperfect estimates of their particular stakes in the outcome, there is seldom a way to structure a public decision that does not unfairly (and inefficiently) privilege at least one alternative over at least one other. If this problem is insurmountable in the small-n world of the public choice theorist, imagine it written across the pages of newspapers around the world. Certainly, the political legitimacy of any such procedure would likely be forfeit before it had resolved its first policy question.

Second, the idea of direct referenda as a solution to the democratic deficit would seem to assume that there is little more to democracy than voting (not to mention the assumption in our present context that majorities are always environmentally rational). As the George W. Bush administration's unhappy experience with Iraqi domestic politics amply demonstrates, ink on your finger doesn't make you a democrat. This is certainly a familiar problem for all who have spent any time contemplating the history of their own country's politics. It is an essential part of the argument in favor of an independent judiciary as a necessary feature of any democratic scheme of government. But even more important for our purposes is the argument that the political culture and practices that constitute genuine democracy can only exist within a framework of constitutional government, which in turn can exist (today, at least) only within the confines of sovereign states (Rabkin 2005). The clear implication is that the stateless environment of global civil society and transnational networks of policy specialists cannot be relied upon to do the one thing that democracy absolutely requires—protect the rights of the individual.

Our response to these admittedly serious difficulties is twofold. First, the problems of collective choice that plague democracy generally are controlled in the juristic model of democracy by asking citizen lawmakers to adjudicate hypothetical concrete cases rather than to formulate general policies. The model depends not on some new mechanism for negotiating rules of right and obligation, but on a method of resolving specific disputes that has been developed and tested over the course of a millennium. This approach benefits not only from the collective rationality that face-to-face deliberation in the jury environment promotes, but also from the impartiality that results from the fact that the dispute being adjudicated is hypothetical. The international law that a procedure of this sort would yield can best be characterized as "general principles of law," which are necessarily subject to further analysis and refinement by existing international judicial institutions. This, of course, reawakens the issue of democratic legitimacy as government officials begin to manipulate the deliberative input of citizen juries. It also introduces our second concern, the problem of protecting the rights of the individual in the stateless international arena.

Democratic legitimacy and the protection of individual rights pose a challenge to the juristic model of democracy for essentially the same reason. The involvement of officials in international organizations introduces questions of political legitimacy into the process of collective will formation because they have not been elected to occupy offices in the structure of a sovereign government and because they cannot be relied upon to protect the rights of individual citizens for precisely that same reason. But notice two things. As the decisions of citizen juries are accumulated and analyzed, the nature of the process shifts from one of data gathering, through a "restatement" procedure that identifies the continuities that emerge from citizen decisions, to a stage at which these restated conclusions are codified and become the raw material of international negotiation and adjudication.

Recalling our discussion of international judicial procedure, the work of international courts (when effective) is generally the result of a prior agreement by sovereign governments to be bound by a particular act of adjudication. It resembles less the work of an Article 3 court in the American federal system than it does a process of negotiated regulation in administrative law. The legal "precedents" generated by the deliberations envisioned by juristic democracy would enter into the legal system in the same way that "customary" international law now does. Sovereign nations, on behalf of their citizens, would have a continuing opportunity to disavow the general principles of law that juristic democracy would create. As a final observation, the sovereign state (as a global/historical institution) is often something less the champion of individual rights than its boosters would have us believe. Indeed, an area of international law where the application of juristic democracy would seem to be both natural and needed is the realm of human rights. As a practical matter, problems of environmental protection and human rights often present themselves joined at the hip, as the environmental justice movement has amply demonstrated.

Local Knowledge and the Problem of Diversity

The second of our fundamental observations about the future of international environmental law is that to be both effective and genuinely democratic it will need to incorporate local ecological knowledge into its information core. There are a number of ways in which this necessity might be in tension with the methods of juristic democracy. It has been argued, for example, that jury-based processes privilege a certain kind of thought and communication that disadvantages the emotive, the instinctive, and the sensual. Much of this complaint is based upon claims about the dynamics of actual juries. Jury deliberation, so the complaint goes, discriminates against those whose style of reasoning and communication rely on affective judgments and emotional appeals. In the environmental realm, this is supposed to be the unique territory occupied by advocates of deep ecology and ecofeminism as well as those who battle environmental racism. As we have discussed, however, the research on juries does not support the notion that they are dominated by the cold, dead hand of logic. There is also scant evidence to suggest that the ability to persuade (dependent as it is on both a wide array of personal qualities and the specific demands of various situations) is differentially distributed across the population in patterns that distinguish between race, ethnicity, or gender (Vidmar and Hans 2007). As for the various "isms" associated with the environmental movement, we have characterized them elsewhere (Baber and Bartlett 2005) as political metaphysics. It is fair, we believe, that they make do with the influence on environmental law that their representation among stratified random samples of the population provides for them. If that is insufficient to their purposes, certainly the answer is better proselytizing on their part rather than greater deference to their beliefs on the part of others.

A more serious problem with loss of local ecological knowledge is the fact that juristic democracy is critically dependent on the written word. The hypothetical cases that citizen juries would adjudicate would not be presented in courtrooms, but in briefs and pleas provided in writing. Obviously, this will pose significant challenges of translation as multiple iterations of jury deliberation are staged in various countries. The choice of locations for deliberative juries will need to be made carefully so as to include any perspectives on the problem at hand that might be culturally or geographically specific. But an even more fundamental and troubling bias is introduced by this approach—bias in favor of literacy, in favor of the written word over the oral tradition.

The dependence of modern forms of adjudication on the written word is so fundamental as to be virtually invisible. This is particularly true in the case of the common law tradition which, to a far greater degree than civil or roman law, was an integral element of the evolution of England from an oral to a literate society. Indeed, the development of written legal documents memorializing the judgments of juries in late twelfth-century Great Britain was crucial to the establishment of reliable relationships between the Crown and landholders who needed the institutions of purchase, marriage, inheritance, litigation, and gift to establish and maintain a stable society (Cantor 1997). But in today's world, the gulf between the global information society and the oral traditions of Earth's remaining tribal cultures is so vast as to be virtually unimaginable. The problem is not that hypothetical cases cannot be rendered as fables and told to the inhabitants of tribal villages. The problem is, rather, the anthropological challenge of documenting and interpreting the responses of those inhabitants in ways that will allow their perspectives to be related to those of citizens in modern industrial states. It may be small comfort as the difficulty of this is contemplated, but it is at least true that a juristic model of democracy is more amenable to this challenge than aggregative forms of politics that require citizens to be familiar with fully developed questions of public policy and the social and economic circumstances that give rise to them before their views can receive a hearing.

Consensus: Be Careful What You Wish For

The increasingly rich literature on deliberative democracy has performed a number of useful functions over the past two decades. One of the most interesting of these is that it has revived discussion of the idea of consensus in democratic theory. Given up for dead by interest-group liberalism, consensus may be the next big thing. It may, in fact, be the battleground upon which deliberative democrats and communitarians (two closely related but sometimes warring clans) are destined to decide their differences. Can consensus be a practical political objective, or must it remain nothing but a regulative norm of political debate? Or does it remain, as the advocates of aggregative democracy have left it, a burned-out shell—useful only as background scenery for the self-serving performances of political charlatans?

To address this question seriously would require (what else?) another book. Fortunately, that complex problem is not the most important one for our present purposes. To understand why this is true, consider the plight of the preliterate society we have just discussed. Its social and economic circumstances have not yet required it to develop written language. Perhaps its members have not even entered that transitional stage that the anthropological record suggests humans travel on their path to literacy—

they don't even make lists of physical objects conceived of as possessions. How is the rest of humanity to treat the members of such a culture? Are we to decide their fate, either by dragging them into our modern world or walling them off in their own? The committed democrat is likely to suggest that they be given the right of self-determination. But in realistic terms, where will that lead? Experience suggests the answer: to the lingering death of their indigenous language, the slow erosion of their social structures, and the eventual loss of their cultural traditions.

We who think of ourselves as environmentalist democrats are capable of at least two reactions. We may embark on a grand project of environmental tourism in an effort to split the difference between life in a tribal society and modernity. Imagine those small fragments of the ancient world that remain preserved as a global EPCOT center, complete with pennant-wielding tour guides escorting visitors through a new corporate empire of English on which the sun would never set. Humankind has done as much for other endangered species; it certainly could do the same for tribal cousins.

If, however, the environmentalist in us triumphs over the democrat, we may come to a different conclusion. We may decide that all human institutions (including language, culture and social relations) are nothing more than adaptations to the demands of the environment. Human diversity is, in this view, simply another kind of biodiversity. Particular characteristics either have survival potential or they do not. Just as those human characteristics that contribute nothing to our survival are simply weeded out of the human gene pool and never missed, human values and traditions that no longer serve a purpose should be allowed to wither without regret.

But what is a democrat to do if he is neither arrogant enough to think that he can manage the cultures of others as if they were amusement parks nor callous enough to sit idly by while traditional societies disappear like disfavored genes? This is not a question that so limited a tradition as law can reasonably hope to answer in its entirety. But part of the answer must surely be something like this: we should never conclude that the unique perspectives of a preliterate society, borne through time in its oral traditions, could ever be dismissed as of no further use. After all, those of us who are products of the Western tradition will still occasionally refer to the multilayered wisdom of Solomon when asked to adjudicate positions so absolute and incommensurable that no compromise between them is possible. Did that ancient king ever truly hold his sword over a child that two mothers longed to possess? Does that even matter?

The story of Solomon is, first and foremost, a human narrative. Its meaning and continuing relevance is not that it is an account of historical fact, much less the resolution of an actual dispute. It is, rather, a brief entry in the journal of human experience. We refer back to it, when needed, to gain a better understanding of our own lives and the challenges they present. The doctrines of the common law are much like this. Collectively, they represent a vast and continually developing consensus about the dimensions of the just. They provide rules for conduct in the same sense that rules of language allow us to understand each other—imperfectly, but well enough. Moreover, these rules of law and our rules of language come together to tell us stories about ourselves that we use to create our political relations, which are nothing more than narratives that describe the areas of our shared existence in which we engage each other in argument and agreement (Lakoff 2002).

The implications of this perspective for the problem of consensus are clear. The danger associated with consensus is not that we may fail to achieve it. It is, rather, that consensus can so easily be achieved (given enough centuries of shared experience) that there is a danger that it may become so all-encompassing that we no longer notice or question it. That outcome is more likely if we allow culturally specific perspectives on the question of justice to disappear from our intellectual gene pool. Here we find the appropriate mission for the environmental democrat. The environmentalist knows that a species with a narrow gene pool is less adaptable and, consequently, in greater danger of extinction. And the democrat knows that the marketplace of ideas upon which we rely to provide solutions to public problems will produce its best results when the largest number of voices is heard. Are we, then, so sure that the global elite can solve all of the world's environmental problems that we will consign to oblivion the inherited wisdom of a tribal kingdom whose name may be known only to anthropologists and its few remaining subjects? If we choose to, we will certainly be the poorer for it. And it should never be claimed that the deliberative goal of consensus required that we do so.

Notes

1. Realist theorists do so while excusing their own behavior by pointing out that their intentions were pure, their methods nonviolent, and their ends highly desirable.

2. There are detailed summaries of realism as a philosophical perspective (Passmore 1957; Werkmeister 1949), so we will limit ourselves to only the briefest account of this venerable tradition. In its earliest form, realism was an opposing doctrine to nominalism. In this context, realism consisted of the view that universals have a real and objective existence beyond the mind of the knower. Realism was also equally opposed to the materialist doctrine that nothing exists beyond material objects and to the idealist view that nothing exists apart from our knowledge or awareness of it and that our ideas are the most real (perhaps the only) things in our lives.

In its more contemporary manifestations, philosophical realism has become almost exclusively a response to the predicament of egocentrism. This is the problem of finding some ground for understanding the world in a way that is not entirely dependent upon the characteristics of the knowing mind. What is sought is an understanding of reality as it exists apart from our own consciousness. To admit that nothing can be shown to exist apart from a perceiving mind is intuitively unappealing. It suggests, as did W. T. Stace (1934), that when I leave a fire burning in the fireplace and return some hours later, it cannot be shown that the fire continued to burn just as it had the prior evening when I stayed at home. Neither the ashes under the grate nor the residual warmth in the room *prove* (either inductively or deductively) that the wood continued to exist and the fire to burn in my absence.

Such a state of philosophical affairs is clearly unacceptable to anyone of even average common sense. But our common sense rejection of this counterintuitive skepticism need not lead us to accept the view that abstract ideas, like the classes into which we divide objects and the attributes we ascribe to them, enjoy the same ontological status as the objects themselves. Our terms for physical objects belong to the earliest and most basic stages in the development of our language capacities. Moreover, the most successful elements of our conversations tend to be about intersubjectively observable features of the environment, and the words we use in those discussions tend to be learned through direct conditioning by the stimulatory effects of the denoted objects. It is, therefore, no wonder that more confidence should be felt in there being physical objects than in there being classes, attributes, and the like (Quine 1960). In short, one need not subscribe to G. E. Moore's realist refutation of the idea that things cannot exist unperceived in order to warm oneself by the fire (Moore 1959).

One additional variant of contemporary philosophical realism is worth mentioning. Critical realists have argued that our perceptions of physical objects should not be understood as attributes of those objects but, rather, as "character complexes" or features of our own mental states (Drake 1968). It is these intuited mental contents of which we are directly aware when we focus our attention on external objects. Illusions and hallucinations are not nearly so problematic to this form of realism. Neither is it plagued by an unavoidable skepticism. While it is true that our mental contents are merely taken as representative of the primary properties of objects, it is not unreasonable to rely upon them because the hypothesis that those objects actually exist in approximately the form we take them is the least taxing explanation for the generally high level of coherence our view of reality has and our success in discussing it with one another.

This limited and pragmatic approach is consistent with William James's refutation of the nominalist claim that "we really never frame any conception of the partial elements of an experience, but are compelled, whenever we think it, to think it in its totality, just as it came" (James [1890] 1952, 305). James observed that this error was not confined to nominalists. It is a common assumption that "an idea must be a duplicate edition of what it knows" and that "knowledge in any strict sense of the word, as a self-transcendent function, is impossible" (307). Once taken by the notion that "an idea, feeling, or state of consciousness can at bottom only be aware of its own quality" we will find ourselves unable to see how any idea can "become the vehicle of a knowledge of anything permanent or universal" (309). Any general propositions that seem to reach the permanent or universal must be regarded as the result of a conjunction of experiences that, through repetition, take on so high a level of cohesion that any deviation is experienced by us as unpleasant.

This interpretation would, however, leave us blind to an element of our mental structure, which expresses itself in aesthetic and moral principles, neither of which can be explained by the idea of "habitual experiences having bred inner cohesions" (James [1890] 1952, 886). That matters of such singular importance can be communicated in neither formal syllogisms nor empirical propositions underlies the view of many thinkers (Rorty 1989) that literature and other expressive forms of communication, rather than philosophy, can best promote the human solidarity needed for societies to cope with the growing awareness of their historical contingency. This insight leads to the conclusion that philosophical realism is inadequate unless it is supplemented by an aesthetic realism that makes sense of these other forms of communication.

3. Even a sympathetic observer of the arts and letters would have to admit that when the notion of realism fell into the hands of that community it took on a range of possible meanings that "runs from the pedantically exact to the cosmically vague" (Davies 1997). At least three of these possible meanings are worth discussing in our present context.

First, aesthetic realism can refer to accuracy of representation. Often referred to as *mimesis*, this quality of an artistic representation is what we might be searching for if we wanted to portray a historical scene (in an encyclopedia, perhaps) that had occurred prior to the advent of photography. In this context, we would praise an artist for his or her ability to capture an exact likeness of the principal players and place them in surroundings that recall the precise state of things long ago. Mimesis can be contrasted with a second form of aesthetic realism, *verisimilitude*. Here we refer to the artist's ability to render a work that has the appearance of reality (perhaps through the wonders of Hollywood special effects). The subject of realist art, understood in this way, need not have ever existed or may have existed in a form so distant from our experience that a literal representation is impossible. So whereas mimesis can represent to us a world from the distant past, verisimilitude shows us worlds that exist (if at all) only in galaxies far, far away.

A third form of aesthetic realism has, as far as we know, no handy Greek or Latin label. We refer to a form of realism most commonly associated with modern literature rather than with the fine arts. As a literary form, realism has come to be associated with the idea that art cannot turn its back on the sordid and sorrowful aspects of human existence in a constant pursuit of beauty and nobility (Morris 2003). The development of the realist novel, for example, has been characterized by a "democratization of subject matter," a tendency toward "confrontation with authority," and a "continuous experimentation with narrative techniques" (97). These trends have manifested themselves in a literary tradition that values, not the capacity for accurate reproduction, but rather the ability to render the familiar strange. As an example, the realism of Tolstoy has been celebrated for the shocking strangeness of his representations of the ordinary world. His was the art of describing familiar objects as if he were seeing them for the first time (Lodge 1972).

Morris argues that realist literature of the sort we are describing can have a number of important effects (Morris 2003). First, it has an *empirical effect*. Through its widely varied narrative techniques, realist writing has the ability to convey the experienced reality of our existence in social, physical, and temporal space. By continually shifting linguistic acts of "selection" and "combination" (101–103), realist literature is capable of representing our existence to us from angles as numerous as are those sharing that existence. Second, realist literature has a *truth effect*. Despite their frequent "here and now" feel, realist novels seem frequently to offer us more than merely empirical knowledge. They often suggest "truth claims," of a more "universal or ethical nature" than simple empirical generalizations (109). To this extent, they seem to satisfy the apparently ubiquitous human desire to impose meaning on the chaos of existence. Third, for many readers realist literature has a *character effect*, which is often the primary means of entry into the fictional world. By placing fully developed and comprehensible persons (albeit fictional ones) in a meaning-rich circumstance, the novelist employs a form of "psychological realism" (117) that assures the reader that the work as a whole makes available a valuable form of knowledge.

At this point, however, we face a conundrum. Aesthetic realism makes a multiplicity of perspectives available to us and validates them. It also proffers truth claims of a universal nature. But how do we reconcile this apparent conflict between the particular and the universal, between the many and the one? Are we not confronted, finally, with a problem very much like the philosophical question that asks: which is the more real—the objects of our daily experience or the categories and concepts we use to discuss those concrete perceptions? For aesthetic realism, the solution may lie in its character effect. We enter into fictional worlds not merely as individual readers but also as part of an interpretive community. That community is less a reader than it is a writer, drafting texts in ways that are consistent with the community's interpretive strategies (Morris 2003). The different views of texts sometimes held by one individual are accounted for by the fact that, in a pluralistic society, everyone is a member of more than one interpretive community. Differences at the societal level over grand narratives can be explained by this same interpretive pluralism. But we should not regard these differences as evidence of incommensurable points of view. If the languages of those whose differences are fundamental actually were incommensurable, they would have no common ground upon which to stand while pursuing their quarrel (Davidson 1984). While this insight does not give us a formula for resolving interpretive disagreements, it should reassure us that Derrida (1978, 1976) is indeed mistaken to argue that all we poor humans can do is exchange monologues and, ultimately, resort to naked power.

If we allow this same pragmatic light to reflect back upon the philosophical dispute between advocates of nominalism and realism, we may discern in that soft glow the outline of a view rather like Jürgen Habermas's notion of communicative reason. As an example, Habermas (1998d, 1998c) argues that we can accept the proposition that much of the linguistic furnishings of modernism hide unequal power relationships without discarding the universal values of free inquiry and individual autonomy that are modernism's unique contribution to human advancement. Thus, and parallel to a fundamental metaphysical principle of pragmatism articulated by Dewey and many others (discussed in the next chapter), we can see that if our intent is to deal with the practical problems that confront us as a species, we do not need to resolve the question of nominalism versus realism. We need simply to outgrow it. In much the same way, for many similar reasons, it is time for us to outgrow political realism as well.

4. In Truman's magnum opus (Truman 1951), he acknowledges a special indebtedness to the pioneering book on interest group politics, *The Process of Government*, published in 1908 by Dewey's contemporary, Arthur F. Bentley. Ironically, later in 1932, Dewey and Bentley began a correspondence that lasted until Dewey's death and resulted in many coauthored articles and one book (Dewey and Bentley 1949).

5. One might imagine that here would be a point about which Dewey and Charles Peirce might have agreed. It is possible, however, to discern subtle but important differences between the two. It was Peirce's view that scientific inquiry can be authoritative without being authoritarian because its conclusions are understood always to

be provisional and its methodology is subject to criticism and revision (Peirce [1877] 1992). The pronouncements of science are politically acceptable because they are subject to reexamination rather than because they are the result of broadly participatory inquiry. And it is the methodology of inquiry, rather than the mere fact of collaboration, that gives science its authoritative character. The idea of Dewey's that science in a democracy should be broadly participatory would strike Peirce as unreasonable. For one thing, Peirce thought that rigorous philosophical and scientific thinking had little to say regarding questions of morality, politics, and "all that relates to the conduct of life" (Peirce [1898] 1997, 29). Moreover, Peirce apparently thought very little of average citizens, consigning them to service of the intellectual elite with the remark that "if it is their highest impulse to be intellectual slaves, then slaves they ought to remain" (Peirce [1877] 1992, 118).

6. Logging is so place-specific and legal context-specific and so focused on a limited number of stakeholders (who share the desire to keep it local, each for their own reason) that it provides almost the prototypical problem that might be addressed by some version of deliberative democracy. If it never works there, it does not have a prayer anywhere. Global warming, on the other hand, is a textbook example of costs and benefits falling on billions of persons in far-flung places with different languages and cultures and the absence of any higher authority to encourage the development of a consensual resolution. Probably no one other than us is foolhardy enough to suggest that some form of deliberative democracy is even plausible in those circumstances.

7. It may be nothing more than practicing liberal tolerance for nonliberal regimes. You can be tolerant and still assert the superiority of liberalism over nonliberal institutions. That is what Rawls does, which is not much different from advancing a coherent and comprehensive theory of justice but declining to force it on people who do not (yet) follow your reasoning.

8. Realists do not necessarily claim that ethics and morality are irrelevant and unimportant, only that it is "naïve and dangerous to believe that morality, expressed through law and international institutions, can consistently restrain the pursuit of relative advantage" (Lebow 2003, 238). For Morgenthau and classical realists, "morality imposes limits on the ends that power seeks and the means employed to achieve them," but "adherence to ethical norms was just as much in the interest of those who wielded power as it was for those over whom it was exercised" (282–283).

9. For primers on the common law, see Holmes [1991] 1881; Cantor 1997; L. Friedman 2005.

10. By the end of the thirteenth century, three great courts had emerged in English law: the King's Bench, the Common Bench (or Court of Common Pleas), and the Exchequer. Each had its own identifiable sphere, but each extended its reach over time so that, by the end of the Middle Ages, a plaintiff often had a choice between any of these three courts. Each would deal with the plaintiff's case in much the same way using much the same rules. The law administered by these courts was part custom, part statute, and part the law common to all Englishmen that

was neither enacted nor statutory but, rather, developed by judges over centuries. The phrase used to describe this law, the *common law*, was already current by that time. But there was, as yet, no body of rules that bore the name of *equity*.

Of these three courts, the Exchequer was more than a court of law. It was also an administrative bureau from which the modern British treasury takes its name. Within this structure there existed a secretarial department, the Chancery, headed by the chancellor who might be characterized as the king's secretary of state for all departments of government. He kept the king's seal and supervised the great mass of correspondence and other writing that had to be done in the king's name. The chancellor was not a judge, but a great deal of his work brought him into close contact with the administration of justice. He supervised the process of preparing the writs that were required to initiate litigation, and which had to bear the king's seal. In the pursuit of this task, the chancellor was empowered to "create" such new writs as were necessary to meet the needs of new and unique cases as they arose. Innovative writs, which were granted without opposition on the testimony of the plaintiff alone, could later be quashed in courts of law as contrary to the law of the land.

In addition to the issuance of writs, the chancellor had the power to deal directly with contested legal matters. Though three great courts had been established to administer the law, there remained a reserve of justice in the hands of the king. Those who could not get relief elsewhere could present their petitions to him. Already by this time the number of these petitions had grown quite large and the work of dealing with them had fallen to the chancellor. In performing this task, the chancellor drew on two kinds of legal power. The first, the common law, was a body of judge-made law designed originally to resolve issues petitioners might have with the sovereign. These actions often raised points of fact that had to be resolved by jury. When matters such as these arose, the chancellor did not summon a jury or preside at trial. Instead, he sent the matter to the King's Bench. As the number and importance of this kind of proceeding grew, it became accepted practice to bypass the chancellor at the outset in such matters.

The second kind of law administered by the chancellor, in what came to be known as "courts of chancery," was the law of equity. The petitioner in an equitable action sought relief at the expense of some person other than the king. However, he complained that for some reason or another he could not get a remedy in the ordinary course of justice under the common law. The petition was often couched in pitiful terms and sometimes prayed for relief from the king as an act of Christian charity. As the number of these petitions grew, they came to be directly addressed to the chancellor. He had the option, of course, to invent a new writ to accommodate the circumstances of each case. But by the fourteenth century, courts of law had become quite aggressive in quashing innovative writs. Instead of pursuing this fruitless course, the chancellor could call in the defendant to answer the complaint against him.

This kind of extraordinary justice was generally triggered by a plaintiff who argued that he was poor and powerless and his adversary was rich and influential, making the matter inappropriate to the ordinary courts and the common law. As true as this often was, it was never destined to be popular with the rich and influential. Consequently, courts of chancery were increasingly discouraged from taking up matters that the common law governed. In one area of law, however, chancellors did increasingly useful work. Courts of chancery increasingly became the forum in which uses (or trusts) were enforced. Fiduciary relationships presented issues of fact that were so tangled and complex that juries of the time seemed entirely incapable of dealing with them. As the importance of this area of law grew, rules of "equity and good conscience" evolved in chancery courts. It is no coincidence that this approach developed in courts governed by the chancellor. He was, after all, almost always an ecclesiastic. And ecclesiastical courts had long punished breaches of trust by spiritual censures and penance. Unfortunately, this moralistic distance between equity and the common law made for a confusing relationship.

Equity thus plays a strange role in the structure of law, separate from and yet part of existing legal norms. The relationship between law and equity in the modern era has never been clearly established. In the common law, equity is still looked upon (because of its association with a separate system of courts) as an auxiliary system of law, to be used only when other approaches would work a hardship so extreme as to shock the conscience of the court. In the American experience, this perplexity is increased by the fact that the fragmentation of courts that characterized the English experience was not replicated in this country and the same courts administered principles of both law and equity from our earliest years as a people. The rustic conditions of the American colonies created no demand for courts of chancery, which by that time had become elaborate mechanisms for resolving the disputes of wealthy families and large landholders. Moreover, the very idea of equitable discretion in the application of law ran counter to Puritanism, as evidenced by the increasing hostility to courts of equity in England. As a result, the American experience with equitable principles developed within the confines of common law courts. These courts were thus required to administer the continuing development of common law principles, inherited from their British progenitors, and to ameliorate the harshest outcomes generated by those same principles as they were applied to the American experience. See Pound 1999; Maitland 1909; Holdsworth 1956.

11. The Montreal Protocol and its implementation has been widely judged to be effective, but by using a fairly low standard of effectiveness. Depletion of the ozone layer is a continuing problem of policy concern for the ozone regime, which must contend with significant problems of implementation and ongoing problems in securing nation-state agreement to next-generation regulations as the issue of ozone depletion has become progressively less salient after initial successes.

12. Reflective equilibrium is equilibrium in that "our principles and judgments coincide" and it is reflective in that "we know to what principles our judgments conform" (Rawls 1999c, 18). Jurors of good conscience do that all the time, but not by starting with abstract principles and not in so sophisticated a fashion as we might expect of philosophers. Squaring moral judgments with abstract principles

is both an inductive and a deductive process. The whole restatement and codification process is designed to reconcile the fact-specific judgments made in courts and to harmonize the principles that those judgments evidence in such a way that future "litigators" can predict how new disputes will be adjudicated and how those decisions can be explained to the "client." The reason for using hypothetical but concrete cases (as Davis 1969 suggests) is to get judgments about cases that square precisely with the policy questions at hand without introducing extraneous concerns that will confound interpretation of the results and without requiring the adjudicator to wrap his intellect around the policy question in all of its complexity.

Most of the empirical research on the way actual juries operate paints a fairly positive picture of how average citizens tackle real-world problems involving difficult moral problems. Vidmar and Hans (2007), in a review of that research, conclude that, although not perfect, juries do at least as good a job as judges in resolving real-world disputes in ways that comport with the dictates of common sense and reflect reasonable interpretations of the available evidence. Moreover, the verdicts of adequately representative juries are seen as highly legitimate by the public. When looked at in comparative terms, the use of juries constitutes a move away from authoritarian forms of government toward more democratic arrangements. The available evidence indicates that meaningful jury service reinforces the democratic impulse in individual citizens (Vidmar and Hans 2007). This is consistent with the research on the effects of participation on policy jurists. It may be a result of deliberation as a generic experience.

13. The development of the tradition of common law, and the superstructure of statutory law that it supports, was a process of working upward from solutions to concrete problems toward general statements about the structure of disputes per se and the relationships among the principles that one could infer from those general statements. The fact that the process was driven largely by judges during most of that development suggests that judges function as good (thought not perfect) aggregators of the sense of justice shared among members of the communities to which they belong. If not, the structure would not have displayed the durability and flexibility that it has. Judges betray their understanding of this when they concede that they have little to rely on other than the inherent legitimacy of their institution in gaining acceptance of their pronouncements. This is why the judiciary may in fact be the most innately democratic branch of government. It comes closest to reflecting a considered social consensus and relies most heavily on universal acceptance of its decisions.

14. The date of birth of the common law is subject to a certain amount of disagreement. It can be traced back at least as far as the Plantagenet rulers of England in the twelfth century. Winston Churchill, however, sees its seeds planted in King Alfred's Book of Laws in the late ninth century (Churchill 1956). Alfred inverted the Christian principle of the Golden Rule ("do unto others as you would that they do unto you") into the less ambitious injunction "What ye will that other men should *not* do to you, that do ye not to other men." This can be seen as the prag-

matic (indeed, lawyerly) conversion of a maxim of positive religious obligation into a negative statement of individual rights more appropriate to the enforcement competencies of government.

15. Posner notes this would not explain the bargain between sovereign and subject because criminal law is no more effective (generally speaking) than primitive systems of private law when it comes to protecting individuals.

Works Cited

Abdel-Nour, Farid. 1999. "From Arm's Length to Intrusion: Rawls's "Law of Peoples" and the Challenge of Stability." *Journal of Politics* 61 (2): 313–330.

Abrahamson, Shirley S., and Michael J. Fischer. 1997. "All the World's a Courtroom: Judging in the New Millennium." *Hofstra Law Review* 26:273–292.

Abram, David. 1996. *The Spell of the Sensuous*. New York: Vintage.

Ackerman, Bruce, and James Fishkin. 2003. "Deliberation Day." In *Debating Deliberative Democracy*, ed. J. Fishkin and P. Laslett, 7–30. Malden, MA: Blackwell.

Anderson, Benedict. 1983. *Imagined Communities: Reflections on the Origin and Spread of Nationalism*. London: Verso.

Andeweg, Rudy. 1995. "The Reshaping of National Party Systems." *West European Politics* 18 (3): 58–78.

Andree, Peter. 2005. "The Genetic Engineering Revolution in Agriculture and Foods: Strategies of the Biotech Bloc." In *The Business of Global Environmental Governance*, ed. D. Levy and P. Newell, 135–168. Cambridge, MA: MIT Press.

Archibugi, Daniele. 2003. "Cosmopolitical Democracy." In *Debating Cosmopolitics*, ed. D. Archibugi, 1–15. New York: Verso.

Arend, Anthony. 1999. *Legal Rules and International Society*. New York: Oxford University Press.

Austin-Smith, David. 1992. "Strategic Models of Talk in Political Decision Making." *International Political Science Review* 13:45–58.

Austin, John. [1832] 2000. *The Province of Jurisprudence Determined*. Amherst, NY: Prometheus.

Axelrod, Regina S. 2005. "Democracy and Nuclear Power in the Czech Republic." In *The Global Environment*, ed. R. Axelrod, D. L. Downie, and N. Vig, 261–283. Washington, DC: CQ Press.

Axelrod, Regina S., David Leonard Downie, and Norman J. Vig, eds. 2005. *The Global Environment: Institutions, Law, and Policy*, 2nd ed. Washington, DC: CQ Press.

Axelrod, Regina, Norman Vig, and Miranda Schuers. 2005. "The European Union as an Environmental Governance System." In *The Global Environment*, ed. R. Axelrod, D. L. Downie, and N. Vig, 200–224. Washington, DC: CQ Press.

Baber, Walter F. 2004. "Ecology and Democratic Governance: Toward a Deliberative Model of Environmental Politics." *Social Science Journal* 41:331–346.

Baber, Walter F., and Robert V. Bartlett. 2005. *Deliberative Environmental Politics: Democracy and Ecological Rationality*. Cambridge, MA: MIT Press.

Barber, Benjamin R. 2004. *Strong Democracy: Participatory Politics for a New Age*. Berkeley: University of California Press.

Barrett, Scott. 1998. "On the Theory and Diplomacy of Environmental Treaty-Making." *Environmental and Resource Economics* 11 (3–4): 317–333.

Bartlett, John. 1968. *Familiar Quotations*, 14th ed. Boston: Little, Brown.

Bartlett, Robert V. 1986. "Ecological Rationality: Reason and Environmental Policy." *Environmental Ethics* 8:221–239.

Bartlett, Robert V. 2005. "Ecological Reason in Administration: Environmental Impact Assessment and Green Politics." In *Managing Leviathan: Environmental Politics and the Administrative State*, ed. R. Paehlke and D. Torgerson, 47–58. Peterborough, Ontario: Broadview Press.

Bartlett, Robert V., and Walter F. Baber. 2005. "Ethics and Environmental Policy in Democratic Governance: John Rawls, Public Reason, and Normative Precommitment." *Public Integrity* 7 (3): 1–22.

Basso, Keith, and Steven Felds. 1996. *Senses of Place*. Santa Fe, NM: School of American Research Press.

Beck, Silke. 2004. "Localizing Global Change in Germany." In *Earthly Politics: Local and Global in Environmental Governance*, ed. S. Jasanoff and M. L. Martello, 173–194. Cambridge, MA: MIT Press.

Beck, Ulrich. 1992. *Risk Society: Toward a New Modernity*. London: Sage.

Beitz, Charles R. 1979. *Political Theory and International Relations*. Princeton, NJ: Princeton University Press.

Beitz, Charles R. 2000. "Rawls's Law of Peoples." *Ethics* 110 (4): 669–696.

Belshaw, Christopher. 2001. *Environmental Philosophy: Reason, Nature, and Human Concern*. Montreal: McGill-Queens University Press.

Ben-Zeev, Aaron. 1984. "The Kantian Revolution in Perception." *Journal for the Theory of Social Behavior* 4:69–84.

Benedick, Richard. 1998. *Ozone Diplomacy*, 2nd ed. Cambridge, MA: Harvard University Press.

Benvenisti, Eyal. 2000. "Domestic and International Resources: What Role for International Law?" In *The Role of the Law in International Politics: Essays in International Relations and International Law*, ed. M. Byers, 109–129. New York: Oxford University Press.

Best, Geoffrey. 1997. *War and Law since 1945*. Oxford, UK: Oxford University Press.

Birnie, Patricia. 1985. *International Regulation of Whaling: From Conservation of Whaling to Conservation of Whales and Whale Watching*. New York: Oceana.

Blackstone, William. 1979. *Commentaries on the Laws of England (A Facsimile of the First Edition, 1765–1769)*. Chicago: University of Chicago Press.

Bleicher, Samuel A. 1972. "An Overview of International Environmental Regulation." *Ecology Law Quarterly* 2 (1): 1–90.

Bodansky, Daniel. 1999. "The Legitimacy of International Governance: A Coming Challenge for International Environmental Law?" *The American Journal of International Law* 93 (3): 596–624.

Bohman, James. 1994. "Complexity, Pluralism, and the Constitutional State: On Habermas's *Faktizität and Geltung*." *Law and Society Review* 28 (4): 897–930.

Bohman, James. 1995. "Public Reason and Cultural Pluralism." *Political Theory* 23 (2): 253–279.

Bohman, James. 1996. *Public Deliberation: Pluralism, Complexity, and Democracy*. Cambridge, MA: MIT Press.

Bohman, James. 1999a. "Citizenship and Norms of Publicity." *Political Theory* 27 (2): 176–202.

Bohman, James. 1999b. "Democracy as Inquiry, Inquiry as Democracy: Pragmatism, Social Science, and the Cognitive." *American Journal of Political Science* 43 (2): 590–607.

Bohman, James. 1999c. "International Regimes and Democratic Governance: Political Equality and Influence in Global Institutions." *International Affairs* 75 (3): 499–513.

Bohman, James. 1999d. "A Pragmatic Interpretation of Critical Science." *Philosophy of the Social Sciences* 29 (4): 459–480.

Bohman, James. 2001. "Cosmopolitan Republicanism: Citizenship, Freedom, and Global Political Authority." *Monist* 84 (1): 3–21.

Bohman, James. 2003. "Deliberative Toleration." *Political Theory* 31 (6): 757–779.

Bohman, James. 2004a. "Expanding Dialogue: The Internet, the Public Sphere, and Prospects for Transnational Democracy." *Sociological Review* 52:131–155.

Bohman, James. 2004b. "Realizing Deliberative Democracy as a Mode of Inquiry: Pragmatism, Social Facts, and Normative Theory." *Journal of Speculative Philosophy* 18 (1): 23–43.

Bohman, James. 2005. "We, Heirs of Enlightenment: Critical Theory, Democracy, and Social Science." *International Journal of Philosophical Studies* 13 (3): 353–377.

Bottoms, Bette L., and Gail S. Goodman. 1994. "Perceptions of Children's Credibility in Sexual Assault Cases." *Journal of Applied Social Psychology* 24:702–732.

Brooks, R. E. 2005. "Failed States, or the State as Failure?" *University of Chicago Law Review* 72 (4): 1159–1196.

Brown, John, and Paul Duguid. 2002. *The Social Life of Information.* Cambridge, MA: Harvard Business School Press.

Bruner, Jerome. 1962. *On Knowing: Essays for the Left Hand.* Cambridge, MA: Belknap Press of Harvard University Press.

Brunnee, Jutta. 1993. "Beyond Rio? The Evolution of International Environmental Law." *Alternatives* 20 (1): 16–23.

Bryan, Frank M. 2004. *Real Democracy: The New England Town Meeting and How It Works.* Chicago: University of Chicago Press.

Bryner, Gary C. 1997. "Implementing Global Environmental Agreements in the Developing World." *Colorado Journal of International Environmental Law and Policy* (1997 Yearbook): 1–25.

Bryner, Gary C. 2004. "Global Interdependence." In *Environmental Governance Reconsidered: Challenges, Choices, and Opportunities,* ed. R. F. Durant, D. J. Fiorino, and R. O'Leary, 69–104. Cambridge, MA: MIT Press.

Buchanan, Allen. 2000. "Rawls's Law of Peoples: Rules for a Vanished Westphalian World." *Ethics* 110 (4): 697–721.

Buchanan, Allen. 2003. *Justice, Legitimacy, and Self-Determination: Moral Foundations for International Law.* New York: Oxford University Press.

By the People. 2006. *Online NewsHour.* PBS 2005 (cited August 2, 2006). Available at www.pbs.org/newshour/btp/index.html.

Caldwell, Lynton K. 1971. *Environment: A Challenge to Modern Society.* New York: Anchor Books (Doubleday).

Caldwell, Lynton K. 1990. *Between Two Worlds: Science, the Environmental Movement, and Policy Choice.* Cambridge, UK: Cambridge University Press.

Caldwell, Lynton K. 1991. "Law and Environment in an Era of Transition: Reconciling Domestic and International Law." *Colorado Journal of International Environmental Law and Policy* 2 (1): 1–24.

Caldwell, Lynton K. 1998. "Is Humanity Destined to Self-Destruct?" *Politics and the Life Sciences* 8 (1): 3–14.

Caldwell, Lynton K. 1999. "Is World Law an Emerging Reality? Environmental Law in a Transnational World." *Colorado Journal of International Environmental Law and Policy* 10 (2): 227–243.

Camilleri, Joseph, Kamal Malhota, and Majed Tehranian. 2000. *Reimagining the Future: Towards Global Governance.* Victoria, Australia: Global Governance Reform Project.

Cantor, Norman F. 1997. *Imagining the Law: Common Law and the Foundations of the American Legal System.* New York: HarperCollins.

Carr, Edward Hallett. 1946. *The Twenty Years' Crisis, 1919–1939: An Introduction to the Study of International Relations.* London: Macmillan.

Case, Ellen. 1993. "The Public's Role in Scientific Risk Management." *Georgetown International Environmental Law Review* 5:479–501.

Casey, Edward. 1997. *The Fate of Place*. Berkeley, CA: University of California.

Casper, Jonathan D. 1993. "Restructuring the Traditional Civil Jury: The Effects of Changes in Composition and Procedures." In *Verdict: Assessing the Civil Jury System*, ed. R. E. Litan, 414–459. Washington, DC: Brookings Institution.

Caufield, Catherine. 1996. *Masters of Illusion: The World Bank and the Poverty of Nations*. New York: Henry Holt.

Chandler, David. 2003. "International Justice." In *Debating Cosmopolitics*, ed. Daniele Archibugi, 27–39. New York: Verso.

Chasek, Pamela S. 2003. "The Ozone Depletion Regime." In *Getting It Done: Post-Agreement Negotiation and International Regimes*, ed. B. Spector and I. W. Zartman, 187–228. Washington, DC: United States Institute of Peace Press.

Chomsky, Noam. 2005. *Hegemony or Survival*. New York: Metropolitan Books.

Churchill, Winston. 1956. *A History of the English Speaking Peoples*, vol. 1. New York: Dorset.

Cleveland, Harlan. 1993. "The Global Commons." *The Futurist* 27 (3): 9–13.

Cobb, Edith. 1977. *The Ecology of Imagination in Childhood*. New York: Columbia University Press.

Cohen, Joshua. 1997. "Deliberation and Democratic Legitimacy." In *Deliberative Democracy: Essays on Reason and Politics*, ed. J. Bohman and W. Rehg, 67–91. Cambridge, MA: MIT Press.

Colding, Johan, and Carl Folke. 2000. "The Taboo System: Lessons about Informal Institutions for Nature Management." *Georgetown International Environmental Law Review* 12 (2): 413–445.

Craik, Neil. 1998. "Recalcitrant Reality and Chosen Ideals: The Public Function of Dispute Settlement in International Environmental Law." *Georgetown International Environmental Law Review* 10 (551): 551–580.

Crossen, T. 2004. "Multilateral Environmental Agreements and the Compliance Continuum." *Georgetown International Environmental Law Review* 16 (3): 473–500.

Crum, Ben. 2005. "Tailoring Representative Democracy to the European Union: Does the European Constitution Reduce the Democratic Deficit?" *European Law Journal* 11 (4): 452–467.

Cumberland, John. 1979. "Interregional Pollution Spillovers and Consistency of Environmental Policy." In *Regional Environmental Policy: The Economic Issues*, ed. H. Siebert, 255–283. New York: New York University Press.

Curtin, Deane. 1999. *Chinnagrounder's Challenge: The Question of Ecological Citizenship*. Bloomington: Indiana University Press.

Davidson, Donald. 1984. *Inquiries into Truth and Interpretation*. Oxford, UK: Clarendon.

Davies, Tony. 1997. *Humanism*. London: Routledge.

Davis, Kenneth C. 1969. *Discretionary Justice: A Preliminary Inquiry*. Baton Rouge: Louisiana State University Press.

Dawson, John P. 1960. *A History of Lay Judges*. Cambridge, MA: Harvard University Press.

Demmke, Christopher. 2004. "Implementation of Environmental Policy and Law in the United States and the European Union." In *Green Giants? Environmental Policies of the United States and the European Union*, ed. N. J. Vig and M. G. Faure, 135–157. Cambridge, MA: MIT Press.

Deng, Francis M., and I. William Zartman. 2002. A *Strategic Vision for Africa: The Kampala Movement*. Washington, DC: Brookings Institution Press.

Derrida, Jacques. 1976. *Of Grammatology*, trans. G. Chakravorty. Baltimore, MD: Johns Hopkins University Press.

Derrida, Jacques. 1978. *Writing and Difference*, trans. A. Bass. London: Routledge.

Dewey, John. [1910] 1997. *How We Think*. Mineola, NY: Dover Publications.

Dewey, John. [1916] 1944. *Democracy and Education*. New York: Free Press.

Dewey, John. [1927] 1954. *The Public and Its Problems*. Athens, OH: Swallow Press.

Dewey, John. 1929a. "America—By Formula." *New Republic* 60:117–119.

Dewey, John. 1929b. *The Quest for Certainty*. New York: Capricorn.

Dewey, John. [1929] 1958. *Experience and Nature*. New York: Dover Publications.

Dewey, John. [1935] 2000. *Liberalism and Social Action*. Amherst, NY: Prometheus Books.

Dewey, John. 1938. *Logic: The Theory of Inquiry*. New York: Henry Holt.

Dewey, John. 1973a. "The Experimental Theory of Knowledge." In *The Philosophy of John Dewey*, ed. J. J. McDermott, 175–193. New York: G. P. Putnam's Sons.

Dewey, John. 1973b. "The Influence of Darwinism on Philosophy." In *The Philosophy of John Dewey*, ed. J. J. McDermott, 31–41. New York: G. P. Putnam's Sons.

Dewey, John, and Arthur F. Bentley. 1949. *Knowing and the Known*. Boston: Beacon Press.

Dhanapala, Jayantha. 2002. "Globalization and the Nation-State." *Colorado Journal of International Environmental Law and Policy* 13 (1): 29–38.

Di Chiro, Giovanna. 1998. "Environmental Justice from the Grassroots: Reflections on History, Gender, and Expertise." In *The Struggle for Ecological Democracy: Environmental Justice Movements in the United States*, ed. D. Farber, 104–136. New York: Guilford Press.

Diggins, John P. 1994. *The Promise of Pragmatism: Modernism and the Crisis of Knowledge and Authority*. Chicago: University of Chicago Press.

DiMento, Joseph F. C. 2003. *The Global Environment and International Law.* Austin: University of Texas Press.

Dorf, Michael, and Charles Sabel. 1998. "A Constitution of Democratic Constitutionalism." *Columbia Law Review* 98:267–473.

Downie, David Leonard. 1995. "UNEP and the Montreal Protocol." In *International Organizations and Environmental Policy*, ed. R. V. Bartlett, P. A. Kurian, and M. Malik, 171–185. Westport, CT: Greenwood Press.

Downie, David Leonard. 2005. "Global Environmental Policy: Governance Through Regimes." In *The Global Environment: Institutions, Law, and Policy*, ed. R. S. Axelrod, D. L. Downie, and N. J. Vig, 64–82. Washington, DC: CQ Press.

Downie, David Leonard, Jonathan Krueger, and Henrik Selin. 2005. "Global Policy for Hazardous Chemicals." In *The Global Environment: Institutions, Law, and Policy*, ed. R. S. Axelrod, D. L. Downie, and N. J. Vig, 125–145. Washington, DC: CQ Press.

Drake, Durant, James Bisset Pratt, Arthur K. Rogers, George Santayana, Roy Wood Sellars, and C.A. Strong. 1968. *Essays in Critical Realism.* New York: Gordian Press.

Driesen, David M. 2003. "Thirty Years of International Environmental Law: A Retrospective and Plea for Reinvigoration." *Syracuse Journal of International Law and Commerce* 30 (2): 353–368.

Dryzek, John S. 1983. "Ecological Rationality." *International Journal of Environmental Studies* 21:5–10.

Dryzek, John S. 1987. *Rational Ecology: Environment and Political Ecology.* London: Basil Blackwell.

Dryzek, John S. 1996. *Democracy in Capitalist Times.* New York: Oxford University Press.

Dryzek, John S. 2000. *Deliberative Democracy and Beyond: Liberals, Critics, Contestations.* New York: Oxford University Press.

Dryzek, John S. 2005. *Politics of the Earth*, 2nd ed. New York: Oxford University Press.

Dryzek, John S., David Downes, Christian Hunold, David Schlosberg, and Hans-Kristian Hernes. 2003. *Green States and Social Movements: Environmentalism in the United States, United Kingdom, Germany, and Norway.* New York: Oxford University Press.

Dryzek, John S., and David Schlosberg, eds. 2005. *Debating the Earth.* New York: Oxford University Press.

Durant, Robert F. 1995. "The Democratic Deficit in America." *Political Science Quarterly* 110 (1): 25–48.

Dworkin, Ronald. 1986. *Law's Empire.* Cambridge, MA: Harvard University Press.

Eckersley, Robyn. 1996. "Green Liberal Democracy: The Rights Discourse Revisited." In *Democracy and Green Political Thought*, ed. B. Doherty and M. d. Geus, 212–236. London: Routledge.

Eckstein, Gabriel. 2005. "Access to Water: Protecting a Hidden Treasure: The U.N. International Law Commission and the International Law of Transboundary Water Resources." *Sustainable Development Law & Policy* 5:5–11.

Ehrlich, Paul, and Anne Ehrlich. 1996. *Betrayal of Science and Reason: How Anti-Environmental Rhetoric Threatens Our Future*. Washington, DC: Island Press.

Ehrmann, Markus. 2002. "Procedures of Compliance Control in International Environmental Treaties." *Colorado Journal of International Environmental Law and Policy* 13 (2): 377–443.

Esty, Daniel. 2005. "Economic Integration and Environmental Protection." In *The Global Environment: Institutions, Law, and Policy*, ed. R. S. Axelrod, D. L. Downie, and N. J. Vig, 146–162. Washington, DC: CQ Press.

Evans, Mark. 1999. "Is Public Justification Central to Liberalism?" *Journal of Political Ideologies* 4 (1): 117–136.

Faga, Barbara. 2006. *Designing Public Consensus: The Civic Theater of Community Participation for Architects, Landscape Architects, Planners, and Urban Designers*. New York: John Wiley & Sons.

Falk, Richard. 1989. *Revitalizing International Law*. Ames: Iowa State University Press.

Falkner, R. 2005. "The Business of Ozone Layer Protection: Corporate Power in Regime Evolution." In *The Business of Global Environmental Governance*, ed. D. Levy and P. Newell, 103–134. Cambridge, MA: MIT Press.

Fatout, Marian, and Steven Rose. 1995. *Task Groups in the Social Services*. Thousand Oaks, CA: Sage.

Faure, Michael, and Jürgen Lefevere. 2005. "Compliance with Global Environmental Policy." In *The Global Environment: Institutions, Law, and Policy*, ed. R. S. Axelrod, D. L. Downie, and N. J. Vig, 163–180. Washington, DC: CQ Press.

Featherstone, Kevin. 1994. "Jean Monnet and the 'Democratic Deficit' in the European Union." *Journal of Common Market Studies* 32 (2): 149–171.

Feld, Lars P. 2005. "The European Constitution Project from the Perspective of Constitutional Political Economy." *Public Choice* 122 (3–4): 417–448.

Feyerabend, Paul. 1987. *Farewell to Reason*. London: Verso.

Firestone, Laurel A. 2003. "You Say Yes, I Say No; Defining Community Prior Informed Consent under the Convention on Biological Diversity." *Georgetown International Environmental Law Review* 16 (1): 171–207.

Fischer, Frank, and John Forester. 1993. *The Argumentative Turn in Policy Analysis and Planning*. Durham, NC: Duke University Press.

Fishkin, James. 1991. *Democracy and Deliberation: New Directions for Democratic Reform*. New Haven, CT: Yale University Press.

Fishkin, James. 1995. *The Voice of the People: Public Opinion and Democracy*. New Haven, CT: Yale University Press.

Fishkin, James. 1999. "Toward Deliberative Democracy: Experimenting with an Ideal." In *Citizen Competence and Democratic Institutions*, ed. S. L. Elkin and K. E. Soltan, 279–290. University Park: Pennsylvania State University Press.

Fishkin, James, and Robert Luskin. 1999. "Bringing Deliberation to Democratic Dialogue." In *A Poll with a Human Face: The National Issues Convention Experiment in Political Communication*, ed. M. McCombs and A. Reynolds, 3–38. Mahwah, NJ: Lawrence Erlbaum.

Fogel, Cathleen. 2004. "The Local, the Global, and the Kyoto Protocol." In *Earthly Politics: Local and Global in Environmental Governance*, ed. S. Jasanoff and M. L. Martello, 103–125. Cambridge, MA: MIT Press.

Foley, Linda A., and Minor H. Chamblin. 1982. "The Effect of Race and Personality on Mock Jurors' Decisions." *Journal of Psychology* 112:47–51.

Foreman, Christopher. 2002. "The Civic Sustainability of Reform." In *Environmental Governance*, ed. D. Kettl. Washington, DC: Brookings Institution Press.

Forsyth, Tim. 2003. *Critical Political Ecology: The Politics of Environmental Science*. New York: Routledge.

Forsyth, Tim. 2004. "Social Movements and Environmental Democratization in Thailand." In *Earthly Politics: Local and Global in Environmental Governance*, ed. S. Jasanoff and M. L. Martello, 195–215. Cambridge, MA: MIT Press.

Fossum, John Erik, and Agustin Jose Menendez. 2005. "The Constitution's Gift? A Deliberative Democratic Analysis of Constitution Making in the European Union." *European Law Journal* 11 (4): 380–440.

Frank, Jerome. 1949. *Courts on Trial: Myth and Reality in American Justice*. Princeton, NJ: Princeton University Press.

Frank, Jerome. 1963. *Law and the Modern Mind*. Garden City, NY: Doubleday.

Frankel, Benjamin. 1996. "Restating the Realist Case: An Introduction." *Security Studies* 5 (3): ix–xx.

Fried, Charles. 2000. "Scholars and Judges: Reason and Power." *Harvard Journal of Law and Public Policy* 23 (3): 807–832.

Friedman, Lawrence M. 2005. *A History of American Law*, 3rd ed. New York: Touchstone.

Friedman, Richard. 1973. "On the Concept of Authority in Political Philosophy." In *Concepts in Social and Political Philosophy*, ed. R. Flatham, 121–146. New York: Macmillan.

Fuentes, Ximena. 2002. "International Law-Making in the Field of Sustainable Development: The Unequal Competition between Development and the Environment." *International Environmental Agreements: Politics, Law and Economics* 2 (2): 109–133.

Fukurai, Hiroshi, Edgar Butler, and Richard Krooth. 1993. *Race and the Jury: Racial Disenfranchisement and the Search for Justice*. New York: Plenum.

Gardner, Richard. 1992. *Negotiating Survival: Four Priorities after Rio*. New York: Council on Foreign Relations.

Garrett, Nathaniel. 2005. "Life is the Risk We Cannot Refuse: A Precautionary Approach to the Toxic Risks We Can." *Georgetown International Environmental Law Review* 17 (3): 517–562.

Gaus, Gerald F. 1997. "Reason, Justification, and Consensus: Why Democracy Can't Have It All." In *Deliberative Democracy: Essays on Reason and Politics*, ed. J. Bohman and W. Rehg, 205–242. Cambridge, MA: MIT Press.

Geddes, Andrew. 1995. "Immigrant and Ethnic Minorities and the EU's 'Democratic Deficit.' " *Journal of Common Market Studies* 33 (2): 197–218.

Gibson, James. 1979. *The Ecological Approach to Visual Perception*. Boston: Houghton Mifflin.

Gieryn, Thomas F. 1995. "Boundaries of Science." In *Handbook of Science and Technology Studies.*, ed. S. Jasanoff, G. E. Markle, J. C. Petersen, and T. Pinch, 393–443. Thousand Oaks, CA: Sage.

Gilles v. Department of Human Resources Development. 1974. 11 Cal.3d 313; 113 Cal. Rptr. 374, 380; 521 P.2d 110.

Gilpin, Robert. 1986. "The Richness of the Tradition of Political Realism." In *Neorealism and Its Critics*, ed. R. Keohane, 301–321. New York: Columbia University Press.

Gilpin, Robert. 1996. "No One Loves a Political Realist." *Security Studies* 5 (Spring): 3–26.

Gindin, Sam. 1994. "The Democratic Deficit." *Canadian Forum* 72 (827): 5–6.

Giorgi, Liana, and Ronald Pohoryles, J. 2005. "Challenges to EU Political Integration and the Role of Democratization." *Innovation* 18 (4): 407–418.

Gismondi, Michael, and Mary Richardson. 1994. "Discourse and Power in Environmental Politics: Public Hearings on a Bleached Kraft Pulp Mill in Alberta, Canada." In *Is Capitalism Sustainable? Political Economy and the Politics of Ecology*, ed. M. O'Connor, 232–252. New York: Guilford Press.

Goldsmith, Jack L., and Eric A. Posner. 2005. *The Limits of International Law*. New York: Oxford University Press.

Goldstein, Judith L., Miles Kahler, Robert O. Keohane, and Anne-Marie Slaughter, eds. 2001. *Legalization and World Politics*. Cambridge, MA: MIT Press.

Gormley, William T. 1987. "Intergovernmental Conflict on Environmental Policy: The Attitudinal Connection." *Western Political Quarterly* 40:285–303.

Graefrath, B. 1991. "The International Law Commission Tomorrow: Improving its Organization and Methods of Work." *The American Journal of International Law* 85 (4): 595–612.

Gray, Kevin. 2000. "International Environmental Impact Assessment: Potential for Multilateral Environmental Agreement." *Colorado Journal of International Environmental Law and Policy* 11 (1): 83–128.

Greenwood, Justin. 2002. "EU Public Affairs and the White Paper on Governance." *Journal of Public Affairs* 1/2 (4/1): 423–435.

Guinier, Lani. 1994. *The Tyranny of the Majority: Fundamental Fairness in Representative Democracy.* New York: Free Press.

Gupta, Aarti. 2004. "When Global Is Local: Negotiating Safe Use of Biotechnology." In *Earthly Politics: Local and Global in Environmental Governance,* ed. S. Jasanoff and M. L. Martello, 127–148. Cambridge, MA: MIT Press.

Gupte, Manjusha, and Robert V. Bartlett. 2007. "Necessary Preconditions for Deliberative Environmental Democracy? Challenging the Modernity Bias of Current Theory." *Global Environmental Politics* 7 (3): 94–106.

Guruswamy, Lakshman. 2003. "Cartography of Governance: An Introduction." *Colorado Journal of International Environmental Law and Policy* 13 (1): 1–4.

Gutmann, Amy. 1999. *Democratic Education.* Princeton, NJ: Princeton University Press.

Gutmann, Amy. 2003. *Identity in Democracy.* Princeton, NJ: Princeton University Press.

Gutmann, Amy, and Dennis Thompson. 1996. *Democracy and Disagreement.* Cambridge, MA: Belknap Press of Harvard University.

Gutmann, Amy, and Dennis Thompson. 2004. *Why Deliberative Democracy?* Princeton, NJ: Princeton University Press.

Haas, Peter M. 1990. *Saving the Mediterranean: The Politics of International Environmental Cooperation.* New York: Columbia University Press.

Haas, Peter M. 1992. "Introduction: Epistemic Communities and International Policy Coordination." *International Organization* 46 (1): 1–35.

Habermas, Jürgen. 1970. *Toward a Rational Society.* Boston: Beacon Press.

Habermas, Jürgen. 1971. *Knowledge and Human Interest.* Boston: Beacon Press.

Habermas, Jürgen. 1979. *Communication and the Evolution of Society.* Boston: Beacon Press.

Habermas, Jürgen. 1987. *The Theory of Communicative Action, Volume 2: Life-World and System.* Boston: Beacon Press.

Habermas, Jürgen. 1988. *On the Logic of the Social Sciences.* Cambridge, MA: MIT Press.

Habermas, Jürgen. 1990. *Moral Consciousness and Communicative Action.* Cambridge, MA: MIT Press.

Habermas, Jürgen. 1995. "Reconciliation through the Public Use of Reason: Remarks on John Rawls's *Political Liberalism.*" *Journal of Philosophy* 92 (3): 109–131.

Habermas, Jürgen. 1996. *Between Facts and Norms: Contributions to a Discourse Theory of Law and Democracy.* Cambridge, MA: MIT Press.

Habermas, Jürgen. 1997a. "Kant's Idea of Perpetual Peace with the Benefit of Two Hundred Years' Hindsight." In *Perpetual Peace: Essays on Kant's Cosmopolitan Ideal,* ed. J. Bohman and M. Lutz-Bachman, 113–153. Cambridge, MA: MIT Press.

Habermas, Jürgen. 1997b. "Popular Sovereignty as Procedure." In *Deliberative Democracy: Essays on Reason and Politics*, ed. J. Bohman and W. Rehg, 35–65. Cambridge, MA: MIT Press.

Habermas, Jürgen. 1998a. "Beyond the Nation State?" *Peace Review* 10 (2): 235–240.

Habermas, Jürgen. 1998b. *The Inclusion of the Other*. Cambridge, MA: MIT Press.

Habermas, Jürgen. 1998c. *The Philosophical Discourse of Modernity*. Cambridge, MA: MIT Press.

Habermas, Jürgen. 1998d. *The Structural Transformation of the Public Sphere*. Cambridge, MA: MIT Press.

Habermas, Jürgen. 1999. "The European Nation-State and the Pressures of Globalization." *New Left Review* 235:46–59.

Habermas, Jürgen. 2001a. "A Constitution for Europe?" *New Left Review* 11:5–26.

Habermas, Jürgen. 2001b. *The Postnational Constellation*. Cambridge, MA: MIT Press.

Habermas, Jürgen. 2001c. *On the Pragmatics of Social Interaction: Preliminary Studies in the Theory of Communicative Action*. Cambridge, MA: MIT Press.

Habermas, Jürgen. 2002a. *Religion and Rationality*. Cambridge, MA: MIT Press.

Habermas, Jürgen. 2002b. "Toward a European Political Community." *Society* 39 (5): 58–61.

Habermas, Jürgen. 2003a. *The Future of Human Nature*. Cambridge, UK: Polity.

Habermas, Jürgen. 2003b. "Toward a Cosmopolitan Europe." *Journal of Democracy* 14 (4): 86–99.

Habermas, Jürgen. 2003c. *Truth and Justification*. Cambridge, MA: MIT Press.

Habermas, Jürgen. 2008. *Between Naturalism and Religion: Philosophical Essays*. Cambridge, UK: Polity Press.

Hafner, Gerhard. 1996. "The International Law Commission and the Future of Codification of International Law." *ILSA Journal of International & Comparative Law* 2:671–677.

Hajer, Maarten, and Hendrik Wagenaar, eds. 2003. *Deliberative Policy Analysis: Understanding Governance in the Network Society*. New York: Cambridge University Press.

Hamilton, Alexander, James Madison, and John Jay. 2005. *The Federalist*, ed. and annot. J. R. Pole. Indianapolis: Hackett Publishing.

Handl, Gunther. 1994. "Controlling Implementation of and Compliance with International Environmental Commitments: The Rocky Road from Rio." *Colorado Journal of International Environmental Law and Policy* 5 (305): 305–331.

Hanson, Mirja. 2005. *Clues to Achieving Consensus: A Leader's Guide to Navigating Collaborative Problem Solving*. Lanham, MD: Rowman & Littlefield.

Hanson, Norwood. 1958. *Patterns of Discovery*. Cambridge, UK: Cambridge University Press.

Harding, Sandra. 1998. *Is Science Multicultural? Postcolonialisms, Feminisms, and Epistomologies.* Bloomington: Indiana University Press.

Hart, H. L. A. 1994. *The Concept of Law.* Oxford, UK: Clarendon.

Harvey, Adrian. 2004. "Monarchy and Democracy: A Progressive Agenda." *The Political Quarterly* 75 (1): 34–44.

Hastie, Reid, Steven Penrod, and Nancy Pennington. 1983. *Inside the Jury.* Cambridge, MA: Harvard University Press.

Held, David. 1995. *Democracy and the Global Order.* Stanford, CA: Stanford University Press.

Held, David. 2003. "Violence, Law, and Justice in a Global Age." In *Debating Cosmopolitics,* ed. D. Archibugi, 184–202. New York: Verso.

Herz, John H. 1976. *The Nation-State and the Crisis of World Politics: Essays on International Politics in the Twentieth Century.* New York: D. McKay.

Hierlmeier, Jodie. 2002. "UNEP: Retrospect and Prospect—Options for Reforming the Global Environmental Governance Regime." *Georgetown International Environmental Law Review* 14 (4): 767–805.

Hiskes, Richard. 1998. *Democracy, Risk, and Community.* New York: Oxford University Press.

Hix, Simon. 1998. "Elections, Parties and Institutional Design: A Comparative Perspective on European Union Democracy." *West European Politics* 21 (3): 19–52.

Hix, Simon. 2005. *The Political System of the European Union.* New York: Palgrave.

Holdsworth, William. 1956. *A History of English Law.* London: Sweet and Maxwell.

Holmes, Oliver Wendell, Jr. [1881] 1991. *The Common Law.* New York: Dover.

Hunold, Christian. 2005. "Green Political Theory and the European Union: The Case for a Non-Integrated Civil Society." *Environmental Politics* 14 (3): 324–343.

Hutchins, Edward. 1995. *Cognition in the Wild.* Cambridge, MA: MIT Press.

Iles, Alastair. 2004. "Patching Local and Global Knowledge Together: Citizens Inside the U.S. Chemical Industry." In *Earthly Politics: Local and Global in Environmental Governance,* ed. S. Jasanoff and M. L. Martello, 285–307. Cambridge, MA: MIT Press.

Ingehart, Ronald. 1977. *The Silent Revolution: Changing Values and Political Styles among Western Publics.* Princeton, NJ: Princeton University Press.

James, Henry, Jr. 1879. *Hawthorne.* New York: Harper & Brothers.

James, William. [1890] 1952. *The Principles of Psychology.* Chicago, IL: Britannica.

Janik, Allan, and Stephen Toulmin. 1973. *Wittgenstein's Vienna.* New York: Touchstone.

Jennings, Cheri Lucas, and Bruce H. Jennings. 1993. "Green FieldsBrown Skin: Posting as a Sign of Recognition." In *In the Nature of Things*, ed. J. Bennett and W. Chaloupka, 173–194. Minneapolis: University of Minnesota Press.

Johal, Surjinder, and Alistair Ulph. 2002. "Globalization, Lobbying, and International Environmental Governance." *Review of International Economics* 10 (3): 387–403.

John, DeWitt. 1994. *Civic Environmentalism: Alternatives to Regulation in States and Communities.* Washington, DC: CQ Press.

Jordan, Andrew. 1994. "Paying the Incremental Costs of Global Environmental Protection: The Evolving Role of the GEF." *Environment* 36:12–20, 31–36.

Kalvern, Harry, and Hans Zeisel. 1966. *The American Jury.* Chicago, IL: University of Chicago Press.

Kant, Immanuel. [1795] 1939. *Perpetual Peace.* New York: Columbia University Press.

Karp, Jeffrey A., Susan A. Banducci, and Shaun Bowler. 2003. "To Know It Is to Love It? Satisfaction with Democracy in the European Union." *Comparative Political Studies* 36 (3): 271–292.

Kassin, Saul M., and Lawrence S. Wrightsman. 1988. *The American Jury on Trial: Psychological Perspectives.* New York: Hemisphere Publishing.

Katz, Jerrold. 1998. *Realistic Rationalism.* Cambridge, MA: MIT Press.

Kelly, Michael. 1997. "Overcoming Obstacles to the Effective Implementation of International Environmental Agreements." *Georgetown International Environmental Law Review* 9:447–488.

Keohane, Robert. 1986. "Theory of World Politics: Structural Realism and Beyond." In *Neorealism and its Critics*, ed. R. Keohane, 158–203. New York: Columbia University.

Keohane, Robert. 2005. *After Hegemony: Cooperation and Discord in the World Political Economy.* Princeton, NJ: Princeton University Press.

Keohane, Robert, and Joseph Nye. 1977. *Power and Interdependence: World Politics in Transition.* Boston: Little, Brown.

Kerr, Norbert L. 2001. "Is It What One Says or How One Says It?: Style vs. Substance from an SDS Perspective." In *Group Consensus and Minority Influence: Implications for Innovation.*, ed. K. W. D. D. Carsten and N. De Vries, 201–228. Oxford, UK: Blackwell.

Kirkman, Robert. 2002. *Skeptical Environmentalism: The Limits of Philosophy and Science.* Bloomington: Indiana University Press.

Kluger, Richard. 1976. *Simple Justice: The History of Brown v. Board of Education and Black America's Struggle for Equality.* New York: Alfred Knopf.

Knight, Jack, and James Johnson. 1994. "Aggregation and Deliberation: On the Possibility of Democratic Legitimacy." *Political Theory* 22 (2): 277–296.

Knox, John H. 2002. "The Myth and Reality of Transboundary Environmental Impact Assessment." *The American Journal of International Law* 96 (2): 291–319.

Ku, Charlotte, and Paul Diehl, eds. 1998. *International Law: Classic and Contemporary Readings.* Boulder, CO: Lynne Rienner.

Kuper, Andrew. 2000. "Rawlsian Global Justice: Beyond the Law of Peoples to a Cosmopolitan Law of Persons." *Political Theory* 8 (5): 640–674.

Kurian, Priya A. 1995. "The U.S. Congress and the World Bank: Impact of News Media on International Environmental Policy." In *International Organizations and Environmental Policy*, ed. R. V. Bartlett, P. A. Kurian, and M. Malik, 103–113. Westport, CT: Greenwood Press.

Kurian, Priya A. 2000. *Engendering the Environment? Gender in the World Bank's Environmental Policies.* Aldershot, UK: Ashgate.

Lachmund, Jens. 2004. "Knowing the Urban Wasteland: Ecological Expertise as Local Process." In *Earthly Politics: Local and Global in Environmental Governance*, ed. S. Jasanoff and M. L. Martello, 241–261. Cambridge, MA: MIT Press.

LaDuke, Winona. 1994. "Traditional Ecological Knowledge and Environmental Futures." *Colorado Journal of International Environmental Law and Policy* 5 (127): 127–148.

Lahsen, Myanna. 2004. "Transnational Locals: Brazilian Experiences of the Climate Regime." In *Earthly Politics: Local and Global in Environmental Governance*, ed. S. Jasanoff and M. L. Martello, 151–172. Cambridge, MA: MIT Press.

Lakoff, George. 2002. *Moral Politics: How Liberals and Conservatives Think.* Chicago: University of Chicago Press.

Lankowski, Carl. 2004. "The Transatlantic Environmental Dialogue." In *Green Giants? Environmental Policies of the United States and the European Union*, ed. N. J. Vig and M. G. Faure, 329–344. Cambridge, MA: MIT Press.

Laslett, Peter. 2003. "Environmental Ethics and the Obsolescence of Existing Political Institutions." In *Debating Deliberative Democracy*, ed. J. Fishkin and P. Laslett, 212–224. Malden, MA: Blackwell.

Le Prestre, Philippe G. 1995. "Environmental Learning at the World Bank." In *International Organizations and Environmental Policy*, ed. R. V. Bartlett, P. A. Kurian, and M. Malik, 83–101. Westport, CT: Greenwood Press.

Lebow, Richard Ned. 2003. *The Tragic Vision of Politics: Ethics, Interests and Orders.* Cambridge, UK: Cambridge University Press.

Leib, Ethan. 2004. *Deliberative Democracy in America: A Proposal for a Popular Branch of Government.* University Park: Pennsylvania State University Press.

Leiter, Brian. 1997. "Rethinking Legal Realism: Toward a Naturalized Jurisprudence." *Texas Law Review* 76 (2): 267–315.

Leiter, Brian. 2001a. "Classical Realism." *Philosophical Issues* 11:244–267.

Leiter, Brian. 2001b. "Legal Realism and Legal Positivism Reconsidered." *Ethics* 111 (January): 278–301.

Lewontin, Richard. 1992. *Biology and Ideology.* New York: Harper Perennial.

Lindell, Michael, and Ronald Perry. 2004. *Communicating Environmental Risk in Multiethnic Communities.* Thousand Oaks, CA: Sage.

Lippman, Walter. 1925. *The Phantom Public.* New York: Harcourt Brace.

Llewellyn, K. N. 1962. *Jurisprudence.* Chicago: University of Chicago Press.

Locke, John. [1689] 1952. *An Essay Concerning Human Understanding.* Chicago: Encyclopedia Britannica.

Lodge, David, ed. 1972. *Twentieth Century Literary Criticism: A Reader.* London: Longman.

Lodge, Juliet. 1995. "Democratic Legitimacy and the EC: Crossing the Rubicon." *International Journal of Public Administration* 18 (10): 1595–1638.

Lord, Christopher. 2001. "Assessing Democracy in a Contested Polity." *Journal of Common Market Studies* 39 (4): 641–661.

Lowi, Theodore. 1979. *The End of Liberalism: The Second Republic of the United States*, 2nd ed. New York: W. W. Norton.

MacRae, Duncan, and Dale Wittington. 1997. *Expert Advice for Policy Choice.* Washington, DC: Georgetown University Press.

Magnette, Paul. 2003. "European Governance and Civic Participation: Beyond Elitist Citizenship?" *Political Studies* 51 (1): 144–161.

Magraw, Daniel. 1986. "The International Law Commission's Study of International Liability for Nonprohibited Acts as It Relates to Developing States." *Washington Law Review* 61:1041–1060.

Mainhardt, Heike. 2002. "Capacity Building Strategies in Support of Multilateral Environmental Agreements." In *Transboundary Environmental Negotiation: New Approaches to Global Cooperation*, ed. L. Susskind, W. Moomaw, and K. Gallagher, 252–275. San Francisco: Jossey-Bass.

Maitland, Frederick W. 1909. *Equity.* New York: Macmillan.

Manheim, Bruce S., Jr. 1994. "NEPA's Overseas Application." *Environment* 36 (3): 43–46.

Mansfield, Bill. 2002. *Establishing the Ground Rules of International Law: Where to from Here?* Wellington: NZ Centre for Public Law, Victoria University of Wellington.

Markell, David L. 2000. "The Commission for Environmental Cooperation's Citizen Submission Process." *Georgetown International Environmental Law Review* 12 (3): 545–574.

Marong, Alhaji B. M. 2003. "From Rio to Johannesburg: Reflections on the Role of International Legal Norms in Sustainable Development." *Georgetown International Environmental Law Review* 16 (1): 21–76.

Marshall, Dena. 2002. "An Organization for the World Environment: Three Models and Analysis." *Georgetown International Environmental Law Review* 15 (1): 79–103.

Martin, Andrew, and George Ross. 1999. "Europe's Monetary Union: Creating a Democratic Deficit?" *Current History* 98 (627): 171–175.

Mazzella, Ronald, and Alan Feingold. 1994. "The Effects of Physical Attractiveness, Race, Socioeconomic Status, and Gender of Defendants and Victims on

Judgments of Mock Jurors: A Metanalysis." *Journal of Applied Social Psychology* 24:1315–1344.

McCaffrey, Stephen C., Daniel Barstow Magraw, Paul C. Szacz, Robert E. Lutz, and Edith Weiss Brown. 1998. *International Environmental Law and Policy*. Gaithersburg, NY: Aspen.

Meadowcraft, James. 2004. "Deliberative Democracy." In *Environmental Governance Reconsidered: Challenges, Choices, and Opportunities*, ed. R. F. Durant, D. J. Fiorino, and R. O'Leary, 183–217. Cambridge, MA: MIT Press.

Meadowcroft, John. 2002. "The European Democratic Deficit, the Market and the Public Space: A Classical Liberal Critique." *Innovation* 15 (3): 181–192.

Mearsheimer, John J. 1990. "Back to the Future: Instability in Europe after the Cold War." *International Security* 15 (Summer): 5–56.

Mearsheimer, John J. 1994–1995. "The False Promise of International Institutions." *International Security* 19:5–49.

Mearsheimer, John. J. 2001. *The Tragedy of Great Power Politics*. New York: W. W. Norton.

Miles, Edward L., Arild Underdal, Steinar Andresen, Jorgen Wettestad, Jon Birger Skjaerseth, and Elaine M. Carlin. 2002. *Environmental Regime Effectiveness: Confronting Theory with Evidence*. Cambridge, MA: MIT Press.

Miller, Clark A. 2004. "Resisting Empire: Globalism, Relocalization, and the Politics of Knowledge." In *Earthly Politics: Local and Global in Environmental Governance*, ed. S. Jasanoff and M. L. Martello, 81–102. Cambridge, MA: MIT Press.

Mitzen, Jennifer. 2005. "Reading Habermas in Anarchy: Multilateral Diplomacy and Global Spheres." *American Political Science Review* 99 (3): 401–417.

Moore, G. E. 1959. *Philosophical Papers*. London: Allen & Unwin.

Moravcsik, Andrew 2002. "Reassessing Legitimacy in the European Union." *Journal of Common Market Studies* 40 (4): 603–624.

Morganthau, Hans J. 1946. *Scientific Man vs. Power Politics*. Chicago: University of Chicago Press.

Morganthau, Hans J. 1951. *In Defense of National Interest*. New York: Knopf.

Morganthau, Hans J. 1978. *Politics among Nations: The Struggle for Power and Peace*, 5th ed. New York: Knopf.

Morris, Pam. 2003. *Realism*. London: Routledge.

Morton, Jeffrey S. 2000. *The International Law Commission of the United Nations*. Columbia: University of South Carolina Press.

Mouffe, Chantal. 1996. "Democracy, Power and the Political." In *Democracy and Difference: Contesting the Boundaries of the Political*, ed. S. Benhabib, 245–256. Princeton, NJ: Princeton University Press.

Mouffe, Chantal. 1999. "Deliberative Democracy or Agonistic Pluralism?" *Social Research* 66 (3): 745–758.

Mouffe, Chantal. 2002. "Politics and Passion: Introduction." *Philosophy and Social Criticism* 28 (6): 615–616.

Mouffe, Chantal. 2005. "Schitt's Vision of a Multipolar World Order." *The South Atlantic Quarterly* 104 (2): 245–251.

Murphy, Sean D., ed. 2001. "U.S. Comments on ILC Draft Articles on State Responsibility." *The American Journal of International Law* 95 (3): 626–628.

Myers, Martha A. 1980. "Social Contexts and Attributions of Criminal Responsibility." *Social Psychology Quarterly* 43:405–419.

Najim, Adil. 2002. "International Environmental Negotiation: A Strategy for the South." In *Transboundary Environmental Negotiation: New Approaches to Global Cooperation*, ed. L. Susskind, W. Moomaw, and K. Gallagher, 41–81. San Francisco: Jossey-Bass.

Nathan, Ari. 2002. "Defining the 'Common Heritage of Mankind.'" In *Transboundary Environmental Negotiation: New Approaches to Global Cooperation*, ed. L. Susskind, W. Moomaw, and K. Gallagher, 3–23. San Francisco: Jossey-Bass.

Naticchia, Chris. 1998. "Human Rights, Liberalism, and Rawls's Law of Peoples." *Social Theory and Practice* 24 (3): 345–374.

Neundeither, Karlheinz. 1994. "The Democratic Deficit of the European Union: Towards Closer Cooperation between the European Parliament and the National Parliaments." *Government and Opposition* 29 (3): 299–314.

Nye, Joseph S. 2001. "Globalization's Democratic Deficit: How to Make International Institutions More Accountable." *Foreign Affairs* 80 (4): 2–6.

O'Brien, Robert, Anne Marie Goetz, Jan Aart Scholte, and Marc Williams. 2000. *Contesting Global Governance: Multilateral Economic Institutions and Global Social Movements*. New York: Cambridge University Press.

Offe, Claus. 1997. "Micro Aspects of Democratic Theory: What Makes for the Deliberative Competence of Citizens?" In *Democracy's Victory and Crisis*, ed. A. Hadenius, 81–104. Cambridge, UK: Cambridge University Press.

Olson, Mancur. 1965. *The Logic of Collective Action: Public Goods and the Theory of Groups*. Cambridge, MA: Harvard University Press.

Outhwaite, William. 1987. *New Philosophies of Social Science: Realism, Hermeneutics and Critical Theory*. New York: St. Martin's.

Pagnani, Marissa A. 2003. "Environmental NGOs and the Fate of the Traditional Nation-State." *Georgetown International Environmental Law Review* 15 (4): 791–808.

Palmer, Geoffrey. 1992. "New Ways to Make International Environmental Law." *American Journal of International Law* 86:258–283.

Parris, Thomas M. 2004. "Managing Transboundary Environments." *Environment* 46 (1): 3–4.

Parson, Edward A. 2003. *Protecting the Ozone Layer: Science and Strategy*. New York: Oxford University Press.

Passmore, John. 1957. *A Hundred Years of Philosophy.* London: Duckworth.

Peirce, Charles. [1877] 1992. "The Fixation of Belief." In *The Essential Peirce, volume 1,* ed. N. Houser and C. Kloesel, 109–123. Bloomington: Indiana University Press.

Peirce, Charles. [1898] 1997. "Philosophy and the Conduct of Life." In *The Essential Peirce, volume 2,* ed. N. Houser and C. Kloesel, 26–48. Bloomington: Indiana University Press.

Pevenhouse, Jon. 2003. "Democratization, Credible Commitments, and Joining International Organizations." In *Locating the Proper Authorities: The Interaction of International and Domestic Institutions,* ed. D. Drezner, 77–104. Ann Arbor: University of Michigan Press.

Picciotto, Sol. 1996–1997. "Networks in International Economic Integration: Fragmented States and the Dilemmas of Neo-Liberalism." *Northwestern Journal of International Law and Business* 17:1014–1056.

Pierce, Maureen C., and Richard Jackson Harris. 1993. "The Effect of Provocation, Race, and Injury Description on Men's and Women's Perceptions of a Wife-Battering Incident." *Journal of Applied Social Psychology* 23:767–790.

Pitkin, Hanna. 1967. *The Concept of Representation.* Berkeley: University of California Press.

Plevin, Arlene. 1997. "Green Guilt: An Effective Rhetoric or Rhetoric in Transition?" *Technical Communication Quarterly* 6 (2): 125–139.

Pogge, Thomas. 1994. "An Egalitarian Law of Peoples." *Philosophy and Public Affairs* 23 (2): 195–224.

Polanyi, Michael. 1958. *Personal Knowledge.* Chicago: University of Chicago Press.

Pollack, Mark A., and Gregory C. Shaffer. 2001. *Transatlantic Governance in the Global Economy.* Lanham, MD: Rowman & Littlefield.

Porter, Gareth, Janet Welsh Brown, and Pamela S. Chasek. 2000. *Global Environmental Politics,* 3rd ed. Boulder, CO: Westview Press.

Posner, Richard A. 1981. *The Economics of Justice.* Cambridge, MA: Harvard University Press.

Posner, Richard A. 1992. *The Essential Holmes.* Chicago: University of Chicago Press.

Posner, Richard A. 1995. *Overcoming Law.* Cambridge, MA: Harvard University Press.

Posner, Richard A. 1999. *The Problematics of Moral and Legal Theory.* Cambridge, MA: Harvard University Press.

Postema, Gerald. 1995. "Public Practical Reason: Political Practice." In *Nomos XXXVII: Theory and Practice,* ed. I. Shapiro and J. DeGrew, 345–385. New York: New York University Press.

Poulson, Ronald L. 1990. "Mock Juror Attribution of Criminal Responsibility: Effects of Race and the Guilty but Mentally Ill (GBMI) Verdict Option." *Journal of Applied Social Psychology* 20:1596–1611.

Pound, Roscoe. 1999. *The Spirit of the Common Law*. New York: Transaction.

Powell, Frona M. 1995. "Environmental Protection in International Trade Agreements: The Role of Public Participation in the Aftermath of the NAFTA." *Colorado Journal of International Environmental Law and Policy* 6 (109): 109–127.

Putnam, Hilary. 1995. *Pragmatism: An Open Question*. Cambridge, MA: Blackwell.

Putnam, Hilary. 2004. *Ethics without Ontology*. Cambridge, MA: Harvard University Press.

Putnam, Robert D. 1988. "Diplomacy and Domestic Policy: The Logic of Two-Level Games." *International Organization* 42 (3): 427–460.

Quine, W. V. 1960. *Word and Object*. Cambridge, MA: MIT.

Rabe, Barry G. 1999. "Sustainability in a Regional Context: The Case of the Great Lakes Basin." In *Toward Sustainable Communities: Transition and Transformations in Environmental Policy*, ed. D. A. Mazmanian and M. E. Kraft, 247–281. Cambridge, MA: MIT Press.

Rabkin, Jeremy A. 2005. *Law without Nations? Why Constitutional Government Requires Sovereign States*. Princeton, NJ: Princeton University Press.

Raustiala, Kal, Daniel Bodansky, Susan Leubuscher, and Jacqueline Peel. 2004. "New Directions in International Environmental Law." In *American Society of International Law, Proceedings of the Annual Meeting*, 275–287. Washington, DC: American Society of International Law.

Rawls, John. 1971. *A Theory of Justice*. Cambridge, MA: Harvard University Press.

Rawls, John. 1993. *Political Liberalism*. New York: Columbia University Press.

Rawls, John. 1995. "Reply to Habermas." *Journal of Philosophy* 92 (3): 132–180.

Rawls, John. 1999a. *Collected Papers*, ed. Samuel Freeman. Cambridge, MA: Harvard University Press.

Rawls, John. 1999b. *The Law of Peoples*. Cambridge, MA: Harvard University Press.

Rawls, John. 1999c. *A Theory of Justice*, revised ed. Cambridge, MA: Harvard University Press.

Rawls, John. 2001. *Justice as Fairness: A Restatement*. Cambridge, MA: Belknap Press of Harvard University Press.

Read, John E. 1963. "The Trail Smelter Dispute." *Canadian Yearbook of International Law* 1:213–229.

Reidy, David. 2004. "Rawls on International Justice: A Defense." *Political Theory* 32 (3): 291–319.

Reinecke, Wolfgang. 1998. *Global Public Policy: Governing Without Government*. Washington, DC: Brookings Institution Press.

Reinhardt, Eric. 2003. "Tying Hands Without Rope: Rational Domestic Response to International Institutional Constraints." In *Locating the Proper Authorities: The Interaction of International and Domestic Institutions*, ed. D. Drezner, 25–48. Ann Arbor: University of Michigan Press.

Richardson, Benjamin J. 2000. "Environmental Law in Postcolonial Societies: Straddling the Local-Global Institutional Spectrum." *Colorado Journal of International Environmental Law and Policy* 11 (1): 1–82.

Richardson, Henry S. 2002. *Democratic Autonomy: Public Reasoning about the Ends of Policy*. New York: Oxford University Press.

Rockman, Bert. 2000. "The American Presidency in Comparative Perspective: Systems, Situations, and Leaders." In *The Presidency and the Political System*, ed. M. Nelson, 64–90. Washington, DC: CQ Press.

Rorty, Richard. 1979. *Philosophy and the Mirror of Nature*. Princeton, NJ: Princeton University Press.

Rorty, Richard. 1989. *Contingency, Irony, and Solidarity*. Cambridge, UK: Cambridge University Press.

Rorty, Richard. 1991. *Objectivity, Relativism, and Truth: Philosophical Papers*, vol. 1. Cambridge, UK: Cambridge University Press.

Rorty, Richard. 1995. "Is Truth a Goal of Enquiry? Davidson vs. Wright." *The Philosophical Quarterly* 45 (180): 281–300.

Rorty, Richard. 1999. *Philosophy and Social Hope*. New York: Penguin Books.

Rosenbaum, Walter A. 2002. *Environmental Politics and Policy*, 5th ed. Washington, DC: CQ Press.

Rydin, Yvonne. 2003. *Conflict, Consensus, and Rationality in Environmental Planning*. Oxford: Oxford University Press.

Sanders, Lynn. 1997. "Against Deliberation." *Political Theory* 25:347–376.

Sands, Philippe, and Jacqueline Peel. 2005. "Environmental Protection in the Twenty-First Century: Sustainable Development and International Law." In *The Global Environment: Institutions, Law, and Policy*, ed. R. S. Axelrod, D. L. Downies, and N. J. Vig, 43–63. Washington, DC: CQ Press.

Schachter, Oscar. 1994. "Dispute Settlement and Countermeasures in the International Law Commission." *American Journal of International Law* 88:471–477.

Schlosberg, David. 1998. "Resurrecting the Pluralist Universe." *Political Research Quarterly* 51:583–615.

Schmidt, Vivien, A. 2004. "The European Union: Democratic Legitimacy in a Regional State?" *Journal of Common Market Studies* 42 (5): 975–997.

Scholtz, Astrid. 2004. "Merchants of Diversity: Scientists as Traffickers of Plants and Institutions." In *Earthly Politics: Local and Global in Environmental Governance*, ed. S. Jasanoff and M. L. Martello, 217–238. Cambridge, MA: MIT Press.

Schultz, Kenneth. 2003. "Tying Hands and Washing Hands: The U.S. Congress and Multilateral Humanitarian Intervention." In *Locating the Proper Authorities:*

The Interaction of International and Domestic Institutions, ed. D. Drezner, 105–144. Ann Arbor: University of Michigan Press.

Schwarzenberger, Georg. 1951. *Power Politics: A Study of International Society*, 2nd ed. London: Stevens.

Schweller, Randall L. 1997. "New Realist Research on Alliances: Refining, Not Refuting, Waltz's Balancing Proposition." *American Political Science Review* 91 (December): 927–930.

Sealy, A. P., and W. R. Cornish. 1973. "Jurors and their Verdicts." *Modern Law Review* 36:496–508.

Sen, Amartya. 2001. *Development as Freedom*. New York: Knopf.

Shapiro, Ian. 2003. *The Moral Foundations of Politics*. New Haven, CT: Yale University Press.

Shapiro, Martin. 2001. "Administrative Law Unbounded: Reflections on Government and Governance." *Indiana Journal of Global Legal Studies* 8:369–377.

Shaw, Brian. 2005. "Rawls, Kant's Doctrine of Right, and Global Distributive Justice." *Journal of Politics* 67 (1): 220–249.

Shi, David E. 1995. *Facing Facts: Realism in American Thought and Culture, 1850–1920*. New York: Oxford University Press.

Shrader-Frechette, Kristin S., and Earl D. McCoy. 1994. "How the Tail Wags the Dog: How Value Judgments Determine Ecological Science." *Environmental Values* 3:107–120.

Sjöstedt, Gunnar. 2003. "Norms and Principles as Support to Postnegotiation and Rule Implementation." In *Getting It Done: Postagreement Negotiation and International Regimes*, ed. B. I. Spector and I. W. Zartman, 89–114. Washington, DC: United States Institute of Peace Press.

Slaughter, Anne-Marie. 1997. "The Real New World Order." *Foreign Affairs* 76 (5): 183–197.

Slaughter, Anne-Marie. 2004. *A New World Order*. Princeton, NJ: Princeton University Press.

Smith, Michael Joseph. 1986. *Realist Thought from Weber to Kissinger*. Baton Rouge: Louisiana State University.

Snidal, Duncan, and Alexander Thompson. 2003. "International Commitments and Domestic Politics: Institutions and Actors at Two Levels." In *Locating the Proper Authorities: The Interaction of Domestic and International Institutions*, ed. D. Drezner, 197–230. Ann Arbor: University of Michigan Press.

Snyder, Gary. 1998. "The Place, the Region, and the Commons." In *Environmental Philosophy: From Animal Rights to Radical Ecology*, ed. M. Zimmerman. Upper Saddle River, NJ: Prentice Hall.

Soroos, Marvin. 2005. "Global Institutions and the Environment: An Evolutionary Perspective." In *The Global Environment: Institutions, Law, and Policy*, ed. R. S. Axelrod, D. L. Downie, and N. J. Vig, 21–42. Washington, DC: CQ Press.

Southern Pacific Co. v. Jensen. 1917. 244 U.S. Reports 205.

Speth, James. 2004. *Red Sky at Morning: America and the Crisis of the Global Environment.* New Haven, CT: Yale University.

Stace, W. T. 1934. "The Refutation of Realism." *Mind* 43:145–155.

Stone, Deborah. 2002. *Policy Paradox: The Art of Political Decision Making,* revised ed. New York: W. W. Norton.

Strange, Susan. 1996. *The Retreat of the State: The Diffusion of Power in the World Economy.* New York: Cambridge University Press.

Strauss, Andrew, Richard Falk, and Thomas M Franck. 2001. "Citizens in the International Realm: The New Participatory Demands." In *American Society of International Law, Proceedings of the Annual Meeting,* 162–172. Washington, DC: American Society of International Law.

Sucharitkul, Sompong. 1990. "The Role of the United Nations Law Commission in the Decade of International Law." *Leiden Journal of International Law* 3: 15–42.

Sunstein, Cass. 1996. *Legal Reasoning and Political Conflict.* New York: Oxford University Press.

Susskind, Lawrence E. 1994. *Environmental Diplomacy: Negotiating More Effective Global Agreements.* New York: Oxford University Press.

Thomas, Caroline. 1992. *The Environment in International Relations.* London: Royal Institute of International Affairs.

Truman, David B. 1951. *The Governmental Process: Political Interests and Public Opinion.* New York: Alfred A. Knopf.

United States v. Canada. 1938. 3 *U.N. Rep. Intl. Arb. Awards* 1911.

United States v. Canada. 1941. 35 *Am. J. Intl. L.* 684.

Valadez, Jorge M. 2001. *Deliberative Democracy: Political Legitimacy and Self-Determination in Multicultural Societies.* Boulder, CO: Westview Press.

van den Belt, Marjan. 2004. *Mediated Modeling: A Systems Dynamics Approach to Environmental Consensus Building.* Washington, DC: Island Press.

VanDeveer, Stacy D. 2003. "Green Fatigue." *The Wilson Quarterly* 27 (4): 55–59.

VanDeveer, Stacy D. 2004. "Ordering Environments: Regions in European International Environmental Cooperation." In *Earthly Politics: Local and Global in Environmental Governance,* ed. S. Jasanoff and M. L. Martello, 309–334. Cambridge, MA: MIT Press.

van Niekerk, Anton A. 2004. "Principles of Global Distributive Justice: Moving Beyond Rawls and Buchanan." *South African Journal of Philosophy* 23 (2): 171–194.

Vidmar, Neil, and Valerie P. Hans. 2007. *American Juries: The Verdict.* Amherst, NY: Prometheus Books.

Vogler, Hohn. 1995. *The Global Commons: A Regime Analysis.* New York: John Wiley and Sons.

Vogler, John, and Andrew Jordan. 2003. "Governance and the Environment." In *Negotiating Environmental Change*, ed. F. Berkhout, M. Leach, and I. Scoones, 137–158. Northampton, MA: Edward Elgar.

Waever, Ole. 1997. "Imperial Metaphors: Emerging European Analogies to Pre-Nation-State Imperial Systems." In *Geopolitics in Post-Wall Europe*, ed. O. Tunander, P. Baev, and V. I. Einagel, 59–93. Thousand Oaks, CA: Sage.

Wallace, William. 2001. "Europe, the Necessary Partner." *Foreign Affairs* 80 (3): 16–34.

Waltz, Kenneth N. 1979. *Theory of International Politics*. New York: Random House.

Waltz, Kenneth N. 2008. *Realism and International Politics*. New York: Routledge.

Wapner, Paul. 1996. *Environmental Activism and World Civic Politics*. Albany: State University of New York Press.

Weiss, Edith Brown. 1993. "International Environmental Law: Contemporary Issues and the Emergence of a New World Order." *Georgetown Law Journal* 81 (March): 675–710.

Weiss, Edith Brown. 1999. "The Emerging Structure of International Environmental Law." In *The Global Environment: Institutions, Law and Policy*, ed. N. J. Vig and R. S. Axelrod, 98–115. Washington, DC: CQ Press.

Weisslitz, Michael. 2002. "Rethinking the Equitable Principle of Common but Differentiated Responsibility: Differential Versus Absolute Norms of Compliance and Contribution in the Global Climate Change Context." *Colorado Journal of International Environmental Law and Policy* 13 (2): 473–509.

Werkmeister, H. H. 1949. *A History of Philosophical Ideas in America*. New York: Ronald Press.

Westbrook, Robert. 2005. *Democratic Hope: Pragmatism and the Politics of Truth*. Ithaca, NY: Cornell University Press.

The Western Maid. 1922. 257 *U.S. Reports* 419.

Wettestad, Jorgen. 2002. "The Vienna Convention and Montreal Protocol on Ozone-Layer Depletion." In *Environmental Regime Effectiveness: Confronting Theory with Evidence*, ed. E. Miles, A. Underdal, S. Andresen, J. Wettestad, J. Skjaerseth, and E. Carlin, 149–170. Cambridge, MA: MIT Press.

Wiener, Jonathan Baert. 1999. "Global Environmental Regulation: Instrument Choice in Legal Context." *Yale Law Journal* 108 (4): 677–800.

Williams, David L. 1999. "Dialogical Theories of Justice." *Telos* 114:109–131.

Wittgenstein, Ludwig. 2001. *Philosophical Investigations*, trans. G. E. M. Anscombe, 3rd ed. Oxford, UK: Blackwell.

Wofford, Carrie. 2000. "A Greener Future at the WTO: The Refinement of WTO Jurisprudence on Environmental Exceptions to the GATT." *Harvard Environmental Law Review* 24 (2): 563–592.

Wolin, Richard. 2004. *The Seduction of Unreason*. Princeton, NJ: Princeton University Press.

Wolin, Sheldon. 1989. *The Presence of the Past: Essays on the State and the Constitution.* Baltimore, MD: Johns Hopkins University Press.

Wolin, Sheldon. 2001. *Tocqueville between Two Worlds.* Princeton, NJ: Princeton University Press.

World Commission on Environment and Development, Experts Group on Environmental Law. 1987. *Environmental Protection and Sustainable Development: Legal Principles and Recommendations.* London: Graham & Trotman.

Wysocki, Robert. 2002. *Building Effective Project Teams.* New York: John Wiley & Sons.

Yearly, Steven. 1992. "Green Ambivalence about Science: Legal-Rational Authority and Scientific Legitimation of a Social Movement." *British Journal of Sociology* 43 (4): 511–532.

Yokota, Yozo. 1999. "International Justice and the Global Environment." *Journal of International Affairs* 52 (2): 583–598.

Young, Iris. 1989. "Polity and Group Difference: A Critique of the Idea of Universal Citizenship." *Ethics* 99:250–274.

Young, Iris. 1990. *Justice and the Politics of Difference.* Princeton, NJ: Princeton University Press.

Young, Iris. 1999. "Justice, Inclusion, and Deliberative Democracy." In *Deliberative Politics: Essays on Democracy and Disagreement,* ed. S. Macedo, 151–158. New York: Oxford University Press.

Young, Oran. 1994. *International Governance: Protecting the Environment in a Stateless Society.* Ithaca, NY: Cornell University Press.

Zapfel, Peter. 2002. "Science and Economics in Climate Change and Other International Environmental Negotiations." In *Transboundary Environmental Negotiation: New Approaches to Global Cooperation,* ed. L. Susskind, W. Moomaw, and K. Gallagher, 130–153. San Francisco: Jossey-Bass.

Zartman, I. William. 2001. *Preventive Negotiation.* Lanham, MD: Rowman & Littlefield.

Zolo, Danilo. 1997. *Cosmopolis: Prospects for World Governance.* Cambridge: Polity.

Index

Lethbridge Communit

AGING & SOCIETY

A Canadian Reader

Edited by

MARK NOVAK

Associate Dean
Continuing Education Division
University of Manitoba

Nelson Canada

I(T)P An International Thomson Publishing Company

Toronto • Albany • Bonn • Boston • Cincinnati • Detroit • London • Madrid • Melbourne •
Mexico City • New York • Pacific Grove • Paris • San Francisco • Singapore • Tokyo • Washington

I(T)P ⁻

International Thomson Publishing
The ITP logo is a trademark under licence

Canadian Cataloguing in Publication Data

Main entry under title:
  Aging and society: a Canadian reader

Includes bibliographical references.
ISBN 0–17–604846-4

1. Aging – Canada. 2. Aged – Canada – Social conditions. 3. Gerontology – Canada. I. Novak, Mark W.

HQ64.35.C2A45 1995   305.126'0971   C94–0932193–1

Acquisitions Editor	Charlotte Forbes
Supervising Editor	Rosalyn Steiner
Developmental Editor	Heather Martin
Senior Production Coordinator	Sheryl Emery
Art Director	Liz Harasymczuk
Interior Design	Stuart Knox
Cover Design	Katharine Lapins
Cover Illustration	Susan Leopold
Composition Analyst	Alicja Jamorski
Input Operators	Elaine Andrews, Michelle Volk

Printed and bound in Canada
1 2 3 4   WC   98 97 96 95

Contents

Introduction

An award-winning Canadian author recently calculated that she could read about 50 new books a year. This came to only about 2000 new books in her adult lifetime. Once she realized this, she said, she began to choose her reading more carefully. With so many books already on the market, why publish another one to take up a reader's time? And why publish a book like this one, which contains work published elsewhere?

First, students new to the field of aging will find this book a useful way to sample the literature. A few years ago a reader like this would have been impossible to put together. When I began teaching gerontology courses in 1974, only a handful of Canadian aging studies existed. I had to rely on studies by American or European writers. Today, instructors can draw upon thousands of excellent Canadian papers, books, and articles for students to read. And this literature grows every year. Many good readings lie scattered through the literature, sometimes in obscure reports or journals. A book of readings can save the student and the instructor time and effort in searching for useful material. It can serve as a small library that students and instructors can read and study together.

Second, this book introduces students to some of the best work in the field. Students can make the acquaintance of leading Canadian gerontologists through their original work. The readings should stimulate students to look further at a topic or at an author's writing. Each section in this reader contains suggested readings for more study. These suggestions direct the student to other Canadian sources. I have tried to select sources that a student can find easily in a university library. A collection like this also becomes more than the sum of its parts. The authors in this reader come from varied fields and have varied perspectives on aging. Taken together they present a snapshot of Canadian gerontology today.

Third, I assume that the student has little or no background in gerontology. I put aside many excellent, stimulating, and well-known writings because the authors wrote for a professional audience. These articles assumed a technical knowledge of government policy, research methods, or theory that beginning students would not have.

All of these reasons for producing a reader also argue against producing one. The reader hands the student a predigested collection, someone else's collection. It may create laziness in the student and discourage a visit to the library or a browse through professional journals. The editor of a reader needs to keep these cautions in mind. He or she must have a clear set of goals that guide the selection of sources and the organization of the articles. Below I present the guidelines that I used to create this collection.

First, the readings should present the best work of gerontologists in Canada. I have selected articles that have received professional recognition for their quality. Most of the readings selected here, for example, have appeared in peer-reviewed journals or books by fellow gerontologists.

Second, the readings should provide a blend of current and classic writings, a blend of empirical and theoretical topics. And they should expose students to the wide topical and stylistic range of gerontological writings. Above all, the readings should provide models of excellence in theory and research.

Third, the readings should do more than present empirical data from a research study or describe a program. A reader should give students a perspective on an issue or topic. It should contain ideas that raise issues or explore controversies. I have selected the readings here to complement standard gerontology texts. Texts typically present and summarize research findings from the literature. But readings allow students to look at an issue in depth, to review research findings, or to think about social policies for themselves. The reader can set the student on the path to critical thinking in the field.

Today many excellent papers, studies, and reports exist. And every teacher has his or her own favourite sources. No single collection could include them all. I have tried to find readings that expand the themes found in textbooks, present alternative sides of controversies, new policy options, alternative futures for aging, new programs, and adequate models of successful aging. I hope that these readings will stimulate questions, class discussion, and debate.

I set myself a single goal at the start of this project: to review *everything* written by Canadian authors on aging between 1988 and the end of 1993. To achieve this impossible goal I conducted the following searches of the literature. First, I reviewed the bibliographies in standard Canadian gerontology texts. I then wrote to 50 prominent gerontologists to request their most recent writings and their suggestions for sources. I reviewed Canadian gerontology, public policy, and social issues journals. I then searched the psychology, nursing, and gerontology CD-ROM databases for Canadian writings.

At this point I had reviewed more than 1000 sources. They did not include all of the writings from 1988 to 1993, as I had hoped, but they made up a good sample to choose from. From these I selected about 100 sources for a preliminary table of contents. Whenever possible I chose Canadian sources on a topic. I considered a source Canadian if the author was born or lived in Canada, used Canadian data, discussed a Canadian topic (e.g., the Canadian Pension Plan), or dealt with a topic that had implications for Canadians. Several colleagues reviewed this proposed collection and made suggestions for changes. Their suggestions and further review led to the collection of writings you see here.

I organized the readings according to topics that correspond roughly to the chapters of my own text *Aging and Society: A Canadian Perspective* (Nelson Canada, 1993). Instructors who use this text may want to link the readings with the text chapters. Chart 1 presents the relationship between the text chapters and the sections in the reader.

CHART 1. GUIDE TO USING *AGING AND SOCIETY: A CANADIAN PERSPECTIVE* WITH *AGING AND SOCIETY: A CANADIAN READER*

Aging and Society		*Aging and Society: A Canadian Reader*	
Chapter 1:	What Is Gerontology?	Section 1:	Myths and Realities of Aging Today
Chapter 2:	Theories and Methods		
Chapter 3:	Aging Then and Now	Section 2:	Many Ways of Growing Old
Chapter 4:	Aging in Canada		
Chapter 5:	Personal Health and Illness	Section 3:	Coping With Individual Change
Chapter 6:	The Psychology of Aging		
Chapter 7:	The Social Psychology of Aging		
Chapter 8:	Health Care	Section 4:	Our Changing Health-Care System
Chapter 9:	Finances and Economics	Section 5:	Income and the Challenge of Retirement
Chapter 10:	Retirement and Work		
Chapter 11:	Housing and Transportation	Section 6:	Housing and Living Arrangements
Chapter 12:	Leisure, Recreation, and Service	Section 7:	Lifelong Learning and Fitness
Chapter 13:	Family Life and Social Relations	Section 8:	Family Life and Relationships
Chapter 14:	Death and Dying	Section 9:	Death and Dying
Chapter 15:	Politics and Policy	Section 10:	Politics and Policies
Chapter 16:	The Future of Aging in Canada		

The sections of the reader have the following contents:

Section 1 looks at the myths and realities of aging in Canada. It examines the images of older people in the media, in government, in business, and in the minds of older people themselves.

Section 2 presents writings on older people in other types of societies, and in a variety of cultural groups in Canada today.

Section 3 focuses on normal physical, psychological, and social changes that come with aging. It also considers some of the supports and coping methods needed to create a good old age.

Section 4 looks at change in the health-care system. It includes critical analyses of health care in Canada and articles on alternative approaches to health-care delivery. This section also considers the unmet needs of specific groups for health care.

Section 5 discusses retirement policy and practice. It includes readings on Canada's retirement income system, the retirement decision, and the impact of retirement on the labour force. It also includes readings on the impact of retirement income policies on minority groups in Canada.

Section 6 presents a variety of housing and lifestyle options for older people. This range of options reflects the diversity within the older population and their different needs.

Section 7 considers a number of approaches to education in later life. It describes some new programs for older learners and points toward some future directions in lifelong education.

Section 8 shows that the family forms the centre of life at every age. The readings describe relationships that range from support to abuse. They also describe less well-known options to family life—remaining single or living in a lesbian relationship. Above all, these readings show the deep emotional ties that exist between older people and their family members and friends.

Section 9 explores social, legal, and ethical questions concerning death and dying. These readings pose as many questions as they answer. This seems right for a topic that touches on our deepest feelings and beliefs.

Section 10 discusses alternative policies for an aging society. The readings clarify Canadian policy issues, and they propose a model for senior advocacy and action in the future.

Each section begins with an introduction that reviews the contents of the readings. It also highlights theoretical issues and controversies in the literature and links the readings to one another. The introduction places the group of readings in the context of wider discussions within the field of aging.

At the end of each section is a series of questions for reflection and discussion. Some questions focus on one reading. Others ask students to synthesize the points made in several readings. Students can use these questions to review their understanding of the readings. Instructors can use these questions as the starting point for a lecture or to stimulate class discussion. Each section ends with suggestions for further reading.

This collection will succeed if the readings enrich students' understanding of aging, and if students decide to learn more about the field.

PUBLISHER'S NOTE

The three-dot ellipsis at the beginning or between paragraphs of an article indicates the omission of material from the original work.

Acknowledgments

A book this complex depends on many people for its existence. My gerontology colleagues deserve my thanks for their help. Dozens of colleagues supported the idea of this book and helped in various ways. Some of them agreed to have their work reprinted here. Others suggested readings, sent material for review, or commented on early drafts of the contents. A small group of anonymous reviewers took the time to comment in detail on an early draft of the book. Their work helped make this a better book. I, of course, take responsibility for any of the book's shortcomings.

The manuscript of this work was reviewed at various stages of its development by a great number of my peers across Canada, and I wish to thank those who shared their insights and their constructive criticism. Among them are Hazel MacRae, Mount Saint Vincent University; Anju Joshi, McMaster University; Tamara Horton, McMaster University; Patricia MacKenzie, University of Regina; Donna Hinde, Mount Royal College; Mervin Chen, Acadia University; and Brian Aitken, Laurentian University.

A cast of assistants and helpers deserves thanks. My sons Christopher, Jonathan, and Sean all helped me search for sources in spite of their busy university schedules. They have become my colleagues and friends. I thank them for their dedication to this project. Jerry Holcombe, an administrative assistant in our division, tracked down permissions for many of the articles reprinted here. The librarians at the J.W. Crane Memorial Library at Deer Lodge Centre in Winnipeg helped me find many sources and bits of information I couldn't find elsewhere. My teammates at Nelson Canada gave me advice and encouragement from the start. Heather Martin arranged for reviews of the manuscript. Charlotte Forbes supported the concept for the book, read the proposal, and argued for its production. This book would not exist without her dedicated support. She is an editor with courage and vision. I thank my wife, Mona, and our youngest son, Daniel, for the love and care they gave me throughout this project.

I dedicate this book to my mother. A small repayment for her unconditional love.

Myths and Realities of Aging Today

Robert Butler (1977) coined the term "ageism" to refer to prejudice based on age. He defined ageism as "a deep-seated uneasiness on the part of the young and middle-aged—a personal revulsion to and distaste for growing old..." (1977, p. 132). This prejudice often shows up as stereotyping, which allows younger people to distance themselves from aging. Studies of the media, greeting cards, and jokes show that many negative stereotypes about aging exist.

These stereotypes can lead to discrimination against older workers, create the tendency to treat older people as children, and lead to low expectations of older people. They can also lead older people to have a poor self-image, withdraw from social contact, and feel despair. Comfort (1976) gives the best argument for an end to ageism—self-interest. The values and attitudes toward aging that young people learn today will influence their treatment of older people (ourselves) in the future.

Beneath the issue of ageism lies the tendency to think of older people as a homogeneous group. Stereotypes hold that all older people talk about the past, like to play bingo or cards, and become forgetful. But throughout this book you will read articles that emphasize the diversity among older people. They differ by gender, race, health, lifestyle, and even age. As a group, older people get more diverse with age. Social class, work, and family life shape our characters as we age. Even professionals may forget this.

One well-intentioned nurse in a nursing home wheeled two men side by side so that they could talk. After a minute or two their conversation stopped and they sat next to each other staring into space. The nurse couldn't understand this. She thought these two old men would have a lot in common. But one man was 70 years old, the other in his mid-80s. They came from different generations and had little to talk about. More knowledge about aging will lead to more awareness about the differences between older people. And this may lead to more appreciation of the uniqueness of each older person.

Gerontologists work to dispel myths about aging with facts and information. The federal government set up the National Advisory Council on Aging (NACA) for just this purpose. NACA produces newsletters, position papers, and reports to increase public understanding of aging. The report presented here describes the images of older people in Canada.

NACA reports that older people generally feel respected. And this sense of respect has increased in the past ten years. NACA also reports improvements in the treatment of older people by the government, in the media, and in business. Still, the report says, subtle forms of ageism exist. Business, for example, too often focuses advertising on products related to disability and illness. Advertising may treat older people as a homogenous group with similar backgrounds, interests, and problems. NACA argues for a more balanced view of later life. The NACA proposals call on the entire community, from government to educators to seniors' groups, to combat ageism.

Shou and Chen conducted a systematic study of ageism in Canadian consumer magazine advertising. They asked how often older people appeared in magazine ads, how the ads portrayed older people, and whether the ads portrayed older and younger people differently. They found no characters aged 65 and over in any of the ads analyzed and only a small proportion of people aged 50–64. The study also found fewer women than expected and no nonwhite characters. The researchers found other ageist stereotypes of older people in the ads.

Shack speaks about ageism from her experience as an older woman. She reminds us that women stand the greatest chance of living into late old age. For this reason ageism especially affects older women. Shack reminds us that many older people stay actively involved in society. They teach, serve on community boards, and attend school. These people should lead us to question negative stereotypes about aging.

The NACA paper on ageism reports a positive change in attitudes toward aging in Canada. In part, this reflects improvements in the health, education, and income of older people. It also reflects a greater public awareness of the full picture of aging. Gerontological research and writing has played an important part in educating the public about later life.

Sources Consulted

Butler, R.N. (1977). "Age-ism: Another Form of Bigotry." In *Readings in Aging and Death: Contemporary Perspectives,* ed. S.H. Zarit. New York: Harper & Row.

Comfort, A. (1976). *A Good Age.* New York: Simon and Shuster.

The NACA Position
on the Image of Aging

National Advisory Council on Aging

■■■

OLD AGE IS NOT WHAT IT USED TO BE

Seniors are not only more visible, they are also more vigorous and more vocal than ever before. Succeeding generations of seniors have enjoyed better health, education and economic well-being; this trend will continue into the next century as today's 'baby boom' generation become seniors. Indeed, the distinction between middle age and old age is now blurred; most seniors belong to what gerontologists Bernice and Dail Neugarten have termed the 'young-old', that is, retirees who are healthy, active, independent and well-integrated in their families and communities.[1] Health status and lifestyles are more important than age in identifying 'young-old' seniors, because the description may apply as aptly to an active 80-year-old as to a 55-year-old. According to the two gerontologists, "What was once considered old age now characterizes only that minority of older persons who have been called the 'old-old', that particularly vulnerable group who are frequently in need of special support and care."[2]

> *"Some people confound aging with illness."*
> *"People confuse the 90% of older people who are able with 10% that are not."*

There is evidence that the image that all seniors are frail, disabled or dependent has changed somewhat to correspond to the contemporary reality. Researchers William Gekoski and Jane Knox, of Queen's University in Kingston, have observed that information about chronological age alone elicits fewer stereotypic 'old age' beliefs than information about poor health.[3] Interviews with older children[4] and with adults aged 35-59[5] show that seniors generally are perceived to be active and independent and that the diversity among seniors is better appreciated.

Many seniors report that they usually encounter open attitudes and respect from other people. Negative attitudes were not identified as one of the major obstacles in NACA's consultation on the barriers to independent living in 1988.[6] Other recent reports indicate that seniors usually feel respected by others[7] and that the degree of perceived respect (at least for some groups of seniors) has increased over the last decade.[8]

MYTHS ABOUT AGING IN THE 1990S: VARIATIONS ON THE SAME OLD TUNE

> *"I get tired of the 'good for you' attitude, as if it were surprising that someone 65+ can be involved in a number of physical, intellectual and volunteer pursuits."*
>
> *"I hear: 'Older women shouldn't wear shorts. Older women don't swear or drink.'"*
>
> *"Some people think seniors never worked in their lives."*

Stereotypes and negative attitudes towards older adults have become less prevalent and it may no longer be 'politically correct' to express overt prejudice—as some public speakers have discovered to their chagrin when they were called to task by indignant seniors' groups. Nevertheless, biased attitudes persist in subtler ways, and the majority of seniors consulted by NACA on public awareness about aging considered that action still is required to increase public knowledge and to make attitudes more balanced. Negative attitudes arise from a fear of, and wish to deny one's own mortality; in the words of author Alex Comfort, "We are taught to be prejudiced against what we ourselves will become."[9] It is necessary to break through the fear that results in an unwillingness to learn about aging.

The basic premise of ageism is that seniors form a homogeneous group in society. Specific attributions constituting the stereotype are a mixture of positive traits (such as warmth, kindness or wisdom) and of negative characteristics (for instance, passive, physically weak, slow in thinking, rigid, incompetent). There are more negative than positive attributes composing the public image, and *all seniors* are viewed and treated the same way. Younger adults perceive that old age is fraught with more problems than what many seniors actually report, and few look forward to growing old.[10]

Because seniors are not expected to be competent or productive, their contributions to their families and to society are either overlooked or devalued. When individual seniors are given due credit for their achievements, they may be seen as outstanding exceptions to the norm rather than proof that the stereotypes are false. Moreover, focusing on the allocation of social resources to seniors while ignoring seniors' past and ongoing contributions has led to new, but no less dangerous attributions. The new stereotype is that seniors are parasitical 'whoopies' (well-off older people) or 'greedy gee-zers', who live too long in unproductive leisure at the expense of the State and drain public funds that would be better used to succour poverty-stricken children.[11]

The Harmful Consequences of Stereotyping

"There is too much patronization and being told what is good for you."

"Maintenance staff in the apartment are slower in doing repairs for senior residents because they believe we aren't going anywhere; so there is no rush."

Ageism—in both the old and the new versions—is a serious concern because it limits seniors' options, threatens their current and future well-being, and, more fundamentally, undermines their dignity. Stereotypes influence how people respond to their own aging. Finally, age discrimination deprives society of valuable human resources.

Bias against seniors is evident in many aspects of Canadian life. Mandatory retirement remains an accepted practice in a number of provinces, with the support of many employers and unions. Pressure may be exerted on older workers to take early retirement, in some instances, involuntarily. There are few opportunities available to seniors for activities that carry social recognition; the fact that many seniors find or create valuable and satisfying roles attests far more to their motivation and ingenuity than to society's demand for their abilities. Suggestions have also been made to limit health care using age as the chief criterion,[12] or more generally to restrict public spending targeted to seniors. Finally, prejudice can be reflected in day-to-day hassles experienced by some seniors.[13]

"It is very hard to grow old when people look down on us."

"I hate it when they lower themselves in the eyes of the public by putting up verses on the bulletin board about their false teeth, or when I hear: 'I'm old.'"

"I'm 66 and I feel like I'm being pressured to 'get old' when I sense that young people form a separate group, a group that I still would like to belong to."

Biased attitudes and discriminatory practices can have damaging effects. Some seniors, especially those whose self-esteem is fragile, can internalize the social labels and act in conformity with the negative expectations, thus reinforcing the myths and undermining their own self-worth.[14] Some may defend themselves by trying to deny their age—thus revealing how threatening old age is for them. Yet others resign themselves to being treated as second-class citizens.[15] As researchers Judith Chipperfield and Betty Havens conclude, "To the extent that elders perceive they are disrespected, they may avoid participation in the community, which in turn is likely to promote feelings of 'alienation', 'rolelessness', or of 'being a burden to society'. Perceived disrespect may even diminish the likelihood that elders will request community assistance when needed. Ultimately, then, perceptions of disrespect may undermine elders' well-being and independence."[16]

"There's a difference between your experience and public attitudes."
"I'm not that old!"

Fortunately, the majority of seniors are able to maintain a healthy feeling of self-worth despite negative social evaluations of their age and despite the real physical and social losses they may experience. People of all ages are motivated to see themselves positively and to act in ways that maintain their self-esteem.[17] Thus, seniors may simply disregard or reject stereotypes that are inconsistent with their image of themselves. They may accept the stereotype of age for others but not for themselves. Some seniors stand up for their rights individually or become militant advocates against ageism in society.

In summary, seniors in Canada continue to be seen as belonging to a homogeneous group whose common characteristics, if not entirely negative, are not especially desirable. Most older adults continue to be obliged to retire at 65 and have fewer socially valued opportunities to contribute than younger persons. Ironically, society then castigates seniors for being unproductive and costly. Ageism also can undermine individual feelings of self-worth and can result in disrespectful and discriminatory behaviour by others.

Canadian society cannot afford to allow misconceptions about aging and negative attitudes towards seniors to persist. If, as demographers predict, 20% of the Canadian population in the year 2020 will be 65+,[18] biased beliefs and attitudes will diminish the quality of life of one-fifth of Canadians and will restrict the access to a large human resource pool needed for continued social and economic development. Moreover, many people who now hold negative attitudes towards aging and seniors will themselves be seniors—and potential victims of the very prejudice they helped perpetuate. Through enhanced public awareness, demographic aging will come to be viewed as a measure of our success as a society rather than as a problem.

ENHANCING PUBLIC AWARENESS: AGENTS OF CHANGE AND ACTIONS NEEDED

Because beliefs and attitudes about aging and older adults are part of our cultural currency, they are manifested in the educational system, the media, cultural and social institutions, marketing and business practices and social policy. Combatting ageism thus requires the concerted and consistent efforts of many partners: governments, educators, social, cultural and religious groups, the media, business, professional associations, employers and unions, seniors' organizations and individual seniors. Because the role of professional associations and of employers and unions on changing attitudes has been addressed in previous NACA position papers,[19] these agents of change are not mentioned in this report. Many laudable initiatives have been taken, but more must be done so that age-bias becomes not simply a taboo, but an oddity in our development as a society.

The Role of Governments

Government policies affect all areas of social and economic life. Public officials not only represent the collective will and values of the population; they have a significant role to play in creating social values, in leading people further in the evolution towards a just, tolerant and compassionate society.

Canada has made substantial progress in the affirmation of individual rights and the elimination of discrimination in general. With respect to the image and rights of seniors, federal, provincial/territorial and municipal governments have adopted legislation and/or programs that have made a significant difference.

Among the many achievements initiated by several federal government administrations, it is worth mentioning the creation of the New Horizons Program, the Seniors' Independence Program (SIP) and the establishment of a Minister of State for Seniors, the Seniors Secretariat, the National Advisory Council on Aging and the Secretariat for Fitness in the Third Age. By providing opportunities for seniors to participate in and direct projects that contribute to the well-being of seniors and their communities, New Horizons and SIP have shown to the public the talent, dedication and creative energy of seniors and have enhanced the self-confidence of many individual seniors and seniors' groups. By establishing offices within the federal government structure either to represent seniors' interests or to provide ministerial advice on matters related to the well-being of seniors and to the aging of the population, the federal government has acquired internal vehicles for making elected officials and policy administrators more sensitive to the needs and concerns of seniors and less subject to stereotypes. Research has shown that public officials who have acquired knowledge about seniors are less likely to express ageist biases.[20] These offices also work to promote a realistic image of seniors, to propose guidelines for communicating appropriately with seniors,[21] to develop new knowledge about aging,[22] and to disseminate factual information about aging and seniors.

The *Canadian Charter of Rights and Freedoms* (1981) enshrined the equality of all individuals, "without discrimination based on race, national or ethnic origin, colour, religion, sex, age or mental or physical disability." Finally, the federal government has shown leadership in combatting age discrimination in the labour force by eliminating mandatory retirement for federal employees and by disallowing the use of age as a criterion for employee selection, training or promotion.

Provincial/territorial governments, too, have enhanced the image of seniors in Canadian society. To name some of these initiatives, many public education campaigns have been conducted; seniors' achievements are officially recognized; various seniors' activities are supported; and seniors are more often consulted on policy issues affecting them. Ministerial offices for seniors' affairs, seniors' secretariats and seniors' advisory councils have been created in most provinces, and some provinces have established guidelines for government communication with seniors. In Ontario, extensive educational materials have been developed to educate particular group about aging. In Québec and Manitoba, mandatory retirement on the basis of age has been banned.

In the area of health and social services, all governments are trying at a policy level to promote community-based health care and home support; when these policies are implemented they will favour the continued intergration of seniors in society and enhance the public's appreciation of seniors' autonomy and resilience. Provincial and territorial governments have contributed somewhat to the development of post-secondary educational programs for service-providers to seniors, thereby aiding in dispelling stereotypes and increasing the sensitivity and knowledge of those working with and for seniors. Education about aging is included in the secondary school curricula of several provinces.

Municipal governments have shared in efforts to integrate seniors better in the affairs of the community and to promote a positive image of aging. Local councils or committees on aging that monitor municipal programs and provide advice to officials and administrators have been the chief vehicle used by municipalities.

These considerable advances in government policy and programs need to be maintained, and further measures should be adopted to promote a positive public image of seniors and greater awareness of both the real needs and capacities of older Canadians. To this end,

NACA recommends that:

Governments at all levels strengthen programs that enhance the public image of older Canadians and create policies and programs that promote the full integration of seniors in the community.

Advisory councils to government on aging be established in the provinces, territories and municipalities where they do not already exist, with a mandate to:

- consult with seniors to provide accurate information and advice to government officials on aging and seniors;

- enhance public awareness about aging and modify negative attitudes.

Government and/or seniors' advisory councils develop and widely distribute communications guidelines for print and non-print materials; these guidelines should stipulate that:

- all communications take into account the normal sensory and perceptual changes associated with aging that may affect comprehension;
- communications directed to the general public project realistic illustrations of persons of all ages;
- communications for or about seniors realistically portray seniors' lifestyles and the individual and cultural differences within the older population.

Governments and/or seniors' advisory councils develop and widely distribute resources to educate business, service occupations and professionals about normal aging and the diversity of seniors.

Provincial/territorial ministries of education ensure that educational curricula include education about aging and seniors from the elementary grades through high school; textbooks and other pedagogical materials used in elementary and secondary schools portray seniors more favourably; and education about aging be included in the training of teachers.

The federal and provincial departments and ministries concerned with post-secondary education earmark funds to develop curriculum content on aging in all college and university programs, both to communicate to the public the social relevance of aging and to promote positive attitudes towards seniors by all occupations that serve the public.

Provincial and territorial governments institute flexible retirement policies in lieu of mandatory retirement at an arbitrary age.

The Role of the Media

"Media present a positive image."
"People listen to the radio or watch television and seem to understand better what aging is all about."
"There are certainly more articles in newspapers and magazines pertaining to growing older."

In recent years, older adults have been represented somewhat more frequently in print, as well as on television and radio, and the images of seniors have become more positive.[23] More factual information about aging is communicated in the press and radio and television programming, although these programs may not be aired at prime time. Many newspapers feature columns that offer current information and advice on topics ranging from health concerns to retirement. Television and radio stations are offering some high-quality programs geared to older adult audiences. Another sign of progress is the development by Conseil de presse du Québec of a code for the ethical presentation of groups such as seniors, disabled persons and ethnic minorities in the media.

> *"Television and newspaper coverage should show an older person as a receptionist or a computer programmer looking alert and well-dressed."*
> *"Too many programs are hosted by young people. Get someone with grey hair."*

Despite the real advances in the way older adults are presented in the media, there remain areas where the broadcasting industry, editors and reporters need to make further improvements. Seniors still are not often presented in the media. The image of seniors tends to be oversimplified and one-dimensional; the diverse and complex reality of aging may be lacking, including references to ethnic minorities and aboriginal seniors. Seniors' achievements and contributions to society do not receive adequate coverage and, conversely, there are indications of an overemphasis in the media on the impending social and economic 'crisis' stemming from the seniors' boom.[24] Editors who are usually vigilant against racist or sexist biases may allow at times stereotypes and biased attitudes towards seniors to emerge in cartoons, articles, advertisements or editorials.[25]

NACA recommends that:

> The broadcasting industry and the press present older adults more often; depictions should include older adults from various walks of life and cultural groups, in a variety of roles and situations, and with a wide range of abilities and personality characteristics.

> Guidelines for the realistic portrayal of seniors on radio, television and in the printed press be developed and applied by the broadcasting industry and newspaper publishers.

The Role of Business

> *"There should be more emphasis on advertising geared to the older adult...and not just for laxatives."*

"We need to use seniors in ads like the beer commercials and the travel commercials."

"Stop referring to persons aged 55-70 as elderly!!! Even the name 'golden age' is discriminatory."

Business has discovered the buying power of the increasing numbers and proportion of older adult consumers. Department stores, travel agencies, pharmaceutical and cosmetics companies and financial institutions are among the many business interests vying for a share of the seniors' market. Increasingly, advertisements are geared to older consumers and 'perks' are offered, such as discounts and special services. To the extent that the needs and preferences of seniors are met in the marketplace, NACA welcomes this growing business trend.

Nevertheless, there are problems related to the images of seniors created by business. First, persons 65+ do not like being singled out and labelled; they prefer to be seen simply as 'people'.[26] Using stereotypes of decrepitude and dependency to advertise products or services not only perpetuates ageism, it also results in rejection by senior consumers who do not identify with the negative image.[27] Conversely, over-simplistic portrayals of seniors as 'whoopies' feed false notions that seniors are over-privileged relative to other age groups. Finally, there may be a tendency to underrepresent seniors in advertising products intended for the general public and to over-represent them in marketing only specific products.

"Salespersons can be impatient if you are choosing something and are not swift enough."

"Salespeople will talk to me rather than to my mother who is 85."

Discriminatory practices exist in the marketplace. Sales and service personnel may treat older customers with less courtesy and respect.[28] For instance, younger customers are served before seniors or are given more attention. Salespeople may tend to adopt overly simple vocabulary and sentence structure in dealing with a senior client, especially with a person who has a hearing or a visual impairment, or they may talk as if the senior knows nothing about the service or product.

Through sponsorship and advertisements, business exerts a strong influence on the content of television, radio and publications. Biases or neglect of seniors by business interests are reflected in neglect by the media.

To promote more balanced and accurate images of seniors in advertising and to counter discrimination against seniors in business settings,

NACA recommends that:

Advertisements depict seniors, as well as younger persons, to sell products intended for the general public and avoid using seniors exclusively to publicize a certain small range of products; in advertisements, images of seniors should be as varied and as flattering as those of other age groups.

Business firms consult with seniors to develop marketing strategies that are free of age bias.

Retail outlets and commercial services assure, through staff training and recognition, that personnel treat all clients with equal courtesy and respect, and respond appropriately to clients with impairments, regardless of their age.

Advertisers and sponsors use their influence to increase the favourable depiction of seniors in the media.

The Role of the Arts

Although social education is not an inherent mission of art, some artists convey social messages through their art. The public image of aging has been enriched and elevated in many songs, novels, plays, films, poetry and the fine arts; a few acclaimed Canadian examples are the novel *The Stone Angel* by Margaret Laurence and the play *La Sagouine* by Antonine Maillet; the films *Company of Strangers*—starring senior women of various backgrounds with no previous acting experience—and *Mon Oncle Antoine;* and the song "Poor Old Rose" recorded by Sylvia Tyson. Because art has a lasting and universal power to influence attitudes,

NACA recommends that:

Foundations and organizations concerned with seniors' well-being establish an award to recognize artistic productions that enhance the public's awareness and appreciation of seniors.

The Role of Educators and Community Organizations

Stereotypic views of seniors emerge in early childhood and persist through adolescence into adulthood.[29] Even young children will describe older adults in terms of limited abilities and roles.[30] Narrow and negative attitudes towards aging among children can be changed by providing opportunities for direct contact with seniors, by including information about life at all ages in elementary and secondary school curricula, and by selecting reading and viewing materials that present seniors in a varied and realistic manner.[31]

"Maybe seniors could help in school where a student needs a little extra help."

"Invite grandparents to day care centres to tell stories."
"Students should interview and write essays about seniors and what they know."
"Social studies, history, civics can be used to depict the role of the elderly in their contribution to Canada."
"Seniors can do many things with youngsters, including choral groups, shows and games."

It is easier to acquire and maintain stereotypes about seniors when contact with real older persons is infrequent and superficial, or when the contacts are restricted to seniors who appear to conform to the stereotypes. Positive contact with a variety of older persons, beginning with grandparents, can lead to a better understanding and appreciation of seniors. In school and community settings, including places of worship, intergenerational programs also benefit children's intellectual, emotional and social development. Educators in some regions have made much progress in increasing children's awareness of seniors by creating and supporting a variety of intergenerational activities. Examples of the many successful intergenerational programs are the Grandpal Program, Prime Mentors, G.I.V.E. (Generations in Various Exchanges), Interlink and STAC (Senior Tutors Assisting Children).[32] These initiatives need to be continued and to become more widespread. Intergenerational participation involving adults of all ages, for instance, in community projects and leisure activities, is an effective way to promote the attitude that people are people regardless of age.

NACA recommends that:

Parents, educators and community groups support existing intergenerational activities between seniors and children and organize such activities where they do not exist.

Community and cultural groups encourage and facilitate participation of persons of all ages in their activities.

Although the curriculum and required texts in primary and high school are the responsibility of provincial/territorial ministries of education, teachers have a role in shaping children's attitudes. They can display a realistic awareness and appreciation for seniors, confront stereotypic beliefs and encourage interaction with older adults. The teaching of children extends beyond the classroom; parents themselves play a crucial role in moulding the attitudes of the next generation, as do sports coaches, boy scout and girl guide leaders and other adults directly involved in the education of children.

NACA recommends that:

Educators of children, including teachers' associations, parent-teacher associations, day care staff and recreational leaders, participate in training seminars or workshops to increase their understanding of aging and appreciation of seniors and to acquire skills in transmitting to children favourable attitudes about seniors.

A recent study indicates that depictions of older adults in children's literature have become more detailed and more diverse and that the exchanges between younger and older characters in the stories have become more central to the story and more complex.[33] Writers and publishers of children's literature need to be encouraged to continue this trend.

NACA recommends that:

Educators of children, including librarians, select literature that portrays seniors realistically and that conveys favourable attitudes towards older adults.

The Role of Seniors and Seniors' Organizations

"I try to show that it is important to age gracefully by participating in activities, by getting more involved."
"Seniors themselves can encourage one another."
"By volunteering and taking an active part in things around them."
"We should become more visible and vocal in presenting the positives."
"Be visible and involved with other age groups."

Seniors have a primary role in showing younger generations what it means to grow old. Individually and collectively, seniors have been challenging stereotypes and negative attitudes for some time. Seniors' organizations quickly confront public statements that belittle older adults. They initiate and lead projects, both local and national, and they participate in political lobbies and social action groups. Seniors engage in educational activities, in athletic events and in more volunteer work than most other age groups. They act as consultants to governments and to non-government agencies on matters related to their quality of life. Much of this activity is intergenerational. The novelty of older adults' involvement in university courses, political demonstrations, computer clubs, running marathons, hot air ballooning, and so on, is wearing off gradually, as public awareness of the vigour of many seniors increases. By their words and actions, many of today's seniors are showing that they are as alive as ever and that they reject stereotyping.

Besides continuing to affirm their entitlement to personal autonomy and public respect and full integration in the community, seniors now must challenge the old stereotypes, negative attitudes and condescension that still apply to seniors in poor health who require support in daily living; this may require that healthy, active seniors themselves examine and dispel negative attitudes they may hold towards those who are frail or disabled. They also must militate against the belief that seniors are interested only in themselves and in the benefits they receive from society.

NACA recommends that:

Seniors and seniors' organizations promote favourable attitudes and respectful behaviour towards other seniors who are less able to assert themselves owing to frailty or disability, and take an active role as advocates on their behalf.

Seniors and seniors' organizations become more visibly involved in intergenerational activities that serve the common good, advocate on behalf of other groups in need, and publicize more widely their contributions to the whole community.

CONCLUSION

Several factors have helped to enhance the public awareness of aging in recent years. Among these factors are the aging of the population and the increase in gerontological knowledge, creative and successful government programs and educational campaigns and the responsiveness of the media and the artistic community.

Most of the responsibility—and the credit—for changing attitudes towards aging, however, belongs to seniors themselves. Seniors insist on remaining integral and self-determining members of society. They seek out and create meaningful ways to contribute to the community and to the well-being of all generations. Because they publicly challenge stereotypes and show by their example that it is possible to live life fully at all ages, ageism eventually may be beaten. Eventually, Canadians of all ages will accept aging as a normal part of life to be welcomed and savoured:

"Up to the present, I have found the aging process a rather pleasurable experience; after all, it is a natural process. Getting old is really no different than other transitions in my journey through life."

NOTES

1. Neugarten, B.L and D.A Neugarten. "The changing meanings of age." *Psychology Today* (May 1987): 29-30, 32-33, 94

2. Ibid.

3. Gekoski, W. and J. Knox. "Ageism or healthism: Perceptions based on age and health status." *Journal of Aging and Health*, 2,1 (1990): 15-27

4. McPherson, B.D. *Aging as a Social Process. 2nd Edition.* Toronto: Butterworths, 1990.

5. Tandemar Research Inc. "An exploratory study of quality of life and accompanying attitudes among seniors in Canada." Unpublished paper prepared for Manifest Communications, Inc., Toronto, 1988.

6. National Advisory Coucil on Aging. *Understanding Seniors' Independence: The Barriers and Suggestions for Action.* Ottawa: The Council, 1989.

7. Tandemar Research Inc., *op. cit.*

8. Chipperfield, J.C. and B. Havens. "A longitudinal analysis of perceived respect among elders: Changing perceptions for some ethnic groups." *Canadian Journal on Aging*, 11, 1 (1992): 15-30.

9. Comfort, A. "Real and imaginary aging." *In Proceedings: Governor's conference on the quality of life for our senior citizens.* Raleigh, North Carolina: North Carolina Department of Human Resources, 1977.

10. Secombe, K and M. Ishii-Kuntz. "Perceptions of problems associated with aging: Comparisons among four older age cohorts." *The Gerontologist*, 31, 4, (1991): 527-533.

    Tandemar Research Inc., *op. cit.*

11. Minkler, M. "Generational equity and the new victim blaming: An emerging public policy issue." *International Journal of Health Services*, 16, 4, (1986): 539-551.

    Minkler, M. "Gold in the gray: Reflections on business' discovery of the elderly market." *The Gerontologist*, 29, 1 (1989): 17-23.

12. Callaghan, D. *Setting Limits: Medical Goals in an Aging Society.* New York: Simon and Shuster, 1987.

13. Courchene, T. "Social policy." In T.E. Kierans (ed.), *Getting it Right.* Toronto: C.D. Howe Institute, 1990.

14. Kuypers, J. and V. Bengtson. "Social breakdown and competence." *Human Development*, 16, 3, (1973): 181-201.

    Rodin, J. and E.J. Langer. "Age labels: The decline of control and fall of self-esteem." *Journal of Social Issues*, 36, 1 (1980): 12-29.

15. Pannu, Raghoo (ed.). "The 'designing' woman." *IFA Newsletter*, International Federation on Ageing (1990): 16-17.

16. Chipperfield and Havens, *op. cit.*

17. Breytspraak, L. *The Development of Self in Later Life.* Boston: Little, Brown Inc., 1984.

    Kaiser, S.B. and J.L. Chandler. "Audience responses to appearance codes: Old-age imagery in the media." *The Gerontologist*, 28, 5 (1988): 692-699.

18. Stone, L.O. and S. Fletcher. *The Seniors' Boom.* Ottawa: Supply and Services Canada, 1987.

19. National Advisory Council on Aging. *The NACA Position on Gerontology Education.* Ottawa: the Council, 1991.

National Advisory Council on Aging. *The NACA Position on Managing an Aging Labour Force.* Ottawa: The Council, 1992.

20. Lubomudrov, S. "Congressional perceptions of the elderly: The use of stereotypes in the legislative process." *The Gerontologist*, 27, 1 (1987): 77-81.

21. Government of Canada. Seniors. *Communicating in Print with/about Seniors.* Ottawa: Supply and Services Canada, 1990.

22. The Seniors Secretariat, Health and Welfare Canada, was a major partner in the 1991 survey of the determinants of independence in later life. Statistics Canada. *Ageing and Independence.* Ottawa: Supply and Services Canada, 1992.

23. Dail, P.W. "Prime-time television portrayals of older adults in the context of family life." *The Gerontologist*, 28, 5, (1988): 700-706.

Gage, M. "Age busting." *Today's Seniors* (June 1991): 7.

24. Boucher, D. "Are senior citizens outliving their welcome?" *The Globe and Mail* (August 15, 1990).

25. McCann, D. "Jokes about aging reflect our attitudes, speaker says." *The Whig Standard*, Kingston (January 26, 1987).

The following articles in Canadian newspapers are examples of the pejorative messages conveyed about seniors:

Boucher, D., *op. cit.* Some statements in this article (e.g. "They have lost the art of the graceful exit") are particularly offensive.

Francis, D. "Sickly snowbirds cost us a bundle." *Toronto Sun*, (January 20, 1991).

MacPherson, L. "You're not getting older, just richer." *Star Phoenix*, Saskatoon (September 6, 1990).

26. Ontario Office for Senior Citizens' Affairs. *Age: The Advantage.* Toronto: Queen's Printer for Ontario, 1989.

27. Ibid.

28. Ryan, E.B. "Intergenerational talk to elders. Is there age bias?" Proceedings of Gerontology Forum, Lakehead University, Thunder Bay, May 1991.

29. Mitchell, J. et al. "Childrens' perceptions of age: A multidimensional approach to differences by age, sex and race." *The Gerontologist*, 25, 2, (1985): 182-187.

Doka, K.J. "Adolescent attitudes and beliefs toward aging and the elderly." *International Journal of Aging and Human Development*, 22, 2 (1986): 173-187.

30. McPherson, B.D., *op. cit.*

31. Stephens, B. "Attitudes Toward Aging, Old Age and Older Persons— A Review and Discussion." Edmonton: Senior Citizens' Bureau, Alberta Social Services and Community Health, June 1978.

32. Bryan, C. "Grandpals is a grand program." *Fifty-five Plus* (August/September 1990): 24.

   The Ontario Office for Senior Citizens' Affairs sponsors the publication of a regular newsbulletin, entitled *Between Generations*, to inform students and seniors of intergenerational activities.

33. Ansello, E.F. "Children's first literature and the feast of life." *The Gerontologist*, 29, 1 (1989): 272-277.

Marginal Life After 49

A PRELIMINARY STUDY OF THE PORTRAYAL OF OLDER PEOPLE IN CANADIAN CONSUMER MAGAZINE ADVERTISING

Nan Zhou and Mervin Y.T. Chen

■■■

BACKGROUND AND PURPOSE OF THE STUDY

The use of older persons in advertising, as compared to the amount of effort devoted to other issues on older people such as health care and retirement, is still a relatively new area of study in both social gerontology and marketing. An examination of the literature reveals very few publications on the portrayal of older Canadians in advertising. One study indicated that people over 65 years of age were shown in just over 7 per cent of the advertisements in the two most widely read refereed Canadian medical journals in 1988. These advertisements did not appear to take into account the special drug needs of the elderly, and the ways the elderly were featured were considered a potential factor leading to inappropriate prescribing (Lexchin, 1990). Another study on the portrayal of gender in Canadian broadcasting in 1984 and 1988, commissioned by the Canadian Radio-television and Telecommunications Commission, indicated that relatively few male and even fewer female characters in the 36–65 age range were in both English and French television advertisements, and similar, but very small, numbers of male and female characters beyond the age of 65 appeared in the advertisements (ERIN Research, 1990).

As an attempt to bridge the gap, this paper presents the results of a preliminary study on the portrayal of older Canadians in consumer magazine advertisements. The specific research questions asked were: (1) How frequently did advertisements present older characters? (2) How were older characters portrayed? (3) How did the portrayal of older and younger

Reproduced by permission of Blackwell Publishers from *International Journal of Advertising* 1:343–54.

characters differ? We focused our comparison on people appearing in advertisements who were judged to be 50 years of age and older and that of the 18–49 age group. Unless otherwise specified, the terms older characters and younger characters hereafter represent these two age groups.

METHODOLOGY

Sample

A sample was drawn from Canadian consumer magazines listed in the *Canadian Media Directors' Council Media Digest 1990/91* following a three-stage procedure. First, all geographic editions of all December 1990 issues of the ten largest circulating magazines in Canada were ordered. Second, all national advertisements (i.e. identical advertisements in all editions of each issue) were identified. Third, all national advertisements containing a picture of at least one human character were retained for analysis. All regional advertisements were excluded because those with regional orientation could distort the results of a national study (Zhou *et al.*, 1990).

A total of 198 editions covering seventeen issues from eight magazines were included in the resultant sample because there were no national advertisements in the other two, *Leisure Ways/West World* and *Starweek*. In selecting characters to be analysed, clearly analysable complete human figures and close-up shots were counted, but blurry shots, shadow figures and very small characters in crowded scenes were not. A total of 255 human characters were judged to be analysable and used in the study.

Categories of Analysis

Categories of analysis were formulated after a review of relevant literature and three runs of pilot study. For each category, a character was classified into the proper sub-category through an examination of the whole content of the advertisement, both written and pictorial. The more descriptors could be applied to it, the greater possibility that the character could be classified into a sub-category. If unable to be classified, the character would be put into the "indeterminate" sub-category.

Coding

Two trained coders content-analysed the data. For initial analysis, both coders were given 30 randomly selected, identical characters. Their judgements were compared and disagreements resolved through discussions between themselves and consultations with the authors. The inter-coder agreements were 98 per cent, which was acceptable in this type of study (Kassarjian, 1977). Two important reasons for the high inter-coder agreements were the extensive training and the pilot studies conducted. One coder subsequently analysed the remaining 225 characters during a period of two weeks. One month after the completion of the analysis, 5 per cent of the characters were re-analysed by this coder and the test-retest agreements were 98 per cent.

RESULTS

Presence of Older Persons

Only 6.3 per cent of the advertisements containing analysable characters had older characters in them. Only 5.1 per cent or one in twenty of the characters were identified to be in the 50–64 age group. There was no character identified to be 65 years of age or older at all. In comparison with their proportion in the Canadian population, the 50 and older age groups were significantly under-represented in the advertisements, while the 18–49 segment was much over-represented.

Gender and Racial Compositions

The distribution of the older characters by gender skewed very heavily toward the male, and females were much under-represented in terms of their proportion in the population. The reverse was true for the younger characters.

While 4.6 per cent of the younger characters were non-white, all of the older characters were identified to be white. There were no non-white older characters shown in the advertisements at all. Demographically, however, aboriginal, Asian, and other non-whites alone accounted for 6.25 per cent of the Canadian population in 1986 (Statistics Canada, 1990a).

Occupation

Of the 12.9 per cent of the older and younger characters whose occupations could be determined, older characters were more frequently shown in low-level occupations (50 per cent). In contrast, younger characters were more frequently shown in high- and middle-level occupations (71.4 per cent). No characters were shown in domestic occupations.

Importance to Advertisement Theme

Parallel to these findings, a much smaller proportion of older characters was judged as being cast in the important role to the advertisement's theme or layout. A much greater proportion of older characters played the equally important role. The proportion of both groups playing less important and unimportant roles was about the same.

Place

Not surprisingly, for the 65.7 per cent of the cases where the setting of the advertisements could be identified, a much larger proportion of older characters were shown in residential house settings, while no older ones appeared in business settings.

Activity

Older characters were also portrayed as less physically active, as 61.5 per cent of the older characters were in sedentary activities, compared to only 40 per cent of the younger ones, while 38.5 per cent of the older ones versus 60 per cent of the younger ones were in non-sedentary and high physical activities.

Association With People

For 90.4 per cent of the characters whose social relationship with other people could be determined, 42.9 per cent of the older ones were seen alone, and 57.1 per cent were with family members or other people of the same or younger age groups. In comparison, 40.9 per cent of the younger ones were alone, 28.6 per cent were with family and 30.5 per cent were with others in the same or other age groups.

Product Association

Both older and younger characters were associated with a variety of products/services, although the main products (product categories) associated with both groups were very different.

CONCLUSIONS

Summary and Discussion

The findings of this study indicate that the problem of the portrayal of older people in Canadian magazine advertisements is one of both quantity and quality. In terms of quantity, the most striking finding is the marginal showing of older characters in the advertisements. With only 5.1 per cent of the characters in the advertisement sample judged to be 50 years of age and older and no one 65 or older, there is no doubt that many Canadian advertisers still do not pay much attention to the older population segment and are still aiming more at the younger market. For quite some time, the latter has been considered to have a larger share of consumer purchasing power. In contrast, to a large extent, the older population has been considered an economically disadvantaged group and therefore was given a "cold reception" by the advertising industry. However, many older Canadians have gone through their prime years during the prosperous 1960s and 1970s and accumulated considerable assets. This fact, coupled with improved pension systems, suggests the financial status of older Canadians has greatly improved. While there are still older Canadians living below the poverty line (National Advisory Council on Aging, 1991), the majority of them are no longer "economically disadvantaged". However, even when marketers are convinced that the older population does represent a sizeable market, they may still be unwilling to direct advertising efforts toward the aged, for they fear that it would "hurt their public image" and turn away the more "desirable" younger age group, as indicated in an earlier study by the U.S. National Council on the Aging (Knauer, quoted in Loudon and Della Bitta, 1988, p. 228).

As far as quality is concerned, the portrayal of older people is generally stereotypic, although not blatantly so. Specifically, the findings regarding gender composition of the older age group point to a very unrealistic reflection of the Canadian population in advertisements. It is common knowledge that, from age 50 upward, the higher the age group, the more women than men in each group. However, older female characters were almost invisible in our data. At the same time, non-white characters in the older character group simply did not exist. As Canada has been highly touted as a multicultural and multi-ethnic society, this finding is particularly ironic.

Our results also indicate that older people were portrayed as uncharacteristically less capable in terms of their occupations; they were cast in less important roles to the advertisement's theme or layout; and they were portrayed as tending to stay at home and being less physically active when compared with younger characters. As a whole, the images of the older characters were largely in their negative stereotypes. From the perspective of older people, their insignificance and poor image in advertisements may lead them to think that they are not considered as valuable customers by the marketers or as valuable members by society.

On a positive note, older characters were seen in social and "transgenerational" scenes and not totally socially isolated. Although the patterns on the products (product categories) associated with older and younger characters differ, the older characters were not often seen in advertisements promoting ageing-associated products and were used to feature goods purchased frequently by the average consumer.

In sum, the findings of this study were consistent with many previous studies on the subject in general. Advertisers, as social gerontologists Hooyman and Kiyak (1991, p. 38) have pointed out, may have indeed been slower than other mass media to integrate positive images of ageing into their advertisements.

Given the notion that advertising acts as a reflector of reality, public perception, and stereotypes, the situation is expected to improve as the older segment of the population grows larger and the societal attitudes toward ageing become more positive (Hooyman and Kiyak, 1991). Greco (1988) found that, in general, the attitudes of U.S. advertising executives toward the use of the elderly in advertisements were becoming more positive than in the past. They felt that elderly spokespersons could get their audience's attention and help gain awareness for new products. If Canadian advertisers do not want to fail in the 50 and older market, they also will have to provide better services to older people by "discovering" and increasing the use of older characters in their advertisements, including women and non-whites. "Advertisers who don't learn to reach older consumers effectively", as suggested by Beck (1990, p. 76), "will find themselves out of touch—and perhaps out of business—in the years ahead."

It is important for advertisers to notice, however, that older people are not a homogeneous group and no one approach will work best. Nor are the research findings conclusive. For example, Moschis (1989) presented a number of contradictions regarding our present knowledge about consumer behaviour and marketing practices. It is up to marketers to learn how to cope with the present circumstances.

Advertisers should also notice that since ageing is a natural process, special considerations should be taken into account in advertising to older people, such as using larger type size, printing on non-glossy paper to avoid glare and on light backgrounds with dark print (Seniors Secretariat, Government of Canada, 1991).

LIMITATION AND FUTURE RESEARCH

To the best of our knowledge, this was the first content analysis of magazine advertisements using a truly national advertising sample. A limitation of the study is that, as a preliminary study, it only included a limited number and type of magazines. By using the present study as a baseline, future research could cover other types of magazines such as those specializing in older consumers which could also be used for comparative purposes. Future research could also take a longitudinal perspective.

From the viewpoint of both gerontology and market research, future study could include the following areas: (1) older people's and the public's viewpoints of, and their reactions to, the portrayal of older people in advertising; (2) advertisers' viewpoints on the subject. Only when knowledge in these areas as well as in product and service needs of older consumers is available and used, can the older segment of the Canadian population be better served.

ACKNOWLEDGMENTS

The authors would like to express thanks to the Social Sciences and Humanities Research Council of Canada for a grant which partly supported the project, to the publishers for providing the magazine copies used in the study, and to Michelle Cameron and Kim Purcell for their assistance in analysing the data.

NOTES

1. The order of the authorship is random. Both authors contributed equally to the project.

REFERENCES

Beck, M. (1990) Going for the gold. Newsweek 23 April, 74–76.

ERIN Research (1990) *The Portrayal of Gender in Canadian Broadcasting—Summary Report 1984–1988,* Cat. BC92–46. Ottawa: Minister of Supply and Services.

Francher, J.S. (1973) 'It's the Pepsi generation…'. Accelerated aging and the television commercial. *International Journal of Aging and Human Development,* 4 (3), 245–255.

Greco, A.J. (1988) The elderly as communicators: Perceptions of advertising practitioners. *Journal of Advertising Research* 28 (June/July), 39–46.

Hooyman, N.R. & Kiyak, A.H. (1991) *Social Gerontology: A Multidisciplinary Perspective,* 2nd ed. Needham Heights, MA: Allyn & Bacon.

Kassarjian, H.H. (1977) Content Analysis in Consumer Research. *Journal of Consumer Research,* 4 (June), 8–18.

Knauer, V. (1988) The aging alienated consumer. In *The Aging Consumer,* Occasional Papers in Gerontology, No. 8, Ann Arbor, Michigan: Institute of Gerontology. Quoted in David Loudon and Albert J. Della Bitta, *Consumer Behavior,* 3rd ed. New York: McGraw-Hill, 228.

Lexchin, J. (1990) The portrayal of the elderly in drug advertisements: A factor in inappropriate prescribing? *Canadian Journal on Aging,* 9 (3), 296–303.

Moschis, G.P. (1989) Marketing to older adults: An overview and assessment of present knowledge and practice. Working Paper No. 21–89, Atlanta, Georgia: Georgia State University.

National Advisory Council on Aging (1991) *The Economic Situations of Seniors: A Fact Book,* Cat. H71-3/14-1991E. Ottawa: Minister of Supply and Services.

Seniors Secretariat (1991) *Communicating in Print with/about Seniors,* Cat. H88-3/7-1990. Ottawa: Minister of Supply and Services.

Statistics Canada (1990a) *Market Research Handbook, 1991,* Cat. 63–224. Ottawa: Minister of Supply and Services.

Zhou, N., Sparkman, R. & Follows, S. (1990) Geographic culture, regional advertising, and the myth of the nine nations of North America: A content analysis of Canadian and U.S. magazine advertisements. In *The Proceedings of the Third Symposium on Cross-cultural Consumer and Business Studies* (eds.) Synodinos, N.E., Keown, C.F., Becker, T.H., Grunert, T.G., Muller, T.E. & Yu, J.H., pp. 1–6. Honolulu: University of Hawaii.

3

The Best Is Yet to Be?

CHALLENGING THE MYTHS ABOUT AGING

Sybil Shack

The bag ladies rummaging in the city's garbage and the platinum-haired widows who own their high-rise condominiums, the sprightly bus riders of eighty and their less happy sisters tied into wheelchairs, my mother who presides over our household at ninety-three and I at seventy-three have this in common: we are female and old; we belong to the growing minority in Canada's population which is collectively known as its senior citizens, the elderly, the Golden Agers, all identifying titles given to us to avoid calling us what we are, old.

According to the banks we enter this state of less than grace at sixty, according to the federal government at sixty-five. Whatever the dread boundary, we are likely to remain members of the minority of the old for a greater length of time than we were anything else, longer than we were infants or teen-agers or young or even middle-aged. There are also going to be more of us as we continue to outlive the men and as science learns more about the control of the diseases that kill us off.

Unfortunately we are not always held in high esteem in a society which values youth above all else, except perhaps money. Attitudes have developed about us that are based on misunderstandings and misconceptions. These often have the tenacity and strength of myths and are believed with almost religious fervour.

From the worship of youth has risen the myth that "old" means "bad." Young people and old, male and female, hold firmly to this belief. We go to extremes to avoid the appearance of being old and hence bad. We feel complimented, as the years creep up on us, to be told that we are young in spirit, or that we don't look our age, or that we are only as old as we feel, because obviously we are to be pitied if we look or feel old. So we dye our hair. We dress like our granddaughters. We lie about our age. I am afraid I startle well-meaning acquaintants when I respond to their compliments with "What's

This article originally appeared in *Canadian Women's Studies (Les Cahiers de la Femme)* 5 (3), Winter 1984.

wrong with being old in spirit? What's wrong with enjoying the earned right to be old?" We've lived. We've accumulated experience, skills, knowledge, even wisdom. Why should we have to apologize for, make light of, our assets?

I have little patience with the nostalgia that recalls a past which never was, and so belittles the satisfactions of the present and the future. Old may sometimes be bad; but so is youth, and so was middle age. Surely part of our maturity is the ability to accept ourselves as we are, senior members of the human race, valuable and contributing people, without having to pretend to be what we are not—young. In accepting ourselves we gain the respect of others. After all, they too in time will be old—that is, if they are lucky.

Acceptance by the rest of society means being considered as individuals, not being lumped together in a homogeneous mass, often only as objects of good works. We value our differences as individuals and our independence. Even when we are old and sick we have a right to make decisions for ourselves, to determine our way of life as long as we possibly can. We have a right to be treated without condescension in nursing homes and hospitals, in department stores and restaurants.

We also resent the label of small-*c* conservatism, of rigidity in our thinking, a label I find more often applicable these days to my very young friends. Never has a generation lived through more, greater, and more rapid change than the old people of the 1980s. During our lifetime history has been accelerated; changes that in the past might have taken hundreds of years have occurred within decades. We have seen the domination of the internal-combustion engine; we watched the first heavier-than-air flying machines take to the skies; we caught the first sounds off the airwaves. We survived two world wars and the Depression of the 1930s. We have accommodated ourselves to sweeping changes in manners and morals. Indeed we, this century's old people, have proved the immense adaptability of the human race. We may be unrealistically nostalgic, but we can hardly be described as rigid.

One of the most dangerous misconceptions about us is that we are no longer affordable. Daily we read that we are becoming just too expensive, that the upcoming generation can no longer bear the cost of providing for us. We are made to feel guilty because the sick among us are depriving younger people of hospital beds and medical care; our pensions are draining the treasury; our housing is a problem for the local taxpayers. If we retire early, our pensions are too costly; if we stay on the job after sixty-five, we are contributing to the unemployment of the young.

Are we really no longer affordable? It is true that as we live longer more of us may require medical care. On the other hand, the numbers who are totally dependent on the health-care system are few, relative to the whole population. Most of us probably require no more care than pregnant women, and far less than premature or handicapped babies. Parallelling the increasing needs of the old has been the vast improvement in the health of the young, with a correspondingly lesser demand on the health-care system. Immunization programs have wiped out the communicable diseases that until recently took their toll on children. Research is progressing—we pay part of the cost—to find cures for the crippling diseases that plague the middle-aged and the old. When it pays off there should be even more funds to be diverted to responsible caring for the helpless aged, those who now sit out their last years waiting for a welcome death.

We are not alone in suggesting that the way in which health care is now delivered needs re-evaluation. There must be more economical and more effective means of providing it. We know that we, the old, would benefit from an overhaul of a system which currently serves us expensively yet poorly.

Are we really not affordable?

Let it be a remembered that throughout our working years we made a substantial contribution to the economy, whether we worked at home or in the labour force. We still pay taxes; and even the oldest, the sickest, the most frail, the poorest among us are consumers of goods and services, providers of jobs.

We create jobs *because* of our age. The sciences of geriatrics and gerontology are growing in importance as our numbers increase. A whole industry has developed around the care and handling of us. It employs people to study, counsel, house, feed, and care for us, to educate and re-educate us. Reporters, researchers, professors, social workers, clergy, counsellors, nurses, aides, administrators; cooks, launderers, cleaners—many of them would be out of jobs if it were not for us. Economists predict that the answer to unemployment lies in the service industries. We provide a base for many of them.

The day the Old Age Security and the Guaranteed Income Supplement cheques are in the mail the banks pour out a steady stream of cash, which is immediately converted into consumer goods. The old have no need to save, and thousands must spend every penny we get just to stay alive. Any cutback on our pensions would be felt within days by local merchants and only a little later by wholesalers and manufacturers. Our numbers and our circumstances make us important consumers.

Moreover, the money from which our pensions are paid forms a large pool of capital, all of it available to Canadian enterprises, as are Canada Pension Plan funds to provincial governments. Much of this—annuities, pension and trust funds—is our money, accumulated as personal savings, as deferred salaries in employers' contributions to private and public pension funds, and as tax payments. It is an important economic resource.

So much for the myth that we are a financial burden, a dead weight for the young to carry. And suppose we were. If they deny us, what kind of responsibility will their children and grandchildren accept for them when today's young find themselves in the Golden Age?

Too often the old are perceived as a social as well as a financial problem. Living quarters are cramped; families are mobile; everyone is busy. There is no room and there is no time for elderly relatives, however close. They interfere with "normal" family life, are responsibilities added to an already crowded agenda.

As it happens, most of my generation cherish our independence as much as our relatives cherish their privacy. Given an adequate income and access to the care we may require in times of illness, we ask only to be allowed to continue our own interests, which might occasionally even include a little baby-sitting for our harassed younger relatives.

And we do have interests. In our thousands, women over sixty-five are sharing our expertise quietly and gladly. We work as volunteers in schools, nursing homes, and hospitals. We teach French or English to immigrant women. We staff charity gift shops and volunteer libraries. We are conscientious members of boards of charitable organizations. We are active in churches, temples, and synagogues. We dish out food in soup kitchens, raise money for the United Way and the Red Cross and every worthy cause in the country. We serve our communities in a multitude of ways, often anonymously, seldom recognized for the unpaid work we do. Having been busy, caring people until the age of sixty-five, we do not suddenly abandon a way of life when we pass through the invisible barrier that separates middle from old age.

A phenomenon of the last few years has been the return to schools, colleges, and universities of older women from every walk of life. I am told by their teachers that they are a delight to have, whether as a whole class of "seniors" or as single students in regular classes. The "returning students" are alert, interesting, vocal, and challenging. They are doing much to change the stereotyping of old women, enriching their own lives in the process.

It is sad that so many of us are victims of the misconceptions regarding growing old. We too equate "old" with "bad" and waste these precious years of our lives longing for an impossible youth and dreading the future. Most of us, however, appreciate the fact of our survival. When asked how we feel, we answer cheerfully, "pretty good, thank you," or a more Canadian "not bad, thank you." We may not agree with Robert Browning that "the best is yet to be," but we know that the "last of life" may last thirty years. We want to make those years as productive as possible. We think we can move in that direction by accepting ourselves as we are, by placing value on age instead of trying to deny it.

SECTION ONE

Discussion Questions

1. *Discuss some of the sources of ageism today. Has ageism declined in Canadian society? Has it gotten worse? What can Canadian society do to reduce ageism?*

2. *How do the media treat older people? Does bias against older people exist? If so, how does bias get expressed? What does this say about our stereotyped view of older people?*

3. *List three myths that exist about older people. State the facts that contradict these myths.*

Suggested Readings

Goulet, T. (1986). "The Visibility and Health of the Aged in Canadian Commercials." *Gerontion*, March/April: 21–25.

Kenyon, G., et al., eds. (1991). *Metaphors of Aging in Science and the Humanities.* New York: Springer.

Office of Seniors Issues (1989). *Are You Listening? Essays by Ontario Senior Citizens on What It Means to Be a Senior.* Toronto: Ontario Ministry of Citizenship.

Schonfield, D. (1982). "Who Is Stereotyping Whom and Why?" *The Gerontologist* 22: 267–72.

Many Ways of Growing Old

Section One describes the danger of stereotyping older people. The articles in that section make the point that older people differ as much from one another as they do from younger people. They differ in personal characteristics such as age, gender, and marital status. They also differ in cultural background. Canada has one of the most culturally diverse older populations in the world. Many of Canada's oldest seniors come from Northern and Eastern Europe. Newer immigrants come from Asia, South America, and the Caribbean. Many conditions affect an immigrant senior's experience, including the attitude of their culture toward aging, the norms governing child and parent relations in their culture, how long they have lived in Canada, the size of their ethnic group, and the social supports that their ethnic group makes available to them. The readings in this section give a sampling of the experience of older ethnic Canadians and show some of the issues that these seniors face.

Sociologists categorize societies by their economic systems or means of production. People in the simplest societies must move from place to place as they hunt and gather food. The people in agricultural societies live settled lives, they plant food, harvest crops, and sometimes produce a surplus. People in industrial societies manufacture goods from raw materials and work outside the home for wages. Large proportions of people in postindustrial societies work in service industries. Postindustrial society has a highly developed service sector that includes schools, hospitals, and nursing homes. Older people play different roles in each type of society. Also, the treatment of older people depends on how a culture defines old age and the roles available for older people to play. The readings in this section provide a sample of aging in each type of society and in varied cultures.

Sharp describes aging among the Chipewyan, a former hunting and gathering culture. This type of society puts great emphasis on physical strength and endurance. All members of the society must have the strength to travel as the group hunts for food. All members of the group must stay productive and add to group life. The Chipewyan distinguish between seniority (a positive development over time) and old age (a negative state).

A man who still practises magic and hunts will have seniority. But he will enter old age and lose stature when he stops hunting. This occurs when his strength starts to fail. Chipewyan society offers women alternative roles to play as they age. Women who can no longer gather food can produce crafts and process food. This allows them to stay active and therefore remain respected into late old age. The different experiences of men and women in Chipewyan society show how cultural values can shape later life.

Vanderburgh also looks at a Canadian aboriginal culture, the Anicinabe of Ontario. She compares the role of the older person before and after the establishment of reserves. Before the move to reserves the Anicinabe elders played a role in ritual and passed on sacred information. The Anicinabe linked long life to supernatural powers. Elders commanded respect for their wisdom and served as role models for the young. The meaning of elderhood changed after the Anicinabe moved to reserves. The importance of traditional culture decreased and older people lost their role as keepers of the culture. Vanderburgh reports on the revival of elderhood among the Anicinabe in recent years. She shows that the revival of elderhood depended on finding new ways to use older people's skills and knowledge.

Vanderburgh's article shows that in simpler societies respect in old age depends on a person's usefulness to the group. When older people have useful roles to play, their status stays high. Without these roles, even relatively young older people suffer a loss of status. Tradition and cultural values provided roles for older people in the past. But today, cultures like the Anicinabe's need to recreate roles for older people to play. Vanderburgh notes that this revival of cultural values takes place in a new social context. Today's elders face new challenges and have new opportunities to serve their culture.

An agricultural society has a different social structure than a hunting and gathering society like the Chipewyan's and the Anicinabe's. Status for older people in agricultural societies typically depends on land ownership. Older people with land have high status; those without land have low status. Children often remain close to and show respect for their parents in a traditional agricultural society. Older people in agricultural societies may take on less activity as they age, but they stay active throughout their lives.

Old Order Mennonite families show this pattern. The younger and older generations often live together and work the same land. Bond describes the existence of homes with two main entrances, one for the middle-aged child's family and one for the parents. Older people in this culture rarely retire. They value their independence and work on the farm into late old age. Mennonite elders do less strenuous work as they age. They produce woodwork, make cheese, or repair harnesses. They often earn an income from these jobs and this adds to their sense of self-worth. This society allows older people to do useful work and maintain respect.

Industrial societies define a person's status to a large degree by their work role. A person has social power and influence, in part, by their ability to earn an income. So the older person who leaves work and lives on a pension enters the "roleless role" of retirement. The role of elder, keeper of societal values and wisdom, has little meaning here. Retirement threatens a person with meaninglessness and a loss of self-worth.

This may come as a shock to an older person from a traditional (agricultural) society who moves to Canada. The older person's concept of old age, how younger people should treat them, their rights and responsibilities, all come into question in an industrial society. Sugiman and Nishio present a detailed description of the stresses that older Japanese Canadians face.

Traditional Japanese culture emphasizes familial support, duty to elders, and dependence of the person on the group. Canadian society emphasizes personal development, independence, and individual achievement. Sugiman and Nishio show how older Japanese Canadians adjust their expectations to fit Canadian life. The first generation born in Canada (the *Nisei*), for example, treat their parents differently than they expect to be treated by their children. Sugiman and Nishio show how each generation finds a unique (and different) balance between Japanese and Canadian values. The article illustrates the challenges that face ethnic elders as they age.

McLean and Bonar look at the experiences of ethnic elders in long-term care institutions. They describe three main issues that ethnic elders face in these settings: loss of family, loss of culture, and loss of community. Each of these losses come about because institutionalization cuts the older person off from their cultural community. It also cuts older residents off from their informal support systems. The ethnic elder may need the formal supports of the institution to survive. But, in the cases reported by McLean and Bonar, the strangeness of the institutional environment can lead to the opposite effect: poor health and in some cases death.

Each of these articles shows how ethnic elders attempt to keep their self-esteem and purpose in life. Sometimes their cultures help them do this, sometimes not. In modern Canadian society many ethnic older people display what Paul Tillich calls "the courage to be." They survive and even thrive "in spite of" the challenge to their cultural roots.

Old Age Among the Chipewyan

Henry S. Sharp

Before contact with Western civilization the Chipewyan were a hunting and gathering society specialized in the pursuit of the barren-ground caribou (*Rangifer tandarus*). Their numbers were small, probably less than 3,500, and they occupied an immense stretch of northern Canada in what is today the Northwest Territories. They ranged along the edge of the boreal forest from north of Great Slave Lake to points not too distant from Hudson Bay. Their yearly cycle took many of them far onto the tundra in summer and deep into the boreal forest in winter. Wherever the barren-ground caribou went, the Chipewyan also went.

The Chipewyan were remarkable in a number of ways. Their specialization upon barren-ground caribou led them to ignore or use only secondarily such other food resources as fish, moose, and musk-ox. Their population density was roughly one per 60-100 square miles and their diet was 90 percent or more animal products. Unlike most Canadian Athapaskans, they were an aggressive people who terrorized the Inuit and constantly fought the Cree and other neighbors.

At the time of the population displacements created by the fur trade, the Chipewyan expanded their range to include the north side of the Churchill River drainage in Manitoba, Saskatchewan, and Alberta, as well as the region between Lake Athabasca and Great Slave Lake. They entered the fur trade as traders and middlemen rather than as trappers. In the new areas they became serious trappers, but in their homeland, along the treeline, trapping never replaced hunting as the primary economic activity.

The homeland of the Chipewyan is four hundred miles beyond the northern limit of agriculture and far from the major trade routes of the Northwest Territories. As a result of their isolation, the Chipewyan did not come into extensive contact with Canadian society until after the First World War, when many Euro-Canadians came north to trap. The additional predation pressure of these white trappers, coupled with the culmination of long-

---

Reprinted from *Other Ways of Growing Old: Anthropological Perspectives*, edited by Pamela T. Amoss and Stevan Harrell with the permission of the publishers, Stanford University Press. © 1981 by the Board of Trustees of the Leland Stanford Junior University.

term changes in climate, precipitated a dramatic crash of the caribou herds in the 1940's.

The crash of the caribou herds coincided with a dramatic drop in the fur market. Within a few years the Chipewyan were unable to continue a subsistence life-style in the bush. The Chipewyan in the area where I did fieldwork settled into two villages, Stony Rapids and Black Lake, in Saskatchewan. The population increased rapidly after the measles epidemic of 1948, largely owing to improved health care, and continued to climb until birth control pills became widely used in the mid-1970's.

Population figures for Black Lake and Stony Rapids are presented in Table 1. These figures include only Treaty Indians as of December 31, 1968, updated by my field notes to March 1970. Treaty Indians constitute more than three-quarters of the population and I have no reason to expect any demographic variation between the two groups.

Chipewyan perception of a person's place in the human life cycle is based upon competence in adult economic and social activities rather than age. Competence derives from individual personality factors in women and from *inkonze* (dream power) in men. Social status is separable from chronological age. The relevant factor in determining social status is the ability to perform the tasks associated with that status; if an individual can perform the required tasks he occupies the status. The Chipewyan distinguish between seniority and old age. A person obtains seniority by virtue of genealogical position in a kinship network, which is related to the passage of time (and other factors) but only tenuously to chronological age. A person is considered elderly (hereafter I shall use "elderly" when I mean old as negative Chipewyan value judgment) when he or she can no longer function as a competent adult member of society. This dual sense of the concept of age is a behavioral rather than a linguistic distinction.

In many respects, since Chipewyan culture is so heavily based upon performance and physical capacity, the life cycles of male and female are opposite but symmetrical. Men begin their adult life with a physical strength that allows them to dominate (but not control) their spouses and a structural potential that keeps their wives subordinate. With the passage of time the man's position increases in strength. A woman remains decidedly subordinate to her husband until her children are grown. When the children of marriage begin to function as adults, the relative positions of the husband and wife begin to reverse within the marriage (Sharp 1977). Children are bound to their parents in this system by sentiment; structural relationships with the father are of significance primarily in sorting out relationships between adult sons after they are married. The ability of the father to exercise the influence inherent in his structural position depends upon his remaining active and competent.

As a man's strength begins to fail he loses the ability to exercise this influence, leaving his position with respect to his children weaker than his wife's. At the same time, his loss of strength allows his wife to escape the

TABLE I

Population of the Stony Rapids Band of Chipewyan in 1970, by Age

Age	Number	Percent
9 and under	159	34.0%
10-19	108	23.1
20-29	61	13.0
30-39	45	9.6
40-49	35	7.5
50-59	26	5.6
60-69	25	5.4
70-79	5	1.1
80-89	2	0.4
90 and over	1	0.2
Total	467	99.9%

Source: Treaty List, Band 07 (Stony Rapids,) 672 (Carlton), Department of Indian Affairs and Northern Development, Ottawa, Ontario, pp. 3308–18.
Note: The Stony Rapids Band of Chipewyan includes the residents of both Black Lake and Stony Rapids.

physical domination he has exercised over her and indeed often allows the wife to become physically dominant over her husband. In a real sense, the position of a man within his domestic unit is one of progressive diminution of influence throughout his life while a woman's position in her domestic unit is one of increasing influence until their respective statuses are virtually reversed.

What is true within the domestic unit is generally true of the social world at large, although the variations by sex and age are not as marked within the social world. An old man is morally more valuable in the social world than is an old woman, but the old woman may have a much greater influence than an old man.

The Chipewyan are egalitarian and place a strong emphasis upon competence. Where competence is present, they are remarkably tolerant of other types of failure or deviancy. In the face of incompetence, regardless of cause, they are intolerant. Chipewyan mythology and folk literature—as well as the accounts of explorers, traders, and missionaries—are full of references to the grim treatment of the incompetent, concluding with the abandonment of "elderly" persons during times of stress. Although such treatment has been modified in the last 20 years, largely because government agencies now care for the "elderly," incompetence is still a condition people abhor and try to avoid. In order to understand the status of "elderly" persons, then, we must first consider the status to which this is contrasted, that of competent adults.

THE LIFE CYCLE

The contemporary Chipewyan no longer have rites of passage to mark the transition of individuals or categories of persons from one status to the next beyond the three rites based upon the teachings of the Roman Catholic church—birth (christening), marriage, and funerals. All three have come to have a uniquely Chipewyan character.

The rites surrounding birth and death are of a different order than those surrounding a wedding. Birth and death are obvious and inescapable transition points between the world of the living and the world of the dead. A wedding, however, announces neither the arrival of a new person nor the departure of an old one; as the transformation of an immature person into an adult Chipewyan, it is uniquely a concern of the living. As a transition of two persons into full adulthood, a wedding is a close approximation of a rite of initiation. All unmarried Chipewyan are regarded in some sense as children, even those who postpone marriage into their forties or who never marry.

Women are considered nubile without regard to their capacity for reproduction, so that women are often nubile before they are fertile. On the other hand, the mere ability to reproduce does not make a woman ready for marriage. To be considered marriageable a woman must appear capable of functioning as an adult in economic activities, particularly traditional activities such as sewing garments, beadwork, and cooking. (The ability to care for children is assumed for all females over ten—a function of their long apprenticeship as baby-sitters.) Marriage has traditionally called for a sound assessment.of the economic potential and disposition of possible spouses— an assessment chiefly made by the parents of unmarried Chipewyan rather than by the young people themselves. Though in recent years most marriages have come to be based on love, love is really the stuff of affairs (which need not terminate because of marriage). Extramarital and premarital sexual activity continue, and illegitimate births are not uncommon.

For a male Chipewyan the maturation process is not marked by any dramatic change but instead involves the mastery of the skills needed to wrest a living from the harsh Canadian subarctic. Success in economic activities, especially hunting and trapping, and the display of the implements of his livelihood (dogs, more recently a snowmobile) give evidence of the underlying magical power that, as we will see, is central to the notion of male adulthood. Once a man does marry, he becomes an adult member of the community and will remain such as long as he retains and can use his skills. When he no longer has them, or is not physically able to use them, he will be considered "elderly."

MAGIC

The Chipewyan believe that competence as a man is conferred by magic. This magic derives from unsought visions in which power is given by a supernatural being. The power from these dreams cannot itself be inherited or sold, but with the approval of the supernatural source, specific knowledge gained from dreams may be taught and charms invested with magic properties may be prepared and sold to men who do not have their own magic or who want to augment the power vouchsafed them.

Magical power, with one possible exception I will mention later, is the exclusive property of men. Women with supernatural power appear in myth but never in stories about real women, whether living or dead. This gives quite a different aspect to the aging process of men and women. The Chipewyan concept of magic embraces both knowledge and power. To have magical power is to have knowledge of how to do things. Magic is also secret. One may not talk about it, reveal directly that one has it, display it openly, perform it in public (magical songs may not be sung where they can be overheard), or reveal the source or dream that gives power. To do so will cause the power to vanish.

This threat of loss of power creates a problem for the individual Chipewyan male. Having magical power is useless unless the community knows a man has it, but how does he reveal the presence of something that revelation destroys? The Chipewyan answer is to judge magical power on the basis of performance: because magic brings success, success is the result of having magical power. Hence a determination of whether or not a man possesses magic, and of how much he has if he does have it, is made on the basis of his performance as a hunter, trapper, gambler, etc.

Chipewyan magic extends into areas other than the ones mentioned above, such as healing and sorcery, but ability in these areas is of a slightly different character than ability in more normal activities. Success in healing and sorcery tends to lead to political influence, whereas other forms of success assure a man the status of a competent adult. Magic for the Chipewyan is akin to our notion of "luck" in that it is a causal mechanism producing differences in performance.

The world in which the Chipewyan live is one in which they are singularly passive creatures. They live without fault for their failures or responsibility for their actions. For example, in the native view a Chipewyan hunter never misses a shot at a game animal; failure to hit the target is the result of the animal's refusing to allow the Chipweyan to kill it. The willingness of the target to be killed is a function of the magical power of the hunter, so that what for a Western hunter would be his own failure (missing a target) is for the Chipewyan a failure of his magic rather than of his person. A Chipewyan may be blamed for an error deriving from physical failure; but for a failure of magic he would not bear blame. He might be shamed or humiliated by the refusal of a creature to allow itself to be killed—unless the circumstances were so unusual that they indicated the target itself was a creature of extraordinary magical ability—but he would not be considered to be at fault for his failure.

Magical power has never been felt to prevent a man from death, at least in the Christian period, but it is felt to provide protection from the infirmities of aging. Merely to live to be old in this rugged environment is to demonstrate the possession of some magical ability, but to live a long time without losing competence is a clear indication of superior supernatural power. The older a man becomes without becoming "elderly," the stronger his magical power is believed to be, since the entire community observes his successful resistance to the aging process.

An example of the respect for a man's magical power that develops as he remains active despite growing old can be shown by something my principal woman informant, Beth, said to me in the course of a conversation about a 71-year-old neighbor in the village, George. Beth had always been fond of George's wife, but she disliked George and criticized him at every opportunity. She and I were discussing the relative magic powers of several men and she remarked of George, "Look at that old man, still walking about. He must 'know something.'" This grudging respect apparently stemmed from the fact that George had recently recovered, without hospitalization, from a case of tuberculosis.

THE DIFFERENCE IN AGING FOR MEN AND WOMEN

Magical power does eventually fail, however, and the Chipewyan man either dies or deteriorates physically and becomes incompetent. Unable to hunt or trap, he is forced to rely upon his relatives for subsistence. His decline can be delayed for a time by the efforts of a healthy wife and the use of young Chipewyan obtained by temporary adoption. But when a man can no longer drive his dogs and venture into the bush alone to hunt, his days as a complete adult male are ended, and he must subsist, like a woman or a dog, on meat and fish obtained by others (Sharp 1976). The Chipewyan do not value the telling of myths and tales greatly, and there are no handicrafts or other activities to which a man can turn in compensation. In the traditional bush life an elderly man, like a woman, is restricted to the few dwellings of the camp; in the village there is more room to wander at will, but the only activity with which to replace hunting is gambling, and competence at cards is a poor substitute.

The situation of an old woman in Chipewyan society is quite different. Where a man has a single paramount activity—obtaining food from the bush—a woman has three: reproduction, handicrafts, and processing food. As I mentioned earlier, women do not have magic (though female midwives may use a kind of magic in performing their specialty). Unlike hunting, women's work does not involve continuous walking, violent bursts of energy, or running, so it can still be performed by women in declining physical condition.

Women's role in reproduction is extended after menopause by the common Chipewyan practice of adopting children. Adoption among the Chipewyan does not imply the complete transfer of legal rights over a child as it does in Western society. Instead, the Chipewyan "loan" children for varying periods of time and for various purposes. Grandparents have the right to adopt a child from each of their children's marriages, and almost any woman can obtain a small child to care for without any trouble. This allows a woman to fulfill most of the duties of motherhood and be called mother, "enna," by a child independently of her actual ability to reproduce. Moreover, small children are of great service in the minor tasks of running a household (hauling water, wood, etc.) and are eagerly sought. Since many of the duties of child rearing are assumed by older children, the mother or grandmother who has or adopts several children may find her work load lessened.

The second major aspect of women's work is handicrafts, primarily sewing and beadwork, but also such other tasks as the preparation of hides for leather. This work is demanding and requires both strength and good hand-eye coordination. Even though talent varies greatly among women, a lifetime of experience gives a competent older woman a real advantage over women many years her junior. And if a woman's strength and eyesight fail with age, she can still teach her skills to younger women and supervise their work—an option that men do not have when their strength fails them.

The third aspect of women's work is processing food. Cooking is only a minor part of food processing, a task that can be entrusted to young girls under minimal supervision. Processing food means primarily cutting dry meat and splitting and deboning fish for drying. These tasks are hard, requiring considerable skill and expertise. They must generally be done outside the dwelling under uncomfortable conditions. Fortunately, the demand for food is proportional to the size of the household, and as demand increases, so does the female labor pool available to supply it. Like sewing, food preparation can be done by several women working together, and old women can supervise when they cannot perform much of the actual work themselves.

Because women's work is considered to involve the use of skills acquired through instruction and practice rather than the use of magic, women are able to remain competent adults much longer than men. Since no special powers are involved, women can cooperate in their work without any loss of face. And old women whose physical strength is waning are valued for the advice and expertise they can contribute. If being able to do it all by herself does not confer the same prestige on a young woman as hunting confers on a man, neither does needing some help destroy an old woman's self-respect and reputation as it does an old man's.

As might be predicted from the differences in the tasks of men and women, the character of old age is different for the two sexes. Many more women than men beyond a marker point of, say, 60 are "old" rather than "elderly." The "old" women are able to remain involved in the affairs of the community, and many are influential because of their seniority in various kin groups. Their positions individually are augmented not only by their seniority, but also by the tendency in the Chipewyan family for ties of sentiment to be stronger with females than with the more structurally significant males (Sharp, 1979).

Elderly men are not in a position to command much influence or respect. Men's affairs are centered upon the bush rather than the village or camp. For them, the increasing confinement to the village imposed by the loss of strength with advancing age is a punishment mitigated by few compensating rewards. They are ill-inclined to become involved in the issues of moral conduct or the proposed marriages that are a mainstay of village gossip. For many men the onset of old age begins in their late forties or early fifties with lung or heart disease, and they must wage a more desperate (and dangerous) struggle to be merely "old" instead of "elderly."

A good illustration of the desperation a Chipewyan man feels when his body begins to fail with advancing age is the case of my informant Beth's husband, John. Through 1971 John was able to keep most of his sons together in a hunting unit by suppressing conflict among them and by exploiting his extensive knowledge of the bush, which made them all economically successful. His magical power was well regarded, though he had given up an active curing practice some years before. In late 1971 John had a heart attack in the bush and had to be hospitalized. He recovered from the attack, but it was discovered that he had emphysema. He refused treatment for the disease and refused to stop his heavy use of tobacco. By 1975 he was so weak that he was unable to perform any work requiring heavy exertion or endurance. As his condition worsened a split developed in his hunting unit as the eldest son attempted to take control. John moved to a different hunting area in the fall of 1975 with one son, but even he was becoming increasingly autonomous.

To compensate for his growing weakness John began to spend more time alone in the bush, avoiding the village where Beth wished to remain because of his ill health. Beth considers John's attempts to continue his activities in the bush dangerous, and feels he must be watched and protected from himself as the attempted exertion will kill him. John is aware of this watching over him, but refuses to accept the need for it. To maintain his status, he must constantly risk his life—a risk he is more than willing to take to avoid being categorized as "elderly."

REFERENCES

Sharp, Henry S. 1973. "The Kinship System of the Black Lake Chipewyan." Ph.D. diss., Duke Univ.

— 1976. "Man: Wolf: Woman: Dog," *Arctic Anthropology*, 13, no. 1:25–34.

—1977. "The Chipewyan Hunting Unit," *American Ethnologist,* 4, no. 2:377–92.

—1979. *Chipewyan Marriage.* Museum of Man Mercury Series. Canadian Ethnology Service Paper no. 58. National Museum of Canada. Ottawa.

5

The Impact of Government
Support for Indian Culture on
Canada's Aged Indians

Rosamond M. Vanderburgh

■■■

The data presented in this paper are drawn from ongoing research among the Anicinabe of southern Ontario, and show that the revival of a status of cultural significance for the aged is taking place in Ontario as well as in British Columbia. It remains for future research to document whether such a revival is occurring across Canada among other Native peoples.

THE ANICINABE OF SOUTHERN ONTARIO

Historical Background

The Anicinabe of southern Ontario are a mixed population of Ojibwe, Odawa (Ottawa), and Potawatomi origins, who refer to themselves as *Anicinabe* or "original people." They share a linguistic and cultural heritage and were historically linked in the nineteenth-century migrations, removals, and resettlements of Native peoples in the Great Lakes area. Southern Ontario acted as a refuge area for Anicinabe of American origin during the last part of the eighteenth and the early nineteenth centuries when military conflicts and white settlement pushed them from their various homelands.

The settlement of the Anicinabe onto reserves in southern Ontario took place recently enough (1820–60s) that a significant number of elderly Indians interviewed in the mid-1970s had close childhood contacts with grandparents who had experienced free access to the resources on which

From Eloise Rathbone-McCuan and Betty Havens (eds.) *North American Elders: United States and Canadian Perspectives.* Reprinted with permission of Greenwood Publishing Group, Inc. Westport, CT. Copyright © 1988.

their lives were based before white hegemony was established by treaty over the southern areas of the province. The following review of traditional elderhood refers to the patterns of those prereserve days; our understanding is drawn mainly from informants who were exposed in their childhood to elders who remembered the days "when there were no reserves." The accounts of these informants are supplemented by standard ethnographic and ethnohistorical sources (F. Densmore, 1929; R.W. Dunning, 1959; A.I. Hallowell, 1964; D. Jenness, 1935, etc.).

The Institution of Traditional Elderhood and Its Erosion

The meaning of elder status is difficult to reconstruct, but was apparently not linked to chronological age. The concept of elderhood held a number of meanings within the framework of the life cycle statuses; the individual who was a grandparent, or who belonged to the grandparental generation, tended to be perceived as an elder. Individual contributions to the family group were related to life-cycle status. Parents assumed subsistence functions, leaving child rearing and socialization functions to the elders, usually the grandparents. Although the grandparent/grandchild relationship was notably warm and fraternal in contrast to the authoritarian aspects of the parent/child relationship, elders expected, and generally received, deference and respect. Grandchildren, on the other hand, expected, and generally received, emotional and pragmatic support in growing up within their cultural tradition. The pragmatic support that "grandparents" provided during the socialization process consisted primarily of information about the techniques of managing social relationships. Success in the field of social relationships was a crucial survival factor in traditional Anicinabe times, as the management of both natural and human resources was framed within the concept of kinship.

The powerful spirits that in Native ontology controlled the natural resources upon which the Anicinabe depended were incorporated within the circle of kinship and called by the same terms for grandparents that children learned to apply to human elders (Hallowell, 1964). The skills necessary to maintain good relationships with these "other-than-human" grandparents were passed on by the human grandparents, who taught primarily through the use of oral narratives, and secondarily by example. Elders used two forms of narrative in passing on their skills/wisdom to the younger generation; the Ojibwe language (one of the three glossed as *Anicinabe*) distinguishes the myth/legend or sacred tale (*atiso'kanak*) from the anecdotal narrative (*tabatcamowin*), which Hallowell calls *news or tidings* (ibid.: 56).

The transmission of traditional ritual and sacred information is a key function of the aged in many nonliterate societies. Frequently the aged also tell stories about their life experiences. However, the linguistic evidence for an institutionalized dual structuring of oral narratives among the Anicinabe is particularly significant in understanding the full breadth of the Anicinabe elder's role. Elderhood was an institution charged with responsibility for cultural maintenance through the transmission of the core cultural values (the myths/legends) and with teaching adaptation to cultural change (in the anecdotal narratives). Elders were passing on both received cultural information and new information about how to cope with new situations that they experienced. Traditional elderhood thus embodied tremendous adaptive potential.

Anicinabe elders had things other than tales to pass on. Attainment of personal success depended upon the incremental building-up of supernaturally derived power during the life course through the maintenance of proper relationships with spirit powers. Survival to old age validated the existence of an elder's personal power, which was often shared with children through such institutions as the naming ceremony. Powerful elders might also teach children specific skills in the manipulation of the supernatural.

It is not possible to ascertain from this distance in time whether *all* older Anicinabe in the grandparental generation functioned as elders. However, the old people interviewed in the 1970s stated unequivocally that they had admired, respected, and loved their elders, and this seems to strongly support the view that in traditional times elders served as important role models for the younger generation. In sum, the transmission of survival wisdom and power was entirely in their hands. The young person who roused an elder's wrath risked loss of access to that wisdom and power, and the possibility that the power might be turned against him or her. The force and vitality of traditional elderhood cannot be emphasized too strongly.

When the Anicinabe settled onto reserves, they became more accessible to the efforts of missionaries and educators, and the context of survival changed rapidly and radically. No longer was vital survival information controlled and transmitted by Indian elders, but by missionaries and schoolteachers who mocked the knowledge and power of elders as "superstition." The children were taught in school and church to view the elders' knowledge and skills as dangerous to their health and spiritual well-being. These children, in their turn, grew old urging their own descendants to acquire in school the survival skills demonstrably effective in the larger society. Christian values, literacy and mathematics, farming skills, manual training, and domestic science came to be defined as paramount. White role models were found and the force of the elders' experimental narratives dwindled as their prestige disappeared. The Anicinabe aged were no longer *elders* in traditional terms; their status now approximated that of the aged in the larger society, and in the marginal economy of the reserves they became liabilities.

■ ■ ■

Revival of Cultural Significance for the Aged Anicinabe: A Case Study

In 1973 on Manitoulin Island a group of Native women trained as teachers and teachers' assistants formed the Manitoulin Indian Studies Committee to investigate ways to stop further erosion of Native language and culture. With funding from the Cultural/Educational Centers Program, the committee set up the Ojibwe Cultural Foundation (OCF) on the West Bay Reserve and undertook to discover resources upon which to develop its linguistic/cultural maintenance and retrieval programs.

A review of OCF's first year of operation reveals that, in addition to language, the following activities already established on Island reserves were defined as significantly "Indian," and thus worthy of support and promotion: local pow-wows, a local Indian drum group, crafts, and the Indian Art Club at the Island's high school. The OCF's language concerns were addressed through the organization of a conference on Indian education for local chiefs, band councils, the school committees of those councils, and Indian teachers. Native people involved in Indian education were brought in from across Canada, and part of the dialogue at the conference was carried on in the local Native language.

During its first year of operation the OCF had virtually no involvement with the local elderly. The earliest programmed utilization of the elderly as resource people was in 1975, where both local and imported resource people were involved in the teaching of ritual and legends to the young people who attended the Summer Arts Program. Local elderly were involved primarily in the more mundane areas of caretaking and cooking, but medicine men from western Canada and the United States, elders in the old institutional sense of the term, were invited to introduce authentic Indian rituals, as there were no known local ritual experts.

This first recognition and utilization of elders set the scene for the development of the foundation's emphasis on the revival of traditional spiritual values and ritual, an emphasis subsequently developed into the focal aspect of the OCF's programming and operation. That development has involved not only imported elders but increasing numbers of elderly Anicinabe from Manitoulin Island and vicinity. By 1978 elderhood in the traditional sense had been revived by a few of these aged Anicinabe, although the context in which they were operating was a very different one from the former familial context. In 1978 the OCF sought funding for an Elders' Program, which continued to bring in functioning elders, not only from American Anicinabe communities but also from Sioux (South Dakota) and Cree (Saskatchewan) communities. These outside elders were located in part through the foundation's networks with the Department of Native Studies in Sudbury, other Cultural/Educational Centers across the country, and its delegates to the Indian Ecumenical Conference in Morley, Alberta.

Although approximately three-quarters of the funding for the OCF's program is derived from DIAND's Cultural/Educational Centers Program, support for the foundation's Elders' Program in 1978 was sought and obtained from various ministries of government of the Province of Ontario. By this date the OCF had more or less consolidated its position and gained acceptance among the communities it served, although in interviews some of the local aged were still expressing anxiety about the foundation's emphasis on the revival of Native religious traditions.

Staff of the foundation, under the leadership of the director of the Elders' Program, began to work slowly, with no intent to change spiritual beliefs, toward the involvement of more local elderly. The timing was good; national Indian leaders were beginning to pay lip service to the elderly as elders. Local Catholic missionaries had begun to implement an ecumenical policy, attending the Native ceremonies presented by the foundation and inviting Native spiritual leaders to attend Catholic ceremonies. The Elders' Program opened with intensive work with the few surviving local healers. The link between pragmatic and spiritual healing techniques in the traditional culture meant that these elderly medicine people invariably possessed both spiritual and herbal knowledge. The Elders' Program emphasized a mentoring relationship between healers and staff, modelled upon the traditional elders-as-transmitters-of-cultural-information role. This patterned relationship assured the cooperation of the elderly healers, who were now perceived by those they instructed as acting in traditional elder fashion.

Full realization of the strength of local elder resources made an enormous impact on the island. New understanding of the vital part that story telling had played in the transmission of Anicinabe core values encouraged midlife adults to recall and reevaluate tales their grandparents had told. Local elders passed on tales heard in their youth, a number of which dealt with places of spiritual power, thus giving a new impetus to the reviving ceremonialism. When the foundation declared in its 1978 Annual Report to DIAND that "these elders *are* the culture and with their involvement in all future projects, success is inevitable," the director and staff were affirming a commitment that has guided the OCF ever since.

Elders began to be invited to the foundation's board meetings, and since 1978 have become involved in all of the foundation's programs. Their language skills are utilized in local schools, and they have been active in the Summer Arts Programs, passing on Anicinabe traditions to the young artists. They attend the craft training workshops, where they pass on specific skills and delight in acquiring new ones. They have participated in such varied foundation activities as Medicine Man's seminar, a meeting with Ontario's Lieutenant Governor, and the 1984 Canadian Indian Bilingual Conference. They have acted as expert resources in the preparation of land claims, and for the Native Studies Department at the University of Sudbury. Elder delegates regularly attend the Indian Ecumenical Conference, and in 1983 they attended the World Assembly of First Nations in western Canada. Groups of elders have traveled to Ottawa to take training in methods of genealogical research, and to Harbor Springs, Michigan, to investigate the historical links between Michigan and Manitoulin Anicinabe. In 1983 the OCF established the Elders' Advisory Council to the foundation's board of directors, and one of the first activities of this council was to meet with Iroquoian elders from

Akwesasne (St. Regis Reserve) to arrange a formal covenant of peace and friendship between these two historically hostile Native nations.

At the more immediate level of coping with the kinds of crisis situations that triggered the move toward revitalization, women elders have worked with the foundation and local schools to arrange informal counseling of suicidal teenage girls. These elders have sought to involve the girls in activities such as quilting and cooking for public occasions, where the ladies chat and tell stories as they work. It must be emphasized that although these Manitoulin elders are beginning to again receive cultural attention, they are now operating in the entirely new context of a voluntary association, the OCF.

■ ■ ■

CONCLUSION

The situation for elderly Anicinabe has considerably improved in the last decade. Many of them are rediscovering a pattern encompassed in the institution of traditional elderhood, making it possible for them selectively to function in a more culturally significant fashion. Not all Anicinabe elderly are interested in this kind of participation, but those who are so functioning are worthy of the status of *elder*, as it has been traditionally understood in this culture. This distinction between the elderly and the elders is not, however, made by all Anicinabe. Many of the younger generation tend to view *all* elderly individuals as *elders*. The elderly themselves are generally aware of the distinction, and will articulate it if pressed. For elderly Anicinabe chronological age still is not a criterion of elderhood; rather it is the site of behaviors discussed above, and the exercise of the mandate to speak with authority that determine elder status.

Some Anicinabe elders and elderly are not involved in the revival of traditional spiritual beliefs. Many are deeply concerned with the formulation and practice of an ecumenical life way. The revitalization picture in southern Ontario is a complex one, and the movements that fall into this category of behavior are taking many forms. Significant here is the fact that most of these movements are supported to some extent through funding from various levels of government—funding that has been designated as support for Indian culture; a renewed interest in the traditional elders' role is everywhere emphasized.

The specific context of change for Canadian Indians is marked by the large proportion of their young population, by government support for multiculturalism extending to the support of Indian culture, and by the resulting emphasis upon the maintenance of Indian identity. In this context the elderly have come to be perceived as making a major contribution to the maintenance of Indian identity; they help to formulate that identity and they are its validators, insofar as they have themselves had validating youthful experiences with traditional elderhood.

Whether the institution of elderhood in its contemporary expression will survive the loss of today's elders with these validating experiences and the inevitable aging of the Native population that must accompany the progress through life of today's young population, is problematic. If elderhood can bridge the gap between tradition and change in a model similar to the dual patterning of the Anicinabe elders' narratives, it may remain a vital institution. Certainly more and more elderly Indians are having significant and valuable experiences in modernizing situations involving the move to urban life and coping with alcohol and drug addiction, as well as with the welfare, health, and educational systems (Vanderburgh, 1977; 1982). Some Anicinabe elders are already using such experiences as the basis of their anecdotal narratives. As long as the information that elders transmit remains vital to the context of survival, elderhood should endure as a viable institution.

ACKNOWLEDGEMENTS

The research upon which this paper is based was supported by the Canada Council (Grant S74-0105, 1974–75) and the Social Sciences and Humanities Research Council of Canada, Population Aging Programme (grant 492-82-0010, 1982–83). Erindale College, University of Toronto, has provided ongoing support in the form of travel grants. In addition, I am indebted to Gelya Frank for certain insights into the bases of the elders' mandate to speak with authority.

REFERENCES

Densmore, F. (1929). *Chippewa Customs*. Smithsonian Institution, Bureau of American Ethnology, *Bulletin 86*. Washington.

Dunning, R.W. (1959). *Social and Economic Change among the Northern Ojibwa*. Toronto: University of Toronto Press.

Hallowell, A.I. (1964). Ojibwa Ontology, Behavior, and World View. In S. Diamond, ed., *Primitive Views of the World*. New York: Columbia University Press.

Jenness, D. (1935). *The Ojibwa Indians of Parry Sound: Their Social and Religious Life*. National Museum of Canada Bulletin 78, Anthropological Series 17.

Vanderburgh, R.M. (1977). *I Am Nokomis, Too: The Biography of Verna Patronella Johnston*. Don Mills, Ont.: General Publishing.

Vanderburgh, R.M. (1982). When Legends Fall Silent Our Ways Are Lost: Some Dimensions of the Study of Aging among Native Canadians. *Culture, 2*, 21–28.

6

Old Order Mennonites Provide Support While at the Same Time Preserving the Independence of Their Elderly

John B. Bond, Jr.

Two of the most significant changes of the twentieth century have been an increase in average age of death and an increase in life expectancy from birth.

In 1921 the average age of death of Canadian men was 39 years, while for women it was 41. Sixty years later, these ages had increased to 69.7 years for men and 75.8 years for women. Similarly, life expectancies at birth increased from 60 years (1931) to 71.9 years (1981) for men, and from 62.1 years (1931) to 79 years (1981) for women. These dramatic shifts can be attributed to control of many diseases which cause death in childhood, as well as treatment of a variety of causes of death of the elderly (pneumonia, chronic heart conditions, better medical care for accident victims, etc.).

These changes, however, have caused significant alterations in family life. While families have fewer childhood deaths to confront, the care of elderly family members is now a concern. Earlier in the century, there were few frail older people in society; widowhood occurred at an earlier age, at a healthier time of life, and lasted for fewer years. Children generally did not have very old parents, let alone elderly grandparents. Now, there are significant numbers of older family members, who may live for decades following retirement from the work force and departure of children from the home.

Given these changes, those in the middle years of life have been called the "new pioneers": there has never before been a time when the middle-aged have had significant responsibilities to their elderly parents as well as their children. There are no models of how families can best provide care to

---

Reprinted with permission of the *Mennonite Mirror*, November 1988.

their older members. Each life experience with an older parent seems to be unique.

With these factors in mind, for the last several years Carol Harvey and I have been examining patterns of family life and the elderly in rural communities, first in Manitoba, and now in Ontario on a more restricted basis. We believe that family ties may be more cohesive and stable in rural areas than in urban settings where social and medical services are usually more available.

Of additional interest has been an examination of the family lives of Mennonites for whom strong family linkages have been a concern throughout history. We think that by comparing Mennonite with non-Mennonite families, much can be learned about successful intergenerational relations, and how family interactions can be improved. We have been extremely fortunate that the Social Sciences and Humanities Research Council of Canada (SSHRC) and the Centre on Aging, University of Manitoba, have financially supported the projects. Most important, however, has been the willingness of hundreds of family members to share their views with us. During the past two years, we have collected interviews from almost 200 parents over the age of 65, and have received responses to our questionnaires from more than 650 middle-aged offspring.

Most of the data we have collected are still being analyzed, using fairly complex statistical procedures. I can, however, offer some of my observations on the family life of Old Order Mennonites as it relates to the elderly. The nine families who shared their insights live near Kitchener-Waterloo, Ontario. They were not randomly selected, but volunteer participants, so my observations may not represent all Old Order families. But I believe that these families honestly and openly presented their lives, and to that extent, we can all profit. All of the parents who were interviewed were males; they ranged in age from 67 to 89. Two parents were widowed, for almost 20 years, and all but one had at least one living sibling. The numbers of living children ranged from two to 11.

The communities in which the interviewees live are a few kilometers from a moderately sized city. All of the Old Order Mennonites we contacted live on family farms, each approximately 100 acres in size. The farms generally produce a number of crops, as well as maintaining some livestock. The homes and farm operations are usually non-electrified, with the exception of those who need refrigeration for milk from dairy cattle. In some instances tractors are used, while horse-drawn plows are also common. There are no telephones on home or farm premises. Local transportation is typically by horse and buggy.

Two significant characteristics of the lives of the parental generation are continuity and independence. These themes can be seen in the home, marital, financial, work and spiritual aspects of life.

On the first day that I was to meet a member of the community, to determine whether my research project would be welcomed, I drove to his home and faced a house with what appeared to be two main entrances. In fact, the house contained two separate homes, one for the son and one for the parents (the *doddy* house). After subsequent visits to a number of homes, I observed that in some situations there is an inner passage between the two homes, while in others no passageway exists. The houses are completely self-contained, with no common areas. The homes can be described as side-by-side, but the lives of the families are independent. One elderly mother said that, even though she and her son lived in adjacent homes, she only saw her son once or twice a week during winter. The ability to maintain a separate household, although having family nearby, is a consistent concern of many elderly in North America. Governments are now realizing that the maintenance of older persons in their own home environments is cost-effective and psychologically beneficial to the older person.

RELIANCE NETWORK

A second example of continuity and independence is the reliance on the lifetime marital partner, rather than adult children, to meet the tasks of daily life. It was not uncommon for an older husband to continue to rely upon his wife for meals, although a daughter-in-law lived next door, who could easily set another couple of places at meal time. Keep in mind that the stoves might be wood burning and the pots and pans cast iron. Some modernization has taken place, and propane stoves are accepted by some. Similarly, the elderly wife relies upon her husband for the maintenance of the home, care of the horse and carriage, assistance with canning of food, and other household chores. At the same time, should strength and abilities fail, younger family members step in and provide whatever is needed, careful not to infringe upon the independence of the older parents.

The financial arrangements established between the generations to maintain economic independence of the elderly caught my attention. As a cautionary note, only three families discussed their financial arrangements, so the generalizability of their comments is suspect; the specifics are noteworthy, in any event. When an older father is ready to "retire" from the farm, and subsequently move to the *doddy* house, he sells the farm and the current family house to the youngest son. ("Why the youngest son?" I asked. At the time the eldest son is ready to establish his own farm, the father is typically in his 40s and not ready to leave farming for the next 40 years. So, the father assists all but the youngest son in relocating to another farm.) As the youngest son is not in a financial position to buy the farm outright, the father provides the mortgage, approximating current interest rates, with the son repaying over time; this provides a consistent source of income to the parental generation. The fair market price of the farm is established by an independent assessor. In one case, the father stated that, as part of the land transfer, he and his wife are entitled to unlimited farm crops for personal consumption, and he pays his son a fixed sum each year for meat. The fathers help other sons in the financing of their farms. They repay the fathers over time, thus contributing to later life income.

In addition to the consistent income from the sale of the farm, most of the older fathers still earn an income. One repairs harnesses and horse collars, another assists his wife in production and marketing of cheese, a third is a wood-worker, and a fourth serves as a broker for the community in purchasing horses for the carriages, receiving only a nominal fee for his help. It was clear to me that the income received is far less important than the desire to be a productive member of the community. One gentleman shared his financial "books" with me, which indicated that he earns less than $1 per hour for his work; but it is important to him that he still has a work role, rather than just being an inactive burden on the community.

Faith in God is fundamental to the activities of the older parents as well as their children. Daily prayer and Bible reading are the norm. The religious beliefs and practices are not newly found, as the end of life approaches, but have been consistently verified by a lifetime of experiences. The willingness to do God's work while on this earth is a theme that I heard time and again. Their faith provides a strength to withstand cultural pressures for change in their lifestyle, a tolerance of people different from themselves, and an acceptance of their own frailties.

Given the desires of the parents to remain independent for as long as possible, it would seem that there is little for the middle-aged offspring to provide their parents. This was reflected in the responses to the questionnaires which they returned. Generally, little help is given on a consistent basis for lengthy periods of time. It is not, however, because they are unwilling to give, but because the parents are not viewed by either generation as needing significant help. When the help is needed, however, it is easily forthcoming. Responses to the question "What do you feel is the most important service or support you provide for your parent?" included: "provide a home alongside our family; share and care; care when ill or sick"; "living side by side"; "companionship"; "just being there when they need us."

The motivation to provide care to older parents is simply ascribed to God's instruction to honour one's father and mother, the Golden Rule, or Jesus' love for us all. A more extensive response was provided by one son: "When I was a child, my parents took care of me, and saw to my needs, emotionally as well as others. Now when they are older, it is the turn of the child to help. Where there is mutual love, this is easy; but even where this is lacking, it is a Christian duty to take care of our older people."

As all of the older participants in this study were fairly healthy and independent, our results do not reflect what happens as the older person loses his or her health, and needs substantial care. I was told of a variety of family settings where extensive support was provided by the family. In one instance, the widowed mother was incontinent, and appeared to have reached a stage of Alzheimer's disease which included continual wandering and periods of violence. The family had organized such that, for each day of the week, a different family member was responsible to move into the *doddy* house and care for the older mother. The family size was sufficiently large and nearby that this placed no undue strain on any individual family member. In instances where the family can no longer provide the needed care, a home has been established by some Old Order women to receive the elderly. In cases where hospitalization is needed, the individual must pay for the services, as the Old Order Mennonites are not participants in the Ontario Health Insurance Plan (OHIP). The individual, family and church community collectively pay for the needed medical costs.

It can be seen that the family lives of Old Order Mennonites foster the independence and self-sufficiency of nuclear families. This can be seen in the domestic and economic roles of the families. As health and abilities become problematic, extended family members dutifully provide support to the extent that it is needed. Intergenerational interdependence, maintaining autonomy wherever possible, is the goal. It is only when the family and spiritual community are unable to provide support that assistance is sought from the larger society. Throughout these changes, faith and the desire to do God's work pervade.

The Ethnic Elderly in a Dominant Culture Long-Term Care Facility

Michael J. MacLean and Rita Bonar

INTRODUCTION

It has recently been suggested that micro-scale research with respect to ethnicity and aging in the western world primarily relates to community studies and the development of age-stratified subcultures (Holzberg, 1982). This research has used various anthropological techniques such as participant observation, life history interviews, questionnaire surveys, and interview schedules in such settings as old-age homes (Ross, 1974; Hendel-Sebestyen, 1979), senior centres (Myeroff, 1978), and hospitals for the aged (Holzberg, 1979). These studies have tended to document how the ethnic elderly cope with issues of aging in an organized setting within a community.

Much of this research tends to focus on one ethnic group in one setting. For example, Ross's (1977) excellent participant observation study entitled *Old People, New Lives* focussed on how a particular group of French people adapted to living in a retirement residence in France. Myeroff's (1978) well-known research entitled *Number Our Days* looked at how Jewish elderly addressed issues of aging in a Jewish Senior Citizen Centre in Southern California. Holzberg (1979) did an anthropological study of Jewish elderly in a highly regarded home and hospital for this ethnic group in Toronto. And Hendel-Sebestyen (1979) looked at the elderly in a Jewish Home for the Aged in New York State. These micro-level studies contribute significantly to our knowledge about how the elderly from specific ethnic groups deal with socio-cultural issues of aging. That is, from the research of Myeroff (1978), Holzberg (1979) and Hendel-Sebestyen (1979) we have gained considerable insight into how the Jewish elderly deal with aspects of aging in different

Reprinted with permission from *Canadian Ethnic Studies/Etudes ethniques au Canada*, Vol. XV, No. 3 (1983), 51–59. This is a substantially edited version of the original article.

settings. From Ross's (1974, 1977) research, we know a great deal about how the French organize their lives in a French retirement residence.

While it is very important to study the ethnic elderly in homogeneous settings, this research does not consider another issue in ethnicity and aging that is highly significant for a multi-cultural society such as Canada or the United States. This issue is related to the way ethnic elderly people adjust to institutions that are primarily for the dominant culture. For example, there are many long-term-care facilities in Canada that are organized and administered for the dominant English-Canadian or French-Canadian population that would make up the majority of the residents. A significant question, in terms of research and practice, is how would an elderly person from one ethnic group adapt to living his/her few years in an institution that is organized for another cultural group? For example, how would an elderly Chinese woman cope with being in a hospital or home for the aged of an English-Canadian population? Or how would an elderly German deal with aspects of aging in a French-Canadian nursing home? And what about elderly individuals from many different ethnic groups who are in a long-term care facility of the dominant culture? That is, how would a small number of elderly men or women from Germany, France, Russia, Poland and Italy relate to being in an English-Canadian institution for the aged?

There are several research and practice issues about ethnicity and aging that evolve from the situation of having elderly people from many different ethnic backgrounds in a long-term care facility for the aged. Some of these issues relate directly to the relationship between the staff and the residents of such a facility. Other issues evolve from the relationship between the staff of the institution and the family of the elderly ethnic person. Still other issues deal with the relationship between the staff and the ethnic community of the elderly person.

The purpose of this paper is to discuss some of the issues involving the institutionalized ethnic elderly in a dominant culture long-term care facility. This discussion will be followed by a case study approach (Campbell, 1982) of some elderly ethnic individuals in an English-Canadian nursing home and chronic care hospital for the aged in Montreal to show how some of these issues have been manifested and considered within this facility. The intent of this paper is to suggest that there are many idiosyncratic aspects of aging among different ethnic groups in such a setting that must be addressed by researchers and practitioners in order to develop a comfortable and supportive atmosphere for elderly ethnic individuals in long-term care.

ISSUES INVOLVING INSTITUTIONALIZED ETHNIC ELDERLY

Research has shown that the relocation of any elderly person into a long-term care facility has the potential to produce negative institutional effects (Brody, 1977; Lieberman and Tobin, 1976). The strangeness of the new environment and the loss of familiar support systems at a time when the elderly person's personal resources are low often influences his/her mental health. The elderly person is faced with a substantial reorganization of his/her life under circumstances of great stress which require considerable adjustment and coping. Therefore, any elderly individual entering a long-term care facility such as a nursing home or a hospital for the aged needs much support from all those involved in the institutional process—the person's family, his/her community of friends and relatives, and the staff and administration of the institution.

This support is even more critical for an elderly person entering a long-term care facility of another ethnic group. In addition to all the issues that the elderly person from the dominant culture experiences on entering a nursing home or hospital for the aged, the elderly ethnic person faces several challenges as a result of being a minority group member in such an institution. The special problems the elderly ethnic person would meet in such a setting would probably make it even more difficult for him/her to adapt to institutional living.

The three main difficulties that an elderly ethnic person would face on entering an institution of the dominant culture would be loss of family, loss of culture, and loss of community. For those elderly people who have family, the loss of interaction with this group has different and possibly more profound implications than this loss has for older people from the dominant culture. For those elderly ethnic people who do not have a nuclear or an extended family, the loss of culture and community is undoubtedly more significant than for the elderly residents of an institution based on their cultural heritage.

LOSS OF FAMILY

One of the main social psychological needs for any elderly person is the need for respect and intimacy. For the elderly ethnic individual, this need is most often provided by the immediate and extended family (Markson, 1979). The manifestation of this need is primarily shown by the family taking care of the elderly person in old age. This usually means providing care for the elderly person's physical needs. However, in recent years the nuclear family of the ethnic elderly in North America has experienced new economic and social pressures which have had an effect on the resources it is able to devote to caring for its elderly members. For example, there has been a greater emphasis for the women in ethnic families to find employment outside the home in order to contribute financially to the family. Consequently, there are fewer women in ethnic families available to care for the needs of the elderly members of that family. Therefore, when the needs of the elderly ethnic person exceed the resources of the family, the elderly person may have to be placed in an institution. This could lead the elderly ethnic person to develop feelings of isolation, rejection, dishonour, and disrespect with regard to his/her family. Since most ethnic groups tend not to institutionalize their elderly members, there is a considerable amount of shame experienced by the elderly ethnic individual who has been institutionalized by the family.

Another pressure impinging on many ethnic communities which has considerable significance for elderly members of these communities is a generational shift in ethnic saturation (Kastenbaum, 1979). This means that there is a tendency for each succeeding generation to appear less ethnic in thought and behaviour than its predecessors. This may lead to the younger generation not having the same commitment to caring for elderly people as the elderly anticipate. For example, Lopata's (1976) analysis suggests that some elderly Polish-Americans are quite resentful toward their children who often fail to accord them the respect they feel they deserve. This generational shift could contribute to the institutionalization of some elderly ethnic people who feel they should be cared for at home by their family. This institutionalization would also lead to a sense of dishonour and loss of family respect by the elderly ethnic individual.

In conclusion, the elderly ethnic individual is likely to experience a great sense of family loss by being institutionalized. This loss is probably more severe (and, therefore, more difficult to adjust to) than that experienced by other elderly people who have socialized their children to lead relatively independent lives. Thus, when an elderly ethnic person enters a long-term care facility, he/she undoubtedly has to cope with feelings of shame, disrespect, and dishonour as well as the normal feelings of anxiety related to the institutionalization process.

LOSS OF CULTURE

Elderly ethnic individuals entering a long-term care facility of the dominant culture also tend to suffer a loss of their culture. In such an institutional setting, their daily existence is, more than at any previous time, linked with and organized by a different culture. There is the loss of familiar and favourite foods or drink. There is also the loss of favourite songs, literature, newspapers, and folklore. These losses contribute to a sense of great isolation for the elderly ethnic person because he/she cannot take part in many of the cultural aspects of life that have been significant for so long.

Another major loss for the elderly ethnic person in a long-term care facility of the dominant culture is loss of the ability to communicate in his/her own language. As a result, the exchange of information with staff is limited. Furthermore, there is considerable potential for misunderstanding as patient and staff may misinterpret each others' mannerisms or tone of voice. This inability to communicate in one's own language also contributes to the elderly ethnic individual becoming more and more passive and dependent.

This passive and dependent behaviour is a disadvantage for the elderly person as often his/her physical and mental condition deteriorates as a result. This may lead to the need for further physical or mental status tests which, when conducted in a language other than the person's own, may result in a misdiagnosis regarding the level of competency of the individual. This problem of communication is even more pronounced when the elderly ethnic person is chronically ill and has to rely greatly on the staff. Often, in these cases, the needs of the elderly person are met through non-verbal communication. This adds a dehumanizing element to the interaction with the old person at a time when he/she needs as much support as possible. Their frustrations are often expressed by acting-out behaviours such as constant verbal expression of sounds, complete withdrawal, or the loss of the will to live.

Thus, the elderly ethnic individual in an institution established for people of the mainstream is bound to experience a tremendous loss of culture at a time when the older person is least able to cope with this loss. Kastenbaum (1979), who refers to this as a "fade-out of ethnicity," suggests that the loss of an individual's culture has particularly serious implications for older people when he explains that

> . . .*when the old person becomes institutionalized, then there may be significant environmental forces that operate to reduce the expression and utilization of ethnically-derived resources and the subsequent dying process may be accompanied by even further reductions . . . when this pattern does exist, there is an apparent fade out of ethnicity just when the individual needs whatever strength he or she can muster from every personally relevant source (p. 86).*

LOSS OF COMMUNITY

Elderly ethnic people who are institutionalized in a long-term care facility of another culture also suffer a loss of community. The sense of community is naturally related to the culture of the ethnic group. However, there are enough differences to make the loss of community significant for the elderly ethnic person. For example, Guttman (1979) suggests that positive aspects of living for older ethnic individuals are directly related to the support system provided by the close and strong interaction among members of that ethnic group. Markson (1979) argues that the community also provides a sense of care and respect for the older ethnic individual. The elderly person loses this upon entering an institution of the dominant culture because he/she, in fact, is entering another community. In addition to the rules and behaviours being different in this new community, the people are also different. That is, there is little or no opportunity to interact with people from one's own ethnic group. There is nobody who knows the rules, the political history, the religious traditions, or the community values. There is little opportunity to form any kind of ethnic community due to the varied population, the nature of the particular institution, or the physical and mental limitations of the residents. An elderly person who is physically able and alert can try to mingle or he/she can link up with others in a similar situation to form a group composed of people from different ethnic backgrounds. However, this is not an ethnic community in the true sense of the word.

It appears that the elderly ethnic individual who is in the minority in a long-term care facility certainly runs the risk of losing a sense of community. Markson (1979) has noted the following consequence of institutionalizing ethnic elderly:

> *Few personal relationships based on common ethnic background arose, perhaps because of personal feelings of alienation and despair, perhaps because no effort was made to group people of common ethnicities together (p. 353).*

It is not surprising that a sense of an ethnic community tends not to develop in a long-term care facility. It is difficult to develop new relationships at an advanced age in a foreign environment when physical, social and emotional resources are low. This would tend to lead to the elderly ethnic person developing an even greater sense of isolation and rejection. As a consequence, the elderly person may become hopelessly convinced that there is no one who can offer him/her familiar help at a time when such help may be needed more than it ever has been.

CASE STUDIES OF ELDERLY ETHNIC INDIVIDUALS IN AN ENGLISH-CANADIAN LONG-TERM CARE FACILITY

In order to consider some of these issues for elderly ethnic people in reality rather than simply in theory, this part of the paper will look at case studies of three elderly people of different ethnic groups in Montreal Extended Care Centre (M.E.C.C.). These case studies have been selected to show aspects of loss of family, loss of culture, and loss of community for elderly ethnic people living in an English-Canadian long-term care facility. However, before these case studies are presented, some background on M.E.C.C. will be provided.

M.E.C.C. is an English-Canadian long-term care facility in the east end of Montreal. It consists of both a nursing home and a chronic care hospital for the elderly. There are 280 elderly individuals in the institution and approximately one-third were born in non-English speaking countries such as Austria, Belgium, China, Czechoslovakia, Estonia, France, Germany, Greece, Holland, Hungary, Israel, Italy, Lithuania, Poland, Romania, Russia, Ukraine and Yugoslavia. The other residents are English speaking people born in Canada, England, Ireland, Scotland or the United States. Most of the ethnic elderly have difficulty communicating in English. A majority of the elderly ethnic individuals are women; the men tend to be widowers or bachelors. Most of these residents do not have extended families in Montreal.

Mrs. A.: Loss of Family

Mrs. A., an 84 year old Italian woman, was referred to M.E.C.C. partially because of her physical deterioration and partly because her children were becoming tired of her domineering disposition. The children described her as being a very demanding and manipulating woman who tried to control them and her husband by guilt. When the children referred Mrs. A. to M.E.C.C. they put tremendous pressure on the staff of the institution to admit her to the chronic care hospital rather than to the nursing home. Since Mrs. A.'s health did not require admission to chronic care, it was explained to her children that she would be admitted to the nursing home. However, due to the great negative stigma in the Italian community of placing one's mother in an institution, the family continued to insist on putting Mrs. A. into the hospital section of M.E.C.C. Since Mrs. A. did need some medical and nursing attention, she was therefore admitted to the chronic care hospital of M.E.C.C.

Mrs. A.'s illness was treated and she recovered immediately—thereby becoming a candidate for the nursing home. Again, considerable opposition about this decision came from the family. They complained strongly; they listed several physical limitations their mother still had; and they totally disregarded the opinions of the professionals at the M.E.C.C. who were caring for Mrs. A. Since Mrs. A. could not continue to stay in the chronic care hospital with her relatively good health, the family was given the ultimatum that she be transferred to the nursing home or that she be discharged to their care. Under duress, the family then agreed to allow Mrs. A. to be transferred to the nursing home. However, the decision still remained very difficult for the family to accept and it was evident that they "blamed" her for getting better.

Mrs. A. felt greatly abandoned by her children. They had originally explained to her that the reason she was placed in an institution was because she needed hospital care. She could accept this but when she was transferred to the nursing home rather than being discharged home, she felt rejected. The family continued to be as supportive as possible by visiting her and by including her in family excursions on the week-ends. However, she remained convinced that her children had brought dishonour upon her. She knew of no other Italian family who had institutionalized their mother. She felt she had sacrificed her life for her family and in her hour of need, they had abandoned her. She felt helpless and hopeless. She died within a few months of the transfer to the nursing home.

Mr. B.: Loss of Culture

Mr. B. was an 82 year old Chinese man who was born in China but who had lived in Montreal's Chinatown for 45 years. He did not have any nuclear or extended family but he was well-rooted in his ethnic culture, traditions, and values. He had adjusted relatively well to Montreal because of the familiar support systems within the Chinese culture in the city. Mr. B. spoke only Chinese, was very hard of hearing, and had limited vision. Because of his deteriorating health, he required a chronic-care placement. The Montreal Chinese Hospital was not able to accommodate him and, therefore, he was admitted to the hospital section of M.E.C.C.

The stress of relocating to this foreign environment was experienced as a culture shock by Mr. B. He was not able to communicate with anyone at M.E.C.C. He also refused to eat any food served to him and indicated that he wanted to eat only Chinese food. Because of his refusal to eat and his inability to communicate, his physical and mental condition deteriorated rapidly within the first month of his admission. It became quite apparent that his culture seemed to adopt even greater significance to him as his health deteriorated. He seemed disoriented and confused and he acted as if he had lost his will to live. He responded by withdrawing from interaction with others. A referral was made to the Chinese community to provide him with a source of support and assistance in the expression of his needs. The volunteers from the Chinese Community Service Centre tried to communicate with Mr. B. After considerable effort to get him to talk, they realized his hearing was so poor that he could not understand what they were saying. One volunteer began writing to him in Chinese and from then on some progress was made in terms of his eating and communicating. However, Mr. B. continued to manifest signs of anxiety and depression related to being institutionalized in a foreign environment. He died within two months of his admission date.

Mr. C.: Loss of Community

Mr. C. is a 93 year old Greek widower who has been a resident of the nursing home at M.E.C.C. for approximately twelve years. Mr. C. was born in Greece but he was brought to Canada by his children twenty years ago after the death of his wife. He has several children, grand-children and great-grand-children in Montreal. Mr. C. was admitted to M.E.C.C.'s nursing home because of failing vision and extensive physical handicaps which made it impossible for his family to care for him.

Since his institutionalization, he has had very little contact with his family or the Greek community of Montreal. He spends most of his time in bed, seems to feel that he is not much use to anyone, and tends to be dependent on the staff for most of his physical and social needs. This is probably mainly due to the language barrier that exists between him and the other patients. In short, Mr. C. has very little contact with anyone in the institution.

However, during the past year, Mr. C. has been befriended by a member of the auxiliary staff who is also Greek. She volunteered some extra time to listen to him and to do instrumental tasks for him. During the process, she became aware of his personal circumstances. She became outraged that Mr. C. seemed to have been abandoned by his family and by the Greek community of Montreal. Her anger led her to telephone a popular Greek radio talk show where she identified the individual and his family and expressed her opinion on this kind of behaviour of the Greek community toward one of its older people. This telephone call immediately mobilized Mr. C.'s family to visit him in order to make amends with him and to restore their status within the Greek community. Furthermore, the Greek community felt a sense of responsibility toward Mr. C. and several Greek volunteers now visit him on a regular basis. This has allowed Mr. C. to become re-involved with his family and his community to the extent that his social well-being is considerably improved.

These three case studies show some of the dilemmas and difficulties that the elderly ethnic individual has to cope with when he/she enters a long-term care facility which is organized for the dominant culture. The sense of loss related to family, culture, and community that the ethnic elderly seem to experience appears to be more complicated than that which is felt by other people entering long-term care. This sense of loss may contribute to deterioration in physical and mental well-being for many of these elderly ethnic people in such an institution.

IMPLICATIONS FOR RESEARCH AND PRACTICE

Several points evolving from this paper have implications for research and practice with elderly ethnic people who are in a long-term care facility of the dominant culture. This section of the paper will report briefly on two of these implications—one for research and one for practice.

If the sense of loss for elderly ethnic individuals in a long-term care facility of the dominant culture is more complicated, or greater, than that for the elderly of that culture, their physical and mental deterioration may be accelerated. That is, elderly ethnic individuals in such an institution may experience declining physical and mental health at a faster rate and have greater mortality rates than elderly people of the dominant culture. This research question could be investigated by comparing morbidity rates, mental status, and mortality rates of the elderly ethnic population who enter a long-term care facility of the dominant culture in a given time period with those rates of the elderly of that culture who enter the institution. By controlling for sex differences, health characteristics, mental status differences and family characteristics, we could isolate the variable of ethnicity to determine if there are ethnic differences on these three issues for the two groups of elderly people in a long-term care facility.

An implication for work with elderly ethnic individuals in a long-term care facility of the dominant culture is that the use of volunteers from different ethnic groups could improve the quality of life for these individuals in such an institution. Volunteers from the ethnic community of the individual could perform many valuable services which the staff of the institution would not have the ability to do. These services could be as simple as talking to the elderly ethnic individual in his/her own language or as complicated as acting in an advocacy role for the individual.

The implementation of these suggestions would sensitize the social service and health care professions to the particular stresses that elderly ethnic individuals face in entering a long-term care facility of the dominant culture. The result of this sensitization would probably lead to further research and practice innovations which would contribute to an improved quality of life for the institutionalized ethnic elderly in a long-term care facility of the dominant culture.

REFERENCES

Brody, E.M. *Long Term Care of Older People.* New York: Human Sciences Press, 1977.

Campbell, J. "Comment: A Time to Return to Cases." *The Gerontologist,* 1982, 22, 3, 244–248.

Guttman, D. "Use of Informal and Formal Supports by White Ethnic Aged." In D. Gelfand and A. Kutzik (eds.), *Ethnicity and Aging: Theory, Research and Policy.* New York: Springer Publishing Co., 1979.

Hendel-Sebestyen, G. "Role Diversity: Toward the Development of Community in a Total Institutional Setting." *Anthropological Quarterly,* 1979, 52, 19–28.

Holzberg, C. "Ethnicity and Aging: Anthropological Perspectives on More than Just the Minority Elderly." *The Gerontologist,* 1982, 22, 3, 249–257.

Holzberg, C. "Anthropology, Life Histories, and the Aged: The Toronto Baycrest Center." *International Journal of Aging and Human Development.* In press, 1983.

Kastenbaum, R. "Reflections on Old Age, Ethnicity, and Death." In D. Gelfand and A. Kutzik (eds.), *Ethnicity and Aging: Theory, Research, and Policy.* New York: Springer Publishing Co., 1979.

Lieberman, M.A. and Tobin, S. *Last Home for the Aged.* San Francisco: Jossey-Bass, 1976.

Lopata, H. *Polish-Americans.* Englewood Cliffs, N.J.: Prentice-Hall, 1976.

Markson, E. "Ethnicity as a Factor in the Institutionalization of the Ethnic Elderly." In D. Gelfand and A. Kutzik (eds.), *Ethnicity and Aging: Theory, Research and Policy.* New York: Springer Publishing Co., 1979.

Myeroff, B. "Aging and the Aged in Other Cultures: An Anthropological Perspective." In F.E. Bauwens (ed.), *The Anthropology of Death.* St. Louis: C.V. Mosby, 1978.

Myeroff, B. *Number Our Days.* New York: E.P. Dutton, 1978.

Ross, J.K. "Learning to be Retired: Socialization into a French Retirement Residence." *Journal of Gerontology,* 1974, 29, 211–223.

Ross, J.K. *Old People, New Lives: Community Creation in a Retirement Residence.* Chicago: University of Chicago Press, 1977.

8

Socialization and Cultural Duality Among Aging Japanese Canadians

Pamela Sugiman and H.K. Nishio

...

TRADITIONAL JAPANESE VALUES

The idea that the Japanese Canadian elderly will be taken care of by younger generations can be traced to the value system of traditional Japan, which had many specific norms about age and the elderly. At the level of an individual, Japanese traditional values taught loyalty and diligence. At the level of family, filial piety was much emphasized requiring from each individual an undivided, selfless dedication to parental needs and care as the most fundamental obligation of children.

With this familism, aging was perceived as a blessing—"a period in life when . . . (one) could sit back and enjoy the fruits of his labor while the members of his family sought his advice on important issues and in making decisions" (Kalish and Moriwaki, 1973:201).

Also associated with the concept of filial piety are certain behavioral codes such as self-limitation, moderation and *enryo* modesty. Reserve, reticence, self-effacement, deference, humility, hesitation and denigration of one's self and possessions make up the norm of *enryo*. *Gaman* or forbearance, for instance, signifies the tendency to suppress emotions, which is the ability to keep calm and carry out duties in the face of frustrating circumstances; it also connotes that one should suffer in silence with much forbearance (Kobata, 1979:100).

Another code of ethics, which is closely linked with filial piety, is the notion of *haji* or shame. The concept of *haji* was still widely practiced in postwar Japan. The Japanese stress exemplary conduct at all times, so as not to

Reprinted with permission from *Canadian Ethnic Studies/Etudes ethniques au Canada*, Vol. XV, No. 3 (1983), 17–35. This material is a substantially edited version of the original article.

bring disgrace or shame upon one's family. This is a practice which serves as a very effective social control mechanism for family members (Kobata, 1979:1000).

The ethical foundation of filial piety rests on the feeling of *kansha* or gratitude. *Kansha* may be interpreted to mean a sense of the enormous dependence of the self upon the human, natural, and supernatural worlds, including one's ancestors. However, this concept is generally applied to some concrete, particular object(s) and not necessarily to an abstract concept such as humanity, God or universe. This *kansha* concept reinforces a feeling of gratitude for whatever comes one's way (Kiefer, 1974:169). This concept, incidentally, is very much related to "giri" (duty). *Giri* involves knowing what is expected of a person, and fulfilling such obligations to the best of one's ability (Kiefer, 1974:169). It is with the feeling of *kansha* (gratitude) that a person is expected to fulfill obligations and responsibilities to others. Different from Christian love and asceticism, these concepts which have been explained here are addressed to identifiable social groups, particular individuals and a certain community. In that sense, they represent the Japanese social ethic regulating the fabric of social interactions and relationships.

Such norms are found in the traditional Japanese value system which has been transmitted from one generation to another through socialization. In this value system, the two dominant objects are (1) to maintain group harmony and (2) to stress the primacy of the group, especially the family.

Seen in this way, the Japanese values are, as Kiefer puts it, "eco-centric" rather than "ego-centric"; self-esteem is based not on individual self-worth, but on group worth and the formation of close human bonds (Trela and Sokolovsky, 1979:126). Thus, the Japanese place extreme emphasis on the maintenance of "equanimity and harmony." Because of this, the normative system shunned a deliberate disruption of natural group processes, for such a disruption would be considered foolish.

Both psychological and material security are to be achieved through the cultivation of mutually binding relationships, rather than through the competitive pursuit of abstract ends. The traditional family was based on clearly defined roles, duties and expectations. The intertwining of these norms and values made for a situation in which the elderly Japanese experienced little if any guilt for being dependent and even expected to depend upon and live with their own children.

SOCIALIZATION OF TRADITIONAL JAPANESE VALUES

The *Issei* (first generation) Japanese who were born and raised in Meiji Japan were quite familiar with these norms. Indeed, they sought to protect themselves from the demands of the new and strange ways of life in North America by re-creating that which was familiar to them and by isolating themselves from the new society. Ethnic solidarity subsequently emerged and the Japanese community structure developed. However, the *Issei* Japanese immigrants had social adaptation as a definite goal. When asked, the *Issei* supported the idea that, "The best thing for the Japanese Americans to do is to associate with more Caucasians and identify themselves completely as Americans" (Masuda, 1970:203). It is interesting to note that the *Nisei* (second generation) and *Sansei* (third generation) were neutral on this particular question. At any rate, the *Issei's* dream about "Americanization" appears to have been transmitted to their children. Perhaps, because of this attitude toward acculturation, the Issei made only modest demands on their children to fulfill filial obligations and did not stress the use of the Japanese language at home.

Language retention normally has a very important implication for socialization; it is the indispensable means of communication and cultural transmission. One study indicates that only 15.6% of the *Nisei* could speak it fluently while 85.1% of the *Issei* relied on Japanese to communicate—a generational loss of 70 points. Kitano has also noted this loss of language: some who had attended the Japanese language school for as long as ten years were still unable to speak Japanese with any degree of fluency (Kitano, 1969:25).

The above seems to indicate that the *Issei,* though they themselves adhered to the Japanese traditional values, very much wished their children to become fully acculturated within the North American value system. This, they thought, would ensure their children's future success. Indeed, it is interesting to note that language retention also failed in Brazil among the Japanese immigrants, perhaps for the same reason. There is one common ground which both the Japanese traditional values and the North American values share, that is, socialization for achievement (De Vos, 1973: 239–240; Caudill, W. 1952; Peterson, 1971).

In the following, our *Nisei* respondents explained how they were raised and what factors influenced their attitudes about old age and dependency of the aged. Their perceptual judgement seems to reflect, as we shall see, their basic cultural ambivalence and duality but they have succeeded in formulating a workable synthesis of independence/dependence as a means of reconciling the outside social forces with Japanese values promoting family integration.

When asked about the instillation of norms about respect for elders during their childhoods, Nisei respondents spoke mainly in terms of generalities—the single most popular response being variants of the line, "I learned to respect elders."

One respondent stated,

> *I was taught to respect the elderly, show loving kindness, compassion, and much patience (when they are slow in speech or hard of hearing, repeating stories over and over . . .)*

Another remarked,

I was brought up with the belief to look after aged parents.

Yet another,

Respect your elders. Provide for your parents when in need such as taking care of them when they are unable to do so.

And,

Usually the eldest (married) son lived with parents—taking care of them and respecting their advanced years. Always offer a helping hand to the aged and also listening to their wise advices (and experiences).

One may argue that Westerners would make similar claims; however, many of the *Nisei* indicated that there were distinct differences between traditional Japanese teachings about the aged and those of "hakujins" (Caucasians). Generally, they claimed that the traditional Japanese family was more closely knit, more likely to support aged parents in their own homes, and willing to give of themselves for the benefit of their parents. One man remarked,

Their family ties are stronger than Canadian families (Europeans are close too). They tend to have more responsibility, filial piety, and respect than other Canadians. White Canadians are too independent—more for their own advantage (to each his own) generally.

The internalization of traditional values is also reflected in their interactions with the *Issei*. However, in some cases forms of behaviour have been modified to fit a North American lifestyle. Kobata says that the *Nisei*, on the whole, have embraced the concepts of filial piety. However, they have adopted different forms of carrying out filial duties. Caretaking may not always include the physical care of parents in the *Nisei's* home. Instead many establish separate houses in the rear of family homes, maintain a separate apartment for the elderly parents with expenses assumed by children, rotate parental care among children quarterly or semi-annually, and unmarried children (rather than the eldest son as tradition requires) are often given total responsibility for the care of aged parents (Kobata, 1974:99).

Such findings tend to support the assumption that the *Nisei* will expect similar treatment when they are aged. However, such an assumption is problematic. The first problem is that it adheres to a very static definition of socialization. It adopts the idealist view of socialization as "clay-modelling" process. Implicit in this causal approach is the idea that the socialization of X values during childhood leads to Y behaviour in adulthood and old age.

The fact that the *Nisei* acknowledge many traditional Japanese age norms, and that many even display traditional behaviours toward Issei parents, does not mean that they will internalize or feel such normative constraints or values with regard to their own aging experience. There is then a difference between acknowledgement and acceptance.

The dichotomy between the traditional Japanese value system and that of North American society is often overlooked because Japanese values of hard work, achievement, self-control, dependability, manners, thrift, and diligence fit in quite nicely with Western middle-class values (Kalish and Moriwaki, 1973:195). However, as Kalish and Moriwaki claim, the difference becomes apparent when one looks at the motivations behind such values and behaviour. In the Japanese case, motivations derive from the importance of the family, dependence of the individual on the family group, obedience and duty to elders, whereas the values of self-actualization and independence are at the root of such stresses among North Americans (Kalish and Moriwaki, 1973:195).

Furthermore, it would be inappropriate to imply that North American ideals do not reflect a respect for the aged or reverence for the family. After all, notions of both filial piety and respect for elders are evident, for instance, in such Western maxims as "Honor thy father and thy mother" (Kalish and Moriwaki, 1973:200). The difference, say Kalish and Moriwaki, is that filial piety in Western cultures tends to be undermined by a vast array of conflicting values, while in Japanese or Chinese cultures, it ranks higher in the hierarchy of values. The authors state, "The themes of independence, self-reliance, and mastery of one's own fate are also dominant in Western thought, while Japan and China honored these values little if at all" (Kalish and Moriwaki, 1973:200).

Contemporary Western cultures place emphasis on the values of independence and individualism such that the latter are equated with personal happiness, maturity, adult status and even normal psychological adjustment. The child, especially the male child, who wishes to remain with his parents after the age of twenty-one comes to be regarded as abnormally attached to his "mother's apron strings." The grown man who defies current gender prescriptions and stays home all day is labelled a "moocher," a "leech," or a "bum." Similarly, "welfare mothers" are stigmatized as lazy, irresponsible women who live off the hard-earned efforts of others. Furthermore, North Americans have a strong desire for self-actualization, privacy, and self-fulfillment. Rewards for achievement and productivity go to the individual, not the family or group—a practice which is clearly reflected in the educational system. In addition, policies aimed at increasing the independence of old people are considered to be positive and progressive.

Logically, then, dependency in North America is a negative trait. Solem comments that in the Western world,

> *individual independency is an important social value, it is reasonable to assume that dependency is felt as degrading and negative. A dependent individual is considered more or less without value and the*

dependent individual himself will according to this run great risks of losing his self esteem and morale (Solem, 1976:71).

In accordance with these values is the Western practice of shunning dependency on one's family in old age. Clark and Anderson say that, historically, Americans have shown a preference for transferring responsibility for care of the elderly from families to the elderly themselves—("through early life inculcation of 'habit of industry, temperance, and foresight') the family 'aided,' if necessary, by the state" (Clark and Anderson, 1967:349–50).

These same authors also state that, although the nineteenth-century Utopians proposed non familial means of *economic* support for the elderly and not *social* independence, twentieth-century America has come to see that "the value of financial autonomy has been extended into the social sphere." They conclude that "there now exists in contemporary American thinking considerable discussion of the question as to whether the aged are happier and more content if they are 'disengaged'—this is to say, only minimally involved in the social life of the community" (Clark and Anderson, 1967:350).

Because of this value system, elderly non-Hispanic whites tend to view dependency upon their children as something to be ashamed of. The three-generational household in most contemporary Western societies is by no means as popular as in Japan. In fact, recent data indicate that most old people in such areas live alone (Atchley, 1980:233).

■■■

CURRENT PERCEPTIONS OF THE *NISEI*

Our findings reflect many ambiguities in the *Nisei's* attitudes toward aging. Although traces of their Japanese upbringing are still evident, their attitudes generally coincide with those of Anglo-Canadians. They are similar to the latter on three indices: (1) the subjects perceived themselves as independent and spoke of this independence as something to be proud of; (2) they perceived growing dependency on their children with much doubt; (3) and they displayed a preference for living alone in old age.

All but six out of a total of fifty-one respondents consider themselves as independent, in the general sense of the term. This may not so much reflect a person's actual independence (since a person's perception of reality and objective reality do not always coincide) as it may represent a desire to present one's self as such, and thus suggest that independence is regarded as a virtue.

Furthermore, the majority of respondents stated that they would most likely become more dependent as they grew older (primarily because of physical incapacities), and that this situation would be slightly bothersome to them. Most respondents said they they would experience considerable guilt about having to depend on their grown children.

This finding may be compared to Clark and Anderson's data on the elderly in San Francisco. After studying 435 men and women, Clark and Anderson report that the older person has various personal goals, including independence, social acceptability, adequate personal resources, and to have the ability to cope with both external threats and changes in the self. They also discovered eight sources of low morale among the elderly. In rank order, these were dependency, physical discomfort or sensory loss, loneliness, boredom, mental discomfort, loss of prestige, fear of dying, and the problems of others (Clark and Anderson, 1967:222).

Furthermore, like the San Francisco respondents (Clark and Anderson, 1967:36, 64), the vast majority of the *Nisei* respondents stated that the ideal living arrangement for themselves in old age would be to live alone or with their spouse. Most respondents made this choice on the basis of not wanting to be a burden on their grown children. The same reason was given repeatedly throughout the interviews and in the questionnaires. One respondent claimed,

> *As long as I am able to look after myself, I prefer to live independently on my own. I feel the children have their own lives to live unhampered with obligations that restrict their freedom to make decisions in their everyday lives.*

Another simply stated,

> *I would prefer not to be burden on my children.*

Another remarked with more ambiguity,

> *In a way I would like to live with them to have some company, but in a way no, I don't. I don't want to be a burden. I think the children should have their privacy too.*

Others have clearly made up their minds. One such woman commented,

> *I would like to live in a senior citizens apartment, not with our children or relatives!*

Yet another,

> *They have their children to bring up and I would feel I was imposing on them.*

Those who presently live with their grown children also express doubts about their living arrangements,

If I am welcomed and respected I would be quite happy living with my children (and providing I am not a burden).

Although this same man later added,

If unable to get around on my own then I would consider living in a nursing home or other institutional arrangement.

However, the *Nisei's* responses differ significantly from those of the dominant group in that, although the *Nisei* indicate a preference to live apart from their children, the primary reason is not self-pride or autonomy *per se* (although this is still important). Rather, this response stems mainly from a perception of their children's needs.

The *Nisei's* responses reflect a mixture of values: a North American desire for independence, Japanese self-effacement, and an overall pride in one's offspring. Ishizuka, too, found that the *Nisei's* attitudes toward aging reflect their dual heritage. She reports learned traditional values of filial piety and respect for elderly, Japanese language use and identification, but greater involvement with American society at large (Ishizuka, 1978:38).

The statement, "I do not want to be a burden," exemplifies this. The respondents' tendency to perceive their own needs as secondary to those of their children manifests self-denial and self-reliance. Ishizuka suggests that this pattern of self-reliance suggests a strong sense of ethnic pride. It is illustrated by the proverb, *Bushi wa kuwanedo takayoji*, which means "although you do not have anything to eat, you use a toothpick to give the appearance of just having eaten" (Ishizuka, 1978:28). According to Ishizuka, a sense of pride and a hesitancy to show or admit need, even hunger, are evident in this proverb (Ishizuka, 1978:28). The Japanese phrase *meiwaku o kakenai yoni* also illustrates this pattern. *Meiwaku o kakenai yoni* also illustrates this pattern. *Meiwaku o kakenai yoni* translates "so as not to put a burden on another person" (Ishizuka, 1978:28).

One could also postulate that such self-denial stems partly from the Japanese hyper-sensitivity to criticism and the feelings of others, and from a desire to cause as little trouble as possible. Keifer states that this extreme sensitivity, in turn, has resulted from a structure in which shaming was used as a method of social control (Kiefer, 1974:70).

Much of this self-effacement may also be simply a reflection of the sample's overrepresentation of females. Studies by Rubin (1979), Bernard (1971), Luxton (1980), and many other contemporary authors show that women are caught up in a "love-duty ethos." That is, they tend to continually place the needs of their families over their own. Otherwise, they experience extreme guilt.

Yet aside from elaborate psychological explanations and ideological considerations, one must consider that the *Nisei's* responses reflect a structural reality—an accurate perception of their objective situation. In traditional Japanese culture, care of the elderly by offspring represented a repayment for the former's life work. And, because of this, dependency in old age escaped negative connotations. However, says Kiefer, in order for this system to work, all parties concerned must implicitly recognize it (Kiefer, 1974:184). But this is not the case in North America. Even if the *Nisei* wished to live with their grown children, the latter would also have to be willing and able. Several obstacles prevent this, foremost among these being the rapid acculturation of the *Sansei* (third-generation).

THE *SANSEI*

Makabe notes that language and religion are the key indicators of the extent to which an ethnic group has kept its specific values and customs and the degree to which it has become acculturated and assimilated (Makabe, 1976:47–48). On both these indices, Japanese Canadians show increasing acculturation with each generation (Makabe, 1976:47–57).

Several studies document the rapid assimilation of the *Sansei*. Arkoff, for instance, compared *Nisei* and *Sansei* of the same age and found that the *Sansei* expressed less need for deference, abasement, nurturance, affiliation, endurance and introspection, and a greater need for North American values of dominance, achievement and exhibition as compared to the *Nisei* (Arkoff cited in Kalish and Moriwaki, 1973:199).

Some researchers, such as Kitano, contest these findings, in stating that acculturation has not been a simple linear movement. Kitano makes this claim because of the emerging sense of ethnic identity amongst the *Sansei* (Kitano cited in Kobata, 1979:104). But his assertion neglects qualitative differences. Although many third-generation Japanese Canadians seek their "roots," they try to do so in a totally different fashion than their parents. Kalish and Moriwaki assert that the *Sansei* seek their cultural roots selectively: "Most obviously, they do not attempt to regain the tradition of filial piety, a sense of obedience to the ruler of the nation in which they live. . . . Rather, they look to the arts, the cultural history, some religious involvement. . . ." (Kalish and Moriwaki, 1973:198).

Levine and Montero, in their study of Japanese in the United States, found that although the majority of the Sansei indicate an interest in Japanese ways, they still embrace the primary goals of American society, especially its stress on socio-economic success (Levine and Montero, 1973:33).

The high educational attainments and economic success of the *Sansei* (Makabe, 1976:28–36) have contributed to their rapid assimilation. Most studies on ethnicity conclude that the higher the education and socio-economic status of the ethnic minority, the more assimilated it will be in the ways of the dominant society (Reitz, 1980).

Thus, one can conclude that the *Sansei* have not significantly adopted the traditional Japanese attitudes toward old age. Instead, they have adopted

North American values of independence and individualism. The *Nisei* acknowledged this in their responses. One woman said about her children,

> *They have different ideas, even if I wanted to live with them, I'm not sure I could. I think there would be a lot of conflict—a lot of hidden resentments which wouldn't be good. In such a case, I'd rather be left to die in an old age home.*

In such cases, a restricted and harsh autonomy is preferred to an unwanted dependency.

■ ■ ■

REFERENCES

Atchley, Robert C. *The Social Forces in Later Life*. Belmont, California: Wadsworth Publishing, 1980.

Bernard, Jessie. "The Paradox of the Happy Marriage." In *Woman in Sexist Society*. Eds. Vivian Gornick and Barbara K. Moran. New York: Basic Books, 1971, pp. 145–162.

Caudill, William, "Japanese-American Personality and Acculturation," *Genetic Psychology Monograph*, 1952.

Clark, Margaret, and Barbara Gallatin Anderson. *Culture and Aging*. Springfield, Illinois: Charles C. Thomas, 1967.

De Vos, George A. *Socialization for Achievement*. Berkeley, University of California Press, 1973.

Ishizuka, Karen C. *The Elder Japanese*. San Diego: Centre on Aging, 1978.

Kalish, Richard A., and Sharon Moriwaki. "The World of the Elderly Asian American," *Journal of Social Issues*, 29, No. 2, (1973), 187–209.

Kiefer, Christie W. "Lessons From the Issei." In *Late Life: Communities and Environmental Policy*. Ed. Jaber F. Gubrium. Springfield, Illinois: Charles C. Thomas, 1974, pp. 167–197.

Kitano, Harry. *Japanese Americans*. Englewood, Prentice-Hall, 1969.

Kobata, Fran. "The influence of culture on family relations: the Asian American Experience." In *Aging Parents*. Ed. Pauline K. Ragan. Los Angeles, California: University of California Press, 1979, pp. 94–106.

Levine, Gene N., and Darrel M. Montero. "Socioeconomic Mobility among Three Generations of Japanese Americans." *Journal of Social Issues*, 29, No. 2 (1973), 33–48.

Luxton, Meg. *More Than a Labour of Love*. Toronto: The Women's Press, 1980.

Makabe, Tomoko. "Socio-Demographic Analysis of the Japanese Canadian Community in Ontario." 1976.

Masuda, Minoru, Gary H. Matsumoto, and Gerald M. Meredith. "Ethnic Identity in Three Generations of Japanese Americans," *The Journal of Social Psychology*, 81 (1970), 199–207.

Peterson, William. *Japanese Americans*. New York: Random House, 1971.

Reitz, J. *The Survival of Ethnic Groups*. Toronto: McGraw-Hill, 1980.

Rubin, Lillian B. *Women of a Certain Age: The Midlife Search for Self.* New York: Harper and Row, 1979.

Solem, Erik. "Dependency—Due to Lack of Individual or Environmental Resources?" In *Dependency or Interdependency in Old Age*. Eds. Chris Phillipson et al. London: Croom Helm, 1986, pp. 71–79.

Trela, James E., and Jay H. Sokolovsky. "Culture, ethnicity, and policy for the aged." In *Ethnicity and Aging: Theory, Research, and Policy*. Ed. Donald E. Gelfand and Alfred J. Kutzik, pp. 117–136. New York: Springer, 1979.

SECTION TWO

Discussion Questions

1. *Discuss how social organization, values, and social roles create different opportunities for Chipewyan men and women in old age. Do industrial societies also offer different opportunities to men and women in old age? Discuss.*

2. *What do the Anicinabe mean by "elderhood"? How is it related to old age? What role did elders traditionally play in this society? How did that role change with the move to reserves? What recent developments suggest the revival of elderhood among the Anicinabe?*

3. *Describe the relationship between the younger and older members of Old Order Mennonite society. Link this relationship to the social structure of an agricultural society and the culture's religious tradition.*

4. *What three main losses do ethnic older people experience when they enter a health-care institution? Give some examples of successful and unsuccessful attempts to help ethnic older people overcome these losses.*

5. *What values in Japanese culture and tradition shape relations between the generations? How does North American culture influence these relations? Why do we need to look at the motivations behind values in Japanese and North American society to understand the differences between these cultures?*

6. *Describe the influence of social structure, tradition, norms, and values on old age in at least three different cultures.*

Suggested Readings

Blandford, A.A., and N.L. Chappell (1990). "Subjective Well-Being among Native and Non-Native Elderly Persons: Do Differences Exist?" *Canadian Journal on Aging* 9 (4): 386–99.

Bond, J.B., and C.D. Harvey (1991). "Ethnicity and Intergenerational Perceptions of Family Solidarity." *International Journal of Aging and Human Development* 33 (1): 33–44.

Driedger, L., and N.L. Chappell (1987). *Aging and Ethnicity: Toward an Interface.* Toronto: Butterworths.

Wong, P.T.P., and G.T. Reker (1985). "Stress, Coping, and Well-being in Anglo and Chinese Elderly." *Canadian Journal on Aging* 4 (1): 29–37.

Coping With Individual Change

People age at different rates. At age 60 some people have the skin of a 40-year-old, others have the skin of an 80-year-old. Also, each system of the body ages at its own rate. A person may have the lungs of a 30-year-old, the skin of a 50-year-old, and the liver of a 70-year old. Our genes play a role in the aging process. A person with long-lived, healthy ancestors has a good start on a healthy old age. Likewise, personal habits and the environment shape individual aging. Research has found that people can control the pace of aging to some degree. Changes in diet, exercise, and the environment, for example, can slow the rate of aging. A positive self-image and good relations with others leads to increased satisfaction in later life.

Today Canadians live longer than ever before. But recent studies show that longer life can also mean more years of disability. Can exercise help to extend Canadians' disability-free years? Shephard reports that it may. He shows that exercise, even in people aged 75 and over, can lead to improvements in health, social relations, and mental ability. Exercise can reduce disability and help keep people out of institutions. It can also improve the quality of life by decreasing insomnia, constipation, and osteoporosis. Volumes of research show the value of exercise for older people. But only a small proportion of older people take part in exercise programs. Those that start these programs often quit after a short time. Shephard suggests some ways to get older people into exercise programs and to keep them coming back.

Sections 1 and 2 of this book dealt with societal ageism and socially structured role loss. Breytspraak describes ways that individuals can cope with these challenges. For example, people can confront and sort out negative images of aging. They can take up new projects in spite of physical decline and role loss. Breytspraak reviews a number of other challenges including nearness to death and coping with failure. This focus on self-development puts the responsibility for well-being solely on the older person. But Breytspraak notes that self-development also requires a supportive social context. The social environment must provide positive images of aging, give older people control of situations, and promote activities that lead to wholeness of the self. Given a supportive environment, Breytspraak says, we may see new expressions of psychological well-being in old age and new models of aging.

Reker notes that only some social environments support creativity in old age. But, he says, older people can "create their own environment, if they want to." Reker describes some ways that older people can act creatively. All of them include an expansion of options, an openness to new possibilities, and a sense of optimism about the future. Reker concludes by noting the importance of "discovering/creating a sense of personal meaning and purpose in life."

The National Advisory Council on Aging (NACA) reading on spirituality and meaning in old age develops this point. The article places the discovery of meaning at the heart of thought and action in old age. The discovery of meaning, the article says, can take place with or without religious faith.

Novak's work supports the idea that older people must play an active part in discovering meaning for themselves. He presents the results of a study of older people who displayed self-actualization. These people, he reports, went through a process—challenge, denial, acceptance, and affirmation—to achieve an integrated personality. The article describes one woman's journey toward a good old age. In the end this woman accepts and even affirms her status as an older person.

The articles in this section show that modern culture offers few supports or models for good aging. Older people today must discover a good age for themselves and with one another. Discovery can take many paths: exercise, social action, creative work, commitment to others. This makes old age an exciting time of life. And it makes today's seniors pioneers in the field of aging.

9

The Scientific Basis of Exercise Prescribing for the Very Old

Roy J. Shephard

Older people are heterogeneous in physical ability. Calendar age offers some basis for categorization, but a functional classification is more useful. We may recognize the young-old, with no restriction of physical activity, the middle-old, with a slight limitation, and the very old or old-old, who face severe limitations.[1] In one study 80% of a North American sample of people at 65 years of age move without difficulty, but by the age of 80 years a high proportion are limited by cardiac or mental problems.[2] Death is usually preceeded by eight to 10 years with some disability and about a year of total dependency.[3] This brief review will discuss why the middle-old and very old should exercise, what forms of exercise should be prescribed, and the likely physiological and psychological responses to such training.

REASONS FOR EXERCISING

Why should a person who has been sedentary for many years suddenly begin exercising at the age of 75 or 80 years? Possible reasons include a potential to improve health, increased opportunities for social contacts, and gains in cerebral function.

Improvement of Health

The goal of improving health is perhaps the most commonly perceived reason why an older person joins a fitness class. Potential gains include reduction in cardiovascular risk,[4,5] control of obesity,[6] and increase in functional capacity.[1] There may also be an improved intake of nutrients[7] and better sleep patterns.[8]

Reproduced with permission of Williams & Wilkins from *Journal of the American Geriatric Society*, Vol. 38, No. 1 (January 1990), 62–70.

Cardiovascular Risk

The risk of cardiovascular disease increases progressively with age,[9] as can be seen from plots of the incidence of acute and sudden death. By 70 years of age, 10% of people have clinically diagnosed coronary artery disease, and community surveys show an even higher prevalence of ECG changes suggestive of myocardial ischemia.[10]

Regular exercise reduces cardiovascular risk, even in the elderly.[4,5] Body mass and body fat content are reduced,[6] the lipid profile is improved,[11,12] insulin sensitivity is increased,[13,14] and resting blood pressure is decreased.[5] A lower heart rate and a lower blood pressure at any given intensity of exercise reduce the cardiac work rate.[16] However, relative to a sedentary person, a fit senior citizen may be more tempted to undertake an occasional bout of overstrenuous activity that could precipitate a heart attack, and perhaps for this reason the extension of lifespan in the oldest age categories is quite limited.

Body Composition

Sidney et al[6] demonstrated a substantial reduction of body fat when 65-year-old subjects participated in a 14-week program of endurance exercise. Regular weight-bearing exercise also slows the rate of osteoporosis.[17] The muscles that are involved in the exercise become stronger[1,18,19]; however, the increase of muscle force may reflect a greater fiber recruitment[20] or a better synchronization of contractions, rather than an increase of lean tissue.

Functional Capacity

An improvement in functional capacity is perhaps the strongest argument for encouraging exercise in the very old. Admission to an institution commonly reflects functional deterioration. Sometimes the precipitating factor is a social or a medical crisis. But in many of the very old, the prime determinant is a lack of functional capacity.

For example, the flexibility of a typical sedentary individual shows a 20 to 30% decrease by the age of 70 years[21,22] and by 80 years of age further deterioration may preclude such important activities as dressing or the climbing of steps. Again, muscle weakening may preclude lifting of the body mass from a toilet seat, while the loss of aerobic power may lead to severe fatigue when carrying out the tasks of a normal day.

Aerobic power typically decreases by about 5 mL/kg . min per decade in a sedentary person, and only a little less in those who have remained physically active.[23] Participation in a conditioning program can increase the aerobic power of the sedentary senior by at least 20%,[24,25] equivalent to a 10 to 20-year reduction of functional age.[1] An active person thus takes 10 to 20 years longer to reach the critical threshold level of aerobic power where institutional support becomes essential.

The secretion of catecholamines at any given rate of working is increased as a person becomes older, but the affinity, if not the density, of the beta-receptors declines. In consequence there is a progressive but variable decrease of maximal heart rate.[26] Older people also have difficulty in sustaining their stroke volume as maximal effort is approached.[27] Diastolic filling, and thus mitral value closure, is delayed by a slowing of calcium uptake in the sarcoplasmic reticulum,[28] and a stiffening of the ventricular wall.[29,30] Preloading is further reduced by varicosities, a decrease in total blood volume, and poor venous tone. The increase of myocardial contractility induced by catecholamines is reduced,[31] whereas after-loading is increased by high systolic pressure, increased aortic impedance, contraction of weakened skeletal muscles at a large fraction of their maximal force, and limitation of the catecholamine-induced vasodilation in the contracting muscles.[29,32]

If subjects with hypertensive and coronary vascular disease are excluded by a combination of stress electrocardiograms (ECG) and thallium scans, an increase of stroke volume compensates for the decrease of heart rate.[28] However, the concept of a frail elderly population free of myocardial ischemia is highly artificial. Moreover, Gerstenblith's hypothesis leaves largely unexplained the age-related decline of aerobic power that occurs in both sedentary and physically active individuals.[23]

Nutritional Benefits

Many old people—particularly those with heavy alcohol intake—have a marginal intake of essential nutrients,[7] especially calcium and some vitamins, but possibly also including protein.[33] By augmenting the total energy intake, regular exercise helps to assure more adequate nutrition. Other nutritional benefits include correction of constipation[34] and reversal of lean tissue loss and osteoporosis.

Sleep Patterns

Sleeplessness is a common complaint in old age.[35] If exercise is performed late at night, it may cause arousal, exacerbating the problem, but moderate exercise done earlier in the day can improve sleep, at least in younger individuals.[16,36]

Increased Social Contacts

Older people tend to withdraw from society[1]; an exercise program counters this trend, offering renewed companionship and joie de vivre. Group activities in a hall, gymnasium, or pool offer more opportunities for social interaction than some endurance-type pursuits such as jogging. However, skilled organization of an exercise class is necessary to ensure that social gains are not made at the expense of functional improvements, or vice versa.

Cerebral Function

Participation in an aerobic conditioning class apparently speeds color recognition and improves other measures of cerebral function in older patients.[37,38] It is possible that exercise increases blood pressure and thus cerebral perfusion. However, any change of blood pressure is quite short-lived, and an exercise-induced increase in cerebral arousal provides a more plausible explanation.

Many people exercise because it "makes them feel better." An increase of cerebral arousal undoubtedly contributes to this sensation. The very old rarely undertake sufficient physical activity to increase the secretion of beta-endorphins,[39] but other possible factors improving mood include an enhanced body image, a greater sense of self-esteem, and stronger feelings of self-efficacy.[40]

Anxiety, depression, and anger may also be reduced, particularly in individuals where mood was initially disturbed.[1,41]

Finally, in young adults exercise reduces cardiovascular responses to psychosocial stressors[40]; however, such studies have yet to be extended to the very old.

WHAT KINDS OF EXERCISE SHOULD BE PRESCRIBED?

When prescribing exercise for the very old, key issues include safety, compliance, and effectiveness of the proposed regimen.

Safety

Safety concerns include sudden death, traumatic and overuse injury, and adverse environmental effects.

Sudden Death

In middle-aged adults (40–49 years), unaccustomed vigorous exercise increases the immediate risk of sudden death by a factor of 5 to 10, although the prognosis for the entire day is improved.[42,43] Interestingly, the relative risk of both nonstrenuous and strenuous exercise is reduced in those aged 50 to 69 years.[44]

Indications of an adverse reaction to exercise include the development of horizontal or down-sloping ST-segmental depression, the appearance of abnormalities of heart rhythm, a peak heart rate that is low for age, a failure of the blood pressure to show the anticipated rise, the onset of chest pain, and a low peak-power output or maximal oxygen intake. Such findings indicate an adverse prognosis, particularly if they are associated with other cardiovascular risk factors.[20]

Depression of the ST segment in itself is an extremely deceptive sign, particularly in women.[45] In middle-aged adults a positive diagnosis of myocardial ischemia is wrong about two times out of three.[42] Bayes' theorem suggests that a positive diagnosis will be correct somewhat more frequently in the elderly, because a higher proportion of patients have clinically significant coronary vascular disease. However, in this age group the diagnosis of myocardial ischemia is frequently obscured by an abnormal resting ECG, while muscular weakness, joint instability, nervousness on the part of the patient or the supervising physician, and the use of beta-blocking medications may all give a false-negative result because testing ceases too soon.

Even if more valid exercise tests were available, how useful would it be to identify an older man who might die while exercising? If he enjoys a weekly game of golf, are we going to tell him to give this up because one day he might die from the excitement of shooting one under par on the 13th hole? What social or personal good will we have achieved if this man lives for an additional five years, but spends four of them paralyzed by a severe stroke, unable to recognize his golfing friends? Would he not prefer to have died on his favorite golf course?

The patient should in any event be told of warning symptoms calling for the halting of a given bout of exercise: severe dyspnea, dizziness, anginal chest pain, extra pulse beats, or abnormal heart rhythms; other suggestions of failing left ventricular performance include nausea, confusion, extreme fatigue, or near syncope; and intermittent calf pain. Indications for caution include a history of arrhythmia, chest pain, congestive failure, or hypertension.[46] Prolonged straining against a closed glottis should be avoided; it tends to provoke a substantial rise of blood pressure.[47]

An increased daily physical activity will not guarantee an old person an extension of lifespan. However, if the prescribed exercise does not provoke symptoms, it is unlikely to be very dangerous for them. Moreover, the quality-adjusted lifespan[48] will almost certainly be increased by the conditioning program. It then seems counterproductive to suggest that exercise is other than normal, reasonable behavior. Insistence upon expensive preliminary laboratory screening tests implies danger, decreases motivation, and can become an unethical component of defensive or even income-generating medicine.

There have been many attempts to develop suitable exercise tests for the elderly.[1] Anxiety, poor coordination, unstable joints, and difficulty in retaining a mouthpiece all make many laboratory tests unsatisfactory for the very old. Functional capacity can be gauged roughly from the self-selected walking pace,[49,50] and at this age it is possible that no better information may be derived from a treadmill or a cycle-ergometer test.

Injuries

More than a half of age-class (Masters') athletes sustain a musculoskeletal injury every year.[51] However, the risk of injury seems roughly proportional to the amount of exercise that is undertaken per session and per week.

Because the elderly are less ambitious exercisers, both traumatic and overuse injuries are less frequent than in middle-aged people who are preparing themselves for major competitions.[52]

Preventive measures are simple. Muscles should be strengthened around weakened joints. Other joints should be taken gently through their full range of motion, using light stretching movements,[53] before more vigorous rhythmic exercise begins. Exercise on hard surfaces should be avoided. Footwear should include shock-absorbing soles with good traction; walking is preferable to jogging, as the impact stress on the knee joints during walking is only a third to a sixth of that during running.[54] The risk of slipping or of twisting an ankle is also much lower for the walker than for the runner. If the weather is icy, exercise should be done indoors (e.g., a shopping mall or a hospital corridor). If balance is poor, it is advisable to avoid such activities as cycling and skiing, and if there is degeneration of the knee joints or vertebrae, weight-supported activities (swimming, aquabics, or chair exercises) should be considered.[55–57]

Adverse Environmental Effects

The very old have difficulty in adapting to extreme environments. They risk death from heart failure[58] or heat stroke[16,59] if they attempt vigorous exercise under hot conditions. The added stress can be assessed quite simply by noting the increase in heart rate at any given rate of performance. The failure of thermoregulation is exacerbated by such common medications as beta-blocking agents.[60] During a hot spell, exercise should be taken in an air-conditioned facility or in the water.

In a severely cold environment cutaneous vasoconstriction, a rise of blood pressure, and reflex coronary vasoconstriction can provoke myocardial ischemia.[61] A poor peripheral circulation increases the risk of chilblains and frostbite.[16] Again, the remedy is to move the exercise indoors.

Underwater exploration is inappropriate for the very old, as even a brief loss of consciousness in the underwater environment is likely to be fatal. Normal swimming or pool exercises may be followed by hypotension, particularly if a patient is receiving antihypertensive medication. It is thus important to ensure that pools have adequate handrails and nonslip decks.[56]

The moderate hypoxia encountered at mountain resorts (altitudes of 3,000–4,000 meters) may be sufficient to precipitate myocardial ischemia in patients with an impaired coronary circulation.[16]

Finally, older people are particularly vulnerable to episodes of severe air pollution,[62] particularly if the respiratory minute volume is increased by exercise, and the normal filtering and scrubbing mechanism of the nose is bypassed by mouth breathing.[63]

Compliance

The major challenge of any exercise program is sustaining exercise compliance.[64] As many as 50% of participants may defect over the first six months of an exercise class.[65] The intention to exercise depends on personal attitudes and social norms.[66,67] Translation of the exercise intention into an overt behavior is limited by barriers to the intended action, motivation to alternative behaviors, situation, and role-playing influences. Attitudes are shaped by beliefs and a personal evaluation of those beliefs, whereas social norms reflect the perceived values of significant others and the motivation to comply with such norms. Habit is a final factor exerting strong pressures at various levels in the behavioral model.[66]

The lessons for encouraging exercise compliance are plain. Rather than attempting to introduce the very old person to novel forms of physical activity, it is desirable to build on previous habits, using existing skills and equipment. As recent memory is often poor, frequent reminders about formal activity sessions are needed. Much of the recommended activity can also be built into the normal day, where it is less easily forgotten: the walk to the store for a newspaper or to the dining hall for lunch and supper. Potential barriers, such as lack of a suitable companion or absence of transportation, must be recognized and overcome. Feedback should be based on personal beliefs and needs (e.g., "regular participation in the exercise class will improve my health"). Finally, the social norm that old age is a time to slow down and take a well-earned rest must be corrected. It is important that the family physician becomes a "significant other," encouraging exercise and other forms of lifestyle modification[68]; too often, the doctor is more conservative than the patient, and there is then little motivation to comply with medical advice.[69]

A person is usually motivated to exercise if the activity is seen as rewarding. Patients may be seeking health, fun, or new experiences. Depending on the needs of the individual, exercise can be presented as a means of escaping from physical dependency, of earning the respect of significant others, or of experiencing personal fulfillment.[70] An older class-leader may be a helpful role model. Failure to meet the unrealistic expectations of a very fit young leader can have a negative impact upon both self-image and motivation.

Effectiveness of Prescribed Regimen

There is only a small margin between an effective and a dangerous exercise prescription for the very old person. However, a sedentary lifestyle leads to a much lower training threshold than in a young adult. Some conditioning may occur with an exercise prescription that demands no more than 30 to 40% of maximum oxygen intake.[1] Although gains of physical condition develop more rapidly with a higher-intensity regimen, conditioning eventually occurs with frequent repetition of a low-intensity program.[25] The patient should thus not be discouraged if general frailty or coexisting clinical disorders limit exercise participation. The optimum duration of training can be related to the required intensity of effort in METS (ratios to resting metabolic rate), using the formula:[71]

$$\text{duration (min)} = 218 \,/\, \text{MET} - 60$$

If the intensity is 2 METS, the prescription would call for 49 minutes of exercise per day. Many old people are unable to sustain physical activity for this length of time. The required prescription is then broken into several feasible segments of vigorous effort, with alternating periods of rest or light activity. Some authors find a good response to circuit training, one- to two-minute periods of light activity being interspersed between five-minute bouts of exercise at several different tasks. As physical condition improves, the intensity and the duration of individual exercise bouts are progressively increased. Since two days are needed for full recovery, the optimal training plan calls for three formal exercise sessions per week, with light walking on intervening days.

The ideal program includes an extended warm-up to minimize the risk of inducing cardiac arrhythmias[72] or musculoskeletal injuries,[53] flexibility exercises, endurance activity, weight-bearing if possible (to strengthen the major bones), some strengthening of major muscles by low-resistance, frequently repeated movements, and an extended (10–15 minute) cool-down. Swimming, aquabics,[55,56,73] and chair exercises[57] may all be modified to contribute to these requirements in the very old.

TRAINING RESPONSE

The likely extent of physiological and psychological responses to a conditioning program depend on the individual's compliance with the exercise prescription and on a regular upward adjustment of the prescription by the program supervisor.

Is it less easy to train the very old? Functional adaptations to most types of stress are reduced,[1] and slower rates of protein synthesis might well reduce the likelihood of morphological adaptations such as muscle hypertrophy.[33] On the other hand, training is facilitated by a low initial fitness level,[74] even though the physiological gap between the sedentary person and the continuing athlete seems to be unchanged by age[1]; an old person may move more slowly from a sedentary to a trained state, but the ultimate conditioning response is apparently not reduced.

Finally, training has a potential impact on immune function[76]; while exhausting training depresses immune function, more moderate regular activity has a positive effect.[77] Training may thus help to counter the age-related deterioration of immune function,[76] which probably contributes to the increased incidence of and mortality from neoplasms and infectious disease in older people.[79,80] There is evidence that an active lifestyle reduces the incidence of both colonic and breast cancers.[81–83] It is less certain whether an improvement of immune function is responsible for this protection, but it is clearly established that regular exercise can increase natural killer-cell activity just as effectively in old as in younger subjects.[84]

CONCLUSIONS

Training cannot restore tissue that has been destroyed by disease, but it may offer some protection against the diseases of old age, and it can make a major contribution to the quality of life by maximizing residual function. It is no mean prize to enjoy the strength, the flexibility, and the aerobic power equivalent to a sedentary person 20 years younger.[1] Given such physical rewards, it is hardly surprising that the exercise-class member will report that exercise makes him or her feel better. On this basis alone, regular exercise merits commendation to the frail elderly patient.

REFERENCES

1. Shephard RJ: Physical Activity and Aging. London, Croom Helm, 1987
2. Heckler MM: Health promotion for older Americans. Public Health Rep. 100:225–230, 1985
3. Canada Health Survey. Ottawa: Health and Welfare Canada, 1982
4. Paffenbarger RS, Hyde RT, Wing AL, Hsieh CC: Physical activity, all-cause mortality and longevity of college alumni. N Engl J Med 314:605–613, 1986
5. Pekkanen J, Marti B, Nissinen A, et al: Reduction of premature mortality by high physical activity: a 20-year follow-up of middle-aged Finnish men. Lancet 1:1473–1477, 1987
6. Sidney KH, Shephard RJ, Harrison J: Endurance training and body composition of the elderly: Am J Clin Nutr 30:326–333, 1977
7. Tiidus P, Shephard RJ, Montelpare W: Overall intake of energy and key nutrients: data for middle-aged and older middle-class adults. Can J Sport Sci (in press)
8. Shapiro CM, Warren PM, Trinder J, et al: Fitness facilitates sleep. Eur J Appl Physiol 53:1–4, 1984
9. Romo M: Factors related to sudden death in acute ischaemic heart disease: a community study in Helsinki. Acta Med Scand 547(Suppl):7–92,1972
10. Montoye HJ: Physical activity and health: an epidemiological study of an entire community. Englewood Cliffs, NJ, Prentice Hall, 1975
11. Matter S, Stanford BA, Weltman A: Age, diet, maximal aerobic capacity and serum lipids. J Gerontol 35:332–336, 1980
12. Yano K, Reed DM, Curb JD, et al: Biological and dietary correlates of plasma lipids and lipoproteins among elderly Japanese men in Hawaii. Arteriosclerosis 6:422–433, 1986
13. Holm GL, Krotkiewski MJ: Exercise in the treatment of diabetes mellitus, *in* Welsh P, Shephard RJ (eds): Current Therapy in Sports Medicine, 1985–1986. Burlington, Ontario, BC Decker, 1986

14. Hughes VA, Meredith CN: Effects of aging, exercise and diet on glucose metabolism, *in* Harris R, Harris S (eds): Physical Activity, Aging and Sports. Albany, NY, Center for the Study of Aging, 1986

15. Tipton CH: Exercise, training and hypertension. Exerc Sport Sci Rev 12:245–306, 1984

16. Shephard RJ: Physiology and Biochemistry of Exercise. New York, Praeger Publications, 1982

17. Chow RK, Harrison JE, Sturtridge W, et al: The effect of exercise on bone mass of osteoporotic patients on fluoride treatment. Clin Invest Med 10(2):59–63,1987

18. Davies CTM, White MJ: Effects of dynamic exercise on muscle function in elderly men, aged 70 years. Gerontology 1:26–31, 1983

19. Chow R, Harrison JE, Notarius C: Effect of two randomized exercise programmes on bone mass of healthy post-menopausal women. Br Med J 295:1441–1444, 1987

20. Wolfel EE, Hossack KF: Guidelines for the exercise training of elderly healthy individuals and elderly patients with cardiac disease. J Cardiopulm Rehab 9:40–45, 1989

21. Adrian MJ: Flexibility in the aging adult, *in* Smith EL, Serfass RC (eds): Exercise and Aging: The Scientific Basis. Hillside, New Jersey: Enslow Publishing, 1981, pp 45–58

22. Canada Fitness Survey: Fitness and Lifestyle in Canada. Ottawa: Canadian Fitness and Lifestyle Research Institute, 1983

23. Shephard RJ: The aging of cardiovascular function, *in* Eckert H, Spirduso W (eds): The Academy Papers. Champaign, Ill, Human Kinetics Publishers, 1989

24. Barry AJ, Daly JW, Pruett EDR, et al: The effects of physical conditioning on older individuals: I. work capacity, circulatory respiratory function and work electrocardiogram. J Gerontol 21:182–191, 1966

25. Sidney KH, Shephard RJ: Frequency and intensity of exercise training for elderly subjects. Med Sci Sports 10: 125–131, 1978

26. Andersen KL, Shephard RJ, Denolin H, et al: Fundamentals of Exercise Testing. Geneva, WHO, 1971

27. Niinimaa V, Shephard RJ: Training and oxygen conductance in the elderly: II. The cardiovascular system. J Gerontol 33:362–367, 1978

28. Schulman SP, Gerstenblith G: Cardiovascular changes with aging: the response to exercise. J. Cardiopulm Rehab 9:12–16, 1989

29. Strozzi C, Cocco G, Destro A, et al: Disorders in peripheral arterial system in asymptomatic elderly: plethysmographic semiology at rest, during postural effort and pharmacological tests. Gerontology 25:24–35, 1979

30. Nixon JV, Hallmark H, Page K, et al: Ventricular performance in hearts aged 61 to 73 years. Am J Cardiol 56:932–937, 1985

31. Weisfeldt ML, Gerstenblith G, Lakatta EG: Alterations in circulatory function, *in* Andres R, Bierman EL, Hazzard WR (eds): Principles of Geriatric Medicine. New York, McGraw Hill, 1985, pp 249–279

32. Van Brummelen P, Buhler FR, Kiowski W, Amann FW: Age-related decrease in cardiac and peripheral vascular responsiveness to isoprenaline: studies in normal subjects. Clin Sci 60:571–577, 1981

33. Zackin MJ, Meredith CN: Protein metabolism in aging: Effects of exercise and training, *in* Harris R, Harris S (eds): Physical Activity, Sport, and Aging. Albany, NY, Center for the Study of Aging, 1989, pp 271–286

34. Keeling WF, Martin BJ: Gastrointestinal transit during mild exercise. J Appl Physiol 63:978–981, 1987

35. Dement WC, Miles LE, Carskadan MA: "White paper" on sleep and aging. J Am Geriatr Soc 30:25–50, 1982

36. Horne JA: The effects of exercise upon sleep: a critical review. Biol Psychol 12:241–290, 1981

37. Spirduso WW: Physical fitness, aging and psychomotor speed: a review. J Gerontol 30:850–865, 1980

38. Tomporowski PD, Ellis NR: Effects of exercise on cognitive processes: a review. Psychol Bull 99:338–346, 1986

39. Harber VJ, Sutton JR: Endorphins and exercise. Sports Med 1:154–171, 1984

40. Emery CF, Pinder SL, Blumenthal JA: Psychological effects of exercise among elderly cardiac patients. J. Cardiopulm Rehab 9:46–53, 1989

41. Ingebretsen R: The relationship between physical activity and mental factors in the elderly. Scand J Soc Med 29:153–159, 1982

42. Shephard RJ: Ischemic Heart Disease and Exercise. London, Croom Helm, 1981

43. Siscovick D, LaPorte R, Newman G: The disease-specific benefits and risks of physical activity and exercise. Public Health Rep 100:180–188, 1985

44. Vuori I, Suurnakki L, Suurnakki T: Risk of sudden cardiovascular death (SCVD) in exercise. Med Sci Sports Exerc 14:114–115, 1982

45. Sidney KH, Shephard RJ: Training and ECG abnormalities in the elderly. Br Heart J 38:1114–1120, 1977

46. Sparling PB, Cantwell J: Strength training guidelines for cardiac patients. Phys Sportsmed 17(3):190–196, 1989

47. Nilsson S, Stranghelle JK, Simonsen K: Cardiovascular responses to static-dynamic work in young men, middle-aged athletes, and coronary patients. Intern Rehab Med 5:202–205, 1983

48. Kaplan R: Quantification of health outcomes for policy studies in behavioral epidemiology, *in* Kaplan R, Criqui MH (eds): Behavioral Epidemio-logy and Disease Prevention. New York, Plenum Press, 1985, pp 31–56

49. Cunningham DA, Rechnitzer PA, Donner A: Exercise training and the speed of self-selected walking pace in retirement. Can J Aging 5: 19–26, 1986

50. Bassey EJ, Fentem PH, MacDonald IC, Scriven PM: Self-paced walking as a method for exercise testing in elderly and young men. Clin Sci Mol Med 51:496–502, 1976

51. Kavanagh T, Shephard RJ: The effects of continued training on the aging process. Ann NY Acad Sci 301:656–670, 1977

52. Matheson GO, MacIntyre JG, Taunton JE, et al: Musculoskeletal injuries associated with physical activity in older adults. Med Sci Sports Exerc 21:379–385, 1985

53. de Vries H: Physiology of Exercise for Physical Educators and Athletics. 4th ed. Dubuque, WC Brown, 1986

54. Pascale M, Grana WA: Does running cause osteoarthritis? Phys Sportsmed 17(3):157–166, 1989

55. Lawrence G: Aquafitness for women. Toronto, Personal Library Publishers, 1981

56. Shephard RJ: Physical activity for the senior—a role for pool exercises? CAHPER J 50(6):2–5, 20, 1985

57. McNamara PS, Otto RM, Smith TK: The acute response of simulated bicycle and rowing exercise on the elderly population. Med Sci Sports Exerc 17:266, 1985

58. Ellis FP: Mortality from heat illness and heat-aggravated illness in the United States. Environ Res 5:1–4, 1972

59. Wyndham CH, Strydom NB: Körperliche Arbeit bei hoher Temperatur, *in* Hollman W (ed): Zentrale Themen der Sportmedizin. Berlin: Springer Verlag, 1972

60. Gordon NF, Myburgh DP, Schwellnus MP, Van Rensburg JP: (Effect of β-blockade on exercise core temperature in coronary artery disease patients. Med Sci Sports Exerc 19:591–596, 1987

61. Shephard RJ: Adaptation to exercise in the cold. Sports Med 2:59–71, 1985

62. Phair JJ, Carey GCR, Shephard RJ: Measuring human reactions to air pollution. J. Franklin Inst Mon 4:37–51, 1958

63. Niinimaa V, Cole P, Mintz S, Shephard RJ: The switching point from nasal to oronasal breathing. Respir Physiol 42:61–71, 1980

64. Fitness Ontario: Those who know but don't do. Toronto: Ministry of Culture and Recreation, 1981

65 Shephard RJ: Motivation: the key to compliance. Phys Sportsmed 13:(7)88–101, 1986

66. Godin, G, Shephard RJ: Prediction of leisure-time exercise behavior: a path analysis (Lisrel V) model. J Behav Med 10:145–158, 1987

67. Fishbein M, Ajzen I: Attitudes towards objects as predictors of single and multiple behavioral criteria. Psychol Rev 81:59–74, 1974

68. Wechsler H, Levine S, Idelson RK, et al: The physician's role in health promotion—a survey of primary care practitioners. N Engl J Med 308:97–100, 1983

69. Godin G, Shephard RJ: An evaluation of the potential role of the physician in influencing community exercise behavior. Am J Health Prom (in press)

70. Maslow A: Towards a Psychology of Being. Princeton, NJ: Van Nostrand, 1962

71. Barry HC: Exercise prescription for the elderly. Geriatrics 34:155–162, 1986

72. Barnard RJ, MacAlpin RN, Kattus AA, Buckberg GD: Ischemic response to sudden strenuous exercise in healthy men. Circulation 48:936–942, 1973

73. Koszuta LE: From sweats to swimsuits: is water exercise the wave of the future? Phys Sportsmed 17(4):203–206, 1989

74. Shephard RJ: Intensity, duration and frequency of exercise as determinants of the response to a training regime. Int Z Agnew Physiol 28:38–48, 1968

75. Paffenbarger R: Contributions of epidemiology to exercise science and cardiovascular health. Med Sci Sports Exerc 20:426–438, 1988

76. Keast D, Cameron K, Morton AR: Exercise and the immune response. Sports Med 5:248–267, 1988

77. Verde T, Thomas SJ, Shephard RJ: Influence of heavy training on immune responses to acute exercise in elite runners. Med Sci Sports Exerc 21:S110, 1989

78. Makinodan T, Yunis E: Immunology of Aging. New York, Plenum Press, 1977

79. Makinodan T, James SJ, Inamizu T, Chang M-P: Immunologic basis for susceptibility to infection in the aged. Gerontology 30:279–289, 1984

80. Maciera-Coelho A: Cancer and aging. Exp Gerontol 21:483–495, 1986

81. Gerhardsson M, Norell SE, Kiviranta H, et al: Sedentary jobs and colon cancer. Am J Epidemiol 123:775–780, 1986

82. Frisch RE, Wyshak G, Albright NL, et al: Lower prevalence of breast cancer and cancer of the reproductive system among former college athletes compared to non-athletes. Br J Cancer 52:885–891, 1985

83. Kohl HW, LaPorte RE, Blair SN: Physical activity and cancer: an epidemiological perspective. Sports Med 6:222–237, 1988

84. Fiatarone MA, Morley JE, Bloom ET, et al: The effect of exercise on natural killer cell activity in young and old subjects. J. Gerontol 44:M37–M45, 1989

85. Shephard RJ: Exercise Physiology. Burlington, BC Decker, 1987

86. Shephard RJ: Alive, Man! The Physiology of Physical Activity. Springfield, IL, CC Thomas, 1972

The Development of Self
in Later Life

Linda M. Breytspraak

Through my career I have found the self to be a very useful focus for understanding the process of aging. The seeds of my interest were planted long before I had any academic credentials. As a young college student, I spent a summer as part of a housekeeping staff in a retirement home. There I found myself asking questions about how it was that some of the older people I met were seemingly quite comfortable with who they were and with the sometimes very visible effects of their aging, while others showed considerable discomfort. Later, as a graduate student at Duke University, I had an opportunity to consider some of these matters more systematically, and I chose to do my doctoral dissertation research on the question of how older adults make sense of their achievements and failures in life in relation to their aspirations, and how this bears on the self-concept. It was instructive to find how differently people describe and value themselves in relation to what might appear objectively to be similar circumstances, which clued me in to the idea that interpretations of our situation play such an important part in who we are. Several years later, I had an opportunity to bring this early interest in aging and self-concept together with some extensive examination I had done of research instruments pertaining to the self and aging, and I crystallized some of my ideas on the potential for self-development in later life into a book, *The Development of Self in Later Life* (Breytspraak, 1984). Although I have taken on a number of other related interests in gerontology since that time, I have found myself returning again and again to the self as a helpful way of conceptualizing the process of aging—particularly what are some of the potentials of later life in a society where old people often are not highly valued and where the dramatic extensions of life expectancy may actually result in prolonging the period of social and physical loss experienced by elders. My theme has been that even though aging often brings with it significant change and loss, it is a natural human tendency to do everything possible to preserve the integrity of the self. This view requires an image of the self as active and creative and not simply reacting to the changes of later life.

. . . I will begin by sharing with you some thoughts about the nature of the self and why it is a helpful concept around which to organize discussion of the aging process. Second, I want to look at some of the challenges to the self that may be particularly evident in later life. In this context I will consider some of the opportunities for self-development that each of these challenges provides. Finally, I will suggest some ways in which the general concepts I am discussing might bear on the perspectives and activities of those who work with the older population, either in the formal service structure or as informal caregivers.

THE NATURE OF THE SELF

We can perhaps begin to identify—at least at an affective level—what the self is about when we think about some everyday situations where it may be challenged or threatened. Consider my friend who told me that he had never thought of himself as old until he was renewing his driver's licence, and the examiner recorded his hair colour as grey—this was the first time he had realized that he did indeed have grey hair! Or consider another friend—a physician—who had to come to terms with the fact that he no longer could keep the extremely long hours that had always been a part of his practice of medicine. Yet, in facing this realization, he has been able to open up important new dimensions of his self, both through his medical practice and his personal life. Imagine a 60-year-old woman whose identity, activities, and lifestyle have been highly intertwined with her husband's work as a parish minister, and suddenly she becomes a widow. You can perhaps feel how these situations may threaten the person's selfhood and definitions of who she or he is. For some the impact is negative, whereas for others the experience may be a turning point in moving to another level of self-awareness.

The self is a construct that has been used for centuries by philosophers and theologians and, in the last century, by sociologists and psychologists. For the purposes of this discussion, I want to propose that the self or selfhood refers to that which is uniquely human: the ability to be aware of one's own boundaries and individuality and to reflect upon these. It has to do with our own formulations and theories about ourselves as personal and social objects. The newborn infant apparently has no sense of self, and it is only as the child gradually begins to interact with important others that it differentiates from others and the self begins to take shape. Thus, the self necessarily only comes about in the context of social relationships. Much of our understanding of who we are is derived from our sensitivity to the appraisals and feedback of those around us; hence, social communication is at the root of the self.

The self also involves the sense of having a body. As with other aspects of the self, this bodily self is much more than simply describing a set of physical characteristics: it involves our interpretation and response to perceived characteristics. Two people may have identical physical or health conditions, but for one, this may become the basis for a positive sense of self, while for the other, it may be rather negative.

Finally, a sense of time is always integral to the self. Our selfhood grows out of a knowledge of where we began and how we will end; in other words, our sense of mortality and time must be an inevitable part of who we are. Through the self we have a sense of continuity or sameness as we move throughout time. At each moment in time we have an altered past and future so that we are potentially always reinterpreting who we are. Hence, we must regard the self as a process rather than as a state. We should not think of the self as something that is reified, or as a sort of lump within the person.

Perhaps we can better appreciate the significance of the self when we consider the possibility of the person without a self. In today's world, with so many people living into old age, there is no disease that any more clearly represents the loss of self than Alzheimer's disease. For many it is the deepest, darkest fear about getting old—to be in a body without having cognitive or social anchors. Likewise, as medical technology has made it more and more possible to prolong life until there is nothing left but the shell of the person ticking away, we are being forced to come to grips with how we defend against such assaults on the self.

It is my contention that we each actively work to preserve the sense of self that we have built up over time, and that we may even develop new aspects to the self in later years. Let me explain. People seem to be driven by two basic motivations. The first is to look good. People want to view themselves positively. None of us wants to look bad, either to ourselves or to others. Sometimes we may even distort reality or use various defensive strategies in order to protect the self-image. We are able to keep a positive self-esteem as long as we are able to keep a favourable relationship between our ideal self—what we aspire to be—and our actual self or our perceptions of our accomplishments. The psychologist William James defined self-esteem as the favourable ratio of our achievements to our aspirations.

The second motivation is to have a certain consistency and continuity in who we see ourselves to be over time. We do not easily incorporate a radically different image into an existing self. Consider, for example, the person who has dieted and lost a tremendous amount of weight. There is much evidence to suggest that such persons often continue to think of themselves as "fat" long after they have shed the pounds. Seymour Epstein (1973) has talked about how we develop theories about our self—who we are, how we behave in various situations, and how we look to others. We get quite proficient at explaining to ourselves why we do and believe certain things, and major challenges to this theory are not easily incorporated. Erik Erikson (1963) has talked about this phenomenon in somewhat different terms in relation to old age when he describes the psychosocial crisis of the elder as being that of integrity vs. despair. In his view, as we look ahead to death, we necessarily want to look back and see that our life took on a pattern, that it made sense. In order to see the patterns and the consistency, we may selectively perceive information and attend only to that which supports our view of self.

Given that we operate with these two motives toward maintaining positive self-esteem and toward self-consistency, we may use a variety of techniques to see that these motives are fulfilled. These include attributing our failures to external causes, de-emphasizing certain goals for others that seem more attainable, or making social comparisons with others who are doing less well in order to build our own self-esteem.

Having defined in the most general sense what we mean by self, let us turn to some challenges to the aging self, at least as they are represented in our culture.

CHALLENGES TO ELDERS AND THEIR SELFHOOD

Let me suggest to you five areas which may represent sources of challenge to the aging person. There are, of course, others, but these are ones to which everyone can relate. They are both social and individual in nature. They include:

1) elderhood as a devalued social status,
2) physical decline,
3) the proximity of death,
4) balancing achievements with aspirations, and
5) loss of certain social roles.

In particular, I want to relate each of these to the selfhood of the person.

Devalued Status of the Elderly

Elderhood is seldom regarded as truly a desired state—one to be aspired for—in any culture, although it is certainly easier in some cultures than others. In western culture, we have had a long strain of denigration of the elderly as juxtaposed against the preference of youth. John Milton in *Paradise Lost* talked of the strength and beauty of youth changing to "withered weak and grey," while Shakespeare in describing the seven ages of man concluded dismally with old age when we are "sans teeth, sans eyes, sans taste, sans everything." The devalued status of the elderly in modern times must be related at least in part to the growing segregation of different stages of life, as well as to the segregation of different sectors of our life (as in the way that we have segregated work from the family).

The challenge to the self of the aging person comes back to the fact that our selves are constructed in the context of our social relationships. The degree to which these negative social messages can reach the core of the self surely varies, but as Kuypers and Bengtson (1973) have shown in their portrayal of the social breakdown syndrome, our susceptibility is greater as we experience the loss of social supports through role exits and deaths of significant others. Often we can defend against these assaults through some of the methods already mentioned: social comparison with others our own age, making attributions to factors beyond our control, or rearranging what is most central to our identity.

Physical Decline

Unless we are struck down by an accident or a rapid illness, sooner or later we must face our own physical decline. Loss of our youthful vigour and attractiveness upsets us at a profound emotional level, and it may result in depression and despair. It is not enough to respond by simply attacking the cult of youth. We must confront our true feelings about this physical decline, since our bodies are so integrally connected with who we define ourselves to be. Imagine the possibility for despair in a person whose career has been highly dependent on his sight when he experiences macular degeneration of the retina and no longer has a central visual field. Or consider the woman who has prided herself on her independent life style and ability to provide for most of her own needs and who is suddenly incapacitated by a hip fracture which may never completely heal. Or consider the case of the elderly woman whom I heard about recently who worked at a church switchboard and was gently told that her services were no longer useful because she garbled some life and death phone messages.

Proximity of Death

While most people become much more aware of their mortality in their middle years, in old age death has become a proximate reality. It is the ultimate loss of self. Even if death isn't feared, the process of dying is likely to be. The approach of death confirms the self's inability to control personal reality. We are caught in the tension of a desire to somehow escape the death of the self (note the interest in cryonics and near-death experiences), while at the same time realizing that it is our mortality that ultimately gives meaning to the self. Swift in *Gulliver's Travels* reminds us of the futility of the quest to avoid death in his portrayal of the Struldbrugs, who were selected persons destined to live forever. Their life became a living hell. The challenge then to the self is to heal the illusion of immortality that we may have earlier in our lives and to open up the possibilities of our finiteness.

Successes and Failures

The literature on the self has shown that an important aspect of it is ideal self-image. We begin to construct this ideal self as young children and revise it a number of times throughout life. Daniel Levinson (1978) has suggested that in mid-life we are often confronted with the need to give up or greatly revise a dream that we had about how our life would be and what we would achieve in our work and in our families. The elderly person likewise must come to terms with how well achievements matched even revised aspirations. In the childhood and young adulthood years, the self-concept may actually be formed more on the basis of capabilities than accomplishments, because these indicate something of what can be expected in the future. As the future perspective is foreshortened, the person must somehow come to terms with the fact that some goals will be left forever unachieved.

Loss of Roles

Old age has often been discussed in terms of the loss of important social roles, that of productive worker, spouse, parent, or community leader. The gerontologist Irving Rosow (1973; 1974) has argued that our self-concepts must inevitably be seriously impaired when our roles are lost. While I disagree with some aspects of his analysis, it is true that these role changes in later life must certainly call for some revision in the self. The perspective among some gerontologists has been that the obvious way to cope with role loss is by replacing these roles with other ones. While this no doubt works out for some people and their self-esteem is preserved, I want to suggest that there are other ways in which people may go about reconstructing their selves in the face of role losses.

Let us now take these five areas of challenge (devalued status, physical decline, proximity of death, successes and failures, and loss of roles) and consider wherein may also lie some of the opportunities of aging. More specifically we want to consider how it is that the self of the person may continue to develop and achieve its potential in the face of these challenges.

OPPORTUNITIES FOR SELF-DEVELOPMENT IN LATER LIFE

Devalued Status of the Elderly

Let us take first the matter of how the older person deals with the negative images of aging that may be pervasive in the society. Here I want to return to the perspective I suggested at the beginning of this presentation, that the construction of the self is always an active process. As the social breakdown model suggests, some people do give in to these negative images. But some apparently can distance themselves from them. One way in which this occurs is simply to not identify with older people in general. Two national surveys in the U.S. by Louis Harris (1975; 1981) found that even though older respondents agreed with younger adults that a list of problems (crime, health, etc.) were serious ones for older adults, they did not see these problems as applying to themselves nearly to the extent that they did for older people in general. Another approach is through the process of making social comparisons with others one's own age. Inevitably, a person can find several or many others of similar age who are worse off—a phenomenon that Arlie Hochschild (1973) called the poor dear hierarchy. By seeing that one is not at the bottom of this hierarchy, the self is protected.

Yet another way to deal with the matter of societal attitudes and stereotypes is to recognize the degree to which one has internalized these attitudes so that we can divest ourselves of them. The potential contributions of the elderly cannot be realized as long as these stereotypes hamper self-images and self-esteem and risk becoming self-fulfilling prophecies. Let me share with you the example of Elizabeth Layton (also known as Grandma Layton), the 80-year-old Kansas artist who began doing contour drawing at the age of 68 as a means of coping with a life-long depression. She was able to release through drawing what a myriad of other therapies had not been able to accomplish. I will say more about her in a few moments, but the point I want to make now is that Grandma Layton through her self-portraits has confronted nearly every negative image of aging in the book and then laughed at them. She is meticulous in pointing out every single physical deformity— the liver spots, the varicose veins, and the arthritic fingers—claiming that she uses herself as a model so that she does not have to risk offending anyone else. What is important is that in her confrontation with and laughter over these realities of aging, she has been able to go beyond them to commentaries on a multitude of social issues such as AIDS, the environment, women's rights, the right to die, and many others.

It seems then that people deal with the devalued status of the elderly in two basic ways, both of which may promote continued self-development. One is to distance themselves psychologically from the so-called problems of the elderly, and the other is to directly confront the stereotypes and sort out which ones do and don't fit.

Physical Decline

We have talked earlier about the urgency of coming to terms with the loss of youthful vigour and attractiveness, as well as the onset of specific disabilities. This is a very tall order, but the challenges with respect to these changes is to find significance in these diminishments, and to recognize that out of loss can come the release of new forces in the person. Let me give you several illustrations of what I mean.

In my book (Breytspraak, 1984), I discussed the self-development of the poet William Butler Yeats in his later years. Yeats, in his younger adult years, was deeply discontented by his inability to bring emotion into his poetry. He was confident of his intellectual ability and aesthetic sophistication, yet he seemed out of touch with his instinctive drives. Yeats suffered a number of physical illnesses as he grew older which greatly limited him, and it apparently was these very infirmities that helped release an incredible power and emotion in his poetry in his final years that far exceeded anything that had come before. He railed and screamed about the terrible things aging does to the body, but he also defied and used his aging to reach new levels of understanding and his personal goal of being able to convey his emotion.

Or take the case of a well-known dermatologist who in his late 60s experienced macular degeneration of the retina which seriously threatened his ability to continue to work. Ultimately, the eye condition progressed so far that he had to give up his practice, and he entered into a period of depression. One of the major areas on which his self was built was gone. But then the tremendous loss which he had encountered became the basis for a new chapter in his life as he put his medical knowledge and his own personal experience with blindness together to help found a low-vision clinic, where he continues to spend time even into his late 70s, counselling people about coping with their vision problems.

For Grandma Layton, the occasion for new growth in her later years was the recognition of the profoundness of her depression, but it also became the vehicle by which she has delved into many of the social issues of the day. Sally Gadow (1983) has suggested that we think of the relationship between one's frailties and one's energies as a dialectical one "where they no longer merely limit and define one another negatively, but also are mutually affirming..."

Some people may actually begin significant new projects in old age, even though they know they must depend on others to carry them on. Gandhi was 72 when he led the final movement for Indian independence one year before his death, and Pope John XXIII in his late 70s launched the Second Vatican Council. Bertrand Russell campaigned for nuclear disarmament and other social commitments into his 90s. Hence, the very fact of aging and infirmity can be the source of new ideas and energies that would not have emerged apart from the aging process.

Proximity of Death, and Balancing Successes and Failures

I want to group two of the challenges I discussed earlier together—the challenge of coming to terms with the likely near end-of-life, and making sense of successes and failures. While there are a number of self issues connected with each, I want to use them as the occasion to consider reminiscence and life review as a process that may encourage continued self-development in the later years. Societal stereotypes have not been especially supportive of reminiscence as a modality for relating to aging, in that there often is worry about those who "live in the past." Gerontologists, on the other hand, have speculated that this tendency to reminisce is a natural and healthy one, especially when death is probably close. Erik Erikson has laid the groundwork with his suggestion that the final psychosocial crisis in old age is that of integrity vs. despair. It is important to our self to have a sense of integration, of wholeness. Victor Marshall (1980) has written about the tendency in later life to want to make one's life story a good one—one that makes sense and is meaningful. The construction of our autobiography is an active and selective process. As Greenwald (1980) has noted, we often act as revisionist historian with regard to ourselves; that is, we rewrite our memories in such a way that we look the best we can. Indeed, this process may figure heavily in to how we confront our mortality—it may be much easier to do when through the process of reminiscence we have been able to put our life into a larger perspective, perhaps diminishing the failures and increasing our remembrance of the successes. So we see that reminiscence has the possibility of being a highly engaging, active process that helps the person come closer to his or her image of self.

Role Loss

And finally, where are the opportunities for one's selfhood in the loss of role? This question elicits for me a variety of responses. One is that we not assume that people do not already have at least some way of making sense of important role changes. Often, it is possible to maintain some identity with the lost role—e.g., people may stay in contact with the profession from which they have formally retired by continuing to be involved with selected activities that support that identity (going to conferences, doing volunteer activities using skills from that role, etc.). The widow may continue to maintain her self-identity as wife by still referring to herself as Mrs. John Jones or by continuing to participate in an activity, such as an auxiliary that may have been related to her husband's work.

Another response is to recognize that the very fact of exiting a role can open up new possibilities for self-growth. When one is less caught up in routine responsibilities of earlier years, there is more discretionary time and less concern about career advancement. This may mean that the person can more easily begin to uncover what Carl Jung and others have talked about as the inner self. There may be unfulfilled longings and untapped reservoirs that finally can find their way to the surface.

The final issue on my agenda is to consider how professionals, as well as persons in the formal networks (family) of the older person, can respond so as to best foster potentials for self-development in the later years. I can suggest only some broad guidelines based on my studies of some of the issues to be faced in the continued development of the self. I must turn to those of you who are practitioners and family members for specific examples of how these principles can be applied.

It is important to remember the two basic motivations of the self which I discussed earlier: the motive to look good (self-esteem) and the motive for consistency and continuity of the self through time. It is also important to remind ourselves that the self is never formed in isolation, but rather is always embedded in the social context. I want to suggest three principles or guidelines which we can derive from our discussion.

First, wherever possible, we should help older people to avoid being drawn into the negative images of aging that pervade our society. So often the result of these negative images is that the older person attributes to himself responsibility for situations that are really at least partially the result of societal pressures. For example, if we assume that people are not capable of being productive, creative, and contributing workers, or that older people cannot learn, then we almost ensure that this result comes about by the structures we set up in society. Part of the task, of course, is for all of us to become fully aware from studies of the aging process of what is possible and under what conditions, but the other side is to help prevent the older person from buying into stereotypes in the first place. One way to do this may be to work with the person to help him or her understand that the source of a problem may not be with an individual, but rather with the situation. In one study (Rodin & Langer, 1980), the researchers experimented in a nursing home with getting a group of patients to make attributions about physical problems to the environment rather than to old age. For example, to keep them from attributing slipping on floors to weak knees and poor movement, they were told that the floors were slippery because they were tiled to keep them clean and that even young people slip on them. As attributions for conditions were directed more to external causes and less to aging itself, the experimenters found greatly improved behaviour, better health, and reduced perceptions of stress. The point for the person doing intervention with the older adult is to get away from a blaming-the-victim orientation to old age by helping people shift their attributions of causality to other areas that have more enhancing effects for the self. I must add that this is not necessarily a matter of deceit, for so often the environments in which people live are full of barriers that could be modified relatively easily so as to promote better individual functioning.

The second guideline or principle that I will discuss is very much related to the first. It is that we make conscious efforts to return control of personal situations to elders wherever possible. Underlying a positive sense of self is a feeling that we are in charge of our destiny and that we can bring about at least some of the effects we desire. The research literature has shown repeatedly how important a sense of control is to happiness, adjustment, and self-concept, and this is just as true for older people as younger people. Yet there are many situations where we as professionals or as family members unnecessarily take control away—or take away more than is necessary—from the older person. Kuypers and Bengtson (1973) propose that those who serve the elderly should divest themselves of as much power and control as possible and give it back to the elderly. In an institutional setting, it has been shown that wherever older people can be given greater control of the policies and administration affecting them, the evidence is strong that they will feel a much greater sense of competence and will perform more effectively.

A third guideline is that we be conscious of and even actively promote activities in the older person that encourage a sense of integration and wholeness in the self. Many of the challenges to the self in the later years, including various role losses and awareness of death as a proximate event, can be at least partially addressed through the encouragement of reminiscence activities. Studies of reminiscence have shown that people experiencing losses are more easily able to move on into the future and other avenues of development if they have been able to review their life and events leading up to the loss and to put them into some perspective.

A study reported by Kahana and Coe (1969) made an impression on me. They studied self-concepts of residents in a home for the aged by comparing their responses to a Twenty Statements Test (where they were asked to respond to the question "Who Am I?") with staff responses to the question of "Who is this resident?" New residents generally tended to describe themselves by their various roles in the family and community, whereas staff generally defined them in terms of interpersonal characteristics, usually referring to some aspect of adjustment or manageability. Among those residents who had been in the home for at least two years, the tendency was to define themselves (as the staff did) by their interpersonal relations and manageability and with very few references to their past roles. In a sense, a kind of depersonalization process unwittingly went on that must have struck at the core of the self.

There may be a variety of ways that we can respond to this suggestion that we encourage integration and wholeness, but one possibility is to establish structured or semi-structured occasions for reminiscing or life review. The University of Southern California developed a continuing education class for older adults where a technique called "guided autobiography" (Hately, 1982) was used in which persons wrote stories related to various areas of their life (e.g., family, health, work, sexual development, experiences with death). They were then guided in looking for underlying themes that might connect the various stories.

I have suggested three areas where we might undertake activities that would further encourage self-development in the later years:

1) helping older people directly confront the negative images of aging that are pervasive in our society,

2) returning control to the person wherever possible, and

3) providing opportunities for life review and integration of one's past.

In essence, what I am advocating is a more active and proactive view of the aging process. Too often we take the view (old and young alike) that aging is something that happens to you. When we concentrate our concern on how a person is adjusting to aging, we are putting everything in a somewhat passive mode. It seems to me that the whole thrust is to identify those areas where change is possible when people take charge of their lifestyles and their lives so as to maximize the opportunities for continued development of the self into later life. In this way, the elderly may move us toward unexplored boundaries and help create new models of aging.

REFERENCES

Breytspraak, L.M. (1984). *The Development of Self in Later Life.* Boston: Little, Brown & Company.

Epstein, S. (1973). The Self-Concept Revisited: Or a Theory of a Theory, *American Psychologist, 28,* 404–416.

Erikson E.H. (1963). *Childhood and Society,* 2nd ed. New York: W.W. Norton.

Gadow, S. (1983). Frailty and Strength: The Dialectic in Aging, *The Gerontologist, 23,* 144–147.

Greenwald, A.G. (1980). The Totalitarian Ego: Fabrication and Revision of Personal History, *American Psychologist, 35,* 603–618.

Hately, B.J. (1982). Guided Autobiography: An Approach to Human Development, paper presented at the annual meeting of the Gerontological Society of America, Boston, November.

Hochschild, A.R. (1973). *The Unexpected Community.* Englewood Cliffs, N.J.: Prentice-Hall.

Kahana, E., and R.M. Coe. (1969). Self and Staff Conceptions of Institutionalized Aged, *The Gerontologist, 9* (Winter), 264–267.

Kuypers, J.A., and V.L. Bengtson. (1973). Social Breakdown and Competence: A Model of Normal Aging, *Human Development, 16,* 181–201.

Levinson, D.J., C.M. Darrow, E.B. Klein, M.H. Levinson, and B. McKee (1978). *The Seasons of a Man's Life.* New York: Knopf.

Marshall, V.W. (1980). *Last Chapters: A Sociology of Aging and Dying.* Monterey, Calif.: Brooks/Cole.

Rodin, J., and E. Langer (1980). Aging Labels: The Decline of Control and the Fall of Self-Esteem, *Journal of Social Issues, 36,* 12–29.

Rosow, I. (1973). The Social Context of the Aging Self, *The Gerontologist, 13* (Spring), 82–87.

_____. 1974). *Socialization to Old Age.* Berkeley: University of California Press.

Creative Aging
THE POWER OF YEARS

Gary T. Reker

We are all conceived, live a life, and die. All things change through time. When looked at from the beginning of time, this change is called development; when viewed from the perspective of the ending, it is called aging.

Development and aging both deal with age change. From a psychological perspective, age change is seen as a single process. Development and aging simply describe changes that occur with the accumulation of time. Development is aging and aging is development. This concept allows both growth and decline to take place at any point in time. Whether you call it development or aging depends on your vantage point.

WHEN DOES AGING BEGIN?

Many lay people believe that aging begins at some magic age such as 65. Biologists believe that aging begins at physical maturity, when things start to go downhill. The magic number is anywhere between 35 and 45 years. From a psychological perspective, aging begins at conception, the same time that development also begins. Thus, aging describes phenomena that apply to everybody, from "day one" onward. However, for relevance and focus, the particular vantage point here is the later years of life, mid-life and onward.

WHAT IS "CREATIVE AGING"?

Webster's Dictionary (1977) defines "creative" as "marked by the ability or power to produce through imaginative skill." Creativity can take at least two forms: attitudinal and product-oriented. Most people tend to think of creativity as product-oriented as revealed in the great works of highly gifted individuals. For the purposes of this paper, ordinary aging individuals who

Reproduced from *Perspectives: The Journal of the Gerontological Nursing Association,* Vol. 14, No. 4 (Winter 1990), 6–9.

engage in predominantly attitudinal forms of creativity are the foci. Attitudes are reflected in the cognitive processes of imagination, contemplation, self-evaluation, or reflection. The term "creative" envisions an active, vital process. From a developmental point of view, it is an active, vital process of adaptation to life circumstances over time (Ager, White, Mayberry, Crist, & Conrad, 1981–82).

There is no denying the biological reality of aging—hair turns grey or falls out, m-o-v-e-m-e-n-t s-l-o-o-o-w-s, bodies become frail. Psychologically, however, in terms of knowing, thinking, feeling, and being, there is no basis for inevitable decline. Indeed, there is now increasing evidence for continued growth in these areas as we age (Bond & Rosen, 1980).

This is a remarkable turn-around in our stereotypical images of the elderly. The elderly were once perceived as unproductive "has-beens", a drain on society's medical and social security systems, confused, feeble-minded, cranky, crotchety, rigid "old fogies". The worst enemy of the elderly is not the fact of biological aging, but the stereotypes and prejudices *about* growing old! Fortunately, these myths have been debunked. The potential for continued growth, given a relatively healthy body, is virtually unlimited. It is argued here that because of the accumulated experiences of a life-time, humans are psychologically at their most highly developed state when they are old. This state is reflected in wisdom, the expression of which our society, until very recently, has failed to encourage or facilitate in our elderly.

Aging is an active, creative process. There is no such thing as "the typical experience of old age"; there is no such thing as the "typical older person". Humans are self-constructing. They have the power to influence their destiny. They are not victims of their own age. They can create their own environment, if they want to. Creative aging is based on the premise that "you *can* teach an old dog new tricks". Creative aging is taking advantage of personal resources that will actualize one's potential for psychological growth. Society's image or ideal of old age must be re-examined and restructured so that a broader social framework can support and reinforce an aging individual's creative endeavors.

PERSONAL RESOURCES

The object of creative aging is the prevention of illness and the promotion of high levels of physical and psychological well-being. Being in good health means more than simply the absence of illness. It means moving beyond the neutral state toward high level wellness.

How can high level wellness be achieved? There are several possible ways. Some are the result of external conditions or circumstances such as being born into an upper or middle-class family; having adequate finances; having a good education, etc. Many other ways are under the control of the individual. They are called "personal resources". Personal resources are available to anyone. All that is necessary is the motivation to pursue or invoke them.

An Attitude of Exploration

The key here is to create opportunities, options, or alternatives. A greater repertoire of diverse experiences can lead to better adaptation to life circumstances. This is particularly important for the elderly who face personal losses, physical decline, and environmental changes with increasing age (Sissons, 1984). An exploratory attitude is based on the philosophy that one should not impose one's own "values" of successful aging on the elderly. Instead, the elderly should be allowed to create their own definitions of successful aging.

Pursuing Meaningful Activities and Relationships

One way to create options is to pursue a variety of meaningful activities and relationships. Sources of meaningful activities and relationships include leisure/recreation; creative activities such as music, painting, or writing; personal relationships with family members, neighbors, or friends; service to others; involvement in social causes; and religious beliefs or practices. These are all life-affirming activities. In a recent study, a variety of meaningful activities was found to contribute to a greater sense of personal meaning and to higher levels of physical and psychological well-being in older adults (Reker, 1988).

Anticipating Future Potentialities

Planning and goal-setting now, in anticipation of future potentialities, is important at all stages of life. However, it becomes increasingly more important with age, as change necessitates new means of coping. In creative planning, each individual commits time and energy to future projects according to personal priorities. This could range from financial planning to planning against future stress, such as the possibility of widowhood, forced retirement, and physical decline.

Planning for change offers the benefit of better preparation for that eventuality before it suddenly happens. Such planning is known as anticipatory socialization. For example, a middle-aged psychology professor who enjoys a good game of hockey knows that at some future time, he will no longer be able to keep pace. In preparation for that eventuality, he gets involved with an alternative sport such as golfing, an activity which is under self-paced personal control. When his legs give out, he can still "putter a round". Hence, one can inoculate oneself against future stress by anticipating its occurrence and by exercising the options available to deal with it, if and when it should arise.

Meaningful activities and relationships deal with the present, the "here and now". An attitude of exploration must also extend into the future. Looking forward to a diverse number of desirable events and being extremely confident that such events will take place is an index of a high degree of personal optimism. This process might be called anticipating future potentialities. Optimists have a positive outlook on life. They interpret negative events more positively. The hope of better things to come helps them to accept present circumstances. Optimists have a clear future vision.

The importance of personal optimism in promoting physical and psychological well-being has been extensively documented in the literature (Reker & Wong, 1983, 1985; Scheier & Carver, 1987). In a recent prospective study, it was found that highly optimistic older adults at the beginning of the study reported significantly fewer health symptoms two years later (Reker & Wong, 1983). In another study, optimistic seniors were found to be physically and mentally healthier than their pessimistic counterparts. They also suffered less from depression, were more committed, and found greater meaning and purpose in their lives (Reker & Wong, 1985). In a recently completed study of middle-aged adults, a high degree of optimism acted as a "buffer" to reduce the impact of negative life events on physical well-being (Reker & Wong, unpublished manuscript).

Creative Coping

Creative coping refers to cognitive and behavioral attempts to reduce or remove actual and anticipated demands appraised by the individual as potentially stressful. Cognitive coping attempts include (1) cognitive restructuring, (2) adopting an attitude of acceptance, and (3) discovering/creating a sense of meaning and purpose.

Cognitive restructuring refers to attempts to restructure, redefine, or re-evaluate stressful situations in order to reduce the impact of the stress. The goal is to de-emphasize the negative and to focus on the positive. Ways of focusing on the positive include finding side benefits of negative experiences, comparing oneself with others who are not doing as well, imagining a worse alternative and feeling "lucky", or constructing a better match between expectations and what is possible. In a study of people whose houses were destroyed by fire, Thompson (1985) found that positive re-evaluators (i.e. optimists) reported better coping, more positive emotions, and fewer physical symptoms.

Adopting an attitude of acceptance means acceptance of things that are perceived as unchangeable, uncontrollable, or not worth one's while to change. Why continuously bang your head against the wall? This is not a passive or pessimistic acceptance, but rather, it reflects a realistic, healthy attitude. An attitude of acceptance was found to be a primary coping mechanism employed by a group of older adults defined as "successful agers" (Wong & Reker, 1984).

Discovering/creating a sense of personal meaning and purpose in life is realized through alternative interpretations that provide a sense of order or coherence to situations that are incomprehensible or undesirable. An elderly gentleman who had lost his spouse through death confided that he coped with this loss by viewing the situation not as a loss but as a loved one "having gone before him". This is a comforting mental attitude that gave meaning to his personal suffering.

Research involving young, middle-aged, and older adults has demonstrated that a high degree of meaning and purpose in life is related to high levels of physical and psychological well-being in all three age groups (Reker, Peacock, & Wong, 1987). In a related study of older adults, a sense of personal meaning was associated with higher self-esteem and fewer physical symptoms (Butler, 1988). In addition, personal meaning was found to play a "dual" health-protecting (buffering) and health-enhancing role, underscoring its importance as an adaptive coping resource for older adults. In a third study, a group of older adults, defined as "successful agers"; that is, aging creatively, made more frequent use of creative coping strategies, such as finding meaning and purpose in life, compared to elderly who were not aging as successfully (Wong & Reker, 1984).

CONCLUSION

This paper has taken the position that, from a psychological perspective, the aging process is marked by continuous growth and development. The aging individual plays an active, vital role in this process by taking advantage of personal resources to actualize the human potential. By developing an attitude of exploration, by pursuing meaningful activities and relationships, anticipating future potentialities, and coping creatively, the aging person successfully negotiates the life course and adapts to life circumstances. The experiences of a lifetime culminate into a highly developed psychological state reflected in wisdom. It is important, then, to begin to defuse the stereotypical attitudes about the aging process that hold elders back, and to promote the concept of "old age" as a stage of development with its own unique challenges.

REFERENCES

1. Ager, C.L., White, L.W., Mayberry, W.L., Crist, P.A. & Conrad, M.E. (1981–82). Creative aging. *International Journal of Aging and Human Development, 14,* 67–76.

2. Butler, B. (1988). *Personal meaning, stress, and health in older adults: A test of the moderator model.* Unpublished Honors Thesis, Trent University, Peterborough, ON.

3. Bond, L.A. & Rosen, J.C. (1980). *Competence and coping during adulthood.* Hanover: The University Press of New England.

4. Reker, G.T. (November, 1988). *Sources of personal meaning among young, middle-aged, and older adults.* Paper presented at the Gerontological Society of America, San Francisco, CA.

5. Reker, G.T., Peacock, E.J., & Wong, P.T.P. 1987). Meaning and purpose in life and well-being: A life-span perspective. *Journal of Gerontology, 42,* 44–49.

6. Reker, G.T., & Wong, P.T.P. (April, 1983). *The salutary effects of personal optimism and meaningfulness on the physical and psychological well-being of the elderly.* Paper presented at the 29th Annual Meeting of the Western Gerontological Society, Albuquerque, New Mexico.

7. Reker, G.T. & Wong, P.T.P. (1985). Personal optimism, physical and mental health: The triumph of successful aging. In J.E. Birren and J. Livingston (Eds.), *Cognition, stress and aging* (pp. 134–173). Englewood Cliffs, NJ: Prentice-Hall.

8. Reker, G.T. & Wong, P.T.P. (unpublished manuscript). *Personal optimism and positive life events: Moderators of life stress in adulthood.* Trent University.

9. Scheier, M.F. & Carver, C.S. (1987). Dispositional optimism and physical well-being: The influence of generalized outcome expectancies on health. *Journal of Personality, 55,* 169–210.

10. Sissons, A. (1984). *Options.* Toronto: Ontario Ministry of Tourism and Recreation.

11. Thompson, S.C. (1985). Finding positive meaning in a stressful event and coping. *Basic and Applied Social Psychology, 6,* 279–295.

12. *Webster's New Collegiate Dictionary.* (1977). Springfield, Massachusetts: G and C Merriam Company.

13. Wong, P.T.P. & Reker, G.T. (March, 1984). *Coping behaviour of successful agers.* Paper presented at the Western Gerontological Society, Anaheim, CA.

Spirituality and Meaning

National Advisory Council on Aging

At the heart of every religion and of contemporary growth psychology is the conviction that human life has a spiritual dimension, that life must be dedicated to the fulfilment of meaning. According to psychoanalyst Erich Fromm, there is a fundamental human need for "a frame of orientation and an object of devotion." In his words, "All men are 'idealists' and are striving for something beyond the attainment of physical satisfaction."[1] For psychologist Paul Wong, personal meaning has three components: intellectual beliefs which help the individual make sense of life experiences; motivation to pursue goals consistent with one's values; and an emotional state of satisfaction because one's life is worth living.[2] In a broad sense, to be spiritual is to be sensitive to the dimension of meaning in one's life.

AGING AND THE NEED FOR MEANING

Having a strongly felt meaning to life contributes in many ways to seniors' well-being. Better morale, less loneliness and a positive attitude towards aging are found among seniors who have a sense of life purpose. They also are more likely to be satisfied with their health and to become less depressed if their health deteriorates. It appears, too, that having a meaning in life helps prevent stress-related illnesses. Similar patterns of well-being are found among those whose life meaning is expressed through a religious faith and those with a sense of life purpose that is not necessarily religious.

A strong sense of life meaning plays a positive role in helping seniors cope with life problems. In the National Advisory Council on Aging (NACA) consultation on the strategies used by seniors to cope with barriers to independent living, several seniors reported that they prayed for strength or tried to accept some difficulties as being "God's will."[3] Psychoanalyst Viktor Frankl survived five years in a Nazi concentration camp in the hope of seeing

Reproduced with the consent of the National Advisory Council on Aging (NACA) and with the permission of the Ministry Supply and Services Canada, 1993.

his wife again and with the desire to write a book.[4] According to Dr. Edward Stieglitz, "Having a purpose distinguishes those persons who grow old from those who get old."[5]

RELIGIOUS MEANING

Inasmuch as religion, as a shared system of personal meaning, is a social reality, religious symbols and rituals form the basis for common values, for social support, for celebration and for mourning. Religious people are propelled by an awareness that there is an ultimate purpose in the Universe in which they participate, or a Higher Power with whom they have a unique relationship. Religion creates solidarity among believers and makes life special.

According to researchers Dan Blazer and Erdman Palmore, the link between emotional well-being and religious commitment is strongest among seniors aged 75 and older.[6] A plausible explanation offered by Harold Koenig, James Kvale and Carolyn Ferrel is that as health, social and financial resources diminish in the later years of life, religion remains a durable source of support and comfort; for seniors 75+, religiousness contributes more to well-being than does financial status or social support.[7]

As a resource for overcoming problems and for adapting to situations over which a person has little control, religious faith works well. Religious seniors afflicted with serious diseases seem to have better chances of recovering, prolonging their life or suffering less physical pain than do people without a sustaining faith. As far back as 1910, Sir William Osler, the famous physician, wrote about "the faith that heals."[8] Comparing religious and non-religious ways of coping with stressful events, researchers Harold Koenig, Linda George and Ilene Siegler observed that religious coping behaviours were mentioned most frequently. These behaviours included prayer, faith and trust in God, reading the Bible and seeking help from the minister, from church friends or from church activities.[9]

RELIGIOUS PRACTICE IN LATER LIFE

Although not all seniors claim to have a strong religious faith, many more seniors are religious than any other age group. Moreover, seniors who have been religious in the past tend to become more committed to their faith as they get older. Attendance at services and other organized religious activities remains high until many seniors reach their mid-seventies, after which health problems may limit their ability to engage in activities outside the home. Nevertheless, these seniors remain committed to their faith and continue to engage in private spiritual activities, such as prayer, Scripture reading and listening to or watching religious programs on radio and television.

MODERNIZATION, MULTICULTURALISM AND FAITH

The influence of organized religion is less extensive than in the past in Canada and other modern industrialized societies. Greater educational opportunities and mobility, the presence of mass communication, the weakening of family and community structures, and the enhanced values placed on individualism and on science as a basis for knowledge have led to a transformation of religious belief and practice. Some religious traditions have adapted their teachings and practices to make their spiritual message more relevant to the modern world. A number of persons claim a religious affiliation but seldom practice their faith; still others meet their spiritual needs in non-religious ways. Moreover, our society has become increasingly multicultural and multireligious; many new Canadians espouse faiths such as Islam, Hinduism, Sikhism, Confucianism, Buddhism and Taoism.

Spirituality holds a special place in the traditional aboriginal cultures in Canada. A poem by Anna Lee Walters, painted at the entrance of Wanuskewin Heritage Park, north of Saskatoon, testifies to the importance of the spiritual dimension of the lives of aboriginal Canadians:

The nations live!
My spirit lives!
The spiritual world is everywhere!
If you listen, you will hear!
In the distance,
I hear one of a thousand songs
Of an ancient spiritual man. . .

For seniors who hold to the religion in which they were raised, religious change and multiplicity can be bewildering. They may feel isolated within their own place of worship, their communities, and even within their own families. Respecting generational and cultural differences in religious belief and communicating about important life matters with seniors whose beliefs, values or religious practices are different pose a challenge to families, faith communities, religious leaders and service-providers.

SPIRITUAL INTERVENTION: THE ROLE OF CAREGIVERS

When people face crises that challenge their will to live, spiritual support and guidance may be essential. Religious leaders have a special role to play, but they are not the only people who can respond to seniors' spiritual needs. Any sensitive person can assist another in finding a meaning in life to weather the storm. Knowing how and when to respond appropriately may be difficult, however.

Paul Wong describes four ways of enhancing meaning in seniors' lives:[10]

- **Reminiscence.** Facilitating, through guided discussion, a review of one's life to resolve past conflicts, affirm accomplishments and skills, and transmit the lessons learned from experience.

- **Commitment.** Providing opportunities to seniors to invest their time and energy to a task or to other persons.

- **Optimism.** Offering future events to look forward to and nurturing the hope that something positive will happen. "It is by looking into the future that we have the best chance of surviving present difficulties."

- **Religiosity.** Supporting religious beliefs and meaningful practices. "When everything is lost, including one's health," writes Wong, "the spiritual capability to reach out to God remains an effective weapon to combat meaninglessness and despair."

Health and social service professionals working with older adults may find it necessary to enter into a religious senior's perspective to support healthy coping behaviours. Consultation with a religious leader of the senior's own faith may be useful in this regard. Many physicians consider that they have some responsibility for dealing with religious issues if requested by their patients. Doctors may be willing to encourage patients' religious beliefs, join in prayer, or if asked, share their own beliefs. Koenig advises that "prayer may be appropriate with older patients during times of severe emotional distress or sickness or near death."[11]

"Spiritual distress", as a loss of meaning in life, is recognized as a nursing diagnosis, requiring nursing care no less than physical, social or psychological distress.[12] Nurse Elizabeth Peterson advises that providing spiritual nursing care for older persons involves first a willingness to be present and to share in the struggles and changes in their lives. This presence assures patients of their dignity and worth. To Father Antonio De Sousa, chaplain in an Ottawa chronic care hospital, "The acceptance and full attention of the caregiver becomes a vehicle for communicating the love of God." The simplest actions can have a spiritual significance if they help to strengthen the sense that life is worthwhile; in the words of Carter Catlett Williams, even a gentle back rub to a patient with advanced dementia can be "a quiet moment of giving and receiving that approaches the quality of sacrament."[14]

In responding to seniors who feel that their usefulness is over when they can no longer "do," Ann Squire, a senior and a former moderator of the United Church of Canada, advises that "it is important to help them learn that 'being' is as important as 'doing'."

Caregivers should assist seniors in continuing meaningful religious practices to the extent possible. They can pray with senior patients, or read scriptural passages to them, if asked. The communal bond a religious service can generate and the power of faith symbols should not be underestimated: even persons in later stages of dementia remain able to respond to religious symbols and rituals. For seniors without a strong religious affiliation, music, art, nature and the confirmation that one is cared for and valued can nourish the sense of meaning.

THE ROLE OF RELIGIOUS LEADERS AND FAITH COMMUNITIES

Religious leaders of all faiths increasingly are called to work with older members of their congregations and their families, in the community no less than in institutional settings. These leaders communicate the answers of their faith to the perennial human questions of death and personal suffering. As people get older, these issues are encountered more frequently. Moreover, spiritual leaders may be increasingly called upon to provide guidance to deal with crises of personal meaning in retirement, the stress of informal caregiving or with ethical decisions regarding life-prolonging medical intervention. To provide meaningful theological answers to the life situations of older adults, persons with pastoral responsibilities need to have some knowledge of aging and to be free of negative attitudes towards seniors.

Leaders of congregations may be in a good position to mobilize community support for senior members who experience problems in daily living owing to faltering health. They may assist in finding meaningful roles for seniors within the faith community. They can help to remove the barriers to participation in services, by such actions as making places of worship more accessible or arranging transportation for seniors with impaired mobility and printing large-type reading material. A committee of senior congregants may be helpful in designing "senior-friendly" places of worship. Outreach efforts by faith communities also benefit lonely seniors by making them less vulnerable to unscrupulous "preachers" who use the guise of religion for financial exploitation.

Programs for senior members exist in several religious denominations. Some churches, such as the Anglican Church of Canada, have established diocesan committees on aging to attend the needs of seniors in the church community. Holy Trinity Anglican Church in Toronto has established a hospice movement to assist terminally ill persons; as described in journalist June Callwood's book *Twelve Weeks in Spring*, this initiative came about from the experience of the congregation in helping senior Margaret Frazer die peacefully at home.[15]

A Catholic spiritual movement especially for persons over 55, known as La Vie Montante, has become popular in many francophone dioceses. In Vancouver, some parishes are considering a Pray and Ride service, where people would drive seniors to church and in return, the seniors would say a prayer for the drivers. In Elliot Lake, Ontario, seniors and religious leaders met for a workshop this year to address the spiritual needs and issues of self-worth and self-esteem among older people.[16]

The United Church of Canada offers pastoral care workshops that teach volunteers how to visit and how to provide support. An inter-generational program is the Secret Pal project; seniors are matched as "secret pals" with children in the church school program and letters are exchanged during the year. At the end of the church school year, a party is held where "pals" meet. In Saskatoon, the United Church runs McClure House, an inter-denominational enriched housing complex which allows residents to remain integrated in the life of the local community and of the congregation.

Many faiths, as well as non-religious personal growth movements, offer the opportunity of retreats. A few days in a quiet place, often with guidance for personal reflection, is popular as a means of spiritual renewal.

Finally, religious leaders can celebrate with the entire community of believers the special spiritual qualities that can blossom fully in later life. In the words of the founder of the Gray Panthers, Maggie Kuhn, "Churches and synagogues have a tremendous opportunity...for creative new ministries, if they take seriously the experiences, skills, and human resources represented in the older members of their congregations."[17]

SPIRITUAL GIFTS IN LATER LIFE

The major religions of the world recognize a special significance to the latter part of human life. In Hinduism, a person who has fulfilled his or her obligations to family and society can dedicate the years of later life to seeking spiritual enlightenment. In Buddhism, old age attests to the transitoriness of the physical world and to the need to find lasting meaning in a participation with the divine Consciousness. According to theologian Brynolf Lyon, the Judeo-Christian tradition also transmits three basic teachings about old age: old age is a blessing of God; it is a period of growth; and old age is marked by a special form of spiritual witness.[18]

The later years of life are considered by many gerontologists to be the period when one takes stock of one's whole life to find meaning and to maintain a sense of identity and peace in the face of one's imminent death. This life review can have a spiritual significance, not only for seniors themselves but for everyone in contact with seniors. Old age is the witness of a lifetime of experience. In the words of Viktor Frankl, now 84, "Old people have their possibilities in the past—the deeds done, the loved ones loved, and last, but not least, the sufferings they have gone through with courage and dignity. In a word, they have brought in the harvest of their lives."[19] For senior Bill Hughes, "Reaping what you have sown throughout life is a joy in the later years." Younger persons can learn from the life journeys of their elders; says theologian Brynolf Lyon, the lives of seniors can provide "a meaningful horizon for the moral becoming of others."[20]

Death becomes more present in seniors' lives, both with the deaths of loved ones and the awareness of the limited time remaining in their lives. For many people, the awareness of death makes life more precious. Theologian Eugene Bianchi suggests that the limits of time in older age can teach us to experience the ordinary as a gift, with emotions of joy and reverence.[21] The present movement can be lived more intensely in old age: the enhanced ability of many seniors to "smell the roses along the way" can serve as a lesson to younger persons to fully experience the present.

Finding the courage to overcome loss and suffering is a challenge to all persons. People who have discovered meaning in their lives are more likely to overcome their suffering; some have realized too that it is possible to find meaning in suffering. A Hindu sage of 72 who had been plagued with chronic illness for many years reflected that "each moment of suffering enables you to understand what it means when others suffer... There is a grace in this, because it brings a widening of consciousness."[22] Seniors who have endured the suffering in their lives with a profound sense of meaning are a source of inspiration to everyone they meet.

SPIRITUALITY AND PUBLIC POLICY

The personal need for meaning is present throughout life, although it may be taken for granted. Certainly, in the modern world, meaning of life questions lie in the private rather than the public domain; it is hard to imagine having a social policy on spirituality, or a Minister of Meaning! In health and social services, spiritual needs may have less precedence; they may be overlooked in planning services or relegated to a minor role. If there is a need to control costs, pastoral care may be sacrificed for more "essential" services. It is necessary for policy-makers, program planners, service-providers and informal helpers to acknowledge the importance of personal meaning to an individual's health and well-being and to use the most appropriate strategies to promote a sustaining sense of life meaning.

NOTES

1.   Fromm, Erich. *Psychoanalysis and religion.* New York: Bantam Books, 1967.

2, 10. Wong, P. Personal meaning and successful aging. *Canadian Psychology,* 30, 3, (1989): 516–525.

3.   National Advisory Council on Aging. *Understanding seniors' independence. Report no. 2. Coping strategies.* Ottawa: The Council, 1990.

4.   Frankl, V.E. *From death camp to existentialism.* Boston: Beacon Press, 1950.

5   Stieglitz, E. Quoted in *Productive Aging News,* no. 66, September 1992, p. 6.

6. Blazer, D. and E. Palmore. Religion and aging in a longitudinal panel. *The Gerontologist*, 16, 1, (1976): 82–85.

7. Koenig, H. et al. Religion and well-being in later life. *The Gerontologist*, 28, 1, (1988): 18–28.

8. Osler, W. The faith that heals. *British Medical Journal*, 1470–71, 1910.

9. Koenig, H. et al. Use of religion and other emotion-regulating coping strategies among older adults. *The Gerontologist*, 28, 3, (1988): 303–310.

11. Koenig, H. Research on religion and mental health in later life: A review and commentary. *Journal of Geriatric Psychiatry*, 23, 1 (1990): 25–53.

12, 13.Peterson, E. Physical...the spiritual...can you meet all of your patient's needs? *Journal of Gerontological Nursing*, 11, 10, (1985): 23–27.

14. Williams, C.C. Long-term care and the spirit. *Generations*, 15, 4, (1990): 25–28.

15. Callwood, June. *Twelve weeks in Spring*. Toronto: Lester & Orpen Dennys Publishers, 1986.

16 Pilon, C. Caregivers, clergy meet with seniors. *Elliot Lake Standard*, October 12, 1992, A3.

17. Hessel, D. *Maggie Kuhn on aging*. Philadelphia: Westminister Press, 1977.

18, 20.Lyon, K.B. *Toward a practical theology of aging*. Philadelphia: Fortress Press, 1985.

19. Frankl, V. Facing the transitoriness of human existence. *Generations*, 15, 4, (1990): 7–10.

21. Bianchi, E. *Aging as a spiritual journey*. New York: Crossroad, 1984.

22. Eugene, T.L. Dialogues with three religious renunciates and reflections of wisdom and maturity. *International Journal of Aging and Human Development*, 32, 3, (1991): 211–227.

Successful Aging

Mark Novak

•••

W hat *does* it take to age well? How do people discover a good age?

Writers in the past have seen aging as a time to turn inward. Carl Jung, for instance, says that "aging people should know that their lives are not mounting and unfolding, but that an inexorable inner process forces the contraction of life."[1] Erik Erikson, one of the keenest students of the life cycle, sees old age as a time to sum life up, a time to look back over the past, tie up loose ends and see life as good. Integrity—the sign of a good age, he says—requires "the acceptance of one's one and only life cycle as something that had to be and that, by necessity, permitted of no substitution."[2]

Psychoanalytic theory describes old age as a time to look back. But it ignores the fact that older people go on living. More recent work has begun to correct this narrow view of old age. Robert Butler, for instance, takes issue with the idea that a person in old age can only accept who they are and what they have been. "People are locked in by such a theory," he says. They may look healthy from Erikson's point of view, but they suffer because they are trapped by their work, marriage or life-style. "Excessive or exaggerated identity seems clearly to be an obstacle to continued growth and development through life and to appreciation of the future. . . . Human beings need the freedom to live with change, to invent and reinvent themselves a number of times throughout their lives."[3]

My own conversations with highly self-actualized older people support Butler's view. The people I talked to did not live serene, content, closed lives in old age. Instead they lived thoughtful, issue centred, active lives, open to the future. In every case they remained engaged in the discovery of who they were, not by looking into the past but by facing specific challenges that came as they aged. Sometimes these challenges came from within. Sometimes they came from outside: widowhood and retirement force people to rethink who

From *Successful Aging: The Myths, Realities and Future of Aging in Canada.* Copyright © Mark Novak, 1985. Reprinted by permission of Penguin Books Canada Limited.

they are. The most actualized older people in every case faced and took up these challenges, and this led the way to further growth as they aged.

After talking to dozens of these people a pattern began to take shape. I found that self-actualized older people discovered a good age through a series of stages. First, they faced a problem or moment of crisis—a *challenge*. Second, they saw that this problem demanded some response from them—I call this the stage of *acceptance*. Finally, they responded to this challenge and moved into the future—I call this *affirmation*. These three stages in the passage to later life all take place in the face of *denial*. As I use the word here, it simply means that a person wants to remain the same. A person engaged in denial tries to hold on to what is or has been.

DISCOVERING A GOOD OLD AGE

■■■

The Challenge

Let me give an example of this process.

I am sitting on a sofa sipping tea with Joanna in her living-room high above the city, in one of the wealthiest sections of town.

From where I sit I can see into the guest-room. Since Joanna lives alone, the second bedroom of this two-bedroom suite is pure luxury. It serves as a study and a guest-room when her children or grandchildren come to stay. Here she has hung an enormous acrylic painting of daisies. "I happen to like it, so I bought it," she says, as if to apologize for its size and bright colour. I happen to like it too, and I tell her so.

Joanna's comment about the daisies tells me in an offhand way that she intends to be her own person, now that she has found herself again after the years of turmoil following her husband's death. Once again she is beginning to discover who she is, and her home, her activities, her likes and dislikes, all say, "This is who I am. Take it or leave it. But don't ask me to live by your rules."

She tried living by someone else's rules after her husband's death twelve years ago. They had lived a comfortable middle-class life—two cars, a cottage, a house, children and friends. They were involved in everything.

Then he became ill with cancer of the brain. "Well," she says, "it was a matter of carrying on. I was going to stop working in real estate and be with my husband when he was sick, but I didn't. My supervisor thought it wasn't a good thing to dwell on it, to be at home a lot. He was right. So I carried on with my job. Of course, I had to do it well. It's part of the picture. You have to do it all well. It has to be perfect.

"I seemed to have this idea that I was going to carry it all on, that I could do it. I did it for two years, and I ran myself into the ground, running up to the hospital at noon and helping him with his lunch, going up again after work and then at night just sacking out so I could go on with another day. It was very hard."

■ ■ ■

This rigid adherence to an idealized picture of what she should be eventually had a serious effect on Joanna.

"I think all this running up to the hospital constantly wasn't really genuine. I did it. I cared for his suffering. But I was human. I wished someone else could be doing it. So I was not being true to myself. I think that led to a lot of things later.

"Also, the year my husband died I got my master's degree. I took my oral exam when he was already in the hospital. My advisor suggested that we postpone it due to the circumstances, but I said no and I did it. I did everything. Everything. It was unbelievable."

Even after her husband died she was determined to carry on as though nothing had happened.

"I was so determined that nothing like my husband's death was going to throw me, and I didn't allow myself a grievance time.

"After his death, I travelled. At Christmas I went to Spain, Hawaii, or wherever. At Easter I went somewhere. I went to Europe. There was never a day—I didn't allow myself any time at all. Do you get the picture? No time to breathe."

To any committee that wanted her she said yes. Then, of course, she would take on the chairmanship. She was running to meetings as well as doing things for the real estate board.

"It was unbelievable," she says, looking back. To keep herself going, she eventually turned to drugs and alcohol.

"No wonder I needed something. I didn't want to lean on people. I think I got hooked on a sleeping pill every night when my husband was sick, plus I drank a bit. Well, for a year after he died I was hospitalized off and on. I was using different kinds of pills. The doctor would change prescriptions, but I wouldn't discard the old ones. I took more alcohol than I'd like to admit along with the pills. I was, a very, very confused person.

"That was my way of coping, my way of standing the pain. I needed some kind of anaesthetic."

Meanwhile her world was collapsing.

"Two days after the funeral I went back to work because I knew I had to get out of this, get away from it, get back to work. And I think that was a good thing to do. But the next day I broke my arm. I was hurrying to get caught up with my work, and I slipped running for the car and a few bones snapped. Meanwhile I was still coping with a couple of courses at the university. Then three weeks after my husband died my daughter and her husband broke up. I think she was waiting until after he died to tell me.

"It all came down on me right then. But it still took two years till I gave in. I was going to deal with it all. I was going to cope with it all. Nothing thrown at me was going to blind me. You finally have to get floored to realize you can't do it alone.

"Well, I finally got floored. The last time I drove my car I drove right into a restaurant—right through the window.

"I had the car washed that day. And I was parked in front of this pizza parlour having a cup of coffee. I thought the sidewalk was quite a distance from the front of the car. I didn't want it sticking out so I put it in low and just eased it up. I drove right through the window.

"I just stepped out of the car—over these shards of plate glass, big pieces of plate glass on the road—and I said, 'I'd like a cup of coffee.' 'Lady,' said the owner, 'you get back in that car.' He was quite certain I was out of my tree. But I didn't get back. I just sat in the booth until the police came.

"That's the last time I drove. That was getting near the end."

For Joanna denial led to a dive into frenetic action. What was she denying? Her loneliness? Her loss? Her fear of her own death? Probably all these feelings drove her at that time.

At the same time it led her to a challenge. "I realized, 'Hey, you're going nowhere but down'.... And that's when I turned it around."

Acceptance

The first stage of the movement into old age, then, is the challenge that comes with the dawning knowledge that one is aging, that one is mortal, that life can't go on as it has.

Arthur Miller starts his play *Death of a Salesman* at just this moment of awakening.[4] Willy Loman, the leading character, is in the process of losing his connection with the life he has built in middle age. As the play opens, he arrives home after cutting short a routine business trip and tries to explain to his wife why he is back early.

> *I was driving alone, you understand? And I was fine. I was even observing the scenery. . .I opened the windshield and just let the warm air bathe over me. And then all of a sudden I'm going off the road. I'm tellin' ya, I absolutely forgot I was driving.*

In the end Willy kills himself because he can't face failure, aging or death. Denial, as Miller shows, turns aging into agony. The alternative is to accept what the coming of age has to tell us, and this is the second phase of growth into later life.

Joanna says this in her own way. "I had to get floored," she says, "before I could stop running." After the car crash she finally took a year off from work, and for the first time her district manager said he agreed with the idea. "I don't know if I did very good work the last year," she says. "Looking back, the strain must have been showing.

"Then I went to A.A. I still go occasionally. They have this theme of surrender to win, and there was a great deal in that. Surrender to win. Yes, let go."

Acceptance may sound like defeat, like giving up, but nothing could be further from the truth. Acceptance does mean a turn *away* from the goals and projects of mid-life, but it also means a turn *toward* an alternative way of being.

In his book *Learning to Grow Old*, Paul Tournier distinguishes between acceptance and resignation. When someone accepts life, he says, they "say yes to life in its entirety. . . . The adult who cannot accept growing old, or the old person who cannot accept his old age, or who accepts it grudgingly, 'because he's got to,' is in the same difficulty, blocked in his evolution against the stream of life."[5]

Oddly, acceptance of aging does not usually lead to a dread of death or decrepitude. The transition may create anxiety but it does not lead to disaster any more than the growth to adulthood leads to the destruction of the adolescent. In fact, it can lead to very positive realizations and the end of potentially harmful fantasies.

"At the time when I had my breakdown," Joanna says, "I thought I was going to get back to real estate. That was my goal when I took a year's leave of absence—to get back there. Because I was the highest paid agent, I got a good salary plus commission, with all these awards, you know. And that was a status claim. I was going to get back.

"Now I'm so glad that I got away from that and got involved in these marvelous things I'm doing now. When I finally retired I found so many things that were more important than sales."

What was the transition like at the time?

"It was terrifying, terrifying. That beautiful job let go. The house too—it was as if the house were sustaining me. I resisted, actually. I resented. And I blamed a lot of people because I had to do these things.

"And it was so hard for me to do that turn around that I did. I think actually the alcohol and the pills that created that collapse really helped because they made it catastrophic. I had to do something or terminate. Getting off them was sort of critical.

"When I went to Alcoholics Anonymous they taught me to find a new pattern. I didn't feel that I belonged anywhere. I felt so out of place everywhere, because I was responding in ways that weren't acceptable, I guess. A.A. was a terrific help. They carry you when there's no one else left. Everyone sort of backed off. I was left alone. I had to get away from the pills every night and the liquor. They carried me until I found a new way up, a new pattern.

"I was, well, inactive for two years, just trying to learn a new way, like learning to walk again. And I disposed of everything—the house, the cottage, the cars (two cars), snowmobiles, boats, everything. And it was like starting again with a bus pass."

"Let me tell you about that, because it's sort of typical of what I was going through. I had never ridden a bus and I didn't trust them. I'd go to the bus shelter and I'd wait, then I'd say to myself, 'It probably won't come. I think I'll call a cab.'

"At my age I had to learn how to ride a bus and to make a connection. I had to learn what bus to take to get to the park or what connection to the St James Hospital. I found it works beautifully. You know, it all fits."

"It was marvellous. Buses are such social places. I used to tend to depression. If I stay in too much I still do. But if I get dressed, get out of here, get on a bus, I'm all right. You get on the Broadway bus, it's a social club. And the West Clarke bus, they're all very serious. Very righteous, probably going to do some very laudable activity. Every bus is different. Good God. It's great fun. Much better than riding in my air-conditioned Lincoln.

"All of a sudden I was thrown into that, and I bought blue jeans and parkas and things for the weather. It didn't matter anymore what I looked like.

"When I was working I used to have my hair back-combed. 'Done.' And then after it was done I'd wear a thing around it at night so it would hold its shape for a week. Now I say, 'Oh the hell with my hair.' It used to be more trouble than it was worth. I just got it cut like this—short, in a pixie cut. I wash it and I blow it, and it feels good.

"Before I was always afraid. I remember one day I was shaking out a new duster and it floated to the balcony on the floor below. I wouldn't go down and get it. That's a very small thing, but I was afraid. Now I'd think nothing of going down and saying, 'Hey, my duster's on your balcony.' I don't know why I would be afraid. I just was.

"I guess for me the change had to come in the form of a crisis. That's the only way I would accept it. I resist change, especially change imposed on me. Now, if I had to let it all go, I know I could do it. I have something here [pointing to herself] that I can be comfortable with."

Joanna speaks about the courage to age. Like Paul Tillich's "courage to be," it requires that a person face the non-being of aging—the loss of beauty, strength, wealth, power, friends, a spouse, and, in the end, life itself. Just as a person grows into adulthood, so they grow into old age. And the key word in both phrases is "growth." The coming of age sets up the condition for this growth. It presents a person with a challenge to affirm life in spite of its limits.[6]

A good age begins when a person first accepts the claim of aging. Only then can they affirm this new stage of life.

Affirmation

And now? "Oh, now I feel a new freedom," Joanna says. "A new happiness. It's a new life. I wish I'd done it before. I'm so glad I finally retired instead of waiting.

"At first I took a leave of absence, but then I didn't go back. Instead I took a second year. After that I left for good. They gave me a lovely letter saying I'd done a very good job and the company president said I could come back any time I chose. But I didn't.

"I began to volunteer at our local school a couple of afternoons a week. I worked with either slow learners or very fast children. I liked the very fast children. I like to see the movement. I guess because I move like that too."

All of this was part of Joanna's attempt to find a new pattern for her life.

"I was keeping my day filled with other things, slowly and painfully trying to fill my life. I found that physical exercise is a must for me, so I joined a health spa and I go there two or three times a week. I also joined a golf club and started golfing. These physical things, along with a lot of meetings, going back to school and working as a volunteer, all helped.

"That took about two years. And after that all of a sudden I found a lot of people wanted my services because I have a lot of training. And I started these two senior citizens' Toastmasters clubs. There are three of them going now. I'm doing youth leadership work in Riverside with fast learning kids. I teach them public speaking, talking on your feet, that sort of thing. I do a couple of those courses every year."

Joanna also sits on the board of directors of a seniors' education centre. She still attends meetings and she still loves to travel.

From the outside her life looks almost the same as before she retired: She is busy, active, involved. But it's not the same. The meaning of life is different for her today.

Paul Tournier speaks of an "inner revolution" in later life. He says that "really to accept retirement is to accept that one no longer gives the orders, that one is no longer in authority. It is to accept that one is no longer a part of the hierarchical society. It means taking part in a different game."[7]

But what game? What are its rules? And most important of all, what is the purpose of playing?

Today Joanna works hard as one of the district lieutenant-governors for Toastmasters International. She visits twenty-four clubs in her district. Two of them, as she said earlier, she started herself.

"It's good fun," she says. "Some are like a poor man's university. Others have lawyers and professors as members. Every club has a different kind of person. I find that very interesting."

I asked her if she planned to go further in the Toastmasters organization.

"I'm thinking no," she says, "that I don't want to do it, because it would be a very time-consuming thing and that's not what I want. It's not a status thing anymore, to be the head guy.

"The year I finally quit real estate I was elected head of the district real estate board, which is really the pinnacle." She smiles at the irony. "I refused that and said, 'No, I can't do anything for a while.'

"I realize now I don't want that at all. It's more the getting there, isn't it? The journey that we like. The journey and not the destination. And once you get there—well—you ask, 'Is this all there is?'"

For Joanna and all the other people I have talked to, neither status nor position matter much in their lives. When I asked people, "What's most important to you today?" in nearly every case they answered "people."

Martin Buber, philosopher and writer, said something like this late in his life. The last chapter of his autobiography he titled "Books and Men."

There he says that in his youth he preferred books to people. But, as he aged, "this has become less and less the case. . . . I knew nothing of books when I came forth from the womb of my mother, and I shall die without books, with another human hand in my own."[8]

But how can people maintain this human bond today in the face of social forces that threaten to tear family and friends apart? Joanna maintains it by caring for others. In addition to her Toastmasters and volunteer work, she has developed a special bond with her teen-age granddaughter.

"My relationship with her is very close," she says, "very open. When she was fifteen, she started having sex with boys, and she told me, not her mother. We talked it through and I got her to go to the clinic for pills. I got her to tell her mother eventually. Now she comes to me with anything. I think it's because I'm not judgmental.

"With my own children I worried too much about their making it in every way. I seemed to think, 'Oh dear, I don't want them to make the mistakes I did.' I was trying too hard and not letting them do their own suffering.

"With my grandchildren, though, I give them a lot more freedom—even the fellow four years old—to let them make their own decisions instead of thinking I know better.

"I say to them, 'How do I know what's right for you? How can I tell you what path to take?' So my grandchildren confide in me where they won't in their own parents. Sometimes I know I can't help them. Very often we'll talk for an hour and I don't do anything. After that hour they'll come to a decision. . . I guess I can be a listener, and I think that's something I owe to my fellow human beings."

I asked Joanna to sum up her life today.

"The grandchildren are wonderful," she says. "I love them dearly. But what really gives my life meaning now is inside. It's not external anymore. I have my inner resources—I always had them, but I didn't use them.

"Now I don't have to run around any more. I'm not at the centre. And death? I don't fear it. I think about it and I think, 'Oh, twenty years from now I won't even be here.' And it's sort of 'What the hell. Who do I think I am?' And it's really great.

"For me getting older was very painful at first because I resisted change. Now I'm changed, and it's okay. I would say I have a new freedom. My granddaughter tells me she's mature at 17. Well, I tell her I'm still maturing. I'm still at it. I thought I had no limits, but for me a great learning was recognizing my limits. It was a complete turnover, almost like a rebirth.

"I guess I've learned we're all weak really. At least we should accept that—being weak—and realize, 'Hey. I'm only a fragile human being.'" Now Joanna can admit her own limits. This was the great lesson aging taught her. She can now affirm her life in spite of loss and change. And she can now move on to a new challenge: to help younger people find meaning for themselves.

■ ■ ■

NOTES

1. Jung, C. "The Stages of Life," in J. Campbell, ed., *The Portable Jung* (Harmondsworth, England: Penguin, 1976), 109.

2. Erikson, *Childhood and Society*, 2nd ed. (New York: W. W. Norton, 1963), 268.

3. Butler, *Why Survive? Being Old in America* (New York: Harper and Row, 1975), 400–401.

4. Arthur Miller, *Death of a Salesman* (1949; New York: Viking Press, 1967), 14.

5. Paul Tournier, *Learning to Grow Old* (London: SCM Press, 1972), 178.

6. Paul Tillich, *The Courage to Be* (London: Fontana Library, 1962).

7. Tournier, *Learning*, 140–41.

8. Martin Buber, *Meetings*, Maurice Friedman, ed. (La Salle, Illinois: Open Court, 1973), 59–61.

SECTION THREE

Discussion Questions

1. *Name three benefits very old people get from exercise. What key issues do you need to keep in mind when designing an exercise program for very old people? How can someone who plans exercise for very old people maximize their participation in the program?*

2. *Describe at least three threats to the self that older people must cope with as they age. What keeps older people from coping well? What opportunities exist for successful responses to the threats of later life? How can professionals and family members help older people enhance their self-development?*

3. *What inhibits creative aging? How can older people overcome barriers to creative aging? What role does a purpose in life and a sense of meaning have in creative aging?*

4. *How has modern society influenced people's sense of spirituality? Does spirituality mean the same thing as religious belief? List some of the ways that older people can enhance the meaning of their lives. How can professionals help in this process?*

5. *What stages does a person go through in discovering a good old age? Why do people sometimes deny that change has taken place in their lives and that they need to adapt? What price may a person pay for this denial?*

6. *Reker says, "Aging is an active, creative process. . . . Humans are self-constructing. They have the power to influence their destiny. They are not victims of their own age. They can create their own environment, if they want to." Discuss this statement in light of the readings in this section.*

Suggested Readings

Chappell, N.L. (1993). "Technology and Aging." *Journal of Canadian Studies* 28 (1): 45–58.

Mac Rae, H. (1990). "Older Women and Identity Maintenance in Later Life." *Canadian Journal on Aging* 9(3): 248–67.

National Advisory Council on Aging (1993). *The NACA Position on Women's Life-Course Events.* Cat. No. H71–2/2–15–1993. Ottawa: Minister of Supply and Services Canada.

Wong, P.T., and L.M. Watt (1991). "What Types of Reminiscence are Associated with Successful Aging?" *Psychology and Aging* 6(2): 272–79.

Our Changing Health-Care System

The medical model dominates Canada's health-care system. This model assumes that health-care service takes place in a doctor's office or hospital, that treatment will take the form of drug therapy or surgery, and that the patient will have an acute, short-term illness. Many writers have criticized this model. First, it suits the illnesses of childhood and youth more than the health problems of old age. Second, it gives the power of treatment and cure to the physician. Third, when applied to older people, it often costs more than more appropriate interventions.

Gerontologists describe at least two other models of health care—the community-care model and the health-promotion model. The community-care model offers many forms of support, including outpatient medical treatment, physiotherapy, and home care. It suits the needs of older people who have chronic, long-term illnesses such as arthritis, heart disease, or osteoporosis. The health-promotion model aims at prevention and life-style change in a variety of settings. Health-promotion programs include exercise classes, nutrition classes, and seniors' centres. These two models can help reduce the cost of health care to an aging population if the current system can contain its costs.

The discussion of health care today often centres on cost. The federal government has cut back on transfer payments to the provinces for health care. The cost of equipment, tests, and health-care workers' salaries increases every year. The medical model leads to costly services that other models of health care may deliver for less. Other models may also provide more appropriate services for older people.

Evans presents a critique of the health-care system. He discusses six issues that confront the system today: cost control, population aging, technology, human resource policy, delivery, and a shift to health enhancement. His article reviews the policies designed to respond to these issues and suggests future directions for policy change. He concludes by making a distinction between a health-care policy and a public health policy. A public health policy would develop a wide range of programs to prevent illness and improve health. It would go beyond the expansion of health services and would extend the opportunity for good health to all socioeconomic groups. But the development of a strong public health program depends on funds now used by the health-care system. Policy would have to reallocate these funds. Evans supports this move. He says that "an overextended health-care system may become a threat to health."

Barer and his colleagues report that Canadians in general feel very satisfied with their present health-care system. Canadians have universal coverage without user fees. They also have a system that costs less to run than the U.S. system, though it provides better coverage. Older Canadians report some of the greatest satisfaction with the current system, and for good reason: seniors in some provinces pay no insurance premiums, and they get free pharmaceutical coverage and low-cost long-term institutional care.

Canada's system needs to change in spite of its success. For one thing, it needs to keep up with the changing needs of an aging society. Shapiro defines long-term care and describes its role in an aging society. She says that long-term care serves a relatively small portion of the older population who have a chronic illness and cannot manage on their own. Long-term care can help keep these people out of institutions. This would reduce costs to the system and provide the kind of in-home care that older people want. Shapiro echoes Evans when she says that the system must reallocate resources. It must reduce the number of institution beds in order to get the maximum savings from community-care programs.

Chappell also asks whether the current system provides services that meet the needs of older people. Health-care expenditures have grown, but older people may still have trouble finding the kinds of services they need. The current health-care system favours medical intervention and tends to provide less community care. Chappell argues for an increase in home-care programs outside the influence of the medical model. She also proposes that increases in home-care budgets come from a redistribution of acute-care dollars.

Evans noted that some groups in Canadian society have easier access than others to health-care services within the current system. Goodwill illustrates this inequality in her description of the health needs of Native seniors, who show physical decline earlier than non-Natives. Poverty, loss of culture, low status, and the lack of fit between the health-care system and Native seniors' needs all lead to decline. Goodwill presents a long list of health problems among Native seniors that the present system fails to solve. She calls for increased resources and improved delivery of health-care services. She notes that Native people and groups must work with the government and health providers to identify and meet Native seniors' needs.

Canada has one of the best and most cost-effective health-care systems in the world. Still, the articles in this section show that the system must change to meet the needs of a diverse and growing older population.

Canada: The Real Issues

Robert G. Evans

■■■

CANADA'S POLICY AGENDA

The functioning of the Canadian health care system is constantly in the forefront of public debate with ministers of health and premiers of provinces, who are held accountable in the provincial legislatures and in the press for any problems or misadventures which occur.

At present, the health care policy agenda in Canada is being driven by a set of interlocked problems, none of which are particularly new, or peculiar to Canada.

These problem areas can be summarized in several categories or clusters. These categories are not conceptually consistent with each other, indeed some turn out to be partial subsets of others. They are, however, the labels that tend to be employed in the public debate, and under which most of the research results are assembled.

1. Cost control
2. Coping with an aging population
3. Coping with the extension of technology
4. Manpower policy—surpluses of physicians and shortages of nurses
5. Improving the effectiveness and efficiency of health care delivery
6. Extending our concern from the delivery of medical care to the enhancement of health

Cost Control

This problem has faced every society in the industrialized world. If the modernization and growth of a country's general economy can outstrip that of its

Robert G. Evans, "Canada: The Real Issues," *Journal of Health Politics, Policy and Law* 17:4, pp. 739–62. Copyright Duke University Press, 1992. Reprinted with permission.

health care system, it need not be overly concerned with health care cost control. This has not, however, been the situation in North America or Western Europe, where all countries have had to wrestle, over the last decade or more, with the problem of moderating the growth of health spending in order to protect resources for other social and private priorities. And any country modernizing its health system must consider how it will deal with the inherent tendency of such systems to expand without limit, in the absence of strongly enforced external constraint (Evans 1990, 1991).

Within the last five to ten years, however, all developed societies, except the United States, appear to have found some response, if not necessarily a permanent solution, to this problem (Schieber and Poullier 1989). Sweden has actually significantly *reduced* its share of national income spent on health care. The process of control, in every country, has been accompanied by considerable difficulties and political conflict, and it is always possible that the health care system will break out of the controls which each society has placed on it, but, for the moment, a degree of stability prevails.

The processes whereby the provincial governments in Canada have imposed this degree of control for nearly twenty years, with the exception of the "recession breakout" of 1982, are three in number. First, as noted above, the nature of the Canadian payment system permits it to function very economically in terms of administrative costs, and these have not been rising over time.

Second, the medical fee schedules negotiated between the provincial medical associations and governments have grown much more slowly than fees in the uncontrolled American environment. Over time, fees in Canada have risen at a rate more or less in line with general price inflation; when physicians can set their own fees freely, fees rise substantially faster. At the same time, the elimination of extra-billing has prevented physicians from exploiting this alternative form of fee inflation.

In response, physicians in Canada do appear to have increased their volumes of billings per physician somewhat faster than in the United States, in order to keep their incomes rising, but they have not been able to offset fully the slower increase in fees (Barer 1988). Fee schedules have helped this process, by limiting the reimbursement of diagnostic services outside hospitals—most physicians cannot simply set up their own laboratories, for example—and also by preventing implicit "fee splitting" between laboratories and referring physicians (Reinhardt 1987).

On the other hand, these controls over the tendency of physicians to engage in "procedural multiplication," particularly when fee inflation is contained, are by no means complete, and Canadian provincial governments are increasingly exploring ways of imposing more explicit "caps" on total outlays for physicians' services. Two provinces—Québec and British Columbia—have already done so, and it is likely that more will follow (Lomas et al. 1989; Evans 1988).

Furthermore, it appears quite clear that the volume of physicians' services billed for in a province rises more or less in proportion to the increasing numbers of fee-for-service physicians. Thus control of cost escalation is directly connected to manpower policy, and in Canada these have been seriously inconsistent.

Finally, a very important part of the control of health care costs has been the system of global budgeting for hospitals, which enables this component of the health budget to be subjected to absolute "cash limits." The result has been a steady decline in acute care utilization, which nevertheless remains high relative to United States experience, and a much less rapid proliferation of new and very expensive high-technology interventions. Canadian provinces do acquire the most recent technology, but such equipment tends to be confined to the teaching hospital centers and does not proliferate throughout the regional hospital system or into free-standing facilities. Thus the availability per capita of such equipment tends to be lower than in countries such as the United States, Germany, or Japan.

The Aging of the Population

This is perhaps the most frequently cited source of serious problems, now and particularly in the future, for the Canadian and most other health care systems. Yet it is the area in which the rhetoric is in fact most misleading. The usual argument is that elderly people require more, and more costly, health care services, on average, than do younger people. At the same time, the population of elderly and, particularly, very elderly people in the population is growing, as birthrates have fallen and life expectancies have risen. Both these observations are true. But the common conclusion, that the costs of caring for the elderly will therefore necessarily exceed the willingness or ability of industrialized economies to pay for them, does not follow.

The aging of the population in Canada and in the rest of the industrialized world is a very important phenomenon over a time span of decades. But its effects on health care use are slow. In Canada, the aging of the population would add about 1 percent per capita per year to health costs, *if* the utilization patterns of each age group remained unchanged, and only the population age structure changed (Woods, Gordon Management Consultants 1984). This is well within the normal, or at least historical, economic growth rates of industrialized economies and could easily be accommodated, with a constant share of such growth being devoted to health care.

However, per capita rates of utilization and costs of health care services for the elderly are rising rapidly for each age group (Barer et al. 1987; Evans, Barer, et al. 1989; Barer, Pulcins, and Evans 1989). Elderly people *are* accounting for a rapidly increasingly share of our health care effort and resources. But the reason is not primarily that there are so many more of them. The real change is in how much is done to and for the elderly—they are being subjected to many more, and more intensive, interventions, often of unproven effectiveness.

The question is what benefits are being derived from the services that are being applied in increasing numbers to the care of the elderly. That brings us to the questions of technology, of effectiveness and appropriateness of care, and indirectly to issues of manpower or personnel. The demographic transition, at least as it applies to the past decade and the next, is in fact a smokescreen that obscures more fundamental questions of the basis on which utilization decisions are made and the costs and benefits of the results.

The Extension of Technology

The extension of technology is simply part of this more general set of issues. Technology per se is neither good nor bad; new knowledge and capabilities in principle merely expand our range of choices. The rhetoric surrounding technology often suggests that we are somehow compelled to apply whatever is discovered, at whatever expense. But the technology does *not* define its own range of application. Some new technologies have the capability to *reduce* significantly health costs—if conservatively applied and limited to areas of demonstrated effectiveness. The real problem of a trade-off between technological "advance" and cost control arises when new and expensive techniques (or for that matter old and not-so-expensive techniques) are employed and paid for in circumstances in which there is no evidence that they will do any good.

Thus the problem posed by new technology is primarily evaluative and organizational, rather than economic. First, how do we determine whether the technique does more good than harm, and for which patients? This requires careful analysis of the biological effect of the associated interventions; it also requires developing techniques for eliciting the preferences and values of potential patients. And second, once such information is available, how do we ensure that utilization decisions by providers and patients actually reflect this information?

A number of students of the benefits and costs of new technology have concluded that there is ample capacity in the health care systems of industrialized societies to support all the new technology that one might want—if one could get rid of the minimally effective, useless, or harmful interventions now being provided and paid for. The problem is to find an organization framework, and decision processes, which will lead to this result—the fifth problem category, detailed below ("Improving the Effectiveness and Efficiency of Health Care Delivery").

Coming back to the Canadian experience with cost control, it has been noted that the intensity of service, or the inflation-adjusted expenditure per person, has risen relatively slowly in Canadian hospitals. The control of hospital costs through global budgets has been associated with a slower rate of increase in the number of procedures performed, and/or their expense, than in the United States.

This raises the question of the appropriateness and effectiveness of the care being provided. Are Canadians being denied potentially effective treatments that would increase the length and/or improve the quality of their lives? Or are they being protected against the overenthusiastic application of interventions that would be useless at best, quite possibly harmful, and certainly expensive? One can find advocates of both points of view.

The second point of view has the assumptions which underlie the use of global budgets, namely that (1) physicians and hospital administrators, when they do not have enough resources to do all that they would like to do, react by eliminating the least useful or most harmful services first; (2) although they will always claim the contrary, they really do have enough resources to do all that is worth doing and probably more besides; and finally (3), if (2) should cease to be true, other sources of information will bring this fact into the open, so that budgets can be adjusted as needed.

On the other hand, detailed information on the effects both of the care that is being provided in Canadian hospitals and of the care that is *not* being provided is remarkably scarce (as it is in most other countries). We should study this area much more closely—the same point emerges when one looks closely at the changing patterns of care of the elderly. But the growing evidence of the very substantial use of inappropriate and actually harmful high-technology procedures in the more richly endowed United States emphasizes that the relative limitation placed on the diffusion of technology by the Canadian funding system may very well be a benefit of that system.

Manpower Surpluses (Physicians) and Shortages (Nurses)

The least successful area in health care policy in Canada has been the formulation and execution of manpower policy. As noted above, the supply of physicians has been rising steadily relative to the population and is projected to do so for the foreseeable future, on the basis of the training capacity now in place. There are now nearly 60,000 "active civilian" physicians in Canada, or about one for every 450 people, and the ratio of physicians per capita is rising about 2 percent per year. This growth places continuing pressure not only on the budgets for physicians' services, but also on the available hospital bed space and associated facilities (Barer, Gafni, and Lomas 1989). The "physicians per bed" ratio is rising steadily, so that each physician *perceives* a growing shortage of capacity, available to him or her.

This problem was easily foreseeable, and was in fact foreseen, in the early 1970s. The collapse of the birth rate in the mid-1960s has been followed by a continuing decline ever since. The population forecasts of the early 1960s were grossly in error, but were the basis for a significant increase in medical school capacity in the late 1960s and early 1970s. These increases were not scaled back when it became apparent that there had been a permanent and large change in population trends, although as early as 1975 changes were made to reduce drastically the rate of physician immigration.

Medical school representatives cloud the political issue with numerous false claims (Lomas et al. 1985): more physicians, they claim, are needed for an aging population. True; but aging is currently adding only about one-third of 1 percent per year to use, not 2 percent (Woods, Gordon Management Consultants 1984). In fact, the increasing physician supply is resulting in the increase in servicing rates among the elderly, as more and more physicians struggle to keep busy and maintain their incomes. They also claim that increasing numbers of female physicians and changing life-styles will lead to more physicians being needed to provide the same services. This would result in a fall in gross fee billings per physician, after allowing for changes in the level of fees, and this is not happening.

Thus Canada's present medical school capacity was put in place to serve a population which was forecast to be, by 1991, nearly 10 million people larger than that which is actually here.

Some reductions in training places are occurring, but slowly and painfully, because the benefits of reduction, in terms of savings, accrue over a number of years, while the political costs are immediate.

Nursing manpower presents the opposite picture, of growing shortages. Nursing shortages and surpluses alternate from year to year, or even month to month, depending upon the provincial government electoral and budget cycle. When funds for hospitals are plentiful, there is usually a "shortage" of nurses to fill the new jobs created. When fiscal times are tougher, the "shortage" disappears, along with the jobs. All that is happening is that the process of supply adjustment is less flexible than hospital budgets. But over the long run, larger forces are at work.

There are nearly a quarter of a million nurses registered in Canada, or about one per 100 persons, but only about one-half are employed full time in nursing. There are another 80,000 nursing assistants, but only about half were employed in hospitals in 1986, and their numbers are falling. Nursing manpower has been barely keeping up with population growth, though the adjustment for aging has more impact on need for nurses than for physicians.

The collapse of births in the mid-1960s has just reached the twenty- to twenty-five-year-old age cohort, from which nursing has traditionally recruited. A greater proportion of the population now works, but not enough to offset the decline; and career opportunities for females are increasing all the time. The demographic change has, in fact, resulted in a long-run shortage situation for nursing, which has become apparent only very recently. (Though it, too, could easily have been forecast from the 1960s birth data.)

The lack of cooperation, and sometimes even communication, between the educational and health care systems, located in different ministries and institutions, has been a major source of the serious inadequacies in health manpower policy. In this field, errors can have consequences for a whole generation.

Improving the Effectiveness and Efficiency of Health Care Delivery

Throughout the discussion above, we have noted that a number of apparently separate problems—population aging, the extension of technology, manpower—actually reduce to special cases of the more general issue: What sorts of health care services do we wish to have produced, and for whom?[1] These questions, as noted, ultimately turn on a combination of technical and value information: What will particular services actually *do*, in the way of good or harm? and, What do actual or prospective patients want?[2]

To date the Canadian health care system has addressed these questions only indirectly. "All medically necessary" services are free, implying that effectiveness, somehow defined, is the overriding criterion. But, as noted earlier, this has been determined implicitly as whatever a physician is willing to offer and a patient to accept. We have discovered, as has every other industrialized nation, that (1) the indirect definition of "need" is indefinitely expansible within the relevant range, particularly for elderly people, and (2) overall utilization rises with the availability of facilities and personnel and presses against any resource constraints, but (3) the aggregate levels and patterns of utilization that result are highly variable and bear no identifiable relation to any external definition of the "needs" of the population served.

The Canadian response has been to try to impose capacity constraints on the availability of facilities, sources of payment, and (much less successfully) personnel. The assumption, as noted above, is that when subjected to these constraints, the providers of health care will themselves choose to provide the services which respond to the greatest needs. Thus, the payers for services can avoid the very difficult and politically very dangerous task of establishing explicit priorities and protocols, and the fiercely defended autonomy of the physician need not be challenged.

This approach is slowly changing, however, in the face of accumulating evidence that patterns of care use in Canada bear no more systematic relation to indicators of need than they do in any other jurisdiction, and increasing pressure for more resources from the providers of health care themselves—the consequences of the physician supply increase and the extension of technology. As the relatively arbitrary limitations on facilities and resources are challenged more and more intensely by providers, provincial governments are becoming increasingly interested in the extensive research evidence of ineffective and inefficient care delivery as a basis for counterattack.

From the Delivery of Medical Care to the Enhancement of Health

The Canada Health Act of 1984 defines the objective of Canadian health care policy as "to protect, promote, and restore the physical and mental well-being of residents of Canada, and to facilitate reasonable access to health services without financial or other barriers" and refers to "outstanding progress" through the system of insured health services. But it also declares that further improvements will depend on a combination of improved individual lifestyles and "collective action against the social, environmental, and occupational causes of disease."

Equalizing access to health care, or at least removing the financial barriers, and significantly increasing the overall quantity of resources available have not equalized health status across the population. There remain significant inequalities in life expectancy and health status across different socioeconomic groups. Furthermore, there are sources of mortality and morbidity which are beyond the reach of health care services as conventionally defined. A public *health* policy, as different from a *health care* policy, would have to go much deeper into the determinants of health and illness, and carry out a much wider range of interventions than simply the expansion (or contraction) of particular health care services.

This is clearly recognized within the federal Department of National Health and Welfare. Most provincial ministries of health have a similar understanding, although they are so heavily involved in the day-to-day and year-to-year operations of the health care system that they do not always have the luxury of pursuing the broader issues. In general, however, these broader issues of inequalities in determinants of health have been honored with much rhetoric and careful thought, but very little money.

The problem is that the relentless pressure for expansion from the health care system, independently of any contribution it may be demonstrated to make to the health of the population, absorbs the lion's share of both current resources and any additional that may become available. Thus, cost containment in health care becomes a precondition for any new initiative in other areas of health. By a cruel irony, an overextended health care system may become a threat to health.

CONCLUSION

In summary, the Canadian approach to health care funding has been very successful in equalizing access to health care services, though less so in equalizing access to health. This appears to be a common experience in the industrialized countries, reflecting the fact that population health is not determined simply by the availability or use of health care. The health status of the Canadian population, insofar as that is known, compares well on the usual indicators of life expectancy and infant mortality with the rest of the industrialized world, and continues to improve (though not as fast as Japan!).[3]

The public insurance system has not only assisted access to health care, it has also played a very important role in "nation building" and community solidarity, as it emphasizes a fundamental equality among citizens. Greater wealth or position buy many things, but they do not buy more or better health care. Moreover the economic burden of this system is shared, through the general tax system, according to ability to pay. Since there are no direct payments, people who must bear the burden of illness and injury do not have to carry an additional economic burden as well.

Going beyond assuring access and improving the lives of individual citizens, the Canadian system has managed to contain the costs of health care for an extended period of time. Equilibrium is a crucial test of the sustainability of a funding system. Furthermore, it has done so in a way that has reconciled the interests of citizens as payers and citizens as patients and is consequently overwhelmingly popular politically. Even most physicians working in the Canadian system prefer it to the known alternatives—they would just like more money (and more hospital facilities and more equipment and the right to extra-bill patients, etc.). But one should not always infer the views of the ordinary physician from the rhetoric of professional associations.

On the basis of this experience, which is not so different from that of a number of European countries, we can conclude unequivocally that centralized, public funding systems "work," although they will require an increasing degree of explicit collective intervention in the determination of the content of medical practice. Whether this will be "public" or "private" or, more realistically, a balance between the two, depends upon whether the medical profession can bring itself to develop and *enforce* scientifically based standards upon its members, or whether the public sector will have to take on this role by default.

On the other hand, we can conclude, equally unequivocally, from the United States experience that a private or pluralistic funding system does not work; it produces neither effective health care, nor equity, nor public satisfaction, and cannot even meet the most fundamental test of stable and sustainable cost. It is conceivable that some pluralistic system might be developed in the future that would be capable of harnessing competitive forces to improve health care system performance. But at present such systems exist only in the imaginations of those with an overriding ideological commitment to the private marketplace—they cannot be shown to have been seriously tried, much less to have succeeded, in the real world.[4] What has been tried, in the United States, has failed.

NOTES

1.   The struggle over income shares (how much we will have to pay the producers) is largely—though not entirely—a separate question, though providers try hard to confuse the two. For example, it is claimed that aggressive bargaining over fees by provincial governments will threaten the quality of care of patients. More generally, the economic and professional objectives of providers are virtually always framed in terms of ill-specified but very important effects on "quality of care."

2. The latter is not in itself wholly decisive. Since in every industrialized nation, most or all of health care is collectively funded and could not in fact be funded any other way, it also matters what the rest of us are willing to pay for. But that will presumably be heavily influenced by the answers to the first two questions.

3. Life expectancy for Canadians at birth is about eighty years for females and seventy-three for males. Infant mortality is about 7.3 deaths per 1,000 births.

4. The work of Enthoven should be excluded from this generalization. His proposals represent the most thoughtful and carefully worked out example of a competitive system that takes account of the sources of failure in ordinary conceptions of "market" systems of health care funding and attempts to develop realistic ways of dealing with them. But his scheme is very subtle and sophisticated, and its feasibility of implementation in a highly adversarial (and often ignorant) environment is very far from clear. In any case, even he offers a totally untried alternative, which may appeal where the status quo is generally recognized as intolerable, and where such admittedly imperfect but battle-tested systems as the Canadian one are ruled out on ideological grounds.

REFERENCES

Barer, M.L. 1988. Regulating Physician Supply: The Evolution of British Columbia's Bill 41. *Journal of Health Politics, Policy and Law* 13 (1): 1–25.

Barer, M.L., R.G. Evans, C. Hertzman, and J. Lomas. 1987. Aging and Health Care Utilization: New Evidence on Old Fallacies. *Social Science and Medicine 24* (10):851–62.

Barer, M.L., A. Gafni, and J. Lomas. 1989. Accommodating Rapid Growth in Physician Supply: Lessons from Israel, Warnings for Canada. *International Journal of Health Services* 19 (1): 95–115.

Barer, M.L., I.R. Pulcins, R.G. Evans, C. Hertzman, J. Lomas, and G.M. Anderson. 1989. Trends in Use of Medical Services by the Elderly in British Columbia. *Canadian Medical Association Journal* 141 (1): 39–45.

Enthoven, A. 1989. What Can Europeans Learn from Americans about Financing and Organization of Medical Care? *Health Care Financing Review,* Annual Supplement: 49–63.

Enthoven, A., and R. Kronick. 1988. A Consumer Choice Health Care Plan for the 1990s (Parts I and II). *New England Journal of Medicine* 320 (1 and 2): 29–37, 94–101.

Evans, R.G. 1988. *Squaring the Circle: Reconciling Fee-for-Service with Global Expenditure Control.* Health Policy Research Unit Discussion Paper 88–8D, University of British Columbia, Vancouver.

_____. 1990. Tension, Compression, and Shear: Directions, Stresses, and Outcomes of Health Care Cost Control. *Journal of Health Politics, Policy and Law* 15 (1): 101–28.

_____. 1991. Life and Death, Money and Power: The Politics of Health Care Finance. In *Health Politics and Policy,* 2d ed., ed. Theodor J. Litman and Leonard S. Robins. Albany, NY: Delmar.

Evans, R.G., M.L. Barer, C. Hertzman, G.M. Anderson, I.R. Pulcins, and J. Lomas. 1989. The Long Good-Bye: The Great Transformation of the British Columbia Hospital System. *Health Services Research* 24 (4): 434–59.

Lomas, J., M. L. Barer, and G. L. Stoddart. 1985. *Physician Manpower Planning: Lessons from the Macdonald Report.* Ontario Economic Council Discussion Paper Series, Toronto.

Lomas, J., C. Fooks, T. Rice, and R. J. Labelle. 1989. Paying Physicians in Canada: Minding Our Ps and Qs. *Health Affairs* 8 (1): 80–102.

Reinhardt, U. E. 1987. Resource Allocation in Health Care: The Allocation of Lifestyles to Providers. *Milbank Quarterly* 65 (2): 153–76.

Schieber, G., and J. P. Poullier. 1989. International Health Care Expenditure Trends: 1987. *Health Affairs* 8 (3): 169–77.

Woods, Gordon Management Consultants. 1984. *An Investigation of the Impact of Demographic Change on the Health Care System of Canada–Final Report.* Prepared for the Task Force on the Allocation of Health Care Resources, Joan Watson, Chairman. Toronto: Woods, Gordon.

On Being Old and Sick

THE BURDEN OF HEALTH CARE FOR THE ELDERLY IN CANADA AND THE UNITED STATES

Morris L. Barer
Clyde Hertzman
Robert Miller
Marina V. Pascali

The fact that Americans spend significantly more than Canadians on health care but are far less content with what they are purchasing has become an important factor in policy discussions on U.S. health care reform. This relatively greater discontent is, in part, the result of a much greater exposure to financial risk: even the elderly face potentially ruinous health care costs, despite the federally funded Medicare program. Yet the literature comparing Canadian and American health care has, to date, not offered any clear picture of the extent of the differences in exposure to financial risk in the two countries.

In this paper we present data on the financial risk faced by the elderly in Canada and the United States for hospital, medical, and pharmaceutical services. These data provide a striking portrait of the impact of being old and sick in the two countries. The role of Canadian public health care programs in preventing poverty among the elderly has no American counterpart.

SATISFACTION WITH HEALTH CARE

The marked contrast between the satisfaction that Canadians and U.S. residents express with their respective health care systems has been extensively described in recent years (Blendon et al. 1990; Blendon and Taylor 1989); Blendon and Donelan 1990; Blendon and Edwards 1991). Most strikingly,

Morris L. Barer, Clyde Hertzman, Robert Miller, and Marina V. Pascali, "On Being Old and Sick: The Burden of Health Care for the Elderly in Canada and the United States," *Journal of Health Politics, Policy and Law* 17: 4, pp. 763–82. Copyright Duke University Press, 1992. Reprinted with permission.

only 10 percent of the U.S. population indicated that on the whole, the U.S. health care system works "pretty well," while the corresponding Canadian proportion was 56 percent (Blendon 1989). The disparity is even greater among respondents over the age of sixty-five. In the United States, 15 percent of the elderly feel that their system "works pretty well"; in Canada the rate is 66 percent. The "satisfaction gap" is smaller for respondents who are "very satisfied" with the system, but the difference remains consistent and considerable (Institute for the Future undated).

In Table 1 we show the proportions of the respective populations who indicated that they were "very satisfied" with particular health care services. These data suggest that the elderly in both countries tend to be more satisfied than younger people. But the largest differences between the countries in reported satisfaction are found among the elderly; particularly striking is the difference in the proportions satisfied with overall health care services. The Canadian elderly who had recently been hospitalized expressed particular satisfaction with that aspect of their health care system.

What these data do not provide is insight into the underlying causes of the wide gaps in degree of satisfaction. A leading candidate may be the different impacts of health care services on the financial security of the elderly in the two countries.

HEALTH CARE ENTITLEMENT IN CANADA AND THE UNITED STATES

Since 1971 Canada has provided universal coverage to its entire population for medically necessary services provided in hospital or by physicians. In addition, all provinces provide some form of coverage for long-term care and pharmaceutical costs.

TABLE I

Percentage of the Public Who Reported They Were "Very Satisfied" With Services, by Type of Service

	Canada		United States	
	Total Population	Population Over 65	Total Population	Population Over 65
Health Care Services	67	77	35	40
Most Recent Doctor's Visit	62	77	54	60
Most Recent Hospital Stay	71	93	57	68

Source: Institute for the Future, undated.

Each Canadian provincial health ministry holds virtually sole responsibility for managing the major components of health care. Funding for hospital, physician, and some long-term care services is shared by the federal government through transfers of tax points and cash to the provincial governments. The costs of pharmaceutical benefits are entirely the responsibility of the provinces. The private insurance industry cannot offer hospital or medical care coverage, although it can provide supplementary and amenity (e.g., private hospital room) coverage. Patient financial participation is minimal. There are no user fees (deductibles or coinsurance) for hospital or medical care. Alberta and British Columbia are the only provinces which retain health insurance premiums, although the universality provision underlying all provincial plans prevents even these provinces from denying care to those whose premium payments may be in arrears.

As we note in more detail below, coverage for the elderly in Canada is, if anything, even more generous. For those residents over sixty-five, the Alberta medical premiums are waived, and the patient copayments in a number of provincial pharmaceutical programs are reduced or eliminated.

Canadian public universal coverage stands in marked contrast to the public entitlement to health care benefits in the United States provided through Medicare and Medicaid programs. Medicare is limited to a certain segment of the population; it does not cover all medically necessary hospital and physician services; and it requires substantial beneficiary copayments.

The majority of the elderly American population (96 percent) is covered by Medicare and about 77 percent purchase supplementary health insurance (P. W. Ries, personal communication, June 1991). Health care benefits may also be obtained through state-administered Medicaid programs which provide coverage for elderly individuals who have depleted both income and assets on health care costs.

THE COST OF UNIVERSALITY

As one might expect, health care costs in the two countries have diverged dramatically, in line with their divergent approaches to entitlement since 1971. But despite the more complete and comprehensive coverage in Canada, the American system has emerged as the more expensive. By 1989, Canadians were devoting 8.9 percent of their gross national product (GNP) to health care services (Canada 1991). The equivalent American figure was 11.6 percent (Lazenby and Letsch 1990), and preliminary indications are that the gap is still growing.[1] Put differently, if the United States had spent the Canadian share of economic activity on health care in 1989, it would have had close to $150 billion available for other uses. This increasing relative commitment to health care in the United States has not, at least to date, been reflected in improved health status (Evans et al. 1991).

The difference in cost experience rests entirely with three types of activity: medical services, hospital care, and administration. More specifically, the share of GNP going to *medical* services has not increased in Canada since 1971. The difference in Canadian/American experience is attributable to a relatively more rapid growth in physician fees in the United States (Evans et al. 1989). For *hospital* care, the difference has been found to rest with more intensive daily service provision in the United States and higher provider-related administrative costs (Newhouse et al. 1988; Woolhandler and Himmelstein 1991). But the most dramatic difference occurs in insurer-related *administration* costs, where, in 1987, Canada spent 0.1 percent of GNP, while the United States spent about 0.6 percent.

Ironically, Canada's relative success with cost control has emerged *because of* its approach to providing universal coverage. A single government agency in each province not only acts as insurer but also takes on the negotiation and payment for the largest program components. Provincial ministries (or departments) of health negotiate provincial medical fee schedules (and, increasingly, global medical expenditures) and global hospital budgets and retain majority control over capital acquisitions (Barer and Evans 1992). Furthermore, administrative activity is largely centralized within those ministries.

TAKING CARE OF THE ELDERLY

As noted above, this general picture of coverage and financial participation for the Canadian population holds for the elderly. In fact, when Canadians turn sixty-five years of age, their entitlements increase. The premiums in Alberta disappear. More significantly, all provinces provide some form of noninstitutional pharmaceutical coverage for the elderly, and, in those provinces where programs exist for the entire population, deductibles and copayments decline markedly at age sixty-five. In addition, each province has developed its own system for chronic or long-term care that facilitates movement across the spectrum of institutional and community care, although some of these systems are more developed than others. The funding of these long-term care systems is derived from a combination of public budgets and private out-of-pocket payments, where the latter are tied to a de facto minimum retirement benefit and are intended to pay in part for room and board.

In contrast, public entitlement to non-means-tested-health care coverage in the United States *begins* at age sixty-five with Medicare, extends only to hospital and medical care, and involves considerable private financial participation. Coverage for pharmaceuticals and long-term care for those over sixty-five varies considerably across states and is generally means-tested. No state covers nursing home stays, other than through the Medicaid program, which requires the recipient to prove that (s)he has virtually no nonhousing assets and a below-poverty level of income.

In the following sections of this paper, we describe in more detail the implications of hospital, medical, and pharmaceutical care for the financial security of the elderly in the two countries.

COVERAGE AND COSTS FOR THE ELDERLY IN CANADA

There are no deductibles or copayments for necessary medical services in Canada. Provincial medical plans are financed largely from general revenues. Medical premiums for the elderly exist only in British Columbia, and can be as high as $35 per person or $62 per couple per month (1991 rates, in Canadian dollars). But there is a relatively generous system of reduced charges tied to income. For the most indigent, premiums are less than $2 per month. In general, there are no user fees for services provided by physicians.

There are no hospital premiums or user fees for elderly acute hospital care anywhere in Canada. Room and board charges for continuing hospital care following an acute episode take effect under varying conditions in different provinces. A general principle is that these are levied at the point where the institution is deemed to be the patient's permanent residence. For example, in the province of Manitoba, a seventy-year-old admitted to acute care with a stroke will be provided with free acute care coverage until such time as the attending physician determines that no further physical recovery is likely, but the patient still requires in-hospital care. At that point the patient becomes responsible for room and board charges amounting to 85 percent of the minimum public income support,[2] which in 1991 was equivalent to leaving a minimum $130.85 comfort allowance for the elderly with the least income. Residential charges in most provinces are set as a fraction of the elderly's minimum income (never more than 85 percent of OAS/GIS/provincial supplement, where applicable),[3] and are designed to leave the lowest-income patients with a living allowance, which in 1991 ranged from about $110 to $130 per month. In a few of the provinces and territories, there are no charges for the hospital-based extension of acute episodes.

There is greater variation in the extent and nature of the cost of drugs to outpatients. This is most likely due to the fact that the provinces have full financial responsibility for "Pharmacare" programs, whereas the evolution of the provincial medical and hospital programs was governed by uniform terms and conditions necessary for federal government cost sharing. The patient's share of the cost is a combination of deductibles and copayments.

The most generous provincial or territorial programs (Ontario, Québec, the Northwest Territories, and Yukon) involve no user fees of any kind. For low users, the least generous program (Manitoba) involves an annual deductible of $92.75 as well as a 20 percent copayment for each prescription. The Prince Edward Island program, which requires the patient to pay a $4 deductible plus the entire dispensing fee for each prescription, would appear to be the most financially punitive for high users, although comparisons of Manitoba and Prince Edward Island are incomplete in the absence of more detailed information on the distribution and relative sizes of dispensing and ingredient costs in the two provinces. In between, we find a variety of combinations, such as that in British Columbia, where those over sixty-five are responsible for 75 percent of the dispensing fee to an annual ceiling of $125.

One can piece together an overall picture of financial exposure for the Canadian elderly for hospital, medical, and pharmaceutical care. In Ontario, Québec, the Yukon, and the Northwest Territories (representing, in total, almost two-thirds of the country's population), the individual patient is at no financial risk for any of these services. In British Columbia, the combination of *maximum* medical premium plus *maximum* out-of-pocket pharmaceutical costs amounted to $545 per year in 1991.[4] The mean will be much lower (the minimum, for the very indigent using no drugs, is about $20 per year). Very high users of pharmaceuticals in Manitoba or Prince Edward Island will incur costs in excess of the British Columbia figure, but these individuals represent the far right-hand tail of the pharmaceutical cost distribution.

COVERAGE AND COSTS FOR THE ELDERLY IN THE UNITED STATES

The closest equivalent to Canadian coverage for the elderly in America is the Medicare program, a non-means-tested program that provides hospital coverage (Part A) and offers optional ambulatory medical coverage (Part B (virtually all individuals eligible for Part A enroll for Part B coverage).

Part A–eligible coverage involves no monthly premiums, but there are extensive user charges. In 1991, patients were responsible for the first $628 (U.S.) of hospital costs incurred in each benefit period (defined as the period beginning with an initial hospitalization and ending only after sixty consecutive nonhospital days). In the event that a hospital stay exceeds sixty days, a daily copayment of $157 is normally incurred for each of the subsequent thirty days. Beyond that, patients may draw on a life-time sixty-day reserve of $314 per day copayment days (Committee on Ways and Means 1991).

In fact, few patients will remain in acute care for as long as sixty days. More commonly, patients will be transferred to skilled nursing facilities following hospitalization. There they are fully covered for the first twenty days, after which they are responsible for a copayment of $78.50 per day for the next eighty days.

Those elderly subscribing to Part B must pay a monthly premium of $29.90, and are responsible for the first $200 of incurred costs, and *at least* 20 percent of physicians' "reasonable charges" beyond that deductible.[5] The Medicare program does not include any ambulatory pharmaceutical coverage. Over 75 percent of the elderly purchase private supplemental insurance policies, the majority of which pay for the deductible and copayments for services covered by Medicare (P. W. Ries, personal communication, June 1991). The patient must usually pay any amount billed that is over and above what Medicare deems reasonable. Private supplemental insurance premiums are often substantial, and the average return to these policyholders in benefits is often no more than 60 percent of the premiums paid for the policies (Rice 1987).

The other major source of public health care benefits for elderly Americans is state Medicaid programs. These programs provide coverage for Americans meeting state-determined means-tested eligibility criteria. Eligibility is based on both assets and income, so that individuals generally become eligible for Medicaid benefits only after having exhausted their personal, nonhousing assets and when their disposable income after medical payments is below, often much below, the poverty line. As a result, in 1984 only 6.4 percent of the elderly who lived in the community received Medicaid benefits (Ries 1987). This means-tested program is to be distinguished from the Canadian social insurance–style programs which are designed to prevent poverty (Marmor et al. 1990). In Canada, poverty is prevented by ensuring that health care charges do not exceed a minimum guaranteed *income* for the elderly, as we noted above. For example, the "hotel" charges (room and board) for extended hospital care are set below this minimum income level in all provinces except Québec.

In addition to providing hospital and medical coverage over and above that provided through Medicare (for those elderly unable to shoulder the Medicare deductibles and copayments), state Medicaid programs can provide prescription drug entitlements to eligible elderly Americans. Medicaid coverage of prescription drugs is an optional service and states vary on the extent to which this cost is subsidized—Alaska and Wyoming do not offer any form of coverage (Soumerai and Ross-Degnan 1990). Drug benefits are also available to the poor, near-poor, or middle-class elderly, through some state pharmaceutical assistance programs, which are financed mostly through general funds or lotteries (Soumerai and Ross-Degnan 1990). Since 1977, eleven states have implemented such pharmaceutical assistance programs.

Income restrictions on eligibility for state programs (ranging from $6,400 to $14,000) are generally less stringent than those imposed by Medicaid, and most do not impose asset limits or spend-down requirements.[6] Generally, the beneficiary is required to pay an out-of-pocket share, ranging from $1 per prescription to 40 percent of prescription costs, to reduce program expenditures and discourage overutilization. In Illinois there is no copayment, but the pharmaceuticals and products covered are severely restricted (Soumerai and Ross-Degnan 1990).

The largest of these programs (the Pennsylvania Assistance Contract for the Elderly) is income-tested, not asset-tested, and there are no spend-down requirements. All state residents sixty-five years or over with annual incomes of less than $12,000 (single) or $15,000 (married) are eligible (Stuart et al. 1991). Despite these programs, it is currently estimated that about 80 percent of the total costs of over-the-counter and prescription drugs are shouldered out-of-pocket by the elderly in America (Stuart et al. 1991).

While current data sources do not permit the creation of a summary out-of-pocket cost estimate for elderly Americans like that described above for Canada, we can develop a rough picture by cobbling together a variety of sectoral estimates. Waldo et al. (1989) report health care expenditures from private sources by sector for 1987. Hospital expenditures totaled $333 per capita; physician expenditures amounted to $393. These estimates combine private out-of-pocket payments and payments from private insurers and other nongovernment sources. Thus they underestimate total out-of-pocket costs, for two reasons. First, any premium payments to private insurers will exceed expenditures on medical and hospital care by the amount of their retained earnings and administrative expenses. Rice (1987) estimates that the loss ratios for premiums paid to private insurers were approximately 76 percent in 1986. In other words, 24 percent of insurance company premium dollars are retained for administration and profit. Second, premiums paid to Medicare are not included in the above figures (Waldo and Lazenby 1984).

Additionally, these figures do not include private copayments for Medicare-financed stays in skilled nursing facilities, which are short, posthospital stays. Silverman (1991) reports that the average number of Medicare-covered days spent in these facilities by people who had ever used such care was 25.3 in 1987. Since the first 20 days of skilled nursing care involve no copayments under Medicare, this leaves 5.3 days, on average, for which the patient would bear the (1987) $65 per day copayment costs.[7] But only about 1 percent of Medicare enrollees used this Medicare benefit in 1987. Therefore, the average private cost per enrollee in 1987 would have been about $3.50. This would raise our "hospital" estimate from $333 to $337.

We know that the 1987 Medicare Part B premium was $180. Furthermore, Waldo (1987) provides an estimate of out-of-pocket costs for outpatient prescription drugs of $304 in 1987 for those over sixty-five years of age. Piecing these figures together produces a "best underestimate" of average per capita expenditures on hospital, medical, and pharmaceutical services incurred by the elderly—approximately $1,215 (U.S.). This is an underestimate of the mean, for the reasons noted earlier. Furthermore, there will be many elderly for whom private expenditures will be far higher, because costs for all three components are functions of rates of use (they all involve copayments).

Alternative estimates for hospital and medical care, for 1985 and 1990, can be pieced together using data from the Committee on Ways and Means (1991). This source reports 1985 average out-of-pocket expenses (copayments, balance billing, and premiums) for hospital and medical care under the Medicare program of $627. The equivalent figure for 1990 is

$1,002. Subtracting the pharmaceutical component from our best underestimate yields a figure for 1987 of $906. The $627 and $1,002 exclude average payments by the elderly for private supplementary coverage, Even so, our underestimate appears to be in the right ballpark.

UNCLE SAM RETIRES IN VICTORIA: AN ELDERLY AMERICAN IN CANADA

Against this picture of costs incurred by the average elderly American, one can speculate on the costs that same American would incur in Canada. Assuming the individual in question chose to retire in Victoria (or elsewhere in British Columbia), (s)he would have been responsible for an annual medical care premium (tax) of not more than $240 in 1987. If (s)he had used the average number of prescriptions reported by Waldo (1987) for elderly Americans in 1987 (seventeen prescriptions) and we assume the dispensing fee on each prescription was $5, (s)he would have incurred ambulatory pharmaceutical costs of $68 (Canadian).

If instead this individual had retired in Prince Edward Island, (s)he would have incurred greater pharmaceutical costs ($153) but would not have been responsible for medical premiums. In all other provinces, the total out-of-pocket plus premium costs would have been less. In fact, this individual would incur no direct or premium costs in a number of provinces and territories.

More recent data, while incomplete, suggest that, if anything, this Canada–U.S. gap in costs assumed personally has increased rather dramatically. By 1991 our retiree would be paying $10 in British Columbia or $187 in Prince Edward Island. Because premiums have been eliminated in Ontario, these costs in that province would have fallen to zero. But if (s)he had stayed in the U.S., average out-of-pocket pharmaceutical costs for the elderly would have increased to $432 (U.S.) in 1991 (projected) up from $304 in 1987 (Waldo 1987). Furthermore the Medicare premium has doubled over this period, and all the copayments have increased significantly. In particular, the projected total of out-of-pocket and premium costs for Medicare in 1990 is $1,002, up from $627 in 1985 (Committee on Ways and Means 1991).

Lost in this discussion of average cost profiles is the fact that the Canadian elderly are not exposed to catastrophic financial risk. They are not responsible for any direct payments for medical or hospital care. In addition, most of the Canadian pharmaceutical programs for the elderly specify out-of-pocket ceilings and, in any case, ambulatory prescription costs are the smallest, and most predictable, of these three health care components. Even in those provinces without pharmaceutical cost ceilings, the right-hand tail of the total out-of-pocket cost distribution is well to the left of the *mean* equivalent costs in the U.S.

To estimate out-of-pocket costs for high users in Canada, we turned to the British Columbia Pharmacare database. It turned out that in 1988/89, 0.5 percent of British Columbia's elderly generated more than $2,200 in ambulatory pharmaceutical billings, and about 2 percent received more than fifty prescriptions. What financial responsibilities would this level of drug use create in provinces with the least generous pharmaceutical coverage? In Manitoba it would have translated into less than $600 per year total out-of-pocket costs for the tiny segment of very high users of prescription drugs. In Prince Edward Island, sixty prescriptions would also generate out-of-pocket costs of about $600.[8]

In marked contrast, elderly Americans without comprehensive private health insurance face potential economic ruin from hospital, medical, and pharmaceutical costs. In order to qualify for public health coverage beyond that offered by Medicare, they must first deplete both income and assets to pay such costs. The *maximum* imaginable out-of-pocket costs in Canada are in all likelihood less than half the *mean* equivalent costs in the United States.[9]

■ ■ ■

NOTES

1. Some American analysts have suggested that the comparison of shares of GNP is inappropriate in this context, and that the relative comparison should be to relative experiences with real per capita costs (Neuschler 1990; Feder et al. 1987). This position finds no support either in theory or empirical evidence (Barer et al. 1991), a fact that has been lost in a recent deluge of anti-Canada propaganda (*Consumer Reports* 1992).

2. The elderly in all provinces are entitled to a minimum income deriving from a variety of programs. These include federal Old Age Security (OAS) and Guaranteed Income Supplement (GIS) and provincial need-based supplements, e.g. Guaranteed Annual Income for Need (GAIN). All residents over sixty-five are entitled to OAS; GIS is an income-tested supplement; and most provinces administer a variant of a GAIN program. Québec, New Brunswick, Prince Edward Island, and Newfoundland do not offer a provincial need-based supplement (Canada 1989).

3. Charges for long-term care in non-hospital-program facilities can, in some provinces, exceed this maximum for those with sufficient means.

4. Even this is misleading, however, because the medical premium is a compulsory *tax,* unrelated to risk status or use of services, and not intended to cover the entire expected cost of medical care.

5. For physicians who "accept assignment," the maximum charge for which the patient is responsible is 20 percent of the Medicare-approved charge. For physicians not on assignment, the patient is responsible for any difference that may exist between the approved and actual charge, although such physicians may elect to accept the Medicare-approved charge as payment in full.

6.   Spending down under Medicaid is a two-step process. First, the individual must meet the assets test: the value of the individual's resources (generally defined as liquid assets) must be less than a state-determined dollar standard. Second, once an individual has depleted virtually all accumulated resources on health care costs, income standards are then considered (Committee on Ways and Means 1991).

7.   Of course, these figures refer only to "covered" days of care in a skilled nursing facility. As Rice and Gabel (1986) noted, the average length of stay may exceed Medicare-covered days by a considerable margin, leaving the patient fully responsible for the costs of uncovered days.

8.   We apply British Columbia utilization data to the copayment provisions in the provinces with the most costly programs because utilization data from Manitoba and Prince Edward Island were not readily accessible to us, and the time and cost involved in accessing and processing those databases were well beyond the scope and intent of the present paper.

9.   Two relatively unexplored frontiers are the costs of assistive devices and indirect payments for health care through taxes. In both countries there are a welter of fragmented programs that provide assistive devices for the disabled, from prostheses to home renovation for those needing wheelchair accessibility, electric staircases, and other environmental modifications. The issue of taxation is also very important because, although the elderly in Canada pay far less for health care in direct out-of-pocket costs, we would expect that some of this difference would be made up from the elderly's contribution to health care through income, sales, and other taxes. At present, there is no well-organized information on either of these costs.

REFERENCES

Barer, M. L., and R. G. Evans. 1992. The Meeting of the Twain: Managing Health Care Capital and Costs in Canada. In *Technology and Health Care in an Era of Limits,* ed. A. Gelijns. Washington, DC: National Academy Press.

Blendon, R. J. 1989. Three Systems: A Comparative Survey, *Health Management Quarterly* 11 (1): 2–10.

Blendon, R. J., and K. Donelan. 1990. The Public and the Emerging Debate over National Health Insurance. *New England Journal of Medicine* 323 (3): 208–12.

Blendon, R. J., and J. N. Edwards. 1991. Conclusion and Forecast for the Future. In *Systems in Crisis: The Case for Health Care Reform,* ed. R. J. Blendon and J. N. Edwards, New York: Faulkner and Gray.

Blendon, R. J., R. Leitman, I. Morrison, and K. Donelan. 1990. Satisfaction with Health Systems in Ten Nations. *Health Affairs* 9 (2): 185–92.

Blendon, R. J., and H. Taylor. 1989. Views on Health Care: Public Opinion in Three Nations, *Health Affairs* 8 (1): 149–57.

Committee on Ways and Means, U.S. Congress, House of Representatives. 1991. *Background Material and Data on Programs within the Jurisdiction of the Committee on Ways and Means,* Washington, DC: U.S. Government Printing Office.

Evans, R. G., M. L. Barer, and C. Hertzman. 1991. The Twenty-Year Experiment: Accounting for, Explaining, and Evaluating Health Care Cost Containment in Canada and the United States. *Annual Review of Public Health* 12: 481–518.

Evans, R. G., J. Lomas, M. L. Barer, R. J. Labelle, C. Fooks, G. L. Stoddart, G. M. Anderson, D. Feeny, A. Gafni, G. W. Torrance, and W. G. Tholl. 1989. Controlling Health Expenditures: The Canadian Reality. *New England Journal of Medicine* 321:571–77.

Institute for the Future. Undated. Unpublished data from the *Three Nations Study* (1989). Menlo Park, CA: Institute for the Future.

Lazenby, H. C., and S. W. Letsch. 1990. National Health Expenditures. *Health Care Financing Review* 12 (2): 1–26.

Marmor, T. R., J. L. Mashaw, and P. L. Harvey. 1990. *America's Misunderstood Welfare State: Persistent Myths, Enduring Realities.* New York. Basic.

Newhouse, J. P., G. M. Anderson, and L. L. Roos. 1988. Hospital Spending in the United States and Canada: A Comparison. *Health Affairs* 7 (5): 6–16.

Rice, T. 1987. An Economic Assessment of Health Care Coverage for the Elderly. *Milbank Quarterly* 65: 488–520.

Ries, P. W. 1987. *Health Care Coverage by Socio-Demographic and Health Characteristics, United States,* 1984. National Center for Health Statistics, Vital and Health Statistics, Series 10, no. 162. Washington, D.C: U.S. Government Printing Office.

Silverman, H. A. 1991. Medicare-covered Skilled Nursing Facility Services, 1977–1988. *Health Care Financing Review* 12 (3): 103–8.

Soumerai, S. B., and D. Ross-Degnan. 1990. Experience of State Drug Benefit Programs. *Health Affairs* 9 (3): 36–54.

Stuart, B., F. Ahern, V. Rabatin, and A. Johnston. 1991. Patterns of Outpatient Prescription Drug Use among Pennsylvania Elderly. *Health Care Financing Review* 12 (3): 61–72.

Waldo, D. R. 1987. Outpatient Prescription Drug Spending by the Medicare Population. *Health Care Financing Review* 9 (1): 83–89.

Waldo, D. R., and H. C. Lazenby. 1984. Demographic Characteristics and Health Care Use and Expenditures by the Aged in the United States: 1977–1984. *Health Care Financing Review* 6 (1): 1–29.

Waldo, D. R., S. T. Sonnefeld, D. R. McKusick, and R. H. Arnett III. 1989. Health Expenditures by Age-Group, 1977 and 1987. *Health Care Financing Review* 10 (4): 111–20.

Woolhandler, S., and D. U. Himmelstein. 1991. The Deteriorating Administrative Efficiency of the U.S. Health Care System. *New England Journal of Medicine* 324:1253–58.

Long-Term Care and Population Aging

Evelyn Shapiro

...

WHAT IS LONG-TERM CARE?

Long-Term Care provides care and support services to persons whose health deficits impede their capacity to function independently and whose informal network is insufficient to meet their needs. These formal services may be provided in the home, in the community or in a long-term care facility. Services run the gamut from a bed in a facility to home help, personal care, medical and other services delivered at home or in other settings (e.g., adult day care or respite care).

The most important difference between community and facility care is the critical role played by family in home care and the relatively peripheral, although meaningful, role of the family in facility care. In facilities, the primary care providers are nurses and auxiliary nurses. In the community, 85 percent of the help is provided by families, supplemented, in some cases, by formal service providers such as home helpers, social workers, nurses, auxiliary nurses and therapists. Because the home and community setting maximizes the individual's autonomy, social integrity and familiarity, most persons needing help prefer to remain at home and in the community as long as they can.

THE DIFFERENCE BETWEEN ACUTE AND LONG-TERM CARE

The long-standing preoccupation with acute care among health care policymakers and planners has spawned unwarranted assumptions about long-term care. One major misconception is that the main difference between acute and long-term care is exclusively or primarily the length of time services are required. This assumption ignores major differences in the reasons for admission and in the types of persons served. A hospital admission is based on a clinical diagnosis denoting the need for hospital-based medical or surgical intervention whereas the primary reasons for long-term use are functional dependency and inadequate informal resources. Therefore, the reason for admission to long-term care and the intensity of service required vary by individual and family circumstances. Long-term care models based on this misconception risk increasing costs by medicalizing disability and providing inappropriate services.

Other differences between acute and long-term care have been noted. Gomez[1] highlights four: the variability of unobserved clinical characteristics of long-term care recipients, the complexity of their medical histories, the preponderance of chronic conditions and the uncertainty surrounding their prognoses. Rosalie Kane[2] adds the following: the difference in technologies and personnel-mix used and individual variations in the purpose of the provided care.

In summary, long-term care is not a longer form of acute care. Awareness of its uniqueness provides the context for reviewing recent developments.

■■■

WHO NEEDS LONG-TERM CARE?

About 75%-80% of persons who receive long-term care services are aged 65 or more. Researchers have, therefore, focused their attention on the factors which affect the use of these services by the elderly. The proportion of elders requiring such care increases with advancing age.

These vulnerable elders can be divided into three groups: (1) those whose characteristics place them at risk of requiring long-term facility care; i.e., at risk of losing their capacity to remain in the community; (2) those whose characteristics place them at risk of requiring community care, i.e. at risk of losing their capacity to manage at home on their own even with informal help; and (3) those whose caregivers find the cumulative strain of caring too much to continue helping a family member stay at home unless they have some help.

Canadian research indicates that the significant predictors of institutionalization are, in descending order of importance, advanced age, no spouse at home, residency in Senior Citizens Housing, a hospital admission two years earlier, one or more problems with the basic activities of daily living (e.g. washing, getting in and out of bed) and having a mental functioning problem.[3] However, it is the combination of these factors, not each individual factor, which is important. Just being a male 85 years or more means having a 16 percent chance of being institutionalized whereas having all the risk characteristics brings the probability up to 62 percent. The difference just between not having or having a spouse at home in this age group lowers the probability of institutionalization from 19 percent to 7 percent.[4]

The predictors of home care use[5] and the risk profiles are similar to those for nursing home use except for two important differences. Home care users are significantly more likely to have mental functioning problems than non-users but cognitive impairment is not a significant predictor of home care use when all other factors are taken into account, probably because safety at home demands sound judgement unless there is a resident family member. And one or more problems with the instrumental activities of daily living (e.g. making a meal, doing laundry) is the next strongest predictor of home care use after age and health status but not of institutional use, probably because managing day-to-day needs is a requisite to being able to remain at home.

■■■

The elderly are the predominant users of long-term care but the data provided in the next sections indicate that only a very small minority of them use these services.

THE DATA ON LONG-TERM CARE

There is a growing Canadian literature on community and long-term facility care. Published Canada-wide studies, for the reasons already mentioned, are still scarce so most published studies on Canadian long-term care are often based on analyses of province-specific data, raising the question of generalizability. These studies, however, are usually careful to point out the policy context in interpreting their findings.

Before proceeding, however, it is important to note that all data presented here on community care include both short and long-term home care.

UTILIZATION

The results of a 1988 survey[6] of long-term care facilities indicate that, when every category of long-term facility care is included, the percentage of elderly in these facilities by province ranges from 5.8 percent to 8.6 percent. The assumption that anyone who can pay the full cost has access to a long-term facility bed is unwarranted. In most parts of Canada, as has been shown, access to such facilities is not based on demand or on the ability to pay.

Age, sex and the level of care required by long-term facility care residents are the major contributors to lengths of stay.[7] Being older, male and more dependent reduces stays. Differences in lengths of stay as a result of these three resident characteristics can be as much as 15 years. With community care costing about 10 percent of facility care, maintaining younger and less dependent persons in the community as long as possible and financially feasible can provide access to more persons with a given supply of beds.

Research data[8] based on a 1971 representative sample of Manitoba's elderly indicate that 4.5 percent of the elderly were admitted to the community care program (short- and long-term care) in 1976 and 9.9 percent received services some time during the year. A later study currently in the process of completion by the author shows that, of a 1983 representative sample, 5 percent of the elderly were admitted to community care that year and 10.4 percent used the service during the year. This indicates, as do the findings by Kane and Kane[9], that the rates of use tend to remain stable if external factors remain relatively stable. This latter study also found that elderly with arthritis (a chronic condition which is prevalent among the elderly and which entails varying degrees of functional limitations) had a higher utilization rate than those without this condition, suggesting that assessments for admission differentiate between those who need and those who do not need service.

About two-thirds of community care recipients receive support services variously referred to by nomenclatures such as home help, home aide or personal care attendant. A minority of service consumers receive nursing services (30%-40%, depending on the province) and an even smaller minority (5%-10%) receive therapy services.

WHO PROVIDES CARE? THE ROLE OF INFORMAL CAREGIVERS

Research shows that informal sources, i.e. help from family, friends and neighbours, provide most of the help the elderly receive. Kane[10], reviewing 26 international studies, found that 75%-85% of all personal care to elders was provided by informal sources whether or not the countries provided comprehensive health care insurance. Canadian studies by Chappell[11] and by Chappell and Havens[12] report that over 90 percent of the elderly who get help at home get it from their informal network. A decrease in the availability of these resources could, therefore, be expected to increase the need for formal care.

Women, mostly spouses and daughters, provide most of the informal services. They constitute 72 percent of the caregivers.[13] In view of demographic trends which will be discussed later, it is useful to know that siblings, primarily sisters, provide substantial help.[14] Some elders without families get some support from others[15] but they are more likely than those with families to be admitted to a long-term care facility.

SUBSTITUTION EFFECTS

Canadian research shows that admission to a long-term care facility reduces hospital admission[16] and that this substitution effect is most marked for persons aged 75 or more who make up most of the institutionalized population.

Two studies done in provinces with a single-entry system show that community care substitutes for long-term facility use.[17,18] These findings are reinforced by the evaluations of experiments in Alberta and New Brunswick. Furthermore, nursing home beds per 1,000 elderly aged 75 or more in Manitoba have been reduced from 167 in 1974/75 when the community care program with its single-entry system was implemented to 134 in 1990/91.[19] Evidence from these reports also shows a reduction in the proportion of persons requiring the lightest level of care from about 20 percent in 1974/75 to 3.5 percent in 1990/91, with a proportionate increase among those requiring the highest levels of care.

A study by Chappell and Blandford[20] indicates that adult day care, a long-term care community care service which, in the province studied, restricts admission to those assessed as eligible by the community care program, reduces hospital use by the elderly.

In summary, Canadian research indicates that:

- community care substitutes for long-term facility use
- long-term facility admission and adult day care, where it is a component of community care, substitutes for hospital admission;
- community care costs average about 10 percent of long-term facility costs;
- long-term facility costs are lower than hospital costs;
- a given supply of long-term beds can provide access to more people if the system favours the admission of older and more dependent persons.

The implications of these findings are that expenditures of additional funds for the expansion of long-term community care can reduce the rate of institutionalization and at reasonable cost savings but several caveats have to be borne in mind. First, the long-term care facilities would, as experience has shown, absorb some of the savings because they would have a higher proportion of more dependent and, therefore, higher cost residents. Second, there is a limit to the substitutability of community care for facility care because some dependent persons cannot be maintained safely or economically at home. However, the substitution of nursing home admission for hospital use indicates that it might be possible to pay for the higher levels of facility care by closing hospital beds.

NOTES

1. C. F. Gomez, "The Elusive Pursuit of Quality in Nursing Homes," The Public Policy and Aging Report 2 (No. 3, May/June 1988): 1–11. (South Ridgewood Court, Chicago: Policy Research Associates Inc.)

2. R. A. Kane, "Assessing Quality in Nursing Homes", *Clinics in Geriatric Medicine* 4 (No. 3, August 1988): 655–666.

3. E. Shapiro and R. Tate, "Predictors of Long-Term Facility Use Among the Elderly," *Canadian Journal on Aging* 4 (No. 1, 1985): 11–19.

4. E. Shapiro and R. Tate, "Who Is Really at Risk of Institutionalization?", *The Gerontologist* 28 (No. 2, 1988): 237–245.

5. E. Shapiro, "Patterns and Predictors of Home Care Use by the Elderly When Need is the Sole Basis for Admission," *Home Health Care Services Quarterly* 7 (No. 1, Spring, 1986): 29–44.

6. L. W. Chambers et al., *The Organization and Financing of Public and Private Sector Long Term Care Facilities for the Elderly in Canada. Report on Part I: Survey of the Provinces* (McMaster University Centre for Health Economics and Policy Analysis Working Paper #92–13, April 1992).

7. E. Shapiro and R. Tate, "Survival Patterns of Nursing Home Admissions and Their Policy Implications," *Canadian Journal of Public Health* 79 (No. 4, 1988): 268–274.

8. E. Shapiro, "Patterns and Predictors of Home Care Use by the Elderly When Need is the Sole Basis for Admission," *Home Health Care Services Quarterly* 7 (No. 1, Spring, 1986): 29–44.

9. R. A. Kane and R. L. Kane, "The Feasibility of Universal Long-Term Care Benefits," *New England Journal of Medicine* 312 (1985): 1357–64.

10. R. L. Kane, "Introduction," in R. L. Kane, J. G. Evans, and D. MacFadyen, eds., *Improving the Health of Older People: A World View* (New York: Oxford University Press, 1990).

11. N. L. Chappell, "Social Support and the Receipt of Home Care Services," *The Gerontologist* 25 (No. 1, 1985): 47–54.

12. N. L. Chappell and B. Havens, "Who Helps the Elderly Person: A Discussion of Informal and Formal Care," in W. Peterson and J. Quadagno, eds., *Social Bonds in Later Life* (Newbury Park, California: Sage Publications, 1985).

13. R. Stone, G. L. Cafferata, and J. Sangl, "Caregivers of the Frail Elderly: A National Profile," *The Gerontologist* 27 (1987): 616–626.

14. A. Martin Matthews, "Widowhood as an Expectable Life Event," in V. W. Marshall, ed., *Aging in Canada: Social Perspectives*, 2nd ed. (Markham, Ontario: Fitzhenry and Whiteside, 1987).

15. L. R. Fischer, L. Rogne and N. N. Eustis, "Support Systems for the Familyless Elderly: Care without Commitment," in J. F. Gubrium and A. Sankar, eds., *The Home Care Experience: Ethnography and Policy* (Newbury Park, California: Sage Publications, 1990).

16. E. Shapiro, R. B. Tate, and N. P. Roos, "Do Nursing Homes Reduce Hospital Use?" *Medical Care* 25 (No. 1, January 1987): 1–8.

17. E. Shapiro and R. Tate, "Is Health Care Use Changing? A Comparison Between Physician, Hospital, Nursing Home and Home Care Use of Two Elderly Cohorts," *Medical Care* 27 (No. 11, November, 1989): 1002–1014.

18. M. J. Hollander and P. Pallan, "A New Planning and Resource Allocation Framework for Institutional and Community Based Long Term Care Services" (Paper presented at the II European Congress of Gerontology, Madrid, Spain, September 11–14, 1991).

19. Manitoba Health Services Commission, *Annual Report 1974/75* and *Annual Report 1990/91* (Winnipeg: Manitoba Health Services Commission, 1974/75 and 1990/91).

20. N. L. Chappell and A. A. Blandford, *Adult Day Care: Its Impact on the Utilization of Other Health Care Services and on Quality of Life,* Final Report. (Ottawa: NHRDP, Health and Welfare Canada, 1983).

17

Health Care in Canada

Neena L. Chappell

■ ■ ■

ADDING COMMUNITY SERVICE

One of the major shortcomings of the formal Canadian care system is its failure to meet the needs of the chronically ill elderly (Chappell et al., 1986). A small proportion of elders are in long-term care at any one time. In 1986, 8.9% of elderly individuals lived in long-term care institutions in Canada (nursing homes and institutions for elderly and chronically ill persons). However, fully 17% of those 75 and over lived in long-term care institutions in that year (Statistics Canada, 1987). While the proportion in facilities at any one time is small, one-quarter of elderly persons can expect to spend some time in long-term care institutions before they die.

Community care, however, is a relatively neglected aspect of the system. It was not until the 1970s that there was substantial growth of home health services. It was recognized that residential services were best able to meet the needs of the very sick (nursing homes) and the very well (housing units). Meeting the needs of those who were intermediate between these two extremes had not been given priority. Early home care programs tended to offer medically oriented services as a means of shortening hospital stays. They were not considered a means of treating and maintaining people needing chronic or long-term care in the community. In the late 1970s, it was documented that almost half (45%) of the residents in nursing homes were in self-sufficient or Level 1 care and that most of these people could remain in the community with proper supports (Dulude, 1978). In addition, intermediate levels of community support were considered less expensive than institutional care (Lalonde, 1974). The search for alternatives was fueled by the increasing aging of the population which raised concerns that greater demands would "bankrupt" the health care system.

Reprinted from *Geriatric Care, Distributed Justice and the Welfare State: Retrenchment or Development* by S. Ingman and D. Gill (eds.), 1993, by permission of the State University of New York Press.

Even though the Department of National Health and Welfare had established a committee for developing pilot home care programs as early as 1957, there were only 26 programs operating in six provinces one decade later in 1967. A federal/provincial working group on home care was established in 1974. In the next year it reported that the number and variety of home care programs was growing but there was little consistency in objectives, eligibility criteria, services offered, staffing, terminology, or funding. The report (National Health and Welfare, 1975) argued for federal/provincial initiatives to correct this lack of uniformity. At that time Manitoba was the only province providing a universal home care program, one which was part of the provincial health care system but not dependent on medical authorization.

It was during the mid to late 1970s that home care programs developed more rapidly and a broad definition of services evolved. Home care was viewed as a service in its own right rather than primarily as a means of shortening hospital stays. This is reflected in the broad definition accepted by the working group as the guideline for home care programs:

> *Home care should be regarded as a basic mode of health care that coordinates and/or provides the variety of personal health and supportive services required to maintain or to help function adequately in the home, those persons with health and/or social needs related to physical or mental disability, personal or family crises or to illness of an acute or chronic nature. A prerequisite is that the home is judged to be a viable place where treatment or care can be provided. Supportive services include social services and other services to assist such persons and their families. (National Health and Welfare, 1975:13)*

The types of needs that can be met through home care are frequently classified as: basic (necessary for the maintenance of the person and include assistance, for example, with preparing food or bathing), supportive (helping the individual to cope with the indirect effects of illness such as providing personal attention, company, or reassurance), and remedial or therapeutic (requiring professional intervention and treatment such as medical, nursing or family counselling) (Shapiro, 1979). In the recent past, basic and supportive needs have usually been met by the individual or by family and friends, while remedial needs have been provided by professionals.

An example of a community-based program is the Manitoba home care program which has a coordinated entry point and offers a range of services available after an initial assessment by a nurse and/or a social worker. There is no unilateral restriction by medical, nursing, social, or financial condition. Services are provided at no cost to the recipient. Home care in Canada, as in other industrialized countries, has been accepted as a necessary component within a continuum of care (Kammerman, 1976). Social services are considered necessary in addition to medical services and the need for coordination with other health care services accepted.

Despite increasing awareness of the importance of community services, the decentralized Canadian system and the lack of national coordination makes the compilation of utilization statistics difficult. The independent jurisdiction of the provinces relative to health matters makes generalization to the entire country problematic. At the current time, the provinces and territories offer some services but vary in terms of the services offered, the need for physician certification, age restrictions, and user fees. That is, inter-provincial diversity in both availability of and access to services is evident.

Support for community services is evident in the recent federal document *Achieving Health for All* (Minister of Supply and Services Canada 1987). This document embraces the World Health Organization definition of health which includes social, psychological, economic, and environmental aspects in addition to medical aspects of health. It recognizes the role of societal structural constraints to individual action as well as the individual's responsibility in choosing among various lifestyles. It recognizes the role of community support. The importance of this report is the further acceptance of a broad definition of health which is not restricted only to medical intervention. Current discussions to implement such a health promotion framework are laudable and far-reaching. They are, however, primarily discussed as add-ons to the existing medical care system with little discussion of changing the current medical care system.

■ ■ ■

APPROPRIATENESS

Services can be equitable or accessible but if they are not appropriate they will not lead to a healthy society. The major illnesses of old age are chronic conditions or acute flare-up of chronic conditions. That is, the greatest need among elderly persons is for services to help them cope with chronic conditions and functional disability. Yet community care programs have tended to develop as add ons to existing institutional and medical care services in Canada. New monies have to be found in order to fund community services. They have not been implemented in a fashion whereby dollars from existing physician and acute care services are being transferred over. This detracts from their desirability when viewed through government eyes.

While there is an increasing recognition of the importance of community and social services for an aging population, this is occurring when a powerful, expensive and complex medical/pharmaceutical/industrial system is already in place. That basic system in Canada has not undergone major transformation even though McKeown and Lowe (1966), McKeown et al., (1975), Dubos (1963), and McKinlay and McKinlay (1977) have demonstrated that medical intervention is not the primary cause of declines in mortality in this century; Maxwell (1975) and Weller and Manga (1982) have shown that the major diseases of old age are chronic not acute illnesses and health care expenditures are not necessarily correlated with health outcomes; Syme and Berkman (1981) and Grant (1984) have shown that social class and poverty are significantly correlated with health; and others (Coddington et al., 1990) report estimates anywhere from 25% to 60% of physician services to seniors are unnecessary or inappropriate.

Amid such established findings questioning the value of extending medical care, there is recent Canadian evidence that medical treatment of the elderly is increasing at a faster rate than the proportion of elderly within the society. Evans (1988) and Barer et al. (1986) argue convincingly that the aging of the Canadian population will not place a significant strain on the health care system. There will be a slow and steady increase with certain sectors increasing more than others, such as long-term care, home care, etc. but that society can handle that gradual increase. Nor is there any evidence to suggest that changing morbidity patterns among elders will lead to drastically increased utilization.

However, there is evidence of dramatic increases in the utilization patterns of health care services (including medical, acute/rehabilitation hospital care, and long-term care) by elderly persons (in the province of British Columbia where the data are collected). There is an increased servicing which is rising faster than the increase in the proportion of elderly. The increased utilization is not due to the demographic change by itself nor does it appear to be due to changing morbidity patterns. Rather, the relative intensity with which the health care system is treating elders is rising dramatically.

As Gill and Ingman (1986) have pointed out, with the explosion in biomedical knowledge it is hardly surprising to see such an increase in service provision. However, since this can continue indefinitely and given the growing opportunities for intervention during old age, there has been growing doubt about the effectiveness and ultimate value of these treatments. Given the biomedical focus of physicians, and the chronic and disability needs of old age, together with a recognition that the system is provider driven and not patient driven, it is a distinct possibility that increased medical servicing is escalating in an unwarranted fashion. As others have pointed out, the medical care system is driven primarily by physicians, not patients (see for example Walker, 1986). Other than the initial visit, patients return to the physician on the physician's advice. Physicians and only physicians have admitting privileges to hospitals, physicians control the tests that will be ordered, the drugs that will be prescribed, the services that will be received, and when the patient will be released from the hospital. These decisions are by and large out of the control of the patient.

The power and strength of the medical/industrial complex is reflected in society's acceptance of those services as more important than social services. Community and social services tend to be equated with tasks normally done for oneself or by family or friends. These tasks, such as homemaker, handyman, and meal services, are seldom thought of in terms of formal agencies. When they are provided formally there is an historical tendency to equate them with welfare and to make them means tested, stigmatizing recipients (Tenhoor, 1982). As economic constraints tighten, Estes and Wood (1986) note that the United States is turning to a medicalization of community care as a result of their medically oriented reimbursement policies.

This has not been the tendency in Canada to date. Indeed the move has been away from home care programs requiring physician certification to those accepting any referral source. However the report of the Canadian Medical Association (1987) on health care for the elderly recommends that while there be both a medical and a social component to assessment prior to entry into the system, the "physician should play a central role" in subsequent coordination of health care. If community care develops under medical dominance, either to receive legitimacy earlier or to tap into the existing national health insurance system, it will not provide necessary broadening of the medical system to a health care system. By definition, a physician dominated community care program will be medical rather than health-oriented. It is only by embracing a broad definition of health, which includes social, economic, psychological, and environmental aspects of health, in addition to the medical, that the health care needs of Canadians will be met.

There is little research on the demand for community services should they be offered as add ons to the existing system. Kane (1985) reports that in British Columbia the demand curve for community services plateaued after two years. He argues that the key to control is a universal system administered from a single entry point with a fixed budget. The experiences in British Columbia, Manitoba and Ontario all suggest that services can be provided within a fixed budget. With about 10% of the nursing home budget, these provincial governments have offered a desirable package of home care services (Kane and Kane, 1985).

Part of the rationale for establishing these services is that they will reduce the use of more expensive forms of care, i.e., physician services, hospital and long-term institutional care. Kane and Kane (1985) did not find evidence of institutional care displacement in the aggregate. However they do argue that the presence of an alternative system of care makes it more feasible to implement a policy to restrict building more institutional beds. Havens (1985) notes that savings in a mature system occur primarily in less use of acute care hospital beds by long-term care patients. Supporting this argument are data from Manitoba adult day care users (Chappell and Blandford, 1983). Furthermore, Levin (1985) points out that while there has been a continued growth in long-term care beds, it has been less than expected by the increase in the number of elderly. The continued increase of 2% per year of elderly individuals and the fact that they use the bulk of long-term care mean that large decreases in the use of other sectors cannot be expected. If the system continues without major re-organization, limited supplies of community services with low overall budgets can be expected.

There is also a growing acceptance that funding for long-term community care should come from a redistribution of health dollars from the acute care sector. The recent federal report of the Standing Committee on Health and Welfare, Social Affairs, Seniors and the Status of Women (Porter, 1991) recommended that a framework be developed for the gradual shift of resources from the institutional sector to community home care, and social support services. National expenditure on hospitals did decrease slightly from 44.4% in 1975 to 39.2% in 1987 with expenditure on home care increasing slightly from 0.3% to 0.8% in the same period. The Ontario government (Ministry of Community and Social Services, Ministry of Health, and Ministry of Citizenship, 1991) has just proposed transferring $37.6 million annually into long-term care and support services. This constitutes less than 1% of hospital expenditures.

It is evident from this discussion that while Canada offers a universal and reasonably equitable medical care system, it falls short in terms of a health care system for elderly persons.

■■■

REFERENCES

Barer, M.L., Evans, R.G., Hertzman, C. and Lomas, J. (1986). "Toward Effective Aging: Rhetoric and Evidence," paper presented at the 3rd Canadian Conference on Health Economics, Winnipeg, Manitoba, May.

Canadian Medical Association. (1987). *Health Care for the Elderly: Today's Challenges, Tomorrow's Options.* Ottawa, Ontario: Department of Communi-cations and Government Relations, Canadian Medical Association.

Chappell, N.L. and Blandford, A.A. (1983). *Adult Day Care: Its Impact on the Utilization of Other Health Care Services and on Quality of Life.* Ottawa, Ontario: NHRDP, Health and Welfare Canada.

Chappell, N.L., Strain, L.A. and Blandford, A.A. (1986). *Aging and Health Care: A Social Perspective.* Toronto, Ontario: Holt, Rinehart & Winston.

Coddington, D.C. et al. (1970). *The Crisis in Health Care.* San Francisco, CA: Jossey-Bass Publishers.

Dubos, R.J. (1963). "Infection into Disease." In D.J. Ingle (Ed.), *Life and Disease.* New York, NY: Basic Books.

Dulude, L. (1978). *Women and Aging: A Report on the Rest of Our Lives.* Ottawa: Advisory Council on the Status of Women.

Estes, C.L. and Wood, J.B. (1986). "The Non-Profit Sector and Community-Based Care for the Elderly in the U.S.: A Disappearing Resource?," *Social Science and Medicine,* 23(12): 1261–1266.

Evans, R.G. (1988). "Plenary Address." Paper presented at Connections '88, International Symposium on *Research and Public Policy on Aging and Health,* Saskatoon, Saskatchewan, February.

Gill, D.G. and Ingman, S.R. (1986). "Geriatric Care and Distributive Justice: Problems and Prospects," *Social Science and Medicine,* 23(12): 1205–1215.

Grant, K.R. (1984). "The Inverse Care Law in the Context of Universal Free Health Insurance in Canada: Toward Meeting Health Needs Through Social Policy," *Sociological Focus,* 17:137–155.

Havens, B. (1985). "A Long-Term Care System: A Canadian Perspective." In *The Feasibility of a Long-Term Care System: Lessons from Canada.* Tampa, FL: International Exchange Center on Gerontology, 19–27.

Kammerman, S.B. (1976). "Community Services for the Aged: The View from Eight Countries," *The Gerontologist,* 16: 529–537.

Kane, R.L. (1985). *The Feasibility of a Long-Term Care System: Lessons from Canada.* Tampa, FL: International Exchange Center on Gerontology, 1–19.

Kane, R.A., and Kane, R.L. (1985). "The Feasibility of Universal Long-Term Care Benefits," *New England Journal of Medicine,* 312: 1357–1364.

Lalonde, M. (1974). *A New Perspective on the Health of Canadians.* Ottawa, Ontario: Health and Welfare Canada.

Levin, P.J. (1985). "A Comparison, from a Hospital Administrator's Viewpoint, Between Three Canadian Provinces' Long-Term Care Programs and the U.S. Non-System." In *The Feasibility of a Long-Term Care System: Lessons from Canada.* Tampa, FL: International Exchange Center on Gerontology, 28–36.

Maxwell, R. (1975). *Health Care: The Growing Dilemma.* New York, NY: McKinsey & Company.

McKeown, T. and Lowe, C.R. (1966). *An Introduction to Social Medicine.* Philadelphia, PA: F.A. Davis.

McKeown, T., Record, R.G. and Turner, R.D. (1975). "An Interpretation of the Decline of Mortality in England and Wales During the Twentieth Century." *Population Studies,* 29: 391–422.

McKinlay, J.B. and McKinlay, S.M. (1977). "The Questionable Contribution of Medical Measures to the Decline of Mortality in the United States in the Twentieth Century," *Milbank Memorial Fund Quarterly,* summer.

Minister of Supply and Services Canada. (1987). *Active Health Report.* Ottawa, Ontario: Minister of Supply and Services, Catalogue H–39–106/1987E.

Ministry of Community and Social Services, Ministry of Health and Ministry of Citizenship. (1991). *Redirection of Long-Term Care and Support Services in Ontario: A Public Consultation Paper.* Ontario: Community Support Services Area Offices.

National Health and Welfare. (1975). *Report on the Federal-Provincial Working Group on Home Care Programs to the Advisory Committee on Community Health.* Ottawa, Ontario: National Health and Welfare.

Porter, B. (1991). *The Health Care System in Canada and Its Funding: No Easy Solutions* (First Standing Report on the Standing Committee on Health and Welfare, Social Affairs, Seniors and the Status of Women). Ottawa, Ontario: Canada Communication Group—Publishing, Supply and Services Canada.

Shapiro, E. (1979). *Home Care: A Comprehensive Overview.* Ottawa, Ontario: Policy, Planning and Information Branch, Health and Welfare Canada.

Statistics Canada. (1987). *The Daily.* Ottawa, Ontario: Minister of Supply and Services.

Syme, S.L. and Berkman, L.F. (1981). "Social Class, Susceptibility and Sickness." In P. Conrad and R. Kern (Eds.), *The Sociology of Health and Illness: Critical Perspectives.* New York, NY: St. Martin's Press, 35–44.

Tenhoor, W.J. (1982). "United States: Health and Personal Social Services." In M.C. Hokenstad and R.A. Ritvo (Eds.), *Linking Health Care and Social Services.* Beverly Hills, CA: Sage Publications, 25–59.

Walker, G.K. (1986). "Reforming Medicare: The Limited Framework of Political Discourse on Equity and Economy," *Social Science and Medicine,* 23 (12): 1237–1250.

Weller, G.R. and Manga, P. (1982). "The Reprivatization of Hospital and Medical Care Services: A Comparative Analysis of Canada, Britain and the United States." Revised version of the paper presented at the 10th World Congress of Sociology, Mexico City, Mexico.

18

Native Seniors' Health Needs

Jean Goodwill

The health needs of the native elderly are unique, an often uncomprehended fact to most people in Canada. Generally, native people age more quickly, their illnesses are more severe, and more of them are afflicted by disease than the average person—facts I will illustrate later in this discussion. Prior to 1988, little research was conducted to define why this is the case until a survey and subsequent supplement was undertaken by the Saskatchewan Senior Citizens' Council. The results of the survey were then published and entitled *A Study of the Unmet Needs of Off-Reserve Indians and Métis Elderly in Saskatchewan.* I have drawn from, and quoted most of my data from, this much-needed study. While it is focused on my home province, as President of the Indian and Inuit Nurses of Canada for six years, I feel that the information revealed in this study is true of the majority of native Elders across Canada. This seems to apply, regardless of where they are situated, in urban centres, on reserves, or in northern settlements and isolated regions where some of the traditional ways of life can still be pursued.

In this discussion, I refer to all Elders who are of Canadian Indian ancestry, Status Indians, Non-status Indians, and the Métis people. Some of us here are all too familiar with the frailties, in some degree, that are a part of the process of aging. Health deteriorates, the old energy we once knew is not what it used to be. With the loss of loved ones and friends, we grow increasingly lonely; we cannot get around like we once could; we must somehow adapt to modern concepts and technology and conflicting value systems between the generations. If we do, there is usually mental stress involved, and if we fail to do so, there is a loss of self-worth and self-esteem. Many seniors must learn to cope with a reduced income. Some seniors do manage to stay "39 and holding." They are the fortunate ones in excellent health for the most part. Good health plays a major role for enjoyment of the "golden years."

Reprinted by permission of Jean Goodwill.

This paper was originally presented at a conference on gerontology in Ottawa, April 18–21, 1990. It was presented without formal bibliographical material and subsequently published in *Aging Into the 21st Century*.

But native seniors must face what one writer has termed a "double jeopardy," in that they suffer an earlier old age. According to a Winnipeg study (Young, 1984, 9), "native people aged 50 and over tend to reveal similar deterioration as is evident for the rest of the population aged 65 and over." The life expectancy for native people is ten years less than that of the general population, and statistics show that natives have more health-related problems and often more severe ones than non-native people. Only three per cent of the native people are aged 65 and over as compared to 12 per cent of the general population of Saskatchewan. On the other hand, fully 42 per cent of those living on reserves are under the age of 15, while in the general population, that figure drops to 23 per cent.

A reduced income is one thing, outright poverty is quite something else. In 1983, the Task Force Committee on Mental Health Services in Saskatchewan noted that the pressures experienced by significant numbers of native households as a consequence of conflicting value systems, poor living conditions, and poverty can cause internal friction and "produce intense reactions of anger, anxiety, depression and hostility." In 1980, the average income of native people was approximately two-thirds that of other Canadians (Statistics Canada, 1984).

While many Canadian seniors do experience conflicting value systems between generations, native seniors must additionally face the complication of loss of culture, traditions, and the native languages in the education processes of young people. In a recent report by Max Yalden, Chief Commissioner of the Canadian Human Rights Commission, he states, "The role of Elders in the community has suffered for several reasons, one being the reluctance of many young people to submit to their authority in the face of other influences."

Since many native seniors do not speak English, communication on any satisfactory level is close to impossible. Holzberg (1982), 253) notes that the "supposition that successful adjustment to old age is based upon a continuity of life patterns is fast emerging as one of the most promising theories in social gerontology." And as the Saskatchewan study points out, "it can be hypothesized that one of the most critical problems facing the native elderly is the loss of continuity in their lives." This is why I describe the situation of native Elders as unique. They face all the difficulties presented by increasing age but to a more severe and complicated degree. As the report points out, "these factors...would challenge the resources of even the most able-bodied individuals."

Why do native people have so many and more severe health problems than other Canadians, especially when the promise of the right to health care was written into the treaties (particularly Treaty #6 in Saskatchewan and Alberta) well over a century ago? Our ancestors had seen the dreadful effect the newly introduced diseases of smallpox, influenza, tuberculosis, and measles were having on native people, and our leaders (my own ancestor, Poundmaker, was a spokesman for this concern) insisted that the right to health care must be included before they could sign the treaty. They had medicine men and women skilled in treating ordinary illness, but the raging epidemics that decimated entire tribes of people were beyond their skills. To conclude their treaties, the representatives of the Canadian government had to revise the planned documents to include the right to health care.

But when we consider the substandard state of Indian health today, we can only arrive at the conclusion that, for various reasons, the health care system, as it was set up to serve the native people, did not effectively meet their needs. No thought was ever entertained then of consulting with native health practitioners. The European health care providers had no idea of the native culture, traditions, or language and did not seem to think they needed it. Since few of their clients could speak English—and a number of them still cannot do so—there was, and often still is, very poor communication between the medical and nursing personnel and their native clients. The idea seems to have been that what works for non-natives should also be successful with native people. This assumption did not take into account the psychological or emotional factors which are now recognized as having a decided impact on the well-being and recovery rates of all ill people. To this day, some native seniors can be found who have undergone many different types of treatments, yet have no idea of what these treatments are, nor why they were performed on them. One interviewer for the Saskatchewan study says of a northern senior who had been in a city hospital two years ago: "She thinks it was a bladder operation, but she doesn't really know." Another respondent said: "I go and see the doctor...all the time and they don't say what problem is upon me."

The need for native medical personnel and/or interpreters has lately been recognized. The new Indian Health Policy of the Medical Services Branch, Health and Welfare Canada, in 1979, recognized the need for the promotion and development of health careers for native people. However, in spite of educational assistance available from Indian Affairs and other sources, the number of Indian medical doctors and students is approximately 20, and there are only about 300 native nurses, two nutritionists, and three dentists. There are no pharmacists, health educators, and other native health-related professionals. But there is still a constant shortage of nurses in the native health field, and the high turnover rate of community health nurses makes for minimal continuity in the provision of health care for the native population.

The Indian and Inuit Nurses of Canada, the first professional native organization in Canada, was formed in 1974 in answer to the need to encourage and facilitate native input into decision making and implementation of programs designed to improve native health and to recruit more people of native ancestry into the medical and related health professions. We stand ready to offer assistance to government and private agencies dealing in matters of native health. We conduct studies and maintain the reporting and compiling of information, and publish and promote material and activities on native health, culture and medicine.

The Saskatchewan study found that six out of every 10 native Elders rated their own health as "fair" or "poor." The survey feels "the importance of self-rated health cannot be underestimated, as self-rated health as been shown to closely predict measures of stability, the need for mobility aids, assistance in the home and assistance when leaving the home."

Poverty, of course, plays a leading role affecting the health of native and non-native people alike. Often, this is directly related to undereducation and lack of language skills which make it increasingly difficult to find employment in the modern world of technology. Almost one quarter of the native households in the southern part of the province sampled by the survey reported incomes for themselves and their spouses of under $500 monthly or less than $6,000 a year. Poverty results in poor nutrition and substandard living conditions, major causes of ill health. It is mentally stressful and creates feelings of worthlessness, rejection, isolation, and resentment.

The most frequently reported health problems among the sampled native seniors in Saskatchewan and other Manitoba surveys of native Elders in both on-reserve and urban settings (Indian and Northern Affairs, Canada, 1986, 38; Young, 1984, 24) bear out evidence that arthritis, diabetes, heart conditions, and back, leg, and foot impairments predominate. We can add to this the notoriously low native resistance to tuberculosis, which even today, with better treatment drugs and facilities, is still nine times higher among native people than it is among non-natives.

Failing eyesight, loss of hearing, and dental problems are common to all seniors, but when so many native seniors have incomes well below the poverty line as identified by the *Canadian Senate Report on Poverty*, they frequently cannot obtain the glasses, hearing aids, or the treatment to alleviate such problems. Status Indians do receive help with some or all of the costs of some of the debilities, but for the rest of the native population, such assistance is not provided. Twenty-nine percent of the survey respondents in the north stated they had difficulty getting medical care. Certainly the greatest problem in obtaining proper care is affordability. As an example, one native senior interviewed suffers from a skeletal deformity as the result of a fall down some stairs several years ago. Although nurses have told her that the deformity can be corrected, the air cost to the hospital is several hundred dollars, or about half of the family's total monthly income. If a friend or a family member is to travel with the ill senior and private transportation is not available, costs can be doubled.

Respiratory diseases are the leading cause of hospitalization for natives, but the surprising statistic that about 25 per cent of the native people in the urbanized areas of the province are afflicted by diabetes, as compared to only five to eight per cent of non-native Elders, has alarming implications. As the survey points out: "Left uncontrolled, diabetes may lead to heart and vision problems and can result in gangrene that may require amputation of a limb" (Markides and Mindel, 1987, 90). Diabetes is a disease where the prognosis and avoidance of complications depend upon adherence to dietary and medical instructions. The significant proportion of native elderly who are unable to read English or have great difficulty in reading dosages or in understanding the relationship between the substance in a syringe and physical health can cause difficulty in the administration of insulin.

The provision of home care or long-term health care is never easy, especially in isolated areas. In her 1985 study, *The Canadian Indian Elderly and Long-Term Care Services,* Anne H. Weiler states: "A comprehensive program is usually expected to include medical and nursing care, social support services, day care, meals on wheels and homemakers. At present, neither the Department of Indian Affairs, nor Health and Welfare Canada have a home care program as such. The Department of Indian Affairs is limited to certain support services...and, in order to denote this difference, refers to its program as 'In-Home-Care.'" She also points out that, "Because most programs are under-funded and lack sufficient resources to provide the level of care needed, the existing long-term services for the elderly in no way satisfy their need for services." Eighty per cent of the native elderly in the south of the province have a chronic or acute health problem, treated or untreated. The mortality rate of registered (or Status) Indians is cited as almost twice that of non-native people, and the number of hospitalizations is three times greater than that of the non-native population.

There is a great need for institutional placement. As Ms. Weiler points out (1985, 22) "...the current long-term care services for the Indian elderly are fragmented, incomplete and institutionally biased. Linkages to other programs are essential... Coordination of the responsible federal and provincial departments is essential for maximizing benefits to the...recipient of services."

But here again we run into difficulties unique to native seniors. Ms. Weiler puts it clearly: "All native people share a common opinion about institutionalization—it is viewed with distaste, not only because it makes them feel transplanted in a totally foreign environment but, above all, it forces them to abandon their natural environment. Placement in non-native nursing homes creates many problems for the person and for the family members. Distances from 'home,' infrequent visits from family and friends, an unfamiliar institutional environment with non-native personnel, strange diet and 'rules' that regulate one's life—all can contribute to the loneliness, depression and sense of isolation of the elderly Indian."

The World Health Organization has recognized this need—the involvement of the indigenous caregivers and spiritual leaders along with modern methods of medical treatment. It is the holistic approach, taking into consideration the mental, social, and cultural concepts of ill people as well as their physical needs. This is especially important now when the Department of Indian Affairs and Northern Development and Health and Welfare

Canada are both committed to community control of health services. Because of the serious problems of alcoholism and substance abuse in many native communities, the National Native Alcohol and Drug Abuse program must continue intensive efforts to pinpoint the causes and treatment of alcohol and drug abuse among native people.

In the field of health, community services, housing and income support, government representatives should meet with native organizations to share program information and to plan appropriate responses. While a first priority should be that the needs of native Elders are met within existing programs, where this is not possible, the development of special programs and services may be required.

Federal and provincial departments should continue to provide information and easy access to their income security programs so that all seniors, including natives, are made aware of, and can apply for, all the benefits to which they are entitled. Due to the lack of formal education of a large number of native people, this information should not depend on the printed word alone, but could be illustrated by the use of posters as well as communicating by radio and television (in the local native language if possible) and through native organization meetings and cultural events. The same holds true in the promotion of good health practices and information on available health care facilities and local medical personnel.

Transportation is a major difficulty for many native seniors. Only 25 per cent of our seniors in urban areas and 10 per cent of those in the north have access to transportation by car as compared to 65 per cent of Elders in the general population. This makes access to required treatment very expensive or simply impossible as illustrated in my example of the northern senior with the skeletal deformity. The Saskatchewan survey recommends that native organizations, seniors' groups, church organizations, and service clubs explore the possibility of developing volunteer driving services to assist the elderly with transportation needs. Where this is not possible, mechanisms for subsidizing transportation costs for the native elderly need to be established.

Another very pertinent recommendation from the Saskatchewan study suggests that native counselling programs modelled on the program at the Regina General Hospital be established in all medical facilities where there is a high utilization of services by native people. The anguish, fear, and isolation of such patients would be immeasurably eased by counselling.

Many natives in the north have never received proper dental care in the past. The dental care of Status Indians, as presently provided, should be extended to all low-income native Elders. Help in paying for glasses should also be considered. In some cases, this aid would increase their ability to produce handicrafts and work in other cottage industries to augment marginal incomes and to increase independence. Resources to extend the availability of home care services in the north must also be considered. Where health services on reserves need to be improved, the development of specific services by the band councils will be necessary.

I hope that the material I have presented so far in this discussion, while it barely scratches the surface of the complex and unique health problems of native seniors, helps to illustrate the critical need for increased and improved health care delivery to all native people. The Senior Citizens' Provincial Council of Saskatchewan identified the need for society as a whole to work together to develop programs and services which are relevant in the field of native health. Statistics prove the very real and critical health needs of all native people, on or off reserves, and call for more specific and relevant health care and funding. I also hope that I have outlined some of the possible solutions as perceived by native organizations, health care providers, and recent studies and surveys on implementing and on improving such specific and relevant health care. The input of those native organizations is of vital necessity here, working along with other seniors' groups and the administrative federal and provincial departments concerned.

Our people are a very powerless and small minority within the general population of our country. But I believe that because of compassionate, moral, ethical, and legal obligations and ideals, we all must do everything possible to assist our original people to achieve the present levels of health and life expectancy as it exists for the rest of our fellow Canadians.

SECTION FOUR

Discussion Questions

1. List three problems that currently drive the health-care policy agenda in Canada. Why is rhetoric around population aging misleading when it comes to health-care policy?

2. How do Canadians and Americans differ in their satisfaction with health care in their respective countries? Do Canadians and Americans have reason to feel the way they do based on the costs and benefits of health care in each country?

3. How does long-term health care differ from acute health care, beyond the fact that one takes place over a longer time? What types of older people typically need long-term care? Who uses and who provides long-term care?

4. What needs does home care best meet? Is this an appropriate form of care in an aging society? How can the Canadian health-care system best fund this type of care?

5. What social and economic forces influence Native seniors' health? How do these forces influence the health services Native seniors have access to and use?

6. State three changes that will likely take place in the delivery of health-care services in Canada in the years ahead. Give three conditions that will lead to these changes.

Suggested Readings

Clark, P.G. (1991). "Geriatric Health Care Policy in the United States and Canada: A Comparison of Facts and Values in Defining the Problems." *Journal of Aging Studies* 5 (3): 265–81.

Dawson, J.I., and L. Critchley (1992). "Community-Hospital Partnerships: The Quick Response Team." *Journal of Nursing Administration* 22 (11): 33–39.

Epp, Jake (1986). *Achieving Health for All.* Ottawa: Ministry of Supply and Services Canada.

Levesque, L. (1993). "Quebec Home-Care Services: A Program at the Local Community Level." In *Caregiving Systems: Informal and Formal Helpers,* eds. S.H. Zarit, L.I. Pearlin, and W.K. Schaie. Hillsdale, New Jersey: Lawrence Erlbaum Associates.

McKim, W.A., and B.L. Mishara (1987). *Drugs and Aging.* Toronto: Butterworths.

Powell, C., L. Mitchell-Pedersen, E. Fingerote, and L. Edmund (1989). "Freedom from Restraint: Consequences of Reducing Physical Restraints in the Management of the Elderly." *Canadian Medical Association Journal* 141 (September 15): 561–64.

Income and the Challenge of Retirement

Retirement is an individual life event. People save for it through pension plans, they take preretirement courses, and they explore second careers. The government even offers incentives for retirement planning through registered retirement savings plans (RRSPs). Studies show that planning for retirement pays off. A good income, good health, and a strong support system lead to personal satisfaction in retirement.

Retirement is also a social institution. Policies decide the timing of retirement, entitlement to a public pension, and the claim on pensions by different social groups (e.g., widows or homemakers). Social policies, as much as individual decisions, shape a person's experience of retirement. Myles (1989), for example, says that public pensions and the "retirement principle" (the idea that people can leave work and still receive an income) create old age as we know it today. He goes on to say that our present concept of old age would disappear without these social inventions.

Myles, in his article here, describes the recent history of pension policy in Canada. He begins with a discussion of the Great Pension Debate that began in 1975. This debate centred on the structure of the Canada Pension Plan and the control of the money that the plan would collect. Myles shows how the structure of the CPP today reflects the struggle between certain powerful groups in Canadian society.

Myles reviews a number of other issues related to public pensions. These include the proposed provision of homemaker pensions, the attack on universality in May 1985, and the promotion of RRSPs as a retirement income option. Myles analyses changes that may transform the public pension system in the future. The new policies that encourage RRSPs, for example, will pull the support of the working and middle classes away from public pension plans. Myles sees this as the development of a welfare state for the wealthy and a potential abandonment of poorer old people.

Guppy looks at the recent debate over mandatory retirement. This debate raises the question of a person's right to work past a certain age. But it also raises the issue of fair access to jobs for younger workers. The Canadian Charter of Rights and Freedoms appears to protect a person's right to work regardless of age. But a finer reading of the Charter raises questions about the fairness of applying this principle. The elimination of mandatory retirement might, for example, hurt younger people in their search for jobs. Mandatory retirement can be seen as a method to ensure intergenerational fairness. A recent Supreme Court of Canada ruling (handed down after Guppy published his article) has upheld mandatory retirement for public employees in Canada (this applies to all provinces that do not have specific laws to prohibit it).

This debate will continue in the future because it raises issues of social justice and intergenerational fairness. But practical concerns will also shape the outcome of this debate in the years ahead. McDonald and Chen place retirement policy in the context of Canada's growing labour-force shortage. First, lower birth rates in recent years mean that smaller groups of young people will enter the labour force in the future. Second, given a good income, workers tend to retire as soon as they can. Third, the recent Supreme Court ruling supports mandatory retirement, a policy that will remove older workers from the labour force. These trends may make the labour-force shortage worse in the future. Canada seems faced with contradictory demands: (1) the demand to move older workers out of and younger workers into the labour force and (2) the demand for more workers than the population of young people can meet. McDonald and Chen focus on the second demand and consider ways that Canadian society can lure older workers to stay at work.

A good retirement income often leads to an early and satisfying retirement. But not everyone has the same chance to receive a good pension. Unattached older women, for example, have one of the highest rates of poverty among older people. And this rate increases with age. The National Council of Welfare traces this high rate of poverty to a combination of things. First, federal income security programs provide too little money to keep single people out of poverty. Second, the Canada Pension Plan pays too little to surviving spouses. Third, most single older women have no private pension. The National Council of Welfare describes some of the problems that poverty causes for older single women. The report ends by describing the social pressures that older single women face as they try to age with dignity.

The National Council of Welfare shows how being old and female, sometimes called double jeopardy, leads to poverty in old age. Gerontologists speak of triple jeopardy when they speak about older immigrant women in Canada. These women have higher rates of poverty than older women born in Canada. Boyd shows how immigration and income-security policies work against these women. She raises the question of what rights older immigrant women should have in Canada beyond the right to live here. Shouldn't these women have the right to the same minimum income that native-born older women have?

The articles in this section focus on social policies that shape retirement today. They show that large social forces like labour-force needs and inter-generational competition shape our definitions of retirement and old age. Policies, as much as or more than personal planning, influence the chance to have a good old age. These readings also show that some policies make old age more difficult for older women than for older men in Canada.

Sources Consulted

Myles, J. (1989). *Old Age in the Welfare State: The Political Economy of Public Pensions*, rev. ed. Lawrence, Kansas: University Press of Kansas.

19

Social Policy in Canada

John Myles

INTRODUCTION

Canadians who have followed debates on social policies for the elderly during the past decade might well be excused if they are now somewhat confused. In the late seventies and early eighties there was a broad consensus that Canada's old age security system was inadequate. The *Great Pension Debate,* as it was called at the time, was not a debate about the facts of the matter but about the choice between public and private solutions to the problem. As the recession deepened in the early eighties, however, talk of reform was replaced by talk of restraint and cutbacks. By 1984, the Great Pension Debate, a debate over how to enhance the system, had been replaced by the debate over universality—whether to restrict Canada's universal Old Age Security benefits to those in need.

Making sense of these debates is no easy task. The first reason is because the policies are complex. Michael Prince (1985) lists over twenty public revenue and expenditure programs for the elderly. Even more confusing are the competing claims about the relative merits of these programs. For some, universal social benefits are the foundation of the "good society"; to others, these benefits provide unneeded and unwarranted subsidies to the rich.

An understanding of these matters is important for several reasons. In Canada, as elsewhere, public programs for the elderly represent the single largest component in the budget of the modern welfare state. As a result, old age policies are a major public issue. As the population continues to age, Canadian political life will be increasingly affected by what Hudson (1978) has called the *graying* of the state budget. Equally important, these programs are the main source of income for the elderly. In 1981 government programs provided 45.5 percent of the income going to aged couples and for single retirees. Trends in poverty in old age confirm this pattern. The poverty rate among elderly couples declined from 41.4 percent in 1969 to 11.1

From Eloise Rathbone-McCuan and Betty Havens (eds). *North American Elders: United States and Canadian Perspectives,* 43–53. Reprinted with permission of Greenwood Publishing Group Inc., Westport, CT. Copyright © 1988.

percent in 1983. The rate among unattached individuals also declined but was still 57.5 percent in 1983 (National Council of Welfare, 1985b).

Women and Pensions

The high poverty rate observed among the *unattached elderly* is rooted in the gender-specific character of the aging process: most of the unattached are elderly widowed females. Retirement is the first major event of the aging process; the second is widowhood. Because of gender differences in longevity, most widowed persons are women and most women become widows. Accordingly, we must also assess the system's capacity to prevent poverty and to provide income security in the face of this second major event in the aging process.

The results are startling. All widows can expect a sharp drop in income to levels well below the low income cut-off. The failure of OAS and C/QPP to provide adequate income security has a cumulative effect on elderly women. The GIS improves the situation somewhat but still leaves a substantial poverty gap.

These are the major failings of the retirement income system in Canada. A system that provided real income security would make the Guaranteed Income Supplement and other social assistance measures redundant. Instead, over 50 percent of Canada's elderly are eligible for such assistance. The Canadian system does better in meeting the antipoverty objective for couples, but fails miserably when the spouse (usually male) dies. In a ten-nation comparison of the support provided to elderly survivors in the mid-seventies (Union Bank of Switzerland, 1977), Canada ranked last. It is from this context that the policy debates of the seventies and eighties emerged.

THE POLITICS OF INCOME SECURITY

The Great Pension Debate: The Failure of Reform

The Great Pension Debate was launched in 1975 when the Canadian Labour Congress proposed that C/QPP benefits be doubled. The debate was not over the antipoverty objectives of the system. There was general consensus that targeted benefits to the low-income elderly, especially elderly women, should be improved. The main point of confrontation was over the use of the public system to improve income security. A review of the debate is useful not only for what it tells us about old age policies but also the insight it provides into the forces shaping policy in Canada.

The core of the debate was rather simple: whether to meet the income security needs of Canada's workers through expansion of the C/QPP, or through improving private sector plans. The cleavages in the debate were also clear. The public sector option was promoted by organized labor, women's rights groups, a variety of social reform lobbies, and the antipoverty lobby. It was recognized that the major reason persons required GIS was the inadequacy of private pensions and the C/QPP. The major opposition came from Canadian business.

As Banting (1985) points out, this societal cleavage was overlaid by a second conflict system within the state. The two major antagonists in the area of pension reform have traditionally been Canada's two most populous provinces, Ontario and Quebec. Quebec took a leadership role in the initial C/QPP legislation while Ontario opposed it. Conflict between the two provinces over additional reforms has continued. On balance, the federal government has leaned toward public sector solutions, especially in the early periods of the debate, as evidenced by the Lazar Commission proposals made by senior federal officials (Task Force on Retirement Income Policy, 1980).

On the face of it, the public sector solution would seem to have been irresistible. The C/QPP already had all of the qualities lacking in private sector alternatives: universal coverage of the labor force, immediate vesting of benefits, portability, indexing, and survivors' benefits. Most ironic, in view of the usual business attacks on public sector "inefficiency," it had the advantages of ease of administration and low overhead costs. By almost any standard it was judged superior to private sector alternatives (Task Force on Retirement Income Policy, 1980).

An additional factor favoring a public sector solution was the lack of consensus by business on improvements to private sector plans (Banting, 1985). Large firms were prepared to accept mandatory private pensions to solve the coverage problem, but small business was not. The financial sector urged modest indexing based on *excess interest,* but the large industrial firms were opposed. What then led to the eventual failure of the public sector reform coalition? To answer the question, it is necessary to examine the nature of the opposition.

To find the business community lurking behind the failure to reform Canada's old age security system is far from self-explanatory. In 1951 big business supported legislation to abolish the means test and introduce universal benefits (Murphy, 1982). In the sixties the insurance industry fought the C/QPP reforms, but received only tepid support from the industrial sector. In the late seventies a more cohesive business coalition, with major industrial firms as the dominant partner, emerged to oppose further public sector expansion. The reason for this, Banting observes, was that the "battle over public pensions had become a battle over one of the commanding heights of the Canadian economy" (1985:59). By the mid-seventies the accumulated assets of the private pension funds were the largest source of new investment capital in the Canadian economy (Calvert, 1977). Any expansion of the C/QPP would transfer the economic power of the pension funds from the private sector to the state. It was no longer a matter of protecting the pension market for insurance and trust companies; expansion of the public system was a threat to the entire business community.

Interprovincial conflicts were also rooted in issues of capital formation. In the 1960s Quebec took the lead in promoting the C/QPP not merely to provide better pensions but also to create a capital pool to finance Quebec's economic development and reduce financial dependence on English Canada. And it was the promise of a cheap source of capital that swung the other provinces behind the plan. As one provincial official remarked: "The main reason for us was the creation of a large fund. It would provide money for development here and give us more liberty in the money markets. The fund was certainly the main reason for me; it was the reason" (R. Simeon, 1972:175–76). The funds of the Canada Pension Plan soon became the major source of provincial borrowing. In Quebec the government agency through which the QPP funds are channelled became the largest purchaser of common stocks in Canada.

But despite the importance of the funds, the government of Ontario continued to oppose expansion of the C/QPP and had the veto power to do so. Governed from 1943 to 1985 by the Conservatives, Ontario is the headquarters of Canada's major financial and industrial corporations. Its power of veto made the Ontario government the private sector's most important and reliable ally.

Thus the reform coalition favoring a public sector solution faced formidable obstacles: a broad alliance of business interests that became increasingly cohesive as the debate evolved; and a federal structure that allowed the government of Ontario to veto reform. Whether the reform alliance would have been able to overcome these obstacles is a question now lost to history. As the recession deepened, the forces for reform began to dissipate. Labor did not give up its objectives; but as unemployment began to rise, attention turned to other matters and resources were deployed to defend past achievements. At the same time a profound cleavage emerged within the federal government. Monique Begin, minister of health and welfare, continued to press for public sector reform, but faced growing opposition from the powerful Finance Department where the concern was to restore "business confidence" and to encourage investment. Neither objective would be enhanced by expansion of the C/QPP.

The erosion of the reform movement was also hastened by the emergence of a break between organized labor and the women's movement over the appropriate method of dealing with the problems of elderly women. This was clearly the most critical issue facing the pension system and the one most likely to arouse broad public sympathy for the reform movement. The focus of the cleavage was on the issue of *pensions for homemakers*.

Pension for Homemakers

The poverty of elderly women is associated with several factors. First, limited participation in the labor market means that they acquire few pension credits during their working lives and those acquired are worth less because of the low wages earned by women. Second, survivor benefits depend entirely on the value of pensions earned by men. If these benefits are low, survivor benefits will be even lower. The major thrust of the reforms advanced by labor and antipoverty organizations was to improve the value of benefits that both men and women earn from their time in the labor market. This would improve the situation of women in the paid labor force and also result in higher survivor benefits.

Women's organizations supported this thrust, but sought to go further to recognize the economic and social value of domestic labor by including a pension for homemakers (L. Dulude, 1981) in the C/QPP. Currently, the only recognition of domestic labor is the *child dropout provision* under which women are not penalized for years out of the labor force raising small children when C/QPP benefits are calculated. The proposal also sought to end survivor benefits—on the grounds that they entrench the dependency of wives—and mandatory splitting of accumulated pension credits between husbands and wives. A form of credit splitting has been enacted. As of January 1, 1987 either spouse in a continuing marriage can apply to divide C/QPP retirement pensions earned during their life together. After a one-year separation divorced spouses may apply for a division of all pension credits acquired during their life together. But it was the homemakers' pension proposal that became most controversial and resulted in the split in the reform movement.

Though opposed by some women's organizations, the proposal won increasing support in the women's movement, particularly from the National Action Committee on the Status of Women representing 250 member organizations, and was included in the recommendations of the Parliamentary Task Force on Pension Reform (1983). The proposal would allow families whose main wage earner earns above the average wage to make contributions to provide C/QPP benefits for a spouse who is not in the labor force or who earns less than half the maximum annual pensionable earnings. Single parents, adults caring for the aged or the infirm, and low-income families would be included but exempt from making contributions. Contributions and benefits would be based on the assumption that the domestic labor of an unpaid homemaker is equal to half the average wage.

Critics in the labor movement and other reform lobbies pointed out that the proposal did not provide a pension for homemaking but a subsidy to homemakers not in the paid labor force. The majority of women in the paid labor force are also homemakers, doing their domestic labor evenings and weekends. If these women earn less than half the average wage, their final benefits would be lower than those received by women not in the labor force. Nor was the presence of children or other dependents a condition of the proposal. Nonlabor force spouses who perform no domestic labor (e.g., those with paid housekeepers) would also be eligible. In effect, the scheme would not be a payment for domestic labor but a benefit for families where one spouse is not in the paid labor force. As the National Council of Welfare (1984b) demonstrated, the majority of elderly women would do better financially with a 50 percent increase in the earnings replacement rate of the current plan. The proposal was significant because it received support of both major parties and thus has some prospect of being enacted into law. By appearing to address the most important problem among Canada's elderly—poor elderly women—it defused much of the political pressure for a broader reform of the system.

The Attack on Universality

With the deepening recession of the early eighties, debates over social policy took on a new complexion. Rising unemployment and a general decline in economic activity meant more social expenditures and a rising federal deficit. As a result, discussions turned from expansionary reforms to reducing expenditures. Canada's universal social programs, including Old Age Security, became an immediate target. Soon-to-be Prime Minister Brian Mulroney gave the attack its classic formulation. In the 1984 election campaign he questioned the practice of providing universal social benefits to bank presidents and other well-to-do individuals when the funds could be used to relieve the poverty of the needy.

To Mulroney's surprise, the right of bank presidents to Old Age Security benefits was defended by virtually everyone except bank presidents. This included not only labor, women's, and old age organizations but also the antipoverty lobbies. Their defense of universality was based on the *middle class incorporation thesis,* i.e., it is necessary to include the middle class in social programs or it will not defend them when they come under attack. In the end the prognosis proved to be accurate. Faced with mounting criticism, Mulroney backed away and announced that universal social benefits were a "sacred trust" to be defended at all costs.

The attack on universality went through two more phases. Once in power, Mulroney allowed his finance minister and leading conservative ideologue, Michael Wilson, to reopen the debate. Wilson announced his personal opposition to universality, implying that some income test would be included in his first budget. Public outcry forced Mulroney to repudiate Wilson, his most important cabinet minister.

Unable to dismantle universal benefits, Wilson turned to the more traditional conservative strategy of slow erosion. In his May 1985 budget, he announced partial deindexation of both family allowances and old age security to save the federal treasury some 4 billion dollars over the next five years. Public outrage was worse than before. After two months during which the threat to deindex old age benefits monopolized parliamentary and public debate, Mulroney forced his finance minister to retract.

The core of the Conservative critique was that universal social benefits were subsidizing the well-to-do. There is considerable irony in this since, historically, universal flat benefits were seen as providing income security that would enhance equality (K. Bryden, 1974). In the discussions that led to the reforms of 1951, there was a clear preference in government for an earnings-based system in which benefits would reflect contributions. In contrast, a flat pension paid from a progressive tax system would result in considerable redistribution. OAS proved to be inadequate to the task, but it became the first element and most redistributive component of an emergent income security system. The attack on universality was intended to remove OAS from the income security system and restore it to the status of poor relief it had prior to 1951. The result would be to erode an income security system that the studies of almost a decade had shown to be inadequate.

On the face of it, the more conservative forces in the new government had suffered an enormous defeat, and this was the way its first year in power was interpreted by the popular press. What went unnoticed was that by 1985 the Great Pension Debate of the preceding decade had entirely dissipated. Proposals to expand the C/QPP disappeared from the political agenda and a modest set of reforms for those already covered by private plans was introduced in December 1985. After almost a decade of debate, the result was to reinforce the economic divisions that had generated the debate in the first place: better pensions for those covered by private plans and nothing for the majority who are not. Even more remarkable was the success of the new government in expanding Canada's welfare state for the rich.

Income Security for the Rich

The proposal to deindex OAS was only one of two proposals to "reform" Canada's old age security system in the Wilson budget. The second was to expand the old age security program for upper-income Canadians, the Registered Retirement Savings Plans (or RRSPs). RRSPs have become a major component of Canada's retirement income system. Though not usually considered part of the public system, the public costs of the program are great. Individuals are encouraged to save for retirement by allowing them to make tax-deductible contributions into a registered retirement savings plan. Returns on these investments are then allowed to accumulate free of tax.

Before the 1985 budget, individuals who belonged to a private pension plan (RPP) to which they contributed less than $3,500 were able to contribute the difference to an RRSP up to a combined ceiling of 20 percent of earned income. Those not in a private plan could contribute 20 percent of earned income to a ceiling of $5,500. High-income earners are able to contribute more (sheltering more income from taxes) and, given the tax structure, they receive a larger tax subsidy for each dollar contributed. A high-income earner in the 50 percent marginal tax bracket receives a benefit of $500 for a $1,000 contribution, whereas a modest-income person with a marginal tax rate of 20 percent receives a $200 benefit. As a result, low-income earners have less opportunity to contribute and receive a lower subsidy when they do.

This initial advantage is subject to the magic of compound interest. The Canadian Council on Social Development (1985) points out that a $5,000 investment at 10 percent interest accumulating tax-free will grow to

$150,000 in 30 years or about $110,000 when taxes are paid on withdrawal. If tax were paid on the interest by an upper-income earner as it was being earned, the same investment would grow to $20,000. "Thus," the Council concludes, "the majority of money in RRSPs is the tax assistance, not the original contribution" (1985:11).

The major change in the May 1985 budget expanded this income security system for Canada's well-do-do. The ceiling on contributions was raised from $5,500 to $15,500. It was clearly a windfall for the rich. The estimated cost of the change for the year 1990–91 will be an additional $235,000,000 in lost revenues (National Council of Welfare, 1985a). Ironically, a decade of debate that began to ensure adequate income security for Canadian workers ended by enhancing income security for the well-to-do.

CONCLUSION

The major thrust of postwar social legislation in all capitalist democracies was away from the *poor law conceptions* of the welfare state toward income security programs that incorporate the stable working class and middle-income earners. The consequences were both political and economic. Programs built on the twin pillars of universality and income security provided a political foundation for a broadly based coalition of lower- and middle income earners supportive of welfare state expansion and resistant to cuts. This process of *middle-class incorporation* did not go as far in Canada as in some countries, but its consequences were significant, the failure of the new Conservative government to change Old Age Security being a case in point.

The neoconservative attack on the welfare state has sought to reverse this trend and has proceeded on two fronts. The first is an attempt to return to the *social assistance tradition* of the prewar period. The attack has not been on the welfare state for the poor but rather on the incorporation of the stable working class and middle-income earners into the welfare state. The key word in the neoconservative lexicon is *rationalization*: transfer dollars should be spent "efficiently" for those most in need. The object is to return the field of income security to the marketplace. The state would prevent starvation but not provide the means for workers to maintain continuity in their standard of living when they leave the market as a result of illness, unemployment, and old age.

This does not mean the middle strata are being abandoned. Rather they are being weaned away from the postwar welfare state and incorporated into a new "welfare state" that subsidizes wealth accumulation. Workers with average and above average incomes are being encouraged to rely on private pensions (RPPs) and personal savings (RRSPs) for income security. The political and economic consequences of such programs are the obverse of the public programs. The public system redistributes income in favor of low-income earners and creates solidarity between middle- and low-income earners. Private plans and RRSPs redistribute income to high-income earners and build alliances around the ownership of wealth. The more the middle classes become dependent on these programs the more ready they will be to support the expansion of the welfare state for the rich and to abandon traditional alliances with the less fortunate.

REFERENCES

Banting, K. (1985). Institutional Conservatism: Federalism and Pension Reform. In J. Ismael, ed., *Canadian Social Welfare Policy: Federal and Provincial Dimensions.* Kingston and Montreal: McGill-Queen's University Press.

Bryden, K. (1974). *Old Age Pensions and Policy-Making in Canada.* Montreal: McGill-Queen's University Press.

Calvert, G. (1977). *Pensions and Survival: The Coming Crisis of Money and Retirement.* Toronto: Financial Post.

Canadian Council on Social Development. Analysis of the May 1985 Budget. *Social Development Overview Supplement, 3,* 1985.

Dulude, L. (1981). *Pension Reform with Women in Mind.* Ottawa: Canadian Advisory Council on the Status of Women.

Flora, P., and Alber, J. (1981). Modernization, Democratization and the Development of Welfare States in Western Europe. In P. Flora and J. Alber, eds., *The Development of Welfare States in Europe and America.* New Brunswick, N.J.: Transaction Books.

Hedstrom, P., and Ringen, S. (1985). *Age and Income in Contemporary Society: A Comparative Study.* Stockholm: Institute for Social Research.

House of Commons, Canada (1983). *Report of the Parliamentary Task Force on Pension Reform.* Ottawa: Ministry of Supply and Services.

Hudson, R. (1978). The 'Graying' of the Federal Budget and Its Consequences for Old Age Policy. *The Gerontologist, 18*(5), 428–40.

Leacy, F.H. (1983). *Historical Statistics of Canada.* Ottawa: Ministry of Supply and Services.

Murphy, B. (1982). *Corporate Capital and the Welfare State: Canadian Business and Public Pension Policy in Canada Since World War II.* Master's thesis, Carleton University, Ottawa.

National Council of Welfare (1984a). *Sixty-five and Older: A Report by the National Council of Welfare on the Incomes of the Aged.* Ottawa: Ministry of Supply and Services.

National Council of Welfare (1984b). *Better Pensions for Homemakers.* Ottawa: Ministry of Supply and Services.

National Council of Welfare (1984c). *A Pension Primer.* Ottawa: Ministry of Supply and Services.

National Council of Welfare (1985a). *Giving and Taking: The May 1985 Budget and the Poor.* Ottawa: Ministry of Supply and Services.

National Council of Welfare (1985b). *Poverty on the Increase*. Ottawa: Ministry of Supply and Services.

Perrin, G. (1969). Reflections on Fifty Years of Social Security. *International Labour Review*, 99(3), 249–90.

Prince, M. (1985). Startling Facts, Sobering Truths, and Sacred Trust: Pension Policy and the Tories. In A. Maslove, ed., *How Ottawa Spends: Sharing the Pie*. Toronto: Methuen.

Simeon, R. (1972). *Federal-Provincial Diplomacy: The Making of Recent Policy in Canada*. Toronto: University of Toronto Press.

Task Force on Retirement Income Policy (1980). *The Retirement Income System in Canada: Problems and Alternative Policies for Reform*. Ottawa: Ministry of Supply and Services.

Union Bank of Switzerland (1977). *Social Security in Ten Industrial Nations*. Zurich: Union Bank of Switzerland.

20

The Magic of 65

ISSUES AND EVIDENCE IN THE MANDATORY RETIREMENT DEBATE

Neil Guppy

Obstacles to individual justice and equality are anomalies increasingly under attack in Western democratic nations. Concern about such barriers is especially poignant in situations where individual merit is ignored, and inaccurate, stereotyped presumptions of ability inferred on the basis of a person's group membership (e.g., sex, race, weight). Indeed, one frequent measure of social progress is the pace at which ascribed stereotypes are superseded by the use of performance and ability indicators in judging individuals.

Age-based discrimination is the most recent social practice to be examined as an unjust violation of individual rights. Such discrimination occurs when decisions ignore the principle of justice according to merit, and rely instead on chronological age as a basis for judgement. Years of life is used as a proxy measure for individual merit. As Flanagan (1985: 23) notes, the "Orwellian" language of "mandatory" or "compulsory" in debates over fixed-age retirement implies this basic contravention of individual freedom.

Opposition to this call for individual justice stresses the equally fundamental principle of group rights. In this line of argument individual justice is contrasted with collective rights, the freedom of individuals counterposed with the rights of groups. Advocates of collective rights assert the importance of fair shares or fair opportunities for the members of diverse groups. This logic lies at the heart of debates over affirmative action (e.g., Abella, 1984).

Historically, age has not been a major basis for group formation, there being little previous age-based conflict (see Davis and van den Oever, 1981). In fact, it is only in the last one hundred or so years that people have seen finely graded age categories as socially meaningful. Now, however, age-graded practices and intergenerational justice are debated, particularly around the costs versus benefits of mandatory retirement.

Reprinted with permission of *Canadian Journal on Aging*, Vol. 8: 2 (1989), 173–86.

Of immediate concern here is the issue of a fixed retirement age at which individuals, regardless of merit, are denied the right to paid employment. First, I review briefly the legal framework within which this debate is being conducted. The importance of the Charter, particularly as it influences human rights legislation, is stressed. Second, I present evidence pertinent to the debate. The evaluation of labour force trends in jurisdictions where there has been a mandated change in retirement provisions is crucial. Finally, I review the basic issues which have been debated. These include discussions of *bona fide* occupational requirements, opportunities for young people, and collective bargaining and labour relations.

THE CHARTER AND HUMAN RIGHTS

The Canadian Government recently signalled its intention to eliminate age-graded practices which prescribe fixed-age retirement (Crosbie, 1986) and as of June 1986 mandatory retirement has been abolished in the federal public service (Eddy, 1986). While more universal legislation has been planned (via changes to the Canadian Human Rights Act) it is still unclear as to when—if ever—these amendments will come into force, even though an all-party federal committee has unanimously recommended that mandatory retirement be abolished (Boyer, 1985: 20).

The Canadian Charter of Rights and Freedoms provides one legal framework within which age discrimination is debated. Section 15(1) of the Charter specifies that:

> *Every individual is equal before and under the law and has the right to the equal protection and equal benefit of the law without discrimination and, in particular, without discrimination based on race, national or ethnic origin, colour, religion, sex, age or mental or physical disability.*

This wording appears to provide for the elimination of mandatory retirement since it is a social practice relying on age discrimination.

The inclusion of age in Section 15(1) presents two interesting aspects. First, as opposed to race, sex, and other attributes listed in this Section, age is a universal characteristic—it is something all Canadians experience and does not constitute a basis for distinct group membership. If we enjoy a normal lifespan, we will all pass age 65. Since age is unique in this regard, it should not be surprising that heated argument has been generated. There is also historical precedent here since age was not included in the 1960 Canadian Bill of Rights whereas most of the other items in Section 15(1) were. This is another reason the debate over age is now so intense (witness the recent spate of court cases).

A second distinctive feature is that age is not defined. The Charter is one of the first legislated packages in this country not to provide some limitation on age protections. Traditionally, anti-discrimination provisions have introduced either a minimum age, "the age of majority", and/or a maximum age beyond which the provision did not apply. For example, in many of the provincial human rights codes, employment protections against age discrimination do not extend past the age of 64. Since the Charter does not "define" age, its application is presumably boundless.

However, other sections of the Charter inhibit any clear interpretation of the range of applicability. First, Section 32 acknowledges that while the Charter prescribes how federal power is exercised, it is not intended to regulate private conduct. It applies specifically to federal legislation and to the federal public sector, and individually or collectively endorsed retirement provisions in the private sector may not fall within the ambit of the Charter. Hence, judgements rendered by the courts in B.C. found that a hospital was undertaking government functions whereas a university was not. Consequently, in the latter case, Section 15(1) did not apply (see McClean, 1987).

But, provincial Human Rights Legislation must be in accord with the basic provisions of the Charter. Some provinces have human rights legislation prohibiting age discrimination, thereby being compatible with the Charter (Alberta, Manitoba, New Brunswick, and Quebec). Other provinces have provisions incorporating age discrimination and could be stricken down by the courts as being incompatible with Section 15(1).

On the other hand, section 1 of the Charter could be used to prevent such court action or more generally to protect fixed-age retirement. This Section "guarantees the rights and freedoms set out [herein] subject only to such *reasonable limits* prescribed by law as can be *demonstrably justified* in a free and democratic society" (emphasis added). Here the argument turns on whether or not an infringement of rights and freedoms is beneficial for the whole of society. Does fixed-age retirement constitute a reasonable limit, beneficial to the larger public even if detrimental to the aspirations of some individuals? Applying a fixed-age retirement policy to all might be an arbitrary but fair way to ease people out of the labour force—at age 65 we all face the same rule. This is one form in which the idea of distributive or intergenerational justice has been argued.

LaSelva (1987): 160–161) offers an alternative approach stressing justice between generations. His argument turns not on the "reasonable limits" clause, but on the distinction between group rights and individual rights. All Canadians would not be treated equally, LaSelva argues, if the courts ignored the issue of justice between generations and focused only on the rights of older workers. If older workers were permitted to keep their jobs indefinitely (so long as they remained competent), then young individuals would be denied the opportunity to compete for those positions. Young people would not have *"equal benefit of the law"*, a key component of Section 15(1).

The Charter does not—as the above reveals—offer a clear formula to follow in deciding the future of mandatory retirement. Until such time as the federal government enacts new legislation eliminating fixed-age retirement, and specifying the scope of application, the courts will be busy with new cases and old appeals. The range of arguments may be limited, but the combinations are so varied that no clear precedents or directions are apparent (reviews of recent legal cases appear in Atcheson and Sullivan, 1985; McClean, 1987; and Richmond, 1987).*

■■■

JUSTIFYING MANDATORY RETIREMENT

The government has signalled its intention to introduce legislation curtailing the use of age 65 as a trigger for mandatory retirement. Given this, I pay particular attention to arguments which support the existing system, and assess the robustness of this position. If individuals wish to continue working after age 65, are there reasonable objections to legitimately discourage such a practice? The following, reviewed in turn, are the common objections found in the social science literature and debated in recent court cases.

i)   organizations need fresh recruits with new ideas

ii) job market crowding

iii) increases in acrimonious grievances

iv) public safety, performance, and older workers

v)   collective agreements and negotiated retirement provisions

i) Fresh Recruits
All organizations need some method of rejuvenation facilitated by a process allowing for the smooth turnover of personnel. This is especially true, it is often argued, for organizations or occupations intimately connected to contemporary science and for businesses operating in highly competitive markets. In a modern world where the pace and diffusion of technological change is accelerating, all organizations must keep abreast of new techniques. Flanagan (1984 : 26–27) summarizes this argument in the context of universities:

> *older researchers will undoubtedly read about the latest advances, but they are unlikely to adopt them as enthusiastically as the new generation learning them in graduate school. Fixed retirement seems to be a reasonable way of ensuring the necessary circulation of personnel.*

---

* Editor's note: On December 7, 1990, the Supreme Court of Canada ruled in favour of mandatory retirement for public service employees. The court found that mandatory retirement constituted age discrimination. But it was a "reasonable limitation" and a "minor" infringement that would lead to greater public good.

To remain vibrant and efficient, organizations need the enthusiasm and zeal that only comes with a sufficient influx of young people.

Objections, however, can be raised against this line of argument. First, eliminating fixed-age retirement does not mean an end to the circulation of personnel. Older workers will still retire, and as noted above, many will do so before age 65, allowing circulation to continue. Second, the argument presumes a fixed supply of jobs, so that new entrants can only be accommodated as older workers retire. This presumed constancy may occur in some areas, but historically the absolute number of jobs in the Canadian economy has expanded, with 1982 being the sole recent exception (Duchesne, 1987:32). Third, there is no evidence to justify singling out people over the age of 65 as the group who will not remain up-to-date. Given the emphasis on upgrading and review courses offered in many fields, there is ample opportunity to remain informed. Learning new ideas or techniques is an ongoing part of many jobs. Finally, nothing prohibits management from instituting positive incentives for employees to retire early, and this practice has of course been followed by numerous firms (e.g., Ontario Hydro).

ii) Job Market Crowding

If older workers choose to remain in their work roles for extended periods beyond age 65, this will clog the upper echelons of organizations, restricting both job and promotion opportunities for young workers. Whereas the "fresh recruits" point is often articulated from an organizational perspective, the "crowding" argument is usually made from the viewpoint of young job aspirants. This latter emphasis captures more fully the argument for intergenerational justice, seeking to insure that there are opportunities for all age groups.

LaSelva (1987) argues that while individual justice is important, earlier and later generations exist together, and one generation's happiness may thus encroach on the happiness of another. Should people be entitled to keep things for themselves if it limits the opportunities of others? As he argues, the principle of equal opportunity, "when applied to generations,...insists that one generation must not be arbitrarily excluded from opportunities that another generation has." This is so, he continues, "because no one [should be] denied valuable opportunities on the basis of irrelevant considerations" (*Ibid.:* 156-7). In this case age is the irrelevant consideration and those born of a certain generation may be denied jobs as the result of "the merely contingent fact of being born when they were" (*Ibid.:* 156).

The job market crowding thesis has a particularly current appeal because of the high rates of unemployment among young people (in 1987 the overall Canadian unemployment rate was 8.9%, while for workers aged 15–24 the rate was 13.7%). The *general* argument has been addressed by economists, and Gunderson and Pesando (1980: 358) have concluded that "banning mandatory retirement *may* decrease opportunities for younger workers...[or] it may also *increase* job opportunities for younger workers" [emphasis in original]. In short, no consensus has emerged.

The crowding argument also faces some quite specific objections. First, while there may not be enough jobs for everyone, it is the case that there are positions for which young people do compete. So, contrary to LaSelva's (1987) detailed challenge, opportunities for young people exist, although perhaps not always in sufficient numbers. Second, given the structure of labour markets it is not the case that a one-to-one correspondence exists between the jobs older workers hold and the opportunities sought by the young (e.g., Ashton and Maguire, 1983).

The strength of LaSelva's position vis à vis those who stress only individual justice is his recognition of cohorts and comparative justice. Cohorts do exist together, and different cohorts may have different interests. However, beyond attributes of age and cohort is the factor of history. There is no guarantee of stable cohort interests across periods. If the customary retirement age of 65 should not be retained because youth unemployment is high, should the retirement age change as a function of future shifts in the ratio of applicants to jobs? It should also be recalled that the current generation of older workers did not step into an expansive job market—they first had to fight in a world war. It would seem historical contingencies should not dictate long term social policies, especially when those contingencies fluctuate markedly.

Finally, in different quarters there is a growing concern that there are too few working-age people in Canada (e.g., Foot and Li, 1986; Seward, 1986). In sharp contrast to the crowding argument, they suggest we need a larger workforce.

iii) Acrimony and Grievances

With fixed-age retirement policies everyone is spared the acrimony and cost of disputes concerning the appropriate timing of individual retirements. I will deal here only with the social costs of "messy" grievance contests, leaving the issue of monetary costs to a discussion of performance evaluation (point "iv" below).

The removal of mandatory policies governing retirement would require, in instances where a person does not choose early retirement, some new method of determining when an individual should retire. Our personal performance and productivity does decline at *some point* in our lives (but see McDaniel, 1986: 81–82), and with mandatory retirement age operates as a proxy for performance evaluation. As Friedman (1984: 99) argues the point, "it is no shame to leave a job because you are 70 and forced to go, like everyone else. But it is humiliating to be fired as a doddering fool." An automatic, one-age-fits-all policy removes the possibility of messy disputes over competence and allows older workers a graceful exit, or so the argument often goes.

This objection to abolishing a fixed retirement age has also been linked to the idea of testing. Currently, benevolent employers "carry" older workers out of loyalty and in order to avoid acrimony. If there were no arbitrary limit on when these workers were to retire, then employers might dismiss them earlier if indeed their performance had noticeably deteriorated.

Several objections undercut the full force of this line of argument. First, there is no evidence to suggest this is anything more than a theoretical point. The experiences noted above for Manitoba and the U.S. do not provide the numerous examples of acrimonious disputes which some proponents of mandatory retirement imply would be the consequence of its elimination. For example, Cabot (1987) notes that in the U.S., where 16 states have prohibited retirement limits in the private sector, there is no evidence of an increase in age discrimination law-suits as one might expect if grievances and acrimony were to increase after the abolition of mandatory retirement (see also Ianni, 1988).

Second, many competent individuals who wish to continue working are denied the opportunity to do so by fixed-age retirement policies. The psychological costs to people forced out by mandatory procedures (e.g., Foner, 1986) *may* be greater than the social acrimony and friction which theoretically could result from eliminating fixed-age retirement.

Third, because competent people are forced out, the system or organization loses skilled, experienced workers. Fourth, the argument assumes older workers are poor judges of their own ability, prone to overestimate their skills. It is difficult to know how common this overestimation is. However, Flanagan (1984: 31) claims "the literature suggests that, given the prospect of financial security, employees will make realistic decisions about retirement if they are given realistic appraisals of their performance." Finally, while chronological age and performance capacity are positively correlated, the correlation is far from perfect.

A supplementary point must be addressed here. It is not just employers who might be concerned with easing workers out of the workforce. For example, insurance companies also have a vested interest in the age at which a person retires. Workers receiving long term disability insurance currently have their payments adjusted once they reach retirement age. If a fixed retirement age were eliminated, one alternative might be to continue such benefits until death, but if this were the option of choice, then disability premiums would rise substantially. This and other obstacles of a policy nature might be overcome with ingenuity and effort—although the solutions could not invoke age triggers.

iv) Public Safety

An important combination of arguments favouring the retention of mandatory retirement cohere around the issue of individual performance and ability. As people age, so the argument proceeds, their capacities decline. Especially in areas where public safety is at risk, this could have serious consequences for many people. Flanagan (1984: 25–26) claims "when hundreds of lives may be at stake, we want to ensure that drivers and pilots are in top mental and physical condition." Mandatory retirement safeguards the public by insuring that older workers are not put in positions where their decisions or actions could harm others. In short, there may be bona fide occupational qualifications or requirements necessitating mandatory retirement policies.

Certainly some jobs, such as flying passenger airplanes, are more likely than others to put lives at risk. However, public safety is an issue for pilots of *all* ages, and it seems incongruous to worry about it when a pilot passes middle age. And, of course, we do not, since a pilot's performance is routinely monitored throughout his or her career. In those occupations where public safety is at risk and where high standards of practice constitute a *bona fide* occupational requirement, we possess performance appraisal systems.

To the extent that performance appraisal systems are effective, then they should function to insure public safety. If such systems are ineffective, then the evaluation mechanism requires overhauling, rather than creating arbitrary fixed-age retirement policies.

An additional argument sometimes used to support mandatory retirement in this specific context claims that testing is expensive. Two points must be stressed here. First, in jobs where competence is important for public safety (e.g., airline pilots, physicians), performance appraisal is currently in place and no additional costs would accrue (assuming young, inexperienced workers would be tested as frequently as older workers). Second, evidence from other jurisdictions suggests the concern is misplaced. Commenting on the U.S. experience, the Canadian Parliamentary Committee on Equality Rights noted "the additional costs of performance evaluation systems, to replace mandatory retirement policies, had not proved significant" (Boyer, 1985: 20).

v) Collective Agreements

Only in a small minority of cases is retirement at a specific age actually enshrined in law. Typically, public retirement provisions have arisen as governments have expanded the social welfare system to provide economic security to older people (from 1927 in Canada—see Myles, 1984). An alternative route, and one that has become more widespread only after the Second World War, has been via the introduction of retirement provisions in collective agreements. Since the majority of Canadian workers are covered by collective agreements which were mutually agreed upon by labour and management, retirement is not coerced. Retirement provisions are a component part of contracts to which workers voluntarily agree. Abolishing mandatory retirement would thus confound collective agreements.

There has been little counter argument on this point, although some objections are possible. While retirement provisions are an important component of collective agreements, such agreements always incorporate a variety of factors. It is unlikely that workers see retirement age as a major component of such packages. There have been many more strikes over wages than over retirement dates. It is retirement benefits that have traditionally been the more contentious issue. This suggests that relatively less attention has been paid to the actual age at which people retire (see Krashinsky, 1988).

Two final points can be made about the voluntary nature of collective agreements. For many years unions "voluntarily" negotiated contracts wherein women were paid less than men, but that did not mean such contracts were necessarily just. Furthermore, voluntary acceptance of the status quo does not preclude the possibility that better, more just arrangements could be concluded. For example, Gunderson and Pesando (1988) have recently argued that we should institute policies which *allow* negotiated mandatory retirement provisions, as opposed to the current legislative thrust of a blanket elimination of forced retirement.

CONCLUDING REMARKS

Five major objections to the elimination of fixed-age retirement provisions have been considered—the need for "fresh recruits", the potential of "job market crowding", the increase in "acrimonious grievances", the threat to "public safety", and the abrogation of "collective agreements". After reviewing relevant literature and considering the evidence which is available, it is clear that this is a social issue of complexity and weight. The evidence is not clearcut and there are good arguments on both sides.

Two aspects of the debate deserve special emphasis. First, the court decisions rendered to date do not provide decisive guidance as to how the judiciary views mandatory retirement (McClean, 1987). With no clear legislation in place to deal with the complexities discussed above, the courts cannot be expected to produce definitive judgements and so the variable interpretations of competing arguments will undoubtedly continue (Eddy, 1986).

Second, mandatory retirement is not an isolated social issue, although the debate is sometimes conducted as though it were. Without adequate pension revisions a substantial portion of elderly Canadians will continue living in poverty. Especially among women, where the increasingly early retirement of men finds no parallel, and where inadequate pension provisions persist, the idea of retirement age must be seen in the context of future economic prospects. Debate over fixed-age retirement must address other aspects of employment policies including benefits for the growing part-time labour force, and reforms of both public and private pension packages (e.g., portability, vesting, survivor benefits—see Myles, 1984). The courts, by the nature of our legal system, cannot directly address this larger set of employment policies, which is why political leadership, with a broad focus, is crucial to the resolution of this debate.

All the current signals suggest the three political parties agree that in a society committed to the principle of equality of opportunity, the invidious use of chronological age as a measure of ability and competence is anachronistic. By providing individual workers with the right to continue their working lives—as long as they are free from debilitating impairment, can demonstrate the necessary ability, and have sufficient motivation—then there is no reason to deny people the basic right to work. Moreover, the evidence suggests that only a minority of workers will continue in the labour force beyond the age of 65.

Individual as opposed to intergenerational justice underlies the push to abolish a single retirement age. Using age as a magical trigger to force people from the labour force runs counter to the basic thrust of individual rights. What is not clear, however, is how social benefits are to be weighed. Individual freedoms (e.g., freedom of speech) frequently collide with group rights (e.g., freedom from hate mongering). This tension between the freedoms of the individual and the group (or society) stretches beyond retirement debates and continues as one of the profound contradictions embedded within our social system. The mandatory retirement debate requires grappling with this basic tension and our legal system is not an adequate forum in which to satisfactorily resolve this dilemma.

REFERENCES

Abella, Rosalie. 1984. *Equality in Employment: A Royal Commission Report.* Ottawa: Supply and Services.

Ashton, David and M.J. Maguire. 1983. "Competition between Young People and Adults: A Research Note on the Structure of the Youth Labour Market". *International Review of Applied Psychology* 32, 263–269.

Atcheson, E. and L. Sullivan. 1985. "Passage to Retirement: Age Discrimination and the Charter" in A. Bayefsky and M. Eberts (eds) *Equality Rights and the Canadian Charter of Rights and Freedoms.* Toronto: Carswell, 231–292.

Boyer, J. Patrick. 1985. *Equality for All.* Report of the Parliamentary Committee on Equal Rights. Ottawa, October, 1985.

Cabot, S.J. 1987. "Living with the New Amendments to the Age Discrimination in Employment Act". *Personnel Administrator* 32(1), 53–54.

Crosbie, John. 1986. *Toward Equality.* Ottawa: Department of Justice.

Davis, K. and P. van den Oever. 1981. "Age Relations and Public Policy in Advanced Industrial Societies". *Population and Development Review* 7(1), 1–18.

Duchesne, Doreen. 1987. "Annual Review of Labour Force Trends". *Canadian Social Trends,* Summer, 26–32.

Eddy, Paulette. 1986. "Mandatory Retirement Masks Issue". *The Public Sector* 10(45), 1, 4.

Flanagan, Thomas. 1984. "The Future of Retirement in Canadian Universities". *The Canadian Journal of Higher Education* 14(3), 10–34.

Flanagan, Thomas. 1985. "Age Discrimination in Canada". Occasional Paper, Research Unit for Socio-legal Studies, Faculty of Social Science, University of Calgary.

Foner, Anne. 1986. *Aging and Old Age.* Englewood Cliffs: Prentice-Hall.

Foot, David and J.C. Li. 1986. "Youth Unemployment in Canada: A Misplaced Priority?" *Canadian Public Policy* 12(3), 499–506.

Friedman, L.M. 1984. *Your Time Will Come: The Law of Age Discrimination and Mandatory Retirement.* New York: Russell Sage Foundation.

Gunderson, M. and J. Pesando. 1980. "Eliminating Mandatory Retirement: Economics and Human Rights". *Canadian Public Policy* 6(2), 352–360.

Gunderson, M. and J. Pesando. 1988. "The Case for Allowing Mandatory Retirement". *Canadian Public Policy* 14(1), 32–39.

Ianni, Ron. 1988. *Report of the Ontario Task Force on Mandatory Retirement: Fairness and Flexibility in Retiring from Work.* Toronto: Ontario Government.

Krashinsky, M. 1988. "The Case for Eliminating Mandatory Retirement: Why Economics and Human Rights Need Not Conflict". *Canadian Public Policy* 14(1), 40–50.

LaSelva, Samuel. 1987. "Mandatory Retirement: Intergenerational Justice and the Canadian Charter of Rights and Freedoms". *Canadian Journal of Political Science* 20(1) 151–162.

McClean, A.J. 1987. "Mandatory Retirement". *The Canadian Journal of Higher Education* 17(1), 1–6.

McDaniel, Susan. 1986. *Canada's Aging Population.* Toronto: Butterworths.

Myles, John. 1984. *Old Age in the Welfare State: The Political Economy of Public Pensions.* Toronto: Little, Brown, and Company.

Richmond, L.A. 1987. "The Impact of the Canadian Charter of Rights and Freedoms on Pension and Welfare Funds". *Employee Benefits Journal* 12(1), 24–31.

Seward, Shirley. 1986. "More and Younger?" *Policy Options* 7(1), 16–19.

The Youth Freeze and the Retirement Bulge

OLDER WORKERS AND THE IMPENDING LABOUR SHORTAGE

Lynn McDonald and Mervin Y.T. Chen

■ ■ ■

RETIREMENT

Retirement Patterns

Canadian workers want to retire before the expected norm of age 65.[1] Virtually all Canadian studies since the early 1970s have found that Canadians desire early retirement; such a desire remains unabated today.[2] Most recently, the 1989 General Social Survey found that, among employed Canadians, over two-fifths intend to retire before age 65, while about one-third do not know when they will retire. Only 14 percent state they will retire at age 65, seven percent do not plan to retire at all, and one percent want to retire after age 65. When age is considered, almost one-half of the baby-boomers indicated a desire to retire before age 65, a rather startling finding since they will constitute the pool from which potential older workers will be drawn.[3]

The preferences of Canadians have been supported by their actions when the precipitous decline in labour force participation rates are considered. Among the men, participation rates for those aged 55 to 64 years were stable until about 1965 when, until 1980, the rate began to decline annually. From 1980 onward, the rate has fluctuated, while the overall trend has been downward. The most recent available data indicates that as of 1991, 62.6 percent of the men in this age group remain in the labour force.[4] The trend for men over age 65 is even more dramatic; nearly half of the men in this age

Reproduced with permission from *Journal of Canadian Studies*, Vol. 28, No. 1 (Spring 1993).

group were in the labour force in 1946, compared to just over 11 percent 40 years later.

The picture of Canadian women is somewhat different than the pattern for men. As is the case for all Canadian women, the labour force participation rates of women aged 55 to 64 began steadily growing in the 1950s. By 1969, about 30 percent of the women were either working or unemployed, and the rate has increased only marginally since then to 35.7 percent in 1991. Since it is well-documented that the labour force participation rates of all women have increased from the 1970s to the 1980s and that women retire earlier than men, it is reasonable to observe that the apparent stability for women is the result of two offsetting forces: an increasing propensity for women to engage in paid employment and an increasing tendency to retire early. The same might be said of the trend for women aged 65 and over. The percentage of women in this age category in the labour force has never exceeded 6.3 percent in the post-World War II period.

Withdrawal from the labour force is not always synonymous with being retired; however, when the retired population is examined directly, the trend to early retirement is confirmed. Analyzing data from the 1989 General Social Survey, Graham Lowe found that 63 percent of the retirees in Canada retired before reaching age 65, only 17 percent retired at age 65, and another 16 percent retired after age 65.[5]

Perhaps even more telling is the fact that the majority of Canadians are very satisfied with their retirement. Life after retirement may not be smooth sailing for everyone, but few people suffer adverse consequences as a result of the act of retiring.[6]

Therefore, just as a labour force shortage of entry-level workers looms on the horizon, substantial numbers of Canadians are exiting the labour force for ever-earlier retirement. And, if the preferences of the baby-boomers are any indication, the trend will be carried into the next century. In the following sections we consider exactly who is retiring, when they are retiring, and for what reasons. Our goal will be to assess what can be done, if anything, to stem the tide of workers into retirement.

Early Retirement

The enormous number of studies of early retirement in North America are consistent in identifying self-perceived health and unearned income from pensions and assets as the two most important predictors of early retirement. People in poor health tend to retire early as do those who can afford to retire early. Earlier studies of retirement placed more emphasis on the role of health in early retirement while studies in the 1980s found more support for the financial factors, the basic argument being that health is an *ex post facto* rationalization in the face of a strong work ethic.[7]

The Canadian evidence is far from conclusive, but most studies do indicate that health and potential retirement income influence the early retirement decision.[8] The only problem is that researchers are not clear which factor is more important for whom and in what context. There is some indication that health and unearned income seem to be more salient factors for men than for women and that public sector workers are more influenced by work-related stress and financial adequacy compared to poor health for men in the private sector.[9] Forty-two percent of primary blue-collar workers retire for health reasons compared to 11 percent of managerial, professional or technical workers.[10]

Although the precise role of health in influencing retirement behaviour is still debated, the health factor is important from another perspective. The unhealthy appear to self-select themselves into early retirement, leaving the more hardy in the labour force. In fact, Meredith Minkler inadvertently makes a case for this position. When the retired are compared on the health variable to those who continue to work, it is not unexpected that the retired report poorer health, since that is why so many retired in the first place.[11] In some ways, this eliminates concerns about the health of most older workers and helps to explain why absences from work are only slightly higher for older workers than for younger workers.[12] It also calls into question the need for aggressive monitoring and evaluation of older workers by employers which some deem will be necessary with the removal of mandatory retirement.[13]

If early retirement is related to having an adequate income, this indicates that additional remuneration in the work place may not be a sufficiently strong incentive to entice all early retirees to maintain their attachment to the labour force. A recent Gallup survey for the American Association of Retired Persons reveals that the three most frequently cited reasons for working by persons over age 63 (past the early retirement norm of age 62) were that they enjoyed the job and the work, that work made them feel useful, and that work enabled them to contribute to society and help others.[14] Future jobs will have to be viewed by potential early retirees as a source of satisfaction that can compete with the perceived value of leisure pursuits. In some ways this bodes well for Canadians, if the American results pertain to the Canadian situation. Reported job satisfaction is as high or higher than national averages in the non-market and dynamic subsectors of the service sector for both standard and nonstandard work.[15]

These general findings mask, however, the heterogeneity found among retirees. An American study suggests that, at least among managerial, professional and technical workers, financial incentives might induce older workers, even those past age 65, to postpone retirement.[16] Nearly half of the respondents indicated that they would postpone retirement if the United States Social Security system were changed to abolish the earnings penalty on recipients aged 65 to 72 or to accord added benefits for years worked past age 65.

The retirement patterns of women in Canada have always been different from those of men. They have also been under-researched. The only clear factor related to women's early retirement is being married.[17] Marriage may provide opportunities for women to stop working because of the increased economic resources that result from the marital union. As the economic situation of women in the work place improves, it has been found that a married woman's decision to retire is influenced by her own wage level, social security entitlement, pension benefits and age, as well as by her spouse's wage level and his retirement status.[18] It might, therefore, be expected that, as women have more continuous employment histories and are thus more likely to qualify for early pension benefits, they will retire even earlier than they do at present. Moreover, if men continue to retire earlier, women who are influenced by their husband's retirement status may also retire early.

Another factor influencing women's early retirement is eldercare for a dependent elder. Eldercare responsibilities generally appear when workers are in their forties and fifties, the time when early retirement also becomes possible. The most recent data indicate that nine percent of care-givers for the frail elderly were lost to the labour force in 1990.[19]

The preponderance of women in the service sector in both high-skilled (health, education and welfare) and low-skilled jobs (retail trade and other consumer services) presents a difficult situation, if retention is the issue. It is doubtful that women will want to fill the labour market gap created by the shrinking youth cohort because these low-tiered service jobs have low status and low pay. By contrast, we know that only 30 percent of the education, health, and welfare industries offer nonstandard work which is preferred by women and which may become a more pressing need as family responsibilities force women into early retirement. Part-time work, part-year work, flextime, and perhaps job sharing will have to become more widespread in the high-skilled jobs if this source of labour is to be retained.

Individual preferences for early retirement have been strongly reinforced by structural factors, most notably the availability of public and private pensions. Studies of how the social security system influences retirement behaviour have generated a diverse array of findings in the United States. Most find that the timing of retirement appears to be affected by the eligibility requirements of the Social Security Act; in particular, sharp jumps take place at ages 62 and 65.[20] In Canada, several studies have shown that public pension benefits do not influence the early retirement decision.[21]

Most recently, changes to the Canada and Quebec Pension Plans have demonstrated the powerful influence of pensions on early retirement. Implemented in 1966, with the addition of flexible retirement in 1984 (QPP) and 1987 (CPP), the plan permitted access to substantial benefits as early as age 60.[22] The response of Canadians was immediate and dramatic. In 1984, three out of every four persons receiving QPP retirement pensions were, for the first time, between the ages of 60 and 64. Two-thirds of new CPP beneficiaries in 1987 were aged 60 to 64.[23]

At the policy level, the potency of an adequate pension cannot be overlooked. If reducing early retirement is the goal, then public pension plans should be made less attractive, should be delayed, or should have some type of built-in disincentive. This, of course, is easier said than done. For example, simulations in the United States show that reductions in monthly benefits to the tune of 13 percent postpone retirement only by about a month.[24] In restructuring incentives, care has to be taken not to create undue hardship for those who are forced to retire early.[25] For example, blue-collar workers retire early primarily for health reasons that are frequently related to the physically demanding nature of such work.

There is also some evidence that private pension plans contribute to early retirement. For example, in 1989 over one-half of workers with employer-sponsored pension plans wanted to retire early, compared to one-third of those without such plans.[26] Employer-sponsored pension plans (RRPs) have grown and improved over the 1970s. Most notably, the availability of early retirement with and without reduction in benefits has increased. The proportion of RRP members, with an option to retire early on a reduced pension, grew from 87 percent in 1970 to 98 percent in 1989, while 77 percent of the members in 1989 could choose early retirement without employer approval, compared to 35 percent in 1970. In 1970 only 19 percent of members could retire early without reduced benefits, compared to almost 55 percent in 1989.[27] Pension formulas could be redesigned to create strong work incentives; in practice, however, this would be difficult, although not impossible.[28]

The other structural factor germane to the retention of the older worker is the occupational structure. There are occupation-specific retirement patterns, although much more research is required in this area. Looking beyond the blue-collar/white-collar distinction, men formerly employed in clerical, sales or service jobs are less likely than managerial/professional workers to retire early. The reverse holds true for women, as a much higher proportion of females in clerical, sales and service jobs retire before age 65.[29] The main reason for the findings for the men is that managers/professionals are more likely to be employed in large bureaucratic firms or government agencies with orderly career lines and mandatory retirement policies. Self-employment, known to be associated with late retirement, is also more pronounced among men in the clerical, sales, and service occupations.[30] Women, who are less likely to be self-employed in these occupations, probably leave as soon as it is financially feasible, given the substandard conditions of work. In support of this observation, one study found that women work into late retirement mainly because of financial hardship.[31]

Early retirement is a complicated issue, but there is room to manoeuvre if older workers are to be retained in the labour force. Older workers, both male and female, may be attracted by interesting and satisfying work in the high and medium-skilled non-market and dynamic subsectors. Public and private pension plans appear to increase early retirement, but reducing the amount of the pension may not be the issue as much as changing the timing of the benefit for select groups. A disincentive, such as raising the retirement age in the United States, deserves serious consideration. This change should be directed at the managerial/professional and technical occupations, where interest in continued work is expressed and losses are the most damaging to the economy. Delaying the retirement age for these workers and offering financial incentives for continued work may be effective. Women face different circumstances in both work and retirement as a result of family responsibilities. The increased availability of nonstandard work in non-market and dynamic services would be a logical impetus for these women to postpone early retirement. All the evidence suggests that women are not going to remain in or be attracted to the lower-tiered services. Far-reaching changes would have to be made to make these jobs more intrinsically and extrinsically worthwhile.

On-Time Retirement

What effect would the elimination of mandatory retirement have on the labour force participation rate of Canadians? There would be little or no effect. The extent of mandatory retirement in Canada is small. Earlier studies show that mandatory retirement, as a reason for retirement, is given by less than one percent of those under age 65, 17 percent of those age 65, and about 27 percent of those over age 65.[32] The abolishment of mandatory retirement in Manitoba and Quebec has shown that there have been no significant effects on labour force participation rates since the inception of the legislation.[33] The General Social Survey (1989) indicates that just over one-quarter of all individuals retired because of mandatory retirement.[34]

If compulsory retirement is not the major reason for "on-time retirement," what then are the other reasons? The answer is mainly speculative. However, mandatory retirement is, more often than not, linked to membership in a pension plan, so retirement at age 65 could reflect financial considerations. In one Canadian survey it has been reported that those who retired for compulsory reasons were more likely to be in receipt of a job-related pension.[35] What is important is that these jobs are usually the higher-status jobs. For example, S. Ciffin and J.K. Martin found that the main reason for retirement among managerial, professional and technical workers was compulsory retirement policies, with nearly 49 percent reporting it as a reason for retirement. Furthermore, support for mandatory retirement is inversely related to education and income.[36] This indicates that, while mandatory retirement may not have a large effect in the aggregate, its elimination may have an effect on the very occupations where workers are required. Mandatory retirement is within the purview of employers to change since it is part of the employee-employer contract.

In actual practice, mandatory retirement may not have a serious effect on participation rates in the aggregate, but the assumptions behind it do have an indirect effect because they fuel existing negative attitudes towards older workers.[37] The mandatory retirement debate has heated up in the wake of the recent Supreme Court decisions which chose to support the concept of mandatory retirement. At the heart of this debate is the unavoidable assumption that older workers are unproductive as a result of the aging process, despite all the available evidence to the contrary.[38] There is a large body of research showing that on most measures older workers are just as productive as their younger counterparts. Studies in various work environments have shown that the connection between age and individual productivity is very weak and can be changed with the environment.[39] Age alone is not a sufficient criterion to decide on individual competency since there is such a wide variation in the rate at which people age. Although the abandonment of mandatory retirement is probably academic, the very attitudes underpinning the concept can serve as barriers to the employment of older workers and would need to be reversed. Eliminating mandatory retirement may help to soften these views.

Late Retirement

The reasons for late retirement are almost the exact opposite of the reasons for early retirement. Most studies confirm that there is little difference between the working retired (i.e. those who retire and return to work) and those who simply continue to work past age 65. Both groups tend to be well-educated with upper-occupational status; they are married men and single women who enjoy reasonably good health and who are attached to their work. A large proportion of late retirees are self-employed probably because they are not subject to mandatory retirement provisions. There is also a greater propensity for recent immigrants from Third World countries to remain in the labour force after age 65.[40]

Though it seems to go against the evidence that it is upper-occupational status individuals who work beyond age 65, a number of studies have indicated that financial reasons often motivate the working retired and those who retire late.[41] Rachel Boaz showed that work during retirement by both men and women was a response to low or moderate levels of unearned income at the beginning of retirement. For men, it was also a response to a decrease in the real value of income during retirement. A comparable Canadian study supports these results. Canadian men and women who worked past age 65 did so out of financial need, but the need was greater among the women than among the men.[42] The reason was basically similar for immigrants who arrived in Canada after 1977. As newcomers they did not qualify for full pension benefits under Old Age Security and their country of origin did not have reciprocal pension agreements with Canada.

It is important to underscore the findings that those people who continue to work past age 65 have far more successful work histories that those who do not, making them an exceptional and valuable source of labour.[43] Reasonable wages and salaries should have a salutary effect on attracting and maintaining this group of skilled, older workers in the labour force.

The "claw-back" instituted by the federal government in 1989 may inadvertently sustain the trend to late retirement. The claw-back means that persons over 65 years of age, earning more than $50,000 a year, will have to pay back part or some portion of their Old Age Security pension. While this may appear just, the claw-back ceilings are not fully indexed to inflation. Therefore, the number of older persons subject to the claw-back will increase each year.[44] Indeed, it is estimated that persons who retire in 2019 with as little as $20,000 in annual income will have Old Age Security benefits reduced by the claw-back.[45]

This broad review of the retirement patterns of older Canadians and their reasons for retiring indicate that there are certain workers who might be potentially recruited back into the labour force or convinced to remain past normal retirement ages. All the data point to the need to retain those retirees from the managerial/professional and technical occupations who have the skills to offer, an attachment to their work, and the motivation to continue working voluntarily. Further, the conditions of work in these occupations are amenable to nonstandard work forms and would meet the need for job satisfaction and interest. Because these workers will be in high demand, the barriers to their employment such as mandatory retirement policies, the opportunity costs of skill up-grading, and the incentives to retire early found in most pension plans may be reversed in these occupations once employers are confronted with labour shortages.

Those who retire late constitute a very important source of potential labour, especially in light of their successful work histories and upper occupational status. The challenge here will be to make the work available to them financially rewarding and to allow for employment on a part-time, part-year and seasonal basis. Policies that foster self-employment would be an additional incentive.

The retention of older women is only likely to occur in the non-market and dynamic service subsectors where women tend to be rewarded accordingly, where the work is interesting, and where job satisfaction is on a higher level. At the same time, if the trend towards early retirement can be reversed for some men, then there is a higher probability that women may curb their move into early retirement. In both instances, the family responsibilities of women will have to be recognized through special work programs if these women are to remain in the labour force. However, all the data indicate that women vacate the lower-echelon services as early as is financially feasible; thus, they are not likely to be the answer to the "youth freeze." The modifications that would have to be made to these low-skilled service jobs are just too encompassing to be practical or even financially possible, at least in the present economy.

From our perspective some workers should be retained; others, such as unneeded, unskilled and untrainable workers, many who are found in blue-collar occupations and low-level white-collar occupations, should be encouraged into early retirement. The question is how to design retirement policies that provide incentives for the latter to leave the labour force in financial comfort while at the same time providing incentives for the skilled to remain.

■■■

NOTES

1. There is considerable evidence that the determinants of early retirement, prior to age 65, on-time retirement at age 65, and late retirement after age 65, are different, as are the issues surrounding the determinants.

2. See P.L. McDonald and R.A. Wanner, *Retirement in Canada,* for an overview of these studies.

3. Graham S. Lowe, "Retirement Attitudes, Plans and Behaviour," *Perspectives on Work and Income* 3 (Autumn, 1991), 8–16.

4. C. Lindsay and M.S. Devereaux, "Canadians in the Pre-Retirement Years: A Profile of People Age 55–64," *Target Group Projects* (Ottawa: Ministry of Industry, Science and Technology, 1991).

5. Lowe, 14.

6. McDonald and Wanner, 81–95.

7. S. Ciffin and J. Martin, *Retirement in Canada: Summary Report* (Ottawa: Health and Welfare Canada, 1976); G.J. Bazzoli, "The Early Retirement Decision: New Empirical Evidence on the Influence of Health," *The Journal of Human Resources* 20, 2 (1985), 214–34; F.J. Sammartino, "The Effects of Health on Retirement," *Social Security Bulletin 50,* 2 (1987), 31–47; O.S. Mitchell, "Pensions and Older Workers," in M.E. Borus, ed., *The Older Worker* (Madison: Industrial Relations Research Assoc., 1988), 151–68.

8. S. Ciffin and J. Martin, *Retirement in Canada: When and Why People Retire* (Ottawa: Health and Welfare Canada, 1977); C. Kapsalis, "Pensions and the Work Decision," Paper presented at the annual meeting of the Canadian Economic Association, May, 1979; R. Baillargeon, "The Determinants of Early Retirement," *Canada's Mental Health* 303 (1982), 20–22.

9. P.L. McDonald and R.A. Wanner, "Socioeconomic Determinants of Early Retirement in Canada," *Canadian Journal on Aging* 3,3 (1984), 105–16; Baillargeon, 20–22.

10. S. Ciffin and J. Martin, *Retirement in Canada: Summary Report.*

11. M. Minkler, "Research on the Health Effects of Retirement: An Uncertain Legacy," *Journal of Health and Social Behaviour* 22 (1981), 117–30.

12. Earnest B. Akyeampong, "Older Workers in the Canadian Market," *The Labour Force* 43, 1 (Ottawa: Minister of Supply and Services, Nov. 1987), 87.

13. M. Gunderson and J. Pesando, "Eliminating Mandatory Retirement: Economics and Human Rights," *Canadian Public Policy* 6 (1980), 352–60.

14. United States Department of Labour, *Older Worker Task Force: Key Policy Issues for the Future* (Washington, D.C., June 1989).

15. Harvey Krahn, "Quality of Work in the Service Sector," *General Social Survey Analysis Series* (Ottawa: Statistics Canada, 1992), 132.

16. B. Rosen and T.H. Jerdee, *Older Employees: New Roles for Valid Resources* (Homewood, IL: Dow Jones-Irwin, 1985).

17. A.M. O'Rand and J.C. Henretta, "Delayed Career Entry, Industrial Pension Structure and Early Retirement in a Cohort of Unmarried Women," *American Sociological Review* 47 (1982), 365–73.

18. D. Galarneau, "Women Approaching Retirement," *Perspectives on Labour and Income* 3 (Autumn 1991), 28–39.

19. J.L. MacBride-King, *Work and Family: Employment Challenge of the '90s* (Compensation Research Centre: The Conference Board of Canada, 1990), ix.

20. Peter B. Doeringer, *Turbulence in the American Workplace* (New York: Oxford University Press, 1991).

21. R.A. Wanner and P.L. McDonald, "Retirement, Public Pension Policy and Industrial Development: A Time Series Analysis," Paper presented at the annual meeting of the Canadian Sociology and Anthropology Association, Hamilton, Ontario, 1987. M. Gunderson and W.C. Riddell, *Labour Market Economics: Theory, Evidence and Policy in Canada*, second edition (Toronto: McGraw-Hill Ryerson Ltd., 1988).

22. Health and Welfare Canada, *Monthly Statistics: Income Security Programs* (Jan-Dec., 1986), 8.

23. H. Frenken, "The Pension Carrot: Incentives to Early Retirement," *Perspectives on Labour and Income* 3 (Autumn 1991), 18–27.

24. G.S. Fields and O.S. Mitchell, "Economic Determinants of the Optimal Retirement Age: An Empirical Investigation," *Journal of Human Resources* 19 (Spring 1984), 245–62; R. Haveman, B. Wolfe and J. Warlick, "Labour Market Behaviour of Older Men: Estimates from a Trichotomous Choice Model," *Journal of Public Economics* 36 (1988), 153–75.

25. S. Bould, "Factors Influencing the Choice of Social Security Early Retirement Benefits," *Population Research and Policy Review* 5 (1986), 217–36.

26. Membership in employer-sponsored pension plans grew from about 19 percent of all Canadians 18 to 64 years of age in 1960 to 30 percent in 1980 and has remained stable since that time. Frenken, 22. Lowe, 15.

27. Frenken, 23.

28. J. Pesando and M. Gunderson, "Retirement Incentives Contained in Occupational Pension Plans and their Implication for the Mandatory Retirement Debate," *Canadian Journal of Economics* 21 (1988), 246–64.

29. Lowe, 13.

30. P.L. McDonald and R.A. Wanner, "Work Past Age 65 in Canada: A Socioeconomic Analysis," *Aging and Work* 5 (1982), 169–80.

31. *Ibid.*, 20; Lowe, 9.

32. Gunderson and Pesando, 354.

33. F. Reid, "Economic Aspects of Mandatory Retirement: The Canadian Experience," *Industrial Relations* 43 (1) 1988, 101–14; Québec, Rapport triennal sur le efferts de la loi sur abolition de la retraite obligatoire (Québec: Ministère de la Main-d'oeuvre et de la sécurité du revenu, 1989).

34. Lowe, 14.

35. Ciffin and Martin, 52.

36. *Ibid.*, 20; Lowe, 9.

37. The recent rulings of the Supreme Court on mandatory retirement provide ample evidence of ageist attitudes to older workers. For example, one judgment ruled hospital policy reasonable on the grounds that "...older doctors are less able to contribute to hospitals' sophisticated practice." *Discovery*, "A Question of Discrimination," (Jan./Feb., 1989), 39; C. Bird and T. Fisher, "Thirty Years Later: Attitudes Towards the Employment of Older Workers," *Journal of Applied Psychology* 71 (1986), 515–17.

38. See, for example, M. Doering, S.R. Rhodes and M. Schuster, *The Aging Worker* (Beverly Hills, CA: Sage, 1983); X. Gaullier, "The Management of Older Workers in a Flexible Career Cycle: The Case of France," *Ageing International* (Autumn/Winter 1986), 36–38; X. Gaullier, *La Deuxième Carrière: Ages, Emplois, Retraites* (Paris: Editions du Seuil, 1988).

39. N. Charness and E.A. Bosman, "Human Factors and Design for Older Adults," in J.E. Birren and K.W. Schaie, eds., *Handbook of Psychology of Aging*, second edition (San Diego: Academic Press Inc., 1990).

40. See P.L. McDonald and R.A. Wanner, *Retirement in Canada,* Chapter 4 for a review of the studies of late retirement.

41. R.F. Boaz, "Work as a Response to Low and Decreasing Real Income During Retirement," *Research on Aging* 9 (1987), 428–40; A. Fontana and J.H. Frey, "Post-Retirement Workers in the Labour Force," *Work and Occupation* 17 (1990), 355–61.

42. McDonald and Wanner, 179–80.

43. N. Morrow-Howell and J. Leon, "Life-Span Determinants of Work in Retirement Years," *Journal of Aging and Human Development* 27 (1988), 125–39.

44. National Council on Welfare, *Pension Reform* (Ottawa: National Council of Welfare, 1990).

45. M. Townson, "Pensions: Who's Responsible Anyway?" Keynote address presented at the annual meeting of the Canadian Association on Gerontology, Ottawa, Oct. 1989.

22

Women and Poverty Revisited

The National Council of Welfare

•••

UNATTACHED ELDERLY WOMEN

The most important difference between the sexes in old age is that the majority of the men live with their wives while most of the women live alone or with non-relatives. This may seem strange, since it takes a person of each sex to make a married couple, but it is less surprising when we remember that a typical woman marries a man who is older than she is and who has a shorter life expectancy.

Marital status is very important in determining whether or not older Canadians are poor. Married seniors, including three-quarters of the men, had a poverty rate of seven percent in 1987. By contrast, seniors living alone or with non-relatives, where most women are found, had much higher rates of poverty which increased sharply for women with advancing age.[1]

At 75 years and over, 50 percent of unattached elderly women lived in poverty. Their real poverty rate was probably much higher because the Survey of Consumer Finances on which these poverty figures are based excludes people who live in institutions.

Why are the unattached elderly so much poorer than elderly couples? Part of the answer is that federal income security programs are effective in protecting most senior couples from poverty, but fall short of that goal in the case of seniors who live alone.

In 1989, maximum benefits from the Old Age Security pension and the Guaranteed Income Supplement fell $1,867 short of the poverty line for a couple living in a large city. For unattached pensioners living in a large city, the gap amounted to $3,393.[2]

From *Women and Poverty Revisited*, Health Canada, 1990. Reproduced with permission of the Minister of Supply and Services Canada, 1994.

The other reason for the much higher poverty rate of elderly women is that they are less likely than men to receive income from occupational pension plans, the Canada and Quebec Pension Plans and investments.

The federal Old Age Security pension and Guaranteed Income Supplement is the only income source which provides more money on average to women than to men. This is not surprising since the Guaranteed Income Supplement is an income-tested benefit that gives the largest payments to people with the lowest incomes.

The biggest gap is for income from occupational pension plans. The average amount women 65 and over received from that source in 1987 was 31 percent of the average received by men—$1,237 for women compared to $3,975 for men. The difference in Canada and Quebec Pension Plan benefits was also substantial, with women receiving 47 percent of the benefits of men.

Are the pension entitlements of men and women getting much closer as more women join the labour force? It is doubtful at this point.

Neither sex is well served by occupational pension plans, with only 37 percent of employed women and 51 percent of employed men participating in them in 1988.[3] For those who are covered, pension benefits depend a great deal on the level of earnings and the frequency of work interruptions, so women's future income from these plans will probably still be very inferior to men's.

The Canada and Quebec Pension Plans have a lot more potential. CPP and QPP benefits are also based on earnings, but the plans cover all paid workers and include a very important feature for women: allowing them to take time off from their paying jobs without pension penalty while their children are young. The effect of this "child-rearing drop-out" provision, as it is called, is to provide continuous and free CPP and QPP coverage to parents of children under the age of seven at their usual level of earnings.

Unlike most occupational pensions, the Canada and Quebec Pension Plans are fully transferable from job to job, and benefits are completely protected against rises in the cost of living. Both features are very important for women, because they change jobs more often and have longer lives ahead of them in which to suffer from the effects of inflation. Women who survive to age 65 can expect to live another 20.2 years, compared to 15.5 years for men.[4]

The main difficulty with the CPP and QPP, as we already saw in the case of widows aged 55 to 64, is that benefits are much too small. Pensions for surviving spouses aged 65 and over are set at 60 percent of the deceased spouse's retirement benefit, with the maximum survivor pension amounting to $4,005 a year in 1989.

Under new proposals for the Canada Pension Plan put forward by the federal government in 1987, the maximum pension would go only to surviving spouses whose unions had lasted 40 years or longer. Benefits to the others would vary depending on the length of their relationships. This would reduce survivor pensions in a large proportion of cases.

The retirement benefits of the Canada and Quebec Pension Plans are also inadequate. Retirement pensions amount to only 25 percent of a pension's average lifetime earnings up to a maximum pension of $6,675 a year in 1989.

To find out how newly retiring women are doing, we obtained information on Canada Pension Plan recipients aged 65 to 69 in June 1989. The results show that women are still very far behind. Only 57 percent of the female pensioners of that age were receiving retirement benefits from the CPP, compared to 96 percent of the men. For those who received benefits, women's lower earnings produced pensions of $3,120 a year on average compared to an average of $5,340 for men.[5]

A pension of $3,120 from the Canada or Quebec Pension Plan, combined with the Old Age Security pension and the Guaranteed Income Supplement, produced a total income of $10,204 in 1989. This was above the estimated 1989 poverty line for a person who lives alone in a rural area ($8,901), but well below the poverty line for a city with a population of 500,000 or more ($12,037).

How does being poor affect the everyday lives of elderly women? It means they have to sell their homes when their husbands die, because they need the money to live and cannot afford to hire people to do jobs such as cleaning the eavestroughs, shovelling snow and fixing the roof.[6]

Because their old neighbourhoods have few apartments to rent, most of these women have to move elsewhere, leaving their friends behind and paying a higher price for often sub-standard apartments. A lucky few get public housing or housing subsidies, but these are in very short supply. Canada Mortgage and Housing Corporation estimates that 44 percent of unattached elderly women had "core" housing needs in 1985, which means that their housing was either inadequate or cost more than 30 percent of their income.[7]

Being poor also means that most older women cannot afford cars or taxis. Seniors often complain about train and bus services that are less frequent when they need them most, in the evenings and on Sundays. Many also have problems with the physical design of public transport facilities. As one old woman put it, bus steps a foot and a half high are not designed for human beings, let alone for old ladies with stiff joints. After a while, it becomes simpler to stay home, and even trips to the doctor become major expeditions.[8]

Most devastating for seniors is the combination of having no money and no spouse. When men get older and frailer, most of them have built-in housekeepers and nurses—their wives. Women are not so fortunate. In the absence of adequate supports such as visiting nurses, professional homemakers and Meals on Wheels, most widows must do without minimal comforts or must turn for help to the second most important caregivers in families, their daughters.

Middle-aged daughters have been called the "sandwich generation" because they are caught between the needs of their parents and those of their own jobs and families. A national U.S. survey found that a quarter of caregiving daughters had children under 18, 44 percent were employed, and 12 percent had been forced to leave their jobs to care for their aged parents. Most caregivers spent about four hours a day, seven days a week, helping their needy relatives, for periods lasting from less than six months to more than 40 years. [9]

According to demographers, longer life expectancy and delayed child-bearing mean that a growing proportion of women will have to provide care both to children under the age of 18 and to elderly parents in the future. Otherwise, fewer frail elderly people will live with their relatives or in their own homes, and more of them will live in institutions.

There are indications that this is already happening in Canada. Between 1971 and 1986, the number of women aged 75 or more living in institutions increased by 127 percent, far outpacing the 68-percent increase in their population. As a result, the proportion of women aged 75 and over who were in institutions rose from 14 percent to 19 percent. Among those aged 85 and over, 41 percent of the women lived in institutions in 1986, compared with 28 percent of the men. [10]

Good institutions for incapacitated old people are in short supply. Only seniors who can pay top dollar are assured of receiving adequate care in a relatively pleasant environment. For most elderly women, finding a decent place to end their days is life's last game of chance.

NOTES

1. Data in this paragraph from special tabulations, Survey of Consumer Finances.

2. National Council of Welfare, *A Pension Primer,* 1989, pp. 10–11.

3. Statistics Canada, *Pension Plans in Canada 1988.* Cat. 74–401, p. 13.

4. Unpublished figures on life expectancies for 1991 provided by the Demography Division, Statistics Canada.

5. Calculated from unpublished data provided by Health and Welfare Canada.

6. Dulude, Louise, "Getting Old: Men in Couples and Women Alone," in *Women and Men: Interdisciplinary Readings on Gender,* ed. Greta Hofmann Nemiroff (Toronto: Fitzhenry & Whiteside, 1987), pp. 328–331.

7. Unpublished data provided by Canada Mortgage and Housing Corporation.

8. Information in this paragraph and the next from Dulude, pp. 328–331.

9. Information in this paragraph and the next from Stone, Robyn, Gail Lee Cafferata and Judith Sangl, "Caregivers of the Frail Elderly: A National Profile," *The Gerontologist,* Vol. 27, No. 5, October 1987, pp. 615–626.

10. Priest, Gordon E., "Living Arrangements of Canada's 'Older Elderly' Population," *Canadian Social Trends,* Autumn 1988, pp. 26–30; Stone, Leroy, and Hubert Frenken, Canadian's Seniors, Statistics Canada, Cat. 98–121, 1988, p. 46.

23

Immigration and Income Security Policies in Canada

IMPLICATIONS FOR ELDERLY IMMIGRANT WOMEN

Monica Boyd

■■■

ELDERLY IMMIGRANTS AND INCOME SECURITY PROGRAMS

Elderly immigrants share one similarity with their native born counterparts. Old age traditionally means declining income, especially among widowed women. But two factors increase the vulnerability of the foreign born population, and foreign born women in particular, to low incomes in old age. First, movement across international borders can mean a low income status in the host country if migrants leave a low per capita income country for a higher per capita income country and if employment generating income capabilities of the elderly in the host society are slim. Low economic status also may be exacerbated by losses in purchasing power associated with moving from one economy to another. Second, the persistence of low incomes also results from the rules governing eligibility to Canada's old age income security programs.

The major pension system in Canada consists of three federal programs to which are added various provincial supplements: the Canada/Quebec Pension plan (C/QPP); the Old Age Security program (OAS); and the Guaranteed Income Supplement (GIS). Unlike the OAS and GIS, the Canada Pension Plan is an employment related social insurance program in which contributions and benefits are earnings related. The plan covers employed and self-employed persons who are between age 18 and 70 and who earn more than a prescribed minimum level of earnings in a calendar year. The

Reproduced from M. Boyd (1989) ."Immigration and Income Security Policies in Canada: Implications for Elderly Immigrant Women." *Population Research and Policy Review* 9 (1): 5–24. Reprinted by permission of Kluwer Academic Publishers.

plan operates everywhere in Canada except in Quebec which has its own plan. Benefits from the Canada/Quebec Pension Plan (C/QPP) are prorated from an allowable maximum according to the length of the period in which an individual has been a contributor to the plan and the amount of monthly contributions, up to a ceiling (Canada. Health and Welfare, 1987: 10–12). The spouse of a deceased contributor may be eligible for a survivor's pension assuming the deceased made contributions for a minimum time period. If the surviving spouse is aged 65 or older, the benefit is 60 percent of the benefit payable to the contributor at age 65 (Canada. Health and Welfare, 1987: 13–14).

The C/QPP is not a program based on universal coverage. Instead eligibility is determined by earnings related contributions. Elderly immigrants, who as new arrivals have made no contributions, will not receive C/QPP benefits. Immigrants arriving in mid-life will have their benefits prorated for time spent in the Canadian labour force. For several reasons these rules and regulations mean that foreign born women more than foreign born men (and Canadian born women) are disadvantaged as beneficiaries of the C/QPP. First, they receive lower pensions than their male counterparts as a result of their lower labour force earnings and the likelihood of not having worked in the paid labour force full time or for as long a period as men. Second, by definition, neither are premiums purchased nor benefits paid for work in the invisible economy. Yet, many of the jobs as seamstresses and domestics are both located in the invisible economy and employ substantial numbers of women born in Asia, the Caribbean and Southern Europe (Boyd, 1986; Gannagé, 1986; Johnson, 1982). Unless self-employment income is declared and premiums paid, these women will receive no benefits in old age for their employment years. And, third, because they are likely to outlive their husbands, foreign born women will receive survivor benefits based on the decreased spouse's C/QPP contributions. But, if the deceased spouse did not accumulate the maximum years of lifetime earnings necessary for full benefits, the survivor benefits also will be prorated. Because most immigrants enter Canada as adults, immigrant women are more vulnerable than are Canadian born women to receiving prorated survivor benefits.

The Old Age Security program comes close to a program based on universal coverage, but here too immigrants may not be beneficiaries. In order to qualify for Old Age Security, an applicant must be 65 years or older, a Canadian citizen or legal resident on the day before approval of the application, and have lived a minimum of ten years in Canada after age 18. If immigrants meet these criteria, their benefits are prorated at the rate of 1/40th of the full monthly pension for each year of residency in Canada. Thus, an elderly immigrant who has resided in Canada for forty years or more before applying for the OAS benefit will receive the maximum allowable compared to the one-fourth rate paid to an immigrant who has lived in Canada for ten years.[1] Once a par tial pension is approved, the rate may not be increased as the result of additional years of residence in Canada (Canada. Health and Welfare, 1987: 7).

For immigrants residing in Canada, no benefits will be paid if they lived less than ten years in Canada. The only exception to the ten year residency requirement is for elderly immigrants from countries which have signed an International Social Security Agreement with Canada. Effective March, 1988, agreements exist between Canada and: Austria, Barbados, Belgium, Denmark, Finland, France, Federal Republic of Germany, Greece, Jamaica, Luxembourg, Netherlands, Norway, Portugal, St. Lucia, Spain, Sweden and the United States. If their total residence in both countries after age 18 meets the ten year regulation, immigrants will be eligible for a partial OAS amounting to one-fortieth of the maximum pension for each year they lived in Canada.

The third federally administered program, the Guaranteed Income Supplement, is an income assistance program designed to assist persons with little or no income in addition to that received from Old Age Security. Income from other sources (earnings related retirement pensions, investment income, wages, etc.) in combination with the OAS benefit cannot exceed certain limits. Since persons must be eligible for OAS benefits in order to be eligible for GIS benefits, elderly immigrants who do not qualify for OAS benefits are automatically ineligible for GIS benefits regardless of their income levels. Modifications to the overall pension system were made in 1984. Immigrants who were eligible for benefits from the Guaranteed Income Supplement program and who were not receiving a full OAS could bring up the OAS to the full level by funds from the GIS program even if it meant exceeding the usual GIS maximum payments. This 1984 provision ensures that those immigrants who qualify for OAS but who have very low incomes will receive income equivalent to the maximum benefits allowable from the combined OAS and GIS programs[2]. However, the overall income levels generated from both the OAS and GIS are not large and many elderly recipients do not have incomes above the poverty line (National Council of Welfare, 1984a; 1984b).

In sum, these government pension policies are of considerable importance for the economic status of elderly immigrants in Canada. Immigrants with no Canadian labour force experience will not receive benefits from the C/QPP. If treaties do not exist with their previous countries of residence, recent immigrants receive no OAS benefits. The Guaranteed Income Supplement, which is an income security program designed to augment partial OAS payments, does not cover immigrants unless they are receiving OAS payments. And until 1984 it was possible for elderly immigrants not to receive a total OAS/GIS payment equal to that received by economically comparable Canadian born elderly. Overall, these regulations enhance the likelihood of low incomes for elderly immigrants, particularly women.

CONCLUSION AND COMMENTARY

The low incomes of many immigrant women are noteworthy for at least three reasons. First, they illustrate the interplay between gender, income security policy and immigration policy. Second, they point to the existence and persistence of economic inequalities, both between various subgroups in the elderly immigrant population and between the old and the young in families. Third, they highlight, but do not resolve, social policy issues predicated on the social rights of individuals and families.

Most of the existing research focuses on the plight of elderly widows (e.g., Canadian Advisory Council on the Status of Women, 1987; Myles, 1988; National Council of Welfare, 1984a; 1984b). While this research draws attention to the strong link between gender, employment patterns, and pension benefits, it fails to acknowledge the additional impact of migration. Immigration policy governs the type of migrant admitted. The substantial percentages of elderly women who are foreign born are the legacy of past immigration policies which emphasized the admittance of large numbers of adults to meet labour demands, permitted the migration of accompanying family members including spouses, and facilitated family sponsored immigration. More recently, the emphasis on family reunification has meant the arrival of "new elderly immigrants", who are arriving late in life and who often are from Third World regions. While immigration policy on the one hand facilitates their admittance, regulations governing eligibility to income security programs reduce the entitlements of these newcomers. Demographically and sociologically, the results are familiar. Elderly women, many of them widowed, predominate in these flows, and they are most likely to live in a family setting (see Boyd, 1988).

The second issue arises out of the first. If gender, immigration policy and income security policy underline the low incomes of elderly immigrant women, the personal consequences remain unexplored. From the perspective of the double or triple jeopardy model, the overall effect is to heighten the degree of inequality among the elderly female population (see Bengtson, 1979; Ujimoto, 1987). Minority elderly women, who are recent arrivals and/or from Third World regions, are the most likely to have low incomes compared to women who are native born or long term residents, or who are from Europe, the United Kingdom and the United States.

But while studies document the applicability of the double/triple jeopardy theme in which age, ethnicity/birthplace and gender interact to produce income inequalities, other related effects are less certain, and indicate more questions than answers. Low incomes and immigration in old age are linked to living with kin (Boyd, 1988). But do such living arrangements imply an optimal economic and social setting for the elderly foreign born women? Gerontological research tends to assume that family life enhances the social integration of the elderly. Yet, such integration may vary according to cultural specific norms regarding the status of the elderly, the age at immigration, and the presence or absence of an extensive "ethnic" network and support system.

In addition, the economic situation of elderly immigrant women indicates the need for additional research regarding the extent to which economic resources are extended to the elderly in family settings. A popular presumption is that family members pool incomes to enhance the well-being of individuals. This assumption not only exists generally, but is an underlying principle of sponsored family migration. Yet transfer of resources across generations may not occur, leaving the elderly in relative positions of powerlessness and dependency. A second presumption, built into the criteria for Canada's low income cutoffs, is that by pooling incomes, family members avoid poverty. But, additional research is required to document the extent to which the effects of low personal income status of elderly immigrant women are mitigated by living in families whose collective incomes are above the established low income cutoffs.

Finally, the low personal incomes of the elderly which are associated with the intersection of immigration policy and income security policy points to a yet unresolved tension over what should constitute the social rights of elderly immigrants and their families. Both immigration policy and income security policy can be conceptualized as conferring rights on individuals or on their families. Provided certain conditions are met, immigration policy permits the right of residency to individuals and the entitlement of already resident families to experience family reunification. Income security programs can be conceptualized as conferring income assistance and/or income maintenance entitlements to the elderly. They also can be viewed as a form of social protection to the middle age family unit. Income security programs are a mechanism for spreading the risk of the financial burden of caring for the elderly among the younger generation who otherwise would have to support the elderly on an individual basis rather than on a collective one.

But immigration related rights of residency and of family reunification do not necessarily mean full social rights in accessing Canada's income security programs. At the moment, rules governing eligibility and amounts of income security benefits are under the jurisdiction of the Department of Health and Welfare, Canada. The ten year residency requirement associated with accessing OAS and GIS benefits and the contribution requirements of C/QPP increase the likelihood that immigrants may not be eligible for benefits or will receive prorated benefits.

Further, even if these restrictions did not differentiate between the foreign and Canadian born, some elderly immigrants might still be ineligible for income security benefits under Employment and Immigration regulations governing entry into Canada. The intent that governments should not have to economically assist family related immigrants is quite clear in the sponsorship agreement. Sponsors complete a form in which they agree to "...provide financial assistance to the named immigrant(s) so that such person(s) shall not require financial maintenance support from any federal or provincial assistance program...". Under this provision, social assistance benefits may be denied to those recently arrived immigrants who enter as sponsored immigrants in the family and assisted relatives categories (see Boyd, 1987; Employment and Immigration Canada, 1985) and for whom the sponsorship agreement is still in effect (five years in the assisted relatives category and up to ten years in the family class). This principle currently is not the basis for denied or reduced access to income programs targeted at the elderly. But, if those used by Health and Welfare Canada were altered, some immigrants might still be disallowed full OAS and GIS benefits under current Employment and Immigration procedures.

These policies confirm that not all foreign born elderly have full social rights in Canada. The current situation arises from the disjuncture between post-war immigration policies which underlie a sizeable foreign born elderly population and income security policies which deny or prorate income assistance benefits. But this disjuncture raises three questions regarding social welfare entitlements. The first question is what social entitlements should be granted the elderly in Canada? This question is discussed extensively by analysts of Canada's income security/assistance programs (see Myles, 1988).

The second question is who shall receive these entitlements—to whom should social rights be extended? Addressing this question requires determining the criteria for granting citizenship rights, in which access is permitted to resources and to the distribution and enjoyment of such resources. To the extent that place of birth is invoked as a criterion, the most circumscribed criteria governing entitlement are those of legal citizenship. The most generous criteria are those which include the mere presence of individuals in the borders or legal jurisdictions of a given nation state. Canada's criteria of ten years of residency and prorated OAS and GIS benefits situate her somewhere between these two polarities. But such positioning also raises the issue of what is the appropriate location on a spectrum of possible entitlement rights. If nations permit migration, what social rights should be extended to the migrants? Should distinctions exist between types of migrants, defined either by entry class or length of residency? Current Canadian policies provide an affirmative answer to the latter question. Yet as shown in this paper, such policies also are related to the low incomes of elderly immigrants.

The third and final unresolved question is who are the beneficiaries of "citizenship" rights: individuals or collectivities? Income security programs can be viewed as programs targeted at the elderly person and thus as representing rights for aged individuals. But the post-war development of the welfare state must be seen not just as the development of social policies by the state but rather in some policy areas as a shift in the burden of responsibility from the family to the state. From this perspective the denial or prorating of income security benefits are issues because they affect both individuals and families. Elderly foreign born individuals receive OAS and GIS entitlements based on years of residency. Such regulations mean that, unlike the Canadian born, young and middle aged immigrant families may not benefit from policies which spread the financial burden of caring for the elderly among the younger generation.

Currently, the questions regarding the criteria for extending entitlements and who benefits fuse. In Canada, under existing immigration policy and income security policy, the first generation may not fully benefit from income security programs, both because, as young families, their social obligations toward their elderly may also be economic ones, and because, in old age, first generation individuals may not receive income benefits to the same extent as the elderly Canadian born.

ACKNOWLEDGMENTS

This paper is a substantial revision of "The Invisible Poor", presented at the 1988 annual meeting of the Canadian Sociology and Anthropology association. The analysis was conducted at Carleton University and was financed by a faculty account. The paper was written while the author was a Visiting Scholar in the Social and Economic Studies Division, Statistics Canada. The author thanks John Myles (Carleton University), A. Rashid (Statistics Canada), John Samuel (Employment and Immigration) and Edward Tamagno (Health and Welfare) for their very helpful comments and information regarding earlier drafts. The contents of this paper remain the sole responsibility of the author and do not necessarily reflect the views of Statistics Canada, or any other agency or individual. Because immigration and income security policies are subject to change, persons seeking information on Canada's immigration regulations or on accessing income security programs must consult the pertinent government departments for such information.

NOTES

1. Legislation regarding the payment of partial pensions based on the number of years of residency in Canada was enacted in 1977. A provision stipulated that a person who had not resided in Canada for 40 years after age 18 might still qualify for a full OAS pension if he or she met several conditions. The major stipulations were that as of July 1, 1977: a) he or she was age 25 or older; b) was resident in Canada on that date or has resided in Canada prior to that date and after age 18 or possessed a valid immigration visa on that date; and c) had resided in Canada for ten years immediately before the approval of the OAS application (Canada. Health and Welfare, 1987: 6–7).

2. For example, as of July 1988, the maximum allowable benefits were $316 from OAS and $375 from GIS, or a total of $691, for a person who was not currently married and who was eligible for GIS benefits. Under regulations prior to 1984,

an immigrant who also received no income from other sources and who received OAS benefits prorated for ten years of residency would receive $79.00 from OAS, and $375 from GIS. Under the 1984 legislation, the same immigrant would receive a supplement from the GIS program amounting to $237 to bring the total income received from both the GIS and OAS programs to $691. This example is valid only for persons who are not currently married and who have no other sources of income. The amount of the Guaranteed Income Supplement received is adjusted on a prorated basis for non-OAS sources of income (see: Canada. Health and Welfare, 1987: 7–8).

BIBLIOGRAPHY

Bengtson, Vern L. (1979). "Ethnicity and Aging: Problems and Issues in Current Social Science Inquiry," pp. 9–31 in Donald E. Gelfand and Alfred J. Kutzik (eds.), *Ethnicity and Aging: Theory, Research and Policy.* New York: Springer Publishing Co.

Boyd, Monica (1986). "Immigrant Women in Canada." pp. 45–61 in Rita James Simon and Caroline B. Brettell (eds.), *International Migration: The Female Experience.* Totawa, New Jersey: Rowman and Allanheld.

Boyd, Monica (1987). *Migrant Women in Canada. Profiles and Politics.* Report submitted to the subpanel on Migrant Women, OECD-Paris. Ottawa: Employment and Immigration, Public Affairs Inquiries and Distribution.

Boyd, Monica (1988). "Family Migration and Living Arrangements: The Case of Elderly Immigrants in Canada." Paper presented at the 1988 meeting of the Population Association of America, New Orleans. April.

Canada. Employment and Immigration (1985). *The Revised Selection Criteria for Independent Immigrants.* Ottawa: Employment and Immigration WH-5-086.

Canada. Health and Welfare Canada (1987). *Overview: The Income Security Programs of Health and Welfare Canada.* Ottawa: Supply and Services. Catalogue No. H76-49/ 1987.

Canadian Advisory Council on the Status of Women (1987). *Integration and Participation: Women's Work in the Home and in the Labour Force.* Catalogue No. LW31-28/ 1987E.

Gannagé, Charlene (1986). *Double Day, Double Bind.* Toronto: The Women's Press.

Johnson, Laura (1982). *The Seam Allowance: Industrial Home Sewing in Canada.* Toronto: Women's Educational Press.

Myles, John F. (1988). "Social Policy in Canada." pp. 37–53 in Eloise Rathbone-McCuan and Betty Havens (eds.), *North American Elders.* New York: Greenwood Press.

National Council of Welfare (1984a). *A Pension Primer.* Catalogue H68-12/1984-E. Ottawa: Minister of Supply and Services Canada.

National Council of Welfare (1984b). *Sixty Five and Older.* Catalogue H68-11/1984-E. Ottawa: Minister of Supply and Services Canada.

Ujimoto, Victor (1987). "The Ethnic Dimension of Aging in Canada." pp. 111–137 in Victor W. Marshall (ed.), *Aging in Canada: Social Perspectives* (2nd edition). Toronto: Fitzhenry and Whiteside.

SECTION FIVE

Discussion Questions

1. What was the "Great Pension Debate" about? How did the issue of homemaker pensions influence the outcome of this debate? How did changes in Canada's retirement income system create income security for the well-do-do?

2. How does the debate over compulsory retirement expose intergenerational tensions? Do the facts support the case for mandatory retirement? Discuss.

3. Compare and contrast the reasons why people retire early or late. State the different reasons for early retirement by men and women. What trends might keep older workers on the job in the future?

4. What barriers keep older women from having adequate pensions? What social conditions lead to poverty among older women? What pension programs best serve the needs of older women?

5. What social forces lead to the low incomes of elderly immigrant women? Describe the ways that the public pension system disadvantages foreign-born older women.

6. How do Canadian income and retirement policies influence the timing and experience of old age? How do these policies influence older people's quality of life?

Suggested Readings

Brown, R.L. (1990). *Economic Security in an Aging Population*. Toronto: Butterworths.

Gee, E.M. and S.A. McDaniel (1991). "Pension Politics and Challenges: Retirement Policy Implications." *Canadian Public Policy* 17 (4): 456–72.

McDonald, P.L., and R.A. Wanner (1990). *Retirement in Canada*. Toronto: Butterworths.

Matthews, A.M., and K.H. Brown (1987). "Retirement as a Critical Life Event: The Differential Experiences of Women and Men." *Research on Aging* 9 (4): 548–71.

Myles, J. (1989). *Old Age in the Welfare State: The Political Economy of Public Pensions*, rev. ed. Lawrence, Kansas: University Press of Kansas.

National Advisory Council on Aging (1991). *The Economic Situation of Canada's Seniors: A Fact Book*. Cat. No. H71-3/14-1991E. Ottawa: Minister of Supply and Services Canada.

Tindale, J.A. (1991). *Older Workers in an Aging Work Force*. Cat. No. H71-2/1-10-1991E. Ottawa: National Advisory Council on Aging, Minister of Supply and Services Canada.

Housing and Living Arrangements

Housing options range on a continuum from maximum independence (e.g., living in a single-family home) to maximum dependence (e.g., living in a nursing home or hospital). A person should live in the type of housing that best suits their abilities and needs. A married couple, for example, may prefer a single-family home where they can garden and entertain large groups of friends. A widow may prefer an apartment that requires less maintenance than a house. People's needs can change as they age. Changes in health, income, or social supports can lead to a change in housing preference. A person should be able to live in the type of housing that best suits their current needs. This requires that a range of alternatives exist at a cost that people can afford. Many new options in housing have emerged to meet the current and future needs of older people.

Lahaie and Theroux describe a nursing-home program called Le Chez Nous. This program provides around-the-clock care to people with Alzheimer's disease and other cognitive impairments. These patients can pose a risk to their own safety, and they place stress on professional caregivers. Le Chez Nous provides a home-like environment that reduces risk and stress. Le Chez Nous asks what life outside an institution offers people, then it attempts to create those conditions inside the institution. The setting includes flexible schedules, comfortable furniture, and nursing staff who take on many non-nursing tasks. Le Chez Nous offers a cost-effective way to serve cognitively impaired patients' unique needs.

Among other things, life in the community offers adults a chance to engage in sexual relations. But institutions often limit this opportunity. They limit the sexual relations of nonmarried residents and may even limit sexual relations between spouses who live in the same facility. Rapelje and Molloy point to prejudice, fear of legal action, and family pressure as reasons facilities give for control over sexual activity. They also suggest some solutions to these problems. Solutions include changed staff attitudes, a recognition of residents' rights, and guidelines to help staff deal with residents' sexuality.

Granny flats, small portable detached houses placed next to an adult child's home, offer an option for older people who need some support, but can live on their own. Australia pioneered granny flats in 1975, and Canada has begun to explore their usefulness. Lazarowich describes a number of granny-flat demonstration projects in Canada. These projects show that granny flats can succeed in Canada. But Lazarowich concludes that the development of granny flats will depend on government acceptance of this option. Municipalities will have to accept them as an alternative form of housing, and the federal and provincial governments will have to encourage their development.

Single-family homes place the most demand on a person and require the most effort to maintain. Winter in Canada adds to the stress of owning a single-family home. Klinger-Zepic discusses the challenges that face older people who live in this type of housing. Klinger-Zepic also discusses the supports that older homeowners need in a northern climate. Supports include home remodelling, changes in suburban by-laws to allow two self-contained units in one house, and better transportation. Klinger-Zepic reviews programs in Sweden and Iceland that could serve as models for future housing in Canada.

As the population ages, older people will need new kinds of housing. Future cohorts of older people will expect more responsive and more attractive alternatives at every point on the housing continuum. The options described in this section suggest some of the ways that housing will respond to seniors' needs in the future.

24

Le Chez Nous

ACCOMMODATION WITH A DIFFERENCE FOR COGNITIVELY IMPAIRED PERSONS IN RURAL MANITOBA

Ulysses Lahaie and Jacqueline Theroux

INTRODUCTION

Victims of cognitive impairment need appropriate accommodation. As research contributes to our knowledge and understanding of the relationship between cerebral function and behaviour, health care providers acknowledge that individuals with cognitive deficits have unique needs requiring unique solutions.

The traditional conceptual framework for care delivery to the elderly focuses mainly on physical needs. In this model, the allocation of nursing care, measured in units of time, does not factor levels of cognitive function appropriately. While the model serves a major segment of the institutionalized elderly, it ignores the needs of cognitively impaired individuals, an increasingly significant group.

Response to the shelter requirements of a cognitively impaired population is best managed within the parameters of a conceptual framework. With the help of a conceptual framework, a long term care facility can use existing financial and human resources to develop a program that accommodates the needs of mentally frail persons.

This article describes our unit's evolution. It includes geographic and demographic data, a historical overview, an elaboration of its conceptual framework, a description of the physical space, discussion of staffing, education, programming and the role of the family, and an evaluation of the unit's progress.

Reproduced from G. Gutman (ed.) (1992), *Shelter and Care of Persons with Dementia.* Burnaby, B.C.: Gerontology Research Centre, Simon Fraser University. Reprinted with permission.

GEOGRAPHIC AND DEMOGRAPHIC DATA

Notre-Dame de Lourdes lies amidst the rolling hills of the Pembina Mountains in Southwestern Manitoba. It is surrounded by rich agricultural land and provides a picturesque setting that inspires local artists. Farming, education and health care are the mainstays of the economy.

Notre-Dame has a population of 708, 24% of whom are aged 65 and over. This contrasts with the provincial rate of 12.8% and the national rate of 10.7%.

The majority of inhabitants are of Swiss and French ancestry. Some neighboring communities share a similar lineage; others claim Dutch and Belgian extraction. This ethnic mosaic is reflected in the Foyer and Le Chez Nous resident populations.

Foyer and Chez Nous Resident Population

The Foyer Notre-Dame is a 61 bed long-term care facility. Admission is open to anyone meeting eligibility requirements determined by Manitoba Health Services Commission guidelines.

Our alternative care unit, Le Chez Nous, comprises 12 of the Foyer's 61 long term care beds. The term "Chez Nous" translates as "my home" and connotes an ambiance of comfort, trust, and a sense of belonging and being at ease in one's environment.

The mean age of the Foyer's general resident population is 85 (range 66 to 101). The gender split is 57% female and 43% male. Thirty-four (69%) of the Foyer's general area population claim French as their mother tongue. Most residents come from southern Manitoba communities but some are from outside the province.

While the mean age (85) and age range (74–96) is similar in Le Chez Nous, the gender split is different. In Le Chez Nous males outnumber females by 2:1. Most male residents were farmers and most females were homemakers. Other occupations noted in the care plans are mechanic, clerk and restaurant owner. Le Chez Nous is home to four Francophone residents.

The Manitoba Health Services Commission's Personal Care Home Program is based on four levels of care with an assignment to level one indicating minimal dependence on staff and an assignment to level four indicating maximum dependency. In the Foyer's general area, five residents are assessed at level one, 20 at level two, 15 at level three and nine at level four. In comparison, Le Chez Nous has one resident at level one, two at level two, seven at level three and two at level four. All Chez Nous residents suffer some degree of cognitive impairment due mainly to dementia-related illness.

HISTORY/BACKGROUND

Several events prompted us to consider establishing an alternative care unit. In a broad context, changes occurring at the national level set the stage for new approaches to the care and shelter of cognitively impaired persons. For example, in the early 1950s, as the number of mental hospital beds were decreased, older patients with cognitive impairment were transferred to long term care facilities as part of the deinstitutionalization movement. Today, home care maintains elderly persons in their homes longer. But individuals with attendant mental health problems exhaust their home supports sooner than those with only physical problems and seek facility care earlier. The result is a higher rate of facility admissions for this group. Finally, as the demographics of aging change, so does the prevalence of age-related mental health problems. Today, people are living longer and the Canadian population is aging rapidly, resulting in greater numbers of persons with mental health problems (Health and Welfare Canada, 1990).

Locally, the precipitating events included:

- a significant rise in the Foyer's cognitively impaired population. We were admitting more cognitively impaired individuals and more residents within the Foyer were becoming impaired;

- a growing number of staff and resident injuries caused by acts of physical aggression. Abuse to various staff included an eye injury, a concussion and a fractured nose. Aggressive acts among residents, resulting in several fractured hips and a skull fracture, were also documented, as were many incidences of physical fighting. Several staff injuries resulted in extensive use of income protection benefits;

- numerous complaints from lucid residents expressing fear of violent attacks and fear of having their privacy invaded;

- several incidences of aggressive acts toward confused residents in attempts to scare them away or preempt attacks;

- an alarming increase in elopements and injuries that jeopardized residents' safety and raised fears of litigation;

- deterioration of staff morale. Many staff members experienced stress from physical and verbal abuse, fear of losing an impaired resident or seeing residents harmed. High stress levels were also manifested in increased sick time usage;

- a significant rise in complaints from families of lucid residents concerned about their relative's safety;

- an unfavourable image in the community, with visitors misinterpreting impaired residents' behaviours and questioning the staff's response to them.

Collectively, these events highlighted the need for a solution that would improve quality of life for all residents, enhance families' perception of the care rendered, reduce staff stress and reconcile problems generated by an environment that failed to accommodate persons with cognitive limitations.

To Segregate or Integrate?

A search of the literature indicated that the notion of segregation, although not popular initially, is now gaining currency. Novick (1988), for example, cites four studies in which segregation of lucid and confused individuals has proved mutually beneficial. Coons (1987a) cautions against an integration model. She argues that intact persons cannot serve as role models for those with severe memory loss. It is unrealistic, she contends, to assume that the cognitively impaired have the capacity to use the behaviour of others as a prototype for their own response. Also, alert persons who find themselves angry, frustrated and unable to cope with their impaired neighbours will probably provide poor behaviour models.

In deliberating the segregation option, we felt success or failure would be determined by our purpose. If we pursued segregation solely to enhance the quality of life of lucid residents by removing the problem (i.e. the impaired resident), the program would fail its disadvantaged population. But if the philosophy guiding segregation focussed primarily on meeting the needs of cognitively impaired individuals, the attendant needs of lucid residents for personal security and privacy would also be met. The Foyer opted to pursue a segregation model featuring a conceptual framework designed specifically to answer the shelter needs of its mentally impaired population.

LE CHEZ NOUS' CONCEPTUAL FRAMEWORK

Le Chez Nous' conceptual framework is analogous to the structure of a home and comprises three principles:

1. **To enhance residents' lives, we must first consider past lifestyles and plan care accordingly.** This principle is our home's foundation and the basis of all decisions that affect our residents. It is the groundwork upon which all policies rest and the root of all planning.

2. **Individuals with cognitive deficits should not be held accountable for their behaviour.** This second principle frames our home and supports our contention that the burden of behavioural ownership must not be borne by impaired persons.

3. **Losses must be compensated for and residents helped to function within their remaining capacity.** This last principle shelters the frame and foundation of our home and protects the integrity of the first two principles.

These principles are reflected daily in case conferences; in admission, discharge and transfer decisions; in programming and in developing, implementing and revising care plans.

UNIQUE FEATURES OF LE CHEZ NOUS

Alternate care units are becoming commonplace in Canada. Most are linked to research centres, universities, hospitals and large long term care facilities. In contrast, Le Chez Nous is a local product, created by in-house talent, developed with available resources and operated within existing staffing levels.

Funding

Most new concepts in accommodation for the elderly originate as research projects, are funded by endowments from benevolent foundations, or are financially supported by one or more government agencies. We received many words of encouragement from health care funding agencies but financial assistance was unavailable. This motivated us to develop a simple, practical and affordable model. Through fundraising campaigns, we solicited financial support from employees, families, friends and the community. In fact, charitable donations account for all of Le Chez Nous' development costs.

Staffing

An increase in personnel was not required. Rather, nursing staff who opted to work on the unit assumed duties that were traditionally the domain of other job classifications such as housekeeping, activities and dietary. This shift of tasks was negotiated with the supervisors from each department and the staff selected to work on the unit.

A Rural Perspective

Almost all alternative care units for the elderly cited in the professional literature are based in urban settings, but the needs of cognitively impaired persons extend well beyond urban perimeters. Le Chez Nous, a rural unit, offers succor to a mostly rural population.

Development

A final point to note is that in contrast to units initiated as university projects or developed in larger urban health centres that benefit from the expertise of several professions and disciplines, Le Chez Nous was inaugurated by our Director of Resident Services together with a nursing supervisor, staff nurses and nursing aides.

ADMISSION TO LE CHEZ NOUS

Le Chez Nous admissions are processed by a team comprising the nursing supervisor, unit coordinator, social workers and physician. The team functions as an autonomous unit unless disagreement or controversy arises. The Director of Resident Services may then intervene in order to reach a consensus.

The Admission Process

When a room in Le Chez Nous becomes available, first priority is given to candidates from within the Foyer's general population. When an outside applicant is considered, members of Le Chez Nous' selection team visit the applicant in his/her residence and conduct a behavioural and cognitive assessment. At this time, team members discuss with families Le Chez Nous' philosophy and goals. Families must then decide if their needs can be met within that framework.

Most applicants are easily assessed. Others, however, present potential problems. In such cases, admission is conditional. The admitting physician agrees, in writing, to a trial period. After three months, the candidate may become a permanent resident. But if Le Chez Nous determines that it cannot meet the candidate's needs, or if the candidate is not seen to benefit from the experience, he or she may either return to previous accommodations or be discharged to an available room in the Foyer.

Knowing that challenging candidates are admitted with this proviso, Le Chez Nous staff make extra efforts to accommodate them. The written agreement also serves as a morale booster. Staff know they will not be taxed beyond the resources they have to care for individuals they cannot safely accommodate.

Admission Criteria

To qualify for admission to Le Chez Nous, individuals must be ambulatory but impaired to the degree that if they were to leave the building unescorted, they would not be able to return safely. We then ask, "Which candidate would best benefit from admission to Le Chez Nous?" The level of cognitive function is not the deciding factor. Rather, it is the candidate's potential to adapt to Le Chez Nous' environment that determines admissibility.

In the trial period, staff look for clues to positive response to the environment. These may include a decrease in aggressive behaviour, pacing or agitation; better nutritional intake and/or improvements in sleep pattern.

Family input complements the admission process. Families must feel secure that admission is in their relative's best interest. If an individual is assessed as a good candidate for Le Chez Nous but the family disagrees, the individual is not admitted.

PHYSICAL SPACE

Le Chez Nous' physical design incorporated existing structures and required only minor remodeling. A rarely used lounge became a kitchen, dining area and living room. A hairdressing shop was relocated, freeing space for a multipurpose service room. Door hardware was installed for additional security. New furniture, enhanced lighting, fresh paint and wallpaper completed the desired ambiance.

During Le Chez Nous' design and development stage, it was helpful to exercise the home analogy. One question we posed was: *"How is the division of labour structured in a home?"* Managing a home requires the exercise of many talents and most family members develop skills in several areas. Accordingly, our staffing model allows employees to perform various duties in housekeeping, dietary and activities. As we expect family members to pull together to fulfill their assignment, staff are also encouraged to rely on each other to complete their tasks. This doesn't, however, preclude the need to accommodate the many disruptions common to the nature of the unit. Resident care is always given at the expense of other tasks.

"Do homes run on schedules?" Homes may have routines but most do not have schedules. We extend our routines accordingly. Bath times and mealtimes are now more flexible. If a resident chooses to eat outside of a regular time, his or her meal is reheated and served later.

Le Chez Nous' design attempts to recreate the easygoing informality we enjoy in our own home. The kitchen is the favoured room for visiting family and friends and they are encouraged to make and serve themselves coffee and snacks. To promote congregation, the kitchen and day living areas are combined. Baking is a regular activity and residents enjoy participating in food preparation, an activity that promotes reminiscing and stimulates conversation. There is a self-serve cookie jar on a shelf within easy reach, and residents have free access to the refrigerator. They often open the refrigerator doors out of curiosity, but unfortunately, they lack the cognitive skill to serve themselves.

"How do we furnish a home?" Considering the residents' past lifestyles, we sought sturdiness, comfort and familiarity in wooden tables and chairs. Families also participate in furnishing rooms to their relative's taste. Working outdoors was a constant feature of many of our residents' lives. A wall of windows facing the inner court draws in the environment and contributes to a sense of intimacy with nature. Lithographs on other walls depict old time harvest scenes. A variety of plants accent the area.

As in a private home, there is free access to the outside in our enclosed, ground level inner court where residents are protected from wind, glare and temperature extremes. A circuitous path winds by a small elevated garden, fountain and pond. Several rest benches, trees, shrubs and a fragrant garden serve as cues to wayfinding. The inner court is used in spring, summer and fall. A smaller enclosed patio is used in all seasons.

Adequate lighting is important. Incandescent lights in the kitchen, dining and living room area were installed for resident comfort. In residents' rooms, staff and residents can choose between incandescent and fluorescent illumination. Hallway lights are evenly distributed to reduce shadows and glare.

The traditional nursing station—inconsistent with our concept of a home—was omitted in Le Chez Nous' design. The nursing staff chart is kept in the dining room. Files are stored in a locked cupboard, as are pharmaceuticals.

STAFFING

Staffing is a critical feature of an alternative care unit. How staff are selected, how their roles are defined and how they are supported in caregiving efforts determine the success or failure of the unit.

Staffing Pattern

Le Chez Nous' staffing pattern consists of an RN unit coordinator and a nursing aide on weekdays, and two nursing aides on staggered shifts on evenings. The unit coordinator is accountable to the Foyer's nursing supervisor but Le Chez Nous nursing aides are accountable to the Le Chez Nous unit coordinator. On evenings, nights and weekends, when the unit coordinator is absent, Le Chez Nous' nursing aides work with the Foyer registered nurse in charge. Night shifts in the Foyer are covered by one RN and two nursing aides and Le Chez Nous serves as the base for nursing functions during the night. This allows close resident supervision when staffing is at a minimum.

Generic Staffing

One method of effectively distributing personnel and resources is through generic staffing. Generic staffing means that caregivers chosen to work in Le Chez Nous assume some tasks and responsibilities traditionally assigned to other departments. Our nursing budget could not accommodate two nursing staff positions on 24 hour duty, the coverage required to operate Le Chez Nous safely. Therefore, housekeeping duties and some dietary and activity functions were transferred from their respective departments to Le Chez Nous. This transfer of hours and tasks allowed appropriate staff covering to meet fluctuating resident needs. Sweeping, dusting, snack preparation and one-on-one activities are now carried out by Chez Nous staff. It is the Chez Nous unit coordinator's responsibility to ensure that all non-nursing tasks are performed to each departmental supervisor's standards.

We favor the generic staffing concept for several reasons. Chez Nous residents are exposed to fewer personnel; this reduces traffic flow, reduces noxious stimuli, and lessens confusion and agitation. Residents see the same faces, hear the same voices, experience the same routines, see the same smiles and feel the same reassurance from caregivers. This enhances feelings of security and tempers emotional stimulation levels. When residents are awake, staff give basic health care but they also involve residents in performing simple environmental tasks that are part of everyday life such as setting and clearing tables, sweeping floors and folding linen. This approach helps staff accomplish their duties, fulfills some of the residents' programming needs, and validates their contribution to their home's operation. Generic staffing also mitigates regimentation by allowing flexible scheduling. The more complex environmental tasks that residents are unable to participate in are effected when they sleep or rest.

Generic staffing occasionally serves as a safety valve. When staff experience stress in coping with difficult behaviours, they can seek refuge in 15 to 20 minutes of time out performing routine environmental tasks that are emotionally less demanding.

Caregiver Profile

Coping with the demands of caring for persons with dementia presents unique challenges for caregivers. Careful selection of personnel counts as a major determinant of success in ensuring empathetic and compassionate response to resident needs. Selection is partially based on one's possession of desirable attributes or characteristics. The following profile is representative of Le Chez Nous caregivers. They:

- have easy going dispositions;
- are creative problem solvers;
- seek humour in daily events;
- respond calmly to catastrophic reactions;
- adapt easily to an unstructured environment;
- are people oriented rather than task oriented;
- work well with minimal supervision yet exercise their obligations to a team approach to caregiving;
- can readily adapt to immediate and sometimes dangerous behavioural changes.

Approaches

Probably the most valuable characteristic to seek in selecting staff to work with dementia victims is the ability to problem solve. The key feature in effective problem solving lies in selecting appropriate approaches to resident care. Coons and Weaverdyck (1986) offer a repertoire of techniques that staff can use. These include gentle cajoling, affectionate encouragement, diversion, humour, and withdrawing to return later to try again. These techniques are consistent with our concept of behaviour ownership. When staff accept that a moderately or severely impaired resident cannot own his or her behaviour, they free themselves of restrictive and failure-prone approaches such as coercion, rigid application of routines and habitual use of uniform methods such as controlling and enforcing conformity and obedience.

Burnout

Although staff burnout is a potential workplace hazard in an alternative care unit, simple safeguards can mitigate the risks. In Le Chez Nous, staff are allowed a trial employment period during which they and the employer determine their suitability for full time or part time work. The trial period contains a proviso that allows staff to return to their previous job if their experience is not positive.

Unit size plays an important role in stress management. With a small group of employees, irritants surface faster but are handled sooner; decision-making is enhanced and changes relating to resident care and quality of worklife are easily initiated. The responsibility for managing change rests mostly with the individual staff member. However, if one experiences a problem, it is quickly felt by others; group awareness then stimulates the need for timely resolutions. Regular case conferences allow opportunities to voice concerns and help to determine appropriate response to specific problems. A teamwork approach also serves to boost morale.

Resources

Le Chez Nous benefits from the expertise of various health professionals. A local physician visits the Foyer once a week and sees Le Chez Nous residents requiring medical care. A geriatrician is available for consultation on program development and staff education. A psychogeriatric nurse consultant visits on a regular basis as do a music therapist and an occupational therapist. We also turn to a regional psychogeriatric assessment unit for advice on behavioural management issues and for occasional temporary admission of Chez Nous residents with behavioural problems requiring intensive therapy. These services are available to all long term care facilities in our area.

Our experience with Le Chez Nous brought to light a variety of unmet resident needs. Integration of confused and lucid individuals tended to obscure behaviour problems. Within the general population, the nature and extent of the requirements of the confused elderly were not evident. Segregation exposed several needs, in particular our need for the services of a social worker, a recreational therapist, a behaviour therapist and a separate and specific program of activities.

■ ■ ■

ENVIRONMENT

Some aspects of Le Chez Nous experience were unsuccessful. Most pertained to the physical structure.

Water taps were a problem. Occasionally, residents would open water taps and wander away, leaving sinks to overflow. The problem was resolved by installing spring loaded handles that close upon release of hand pressure.

The water fountain in the inner courtyard proved a source of intense interest for residents but their safety was compromised when they approached the small pool out of curiosity. The fountain water jet was disconnected, eliminating the distraction.

While entry and exit to the unit must allow ease of transit for staff and visitors, Le Chez Nous residents must be deterred from leaving. Ordinary door hardware and a disguised bolt action lock requiring simultaneous use of both hands to open the door discourage moderately and severely impaired residents but do not deter mildly impaired residents. We are still seeking a satisfactory solution to this problem.

CONCLUSION

As we approach a new millennium and experience a shift in the demographic curve towards longer lifespans, the percentage of elderly in the general population will rise dramatically. A high risk of cognitive impairment accompanies longevity, especially in the 85 and over age group (Health and Welfare Canada, 1990). Initiatives are required now to ensure health care environments can adjust to these needs.

Our model offers several attractive features:

- it is adaptable to many existing long term care environments;
- it can be implemented with homegrown talent and expertise;
- it can be developed without government funding yet comply with standards of care;
- it can become a focus of community involvement and a source of community pride.

For the smaller long term care facility, Le Chez Nous' conceptual framework offers an innovative, practical and cost effective model that enjoys a wide range of application yet meets present and future accommodation needs of individuals with cognitive losses.

ACKNOWLEDGMENTS

The authors wish to thank the staff of Le Chez Nous and the following individuals who contributed to this chapter: Marcie Plaitin, Recreational Therapy student; Darcy Mosquin, Pharmacist; Gerard Rioux, Social Worker; Simone Comte, Unit Coordinator; Gail Snider, Head Nurse; and Muriel Deleurme, typist.

REFERENCES

Coons, D.H. (1987a). *Designing a residential care unit for persons with dementia.* Prepared for the Congressional Office of Technology Assessment, 1–39.

Coons, D.H. (1987b). Training staff to work in special Alzheimer's units. *American Journal of Alzheimer's Care and Related Disorders and Research,* 2(5), 6–12.

Coons, D.H. & Weaverdyck, S.E. (1986). Wesley Hall: A residential unit for persons with Alzheimer's disease and related disorders. *Physical and Occupational Therapy in Geriatrics,* 4(3), 29–51.

Hall, G., Kirschling, M.V. & Todd, S. (1986). Sheltered freedom: an Alzheimer's unit in an ICF. *Geriatric Nursing,* 7(3), 132–137.

Health and Welfare Canada (1990). Services to elderly residents with mental health problems in long term care facilities.

Kromm, D. & Kromm, Y.H.N. (1985). A nursing unit designed for Alzheimer's disease patients at Newton Presbyterian Manor. *Nursing Homes,* 34(3), 30–31.

Mace, N. (1987). Programs and services which specialize in the care of persons with dementing illnesses—issues and options. *The American Journal of Alz-heimer's Care and Research,* 2(3), 10–17.

Novick, L. (1988). Coping with the intermingling of the lucid and confused. *Healthcare Management Forum, 1(1),* 18–22.

Weaverdyck, S. & Coons, D.H. (1988). Designing a dementia residential care unit: Addressing cognitive changes with the Wesley Hall model. In: G. Gutman & N. Blackie (Eds.) *Housing the Very Old* (pp. 63–85). Burnaby, B.C. The Gerontology Research Centre, Simon Fraser University.

25

Sexuality of Institutionalized Older Adults

A COMPLEX DILEMMA

D.H. Rapelje and B.W. Molloy

Aging is regarded as a demon that heralds approaching death, whereas sex is equated with life. That is why sexuality is especially significant for an older person's morale—it is an affirmation of life and a denial of death. (See Thomas H. Walz and Nancee S. Blum, Sexual Health in Later Life. *Boston, MA: D.C. Heath & Company, 1987, p. 1.)*

There are certain things in life that we value so highly that to deprive people of them or to fail to help people attain them when we can is a violation of our ethical duty. Sexuality is one of those things. Sexuality may be defined as any activity that satisfies desire. It can include hugging, talking, fantasy, touching, masturbation and intercourse. Although sexual activity is healthy, health preserving and contributes to our quality of life, the way sexuality is repressed in many long term care facilities is counterproductive to these beliefs. Older adults who live in these institutions have experienced many losses and suffer from illnesses that have robbed them of their independence. Although many can still enjoy their sexuality and may wish to express it, they are prevented from doing so for a wide variety of reasons.

Our society clings to certain myths about sex: "sex is only for the young," "older adults don't have sexual desires or needs," "geriatric sex is disgusting." Although we are sexual beings throughout the life cycle, society's attitudes restrict the expression of sexuality in old age. Society perpetuates the belief that sex is for the young, and older people are asexual beings. The only type of sexuality that is widely accepted and condoned by society is heterosexual sex in younger adults for pleasure or reproduction.

In the health care system, there is a prevailing sense of fatalism towards older adults. Aging is often regarded as an incurable disease by health care professionals who are committed to "fight the war" against illness. For many, anything less than a "cure" or "victory" in this ongoing battle is unacceptable. Therefore, the elderly with chronic degenerative diseases, suffering from cognitive and functional impairments which are "incurable," are often viewed as "hopeless cases," "old crocks," or "gomers." These myths associated with aging prejudice our attitudes towards the elderly and affect the way older adults are treated.

THE PROBLEMS

A study carried out by the Saskatchewan Senior Citizens' Provincial Council entitled *Love, Sexuality and Aging in Nursing Homes and Public Housing in Saskatchewan,* published in 1984, offers insight into the issue of sexuality in the institutionalized elderly. In the introduction, the authors refer to Butler and Lewis, *Sex After Sixty* (New York: Harper & Row, 1976, p. 114), which helps set the theme of this article:

> *The five percent of persons over sixty five [in the United States] who live in homes for the aging, nursing homes, chronic disease hospitals and other Long Term Care institutions have a very painful problem. In general they are denied the opportunity for any private social sexual life of their own. Visitors are in full view of roommates and staff, and can be overheard by them. Most people in institutions are widowed, and a few are divorced or single. But even those who have marital partners are seldom able to share conjugal visits, where the patient is provided a private time and place with his or her spouse. One older man described how he locked himself and his wife in the bathroom on one of her visits so that they could make love. There was no other place to get away from the other patients and the nursing staff.*

Intimacy of any kind between unmarried patients, even hugging or kissing or holding hands, are frowned on despite the fact that they are consenting adults. Even persons who, understandably, resort to masturbation because they have no other sexual outlet, run the risk of being discovered and reprimanded like children.

Nowhere is the restriction on the liberty of sexual expression as severe as in the institutionalized, dependent older adult. The prejudices of society, families and health care professionals restrict the freedom of older institutionalized adults to demonstrate or enjoy their sexuality. Staff attitudes limit the options available for sexual expression. Institutions often discourage sexual expression or intimacy because they fear it will damage the facility's reputation. The public and families expect the institutions to protect the residents from sexual activity, assault and personal injury and, as a result, institutions are concerned about legal liability.

Older adults in long term care settings are particularly at risk of suffering because of these prejudices. They have lost their autonomy and are bound by the rules of these organizations and facilities which are often managed by individuals who are prejudiced against older adults. Admission to long term care is often involuntary and traumatic and rarely occurs with the active participation of the person. The move to an institution is perceived as complete loss of independence, with loss of control, privacy, personal possessions and freedom of sexual expression. Many view these institutions as places where the elderly are warehoused before they die, ante-rooms or atria to the funeral home.

Lack of privacy or provision for intimacy in these settings may be an insurmountable barrier for many residents to express their sexuality or satisfy their sexual needs. Those older adults who live in homes for the aged, nursing homes, chronic care hospitals and other long term care hospitals are generally denied the opportunity for any private sexual life of their own. Residents often live in two- or four-bed rooms which afford no privacy. For safety reasons, bedroom doors cannot be locked, even for those in single rooms, so the feeling of being secure or comfortable in a sexual situation is not possible. Visitors are in full view of roommates and staff and can be overheard by them.

Most of the institutionalized older adults are women who are widowed, divorced or single. But even those who have spouses are seldom able to enjoy any intimacy because of the lack of private time or space. Residents who attempt to dress attractively and wear make up, to look and feel attractive to the opposite sex, may be ostracized and ridiculed by other residents and staff.

Family members often discourage displays of sexuality or intimacy between residents, even if it involves consenting adults. This is often disguised as "What would dad think about mother doing this?" In some cases they may be concerned about loss of their inheritance. In other cases they cannot or will not view their parents as sexual beings and expect a parent to remain celibate and faithful to a deceased spouse forever. Staff and administrators are often criticized by families for not stopping a marriage between two consenting residents of a home. In another situation, when one partner is institutionalized and the other is not, there is often concern when the institutionalized person becomes romantically or sexually involved with another resident. In these cases the solutions are extremely complex, especially in trying to establish competency for intimacy among the residents.

THE SOLUTIONS

If we believe that sexual activity is healthy, health preserving and contributes to our quality of life, then we are failing to plan for it, and are even actively discouraging it in the institutionalized elderly now. These attitudes deprive residents of basic liberties and human rights to express their sexuality, and negatively affect their quality of life. In many cases we do not have drugs or treatments to cure or ameliorate the decline that these cognitively impaired older adults experience. Yet we can enhance their quality of life and sense of personhood by acknowledging their sexuality and allowing them to express it without fear of ridicule or punishment.

However, there are a number of obstacles that we currently face in permitting institutionalized older adults to express and enjoy their sexuality and fulfill their sexual needs. Solutions must be implemented at many different levels. First, society's attitudes and perceptions of older adults must change. Society must accept that we are sexual beings throughout the life cycle and that older adults have sexual needs. When a person goes into an institution, his/her need for privacy, a drink, enjoying pets, hobbies or sex does not cease. Society must accept that sexuality in the institutionalized older adult is not aberrant or abnormal behaviour.

Second, the health care team and management must recognize that older adults have sexual needs that must be considered. Activities should be designed to allow residents to express their sexuality in a non-threatening way. Petting rooms which provide privacy and comfort for residents or their families should be provided. In most long term care facilities, one third of the residents are men and two thirds are women. Many women cannot find partners who can consent to intimacy. Creative solutions will be needed for these problems.

The way we handle problems sends out powerful messages to families and other residents about our attitude towards sexuality. When residents expose themselves, masturbate in public, grab, pinch or make sexual advances to staff, they may be sending out important messages that are often ignored or misinterpreted. Calling the daughter to warn her that if her father continues with this behaviour, he will be asked to leave, or zombifying him with neuroleptics and/or sedatives, will not solve the problem.

PERSONAL VALUES MUST BE EXAMINED

Finally, we need to examine our own attitudes towards sexuality in older adults and explore these matters personally to increase our understanding and resolve any prejudice so that we may better meet the needs of the institutionalized elderly. We need to improve the environment and provide an opportunity for privacy. We need to develop guidelines to deal with these problems and become more relaxed and open minded to counsel concerned family members about these issues. Education is essential to increase awareness among the residents, their family, volunteers and health care professionals. There is a need for more information and research into this area. There are only five studies that have examined the sexual behaviour of residents in long term care institutions. We have a long way to go to achieve liberty and equality for the institutionalized elderly and the journey only starts when we examine our own attitudes and values.

As Alex Comfort states in his article "Sexuality and the Institutionalized Patient," "The chief sexual problem of the institutionalized...is the projected anxiety, embarrassment and unease of staff—arising mostly from not knowing anything to say or do which might be helpful." It is obvious that the challenge is for administration, on behalf of the staff, residents and families, to take on this leadership role.

A paper entitled "Sexuality Throughout Life: An Unrecognized Need," prepared by the Niagara Interdisciplinary Advocacy Group regarding Aging and Sexuality in 1991, states the following on *What You Can Do to Change the Situation*:

> **All people** *must examine their own values and attitudes towards sexuality in the elderly.*
>
> **All people** *must be aware of the broad range and diversity of sexual expression in older persons.*
>
> **All people** *must be informed on how people's values and attitudes may influence, positively or negatively, acceptance of sexual behaviours of others.*
>
> **All people** *must be empowered to express their sexuality while respecting the rights of others.*
>
> **The elderly** *must be informed of their rights to intimacy, to sexual expression and to the opportunity to fulfill their needs.*
>
> **Advocates** *for older adults must be aware of the need for environments that facilitate the expression of sexuality.*
>
> **Formal care providers and informal caregivers** *(e.g., family, neighbours, friends, volunteers) must be sensitive to people's ongoing sexual feelings and needs for expression of sexuality.*
>
> **Educators** *at all levels must recognize and convey the full spectrum of sexuality throughout the life cycle. Curricula must include the attitudes, values and knowledge needed to deal with the complexity of issues surrounding sexuality and the elderly.*
>
> **Policy makers** *(e.g., trustees, legislators, administrators) must acknowledge the right to sexual expression as an integral part of human rights.*
>
> **Institutions** *must incorporate these principles in their care and service programs.*
>
> **Researchers** *must establish a body of knowledge that identifies facts, myths, assumptions, perceptions, beliefs, values and attitudes about sexuality in the elderly.*
>
> **Research** *must be conducted to demonstrate the effects of sexual behaviour on health, well-being and quality of life.*

26

Granny Flats in Canada

N. Michael Lazarowich

The proportion of elderly persons in Western countries is increasing, and it is expected that by the year 2030, 20 percent of the population will be age 65+. Given that currently only about 10 percent of the population is 65+, this doubling will have serious physical, social and economic implications.

There are few housing options available for the growing number of seniors who are still fairly independent, healthy and mobile and do not require or find it difficult to maintain a large family home. Institutional alternatives may be one of the few options available to seniors. However, in recent years sociologists and psychologists have found that institutionalization can have negative psychological effects on the elderly. In fact, for some elderly persons the psychological stress of entering an institution may be fatal. Furthermore, institutionalization is an expensive economic burden on the members of the work force. As an increasingly larger number of persons retire, fewer workers are left to pay the cost of social welfare. Thus, for economic and psychological reasons institutionalization does not appear to be the best method of housing the elderly. Instead, governments within the last few years have encouraged the establishment of community based services which permit the elderly to remain a part of the community for a longer period of time.

The Granny Flat is a form of housing that facilitates the provision of community and, especially, family based services. The unit is ideally suited for that segment of the population which is no longer able to be totally self-sufficient and yet does not require extensive medical care and supervision. Generally speaking, the Granny Flat is most suitable for the young old (age 65–74) and the middle old (age 75–84). It is housing for independent and mobile pensioned people. The idea is appealing because the unit is located on a relative's or other person's property (host's property), is separate from the main house, connected to the main house utilities, movable and about

50 sq. m. in size. They are government or privately financed, are built for 1 or 2 persons and have a livingroom, kitchen, bedroom and bathroom. The granny flat concept, an innovative housing option for the elderly, commenced as a program in 1975 in Victoria, Australia. The program has grown rapidly in Victoria so that in 1989 there were approximately 2,140 rental units in the metropolitan Melbourne area alone. The Australian experience has fostered granny flat programs in New Zealand, many states in the United States and several provinces in Canada. Small attached houses for elderly, "granny flats," although not fostered by the Australian experience, have been used in Britain for many years....

Granny flats have, for the most part, been successful. Responses that have been made and are being made to changing conditions indicate that the prospects are good for granny flats in the 1990's.

■ ■ ■

The development of granny flats in Canada was due to the efforts of two major actors: Canada Mortgage and Housing Corporation (CMHC) and the Ontario Ministry of Housing (OMOH) with each actor playing a variety of roles. This paper examines and evaluates the roles played by these major actors in the introduction, development and future of granny flats. In this paper, granny flats or garden suites or portable living units for seniors (PLUS), as granny flats are sometimes called in Canada, are defined as a small, detached, self-contained, movable house with all the amenities for one or two persons and located on the property of a relative or another person.

EARLY RESEARCH

The "granny flat" concept as a separate living space for an elderly person has historical precedents, for example, in Great Britain (Tinker, 1976) and in Canada with Old Order Mennonites' (Waterloo County in the Province of Ontario) use of "doddy houses." The modern movable units have only been used to any extent in Victoria, Australia, where a large scale and successful program was started in 1975.

The Australian program has created a lot of interest, Canada included. However, it was not until early 1982 that the first granny flat feasibility study in Canada (Lazarowich and Haley, 1982) was completed. This study examined the British granny annex and Australian granny flat programs, and assessed the key physical, financial, regulatory, taxation and administrative issues that needed to be addressed in a successful implementation of a granny flat program. The study found that the Australian concept was transferable to Canada and specifically to Ontario in technical terms, planning and other regulations.

This study was followed by a marketing study on granny flats (Lazarowich, 1983, 1984a) where the degree of acceptance by potential occupants and host families, amount of demand, obstacles to be overcome in acceptance, granny flat designs and layouts preferred by the elderly were examined. In this random, stratified sample study, 75% of rural elderly and 60% of urban elderly would live in a granny flat if it was available; 80% of rural host families and 50% of urban host families (host families are families that would have a granny flat on their property), would have a granny flat on their lot (Lazarowich, 1984a). This study included many recommendations on marketing, regulations, design and demonstration that proved a basis for subsequent initiatives by CMHC, Canadian Manufactured Housing Institute (CMHI) and OMOH.

CMHC AND CMHI DEMONSTRATION PROJECT

Following a 1984 presentation (based on the marketing study) by Lazarowich to CMHI, the industry proposed to CMHC that the two agencies sponsor a Canada wide granny flat demonstration project but two federal government spending freezes delayed the start of the program. In 1987–88 garden suite (as granny flats are called by the manufactured housing industry) demonstrations were held at 30 locations in ten provinces. Close to 500,000 persons viewed the units. There was "a lively interest in and very positive acceptance of the concept. Visitors' questions and comments tended to focus on—zoning restrictions, installation costs and the availability of units" (DPA, 1989). Installed garden suites have been estimated by CMHI to cost between $30,000 in Saskatchewan and Manitoba to $37,000 in British Columbia and Ontario (DPA, 1989).

OMOH DEMONSTRATION PROJECT

On completion of the 1984 market demand study, Lazarowich submitted to the Housing Conservation Unit of the Ontario Ministry of Municipal Affairs and Housing a proposal for financial support of a granny flat demonstration project in the City of Waterloo (Lazarowich, 1984b). At that time the granny flat concept was one of a number of new housing options considered in the Ministry's study of residential intensification (Klein and Sears, 1983) but it did not have high priority.

Consideration of the proposal and increased public interest in the concept placed higher priority on the concept. In early 1985 the Ministry sponsored a 12 unit comprehensive PLUS (Portable Living Units for Seniors) project in the City of Waterloo (55,000 population) and Ottawa-Carleton and Sudbury (located in northern Ontario) Regional Municipalities. The PLUS project was designed as a market rent program and did not involve rental subsidies. Rents averaged $360 per month in 1985 (plus utilities) and were based on CHMC's market rent survey for a one bedroom apartment. The project was carried out between 1985 and 1988 and involved installation, occupancy, several relations and project assessment.

An attractive architecturally designed modular unit of about $70m^2$ for one or two persons was used. The installed units cost between $46,400 and $61,300 (Dillon, 1988). The units were of high cost because of low volume and deliberate emphasis on attractive, good quality units to avoid tarnishing the image of a good concept with a "cheap" looking unit. Occupants, based on familial relationship and age 55 years and older, were selected by local working committees.

Temporary use bylaws provisions in the Planning Act were used to locate the units on host family properties for three year periods.

The social assessment showed that almost all occupants and hosts were very satisfied with this form of housing (DPA Group, 1987). The real estate appraisal study showed PLUS units had no negative effects on re-sale value, and minimal negative effects on use and enjoyment of adjacent properties (Davis et al., 1986). The planning/regulatory and legal assessment suggested that licenses be used by municipalities to reduce time used by the public notification process (Weir and Foulds, nd). The modular system of building was used in producing the units. The units performed well technically. No major improvements to the design and construction were required. The main issues were the standards and regulations for the installation process (Dillon, 1988). The market demand assessment is discussed in the national survey section.

OTHER CANADIAN DEMONSTRATION PROJECTS

Based on the CMHC and CMHI and OMOH demonstration projects, demonstration projects have been developed in Newfoundland and Alberta.

The Newfoundland and Labrador Housing Corporation had a successful demonstration project with the CMHC garden suite project. Three units were built under non-profit housing in Newfoundland. A garden suite program is scheduled to be introduced in 1990, contingent on CMHC funding becoming available.

The Alberta Department of Municipal Affairs introduced the garden suites pilot project in 1989. The project is scheduled for 3 years and is similar to the Ontario demonstration project. Five units have been installed and a preliminary evaluation of the project is currently being done. It is anticipated that a full program will be developed in two years.

NATIONAL SURVEY

In 1988–89 Gallup Canada Inc. conducted a national garden suite market for CMHC. Approximately 2.66 million properties are potentially available for garden suites across Canada; 213,000 host families were *very* likely to install a garden suite on their property; 45% of the market lies in rural communities of 10,000 or fewer residents and 27% in large urban centres. This national market survey provided further corroboration to CMHC, CMHI and OMOH that there was a strong demand for granny flats across Canada.

GRANNY FLAT PROGRAM ISSUES

The demonstration projects and evaluations have indicated a strong consumer acceptance of the granny flat concept by occupants, hosts, neighbors and regulators. There is a strong market demand and a willingness by hosts to have a granny flat on their properties. Granny flats were found not to have any negative effects on re-sale values of homes. Units are technologically sound and the industry is willing and able to provide quality units.

There are four issues that need to be resolved for granny flats to become a full program. These are: financial, regulatory, information/marketing and political will issues. The financial issue is one that places financing of the building and renting of granny flats on par with other forms of housing available for seniors. The regulatory issue involves regulation of the flat itself on a lot and secondly, regulation of occupancy of the flat. Information and marketing issues involve providing information to sponsors and developers of flats on how to develop and manage the flats, information to potential occupants and hosts on the program and how to acquire a flat. Marketing involves "selling" the concept to municipalities, to local sponsors, and to other implementing agencies. Municipal acceptance and municipal political will are, in the final analysis, the critical factors in making a full granny flat program work.

RECENT DEVELOPMENTS AND FUTURE PROSPECTS

There have been recent developments that are geared to solving the four issues identified above. They provide optimism that a full fledged granny flat program will develop in Canada.

At the federal level, CMHC is being encouraged (DPA, 1989) and is seriously considering expanding its seniors' social housing program (which includes seniors' apartments and coop residences for seniors) to include granny flats. The acceptance of granny flats as a form of housing for seniors would make granny flats eligible for rent supplements, non-profit housing and its cost sharing in unit construction (70% federal and 30% provincial). A trial program should be considered with a review after 3–4 years. If all goes well a full program could be possible.

In 1989, CMHC guaranteed chattel mortgages for garden suites. This was a breakthrough in financing of garden suites because previous financing was only available in the form of consumer loans (and not guaranteed by CMHC). CMHC guarantees increase the amount of financing available from conventional lenders for garden suites. The limitation with the CMHC chattel mortgage guarantee is that it is only available for the first owner and only for as long as the owner lives in the garden suite. When CMHC approves garden suites as a form of seniors' housing then the chattel mortgage guarantee will have to be extended to the garden suite per se. These CMHC initiatives will facilitate the overcoming of the financial obstacles facing garden suite programs.

The Ontario Ministry of Housing also sees its role as facilitator in granny flat programs. The Ministry will facilitate granny flats by providing information and communication and by making it easier for municipalities to regulate granny flats.

The communication/information packages would be geared to municipalities to provide guidelines on how to institute, manage and control granny flats. For inquiring consumers, the communication/information package would provide details on the program.

The regulatory assessment of the granny flats demonstration suggested that the Municipal Act be changed to allow municipalities to issue licenses to reduce public notification time and thus install the units sooner. Licensing may not be attractive because licensing was devised as an instrument to regulate businesses and not housing. Further, the licensing power of municipalities is under review by the Ministry. An option is to allow licensing of granny flats and use the review process that is in place to review and resolve the issue of licensing housing.

The temporary use bylaw in the Planning Act needs to be streamlined so that public notification time is shortened and the units installed sooner. The three year period of the bylaw is too short and is stressful to occupants because of the frequency of renewals. Perhaps the time of the bylaw should be extended to seven years to reflect the length of expected occupancy of Australian granny flats (DPA, 1989). Based on the Australian experience, a special act or special legislation which would permit granny flats "as of right" if certain conditions such as lot size, siting, and neighborhood density were met, would be the best method to legislate their use. Because of the time it would take to enact such legislation, and the political climate, such legislation does not appear to be appropriate at this time in Ontario.

Guidelines on such items as conditions, timing of removal of a unit, siting, and standards need to be provided. The additions of such details in the Planning Act might not be attractive to planners but there is a precedent in the details that are provided for subdivision agreements in the Planning Act.

The other type of regulation that the municipalities will have to consider is regulation of occupancy. The control of occupancy in boarding houses in Ontario based on familial relationship has recently been struck down in the courts (the ruling was based on the Canadian Charter of Rights). Occupancy can likely be more readily controlled on the basis of age. The Charter and provincial statutes favor disadvantaged groups such as elderly and handicapped persons and thus occupancy of granny flats could be controlled on the basis of age.

Innovativeness and political will at the municipal level are encouraging signs for granny flat programs.

The Regional Municipality of Haldimand-Norfolk has amended its official plan and the local official plans so that granny flats are "as of right" in hamlets and agricultural zones. This is appropriate for this primarily agricultural region.

The Regional Municipality of Ottawa-Carleton has been interested and committed to the concept of granny flats since 1984 and has participated in the PLUS demonstration project. The Region has recently attempted to institute granny flats as non-profit housing. In April 1990, a report prepared by regional planners and adopted by regional council strongly recommended that the regional and municipalities' official plans be amended to permit granny flats and to lobby government to provide active assistance in implementing granny flats. There must be strong support of the initiatives taken by the regional municipalities of Ottawa-Carleton and Haldimand-Norfolk and their local municipalities. Data must be systematically collected on the development and maintenance of their programs. As these innovative municipalities develop a track record, other municipalities will join in.

In summary, all the requirements appear to be in place for a full granny flat program to develop in Ontario which can lead to matching programs in other provinces.

The enthusiasm, excitement, commitment and leadership provided in the CMHC and OMOH demonstration projects has made them a success as demonstration projects. Continued and sustained commitment is being provided in the financial and regulatory spheres and at the municipal political-will level. Housing industry initiatives are facilitated by these developments. These developments provide for optimistic prospects for granny flat programs in Ontario in the 1990's.

REFERENCES

Davis, Hicks and O'Brien Ltd. (1986). Report of PLUS Project Effect on Property Values. Toronto: Ontario Ministry of Housing

Dillon Consulting Engineers. (1988). Portable Living Units for Seniors— Technological Research and Assessment. Toronto: Housing Conservation Unit, Ontario Ministry of Housing.

DPA Group Inc. (1987). Social Assessment Component of Portable Living Units for Seniors. Toronto: Housing Conservation Unit, Ontario Ministry of Housing.

DPA Group Inc. (1989). Report on garden suites: An evaluation report with suggestions about implementation. Ottawa: Canada Mortgage and Housing Corporation.

Gallup Canada Inc. (1989). Garden Suites Demonstration, National Survey. Ottawa: Canada Mortgage and Housing Corporation.

Klein & Sears. (1983). Study of residential intensification and rental housing conservation. Toronto: Housing Conservation Unit, Ontario Ministry of Municipal Affairs and Housing.

Lazarowich, M. and Haley, B. W. (1982). Granny flats: Their practicality and implementation. Ottawa, Ontario: Canada Mortgage and Housing Corporation.

Lazarowich, M. (1983). The potential use of manufactured homes for granny flats. Ottawa, Ontario: Canada Mortgage and Housing Corporation.

Lazarowich, M. (1984a). Market assessment for granny flats: A consolidated report. Ottawa, Ontario: Canada Mortgage and Housing Corporation.

Lazarowich, M. (1984b). Proposal to the Ontario Ministry of Municipal Affairs and Housing for financial support of a granny flat demonstration project. Waterloo: School of Urban and Regional Planning, University of Waterloo.

Tinker, A. (1976). Housing the elderly in the community: A study of granny annexes. London: The City University.

Weir and Foulds. (nd). Evaluation Part 4: Planning regulatory and legal assessment. Toronto: Housing Conservation Unit, Ontario Ministry of Housing.

27

Growing Old in a Winter City

A CHALLENGE TO INDEPENDENCE AND INDIVIDUALITY

Xenia Klinger-Zepic

INTRODUCTION

Architects and designers have an important role in understanding the special needs associated with growing old so that they can experiment with new ideas for housing and urban design that are more appropriate to those needs. Without these new ideas, it has become evident that living space designed for people in the prime of their physical and emotional lives will undermine independence and individuality in the later years.

The organization of living space—which covers everything from bedrooms, homes, backyards and neighbourhoods to parks, downtowns and metropolitan regions—should begin with the question of who that space is to be designed for. More often it begins with an assumption, and that assumption does not usually include the elderly.

We have an enormous amount of housing space in Canada, the highest per capita in the world. We also have a high and growing proportion of elderly people in our population. Yet the needs of the elderly have not been taken into account. We built millions of acres of suburbia to house the baby boom generation, but we failed to take into account that baby boom parents would grow old, that people's needs would change, and that the design of our living space would have to change if that generation was going to enjoy their golden years.

Our northern climate adds to the stress of living and to the design challenge facing architects and urban planners in providing truly livable housing and cities for the elderly. This paper identifies specific problems that winter conditions impose on design for a population that is growing older in urban space designed for a younger generation. It also proposes specific ideas for minimizing the hardships of growing old in a winter city.

YOUNG HOUSING AND AGING OCCUPANTS

From the air, Canada looks like a young country. The cities are bright and fresh, and the housing stock is on average younger than the people living in it. That sounds like a positive factor, but it disguises an emerging housing crisis. This crisis has nothing to do with the age or condition of the built structure; rather it concerns the misfit between the housing and its occupants.

The majority of seniors in Canada live in privately owned single-family houses. Those houses are well looked after; they have generally been paid for and represent the reward for a life of hard work and sacrifice. Seniors want to live out their lives in familiar surroundings, but they often cannot. The house built originally for a young active family becomes unmanageable, its maintenance costs and its space become a burden. While there is a strong desire to remain in one's own house and to stay in the neighbourhood, many seniors are forced to move into less expensive and less satisfying accommodations for financial reasons or because they cannot cope with the problems caused by the physical inadequacy of those houses or the lack or services in the neighbourhood.

If those homes could be modified to suit the new needs of their now elderly owners, and if the new demands for higher levels of health and social services could be provided within the neighbourhood, the move to seniors' housing or to a more institutionalized setting could be postponed for many years.

In Canada, with our long winters, low temperatures, winds, ice and snow, any housing conditions that contribute to loneliness, isolation and depression are exaggerated. Extremely simple but essential things, such as visits from friends and relatives, which are taken for granted in more temperate climates, are often major undertakings for Canadians in winter. When special effort is required to cope with the adversities of winter, to get to church or just to the corner store, sometimes the only solution for seniors is to remain at home, imprisoned by the design of their shelter and community. This approach to winter may suit the physiology and lifestyle of bears, but it is not what most people have in mind for their retirement years.

Only recently has professional attention been focused on how cold climate affects human needs and lifestyle and how the built environment can amplify or reduce the negative effects of climate. Because much of modern housing and urban design philosophy and building practice derives from more southerly climates, we experience more hardship than necessary. However, to modify what we have built, now that so many of us are growing older and less able to cope with designs that are poorly adapted to winter climate, will require major co-operative efforts between governments, the building industry, the community at large, and seniors themselves.

If seniors are to retain their independence longer and remain in their own homes, substantial changes will be required in the organization and delivery of health care, community and social services, and transportation in the city and into suburban neighbourhoods.

Funding for home improvement programs to extend the livability of suburban housing for the elderly will be needed. Such renovations will remain the responsibility of homeowners, but new programs, grants and advisory assistance will have to be offered by governments. These public costs will be offset by reduced demand for new seniors' housing and by a growing number of happier and more independent seniors.

GROWING OLD IN THE COLD

Winter can be as beautiful as the postcards, but inevitably winter months mean more time spent indoors, substantially reducing the extent of our living space and reducing our mobility. Outdoor activities are more limited for seniors because of the cold and dark, and because outdoor space has not been designed to take into account seniors' growing sensitivity to the cold and less than optimal strength or co-ordination and balance. Slippery steps without handrails, doors, walkways and driveways drifted with snow, icy corrugated sidewalks, snowbanks created by municipal ploughs all too eager to keep vehicular traffic moving—all of these are discouraging and dangerous.

So the elderly, like the very young, tend to be confined indoors. Less active, and suffering perhaps from aggravating health problems, the elderly need to keep warm—a simple requirement, perhaps, but the cost of heating, often increased by poor insulation, non-functional room layout, and a high proportion of unused space, becomes a major concern of senior owners.

Fewer daylight hours and dull grey days, especially in regions with high precipitation, increase irritability and depression. While the solutions are not as easy as turning up the thermostat to get more heat, we should expect a little more creativity from architects and builders. The elderly, with diminished vision, are more affected by the reduced amount of sunlight. Levels of interior illumination have to be increased to compensate for the loss of vision. Even simpler things, such as the placement of lighting fixtures and their brightness levels, should be one of the concerns of designers doing renovations for seniors.

The individual house is the best and easiest place to introduce changes to improve the quality of life during the winter season. (For example, if getting up and down stairs is becoming a problem, then modifying the interior floor plan to put a bathroom and possibly a bedroom at ground level would be one solution to extend the livability of the house.)

Other less radical and expensive ideas involve rearranging and redesigning individual rooms for greater safety and comfort. Some of the more obvious ideas are

- replacing bathtubs with walk-in showers to reduce slips and falls;

- installing bathbars and rails for the same purpose;
- installing at least one window with a lower sill on a south or west wall to provide more light and sunshine, possibly to be used as a greenhouse;
- enclosing an existing porch or balcony to create a windbreak at the entrance or a greenhouse space where sunlight and flowers could be enjoyed during winter months;
- installing adequate lighting at all major changes of level in the house, such as stairways, and in the kitchen;
- replacing round door knobs, taps and other fixtures with those that are easier to operate, especially for those with arthritis or other problems of strength or dexterity;
- replacing narrow bathroom doors with 30-inch openings to facilitate access by wheelchairs or walkers.

Some owners will be able to undertake these improvements, but many will not be able to afford it. In these cases, special assistance and financial aid will have to be introduced. In Sweden, for example, financial assistance policies enable the elderly to remain independent as long as possible. The elderly are protected from inflation and rising home costs. Grants are available to adapt dwellings to the needs of disabled occupants, and improvement loans are available for owner-occupied housing. France has also initiated policies, including a home rehabilitation program directed primarily at the supply of adequate personal care facilities and heating.

Overall, however, too little public attention has been given to the potential of adapting homes to help older people to remain independent at home. The result has been that the housing problems of the elderly are often misinterpreted as problems of dependency; instead they should be regarded as deficiencies in housing and neighbourhood design that can be rectified. Instead of having to provide extra services, care and surveillance, we should be paying attention to those design factors that contribute to dependency and offer ways to adapt housing to minimize dependence.

STAYING PUT IN SUBURBIA

Most Canadian seniors live in single-family detached dwelling units that they own. Seniors now in their 60s likely bought their homes 30 years ago. Typically these houses have two floors, 3 or 4 bedrooms, a large family or recreation room, and a 2-car garage and are located in one of the many sprawling subdivisions built after the war. These houses were designed to accommodate a young family with a steady income and easy access to bank loans.

Increasingly, these houses are occupied by elderly couples or single people living on reduced incomes and facing growing maintenance costs and municipal taxes. In many cases the house, now free from mortgage, is the only asset and security seniors have. Their dilemma is whether to sell and move to different accommodation that meets their needs more closely, or to stay put and to try to overcome the living problems inherent in the house and neighbourhood. Only with changes in housing design and the introduction of more appropriate neighbourhood services and community support will they be able to stay put.

Most elderly Canadians would prefer to remain in their own neighbourhoods and to avoid the trauma of uprooting and moving out of familiar surroundings. But much of suburbia presents major problems to growing old with independence.

Isolation and loneliness, aggravated by winter immobility, could be relieved considerably by providing ways to enhance companionship. (For example, an additional self-contained unit within a single-family house could be rented out or provided to a live-in companion. The companion would of course also value privacy and independence.) Adapting the suburban house to meet this need for social contact will mean changing zoning bylaws and new sources of low-cost financing for construction. For seniors wanting to remain active, overseeing renovations and being a landlord or landlady could bring considerable satisfaction.

However, most municipal bylaws do not permit two self-contained units within a single-family dwelling. Changes in zoning can only be introduced if support is expressed by the majority of residents. Organizing seniors and neighbourhood support for such zoning changes would be another activity supporting independence and self-interest.

It is one thing to grow older in an area where shops, doctors' offices, churches and transit services are all a part of the neighbourhood. It is another matter to live in suburbs where such services are far removed from homes and may be accessible only by car. But that is where the majority of the elderly in Canada live.

The most difficult problem for seniors living in suburban areas is the lack of adequate transportation services. Spread out development at low densities may once have been the suburban dream, but now it just isolates those who cannot afford or do not want to drive. Many forms of transportation services have been experimented with to provide more convenient mobility in the suburbs, but they tend to be expensive to operate, and few communities have been willing to pay for them. However, with their increasing numbers, seniors should be taking action to modify the way their communities are organized and financed so that their changing needs can be met.

Convenient and safe walking is another consideration that has been neglected. Providing more shelters at transit stops, some of them heated, and well-lit pedestrian pathways should not involve major costs. Where there are no sidewalks along major roads, thought should be given to providing new pedestrian connections to shorten the distance and reduce walking time. Such pathways would be designed to link the neighbourhood together for the senior pedestrian—homes, community centre, fitness club, park and bus stop. The pathways should be protected from strong winds, surfaced with non-slippery pavement, well lit, and supplied with benches at appropriate intervals.

Besides transportation services and good pedestrian facilities, there is a growing need for new community services, health care centres and seniors' parks and recreation if seniors are to stay in suburbia. The reduced scope of activity in old age requires park facilities different from those required when most users are children.

Local parks should be designed to promote social interaction and not be totally activity-oriented. Simple pleasures are important: sitting in the sun, opportunities for birdfeeding, some ice skating, a cleared walking path under pine trees, and a place to sip a cup of tea or coffee in a winter garden would do a lot to make life less dreary in the winter. Again, suburban seniors will have to become politically active if they are to obtain these amenities, because no one else is seeing things from their perspective.

ALTERNATIVES TO SENIORS' PROJECTS

The move away from home and kin is unavoidable for some seniors, but there is growing dissatisfaction with existing forms of senior residences. Until recently this accommodation was provided in the form of high-rise complexes with limited amenities. Only the most expensive and exclusive residences offered an environment that was not institutional and that catered to the independent lifestyle of residents.

The new generation of seniors is used to a much higher standard of living. These seniors are demanding more living space and a wider variety of services, ranging from hair dressing to fitness centres and private dining rooms where they can entertain their guests. Traditional "old folks'" homes will soon become a thing of the past, as is happening throughout Scandinavia.

The current trend in housing for seniors is towards residential hotels and service flats, where much more flexibility in accommodation and facilities is provided to satisfy the needs of individual residents. Even the term "hotel," as used in Sweden, was adopted to avoid association with the institutional character of existing projects. The idea behind service flats is that seniors can lease their units, furnish them with their own furniture, and have access to all medical, food and personal services on a 24-hour basis. In addition they can purchase domestic services if required.

Considering the social needs of seniors opens up an important new area of design. Beyond the new social considerations in designing housing for the elderly, there is a very special need to deal with winter. Adequate expose to sun, daylight, vegetation, animated surroundings, contact with nature—all are absolutely necessary stimuli for everyone living in cold climate countries. These should be primary considerations in the design of new housing for seniors. The new awareness of how climate influences our well-being should be combined with the opportunity to introduce appropriate designs to reduce the negative aspects of winter. This would be a major contribution to the welfare of seniors.

Year-round environments have been created successfully in commercial developments, but they are perceived to be costly and offer low return on investment in residential projects. Glass roofs, atriums, winter gardens, protected outdoor sitting areas, recreational space that can be used year round (but is not totally enclosed)—these design elements can be incorporated in seniors' residences to reduce the amount of time spent indoors in winter and to minimize the adverse effects of winter.

The Scandinavian countries have gained considerable insight into the design of buildings that respond to local climate conditions and seniors' needs. Projects have been designed, built and evaluated on their physical performance (e.g., energy saving and maintenance costs) and the social needs of inhabitants.

A housing project in Eslov, Sweden, built in 1983 has demonstrated the versatility of glass in creating an environment that is livable year round. The 126 dwelling units (2-storey townhouses and apartment units) border a 376-metre glass-covered street. This internal street serves as an extension of individual, private living spaces as well as a meeting place for residents. In Sweden, as in Canada, where people are forced to spend many months indoors, this concept provides an alternative that was embraced enthusiastically. Although the project was not built for seniors exclusively, a large proportion of owners are in fact elderly.

In Iceland, another interesting housing concept involving a round house design was completed in 1987. Units are arranged in a circle, with a glass-covered central space accommodating a communal garden and recreational facilities. The glass roof also covers individual backyards, thus creating all-season greenhouses.

While these examples illustrate creative use of technology in new settings, for most of us the real solution lies in adapting existing housing and reconstructing suburbia.

CONCLUSION

There is considerable opportunity to enhance the quality of life for the elderly in winter cities through design. Ideas range from the very small-scale changes that any homeowner can make to correct obvious deficiencies in housing designed originally for young and growing families, to large-scale architectural ideas for creating more livable year-round space in new seniors' residences.

Underlying all such changes, however, is the need for seniors to identify and express the inadequacies of existing housing, neighbourhoods and public services. Without that expression, there can be no new ideas, no social recognition and no opportunity for the design professions to make their contribution to extending the independence, happiness and fulfillment of the golden years.

SECTION SIX

Discussion Questions

1. What external and internal conditions led the Foyer Notre Dame to set up a separate unit for cognitively impaired residents? Discuss the philosophy that underlies the care of patients in Le Chez Nous.

2. Describe the social forces that lead to repressed sexuality in nursing homes. What can be done to allow older people in nursing homes to express and enjoy their sexuality?

3. What is a granny flat and what purpose does it serve? Describe the outcomes of demonstration projects on granny flats in Canada. What issues does Canada need to resolve before granny flats can develop into a widespread option?

4. What problems do older Canadians face in the winter? What do older people need to do to modify their homes and living environments to cope with winter? What special problems does living in suburbia raise for older people?

5. Many older people want to age in place. What can governments and individuals do to achieve this goal?

Suggested Readings

Gutman, G.M., ed. (1992). *Shelter and Care of Persons with Dementia.* Vancouver: The Gerontology Research Centre.

Gutman, G.M., and N.K. Blackie, eds. (1986). *Aging in Place: Housing Adaptations and Options for Remaining in the Community.* Vancouver: The Gerontology Research Centre.

Joseph, A.E., and A.M. Fuller (1991). "Towards an Integrative Perspective on the Housing, Services and Transportation Implications of Rural Aging." *Canadian Journal on Aging* 10: 127–48.

Keating, N.C. (1991). *Aging in Rural Canada.* Toronto: Butterworths.

Northcott, H.C. (1988). *Changing Residence.* Toronto: Butterworths.

Lifelong Learning and Fitness

Lifelong learning has become a reality for nearly everyone in the work-force. This may take the form of orientation training when a person takes their first job. Or it may take the form of in-service training that keeps a worker up to date. Some people find that they have to go back to school in middle age to retrain. Most of this learning takes place in relation to work. But what does lifelong learning mean to someone in retirement? What purpose does learning serve outside of career training? And what does lifelong learning look like in late old age? What do people want or need to learn at this stage of life? The field of continuing and adult education has only begun to look at learning in later life.

Moody asks about the purpose of learning in old age. He notes that we have few principles to guide the philosophy or practice of education in later life. Moody reviews four perspectives on old age that guide four different views of education. He calls on educators to provide older people with new educational options—options that students themselves may not know they want. Moody concludes by asking whether traditional educational institutions can play this role.

Elderhostel offers one answer to Moody's question about what type of education best suits people in later life. Elderhostel has grown from a pilot project in New England a few years ago to a worldwide network of programs. More than 200,000 North Americans over age 60 enrol in Elderhostel programs each year. Many of these programs take place on university campuses. Almost 13,000 older Canadians took Elderhostel courses in 1989. Programs took place in all of Canada's provinces and territories. O'Brien describes the structure of the programs and a sample of the topics offered.

Elderhostel meets the needs of older people who want to stay intellectually active, but who don't want a degree. The philosophical presuppositions of education for younger people—job training, grading, the assumption that students arrive in class as empty vessels—do not fit the educational needs of older people. Elderhostel challenges students intellectually but has no grading or competition. It assumes that students come to class with a lifetime of knowledge and experience. It also welcomes their participation in the learning process. Older people in the future will have more educational credentials and will demand more of educational institutions. Elderhostel points the way to what future educational alternatives for seniors may look like.

Penning and Wasyliw also describe an innovative program for seniors, Homebound Learning Opportunities (HLO). This program, like Elderhostel, focuses on personal development in later life. And, like Elderhostel, it provides education in a format that suits the needs of a specific group of seniors. Homebound Learning Opportunities developed when its parent educational organization, Creative Retirement Manitoba (CRM), noticed that as people aged they stopped attending on-site programs. CRM decided to provide a program to its former students (and other homebound older people). The program tailors content and delivery to each student's needs. HLO overcomes the physical limits that keep many older people from taking part in education.

Cousins and Burgess discuss the recent surge in interest in physical education among older people. Participaction, yoga, t'ai chi, foot massage, and aerobics classes for seniors have all grown in popularity. The authors discuss the challenges that professional educators face as they develop programs for older people. They discuss, for example, the potential risk to health from vigorous exercise in old age. Cousins and Burgess also discuss types of risk that may keep older people from entering exercise programs. For example, many older people see physical fitness programs as a risk to their self-image. The article discusses how instructors can help older students cope with this risk. The authors say that instructors need to learn more about physical potential from their students. The article points out that instructors and students need to communicate with one another about their concerns and their goals.

Ryan and Heaven explore some of the ways that computers can improve later life. For example, computers offer increased communication and interaction for handicapped older people. Computers offer greater access to information, new opportunities for entertainment, new ways to learn, and health-care monitoring. Relatively few older people today have computers or know how to use them. But in the future this will change. More people will come into old age computer literate, and the lower cost of computers will make them as common as a microwave oven. The future will bring new and unforeseeable applications of computers to education in later life. A grandmother in Winnipeg will be able to play checkers with her grandchild in Vancouver at little cost. A homebound person will take part in a discussion group with colleagues and friends who live thousands of miles apart or across the street. The computer and new ways to use electronic communications will open new opportunities for all of us as we age.

People enter old age today with more education, more income, and more active lifestyles than ever before. They will want more travel, computer, and fitness courses. They may also want new forms of education that do not exist today. These new groups of seniors will work with professional educators to develop options for themselves.

28

Philosophical Presuppositions of Education for Old Age

H.R. Moody

INTRODUCTION

Philosophical reflection is always rooted in the demand for justification of activities that appear problematical, and education for older people must certainly be seen in this light. Education for the older adult, unlike education or training for the young, is not an activity that is in any way functionally required for the maintenance of society. This fact not only explain why education for older people tends to have low priority but also suggests why, at the outset, we have no clear idea of the principles or purposes that guide the activity. The most common pattern is for education of older people to be assimilated into the general field of adult education and for its guiding principles to be taken from what Knowles (1970, 1973) has called *andragogy*—the theory of adult educational practice. However, this solution does not take us very far since it fails to distinguish anything essential about old age that might be distinctive for the educational process. As we shall see, this very question—whether old age is best thought of as a distinctive stage of life or simply as a continuity of adulthood—is itself a crucial philosophical question. To describe it as a "philosophical" question is to say that it is not a question of learning abilities or the efficacy of different pedagogical techniques. It is not a scientific or technical question at all, but a question of how we view human life as a whole, and, in particular, what significance we assign the experience of aging. To put it differently, it is not a question of facts but a question of deciding whether old age constitutes a phase of experience distinct enough for education of older people to have an altogether different set of purposes and criteria than adult education for other members of the population.

From *Educational Gerontology* 1976, Vol. 1, 17–40, by H.R. Moody, Washington, D.C.: Taylor & Francis, Inc. Reproduced with permission. All rights reserved.

For this reason, it is useful to begin by identifying some of the major attitudes or presuppositions that guide the development of programs of education for older people and in each case to indicate the characteristic values, theories of knowledge, and assumptions about human life associated with them. Table 1 sets forth four such "Modal Patterns" or ways society tends to regard old people.

TABLE I

Modal Patterns for Treatment of the Aged

Modal Pattern	Characteristics	Basic Attitude
Rejection	Segregation; mandatory retirement; poverty, neglect; family abandonment	Repression, avoidance
Social Services	Transfer payments (welfare, social security); professional care; senior centers	Social conscience, liberalism
Participation	Second careers (employment or volunteer activity); senior advocacy; autonomy	Social integration, "normalization"
Self-actualization	Individuation, psychological growth, and self-transcendence	Wisdom, ego-integrity

These stages need not be thought of as chronological, although, as the following remarks will make clear, the transition between stages has been associated with historical changes in attitudes and public policy over recent decades. Stage I, the rejection and neglect of the aged, corresponds roughly to the negative consequences of industrialized society's impact on old people, while Stage II is correlated with liberal policies of the welfare state designed to ameliorate those conditions. Stage III in certain ways evokes the "consciousness-raising" efforts of the Gray Panthers and the demand for continued activity in the mainstream of community life as opposed to institutionalized forms of separation. Finally, Stage IV envisages possibilities for humanistic psychological growth in old age which today must appear strictly utopian, but in fact have significant historical precedents.

I. REJECTION

The first stage, rejection, could also be described as "avoidance," "repression," or "neglect" in regard to old people. It is important to realize that this state of affairs is not accidental but flows from the very patterns and assumptions on which modern life is based. In a profound sense, the isolation of the aged in modern societies generally can be said to arise from the fact that old people are, functionally speaking, nonentities. Mandatory retirement and the isolation of the nuclear family casts them more and more into oblivion. Indeed, from the standpoint of what Mumford (1973) calls the "mega-machine" of technocratic society, old people simply need not exist; they are expendable. The entire thrust of modern consciousness is toward growth, change, development, and progress: an overwhelming emphasis on the centrality of knowledge and expansive power, or what Spengler perceptively identified as the "Faustian" ethos of the modern world as a whole. All of this is unalterably opposed to the universal experience of old age—stability, finitude, and recognition of the ultimate limitations of life. Where the modern world prizes productive knowledge, the characteristic virtue of old age is wisdom. Where the imagination of modern man is dominated by the idea of the future, old age looks inevitably to the past. Old people represent our shattered dreams, our limitations, and even the ultimate finality and exhaustion of all our ideals.

Because old age represents the antithesis of the prevailing values of modern life, there is an almost instinctive avoidance of old people, as with the avoidance of death and mortality that Ernest Becker (1973) describes in *The Denial of Death*. We shun and fear old people because, symbolically, they represent our own fate; in their despair, it is really our own that we fear. This intrapsychic process of repression, of unconscious dread and denial, is recapitulated and "writ large" even in the very social institutions and mechanisms that modern life evolves to "deal with" the problem of aging: the enforced segregation of the nursing home and the "gold coast" retirement communities.

Given the negative standpoint of this first stage, which still largely dominates our social institutions and ideology, there can be no rationale for education of older people. If education is viewed as an investment in "human capital," as certain techniques of "human resource accounting," then educational investment in old people makes little sense on economic grounds; the life of the asset is too short, depreciation too far advanced. The implicit assumption here, of course, is that education is a preparation for the future and that its purpose is to be discovered outside of the process itself. That assumption is certainly open to question at all levels of education, but this "instrumental" assumption about learning cannot be separated from an approach to human beings themselves as mere instruments to be set aside and discarded when their usefulness is at an end.

II. SOCIAL SERVICES

The second stage, social services, is best understood as an expression of the ideology of political liberalism and the institutions of the welfare state:

unmet human needs require the intervention of public policy to deal with casualties of industrialized society created by Stage I. Approaches here include transfer payments (food stamps, social security, welfare) as well as substantive programs for nursing home care, senior centers, etc. The assumption is that the target population, in this case old people, requires social services and that government bureaucracies and specialized professions can best provide these services. Typically, as with the poverty programs of the recent past, the target population becomes a kind of constituency, with professionals and bureaucrats advocating ever larger infusions of public funds to support increasingly more complex and differentiated government services and professional roles in the areas of nutrition, recreation, health care, homemaker assistance, etc.

For each of these needs, it is characteristic of the social service mentality to be "pragmatic" in dealing with the symptoms, if not the underlying causes, of the social problems, and to assume that the underlying condition cannot be corrected, for one reason or another. It is also characteristic of social services that a service is something done *for* someone, typically by a professionally certified person (nurse, social worker, physical therapist, etc.). In this way, there is a subtle tendency for the "patient" or the "client" to become progressively more passive in a social situation structured according to the notion of "social services," and this tendency toward passivity makes it understandable why the social service mentality seems to correspond well to the so-called "disengagement theory" of aging. According to disengagement theory, successful aging requires increasing separation from the prevailing roles and activities previously dominant in a person's life (Cumming, 1963; Cumming & Henry, 1961). The social distance between professional and client quickly becomes institutionalized in settings that reinforce an absolute segregation of old people from all aspects of community life, such as in the nursing home or the retirement village. Naturally, wealth and poverty receive vastly different treatment among the old as among other groups, but even in rich retirement communities the appeal of leisure and recreation—"taking it easy"—reveals a convergence of passivity and segregation, whatever the profusion of social services provided by the management. Indeed, it is just this lush undergrowth of services and leisure-time activities that discloses the guiding principle of education for older people under Stage II.

The characteristic educational mode of Stage II could best be described as entertainment or "keeping busy." It may be argued that, with more time on their hands, old people are in a conspicuous position to enjoy life, to pursue different kinds of entertainment (if they have the money), or to enhance themselves through culture and education. For example, it is commonly reported that certain residential communities exclusively for retired adults (especially middle-class enclaves) are virtually teeming with activities such as square dancing, crafts, drama productions, the study of foreign languages, and art appreciation. Such activities are often a source of pride to the residents, apparently as an example of the rich life available to those who live there. What is important for our purposes is to recognize that these recreational and educational activities appeal to older people precisely in terms of the image that seems appropriate and normative for them in old age. Regardless of the enthusiasm, even the frenzy, with which the residents engage in their activities, one fact is conspicuous: these activities are what we generally regard as "leisure-time pursuits." They characterize the human being as a consumer, not as a producer; in the mode of leisure, not the mode of work. Moreover, they are carried out within a framework of segregation and separation from the mainstream of social life in the wider society (the family, the work place, the political community, etc.) Again, the fact that the residents are "happy" or "well-adjusted" is not the issue. The question here, as with each of the stages examined, is strictly philosophical and concerns the distinctive assumptions about the meaning of old age within a view of human life as a whole. On this point, the assumptions of passivity and segregation, "taking it easy" and "keeping busy," are all of a piece. They present a portrait of old age as a time of leisure and curiosity. Old people are portrayed as human beings who have become something less than human, that is, they are not seriously engaged in projects and demands of life that are validated by the entire community as supremely worthwhile, such as work, child rearing, artistic creation, or spiritual devotion.

III. PARTICIPATION

The third stage, participation, constitutes an expanded view of the dignity and autonomy that are possible for old people. Unlike Stage II, which claims attention for old age in the name of conscience and political liberalism, Stage III rejects the passivity of social services and proposes to cure the underlying causes and not just the symptoms of the pathology at hand. The cure proposed is essentially to enable old people, as far as possible, to live their lives in contact with the mainstream of society and to pursue the activities associated with a normal life in that society ("normalization," to use Wolfensberger's (1972) term). Home health care, deinstitutionalization of the mentally ill, and decentralized social services in a community setting are directly in keeping with the theme of normalization. In other words, the answer is not to expand the services currently provided, but to restructure radically those institutions that have contributed to the problem in the first place.

The notion of participation suggests that activity, and not disengagement, be the fundamental criterion of successful aging, and this point has many implications for education for the older adult. First, it suggests that the passivity inherent in the social services model is inappropriate and indeed a reflection of the sense of inadequacy and segregation experienced by other social groups that have been kept out of the mainstream in the past. On this view, education should be designed to avoid these unhealthy aspects of disengagement and instead should focus on second careers and on the discovery of new ways of participating more vigorously in society. As a rule, Stage III would prescribe integration rather than segregation for the different age groups and certainly would propose guaranteed employment opportunities for those who wish to work for as long as they are able. Just as with the boredom, delinquency, and other problems created by ever extended schooling for young people, so the problems of aging would largely be solved by integrating older people into the mainstream of community life.[1]

Interestingly enough, this model goes back to preindustrialized social groups; for example, the aged person was not subject to mandatory retirement at a fixed age on the nineteenth century American farm. As infirmities arose, the older person simply cut down his work load accordingly, without need for bureaucratic age limits or compensating social services. Far from receiving services, such as entertainment or education, the older person was still a functioning member of the household, distinctly needed in caring for young children, cultivating the garden, and doing household chores. The line between "old age" and the rest of society was much less defined, and, one assumes, the feelings of worthlessness or despair were less acute. Many older people, who have rediscovered a sense of meaning through second careers or voluntarism, have testified that to feel alive is to feel needed; the integration of the aged in society is required for this end.

It is significant that this example is drawn from an agrarian, preindustrial setting, where old people *felt* they were needed because in fact they *were* needed. A similar example can be found in contemporary China, where all segments of the population, young and old, are needed to build up a new society. Indeed, from the Maoist or Marxist perspective, the so-called "problem of aging" is simply one more illustration of social disintegration and chronic unemployment in capitalistic societies. In advanced capitalist societies, the aged are useless to an economic system, and the ever declining retirement age indicates a weakness of demand for labor rather than a lack of work to be done (falsely ascribed to "automation") or a lack of a desire to work. From the Marxist standpoint, the "liberal" policy of expanded social services for the aged (Stage II) is just as economically unsound as giving welfare checks to poor people. What people really need are decent jobs and meaningful participation in a wider community. But, because of the dehumanizing effects of modern capitalism, old people are left helpless as family ties are weakened and impersonal mechanisms condemn ever larger numbers of them to poverty and despair (e.g, the earnings test on social security). Simone de Beauvoir reached a similar conclusion in *The Coming of Age*, a book that on the whole may stand as an eloquent statement of the assumptions of Stage III and the demand for a radical restructuring of society.[2]

Despite the prescription of fundamental social change, education clearly must play a role in Stage III. Older people must experience a kind of "consciousness raising" that allows them to adopt a positive attitude toward their situation and to take steps to change it. They need help in shedding the self-hatred caused by stereotypes and the prevailing attitudes of society at large. Educational programs can equip leaders to undertake advocacy for older people to articulate their needs in areas such as employment, social security, and medical care. As individuals, older people must be led beyond passivity and given the option of second careers and new opportunities for genuine participation, regardless of age.

IV. SELF-ACTUALIZATION

At the present time, the cutting edge of social reform is expressed by the goals described in Stage III: a demand for dignity for old people, recognition of sexuality, the right to work, and opportunity of living within the mainstream of society; in short, for "normalization" of the treatment accorded them. Stage IV, "self-actualization," is much harder to describe because in many ways it posits goals of spiritual and psychological growth that are completely outside the prevailing values of modern society. In other words, Stage IV does not yet appear on the agenda of social policy, even of social critics and reformers, although its implications for education of older adults are profound.

In forming a notion of what "self-actualization" in old age might mean, it is helpful to return to the fundamental question we began with: does old age constitute a phase of experience with its own distinct and qualitative demands? If it does, then the demands of old age must somehow be rooted in the experience of aging itself, and not in generalized qualities belonging to all human beings (e.g., the "rights" demanded in Stage III). There must be something *uniquely possible* in old age that is only available at this point in the life cycle. It is difficult to imagine exactly what this consists of, precisely because old age in the modern world has no distinctive or positive features. It is either an invisible void in one's psychological life-space or it is to be "filled up" with activities in common with previous roles and responsibilities. However, clues to answering this question may be found in the values and institutions of other societies.

In ancient India, for example, the Hindu concept of life dictated that the human life span should be seen as a series of changing demands and stages of growth (*āshramas*), each with its own patterns and roles (Zimmer, 1964). Beginning as *students*, young people then grew to take on the role of *householders*, and then, at the conclusion of this phase of life, they were called on to renounce the responsibilities of work and family and to retreat into the forest for *contemplation* and *meditation*. The final stage of this process constituted a mystical absorption into the transcendent goal of human experience, spiritual deliverance (*moksha*). Thus, like each of the earlier stages, old age had its own distinctive dimension of meaning, the supreme meaning of self-realization in the spiritual quest.

In many traditional societies, the respect accorded the old helped reinforce this dimension of meaning, as a reminder to all of the link between generations, the relativity of life and death, and the final destiny of all human beings. In this way, the old person could become a symbol of the "closure" or completeness of the life cycle and even, in the archetype of the "wise old man" (the patriarch, the *guru*, etc.), a symbol of the spiritual goal of existence. Modern societies have no access to this missing dimension of meaning; the symbolic aspect of aging has been lost in a flight from death and in the flight from aging, which stands at the threshold of death (Blauner, 1966).

These traditional views are echoed and confirmed by the concepts of certain schools of modern depth psychology, where the problem of aging is presented in a language more attuned to the modern situation. In *Childhood and Society*, for example, Erikson (1963) presents a typology of psychological development throughout the life cycle and speaks of the last stage of life as being dominated by the polarity between "ego-integrity" vs. "despair." The crucial psychological issue of old age, then, is whether or not the person's life experience can be encompassed and affirmed in its totality. Erikson describes this reconciliation of the past with an awareness of finitude and death in terms of the characteristic virtue of this last phase of life, "wisdom." From a different perspective, Jung (1955) describes the fundamental task of the last stage of life as "individuation"—the disengagement of the transcendent Self from the socially required *persona*, or the "mask" of the various roles and activities required by responsible adulthood. Only when these masks fall away, Jung suggests, can the ultimate question of individual identity be faced in its final form. Indeed, as the path of life narrows progressively with each passing year, as it does for all of us, the question—what remains when everything disappears?—becomes finally unavoidable, and this constitutes the spiritual crisis of old age and the conflict between ego-integrity and despair.

It is at this point that we realize why it is difficult to imagine what Stage IV might signify under the conditions of modern life. As described under Stage I, the values and institutions of modern life seem to have no place for old age, just as families and places of employment have no room for the old people in our midst. More deeply, as Curtin (1972) points out in *Nobody Ever Died of Old Age*, what our culture lacks is an image of life in its wholeness, and this emptiness, this spiritual void, is what lies behind the ultimate despair of old age. It is for this reason that the implications for education at this fourth stage are far-reaching and provocative. The most important conclusion is that education for the older adult should not "entertain" people ("keeping busy") or simply perpetuate a style of activity associated with the sources of ego strength during adulthood. Preparing for a second career, just as much as the pursuit of travel, crafts, and recreation, can be a way of avoiding the fundamental life-task of old age: to encounter who we are. What Stage IV argues for is instead a deepened definition of what psychological growth in old age might consist of, perhaps modeled on the insights of the great world religions or the contributions of humanistic psychology. Indeed, the term "self-actualization" is taken from the work of Maslow (1968) and the humanistic psychology associated with his name. In this new image of psychological growth, disengagement is required but only for the sake of a more meaningful form of activity: contemplation and resynthesis of the self, now disengaged and liberated from the limited forms and social roles required by tasks originating outside the self (work, child rearing, etc.). Thus, neither "disengagement" nor "participation" expresses the distinctive developmental task of old age, which is a breakthrough into new dimensions of meaning and psychological growth.

For educators, the challenge of Stage IV is to make available to older people the great ideas of the humanities and the social sciences that can nourish this psychological development in old age. In the fields of philosophy, religion, psychology, and literature there are elements that can *only* be grasped in all their depth and richness by individuals who bring a lifetime of personal experience to their study. The task of designing an educational experience for old age in these terms has barely begun.

SOME REFLECTIONS ON THE FOUR STAGES

It was mentioned at the outset that the four stages cannot be put in strict correlation with time periods; they are rather, in Weber's sense, "ideal types" that represent a complex of attitudes embodied in varying degrees in individuals, institutions, and historical periods. Stage I, clearly, is based largely on *economic* values and represents the uncorrected abuses of capitalism and technological society in general. Stage II is determined by the values of *liberalism* and the *welfare state:* redistribution of resources to ameliorate the worst excesses of Stage I but no fundamental challenge to the prevailing institutions, whether the family or the corporation. (For example, to abolish mandatory retirement altogether or to reverse the isolation of the nuclear family would be considered "utopian"; the best that can be hoped for are second careers and surrogate families.) Stage III is characterized by predominantly *political* values. It challenges the age-graded distribution of power and status in society by demanding for old people rights that have been denied them, sometimes through the policies alleged to be in the interest of their welfare (as though to "protect" them: the parallels with women's liberation are evident) (see Townsend, 1971).

The political advocacy of Stage III stops short of challenging the ultimate values of modern society (shared by the old as well) and, in fact, desires only a "normalization" in the life of old people, with respect to work, sex, political power, and social living. In Stage III the demand for increased participation in society is predicated on a desire for the equality, freedom, and happiness that are expected from such participation. The irony of Stage III is that it chooses to struggle in terms laid down by the prevailing norms of adult life, those of power and activity. Thus, there is a tendency to create political pressure groups on behalf of the aged by analogy with other self-interest groups and a tendency to deny that aging should signify any diminution of energy and activity. The standard of happiness and self-esteem remains the perpetuation of patterns of success associated with other phases of the lifecycle—the adult roles of power and productivity—which the ancient Hindu view of life would have correlated with the stage of the householder. In this sense, Stage III denies the aging process in the name of continued activity. It is only Stage IV that accepts aging on its own terms and discerns in the experience of growing old not a problem to struggle against but an opportunity to reach deeper levels of meaning. Thus, the prevailing values of Stage IV are inner-directed and are *psychological* and *spiritual* in their orientation.

What are the prospects for change and further evolution between the stages described here, and what role can education play in this process? To answer these questions requires consideration of the way each of the stages is associated with the ideology of major institutions and power groups in society today. For example, the prevailing values of both organized labor and industry are anchored in Stage I, while the social policy of government, on the other hand, tends to be characterized by the values of Stage II. Outside of these concentrations of public and private power, smaller advocacy groups drawn from senior citizens, the consumer movement, and certain professionals have begun to reject the pattern of solutions proposed under Stage II and have argued in favor of more radical changes associated with Stage III. Finally, at the present time, there is no cultural force acting in support of the goals of Stage IV, nor is there a well-developed ideology or view of life that could serve as a point of departure for such a vast mutation of consciousness as it presupposes, for reasons mentioned in the description of Stage IV. To create such a vision of psychological growth in old age will require the contributions of religion, philosophy, and humanistic psychology. Higher education will have a part to play in this development.

As educational institutions move to take a more active role in the education of older people, there needs to be recognition of the difficulty in initiating fundamental change in the present situation. To begin with, groups of older people have rarely been able to exercise effective political pressure in the United States (Putnam, 1970). Public pressure has been effective chiefly for promoting classically liberal solutions such as social security and health insurance (Medicare), standard expressions of Stage II. To imagine a policy of guaranteed employment options for persons over 65, for example, is unlikely in view of the large forces that are opposed to fundamental political and economic change (e.g., both labor and management tend to support mandatory retirement rules, each for their own reasons.) Not surprisingly, educational policy for older people usually supports programs associated with the liberal solutions of Stage II. From a pragmatic standpoint, it seems realistic to offer reduced-tuition leisure-time courses for persons over 65, while to offer them training for second careers assumes that jobs are available for trained people; given the prospects for government national employment policy, this seems unlikely. As with welfare for poor people, expanded education for older adults, without meaningful participation beyond it, represents a "solution" to the problem of aging that fails to confront the underlying causes.

THE ROLE OF HIGHER EDUCATION

We have observed that the ideology of Stage II is most familiar and comfortable for educators, and it corresponds well with the adult education interests of most older people today. More education for older adults may seem intrinsically justified because education is self-evidently a "good thing" or again because old people, with time on their hands and a rising level of education, constitute a "new clientele" (i.e., an untapped market) for higher education in a period facing enrollment declines (Vermilye, 1974). To date, the greatest thrust for educational opportunities for older people has come through community colleges and through divisions of continuing education, where the laissez-faire policy of noncredit programs allows market forces to determine the curriculum (DeCrow, undated; Korim, 1974). Students "vote with their feet" by registering for courses, and in turn success—as measured by enrollment, publicity, growth, etc.—tends to confirm itself, no questions asked.

This situation—"open ended," "learner-directed," "nontraditional" (to use the current jargon)—seems appropriate, since the truth is that in higher education we have no clear conception of the basis of a curriculum for older adults. The notion of "lifelong learning" receives such general endorsement because it remains largely vacuous: a marketing slogan or a sentimental appeal that identifies "more education" with "growth," "curiosity," or "creative use of leisure time," all of which belong to the ideology of Stage II. It is only with Stages III and IV that the question of curriculum and educational goals becomes at all meaningful. When the situation is defined in the terms of Stage II, there is no curriculum at all apart from the choices people actually make, and higher education abdicates any leadership role. Educational policy, as often occurs in continuing education, becomes a branch of market research; it is empirically based rather than value-based. The questions of "where we want to go" and "how we know when we get there"—in short curriculum and evaluation—seem to make no sense at all since these questions are intrinsically value-based. This in turn means that our values about education for older people must be justified in terms of a more far-reaching philosophy, and this has not yet happened.

Certainly one of the most important causes of this situation lies in the funding and administrative structure of continuing education programs in higher education. However, finance, administration, and marketing, in my judgment, are not the source of the problem. The problem, very simply, is that, as educators, we have no clear idea of why older adults should be educated, and this absence of fundamental philosophical reflection is ultimately dangerous for the whole enterprise. We may *feel* that it is a good thing for older people to learn, and the students themselves may agree, but what this feeling really signifies is that we bring with us certain covert goals, such as entertainment, curiosity, or prestige, that tend to remain unexamined. Education for older people is self-evidently "good" only when viewed through the eyes of institutional self-interest (the "new clientele") or through the ideology of Stage II, which serves a latent function in society by promoting disengagement of older people and by failing to challenge the causes of the underlying condition.

The recent emergence of education for older adults has tended to follow patterns of adult education in general without sufficiently questioning whether there is anything distinctive about the role of education in the life-cycle that would make older adults unique. That fundamental question, raised at the beginning of this discussion, has profound implications for every phase of education for older people at the practical level, including needs assessment, program development, instructional methods, and evaluation techniques. By failing to ask this question, we end up instead asking our prospective students what they want to study (Heimstra, 1972; *Never Too Old to Learn*, 1974). They answer us, naturally, in terms of their own past experience and their unconscious expectations about what education can provide. For example, they tend to answer in terms of subject matter rather than in terms of the goals of the process itself. We cannot expect anything else because, as a rule, people are limited by their previous experience as far as conceiving alternative or imaginable situations. Higher education itself is organized around distinct areas of subject matter, so that students' labels and names for what they like and dislike tend to follow the previous patterns of organization. We "like" literature or we "dislike" mathematics; we are "stimulated" by a good lecturer, but we are "turned off" by writing. Tastes and expectations are in turn determined by prior experiences in the educational system, so that, invisibly, all of us are socialized into the requirements and expectations of that system. We have no names for possibilities that fall outside of that system, but within it we have a thousand labels, opinions, and associations linked to what we imagine formal education can and cannot do.

As teachers or as students, the expectations we bring to an educational experience are regulated and limited by these narrowing ideas of what learning is. Institutional inertia reinforces the process until we can conceive of the future only as an expansion or an extension of what we already know. (When the railroad was introduced it was called the "iron horse.") In the evolving field of education for older adults, this describes exactly the situation at the present time. The alternative is to imagine an educational experience from which students would emerge as *different kinds of people*, with a new and enlarged sense of values and deepened understanding of who they are as envisioned in Stage IV (Mason, 1974).

But is this what the students want? someone may ask. How can we know ahead of time? One may reply, how do we know if we like caviar before we have tried it? How can we ask the student about a type of experience—call it "insight," "dialogue," or "self-discovery"—that is a burning sense of novelty, a white-hot pursuit of thought and feeling and an absorption into a process of questioning that discloses its own answer? This is what an educational experience, at its best, can be. Both the political activism of Stage III and the model of self-actualization proposed in Stage IV require just this kind of consciousness-raising. Whether educational institutions can provide this experience remains the critical question.

NOTES

1. In the case of old people, the argument here is strictly parallel to the analysis by Illich (1970).

2. Simone de Beauvoir's (1972) critique is rooted in a Marxist analysis of human society and an existential philosophy of human nature. In both cases, the prescription is the same: self-realization through labor and *praxis*, engagement through the existential "project." Compare: "Freedom and clarity of mind are not of much use if no goal beckons us any more: but they are of great value if one is still full of projects. The greatest good fortune, even greater than health, for the old person is to have his world still inhabited by projects; then, busy and useful, he escapes both from boredom and from decay." (p. 492) and "There is only one solution if old age is not to be an absurd parody of our former life, and that is to go pursuing ends that give our existence a meaning—devotion to individuals, to groups or to causes, social, political, intellectual or creative work. In spite of the moralists' opinion to the contrary, in old age we should wish still to have passions strong enough to prevent us turning in upon ourselves." (p. 540)

REFERENCES

Becker, E. *The denial of death.* New York: Free Press, 1973.

Blauner, R. Death and social structure. *Psychiatry: Journal for the Study of Interpersonal Processes,* 1966, *29,* 378–394. Reprinted in B. Neugarten (Ed.), *Middle age and aging.* Chicago: University of Chicago Press, 1966.

Cumming, E. M. Further thoughts on the theory of disengagement. *International Social Science Journal,* 1963, *15,* 377–393.

Cumming, E. M., & Henry, W. E. *Growing old: The process of disengagement.* New York: Basic Books, 1961.

Curtin, S. *Nobody ever died of old age.* Boston: Little, Brown, 1972.

de Beauvoir, S. [*The coming of age*] (P. O'Brian, trans.). New York: Putnam, 1972.

DeCrow, R. *New learning for older Americans: An overview of national effort.* Washington: Adult Education Association of the U.S.A., undated.

Erikson, E. Eight ages of man. In E. Erikson, *Childhood and society.* New York: Norton, 1963.

Hemstra, R. P. Continuing education for the aged: A survey of needs and interests of older people. *Adult Education,* 1972, *22*(2), 100–109.

Illich, I. *Deschooling society.* New York: Harper, 1970.

Jung, C. The stage of life. In C. Jung, *Modern man in search of a soul.* New York: Harcourt, 1955.

Knowles, M. S. *The modern practice of adult education: Andragogy versus pedagogy.* New York: Association Press, 1970.

Korim, A. *Older Americans and community colleges: An overview.* Washington: American Association of Community and Junior Colleges, 1974.

Maslow, A. *Toward a psychology of being.* Princeton: Van Nostrand, 1968.

Mason, W. D. Aging and lifelong learning. *Journal of Research and Development in Education,* 1974, *7*(4), 72.

Mumford, L. *The myth of the machine.* Vol. 2. *The pentagon of power.* New York: Harcourt, 1973.

Never too old to learn. New York: Academy for Educational Development, 1974.

Putnam, J. K. *Old age politics in California.* Stanford, Calif.: Stanford University Press, 1970.

Townsend, C. *Old age: The last segregation.* New York: Bantam, 1971.

Vermilye, D. W. (Ed.). *Lifelong learners: A new clientele for higher education.* San Francisco: Jossey-Bass, 1974.

Wolfensberger, W. *The principle of normalization in human services.* Toronto: National Institute on Mental Retardation, 1972.

Zimmer, H. [Caste and the four life stages.] In J. Campbell (Ed.), *Philosophies of India.* New York: Meridian, 1964.

29

Beyond the Three R's

Laird O'Brien

The old bus bounces along a dirt road deep in the Boyd Conservation Area, about 15 kilometres northwest of Toronto, and finally lurches to a stop at the edge of a grassy field. Twenty-five passengers offer good-natured applause and climb out. For a Tuesday morning in late August there is a surprising chill in the air. Many of the passengers rub their hands and turn up their collars as they gather around Bob Burgar—easy to spot with his khaki shorts and black beard and a red bandanna around his forehead. Burgar is their guide to the archeological site they are about to visit. As he explained to the group last night over coffee, the site dates back to about AD 1550, when 1,500 to 2,000 Hurons lived there. Over several years the Hurons built eight longhouses with a six-metre tall log palisade around them.

Bob leads the way to the actual work place—a shallow excavation area marked off in neat rectangles by strings tied to small red posts. The group sets to work with shovels and other tools, following carefully explained procedures, its members taking turns sifting buckets of dirt in search of pottery, bones and stone close to 500 years old. The morning's first discovery—a fragment from what was probably a ceramic vessel—brings the group crowding around for a closer look. What seems as remarkable as the relic itself, however, is the fact that these men and women have come here from all over North America to be archeology students for a week and not one of them is less than 60 years of age.

This is an Elderhostel class—a new educational option available to older adults. This year, more than 200,000 North Americans, age 60 and over, will enroll in Elderhostel programs that are available in 10 Canadian provinces and two territories, 50 American states and more than 50 other countries. The prospective students will choose from literally thousands of courses held at almost 1,400 colleges, schools and other institutions.

Some of the subjects are challenging: aquatic ecology, Jungian psychology, German and contemporary Christian thought, for example. Many tie in to hobbies and special interests: arts and crafts, music appreciation, nature,

Reproduced with permission from *The Review* (Spring 1989), 21–25.

photography, sailing, Renaissance art.... Among the most popular courses are those devoted to famous authors, microcomputers, religious and philosophical topics and the history of the area in which the course is held. Among the most unusual: No Porcupines or Snakes, but Lots of Killer Plants, held at Sir Wilfred Grenfell College in Newfoundland; The Art of Storytelling, held at Yavapai College in Arizona; The Method School of Acting, held at Southern Connecticut State University; and Oriental Bookbinding, held at Hawaii Loa College.

This year the fee for a one-week course is about $255, which includes everything except the cost of getting to the campus. Meals and accommodation are usually provided in student residences, and three dollars of every registration fee are set aside for the Hostelship Fund, which helps individuals who otherwise couldn't afford to attend.

The archeology class is typical. There are no credits or exams, neither is there any homework. No previous knowledge or study is required, and while some students may arrive with doctorates, others may never have finished high school. What they share in abundance is curiosity and the desire to be challenged.

Mort Moseman from St. Petersburg, Florida, leans on his shovel and says with a laugh, "Elderhostel keeps people young." He and his wife, Georgia, arrived on Sunday with the rest of the group. This is their ninth Elderhostel trip—a one-week course that has three parts: Peeking into Prehistory offers training in archeological field techniques; Swede Saws and Hard Hats is a program that helps people identify trees and examines their uses through the years (and also includes participation in an active tree-management program); and Native Use of Plants looks at how different plants were once used for food, medicine and tools.

This is the group's second day at the site. The banter is gentle and the work is going well. Bob Burgar finds his students to be enthusiastic and easy to teach. He shares the view of one professor, more accustomed to youthful students, who said, "I'm always impressed with the earnestness of Elderhostelers."

The midmorning break is a chance to visit. Bill and Arline Applegate, 30-year residents of Princeton, New Jersey, now retired to Florida, are typical of many Elderhostelers who combine learning with travel. "Last week we were at Wells College in Aurora, New York," Bill explains. "Took Quaker religion, botany and ceramics. We wanted to see this area, so we picked a course up here." Personal circumstances often play a role in introducing people to Elderhostel. Arline recalls a man they met in Aurora: "He'd been to 26 Elderhostel courses *this year*. He said his wife had died about four years ago and the courses had been a great outlet for him."

Ethel Coleman of Valleyfield, Que., is a first-time student. "I'm a widow," she says, "and really have no ties. Friends had gone to Prince Edward Island and Haliburton, Ont., with Elderhostel. They enjoyed it, so I thought I'd give it a whirl. My friend who is with me has a daughter living in the area, so we'll combine the course with a visit to her place."

Bill Hunter and his wife have driven down from Ottawa. "We're Elderhostel veterans," laughs Bill. "We'd never been to Newfoundland, so we went there last summer and took marine biology."

This movement of seniors to the classroom grew out of an evening meeting in 1974 between Martin P. Knowlton—teacher, research engineer, backpacker, world traveler and social activist—and his friend David Bianco, director of residential life at the University of New Hampshire. Both men share a love of travel and adventure. After a four-year walking tour of Europe, Knowlton had returned to the United States highly impressed with the youth hosteling movement on the continent, which he believed had had a tremendous influence on the young people of Europe, promoting a spirit of adventure and involvement. He was also struck by the more active roles played by older people in most European communities.

That night, convinced that education could effectively guide older citizens to greater fulfillment and feelings of self-worth, they planned "a network of 'elder hostels'...spanning North America." A year later Elderhostel was in operation at five colleges and universities in New Hampshire and soon became a nationwide program. By 1980, more than 20,000 older adults had enrolled in programs at college and university campuses across the United States, and by 1988 enrollment in the United States had climbed to a total of more than 100,000.

The first courses in Canada were held in 1980 and attracted a total of about 250 students, most of them from the United States. By 1986, 4,200 people had enrolled in courses in Canada, and the decision was made to establish a separate Canadian operation. The executive director of Elderhostel Canada is Robert Williston, a round-faced, cheery man in his thirties who has been involved in the program from the beginning. He was assistant director of continuing education at the University of New Brunswick, where the first Canadian classes were held. He fondly recalls that summer of 1980: "One course was called Short Stories of Atlantic Canada. After the second day of classes I met the instructor at the photocopying machine. He said, 'I can't get an undergraduate student to read one short story a class, but this group has gone through six in two days. They show up on time. They want to buy me coffee and talk about Atlantic writers who aren't even on the course. I'm learning more than they are.' Later the housekeeper came up to me and said, 'I think the residence is in much better shape than when they got here.' After the success of the program the first year, we just got bitten by the bug."

Growth has been spectacular. This year the permanent staff of four in downtown Toronto will register almost 13,000 students for courses in Canada, including French programs in six provinces. A bilingual course catalogue, published three times a year, will go out to more than 55,000 Canadians.

Because Elderhostel is completely independent and nonprofit, volunteers play a prominent role. Walter Pitman—a former president of Ryerson Polytechnical Institute, a former executive director of the Ontario Arts Council and now director of the Ontario Institute for Studies in Education—is chairman of the board. He has recruited volunteers across the country to help out with publicity, planning and the development of new courses.

Why is Elderhostel proving to be so popular? There are many answers, some of them quite personal. One woman in the archeology course pauses on the site and says softly, "When I was in high school I wanted to study archeology, but I thought, 'Oh, soon there won't be anything left to dig up.' Wasn't that silly? Look at me now—more than 40 years later I'm finding wonderful things." She smiles and holds up a 300-year-old sliver of pottery.

"We know who we appeal to," says Robert Williston with a certain missionary zeal—"those who are comfortable with education, who see education as a way of participating in the world, who are more than 60 years old and who as a group are growing more healthy and are unwilling to sit and watch television."

Husbands and wives sharing the experience make up 60 percent of the student body, but as Williston points out, "We're also seeing mothers and daughters together and brothers who live far apart meeting for a class and a visit."

Certainly the health and mobility of today's seniors contribute to the booming attendance, but the fascinating subjects and locations of the courses are a big part of the appeal. In Happy Valley-Goose Bay, Nfld., a program on the history and culture of Labrador—including wildlife and handicrafts—attracts visitors from all over the United States, many of whom renew friendships dating back to 1944, when some of the participants served at the U.S. military base in Labrador. Even a course held at Arctic College in Fort Smith, N.W.T. (on the ecology of Wood Buffalo National Park), is filled to capacity every summer with students from all over North America.

Elderhostel's international programs are cooperative ventures, run in conjunction with a variety of organizations and host institutions around the world. Courses are usually three weeks long, with instruction in English. This year, colleges and universities in more than 50 countries, including England, France, Switzerland, Australia, New Zealand, Japan and Brazil, are participating. Here, too, the emphasis is on the experience rather than the accommodation. "We want Elderhostel people to be treated as regular students," Williston explains. "They stay in dormitory rooms, usually with the bathroom down the hall. They pick up their own dishes and make their own beds. It's a little more chicken and spaghetti than it is steak and roast beef. But watching Elderhostelers lining up to get their dinner along with basketball players and summer students is wonderful. That's what education should be."

Elderhostelers seem to agree. No students seem to enjoy themselves more thoroughly. Bob Turnbull, former travel editor of *The Globe and Mail*, now retired, discovered Elderhostel in 1986. He and his wife have taken several courses, and he describes it as "a vacation with a difference—one of the most inexpensive holiday packages, with the bonus of a stimulating learning experience."

Evelyn Baird of Leamington, Ont., is 77 and has traveled with Elderhostel to England and Scotland as well as to various locations in North America. The subjects of her courses have ranged from speed-reading to Shakespeare—given by a retired nun "who could make Shakespeare sing." One of her most memorable trips was to St. Paul, Minnesota, for courses on ancient Egyptian civilization, the Middle East and the Arab-Israeli conflict. Among the speakers were a former aid to Ayatollah Khomeini and the former head of an Iranian hospital.

Being on one's own is no reason to miss out, according to Emma deGroot. A widow recently retired from teaching, she went to Australia and New Zealand with Elderhostel last year. "I didn't know a soul," she recalls in her Mississauga townhouse, "but from the moment I got to the airport I was never alone. Our luggage was color-coded to identify course members from Canada. Two ladies from St. Thomas, Ont, approached me in the airport, and we soon became friends." The trip included one-week courses on the culture, environment and history of the regions around Sydney and Newcastle in Australia and Auckland in New Zealand. She stayed on for a further three-week holiday with friends she had made on the trip and is now planning to register for one of several programs in Hawaii. "Two years ago," she adds, "I'd never heard of Elderhostel. Now I'm being asked to speak about it to some of the teachers' groups."

Keeping up with demand is Elderhostel's biggest challenge. Its traditional summer schedule of classes is expanding into the fall and winter, and experimental programs are taking shape. For example, a rare two-week course offers two perspectives on the War of 1812: the first week will be held at St. Lawrence University in Canton, New York; the second across the border at Queen's University in Kingston, Ont.

To cope with the tremendous popularity of classes that deal with the North, Elderhostel plans to make greater use of private lodges, which tend to be vacant after the fishing and hunting seasons. One program, The Trail of '98—Klondike Gold, takes a class by government ferry on a four-day trip to Skagway, Alaska, and then over land to Whitehorse, where the students complete the program at Yukon College.

Percy Waxer, a retired stock broker who assists the organization with communications and publicity, believes Elderhostel is "still the best-kept secret in Canada." He's trying to change that and detects growing interest among corporations and governments. A number of them now include Elderhostel as a component of retirement planning. "In fact," adds Waxer, "I was asked if an Elderhostel course could be given to an employee as a retirement present. Why not?"

Lunchtime at the archeological site. Shovels are set aside, artifacts collected in small brown bags for their journey to the Royal Ontario Museum in Toronto, and hungry students board the bus for the return trip to the main site facility. The huge stone building was originally the summer home of industrialist Garfield Weston. Today it is a well-integrated collection of dormitory rooms, lounges, libraries, teaching facilities and, of course, a bright cafeteria.

As the group members line up for lunch, chatting among themselves over the din of dishes up ahead, Trudy Hunter of Ottawa talks about the informal network that builds up among the travelers. "We talk about different places and courses," she says. "The rooms are great at one place, courses aren't so hot at another—that kind of thing. Now here, the staff is excellent and the food is really out of this world."

Farther down the line, another student mentions a possible side trip tomorrow to the McMichael Gallery in nearby Kleinberg. "Not many people skip classes," she explains, "but you certainly can if you want to. After all," she adds with a smile, "there are no exams to pass—we are learning simply for our own pleasure."

30

Homebound Learning Opportunities

REACHING OUT TO OLDER SHUT-INS AND THEIR CAREGIVERS

Margaret Penning and Douglas Wasyliw

The majority of older adults are able to maintain health and independence in later life. Over half of those aged 65 and older report no limitations on their abilities to carry out various activities of daily living (Chappell, Strain, & Blandford, 1985). However, the rapidly increasing size of the old elderly population (those aged 85 and over) is also increasing the number of individuals who will be homebound for some period of time, particularly as a result of chronic illness and consequent disability.

Over 80% of the elderly have one or more chronic health problems (Hickey, 1980) and it is estimated that about one in four people aged 65 and over experience moderate or major activity limitations as a result (Statistics Canada, 1987). One-quarter of those aged 75 through 84 and half of those aged 85 and over have one or more chronic health problems that render them at least moderately disabled (Longino & Soldo, 1987).

As disability increases, social opportunities and involvements frequently decline. Findings reported by Longino and Soldo (1987), for example, indicate the vast majority of frail elderly are also socially, economically, and/or environmentally impoverished. According to these authors, the social world of the frail elderly may often be more or less fully defined by the housing space they occupy. The stress induced by involuntary social isolation is likely to contribute to even further declines in health and well-being.

One response to the boredom and isolation often imposed on the homebound community-dwelling elderly is to make opportunities available to them in their own homes. Traditional home care services, while providing indispensable assistance, do not take into account intellectual, emotional,

---

Reproduced from *The Gerontologist*, Vol. 32, No. 5, 704–707 (1992). Copyright © The Gerontological Society of America.

and creative needs that are instrumental to quality of life. Homebound Learning Opportunities is designed to fill this gap in service.

THE SERVICE

Homebound Learning Opportunities (HLO) is a nonprofit health promotion and educational outreach service for older adults and their caregivers over the age of 50 who are homebound on a permanent, temporary, or seasonal basis. HLO provides shut-ins with over 125 topics to choose from for an individualized one-on-one or small-group learning program delivered in their own homes or seniors' residence. An audiovisual lending library and educational television series have been developed to complement the in-home offerings. Peer support counseling is provided for shuts-ins and their caregivers in distress. Finally, HLO attempts to make use of the skills, experience, and knowledge of shut-ins for the benefit of the wider community.

Eligibility
Individuals are considered for participation in HLO if they reside in the city of Winnipeg, Manitoba, are 50 years of age or older, retired, and permanently, temporarily, or seasonally homebound. Individuals are considered homebound if they face significant mobility and/or transportation obstacles restricting their ability to attend more traditional community-based educational events. Given the locale, a significant number of elderly find themselves homebound during the harsh winter months (November–March) each year. The lower age limit of 50 enables those who experience premature retirement as a result of ill health to participate. Older caregivers (aged 50 and over) of persons who are homebound are also eligible to participate in the program as are those who are homebound due to obstacles of a psychological (e.g., agoraphobia) or social nature (e.g., a loss of support systems).

No formal assessment procedures are used to determine eligibility for service. Participants effectively select themselves into and out of the program. Most are initially referred to the program by professionals affiliated with community agencies including seniors' organizations and elderly persons' housing unit or guest home staff. Provincial home care, hospital, and adult day care program staff also make referrals. Still others are referred by family members, friends, or other participants. The remainder contact HLO directly as a result of seeing the service advertised. Increasing numbers of shut-ins watching the HLO television shows call to request classes.

Participants range in age from 50 to 94 with the majority aged 75–84. Participants come from all educational backgrounds, live in all areas of the city, and have a wide variety of health problems.

Development

Homebound Learning Opportunities was initiated in 1988 by Creative Retirement Manitoba (CRM), a nonprofit community-based organization established in Winnipeg, Manitoba, Canada in 1981. CRM focuses on developing programs that will enable older adults to live creatively and to grow and share their knowledge and skills with peers and with society at large. It attempts to encourage people of all ages to prepare for a creative life in retirement as well as to raise awareness of the worth and potential of older adults. Its activities are based on the philosophy that: (1) retirement is a creative opportunity for individuals, groups, communities, and society as a whole; (2) people of all ages have the ability to learn, change, and be useful; (3) people of all ages have the right to access education appropriate to their interests and needs; (4) life-long learning not only promotes intellectual growth but also contributes to physical, psychological, and social well-being; and (5) older people represent a resource for knowledge and experience.

Primary sources of funding for CRM include the provincial (Department of Education, Government of Manitoba) and federal (New Horizons Program, Health and Welfare Canada) governments. Supplemental funding is provided through donations received from the private sector, philanthropic foundations, and service clubs.

In the mid-1980s, CRM recognized that its educational opportunities were not accessible to those unable to attend classes in community-based settings. A needs assessment was conducted to assess the types of educational activities desired by older shut-ins. The results supported the need for an "at home" version of its educational programs: about two-thirds (68%) of those contacted by phone ($N = 123$) said they would likely participate in such a service if it were available. Funding was requested for a 2-year demonstration project. The positive response of shut-ins to HLO resulted in ongoing provincial government support for the service, beginning in 1990.

Content and Delivery

HLO is currently delivered to participants either individually or in groups (of 2 or more) in their own places of residence. Participants select the courses they feel best meet their needs. Only one course can be taken at a time. Special requests are filled where possible. A nominal fee is assessed and any materials required for the course are paid for by the participant. Special arrangements can, however, be made for those who lack the ability to pay. No formal procedures are used to determine eligibility for tuition subsidy. Participants simply state what they can afford to pay. To date, approximately 2% of participants have requested a reduction or waiving of fees.

After field-testing various approaches, organizers selected ongoing course registration throughout the program year (September 1–May 31) as the most efficient and effective way to offer these educational opportunities. Courses meet weekly and continue for an average of 6 weeks. Classes are scheduled at a time mutually agreed upon by the participant(s) and instructor.

Courses cover a variety of areas including arts and crafts, business and computer skills, communications, fitness and bodywork, home management, music, and special interest topics such as bridge, current events, poetry, mathematics, and philosophy. The most popular individual courses include computer courses, artistic expression courses, and communication skills, as well as selections from the audiovisual lending library. The most frequently requested group courses are armchair fitness, painting, t'ai chi, and a "Live, Laugh and Learn" sampler series, designed to acquaint individuals with the HLO program and its offerings.

Provision is also made for courses to be offered by telephone. This allows for greater flexibility in the timing of classes, thereby accommodating those whose health status may fluctuate as well as instructors who are themselves homebound. A coordinator matches clients with instructors who then visit with them in person at least once prior to beginning the course. Conversational language courses tend to be particularly well-suited to this format.

Access to the HLO audiovisual library's specialized educational resources is provided through the mail, with provisions made for pick-up and delivery of tapes. Audio cassette machines are available for loan at no charge. Video cassette machines are also made available for group educational events. Only those residing in the city are eligible for courses taught in person by facilitators. However, shut-ins or their caregivers living in the province can subscribe to the audiovisual library.

An educational television series for and about older shut-ins is also produced and broadcast on local public access television. Topics offered have included: exercise routines for those with special health challenges; nutrition and cooking suggestions for those with special needs or those living alone; information on medical advances that pertain to shut-ins; arthritis management; and coping with isolation. Geriatric hospital and day hospital staff often tape episodes of the series for use with seniors' discussion groups. Residents of personal care home facilities also find the series of interest and value. Copies of the television shows are being made available to rural cable television systems throughout the province.

A peer support counseling service is also available. Early in the development of the HLO service, government continuing care staff suggested that HLO develop this resource to help shut-ins and their caregivers in distress, based on their experiences showing that older adult shut-ins and their caregivers tended not to turn to younger social workers and nursing staff for such support. Counseling is short-term with referrals made to other agencies as appropriate. Volunteer peer counselors tend to be retired social service professionals or others trained to provide counseling to older adults. Matching of shut-ins with a peer counselor is done on the basis of such information as problem area, individual interests, and availability.

HLO is administered and managed by a coordinator with support from volunteer office staff. Seniors are involved in all aspects of the service. The coordinator is assisted by an advisory committee of seniors (i.e., volunteer consultants, facilitators, and participants) as well as relevant professionals in the community.

Service delivery is accomplished using two groups of trained retired volunteers. A team of volunteer consultants provides participants with educational and recreational resource information, encouragement, and assistance with educational needs assessment, course selection, and registration. Consultants also assist with the ongoing monitoring and evaluation of the entire HLO service.

Retired volunteer facilitators deliver the vast majority of courses. Currently, there are 145 volunteer facilitators and 39 paid facilitators associated with HLO. Volunteer facilitators are called upon first, with paid instructors used only if a volunteer is not available to deliver the course. Matching of participants and facilitators is usually done on the basis of availability. Occasionally, however, participants have been able to request a particular facilitator. HLO seeks to make use of the skills, experience, and wisdom of shut-ins for the benefit of the wider community. Therefore, homebound retirees are actively recruited as instructors for other homebound learners and their caregivers. HLO provides free transportation to homebound instructors for this purpose.

HLO courses are generally informal in tone and structure and are paced to take individual participants' interests and capabilities into account. Patience and flexibility as well as skill and experience in the subject area are therefore considered essential. Volunteer orientation and training are extremely important aspects of the service, ensuring quality instruction. Facilitators receive initial orientation upon entry into the program. Thereafter, they are encouraged to participate in continuing education sessions that are arranged each year. These sessions are designed to offer facilitators opportunities to improve their instructional capabilities and to increase their understanding of the challenges faced by those who are homebound. The most popular facilitator seminars have been those dealing with communication disorders among post-stroke victims and instructing shut-ins with visual impairments.

IMPACT AND EVALUATION

To help ensure the quality of the educational opportunities offered within HLO, participants complete an evaluation form at the end of each course. A volunteer consultant also contacts participants once a year to discuss their overall satisfaction with the service. To date, satisfaction ratings have consistently been high. Comments received from participants, volunteers, and others further increase confidence that the service is effective, enhancing self-sufficiency and quality of life:

> *I can now write almost as good as my facilitator. When I started, people could barely understand my writing. (post-stroke participant)*

> *I had not realized the important ingredient that anticipation (of an HLO course) plays in elevating moods and in making the time spent just getting better easier to endure. (post-surgery participant)*

> *Our frail residents definitely show a difference.... They are clearly more talkative and cheerful. They appreciate being led by an older facilitator. If she can do it, they feel they can, too. (guest home facility owner)*

> *Helping someone else in worse circumstances [than mine] is good for me. (facilitator)*

Increases in enrollment over the duration of the program further support its value. In its first year of operation (1988–1989), there were 252 participants in 85 individual and 167 group courses. In 1989–1990, the number of participants increased to 525, particularly as a result of increases in the number participating in group courses (449). Seventy-six individual courses were offered in the second year. Television series audiences are estimated to be between 300 and 500 shut-ins and increasing rapidly as more publicity about the series is done.

Homebound Learning Opportunities has coordinated a number of unique education events for shut-ins. Computer courses for post-stroke, visually handicapped, and polio victims; t'ai chi for students with visual impairment and other significant health challenges; communication skills courses for post-stroke and immigrant shut-ins; and art appreciation and audio cassette programs for hospital-bound seniors are some examples. Of note is the positive change in attitude and self-esteem that shut-ins exhibit when they instruct others or participate in projects of value to their greater community. Volunteers have frequently stated how involvement in HLO has enriched their lives.

Public support for the program has also increased. HLO has attracted considerable attention from local and national media, government sources, and others for its innovative efforts to provide opportunities for the homebound elderly and their caregivers to age in place with enhanced independence.

DISCUSSION

Homebound Learning Opportunities will continue to develop and experiment as it meets the increasing demands for service. Future plans include addressing more fully some of the gaps that remain in service delivery: providing seminars on developing educational services for rural shut-ins and more service to those with significant cognitive impairment.

The use of technology will continue to be explored in an attempt to develop further educational applications for shut-ins. The audiovisual lending library will be expanded to include more self-care and health education resources in areas like pain management, arthritis, and high blood pressure management. Portable computers, with portable printers and modems, will continue to be used. Educational television has proven to be a cost-efficient means to provide easily accessible, relevant information and education to hard-to-reach older adults. The use of community access television as an educational tool for shut-ins will continue to be refined.

The success of HLO indicates that educational opportunities are of genuine interest to older shut-ins and their caregivers. As people age, they maintain a broad range of educational, recreational, and artistic interests and many are willing to experiment and take risks with new areas of learning and creative expression if a nonthreatening, supportive learning environment is maintained. For the homebound, these activities may be the only connections to the community they are able to sustain. Such activities often serve a useful therapeutic function as well, picking up where professional health and social services end.

ACKNOWLEDGMENTS

The authors thank Farrell Fleming, Executive Director, Creative Retirement Manitoba, and Win Lindsay, Life Enrichment Consultant, Creative Retirement Manitoba, for their review of the manuscript. Funding for Homebound Learning Opportunities is provided by the Support Services to Seniors Program, Department of Health, Government of Manitoba, and the New Horizons Program, Health and Welfare Canada.

REFERENCES

Chappell, N. L., Strain, L. A., & Blandford, A. A. (1985). *Aging and health care: A social perspective.* Toronto: Holt, Rinehart, & Winston.

Hickey, T. (1980). *Health and aging.* Monterey, CA: Brooks/Cole.

Longino, C. F., & Soldo, B. J. (1987). The graying of America: Implications of life extension for quality of life. In R. A. Ward & S. S. Tobin (Eds.), *Health in aging: Sociological issues and policy directions* (pp. 58–85). New York: Springer Publishing.

Statistics Canada. (1987). *General social survey analysis series, health and social support.* Ottawa: Minister of Supply and Services Canada.

31

Perspectives on Older Adults in Physical Activity and Sports

Sandy O'Brien Cousins and Art Burgess

INTRODUCTION

The evidence that "exercise is the best medicine" is proliferating across medical, health-care, gerontology, and physical education journals. Indeed, Bortz (1980) claims that there is no single medication that can compete with the range of pathology for which exercise has been prescribed: obesity, depression, diabetes, arthritis, hypertension, coronary heart disease, insomnia, migraine, and smoking cessation. Research suggests that exercise alone can slow the aging process by elevating and maintaining physiological function at levels typical of adults who are decades younger (O'Brien & Conger, 1988; Posner, Gorman, Klein, & Woldow, 1986). Regular, sweat-inducing physical activity appears to be "the one percent solution," that is, a way to reverse the overall average 1% annual decline in many human functions (Bouchard, Shephard, Stephens, Sutton, & McPherson, 1990). Aging mechanisms are not well understood, but evidence has rapidly accumulated that physical fitness and lifelong physical activity do delay many disease processes and can lengthen life by up to two years (Blair et al., 1989; Paffenbarger, Hyde, Wing, & Hsieh, 1986).

For many, exercise provides a level of emancipation from old age. Having socially supportive networks endorsing physical play and obtaining the knowledge and power to be more in control of one's body in late life are liberating forces that more and more aging adults seek (O'Brien & Vertinsky, 1991). As such, finding the older learner in physical-education programming is an example of educational gerontology in possibly its most challenging form.

Cross (1981) argues for the merits of a "blended life plan," meaning that work and education and leisure are worthy of concurrent and lifelong involvement.

From *Educational Gerontology*, 1992, Vol. 18, pp. 461–81, by Sandy O'Brien Cousins and Art Burgess, Washington, D.C.: Taylor & Francis, Inc. Reproduced with permission. All rights reserved.

Age is an especially interesting characteristic because it reveals so clearly certain socialized perceptions about the role of education at various life stages. Sadly the data also reveal the socialized perception that learning is for young people. The feeling of being too old to learn increases steadily with age until it becomes a common barrier to education for older people (Cross, 1981, p. 57).

But fortunately attitudes about aging are changing. New attitudes about lifelong learning are accompanied by new information and changing priorities for adult social and recreational programming (Haley & Hauprich, 1987; Hecox, Levin, & Scott, 1976; Horosko, 1990; Portnoy, Richards, & Roberts, 1989).

Public awareness campaigns aimed at increasing the activity levels of adult Canadians (and ultimately aimed at reducing morbidity rates) are receiving renewed impetus by provincial and federal health agencies such as the Secretariat for Fitness in the Third Age and the 20-year campaign of Participation Canada. After a decade of exposure to the fitness movement, it is not surprising that older Canadian adults are showing increasing interest in physical activity participation. The evidence of this surge in late-life learning is seen in the diversity and numbers of seniors' program offerings at community centers, the appearance of Masters' levels in sport clubs, the creation of Seniors' Activity Centers, and the proliferation of seniors' participation in a wide variety of dance forms. Thousands of seniors are trying to qualify for Seniors' Games across Canada, and the elderly participants, in this late-life pursuit of excellence, seek quality instructional help and supervision.

Evidence exists that supervised exercise programs are indeed superior to unsupervised activities in terms of optimizing the benefits of participation (Kugler, Dimsdale, Hartley, & Sherwood, 1990). Increasingly, there has been a demand for trained instructors, consultants, and supervisors for the older age groups. Although the National Advisory Council on Aging (1991) calls for the removal of barriers that limit access to learning by seniors, it is becoming obvious that insufficient leadership is one of those barriers. Unfortunately, in Canadian communities, few older adults have adequate training to physically assist their peers, and younger leaders who do are usually not prepared to properly adapt recreational programs to aging adults. Surprisingly, little attention has been paid to this leadership void by the various professional groups most likely to be concerned.

The purpose of this article is to identify some important challenges facing prospective physical educators of older adults in sport and exercise training. Further, the article intends to raise an awareness about the role of educational gerontology in the physical setting and recognize that many, if not most, fitness leaders and sport coaches are inexperienced in dealing with the sometimes special needs of older learners. With scientific evidence lacking, it seems worthwhile to share the experiential knowledge of exercise specialists who work with older adults.

The first objective of this article is to identify the kinds of challenges that Canadian educators are experiencing in physical activity and sport settings with the senior population. Although the challenges of older adults in physical activity are significant, the aim of identifying them is not to discourage potential leaders but rather to ready them so that the educational setting might be enhanced. Such challenges include issues of safety and perceptions of risk, intergenerational issues, and ageism. Secondly, the paper discusses approaches to older adult physical education that may optimize learning. Philosophical considerations and a summary conclude the article.

THE CHALLENGES OF PHYSICAL EDUCATION IN OLDER ADULTHOOD

Learning Safely: Old Bodies, Fragile Egos, and Perceived Risk

The development of a safe environment for maintaining and learning physical skill is a necessary accompaniment to quality instruction and enjoyable, low-risk participation at any age. Certainly, by the older years, chronic and acute disease processes do increase risk of pain and aggravation for some adults who require specific exercise modifications. At the same time, older adults do not appear to be more injury-prone (Clarkson & Dedrick, 1988), and the overly cautious nature of disease-free older people may require at times the creation of an instructional climate that fosters risk-taking (Allessio, Grier, & Leviton, 1989).

How do we define risk? Perceived risk, like beauty, is in the eye of the beholder. It involves an evaluation of a situation in terms of its likely physical and psychological outcomes for the individual. Because actual statistical risk is not known for the many things that people do in physical activity, people tend to rely on their own subjective assessment.

Risk, though relative and personal, has absolute factors as well. Certain practices are absolutely risky. A commitment to actions or sequences of actions that must be performed at full strength and full speed is inherently risky for those unprepared for it. Actual risk is exacerbated in situations where the individual is "externally paced" and is forced to respond regardless of their readiness to do so (Anshel, 1989). These situations can potentially cause risk to life and limb at any age.

Another area of risk is possible damage to the ego, in which a negative performance outcome can result in embarrassment and ridicule from peers or onlookers. This loss of self-esteem through failure to live up to expectations is a psychological risk. Failure to meet one's own physical standards as well as the expectations of one's peers and coach can create considerable anxiety and distress. In these situations, continued participation is in jeopardy. Moreover, the aged adult is particularly vulnerable to diminishing returns because real aging decline may exaggerate present inadequacies in an exercise situation. Comparisons between the realities of present ability with past performance are often depressing and in themselves pose a risk to the self-image.

Risk to self-image is highest when the individual has to confront the state of their own decrepitude. Older men recall their youthful muscular body as it was decades earlier, and although sports participation may have delayed some of the aging events, the challenge to maintain one's former performance level may increase. Some older men withdraw completely from exercise activity on the rationale that because they can no longer perform at their youthful level, they would rather not participate at all.

For different reasons, aging females may also be apathetic about exercising. Historically discouraged from sport and vigorous forms of exercise, many older women prefer to hide themselves in stylish clothing and avoid exposing their aging figure. Society, which continues to reinforce the beauty of the young and slim, has given females little possibility to age successfully (Vertinsky, 1991). It appears that women's concern about aging in the physical setting has not been attending so much to declining performance, as it has been paying attention to the "battle of the bulge."

Risk to the self-image also can arise from the mere act of committing to an activity. That an older person would take themselves seriously as an athlete is fraught with psychological risk. Older persons experience considerable social pressure from peers and their families *not* to be involved in what is perceived as unusual and infantile behavior for their age (Arluke & Levin, 1984). When seniors persist in activity despite the discouragement they receive, some question is raised about their judgment. Thus the risk is twofold: the possibility of injury, which may be small, but real, and the likelihood of social sanctions from peers or family if they persist and then are injured or fail to perform ("The old fool, why doesn't she act her age!").

Both physical and psychological risk are increased when peer pressure to perform enters the situation. Participants can find themselves in a situation in which they feel obligated to be active at a level for which they feel unprepared. The presence of someone with whom they must keep up or who, by example, is demanding of them performance levels for which they are unready, not only creates risky situations but undermines the "self" in self-directed learning. An older person can be overwhelmed, for example, in a tennis mismatch or on a long-distance hike with no safe and shorter alternative. In situations such as this all kinds of unspoken expectations are placed on the individual who may perceive no honorable way out. Such events may be devastating to one's self-image and to maintaining confidence in one's personal ability to function at "normal" levels, however normal they already are.

Former athletes are thought to be particularly susceptible to risk in sport situations. These individuals may be accustomed to performing at high-intensity levels—levels no longer appropriate to their needs—and feel pressure to live up to expectations of their peers. At the same time there is an internal desire to measure up to their past performances, however unrealistic these may be. The outcome for aging athletes may be frustration, overstrain, and potential injury—unless sound coaching and respected supervision is available.

In reviewing the many public and personal risks facing older adults, it is easy to understand why many older adults enter sport and physical education settings with anxiety. Moreover, existing anxiety is frequently reinforced by the educator who gives patronage to old notions about overexerting the body and diligently conducts heart-rate monitoring every few minutes. Target heart-rate monitoring is not infallible and may actually increase risk by giving adults a false sense of security (Powles, Sutton, Wicks, Oldridge, & Jones, 1979).

Inexperienced coaches of older adults have been observed to trade ideals of pursuing performance excellence for the ideals of perfect vigilance—ideals demanding dependency of the learner on the educator. This means that no learning or activity can occur without full supervision, not unlike the strict supervisory setting in some nursing homes for the aged, where ambulatory risk is considered to be greater than overmedication and bedsores. Similarly, older adults in exercise settings can be overly restricted; rather they must be given opportunity to explore their own physical limits, and yes, accept an uncertain amount of risk in doing so. However, with proper progression, combined with self-paced advancement, older adult participation in fitness exercise and sport can be essentially injury free, even if unsupervised.

There are situations in which the benefits of participation clearly outweigh the risks. For example, the exhilaration of learning a cartwheel at age 67 or training for a 5-kilometer run at age 73 provides such an adrenalin "rush" that the resulting effect on self-esteem is a benefit that seems to be immeasurable. There are situations of "calculated risk" in which expert instruction is available, identifiable obstacles to safe practice are eliminated, and all available safety features are in place.

The University of Agers gymnastics team, average age of 68, has trained at the University of Alberta since 1986 without serious injury. Some might attribute this safety record to simple good fortune, but a recent injury study indicated that the self-controlled pace of learning may be among the key safety attributes of their program (Burgess, 1990). In addition, the use of quality mats, spring flooring, progressive instruction, supervision, and spotting, and the emphasis placed on preliminary physical conditioning all probably contribute to a safe learning environment. In this program setting, calculated risks are being made with great frequency. Decisions about group readiness for technical information about new skills lie with the educator, whereas decisions about personal participation are in the control of each individual. In this way two safety valves are in place, and the outcomes are predominantly of great benefit to the participant.

To clarify this mutual responsibility for safe learning, each member of the U. of Agers group completes an informal consent form. This form specifies the relationship of the educator to the learner and makes explicit a locus of control that is completely in the hands of the learner. Further, information about any health condition that might contraindicate certain activities is obtained from a modified version of Fitness Canada's PAR-Q (Physical Activity Readiness Questionnaire) form completed yearly by each participant (Burgess, 1991). Certainly, many older people have some kind of condition that requires prudent accommodation. The intent of the forms is to identify these health concerns to educators, and more importantly, to acknowledge a joint understanding of the limits to safe participation.

The Challenge of Heterogeneity

The heterogeneity of the elderly in terms of individual combinations of specific abilities and disabilities is likely to prevent even the most veteran educators from arriving at any simple exercise prescriptions and instructional strategies. Some older adults will be ready to participate at performance levels of adults decades younger, while other adults will be confronting enormous health difficulties. As such, the learners may represent opposite ends of the health continuum and, therefore, should not compare their achievements to others on the same scale. Obviously then, goal-setting must be highly individualized, and "maintaining" rather than "gaining" may be a more realistic objective for those who are already physically fit.

Educators of older adults need to be aware that, at the higher performance levels, they may notice inconsistency in some participants. On some days they function superbly, and other days they can't seem to do anything well. This phenomenon needs further study, but it is perhaps a feature of aging decline that health and energy fluctuations are more apparent from day to day. Such fluctuations can be acknowledged as a "normal" challenge to older adult performance, but persistent downswings should lead to medical attention. One important advantage of training the body at all ages is that less than optimal function can lead to early detection of disease processes and ultimately improved treatment prospects.

Intergenerational Challenges

With the proliferation of segregated fitness and sports activities for adults over age 50, the demand for competent physical educators from the same age range exceeds the supply. This need for older educators has arisen quietly, usually discovered by older adults themselves when they find that they prefer being instructed by their peers. It has been observed in Canadian programs that female fitness instructors, if young, may be regarded with some disdain by older women. The youth, vitality and "lycra leanness" of many younger instructors are probably threatening to many older individuals. Despite certified expertise, youth carries with it an aura of verve and inexperience that, when combined with what seems to be "new fangled" information, can too easily be discredited. No matter how well-trained a young physical educator may be, there is the major hurdle of credibility to leap before young leadership can become effective. And leadership credibility is proposed to be a key ingredient of the skillful educator (Brookfield, 1990).

Youth as a Handicap

Without appropriate training, new physical educators come into the instructional setting with certain inherent handicaps. An insensitivity to the needs of older persons for adapted instructional strategies is a serious gap in the training of younger-aged physical educators and sports coaches. Notable is their approach to instruction that, even when purposely modified, is essentially paced at too high a performance level. Within this is an assumption that all older people function as do youth.

Something as basic as voice projection, diction, and speed of delivery in speaking to older people can pose communication problems just as the use of spoken jargon and slang expressions can create communication barriers. Observation of older people in activity groups can be instructive. Any announcement to them is followed by a buzz of interactions confirming what was said, questioning what was meant, verifying their own interpretation of the announcement. The more crucial the announcement appears to be, the greater the confirmatory buzz. A younger instructor will often speak quickly and somewhat "off the cuff" and having spoken, moves on to the next item, leaving the older listeners in a cloud of half-confirmed ideas.

As a resource person, the younger adult can also fail at the level of basic communication. Brookfield (1986) claims that "a resource person is often seen as someone who assists adults to locate individuals and material resources in order that they may complete learning efforts that they, the learners, have defined" (p. vii). Unless the younger adult identifies the goals of the older learners and locates expertise and material resources appropriate to these goals, respect for the value of those resources may be lacking. Furthermore, material resources need to be age considerate. The use of signs and visual aids should take into account vision problems that are common in older people. Notices should be posted in large type with the expectation that many older persons will be without their glasses in a swimming pool or gymnasium setting. A posted sign can be supplemented with an oral reading of it to the group.

Young physical educators may be "out of synch" with the way older people learn new motor skills. Skill instruction with older people has to be based on a firm link between the present capability of the older person and the possible utility of the skill in the future. Educators who are inexperienced with older adults will often assume that the instruction of a new physical skill will be immediately seen in its overall context within an activity. This quite often is not the case, particularly if the adult is not familiar with the movement requirements of the sport. Though a good teaching strategy may present complex physical skills in small movement units (as in part-whole learning), older learners do not necessarily understand the importance of the parts or their place in the structure of the whole activity. Even when the whole skill is presented, the parts just mastered may not be recognized within it. Research on this phenomenon is needed to explain whether older adults have this perceptual difficulty because they are not accustomed to this instructional approach or are simply not familiar with the learning of complex motor patterns. Self-paced practice is helpful in preventing information overload leading to visible frustration and confusion in the learning process. Further, considering that some skills take months, and sometimes years, to master, it is probably essential to carefully explain the relevance of the movement parts in relation to the final skill.

Culture Shock or Stagnation

A challenge to be faced by adults of different generations is the fact that everyone may sense a culture shock of sorts. How the younger physical educator presents himself or herself—persona, the selection of music, and the respect for ideas and suggestions of the participants—is instrumental in creating a climate conducive to individual improvements. Frustration and helplessness may be felt by both sides if it is realized that a lifetime of experience with one's body may be challenged by contemporary knowledge and unfamiliar techniques.

For all the comfort that age-peer physical educators provide their elderly students, they too have their limitations. This is seen particularly with older leaders whose information and methods are out of date. Often the older educator has continued to teach without ever having been updated on current training information. In most cases, little damage is done, but the effectiveness of a 30-year-old methodology leaves a lot to be desired. The author recalls attending a long-established fitness class conducted at a famous resort beach. The setting, the attitudes, and the method were right out of the post–World War II era. The corps of volunteer instructors were themselves elderly, as were many of the participants. Although the exercises were forceful, regimented, jerky, and hard on joints, the classes still attracted a huge following year after year. Though clearly a case could be made for retaining the nostalgic elements contributing to the program's success, it would be quite difficult to convince program administrators that this class was inherently risky and that the educators needed further training.

That this, and other exercise groups, continue in the face of such apparent malpractice gives pause for consideration. An important feature of these situations was the strong allegiance of the participants for the instructor in whom they had complete confidence. Inherent with this commitment to the older instructor is a sureness that the older instructor still knows best, has their best interests at heart, that she or he will be tolerant of their own individual variation from the prescribed exercise, and that participants can stop whenever they feel it is appropriate. Thus, the participant may sense a better measure of personal control over the situation. This sense of control may provide some protection from the errors of outdated exercise techniques.

Still, issues regarding age-peer leadership need to be addressed. In some provinces, special certification and fitness leadership courses addressing exercise adaptations for older adults have been conducted; ideally, older instructors will continue to be invited to these courses to exchange experiential resources in return for safer program content ideas from contemporary instructors.

Stereotyping and Ageism in Programming

Ageism, or the treatment and organization of learning based on age alone, could be considered poor practice. Although population aging permits certain age-related jokes and comic stereotypes about the capabilities of the elderly to be popular, individual aging is highly unique. Older people have more abilities than they have disabilities—a truth that is evident in the National Film Board of Canada (1990) production of "Age Is No Barrier." Physiologically, it is known that the organ systems of any one person age at different rates, and these rates of aging vary enormously from one person to the next. The implication for exercise programming then, which is directly impacting on human physiological function, is that the exercise leader cannot simply cater to a single level of physical fitness, even in a single adult. One shoulder might be flexible and the other stiff; one hand-grip might be strong and the other weak; the heart may be aerobically fit, but local muscular endurance limited.

Some years back, the author had the experience of conducting fitness programming for adults 50 and older. The initial strategy was to keep the program safe by addressing the needs of the most unfit members of the group. Some months into the program, fitness evaluations indicated that fitness levels in some adults, in some functions, were at the level of 30- and 40-year-old adults—functional advantages that would be quickly lost to aging processes if the class continued to operate at a level below their present capabilities. The instructional problem was explained to the group, and consensus quickly developed that the instructor should proceed at a higher intensity level with each individual controlling their own participation intensity. One woman quipped, "We wondered how long it would take you to figure out most of us could handle much more, but we were too lazy to admit it!"

Overall, a problem of everyone underestimating the interests, the physical capacity, the motivation, and the potential for learning in the later years, particularly with respect to physical activity and sport skill, is likely to reinforce stereotypes of frailty as a natural and inevitable outcome of aging processes.

APPROACHES TO OLDER ADULT PHYSICAL EDUCATION

The Role of Fitness and Learning

An essential requirement for mastery of physical skills is having adequate physical fitness to work through the progressions, attempt the skill, and practice it. Many skills are in themselves quite simple but may require substantial strength and endurance. If conditioning is insufficient, the older person will be unable to sustain the number of practice repetitions that would ensure successful mastery. Thus, it is recommended that skill learning start with elementary movements, requiring a minimum of fitness. Over a longer period, conditioning and learning tend to advance together.

Preliminary conditioning is common in coaching practice, but the need for extra developmental time for stamina to build among older learners is sometimes forgotten or rushed. The maxim, "Make haste slowly," has particular relevance in working with older adults. This calls for a less instructionally intense situation. Less intensity means that more recovery time is available for strenuous activities, and instructional time is less focused on immediate results. Rather a reduced training intensity permits the immediate benefits of physical activities to take priority. Jovial interactions, information sharing, socializing, and submaximal performances of skills are among the immediate benefits of a slower learning pace. The less intense pacing has a twofold advantage: First, it enhances the social aspects of exercise programs that are key determinants of present and future participation (O'Brien Cousins, 1991), and second, stamina for learning is extended and longer activity sessions are possible. Enhancing enjoyment, maintaining regular attendance, and extending stamina for learning are all important aspects of good health practice leading to successful learning in the exercise setting.

The importance of present physical fitness for enjoyable participation was recently illustrated in the introduction of a new Seniors' Games event. Inclusion of shot-put in masters' track and field competition resulted in a rash of hand injuries, particularly among a group of highly fit older women. Even though the women were fit, the instructor may have overestimated their physiological readiness to handle intense practice. Though the leg and back musculature of these older female shot-putters was able to deliver the shot, the hand muscles were disproportionately stiffer and weaker and sustained injury when the women began to throw hard too early in their training. Many were forced to give up throwing altogether because of this chronic injury. This example makes the point that although often older adults must seek the technical training they need from younger professionals, it is often the professionals who do much of the initial learning, usually in hindsight, in these intergenerational situations. Ideally, educators have foresight, rather than hindsight, and are adaptable, creative, and use an individualized approach with older adults, even in the group setting—a monumental task even for experienced educators.

The Role of Sport Technology

Although the high technology currently applied to elite development coaching systems can surely benefit improved performance capacity at all ages and all levels, it is likely that humanistic, more than mechanistic, approaches will first facilitate the older adult learner. It takes time, trial and error, accumulated experience, and practice for adult educators and coaches to develop adaptive and individualized strategies that permit older adults to realize their true performance potential.

Anshel (1989) claims that much activity occurs in short-term memory before, during, and after a motor task is executed. Motor activity is undermined by complex, rapid, and overly abundant information about the activity. Anshel suggests that self-paced tasks, using self-talk as a mental strategy, emphasizing meaningful performance cues, and using mental imagery are valuable strategies to facilitate older-adult motor learning.

Older learners who have access to a physical-education facility may be technically aided in ways they have never experienced, and these advantages can accelerate learning, increase motivation, and heighten overall progress. Exercise mats, indoor exercise bikes with speedometers, bungee cords, hand weights, and pulley systems are frequently available at no extra cost to participants.

If older adults are willing to participate with younger adults and younger exercise leaders, they will likely have access to certified fitness instruction in local community centers, to certified coaching in sport club settings, to anthropometric and fitness assessment at local universities and fitness centers, and to videotape cameras that provide immediate performance feedback in slow motion. Such access to expertise and technology is not the current norm for older adults—yet, but such programs are already being put on trial. An experimental project at the University of Alberta, for example, is currently being conducted in the Department of Athletics, Campus Fitness, and Lifestyle program (Burgess, 1991). This innovative new program for seniors is called "Project Alive and Well" and offers a glimpse of the future in exercise and sport for aging adults. Qualified, age-peer instructors are available at scheduled times in various sport and exercise settings, including ice skating, tennis, elementary gymnastics, aquatic fitness, and social dance. This program quickly reached capacity, and future expansion is desirable, but fiscal restraint, facility scheduling, and limited staffing resources provide significant barriers to additional opportunities for seniors in this community.

Empowerment Versus Control

A bumper sticker sums up the essence of older-adult physical education, "When the people take the lead, the leaders will follow." A prudent educator of older adults will facilitate their initiatives for activity and learning. However, some difficulty may arise in determining the amount of empowerment and control that an older adult may desire. In any group of elderly adults, there is usually a combination of novice, intermediate skilled, and advanced learners. Each has a preference for the amount of supervision and direct assistance to be offered. The creation of a learning climate that encourages and rewards individual striving and at the same time provides technical support upon request is a departure from traditional experiences for many older individuals. Some adults may question the amount of independence given to them in the exercise setting, since they may be accustomed to the former regimens of "P.T." On occasion, the expectations of the older learner and the contemporary adult educator may, and do, clash.

Brookfield (1986) emphasizes the primacy of the learner in controlling their own learning experiences, but cautions, "it is misconceived to talk of the self-directedness of learners who are unaware of alternative ways of thinking, perceiving or behaving" (p. 124).

He eloquently summarizes the complexity of the leader-dominant versus learner-dominant activity as encounters of conflicting purposes and contrasting personality styles that "frequently challenges learners to engage in anxiety-producing reexamination of the self or of previously unchallenged norms (organizational, behavioral, or moral)" (Brookfield, 1986, p. vii). Brookfield claims that the goal of the educator in some settings is to provoke and question, not accept and give comfort. Playing the devil's advocate may place the educator in an apparently unfriendly position to learners.

> *The facilitation of learning—assisting adults to make sense of and act upon the personal, social, occupational and political environment in which they live—is an important, exhilarating and profound activity, both for facilitators and for learners. It is also a highly complex psychosocial drama in which the personalities of the individuals involved, the contextual setting for the educational transaction, and the prevailing political climate crucially affect the nature and form of learning. (p. vii)*

The important issue is that, eventually, physical autonomy is advanced to the older athlete or exercise participant. Ultimately "learning to learn" is a responsibility that most older learners come to appreciate and enjoy.

Program Objectives

One of the significant distinctions between older and younger adults in sports participation lies in their different approaches to competition and training. Older adults are usually concerned with a relative performance standard. As one hopeful older runner put it, "If I can keep my time constant for the next two years, I'll equal the Canadian record because I'll be older!"

Older adults are concerned with where they are not compared to where they might be if they had not trained at all. They recognize the limits imposed on them by the aging process and continue to test themselves against those limits.

Most older people have a better understanding than youth of where participation fits into life and recognize that sport is not life itself. Due to age and experience, older people have a wider perspective from which to view athletic achievement. While youth has a narrower, short-term view of the world, the older adult has seen the broad picture. Youth is more anxious to get on with training and realize achievement. Thus youth is more focused on the pursuit of excellence and, because of its primeness, is able to realize the results of training more directly; a young athlete appears to be able to modify skills and techniques readily. With their experience of sports participation so immediate, young people tend to be more task-oriented and use objective results as the measure of their success.

Older adults, on the other hand, appear to not effect change with as much ease and so could be considered not as trainable. As a result, the training experience for older adults has other facets that are important: the meeting of other "kindred spirits" and "sharing the moment" are essential parts of training. Coaches familiar with training youth are often put off by the apparent lack of discipline in older athletes who like to chat and generally socialize around the training experience. Successful older-adult athletic events are marked by the emphasis on this parallel socializing experience. Coffee parties, dance socials, beer-fests, and singsongs are popular and prevalent at older-adult sports competitions (e.g., Seniors' Games).

Youthful athletes tend to regard the competition from an adversarial perspective. In the "zero-sum" game of competitive sport, for one to win, one must lose. Placement on national teams, public accolades, travel expenses, and scholarships go to the more elite who cannot afford to give "aid and comfort to the enemy" by socializing. At the same time, older people in competition have a less urgent agenda. Although striving to best their opponents, the atmosphere is more friendly and collegial. What they really hope to best is their own performances.

The implications of this for older-adult participants point clearly to enhancing the opportunity to train, compete, and socialize on their own terms. The athletic event must be seen as an opportunity for self-enhancement through participation in the event but also for parallel social interactions. Older-adult educators might better recognize that the post-training coffee break is, in many ways, as important as the workout itself.

With the proliferation of older-adult fitness and sports programs, certain realities about the involvement of older adults in high-level competition are becoming clear. One of these is that coaching older people in sport is not just a scaled-down version of coaching youth. More and more older people are entering competitive sport, and their presence is demanding attention of the coaching community, most of whom come into new coaching relationships for which they are often ill-prepared. Older people are approached as anomalies on which coaches work their training strategies. Little credit is given to the remarkable ability, knowledge, experience, autonomy, and special interests of older people.

Ill-prepared coaches may mask their insecurity in an authoritarian coaching role and adopt a one-sided, parent-child relationship with older learners. In this dependent relationship, all decisions are made or ratified by the coach who sets goals, decides the training regimen, awards praise or blame, and is the source of all information and direction. This coach-centered system usually focuses on the task at hand. It produces very little personal growth or autonomy among the adult learners who are essentially pawns of the coach. Moreover, older adults resent and resist being ordered about. They demand reasons for decisions made on their behalf and question authority seemingly exercised for everyone's benefit. Following is an example of older adults in a sport in which differences in philosophy have had negative results. From this come several conclusions and recommendations.

An older skate-dancing couple, both partners with years of experience in skating, came under the leadership of a quite successful coach of children. From the start of the relationship, they were surprised by the coach's inflexibility and his total disregard for their own previous background. His coaching was a litany of complaint about their various deficiencies and a demand for absolute submission to his authority. This authority included choosing their costumes and keeping iron control of each moment of the practice session. He would brook no discussion of any matter concerning skating. Needless to say, the older couple refused to continue under his direction and later coached themselves to a Provincial Championship.

Several conclusions can be drawn from this example. Foremost is the concept of the maturity and independence of the adult participant. Not a precocious child, not a substandard has-been, the older-adult sports participant is more often an example of successful aging. They bring to the athletic experience a physique and physiology that is declining minimally in vigor. They bring as well their maturity, their experiences, and their wisdom. They bring also a childlike enthusiasm for play. Most of all, they know about life and how it will all end.

Another conclusion comes from the idea of the athletic experience as a source of personal growth. It recognizes that older people who engage in sport do so to meet higher needs. One would assume that the basic needs described by Maslow are met when the older adult sets out to play. Thus the need for affiliation and for self-actualization are likely the operant needs in *the playing situation*[1] (Waldron & Moore, 1991).

If this is true, then the playing situation must have certain features that enhance and strengthen the gratification of these higher needs. Foremost is the idea that the individual is more important than the activity. Activity must be pursued for its self-enhancement value. It is the context for growth of new friendships. It is the location of friendly interaction. It is the arena of personal growth. At the point where the outcome of the activity becomes more important than its effect on the participants—where the score, the game statistics, the style, and precision of the performance overshadows its effect on the players—the value to the older adult disappears. Persons involved in coaching older adults should be aware of these differences in objectives and structure the playing situation of their older participants accordingly.

Fan the Flames or Contain the Fire?

It is clear that, though society continues to think of its oldest members as tired and burned-out entities, many older adults are gearing up to try activities for which they have been waiting all their lives. A single philosophical stance on older-adult learning in physical settings is probably impossible in light of the diversity of older adults. The difficult questions and major issues for practitioners in educational settings are the following: "Should one fan the flames of older-adult enthusiasm for mastery of the body and *augment* the intoxicating high that accompanies late-life skill development? Or should the facilitator be more protective and subdued in light of the potential problems facing the aged? Is the letdown of the inevitable aging decline only made more malicious by elevating late-life performance gains to new heights? What are the risks of snuffing out a blaze of inspired adult learning by reaffirming the realities and time limitations of a finite life span?"

Research on the cognitive strategies that older athletes use to justify the importance of "winning" at the finish line of life's course suggests that many people feel that the clock is indeed running out (O'Brien & Conger, 1991). Many active older adults feel that every minute counts and that they have no time to look back or have regrets. A phrase describing this attitude, and its accompanying acceleration, is "over the hill and speeding up." Sportive seniors report that there are things to do and things to see, and an optimistic outlook gets many of them through each day. O'Brien and Conger's study on the philosophical stance taken by athletes at the Alberta Seniors' Games supports the strategy of educators and coaches fanning the flames of learning as long as possible and helping seniors realize their potential by "going out in a blaze." As one senior quipped, "I hope I die with my sneakers on."...

NOTE

1. *The playing situation* is a generic term to describe training, learning, competing, and socializing subsumed by sports participation. It recognizes that "play" is an important and integral part of sports participation.

REFERENCES

Allessio, H.M., Grier, L.J., & Leviton, D. (1989). Trailblazing recreational programming for the elderly: High-risk activities. *Activities, Adaptation & Aging, 13*(4), 9–16.

Anshel, M.H. (1989). An information processing approach teaching motor skills to the elderly. In A.C. Ostrow (Ed.), *Aging and motor behavior* (pp. 285–303). Indianapolis, IN: Benchmark Press.

Arluke, A., & Levin, J. (1984). Another stereotype: Old age as a second childhood. *Aging, 346*, 7–11.

Blair, S.N., Kohl, W.H., III, Paffenbarger, R.S., Clark, D.B., Cooper, K.H., & Gibbons, L.W. (1989). Physical fitness and all-cause mortality: A prospective study of healthy men and women. *Journal of the American Medical Association, 257*, 3115–3117.

Bortz, W.M. (1980). Effect of exercise on aging—effect of aging on exercise. *Journal of the American Geriatric Society, 28*, 49–51.

Bouchard, C., Shephard, R.J., Stephens, T., Sutton, J.R., & McPherson, B.D. (Eds.). (1990). Exercise, fitness and health: The consensus statement. In *Exercise, Fitness and Health* (pp. 4–28). Champaign, IL: Human Kinetics.

Brookfield, S.D. (1986). *Understanding and facilitating adult learning: A comprehensive analysis of principles and effective practices.* San Francisco: Jossey-Bass.

Brookfield, S.D. (1990). *The skillful teacher.* San Francisco: Jossey-Bass.

Burgess, A.C. (1990). *Injury rate study in older gymnasts and young controls.* Unpublished report. Department of Athletics, Edmonton, AB: The University of Alberta.

Burgess, A.C. (1991). Project alive and well report. In C. Blais (Ed.), *Aging into the twenty-first century.* Ottawa: Captus University Publications.

Clarkson, P.M., & Dedrick, M.E. (1988). Exercise-induced muscle damage, repair, and adaptation in old and young subjects. *Journal of Gerontology: Medical Sciences 43*(4), M91–96.

Cross, K.P. (1981). *Adults as learners.* San Francisco: Jossey-Bass.

Haley, E., & Hauprich, A. (1987). Elderly and able? *Healthsharing, 9*(1), 24.

Hecox, B., Levine, E., & Scott, D. (1976). Dance in physical rehabilitation. *Physical Therapy, 56*(8), 919–923.

Horosko, M. (1990). Senior adults—Your new pupils? *Dance Magazine*, April, 60–61.

Kugler, J., Dimsdale, J.E., Hartley, L.H., & Sherwood, J. (1990). Hospital supervised vs. home exercise in cardiac rehabilitation: Effects on aerobic fitness, anxiety, and depression. *Archives of Physical Medicine & Rehabilitation, 71*, 322–325.

National Advisory Council on Aging. (1991). *Aging and NACA: The NACA position on lifelong learning.* Ottawa: Ministry of Supply and Services.

National Film Board of Canada. (1990). *Age is no barrier.* [Film.] Ottawa: Author.

O'Brien, S.J., & Conger, P.R. (1988). *Physical fitness of women participating in the Alberta Seniors Games.* Unpublished manuscript, the University of Alberta, Department of Physical Education & Sport Studies, Edmonton.

O'Brien, S.J., & Conger, P.R. (1991). No time to look back: Approaching the finish line of life's course. *The International Journal of Aging & Human Development, 33*(1), 75–87.

O'Brien, S.J., & Vertinsky, P.A. (1991). Unfit survivors: Exercise as a resource for aging women. *The Gerontologist, 31*(3), 347–357.

O'Brien Cousins, S.J. (1991). *The description and determinants of late life exercise in women born before 1921.* Unpublished doctoral dissertation, University of British Columbia, Vancouver.

Paffenbarger, R.S., Jr., Hyde, R.T., Wing, A.L., & Hsieh, C. (1986). Physical activity, all-cause mortality and longevity of college alumni. *The New England Journal of Medicine, 314*, 605–613.

Portnoy, F.L., Richards, C., & Roberts, R. (1989). Wheelchair karate. *Geriatric Nursing,* March/April, 76–77.

Posner, J.D., Gorman, K.M., Klein, H.S., & Woldow, A. (1986). Exercise capacity in the elderly. *American Journal of Cardiology, 57*, 52C–58C.

Powles, A.C.P., Sutton, J.R., Wicks, J.R., Oldridge, N.B., & Jones, N.L. (1979). Reduced heart rate response to exercise in ischemic heart disease: The fallacy of the target heart rate in exercise testing. *Medicine & Science in Sports, 11*(3), 227–233.

Vertinsky, P.A. (1991). *Regulating female physicality: Theory and historical evidence.* Unpublished manuscript prepared for Sporting Traditions VIII, Canberra, Australia. Printed in the Faculty of Education at the University of British Columbia, Vancouver.

Waldron, M.K., & Moore, G.A.B. (1991). *Helping adults learn.* Toronto: Thompson Educational Publishers.

32

Promoting Vitality Among Older Adults With Computers

Ellen Bouchard Ryan and Roberta K.B. Heaven

NEEDS OF OLDER ADULTS

Much has been written about the challenges of adapting to old age and of leading a rich and satisfying life in the later years (Fries & Crapo, 1981; Skinner & Vaughn, 1983). Older adults experience a variety of needs upon which their physical and mental well-being depend. Among these are respect and dignity; independence and control over their lives; communication and social interactions; access to information; health care; entertainment and stimulating leisure activities; opportunities for learning; and socially useful roles (Butler & Lewis, 1982; McPherson, 1983).

As computer technology becomes more and more a part of our lives, it becomes increasingly important to address issues concerning the impact of this technology on the well-being of older adults (Hoot & Hayslip, 1983). Hence, the present article focuses upon some specific ways in which computer applications can enhance the health and life style of older adults. In addition, factors inhibiting the widespread use of computers by elders and challenges involved in ensuring that these applications are beneficial are discussed.

IMPACT OF COMPUTER APPLICATIONS UPON OLDER ADULTS

Communication and Social Interactions

By expanding the opportunity to communicate with other people, technology has altered the lives of many handicapped individuals. These advances can also benefit elderly persons who lose some function late in life. For the speech-impaired who retain reading and writing skills, a lightweight electric typewriter that can be carried everywhere would be useful. Or, a small brief-case computer with word-processing skills allows for advance preparation of messages, for storage of frequently used messages, and for a variety of additional uses. Speech therapy exercises can be done with a computer, to complement those done with a therapist or with another helper (Beasley & Davis, 1981; Obler & Albert, 1980; Vaughn, Faucett, & Lightfoot, 1984). Electronic aids which produce words in synthesized or taped speech can enable stroke patients to communicate understandably with those around them, even when they are only able to point to 20 different pictographic symbols for words. Computerized versions of these aids permit the construction and use of oral messages of impressive complexity if the user can learn the symbols and how to remember where they are stored.

For hearing-impaired elderly, technological advances are continuing. Computer-aided testing of hearing and fitting of hearing devices increases the likelihood of an effective aid and its consistent use. Computer-monitored hearing devices which change their settings according to the current situational needs of the user promise to be of great assistance to the older person with some hearing loss. Devices for telephones to enhance the signal are widely available now, and deaf individuals use computer terminals with printouts to communicate by telephone (Popelka, 1984). Picture telephones which send video displays of the speakers will help those who have difficulty hearing effectively on the telephone or following conversation without visual cues. Advantages of the computer printout over the telephone are that a written record of the interaction is available for future reference and that the message can be prepared ahead of time. Advance preparation is important if an individual has difficulty with the language, is uncomfortable on the telephone, or has difficulty with the time pressures of the telephone.

For the visually impaired, computer translation of text into Braille and Braille keyboards and printers can expand their access to information and opportunities for communication. Also, voice entry computer systems which recognize oral commands are available for limited tasks at the present time; and expansion in this area can safely be expected in the near future.

For all older adults, the use of computers for word processing and electronic mail services opens up possibilities that are just becoming apparent. Sending of personal letters can be substantially facilitated with word processing, and electronic mail further increases the likelihood of interchange. Once the typing skills and the few word processing commands are acquired, an individual can communicate in writing much more easily than traditionally. Therapeutic life review can be facilitated with word processing; and life histories, other prose, and poetry can be written for friends, family, and the public with relative ease.

Access to Information

The modern era of technology is often referred to as the Information Age. Computers make it possible to store, manage, and retrieve many kinds of information. Commercial computer database searches are available with which one can identify articles and books addressing almost any topic. Bulletin services provide access to information concerning daily news (local, national, or global) on general topics or only on restricted topics of particular interest to the subscriber. Both the bibliographic searches and the news bulletins offer lists by title, selected abstracts, and opportunities to obtain the original reports. Personal computers make it possible to develop and access databases concerning the local community or concerning a hobby such as medieval music or stamp collecting.

Opportunities for Entertainment and for Learning

Software for personal computers is currently written so that one needs a minimal knowledge about operating the computer to use applications. Programs are available for video games, word games, card games, and chess. Using these programs for entertainment and activity therapy has already been successful among the frail elderly in nursing homes (Weisman, 1983). To help with typical tasks, one can relatively easily use programs to balance the checkbook, set up a budget, complete income tax forms, organize recipes, plan menus, and organize a weekly or daily schedule.

Computer-aided instruction is another option which older adults will find increasingly valuable. Continued education can be conveniently pursued at home, at the Senior Center, or at the library with programs teaching any topic from accounting to art history to music composition. For most content areas, the computer can promote learning by incorporating exercises and graphic illustrations within the presentation of information. The computer is naturally an infinitely patient teacher, provides immediate feedback on learning progress, and can be quite motivating. Computer-assisted learning can also be supplemented with readings, lectures, or televised lectures. Danowski and Sacks (1980) have shown that older adults can learn effectively in this context and that they benefit especially from highly interactive programs. Such programs can also be used to teach specific daily living skills such as how to use automatic bank tellers and preparation for the written or road tests for driver's licenses.

Some older adults become keen to learn to program the computer after working with a number of these application programs. This is an interesting and challenging learning experience which many find satisfying and which expands one's problem-solving skills (Krasnor & Mitterer, in press; Papert, 1980; Sanders, 1981). With programming skills and/or maintenance skills, older adults have a new hobby, a channel for social interactions with other programmers, and prospects for part-time or full-time employment. There is a burgeoning need for new computer programs to carry out specific tasks for individuals and for groups.

Health Care

Within the health domain, the impact of technology in prolonging life and in treating previously fatal conditions comes to mind immediately. In addition to acute care, however, computers and related technological aids can be very helpful in monitoring vital life functions (e.g., heart beat, blood pressure, blood chemistry) for individuals with chronic conditions and in sounding an emergency alarm when necessary.

With regard to the elderly in particular, the various emergency alarm systems available for the home often make it possible for individuals to remain in their own home instead of moving in with a relative, or to remain living with a relative instead of moving to a nursing home (Hess, 1984; Symington et al., 1980). These systems usually involve an emergency button, worn by an individual and pressed in time of need, which activates telephone connections with emergency staff, family and friends, and ambulance in an order determined for each individual. Typically, unless the target individual is listed as especially vulnerable to life-threatening episodes, the service would begin with a return telephone call for additional information about the problem experienced. Other systems require that individuals press the button at scheduled times to indicate that they are O.K. With the support provided by this type of emergency alert system, many older people can have the opportunity of remaining active and in control of their own lives for a longer period of time.

There are difficulties, of course, in acceptance of such a system and in the consequences of its use. On the basis of two unpublished reports (Sherwood & Morris, 1980; Dibner, Lowry & Morris, 1980) Hess (1984) summarizes an evaluation study of the Lifeline system with the aged. Compared to controls, users of the system expressed more comfort in living alone, greater confidence in their ability to remain in their homes, and fewer nursing home days. However, this increase was predominantly observed within a subgroup who were severely impaired and were not socially isolated. The mechanical intervention was reassuring for those with a sense that someone cared, whereas the intervention may have highlighted the vulnerability of individuals who were isolated. Further research concerning the acceptance and consequences of technological aids among the elderly is clearly necessary.

The availability and flexibility of microcomputers open up many possibilities for computer-aided health assessment and health education. The computer can easily be programmed to be supportive, tireless, and systematic in interviewing patients about their health problems as well as lifestyle (Evans, 1984). Evans describes a particular application in which a lifestyle assessment method developed by Wilson and Ciliska (1984) formed the basis of a computer program. The method is based on the mnemonic "FANTASTIC," in which each letter represents a significant component of lifestyle to be examined. The program, written in BASIC for the Apple microcomputer, poses the series of questions in a relaxed, non-threatening manner; and it subsequently provides feedback to people regarding how healthy their lifestyles are and offers some motivational messages concerning possible changes. Of course, people can be less than honest with the computer; but the literature suggests that they may actually provide a computer with more information about themselves than they give to an interviewer (Dove et al., 1977, Skinner & Allen, 1983).

Relatedly, computer programs can be written to offer health education on a diverse set of topics relevant to older adults (Ellis & Raines, 1981; Ellis, Raines, & Hakanson, 1982). For example, they can benefit from learning what to expect as one ages and alternative ways of adapting to changes in physical limitations, residential situations, and social roles (Barr, 1983). As well, they could benefit from learning about uses and misuses of prescription and non-prescription drugs; about the manner in which nutrition and physical exercise can enhance their current and future health; and about ways of coping with depressed moods and feelings of social isolation (Shamansky & Hamilton, 1979; Thurston & Kerr, 1983). For those needing to learn about a newly diagnosed chronic condition, a computer program can be a stimulating complement to pamphlets and talking with experts. The computer's non-humanness can be an advantage when one is worried or embarrassed, not wishing to discuss one's problems. Also, immediate feedback on progress in learning would be particularly helpful when an individual is under stress and likely to exhibit poor concentration. Practical guidelines for the preparation of health education software (Evans, 1984) are available to guide the development of new computer programs in this domain.

A final aspect of health care in which computer assistance can be beneficial is rehabilitation. When an individual has lost some cognitive abilities such as attention, memory, or language skills, systematic practice of increasingly more demanding tasks within the skills domain can be effective in promoting recovery. After a stroke, for example, cognitive and language abilities are frequently recovered gradually. The required therapy is slow, repetitious, and dependent on a high level of motivation. Alternative, interesting and motivating ways of keeping the patient's attention on this type of task can be very valuable complements to traditional therapy.

Playing video games could be just the answer. However, the commercially available game programs typically require relatively rapid and complex responses. In some cases, it is not too difficult to adapt these to allow for slow responses and gradually increasing speeds. If one begins with an analysis of the types of skills that need to be built up, then one can write programs which assess and stimulate the growth of these skills.

For my current research, I have developed a program called Memory for Goblins. Within the memory literature, an important conceptual distinction is made between short-term memory and working memory (Baddeley & Hitch, 1974). The traditional measure of short-term memory is the digit span task, in which one is asked to repeat increasingly long sequences of digits. This measure of memory correlates with more complex intellectual tasks depending upon memory; but it has been argued that a better predictor of complex performance is a memory measure in which storage must occur while information processing takes place (Daneman & Carpenter, 1980; Hitch, 1978). For example, when we read, we must store the meanings of the text while we continue identifying new words and integrating them into sentences. One useful measure of working memory is the Counting Span task (Case, Kurland, & Goldberg, 1982), in which the participant counts dots on a sequence of cards (e.g., 1-2-3-4; 1-2-3-4-5-6-7; 1-2-3-4-5-6-7-8-9) and then reports the count values (e.g., 4, 7, 9). Our program translates the dot counting task into a video game format in which goblins intermingled with squares are counted. The shape of the goblins changes as the difficulty level increases. With this program, we can measure the speed and accuracy of counting goblins as well as the accuracy of recall for number sequences. Since the game terminates as soon as the player reaches a level where he does not succeed, frustration is minimized and reward for improvements as the levels increase is maximized.

The game can be played in two modes. In the immediate mode, the goblin display disappears as soon as the count number is entered, while in the paced mode the display remains until the space bar is pressed. The paced mode thus offers the opportunity for rehearsal, and the program measures the amount of rehearsal time taken. Within the structure of the Memory for Goblins game, there are options for providing strategy instructions to the player. The game could be further modified to address other practice needs. If accurate perceptions were a target task, then the contrast between goblins and non-goblin figures could be gradually modified from obvious to more subtle. If increasing speed were a target task, then the amount of time allowed for counting could be gradually decreased. Hence, practice with more and less challenging variants of the Memory for Goblins game could form a valuable component of a cognitive or motor rehabilitation program.

Independence and Control

Computers and related technology will be playing a larger role in the coming decade in assisting older adults to live in their own homes for as long as possible. In Figure 1, we have presented a schematic diagram illustrating the potential use of home microcomputers in providing further independence and security for the elderly. Individuals who are having some difficulty living independently but are not in definite need of a nursing home placement can be assisted with this system. At the present time, this type of system is possible given some modification of existing hardware and software.

FIGURE I

Schematic of Home Microcomputer Potential

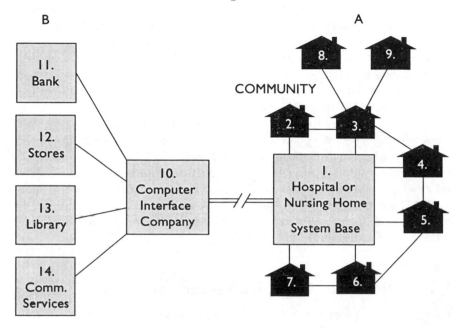

Section A represents the system base, located in a community hospital or nursing home, and its links with 6 elderly clients in their individual homes. Health care staff are available at the base for consultation and for home visits as necessary. The homes, #2 to #7, are outfitted with a personal computer linked by telephone with the base. The potential services provided by the home terminal are practically unlimited. With the system, the individual can contact the base at any time, either by emergency alert or by terminal. Depending upon the individual's needs, these home terminals will be equipped for various aspects of environmental control, such as door security, heat monitoring, telephone answering, and radio/TV operation (see Vasa, 1982). From the base, health staff can contact clients to assess health status (with the aid of additional technical measurement devices in some cases), to give instructions regarding medications, to determine daily needs, and to arrange for any needed consultant services. Clients can use the system to find out about community activities, local news, and other information made available as well as to request transportation arrangements, medical appointments, and the like. Terminal links among clients and with relatives or friends outside the base network facilitate communication among this social group for activities such as information sharing, group projects, and chess games. In addition, all the software mentioned above for entertainment, practicing memory skills, computer-assisted instruction, and money management would be available for use.

Section B represents the further potential of this computer communications system. The system could be used to conduct many aspects of traditional business from the home. Thus, clients could do mail order shopping, order groceries, do their banking, select books from the library, and connect with a variety of community services. The luxury of searching the "card-catalogue" for one's own selections and examining "book covers" to see if the title reflects the content has traditionally been reserved for those who could actually visit the library. Such a system would also allow for client feedback on books read such as suggestions for further reading and short book reviews. This information could then be incorporated into the library database and made available to other readers.

When considering this type of system, the imagination is stimulated to create impressive vistas for the otherwise homebound and dependent older adult. Much of what we can only imagine today can actually come to be tomorrow. Yet, one might raise the legitimate concern of whether these advances will truly benefit the majority of older people.

FUTURE IMPACT OF COMPUTER TECHNOLOGY

Given that computer technology will be increasingly involved in our daily lives, it is important to reflect upon how these advances will affect older adults. As we have outlined, technology can eliminate or reduce some of the important barriers to a good quality of life for adults. Moreover, computers in the home and in the community can be a valued tool for communication, stimulation, information access, and health care.

Nevertheless, some limitations on the full implementation of beneficial uses of the computer for older adults do exist. First, individuals over 65 have been reported to show less use of and less favorable attitudes toward computers (Kerschner & Hart, 1984). Within this overall generalization, however, are some positive signs. In particular, older adults who have used the computer are more favorable; and succeeding cohorts can be expected to be more familiar and comfortable with computers and technology (Kerschner & Hart, 1984; Krauss, Kenyon, Chareets & Hoyer, 1983). Hence, it seems that older adults can best be induced to view computers as useful tools for their purposes through actual experience with some user friendly computer applications.

Another potential limitation to widespread use of computers by the elderly is financial. In the past 5 years, however, the price of personal computers has dropped substantially. Microcomputers are now very affordable and soon will be commonplace in homes, senior centres, physicians' offices, and public libraries. Obtaining appropriate software is still an expensive and time-consuming affair; but availability of inexpensive programs for many applications is rapidly expanding. Finally, computer and technological support to enable an individual to remain at home would involve much lower costs than institutional care.

Another limitation of elder use of computers is the difficulty. As we have discussed, the use of many computer applications does not require more than minimal acquaintance with the computer. More and more programs are being written with the expectation that the user will know very little about the operation of the machine. Explanations are brief, given on the screen rather than in a manual, and intended for a broad audience with varying experience and capabilities. There are, however, some specific adaptations of hardware and software which would make applications more suitable to many of the elderly (Hoot & Hayslip, 1983). For example, such modifications as magnified screens, increased contrast, modified keyboards, and voice entry systems would be of specific benefit to individuals with visual or manual problems. As well, programs which allow the user to set his own pace are much more valuable for older adults than those which speed along at a predetermined rate.

In addition to limitations in availability and use, we must also consider the potential threats posed to the elderly by increased computerization. Because of stereotypes about the ability and willingness of older adults to learn intellectually challenging tasks (e.g., Rubin & Brown, 1975), the interests of this age group might be bypassed as applications are developed. Relatedly, there might be a tendency to assume that older adults can benefit only from passive applications such as emergency monitoring rather than the whole spectrum of other applications. There may also be a tendency for modifications needed by some elderly in hardware or software to receive a lower priority than financially more lucrative advances.

Finally, computerization might replace, rather than supplement, human support for older adults. Likewise, the very technology which can promote independence and a sense of control might also increase dependency and decrease a sense of control. It is clear, however, that this need not be the case. Like the telephone, the computer has the potential capability of decreasing or increasing human interactions. Whether the effects are generally supportive of increased vitality in older people depends upon decisions made by the developers, the social agencies using them, families, and the older adults themselves. The key is to be informed and to use this latest form of technology for the advantage of individual people.

Along with Skolnick (1984), we would argue that social advocacy on behalf of their natural constituency is a necessary and important role for some older adults to adopt. These advocates need to make themselves aware of the benefits and potential dangers of technological advances, to identify areas where the needs of older persons are not being met appropriately, and to argue publicly for improvements. As the next generations of older people, younger advocates can certainly contribute to this process of monitoring the effects of technology.

ACKNOWLEDGMENT

Preparation of this article was partially supported by a grant from the Gerontological Research Council of Ontario.

REFERENCES

Baddeley, A.D., & Hitch, G. (1974). Working memory. In G.H. Bower (Ed.), *The Psychology of learning and motivation, Vol. 8.* New York: Academic Press.

Barr, G. (1983). Educators play crucial role in promoting healthy aging. *Health Education, 23*(3), 2–7.

Beasley, D.S., & Davis, G.A. (Eds.) (1981). *Aging: Communication processes and disorders.* New York: Grune & Stratton.

Butler, R.,N., & Lewis, M.I. (1982). *Aging and mental health.* St. Louis: C.V. Mosby Co.

Case, R., Kurland, D.M., & Goldberg J. (1982). Operational efficiency and the growth of short term memory span. *Journal of Experimental Child Psychology, 33,* 386–404.

Daneman, M., & Carpenter, P.A. (1980). Individual differences in working memory and reading. *Journal of Verbal Learning and Verbal Behavior, 19,* 450-466.

Danowski, J.A., & Sacks, W. (1980). Computer communication and the elderly. *Experimental Aging Research, 1980,* 6, 125–135.

Dove, G.A.W., Wigg, P., Clarke, J.H.C., et al. (1977). The therapeutic effect of taking a patient's history by computer. *Journal of the Royal College of General Practitioners, 27,* 477–481.

Dunkle, R.E., Haug, M.R., & Rosenberg, M. (Eds.) (1984) *Communications technology and the elderly.* New York: Springer.

Ellis, L.B.M., & Raines, J.R. (1981). Health education using microcomputers: Initial acceptability. *Preventive medicine, 10,* 77–84.

Ellis, L.B.M., Raines, J.R., & Hakanson, N. (1982). Health education using microcomputers II: One year in the clinic. *Preventive Medicine, 11,* 212–224.

Evans, C.E. (1984). A computer in the waiting room: Who needs the doctor? *Canadian Family Physician, 30,* 869–876.

Fries, J.F., & Crapo, L.M. (1981). *Vitality and aging.* San Francisco: Freeman.

Grotkowski, M., & Sims L. (1978). Nutritional knowledge, attitudes, and dietary practices of the elderly. *Journal of American Dietary Association, 72,* 499–505.

Hess, B.B. (1984). Social aspects of communication in the later years. In R.E. Dunkle, M.R. Haug, & M. Rosenberg (Eds.), *Communications technology and the elderly: Issues and forecasts* (pp. 46–66). New York: Springer.

Hitch, G.J. (1978). The role of short-term memory in mental arithmetic. *Cognitive Psychology, 10,* 302–323.

Hoot, J.L., & Hayslip, B. Jr. (1983). Microcomputers and the elderly: New directions for self-sufficiency and life-long learning. *Educational Gerontology, 9,* 493–499.

Kerschner, P.A., & Hart, K.C. (1984). The aged user and technology. In R.E. Dunkle, M.R. Haug, & M. Rosenberg (Eds.), *Communications technology and the elderly: Issues and forecasts* (pp. 135–144). New York: Springer.

Krasnor, L.R., & Mitterer, J.O. (in press). LOGO and the development of general problem solving skills. *American Educational Research Journal.*

Krauss, I.K., Kenyon, D.G., Charette, M.R., Familant, M.E., & Hoyer, W.J. (1983). Attitudes toward computers: Age and experience as moderators. Proceedings of the Gerontological Society of America, San Francisco.

McPherson, B.D. (1983). *Aging as a social process.* Toronto: Butterworth.

Midlarsky, E.S., & Kahana, E. (1982). Helping by the elderly: Conceptual and empirical considerations. In M.B. Kleinman (Ed.), *Social gerontology, Vol. 17.* Basel: Karger AG. Ontario Seniors Secretariat (report forthcoming). Teledon project, Toronto.

Obler, L.K., & Albert, M.L. (Eds.) (1979). *Language and communication in the elderly.* Lexington, MA: Lexington Books.

Papert, S. (1980). *Mind-storms: Children, computers, and powerful ideas.* New York: Basic Books.

Popelka, G.R. (1984) Improving the hearing of the elderly. In R.E. Dunkle, M.R. Haug, & Rosenberg, M. (Eds.), *Communications technology and the elderly: Issues and forecasts* (pp. 81–96). New York: Springer.

Rubin, K.H., & Brown, I.D.R. (1975). Life-span look at person perception and its relationship to communicative interaction. *Journal of Gerontology, 33,* 98–102.

Sanders, D.H. (1981) *Computers in society* (3rd ed.). New York: McGraw-Hill.

Shamansky, S., & Hamilton, W. (1979). The health behavior awareness test: Self-care for the elderly. *Journal of Gerontological Nursing, 5* (1), 29–32.

Skinner, H.A., & Allen, B.A. (1983). Does the computer make the difference? Computer vs. face-to-face vs. self report assessment of alcohol, drug, and tobacco use. *Journal of Consulting & Clinical Psychology, 51,* 267–275.

Skinner, B.F., & Vaughn, M.E. (1983). *Enjoy old age: A program for self management.* New York: W.W. Norton.

Skolnick, M.H. (1984). Technology in health care for and by the aged. In R.E. Dunkle, M.R. Haug, & M. Rosenberg (Eds.), *Communications technology and the elderly: Issues and forecasts* (pp. 11–24). New York: Springer.

Symington, D.C., O'Shea, B.J., Batelaan, J., & White, D.A. (1980). *Independence through environmental control systems.* Toronto: Canadian Rehabilitation Council for the Disabled.

Thurston, N.E., & Kerr, J.C. (1983). A nutritional knowledge questionnaire for the elderly. *Canadian Journal of Public Health, 74,* 256–260.

Vasa, J.J. (1982). Electronic aids for the disabled and the elderly. *Medical Instrumentation, 16,* 261–262.

Vaughn, G.R., Faucett, R.A. & Lightfoot, R.K. (1984). Communication outreach: Delivery systems and devices. In R.E. Dunkle, M.R. Haug, & M. Rosenberg (Eds.), *Communications technology and the elderly: Issues and forecasts* (pp. 107–122). New York: Springer.

Weisman, S. (1983). Computer games for the frail elderly. *The Gerontologist, 23,* 361–363.

Wilson, D.M.C., & Ciliska, D. (1984). Lifestyle assessment: Development and use of the FANTASTIC checklist. *Canadian Family Physician, 30,* 1527–1532.

SECTION SEVEN

Discussion Questions

1. *Describe four stages in society's commitment to education for older people. What stages need further expression and support to meet the needs of older people today? What forms might these educational alternatives take?*

2. *Why do you think Elderhostel has attracted so many older people to its programs? What types of people attend Elderhostel programs? Do you think this program will continue to attract older people in the future? Why or why not?*

3. *Why did Creative Retirement Manitoba begin its Homebound Learning Opportunities (HLO) program? What types of courses does it offer? Who takes these courses? Describe some of the unique programs HLO has designed for its students.*

4. *What issues does risk of injury raise in the design of exercise programs for older people? What problems can arise when younger physical education instructors work with older people? What principles of adult education apply to physical and sports programs with older adults?*

5. *Describe some of the benefits that older people can gain from using computers. For example, what health benefits could they gain? What future role might computers play in improving the well-being of older people?*

6. *Discuss some of the ways that educators need to adapt programs for older people. State three principles of late-life education that you draw from the readings in this section.*

Suggested Readings

National Advisory Council on Aging (1990). *The NACA Position on Lifelong Learning.* Cat. No. H71-2/2-10-1990. Ottawa: Minister of Supply and Services Canada.

Novak, M. (1987). "The Canadian New Horizons Program." *The Gerontologist* 27: 353–55.

O'Brien, S.J., and P.A. Vertinsky (1990). "Elderly Women, Exercise and Healthy Aging." *Journal of Women and Aging* 2(3): 41–65.

One Voice, The Canadian Seniors Network (1991). *A National Literacy Strategy for Older Canadians.* Ottawa: One Voice, the Canadian Seniors Network.

Thornton, J.E. (1992). "Educational Gerontology in Canada: Special Issue." *Educational Gerontology* 18(5): 415–31.

Family Life and Relationships

Older people play many roles in their families. They give financial help to younger family members, they give advice, and they look after grandchildren. They also need support from their families. Older people who live alone, for example, may need help with transportation, shopping, and daily chores. People generally turn to their families for support before they use formal health-care and social services. And families accept this responsibility.

Some years ago gerontologist Elaine Brody (1981) wondered whether we would ever kill the "hydra headed myth" that families abandon their older members. Research has shown over and over that older people live rich family lives. Many older people report that they live a relatively short distance from at least one of their children. They say that they see or at least talk with their children and grandchildren regularly. McDaniel presents current facts on family support for older people in Canada. She shows that older people tend to get emotional support from their spouses and children. Seniors also tend to stay in contact with their children. These findings support Brody's view that older people live in an active family network.

Recent gerontological writing on family support for older people has focused on caregiving. Much of this research has studied caregiver burden, but some of this research shows that caregivers feel useful and satisfied with their relationship. Lee-Hoffer shows that caregiving has its good and bad moments. Her story allows us to see the love and commitment that carry caregivers through the good and bad times.

Lee-Hoffer's account shows that she often faced conflict between her roles as mother, wife, and daughter. This role conflict added to or caused feelings of burden. Work outside the home also adds to caregiver burden. Gottlieb and Kelloway document the stresses that caregivers face due to family and work conflicts. They found that caregivers with flexible work assignments felt less stress. Gottlieb and Kelloway project an increase in eldercare among workers in the years ahead. They say that business will benefit from support to employees who have eldercare responsibilities.

The articles on caregiving tend to focus on the feelings of the caregiver. This focus casts the older family member as a receiver of help (and possibly a cause of problems). Rosenthal has produced a series of papers that describe valued roles that older family members play. These include the roles of kinkeeper, ambassador, and family head. Rosenthal's article here describes the role of comforter. Comforters listen to younger family members, give advice, and offer sympathy. Rosenthal describes the type of person likely to play this role, the kinds of things they do, and the ways that people move into and out of this role. This article shows that families create and maintain positions that allow older members to support younger members. These positions make life smoother for young people and give older people the chance to stay useful.

Writings on aging and the family often report on a stereotypical family structure. This structure includes the older person's spouse (though sometimes the older person is widowed), children, and grandchildren. Focus on this structure ignores other family structures in old age—widowed men, gay and lesbian elders, and never-married people. O'Brien describes the experience of a group of never-married older women in Prince Edward Island. These women remained connected to others through many longstanding family and friendship ties. Their support networks included nieces, nephews, brothers, and sisters. Some had made friends with younger women. The close community life of the Island helped provide a stable context for their relationships.

Auger presents one of the first reports on another minority group within the older population, lesbian women. She estimates that more than 150,000 women aged 65 and over in Canada are lesbians. These women face many of the same problems that heterosexual women face as they age: negative attitudes toward physical aging, the stereotype of older women as sexless and ugly, and stress from retirement. But these women also face unique issues. Lesbians in rural areas, for example, face isolation and the lack of understanding of their lifestyles. Lesbians may also lack the emotional supports to help them deal with these issues. Auger's report makes us aware of the diverse needs of older people.

Traditional family relations—spouses living together or an older person living with a child—meet the ideal of family life only if family members get along. When people don't get along or when external pressures cause stress, these living arrangements can lead to violence and abuse. Patterson and Podnieks report on the risk factors associated with abuse, the most common types of abuse, and the prevalence of abuse in Canada. This article and others have increased gerontologists' and professionals' awareness of elder abuse. Prevention will require further education of professionals about detection and early intervention.

Family structures and relationships will change in the years ahead. Serial monogamy (many marriages in a lifetime) will lead to parents with many sets of children, children with many sets of grandparents, and grandparents with many sets of grandchildren. Increased mobility, longer life expectancy, and many generations living together over many years will create new social bonds. Whatever the changes, older people will both give to and depend on their families in the years to come.

Sources Consulted

Brody, E.M. (1981). "'Women in the Middle' and Family Help to Older People." *The Gerontologist* 18: 471–480.

33

Emotional Support and Family Contacts of Older Canadians

Susan McDaniel

Elderly people can no longer expect to spend their senior years living with their families. This is particularly true for older women, who as widows are more and more likely to be living alone. With more seniors living on their own, emotional support from family may not be as easy to come by as in the past. It takes some effort by the individual, as well as by family and friends, to maintain the social contact they want.

Family ties contribute to an individual's well-being. Whom one calls on for help is an indication of how important family members and others are to a person's emotional well-being, and also reveals the social networks that exist. How often people interact with their family is an important factor in maintaining these ties.

EMOTIONAL SUPPORT

According to the General Social Survey, spouses and children were the main sources of emotional support for most of the three million Canadians aged 65 and over in 1990.[1] When asked who they would turn to first when they were a bit down or depressed, older women tended to report a larger variety of sources of support than did men. It is not surprising, therefore, that while a relatively large proportion of married (including common-law) seniors reported that they would turn to their spouse for support, it was more common for men this age (45%) to do so than it was among women (37%). Married women were more likely to seek support from one of their children

Statistics Canada, *Canadian Social Trends,* Catalogue 11–008 (Spring 1993): 30–33. Reproduced by authority of the Minister of Industry, 1994.

Readers wishing further information on data provided through the cooperation of Statistics Canada may obtain copies of related publications by mail from: Publication Sales, Statistics Canada, Ottawa, Ontario, K1A 0T6, by calling 1-613-951-7277, or toll free 1-800-267-6677. Readers may also facsimile their order by dialing 1-613-951-1584.

(25%) or from a friend (10%) than were men (15% and 4%, respectively). This relative isolation of married men when it comes to emotional support is further illustrated by their greater tendency not to seek support from anyone. More than twice the proportion of men (12%) as women (5%) reported they would not seek support from anyone.

Women aged 65 and over not living with a spouse were most likely to say they would turn to a daughter for emotional support (28%), while only 16% of the men without spouses would do so. Both women and men were less likely to turn to a son than to a daughter (12% and 7%, respectively). The lesser tendency for men to turn to a child, whether a son or a daughter, is somewhat underestimated by these percentages, since only 5% of men said they had never had children, compared with 12% of the women. Men, on the other hand, would most likely turn to a friend (24%), whereas this was the case for only 16% of women.

When upset with a spouse or partner, many older Canadians (26%) said they would turn to one of their children, their daughters in particular, for support. More women (31%) than men (21%) would turn to a child for support in these circumstances. A slightly higher proportion of women (8%) said they would seek support from a friend than did men (5%). About 15% of both men and women would seek help from a professional when upset with their spouse or partner. However, many older Canadians (27%) reported that they didn't know to whom they would turn for support and 21% said they would not seek support from anyone. A larger proportion of men (24%) than women (16%) reported they would not talk to anyone when upset.

DISTANCE AND CONTACTS WITH CHILDREN[2]

The personal contact elderly parents had with their grown children who had left home was certainly influenced by how far away they lived, and also likely depended on the quality of the relationship. As the distance from the child increased, the frequency of contact fell. No matter how far parents lived from their child, however, few said they had not seen the child at all in the previous 12 months.

In 1990, older Canadians tended to live close to the child with whom they had the most contact, with about one-half living within 10 kilometres. Among parents living this close to the child with whom they had the most contact, 26% saw their child on a daily basis and 60% saw them at least once a week. Another 22% of the parents lived within 11 to 50 kilometres. More than one-half (53%) of the elderly visited weekly with the child in question. Another 36% had monthly visits. When parents lived over 50 kilometres away, visits were mainly monthly or at longer intervals.

In 1990, just 7% of elderly parents lived over 1,000 kilometres away from the child with whom they had the most contact. Visits over this distance require time, money and motivation. It is therefore not surprising that over two-thirds (69%) reported seeing their child less than once a month, and 23% reported no personal contact at all in the previous 12 months.

Older women, regardless of distance, tended to see their child more often than did men. Men were more likely than women to have had no personal contact at all over the year preceding the survey.

Most men (74%) and women (68%) aged 65 and over thought that the amount of personal contact they had with their adult children was just right. Men were slightly happier than women with the frequency of contact. About one-quarter of married men and one-third of married women said they saw their child less often than they would like. More widowed men (33%) than widowed women (27%) were unhappy about the amount of contact they had. Very few seniors, regardless of gender or marital status, expressed concern about seeing their child more often than they would like.

SISTERS AND BROTHERS

Older Canadians reported large numbers of sisters and brothers relative to younger Canadians. This is not surprising in view of the large family sizes of the older generation. In 1990, more than one-half (54%) of people aged 65 or over reported coming from families where they had five or more siblings. Only 4% of men and 5% of women reported having no siblings, while 8% of men and 10% of women had only one.

More seniors reported having sisters who were still living than brothers. This is expected given that women generally live longer than men. Among those aged 80 or over, about 60% of both men and women reported having a living sister. In contrast, 33% of men and 38% of women in this age group reported having a living brother.

Contact With Sisters and Brothers

Most older Canadians with brothers and sisters still alive had relatively little personal contact with their siblings in 1990. That year, 40% saw them less than once a month and another 18% had not seen their siblings at all. On the other hand, 18% reported monthly contact, 17% reported weekly contact, and 5% saw one of their siblings every day.

Older men and women maintained the same frequency of contact with their sisters and brothers overall. More women (43%) than men (36%) saw them less than once a month. However, more men (22%) than women (15%) reported they had not seen them at all during the previous 12 months.

Older women who had never married reported the most personal contact with their sisters and brothers. As many as 15% saw them daily and another 30% saw their siblings at least once a week. Never-married men were the next most frequent visitors of their siblings: 12% saw their siblings daily and 23% on a weekly basis.

Married men aged 65 and over maintained about the same amount of contact with their siblings as did married women aged 65 and over, with one in five seeing them daily or weekly. Divorced men were more likely to have daily contact than were divorced women. Widowed men and women saw their siblings less frequently than did others.

Women had contact with sisters and brothers by telephone or letter more often than did men. Daily and weekly contact with brothers or sisters by phone or mail was maintained by 39% of women, compared with 25% of men.

DISTANCE AND CONTACT WITH PARENTS

In 1990, approximately one-half of middle-aged Canadians (aged 45–64) reported that at least one of their parents was still alive. This is no surprise in light of the dramatic increase in the odds of living well into old age. Personal contacts with elderly parents reported from the middle-aged child's point of view provides an additional perspective on family ties.

Most middle-aged Canadians (57%) whose mothers were still alive saw their mothers at least once a month. Personal contact declined, however, as distance from mothers increased. About 80% who lived within 10 kilometres of their mothers saw them weekly or daily. The proportion who saw their mothers at least weekly dropped to about one-half (52%) for those living from 11 to 50 kilometres away.

Daughters tended to see their mothers more often than did sons. Middle-aged women (86%) had a greater tendency than men (73%) to visit with their mothers daily or weekly if they lived within 10 kilometres. Men, although frequent weekly visitors of mothers, tended more toward monthly visits. For example, among men who lived 11–50 kilometres from their mothers, 43% saw their mothers weekly and another 43% saw them monthly. Among women living the same distance away, 56% saw their mothers weekly and 35% saw them monthly. With increased distance from mothers, women still saw them more often than men did. For men living 51–100 kilometres away, 14% saw their mother weekly and 63% monthly. However, 39% of the women living this distance away had weekly visits, while 49% had monthly visits.

For fathers, the pattern was different. Fewer respondents had fathers who were still alive because of men's lower life expectancies. Also, men tend to be older than their wives. It was principally the middle-aged children living within 10 kilometres of their fathers who maintained daily or weekly contact (76%). Among children living 11–50 kilometres away from their fathers, 3% saw them daily. Another 19% said they saw them at least once a week and another 47% said at least monthly. For those living 51–100 kilometres away, none saw their fathers daily. However, 3% had weekly contact, and another 69% had monthly contact.

The most frequent of these parent-child contacts were between daughters and mothers (41% of daughters saw their mothers daily or weekly). Ten percent of daughters had not seen their mother in the past year, and the same percentage had not seen their fathers. Personal contact between sons and their fathers occurred the least frequently. Only 20% of sons saw their fathers daily or weekly, 40% saw them less often than monthly, and another 18% did not see them at all. This is consistent with men's greater emotional distance from family members alluded to by the information on elderly men's sources of emotional support, as well as by how often sons and husbands are the first choice for that support. However, one should also consider differences between middle-aged men and women when it comes to how flexible their time is, with more sons than daughters in the labour force. How old or dependent the parent is could also be a factor, since elderly fathers are on average younger and less apt to be alone than elderly mothers.

CONTACTS WITH GRANDPARENTS

Grandchildren are an important part of the elderly's family environment. In 1990, over one-third of Canadians with a grandparent still living saw at least one of their grandparents once a month or more: 3% had daily contact, another 14% had weekly, and another 22% saw their grandparents at least once a month. It was common, however, to see a grandparent less frequently than once a month (41%). Another 20% had not seen their grandparents in over 12 months.

Young adults aged 15–24 saw their grandparents more often than did people aged 25–44. People who had never married reported more frequent contact with their grandparents than others. This may in part be a reflection of age.

The contacts by telephone or by letter that persons aged 15 and over had with their grandparents were quite similar in frequency to personal contacts. As many as 3% had daily contact by letter or phone. Another 13% talked or wrote to their grandparents weekly. Another 22% had this type of contact on a monthly basis, while 33% were in contact by phone or mail less than once a month. However, 29% of Canadians aged 15 or over had no contact with one of their grandparents by letter or phone in the year before the survey.

It is difficult to compare the level of personal contact between those aged 15 years and over and their grand-parents with the level of contact middle-aged children have with their parents. The frequency of personal contact between middle-aged sons and their fathers ranks low compared to the other parent-child relationships, but it closely resembles the frequency of contact between grandchildren and grandparents. Given the greater distance in terms of kinship, grandchildren appear to be doing their part.

Canadians are living longer. With access to pensions and increased mobility, more older Canadians are living alone or living with their spouses and no children. Women continue, on average, to outlive their spouses. With the growth in the elderly population, this means an increasing number of older women are living alone. The extended family household is becoming a thing of the past. Consequently, contacts with family members can no longer be taken for granted as the result of living together. For older Canadians to hold onto the feeling of security that family represents, someone must make the effort to maintain contact.

NOTES

1. The number of seniors surveyed in the 1990 GSS was doubled with the support of the *Seniors Secretariat,* Health and Welfare Canada.

2. The "child" referred to in the discussion of distance and contacts with children is the "reference child" defined by the 1990 General Social Survey. This is the child with whom the respondent reported having the most contact. Only adult children who did not live with the respondent were eligible to be selected as the reference child. In addition, only people who had children (i.e., natural, step, adopted) still alive at the time of the survey were asked to select a reference child and answer questions about this child and their relationship with the child.

Full Circle

EXPERIENCES WITH AN AGING PARENT

Judith Lee-Hoffer

CARE-GIVING

Oh, thank you! You're so good to me." Mom looks grateful as I put her slippers on and bring her a cup of hot coffee in her favorite cup.

I know she appreciates what I do. I also doubt she has any memory of what I did for her yesterday. Tomorrow she will have little recollection of what transpired between us today. We live strictly in the "now."

Mom has almost lost much of her ability to communicate. It is unlikely she will even be able to tell anyone else whether I am gentle or rough with her. She is completely entrusted to my care. Sometimes this responsibility weighs heavily. I feet both powerful and helpless.

I must remind myself I do have the freedom of choice. Do I become a martyr who does what she has to do with resentment? Or, do I view these tasks as privileges and respond with humility and love?

Within the confines of this home, and in the everydayness of my life are challenging opportunities for personal growth. This situation demands I re-examine all my motives for caregiving. It necessitates an honest answer to the question, "Who am I really, when nobody is looking?"

COMMITMENT

We are all dressed up and ready to go. Looking forward to the party—close friends, colleagues, interesting people. It promises to be a most pleasurable evening.

My husband proceeds out to the car while I go to check on Mom one last time before leaving.

Uneasiness creeps over me when I see her. Although not complaining, she does not look very well. Her breathing seems somewhat labored. Immediately I feel disappointed and conflicted.

My husband is already in the driver's seat patiently waiting. He has grown accustomed to my last minute checking. With a heavy heart I explain why I feel I simply cannot attend the party. He offers to stay home too but I decline, urging him to go and enjoy himself.

As the car pulls out of the driveway, I experience a great sense of relief. I go back into the house to reassure Mom, I will be home for the evening.

I am confident, once at the party, my husband will enjoy himself. I am also confident that, although he may prefer my company, he will bear me no resentment. Nor, upon his return, will he shower me with unwanted pity. He knows me well. He understands that tonight I have chosen to be where I most need and want to be.

Thank God for the nature of our marriage.

■■■

Loss

Life is harsh at times. Today I felt criticized and rejected.

The house is quiet when I arrive home. Only Mom was here. She must be in her room. Like a vulnerable youngster with hurt feelings, I find myself seeking her out.

There she is, seated on her rumpled bed. Her unaware gaze warns me not to risk disclosing my pain. Looking at her, I once more feel like an abandoned child. Longing for the comforting mother of earlier years, I sit down and put my arm around her. She remains unresponsive, not noticing my tears. My only solace comes from trusting that locked within her frail body still lives the person who has always loved me. Who, I know, if able to express herself, would reassure me all will be well.

I reach in and take a hankie from her housecoat pocket. For some unknown reason, I am reluctant to leave her side.

The afternoon sunlight gradually fades. The rest of the family will soon be home. I must go and make supper.

■■■

Needed

She sits there in her housecoat. Hands folded idly in her lap. No longer able to walk briskly, wash clothes, mend, cook, or lend a helping hand wherever needed. No longer even able to speak words of wisdom or encouragement.

She sits there staring sadly into space. This daughter, this wife, this mother, this grandmother, this great grandmother who has made her whole purpose in life to serve others, now feels useless. Willing spirit trapped in an aged body.

How can I let her know that despite her limitations, she is still wanted, still needed?

I curl up beside her on the chesterfield. "Mom, my feet are cold. Would you mind if I stretched out and put them in your lap?"

Wordlessly, she lifts the blanket covering her knees. As I tuck my feet underneath, her lotion-smooth hands gently yet firmly grasp my toes. A soft smile of contentment creeps across her dear wrinkled face. She looks knowingly at me. Still wanted, still needed, still useful.

■■■

AN ACCIDENT

I was right there when it happened. Right next to Mom on the stairway. She turned. I knew she was falling and I couldn't catch her. I felt so helpless.

Now she's in pain. No visible broken bones. A cracked rib perhaps? It's the weekend and the doctor's office is closed. Out-patient emergency usually means a long wait. Would it be worth the effort and the suffering? I long for the old days when the doctor made home visits.

I decide to settle for telephone consultation and suggested pills to ease her discomfort. Tomorrow we'll slowly go through all the necessary procedures—driving, getting in and out of the car, undressing, examination, x-rays. We'll do them, unsure of the benefits, but not wanting to omit anything that might be helpful. I dread it.

But today. What about today? She is obviously hurting. Not much I can do … yes, there is one thing I can do. Past experience has taught me being in pain is an isolating, lonely experience.

Sitting here close beside her I feel somewhat better. I trust in even a small way she does too.

■■■

NIGHT VIGIL

How I hate going to sleep at times of great distress! I yearn to stay vigilantly alert for I dread those first moments upon awakening. Those moments when I am flooded with the realization of the actual situation. This morning is no exception. My first thought of making Mom breakfast is immediately overcome with the awareness her room is empty, she's no longer here, she's lying helplessly alone in a hospital bed.

I get up and begin preparing breakfast anyway. Not for me but for Mom. She hasn't been eating. Perhaps if I bring her one of her favorites—a soft boiled egg with butter and pepper and salt—she'll eat a little.

Just as the water begins to simmer, the phone rings. It's the doctor on duty for the weekend. A stranger to me. He admits he was surprised when he noted there was still a CODE on Mom's chart. He wonders if I really want it to remain. There's compassion in his voice. I am upset by the oversight. We both agree, when the time comes, any attempt at resuscitation would only be cruel. Filled with gratitude for his caring I unhesitatingly give him permission to remove the CODE.

I continue preparation to leave for the hospital. Along with the cooked egg, I take a few necessities. From now on I am determined I won't leave Mom's bedside. No more sleep. Tonight God and I will keep watch.

■ ■ ■

Closure

Unannounced, at midnight, our friend arrives carrying doughnuts and hot coffee. She has driven in from her campsite to be with us. I am very grateful for her company.

Not wanting to exclude Mom who is unable to drink from a cup, we attempt to share our coffee with her by soaking her mouth sponge. The snack completed, our friend retreats to an unobtrusive chair in the corner where she maintains her silent vigil.

Shadows loom large in the soft light cast from the towel-covered desk lamp borrowed from the nurses' station.

Past grief experiences have taught me the importance of such a night as this. Between snatches of favorite hymns and comforting Bible passages, I tell Mom what a wonderful mother she has been. I remind her of the dream she once had in which God told her that when she was ready to die she had only to knock and the door would be opened. She was promised that under the darkness she would find the Everlasting Arms. Most importantly, I am able to tell her I am ready to have her leave, I will miss her but she doesn't have to worry, I will be fine.

Morning dawns.

■ ■ ■

35

Eldercare and Employment

Benjamin H. Gottlieb and E. Kevin Kelloway

Mary Carmichael is 47 years old, married and a fulltime accounts clerks at a major financial institution. She and her husband, Bob, have three dependants—a son aged 10, a daughter aged 14, and Mary's mother, aged 73. After Mary's mother was hospitalized for a stroke last year, everyone knew she couldn't go on living alone up north, and so she moved into the spare room. Everyone has had to make adjustments, but Mary shoulders the most responsibility for seeing to it that her mother receives the special care she needs.

For a growing number of Canadian employees, this situation is becoming more common. More and more people are now holding down a job outside the home, while carrying the responsibility for the care of children and one or more elderly relatives. This is because of profound changes taking place in the Canadian demographic landscape, changes which reveal that, as of 1991, 11.6% of our population was composed of people over the age of 65 as compared to 7.8% in 1951. But projections for the next 40 years are even more astounding; by 2031 the proportion of Canadians over the age of 65 will have doubled to 22.7%, while the oldest of the elderly, those over the age of 85, will have almost tripled (Statistics Canada, 1993). In short, due to changes in mortality that now make it possible for most people to reach advanced age, almost a quarter of the Canadian population will be elderly, and more than 10% will be at least 75 years old. Even with lifestyle changes and advances in prevention and treatment that are redefining the age range of old age, this segment of the elderly population will undoubtedly require the greatest care.

And who is called upon to provide this eldercare? For the most part, it is the same segment of the population that will account for the majority of labor force growth in the coming years, namely women. Due to a decline in real wages, most families will need two incomes in order to achieve a reasonable standard of living, and therefore women will enter the labour force in even greater numbers than they have to date. The fact is that the vast majority of all women who are in the age group when they are most likely to be called on to care for the elderly (45-60 years old) will be employed.

Reproduced with permission from *Human Resources Management in Canada* (June 1993).

Recognizing these demographic trends, the Work and Eldercare Research Group of the Canadian Aging Research Network (CARNET) set out to investigate eldercare as a workforce issue, and eventually to identify human resource strategies that meet the needs of employed caregivers and their dependants, while sustaining productivity and morale in the workplace. Accordingly, in collaboration with our corporate partner, Corporate Health Consultants, a survey of over 5000 employees in eight Canadian organizations was conducted in order to answer three major questions: [a] how many employees are providing eldercare, [b] how does eldercare affect employees both personally and on the job, and [c] do flexible work arrangements and certain kinds of employee assistance programs help? Because our research group draws on experts in the fields of social gerontology, sociology, geography, and social and industrial psychology, it reflects the state of the art in measuring the nature and effects of eldercare on organizational and personal performance.

HOW MANY EMPLOYEES ARE INVOLVED IN ELDERCARE?

To measure eldercare, we drew up a list of 18 different kinds of assistance that might be provided to relatives over the age of 65, and asked respondents whether they had rendered such assistance to an elderly relative during the past 6 months. Depending on the type of assistance they had provided, and whether or not they were also involved in caring for a child who was under the age of 19 and living with them at home, we then organized respondents into three groups:

- General Eldercare Providers assisted their relatives with activities such as shopping, transportation, household chores, meal preparation, and home maintenance.

- Personal Eldercare Providers assisted their relatives with nursing-like activities such as feeding, dressing, bathing, and taking medications.

- Dual Caregivers combined either Personal or General Eldercare with the care of children.

The survey findings reveal that almost one-half (46%) of the sample were involved in providing some form of eldercare. Fourteen percent provided General Eldercare, 6% provided Personal Eldercare, and a whopping 26% were Dual Caregivers. More than three-quarters of these Dual Caregivers, sometimes referred to as the "Sandwich Generation," combined childcare with general eldercare, while the remainder shouldered the greatest burden, combining childcare with personal eldercare.

We also asked about the amount of time that these employees invested in aiding their elderly relatives each week, as well as the number of crises to which they had responded in the past six months. General Eldercare consumed an average of three hours per week, while Personal Eldercare involved an average time commitment of nine hours a week. This is probably because those providing this form of intensive caregiving were also responsible for many of the general caregiving tasks as well. Hence, involvement in Personal Eldercare often meant adding an extra workday to the week. Personal Eldercare is also more crisis-oriented, with providers being twice as likely to help in crises as are General Eldercare providers. These findings about the time and crises involved in the two types of eldercare apply equally to the Dual Caregivers, but obviously their dependant care load is increased by virtue of their childcare responsibilities.

Another virtue of the survey is the fact that it was not targeted only to eldercare providers, but includes respondents who have no direct caregiving responsibilities (the No Caregiving group) and those with childcare responsibility only (the Childcare Only group). In this way, it is possible to compare the impacts of different kinds of caregiving involvements with one another and with no involvement at all.

How Does Eldercare Affect Employees?

Employees involved in Personal Eldercare, Dual Caregiving, and Childcare Only consistently reported more impacts of their family responsibilities on their jobs and personal lives. In contrast, those with No Caregiving and those involved in General Eldercare reported much less impact.

The impact of caregiving shows up in several ways. Employees with Personal Eldercare, Childcare, or Dual Caregiving reported more stress, more conflict between their work and family lives, and less job satisfaction than those with No Caregiving or General Eldercare responsibilities. Each of these outcomes was measured through the use of multiple indicators, including a 14-item stress scale, two 4-item work-family conflict scales, and a 7-item job satisfaction scale. Generally, Dual Caregivers reported the highest levels of work-family conflict and stress, and employees in all four caregiving groups reported that their work interfered with their family lives more than their family lives interfered with their work.

The demands of caregiving have equally clear job consequences. Employees with the most onerous caregiving responsibilities, namely Dual Caregivers who combine childcare with personal eldercare, were four times more likely to have unscheduled single day absences and absences of three or more days than those in the No Caregiving group. For example, 17% of these Dual Caregivers reported that their responsibilities outside work had caused them to be absent for at least one day in the past 6 months, compared to 4% of those who had no caregiving obligations. The same trend applied to partial absenteeism, which was measured by questions about interruptions of at least 20 minutes during the workday as well as tardy arrivals at and early departures from work. Those combining childcare with personal eldercare were almost twice as likely to experience these forms of partial absenteeism as employees without any caregiving responsibilities. Fully 50% of these Dual Caregivers reported workday interruptions associated with their dependent care responsibilities.

Equally important, individuals responsible for childcare, personal eldercare or both also report more job-related opportunity costs. Because of their family demands, these individuals miss meetings and training sessions, decline promotions, business travel, and extra projects at work, and are unable to work the shifts they desire. Again, those who combine childcare with personal eldercare are five to seven times more likely to experience these job opportunity costs as employees with no caregiving or general eldercare responsibilities.

The survey also documents the personal opportunity costs resulting from employees' involvements in dependant care. In fact, more employees report having had to curtail their involvement in leisure, continuing education, and volunteer activities than the proportions reporting job opportunity costs. However, the two patterns are consistent; relatively small proportions of those with no caregiving and general eldercare responsibilities are affected in comparison to the percentages of the Dual Caregivers and those engaged in Personal Eldercare who have reduced their involvements in these personal life spheres. Paradoxically, it appears that, in their efforts to balance family demands and job responsibilities, employees are cutting back on those activities that afford relaxation, rejuvenation, and personal or career development.

Considered as a whole, our findings reveal that employees' caregiving responsibilities affect virtually every aspect of their personal and working lives. Most importantly, the strain of constantly juggling conflicting responsibilities is taking its toll on individuals, families, and employers.

Do Flexible Work Arrangements Help?

To date, childcare has largely dominated the agenda of human resource programs aimed to assist employees to harmonize their work and family responsibilities. The results of our survey reveal that approximately the same proportion of employees are involved in eldercare as are involved in childcare. Moreover, the demographic trends reviewed earlier suggest that we are presently on the cusp of an eldercare boom that will see even greater numbers of employees assuming responsibility for the care of elderly relatives.

To recruit and retain valued employees, and to ensure that they do justice to their jobs and their family members, we must identify the kinds of work arrangements and types of assistance that meet the needs of employers and employees alike. To this end, we presented respondents with a list of 11 flexible work arrangements and three types of information and assistance programs, and asked them to indicate whether or not each was available, and if available, whether or not the employee had made use of it. In addition, we asked respondents to identify those initiatives which they would use if they were available at their workplace. The flexible work options included various part-time employment and personal leave arrangements, flextime, telecommuting, job sharing, and a compressed work week, while the three information and assistance programs covered childcare, eldercare, and an EAP.

Details regarding all the findings concerning the availability and use of these arrangements are beyond the scope of this article but are available upon request (The Work and Eldercare Research Group of CARNET: Canadian Aging Research Network, 1993). Several noteworthy findings bear emphasis here. First, perhaps the most encouraging and provocative finding is that employees who reported the availability of flexible work arrangements and assistance also reported lower levels of stress, higher levels of job satisfaction, and less work-family conflict than employees for whom flexible work arrangements were not available. Second, these flexible work arrangements and assistance programs are reaching those who need them most. That is, those caregivers who experience the most stress and work-family conflict are the employees who utilize the supportive arrangements that have been put in place.

Overall, flexible hours, personal days, and time off in lieu of overtime pay were the arrangements most widely used by employees. Shorter work weeks, flexible work hours, and work-at-home arrangements top the list of options that would be used if they were made available.

Despite the fact that 46% of the respondents are involved in eldercare, only 8% have eldercare information available to them. Consistent with our observations about the demands of caregiving, individuals involved in eldercare (general or personal) were most likely to use personal days and those involved in personal eldercare or dual caregiving reported more utilization of Employee Assistance Programs (EAPs) and part-time employment options.

THE FUTURE

The aging of the population means that a much larger proportion of the workforce will have eldercare responsibilities in the future. Our Work and Family Survey reveals that almost 50% of employees have already assumed this responsibility. Coupled with the findings that eldercare involvement impacts on both personal and working lives, eldercare emerges as a mainstream business issue both now and for the future.

Our findings also suggest that flexible work options and assistance tailored to the needs of employees enable them to deal with the challenges involved in balancing work and family responsibilities. We must caution, however, that flexibility goes beyond establishing a corporate policy on flextime, personal days, or other "family-friendly" benefits. Our discussions with Human Resource personnel, senior management, and employees who are involved in caregiving point to several landmarks on the critical path leading to a culture that is genuinely committed to achieving a healthy balance between work and family. Human Resource professionals must leverage support from all strata of the organization. They must build the business case for action. In addition, they must initiate training programs that empower employees and managers to negotiate flexible work arrangements that meets the needs of both the individual and the organization. Our findings and the experience of many companies suggest that flexible work arrangements are not only effective ways of helping employees to harmonize their work and family lives, but also can be used as strategic tools to address work flow issues and organizational restructuring.

As the Work and Eldercare Research Group continues to entertain requests for our survey, and as we proceed in the development of new approaches to management training in the work and family area, we are bound to learn more about the process of transforming organizational cultures in ways that optimize the support of the employees and the competitive position of the company. The instruction gained from our experience thus far has persuaded us that collaborative initiatives to create a more flexible workplace has benefited all three stakeholders—employees, their dependants, and employers.

REFERENCES

Statistics Canada, 1993. *Population Aging and the Elderly.* Catalogue No. 91–533E. Ottawa: Ministry of Industry, Science and Technology.

Work and Eldercare Research Group, 1993. *Work and Family: The Survey Findings.* Gerontology Research Centre, University of Guelph, Guelph, Ontario, N1G 2W1.

The Comforter
PROVIDING PERSONAL ADVICE AND EMOTIONAL SUPPORT TO GENERATIONS IN THE FAMILY

Carolyn J. Rosenthal

This paper presents a novel conceptualization of emotional support in intergenerational families. It is shown that many families have a person who specializes in providing this type of help. This person is recognized by others in the family as being a person to whom family members turn for emotional support and personal advice. In the paper, this person is referred to as the family "comforter." In addition, it is shown that in some families people can identify the person who provided emotional support prior to the present comforter. On the basis of these data, a "position" of family comforter is inferred. The paper investigates the social correlates of the position, the type of activities associated with being the family comforter, and the pattern of succession as different generations in the family move in and out of the position.

EMOTIONAL SUPPORT IN FAMILIES

The importance of emotional support in contemporary families reflects a more general emphasis on affective bonds. This emphasis on the affective aspect of family relationships is said to be a distinguishing feature of inter-generational relationships in the contemporary family, compared to the family of earlier times. Historically, the bonds between generations were related more strongly than today to the economic function of the family. Fischer (1978:59) argues that the economic dependence of younger on older generations, extending well into the younger generation's adulthood, contributed little to the possibility of feelings of closeness, sympathy, or free-flowing emotional support. Laslett (1971:157) and Shorter (1977:5) also contend that the preindustrial family was not a place for emotional succour. Scholars have argued that as the aged lost moral and economic authority

Reproduced with permission from *Canadian Journal on Aging*, Vol. 6: 3, 228-39 (Fall 1987).

within the family, the strength of and/or emphasis on affective bonds increased (Fischer, 1978; Lasch, 1977; Shorter, 1977).

Within social gerontology, research on the emotional quality of relationships between adult generations in families has been relatively rare. The small body of research that exists points to high levels of perceived positive affect in parent-child relationships (e.g., Bengtson, 1971, 1975; Bengtson and Black, 1973; Hill et al., 1970; Troll et al., 1969). The importance of family members in providing moral support has been shown in research on widowhood and confidant relationships (Litman, 1971; Lopata, 1973; Lowenthal and Haven, 1968; Matthews, 1979; Tigges et al., 1980; Treas, 1979). Emotional support is one of the most commonly exchanged types of assistance between parents and adult children (Rosenthal, 1987).

While no previous work has investigated the provision of emotional support in the context of the extended family, the work of Nye (1976) offers some insight. Using the marital couple as the unit of analysis, Nye investigated dimensions of the "therapeutic role," defined as helping the spouse with personal problems. Nye found that over 60% of men and women expressed normative support for this role.

The present study is somewhat similar to Nye's work in that the comforter, like Nye's "therapeutic role," is conceptualized as involving the provision of emotional support and advice. Nye viewed the role as focused on problem-solving and as including the provisions of emotional support, listening, acting as a "sounding board," providing information or insight, and taking action. These activities emerged as characteristic of the comforter position, as the analysis section will show.

Of relevance to the present study, Nye's respondents were asked to whom they talked about their personal problems and were allowed to identify as many persons as they wished. Spouses were by far the most frequently named. However, parents, siblings and other relatives were also identified. Between one-third and three-quarters of the respondents, depending on gender and kinship category, had ever (frequently, occasionally, seldom) talked over their problems with these kin beyond the conjugal family.

The study at hand differs from the work of Nye and associates in that their unit of analysis was the marital couple whereas the present study asked respondents to think in terms of their "side of the family," including all living kin. This study explicitly investigates the provision of emotional support and personal advice within the extended family. While the research described above suggests that families do provide emotional support and that this is an important service families provide to their members, we have little information on how families work in this regard. That is, how does emotional support get provided within families? With this question in mind, I hypothesized that many families might have one person who specialized in this sort of task and that such specialization could be investigated in its own right.

The study employed the concept of a "familial division of labour." It was postulated that a variety of task-specific positions exist within extended families. A "position" in the division of labour was conceptualized as involving a number of roles attached to tasks performed, rather than categories of people served (Bates, 1956). The tasks are related to each other through a common dimension of family life such as, in the present study, affective support.

METHOD

The Generational Relations and Succession Project, in which the author collaborated with Victor W. Marshall and Jane Synge, investigated this and other questions relating to the intergenerational family. Interviews were conducted in 1980 with a random sample of 458 respondents aged 40 and older, living in Hamilton, Ontario, a typical Canadian urban area.[1]

Respondents were asked a number of direct questions about the possible existence within extended families of such positions as kinkeeper, comforter, ambassador, financial advisor, job placement officer, and head of the family. This paper focuses on one of these positions, the comforter (for analyses of other positions, see Rosenthal et al., 1980; Rosenthal, 1985; Rosenthal and Marshall, 1986).

The provision of emotional support was investigated by asking respondents to think about their family in broad terms, including siblings, aunts, uncles, cousins, grandparents, parents, and so forth. Using this kin group as the frame of reference, respondents were asked, "Is there currently any one person among you and any of the relatives on your side of the family with whom other family members particularly like to talk over their troubles—someone they can go to for advice and comfort?" Those who said there was not such a person were asked whether there had been one in the past and, if so, who. Those who said there was currently such a person were then asked a series of questions concerning who that person was, why the person was sought for advice and comfort, the length of time the person had been providing advice and comfort, how and why the person came to be sought out on this basis, and who was turned to for advice and comfort prior to the present person. The position of comforter was inferred from the resulting data.

A possible limitation of the present analysis is that the question included both providing comfort and giving advice as activities defining the position. Greater clarity in future research could be gained by distinguishing among emotional, appraisal and informational support (House and Kahn, 1985) and questioning respondents as to whether the person named as comforter provides these various types of support. Despite this lack of precision in the present analysis, the main purpose of establishing the existence and prevalence of a family "position" of comforter/advisor and of investigating associated features may still be pursued profitably.

The analysis is conducted at both the individual and the family levels. At the level of the individual, the focus is on the identification of the position, and the characteristics of occupants of the comforter position, including gender, age, kinship category, and generational location relative to the respondent. At the level of the family, the analysis pursues the type of activities associated with the position and the factors associated with the passing of persons into and out of the position.

RESULTS

Identifying the Position

In this study, 39% of the 458 respondents said there was someone in their extended family who specialized in providing personal advice and emotional support. A further 17% said that although there was not such a person in their family at present, there had been one in the past. Altogether, then, over half the study respondents said that someone had held the position of family comforter, either now or in the past....

What Comforters Do

Open-ended questions provide details about what the person named as family comfort/advice specialists actually do. (Note that activities were inferred from questions enquiring as to why the person was sought out for advice/comfort and how they came to be sought out for these purposes; for this reason, a number of cases were not codable for activities in the position). They listen and offer sympathy, compassion, and understanding. For example, one man said, "She has a sympathetic ear and listens to you." Another respondent, a woman, said, "She's very sympathetic. She'll give advice and tell you what she's thinking."

Of the respondents who identified a family comforter, half referred to affective activities (giving sympathy, compassion, understanding, concern and love) one-quarter referred to advice-giving, and one-quarter either mentioned a combination of these activities or neither of them. Based on these responses, the comforting aspect of the position appears to be more common than the advice-giving aspect. The affective task appears to be a more vital task of the comforter and, by inference, a more needed service in the family.

Since the wording of the initial question defined the position as including both the providing of comfort and the giving of personal advice, it seemed possible that men might respond to the question in terms of advice and women in terms of comfort. In an effort to gain more precision on this issue, the analysis focused on gender, first with respect to the activities of the position occupant and second with respect to the relationship between the gender of the respondent and the activities described.

The comforter's activities vary according to the gender of the position occupant and are related to the distinction between the advising and comforting dimensions of the position. Personal attributes to do with advice-giving (intelligence, judgment, experience, knowledge, or being able to give good advice) were more frequently mentioned for male than female comforters (74% vs. 40%). In contrast, attributes to do with providing comfort or emotional support (being sympathetic or a good listener) were more frequently offered as descriptions of female than male occupants (60% vs. 26%). These findings suggest that, to some degree, men provide advice and women comfort. This conforms somewhat to the traditional Parsonian instrumental/expressive dichotomy (Parsons, 1955:51) in the division of familial labour between men and women. However, despite the overall tendency, it is important to note that a substantial minority does not conform to gender stereotypes.

When responses were analysed according to the gender of the respondent, it was found that women are more likely to view the position as one of providing emotional support than as one of providing advice, while men do not seem to favour one aspect of the position over the other. Only one-third of the comforters identified by female respondents were described in terms of advice-giving attributes, compared to half the comforters described by male respondents.

Filling the Position

Respondents who said there was someone in their family to whom other members turned for comfort and advice were asked who that person was. From the responses, some conclusions may be drawn about the social correlates of family comforters.

Of those named as past or present comforters, about three-fifths were women, while about two-fifths were men. This female dominance in the task of giving emotional support has been found in other research. For examples, Tigges et. al (1980) studied confidant relationships, viewed as one type of emotional support, among individuals aged 60 and over. Of the confidants who were relatives, the ratio of women to men was three to two. The work of Lowenthal and Haven (1968) also suggests women serve as confidants more frequently than men do.

The relatives most frequently named as comforters were siblings and self-designations (accounting for 41% and 38%, respectively, of all current comforters[2]). Parents accounted for 8%, children for 5% and other relatives (aunts, uncles, spouses, cousins, nephews, nieces) for 8% of current comforters. The relative infrequency with which parents occupy the comforter position relates in part to availability; only 31% of respondents had a living parent. Among respondents who had a living parent, 20% identified a parent as the family comforter. Further, of the people who said there was no one currently filling the comforter position but who named someone as comforter in the past, 39% named a parent; mothers outnumbered fathers three to two.

Data on age of comforters are available only for the 27% of the respondents who designated themselves as comforters. Inferring age of comforters from the data on self-designations, male occupants tended to be between the ages of 50 and 64, or in their 70s. Female occupants tended to be between the ages of 55 and 74, in which age groups about one in five women claim to provide emotional comfort in the extended family.

Length of occupancy of the comforter position was investigated. As is the case for family kinkeepers (Rosenthal, 1985) family comforters occupy the position for a long time: in this position, the median time was twenty years.

Comforters tend to belong to the respondent's own generation. While naming a comforter does not mean, strictly speaking, that the respondent himself/herself personally seeks comfort from the person named, the open-ended question suggest this does, in fact, often occur. For example one person named her cousin as comforter and said, "We all just seem to turn to her. She has the time and the solutions."

To the extent that respondents themselves seek comfort from the person named, it may be inferred that the tendency to name a generational peer as comforter implies that people tend to seek this comfort from members of their own generation. Lopata (1979:195) notes a similar tendency among widows to seek support from a generational peer.

Accession and Succession

To investigate how people begin to occupy the comforter position, respondents were asked how it came about that the person named as comforter had come to be sought out for advice and comfort. Many people offered reasons relating to ascriptive characteristics such as birth order or kinship status, or, more commonly, offered reasons relating to the comforter's personality. However, some of the responses provide data on the dynamics of the accession/succession process.

Accession is often related to some family or individual life course transition. For example, about one-fifth of the comforters were said to have assumed the position in order to fill the vacancy created by the death of the former comforter. Thus, one male respondent said of the person named as current comforter, "He took over when father died." Sometimes the life course transition in question concerned a change in marital status. For example, a male respondent said, "I got married and started raising a family and she gave me a lot of advice." In one-tenth of the cases, comforters stepped into the position in response to a specific need or turning point in the family.

Information on the succession of the position is provided by the 93 respondents who said there was currently a family comforter and also named the person who had been the comforter prior to the present person[3]. Over three-fifths of those named as prior comforters were parents, with mothers outnumbering fathers at a ratio of two to one. Siblings were named in one-seventh of the cases, husbands in about one-tenth, and grandparents a little less often than that[4]. Analysis of the transitions from past to present shows that inheritance of the position moves down the generations along same-sex lines, most commonly from female to female. Same-sex transitions are far more common than transitions from male to female or female to male. (This may well relate to the advice/comfort distinction discussed earlier.)

The comforter task is typically handed down the generations, rather than moving to a new occupant within the same generation. Over three-quarters (78.4%) of the 93 cases in which a past and present occupant was named involved a move from an older to a younger generation. The most common transition is mother to sister, followed by mother to female respondent. Transitions originating with mothers are far more likely to move to a female than a male. While less common than transitions originating with mothers, those originating with fathers are the second most frequent type in the data. These typically move to a male, either a male respondent or a brother.

CONCLUSION

Elsewhere, using data from the same project on which the present analysis draws, it has been shown that emotional and moral support is one of the most common items of exchange between parents and their adult children (Rosenthal, 1987). The present analysis shows that emotional support is not restricted to the nuclear family but is provided commonly enough in the extended family that more than half the people in this random sample said someone in their families, either now or in the past, was recognized as a person to whom other family members turned for this type of support. It has been argued in this paper that the data support the notion of a "position" of comforter/advisor. Occupancy, activity, and succession in this position are patterned by gender. Women predominate as family comforters, although men comprise a substantial minority.

Most people identified someone from their own generation as the family comforter. This tendency calls for comment. First, it suggests that to some extent people wear generational blinkers, perceiving the distribution of family responsibility in generationally homogeneous terms. People likely are in greater contact with same-generation relatives (aside from lineage members) than other-generation relatives, and may simply be better informed about what is going on in the family among their generational peers. The tendency to name a same-generation comforter also points to boundaries between generations. The data are somewhat limited in that we do not know whether the respondent, having named someone as comforter, has ever personally sought advice or comfort from that person. However, to the extent that this may have occurred, the data make clear that the overwhelming tendency is for people to seek personal advice or emotional comfort from someone within their own generation.

The tendency to name a comforter who belongs to the respondent's own generation suggests an "overlap" in the succession process. As the years go by, younger generations may increasingly find themselves providing emotional support in the extended family, while the older generation specialist also continues to be turned to for this type of help. However, the balance is shifting. Thus, a younger generation member may think her sister has become the family comforter while the mother still views herself as the specialist in the family. Or, a middle-aged woman may still feel her mother is the family comforter, but the woman's generational peers have already begun to turn to her as the family specialist in providing comfort/advice. The net result, however, is that eventually a younger generation comes to fully occupy the position.

Many people were able to describe the line of succession of the position of comforter. It was striking that people described this process as following same-sex lines. In most families, the comforter position is passed from mother to daughter, but in a fair minority the position passes from father to son. A number of people said that the new occupant took up the task when the parent, the former occupant, died. In a dramatic illustration of this process, one woman said her sister took on the responsibilities of comforter because "She made a promise to mother." Promises such as this likely represent the hopes and wishes of many aging family members, wishes that their descendants will continue to work at maintaining family bonds.

NOTES

1. The sample was drawn from the 1979 property assessment list, which is an annual census of all occupants of all dwellings. The sample was stratified into six equal frames of males and females in the age categories 40–54, 55–69, and 70 and older. Of 746 eligible contacted persons, 281 refused to be interviewed, yielding a 62% response rate. This is comparable to that obtained in similar Canadian community surveys involving older populations (Chappell, 1983; Connidis, 1983). Five respondents who were interviewed in institutions were excluded from ensuing analyses. The study underrepresents the bedfast and very ill elderly. One-fourth of the sample reported annual family income of $8,000 or less, while 22% reported $25,000 or more. About half the respondents listed British as their main ancestry, while the next largest groups (Irish, Italian, and German) were listed by 7% or less of respondents.

2. The pattern for a substantial minority of respondents to designate themselves as family comforter mirrors the pattern found in the analysis of other familial positions (see Rosenthal, 1985; Rosenthal and Marshall, 1986). It would be interesting to know how self-designated comforters differ from other relatives who are named as comforters with respect to such characteristics as age, family

structure, marital status, and so on. Unfortunately, such an analysis is not possible since this type of data is only available for self-designated comforters.

3. In this paper, I use the term "previous comforter" to refer to those instances in which respondents did not identify a present comforter but said their family had had a comforter in the past. "Prior comforter" refers to persons identified as past comforters by respondents who also identified present comforters.

4. The fact that husbands were named as prior comforters more often than wives reflects sample differences in marital status. That is, more women than men were widowed, and therefore they more frequently identified a spouse as a prior comforter.

REFERENCES

Bates, F.L. (1956). Position, role and status: A reformulation of concepts. *Social Forces,* 34, 313–321.

Bengtson, Vern L. (1971). Inter-age differences in perception and the generation gap. *The Gerontologist,* Part II, 85–90.

Bengtson, Vern L. (1975). Generation and family effects in value socialization. *American Sociological Review,* 40, 358–371.

Bengtson, Vern L. & Black, K.D. (1973). Intergenerational relations and continuities in socialization. In P. Baltes & W. Schaic (Eds.), *Life-Span Developmental Psychology* (pp. 208–234). New York: Academic Press.

Chappell, Neena L. (1983). Informal support networks among the elderly. *Research on Aging,* 5, 77–99.

Connidis, Ingrid (1983). Living arrangement choices of older residents. *Canadian Journal of Sociology,* 8, 359–375.

Fischer, D.H. (1978). *Growing Old in America.* Oxford, London, New York: Oxford University Press.

Hill, R., Foote, N., Aldous J., Carlson, B. & MacDonald, R. (1970). *Family Development in Three Generations.* Cambridge: Schenkman.

House, J.S. & Kahn, R.L. (1985). Measures and concepts of social support. In S. Cohen and S.L. Syme (Eds.), *Social Support and Health* (pp. 83–108). Orlando: Academic Press.

Lasch, Christopher (1977). *Haven in a Heartless World: The Family Besieged.* New York: Basic Books.

Laslett, Peter (1971). *The World We Have Lost, 2nd Edition.* London: Methuen.

Litman, T.J. (1971). Health care and the family: A three-generation analysis. *Medical Care,* 9, 67–81.

Lopata, Helena (1973). *Widowhood in an American City.* Cambridge, Mass.: Schenkman.

Lopata, Helena (1979). *Women as Widows: Support Systems.* New York: Elsevier.

Lowenthal, M.F. & Haven, C. (1968). Interaction and adaptation: Intimacy as a critical variable. *American Sociological Review,* 33, 20–30.

Matthews, Sara H. (1979). *The Social World of Old Women: Management of Self-Identity.* Beverly Hills: Sage.

Nye, F.I. (1976). The therapeutic role. In F.I. Nye (Ed.), *Role Structure and Analysis of the Family* (pp. 111–130). Beverly Hills: Sage.

Nye, F.I., with Bahr, H.M., Bahr, S.J., Carlson, J.E., Gecas, V., McLaughlin, S. & Slocum, W.L. (1976). *Role Structure and Analysis of the Family.* Beverly Hills: Sage.

Parsons, Talcott (1955). Family structure and the socialization of the child. In T. Parsons and R.F. Bales (Eds.), *Family Socialization and Interaction Process* (pp. 35–131). New York: The Free Press.

Rosenthal, Carolyn J. (1985). Kinkeeping in the familial division of labour. *Journal of Marriage and the Family,* 47, 965–974.

Rosenthal, Carolyn J. (1987). Aging and intergenerational relations in Canada. In Victor W. Marshall (Ed.), *Aging in Canada: Social Perspectives, 2nd Edition.* Markham, Ontario: Fitzhenry and Whiteside.

Rosenthal, Carolyn J., Marshall, Victor W., & Synge, Jane (1980). The head of the family: Social meaning and structural variability. *Canadian Journal of Sociology,* 11, 183–198.

Shorter, Edward (1977). *The Making of the Modern Family.* New York: Basic Books.

Tigges, L., Cowgill, D. & Habenstein, R. (1980). Confidant relations of the aged. Paper presented at the 33rd Annual Scientific Meeting of The Gerontological Society of America, San Diego, California, November.

Treas, Judith (1979). Intergenerational families and social change. In P.K. Ragan (Ed.), *Aging Parents* (pp. 58–65). Los Angeles: University of Southern California Press.

Troll, Lillian, Neugarten, Bernice L. & Kraines, R.G. (1969). Similarities in values and other personality characteristics in college students and their parents. *Merrill-Palmer Quarterly,* 15, 323–336.

Never-Married Older Women
THE LIFE EXPERIENCE

Mary O'Brien

INTRODUCTION

Until recently, never-married persons have been included with widowed, separated and divorced persons in research studies. It's only in the past few years they have become the focus of research as an independent group, and as that group emerges, gender and age have not been accounted for. As interest in older never-marrieds grows, particularly never-married older *women*, we are finding more information on gender differences (Braito and Anderson, 1984).

Currently, however, there is very little existing data on the life experiences of never-married older women, and many questions are yet to be addressed: Are they subject to some of the common stereotypes of old age in addition to those associated with being never married? How have they coped with singlehood over a lifetime? How have they handled life changes and the aging process?

To explore these questions, in-depth interviews were conducted with 15 never-married women, 80 years and over, living in community settings in Prince Edward Island. Prince Edward Island is unique in that it has both the highest proportion of elderly (12.5% compared to the national rate of 10%) and of never-married women over 75 (15% according to the 1981 Census). The study had three purposes: to identify the personal, social and economic factors which might influence the never-married older woman's ability to deal with everyday living and the changes which occur with aging; to evaluate some of the common stereotypes of never-marrieds; and to identify the specific needs of this group as an aid to developing appropriate social policies.

Reproduced from M.F. O'Brien (1991). "Never-married older women: the life experience." *Social Indicators Research* 24: 301–15. Reprinted by permission of Kluwer Academic Publishers.

METHODOLOGY

A qualitative approach was used. This utilized the participants' understanding and interpretation of the decision making processes, life events and conflicts which shaped their lives. Further, it allowed for examination of the attitudes and assumptions that lay behind those processes. This study is therefore concerned with subjective indicators regarding life satisfaction and well being as reported by respondents.

An initial questionnaire was administered to gather demographic data. That was followed by a series of three to four interviews of an hour with each participant. Various phases of the women's lives were reviewed, taking into account the historical aspects of the time. The influence of social, economic, religious and political currents, as they related to women in particular, were also examined. These interviews were taped and later transcribed.

Participants were selected through contacts with professionals in the field of aging and through non-professional acquaintances. Contacts were asked to recommend women who were over the age of 80, never married, living independently and perceived as having a positive attitude toward life. The age of 80 was selected as a criterion since it is at this time of life that chronic conditions prevalent in old age begin having the greatest effect on the lives of older persons in general, and older women in particular, who experience more chronic illnesses than do men (Verbrugge, 1976).

Demographic and background data from the initial, structured interviews were summarized quantitatively and examined for typical and unique responses. Transcripts of the open-ended interviews were examined and the following categories were selected for data analysis: Reflections and views on childhood, family and community relationships; work life and career development; self-perceptions as a person and as a single woman; problems and satisfactions experienced; adjustments to life-changes and the experience of aging.

STUDY FINDINGS

About half of the women who were interviewed were between 80 and 85 years of age and the remainder were between 86 and 90. The majority were living alone in their own houses and apartments in one of the two main urban centers on the Island. All but one had spent childhood and early youth in Prince Edward Island and half had grown up in rural areas of the province. Most had come from large families and maintained strong family ties. There was no particular pattern in birth order. While health and mobility problems were common—about half required assistance with shopping and transportation—most of the women considered themselves better off than their peers. Nearly all were satisfied with their friendships and with family relationships in general.

The women who participated in the study came from a broad range of family backgrounds and living situations, yet the similarities in their perceptions of their formative years are more striking than the differences.

The general image of childhood, as seen by the study participants, is one of security, harmonious family life with a clear separation of parental roles, certainty and acceptance of rules and social norms, and a strong sense of belonging to one's community. Perhaps the most frequent impression of childhood that was conveyed was one of being well taken care of by good parents, of a secure, harmonious, close family life:

> *I had a really lovely childhood. My parents were marvelous. I always remember that sort of warmth and assurance that I got from my father and mother.*

Mothers were quite distinct and well-defined in the families of these women. The household was clearly the mother's domain:

> *Mother never worked (outside the home). Those were the days when women just got married...you stayed at home and each day was allotted to different parts of the housework...In those days they weren't working in the community, like they do now, with all these clubs and things. There was nothing else but to run the home and to lead a sort of social life.*

Several of the women expressed strong admiration and affection for their fathers:

> *...he was a fine, smart man, my father...Dad and I were just as thick as peas in a pod.*
> *I always admired my father very much and we were proud of him...*

Participants differed somewhat on which parent was seen as the authority figure in the household. Some could clearly point to their mothers as disciplinarian; others saw father as the boss. Discipline by fathers often took the form of a disapproving glance:

> *...he never said anything cross to me in my life...he just had to look at me...*

Relationships with brothers and sisters were usually described as harmonious, especially in the large, rural families. There were some hints of sisterly conflict:

> *...sister was mother's favorite...*
> *Sister didn't share the housework.*

All seemed to get along with brothers. Family harmony may have been enhanced by a clear division of responsibilities among the children which was apt to be flexible rather than based on rigid criteria such as sex.

None of the women expressed any strong feelings of discrimination against girls in the family; if it occurred, it was accepted or went unnoticed. It is interesting to note that some respondents perceived their brothers as more adventuresome than they and one noted that her brother would occasionally resist parental authority whereas she would not:

> *Boys were more independent. I know my older brother—he's the only one in the family who ever learned to spin. Mother wouldn't let any of us go near the spinning-wheel because we'd spoil the yarn, but my brother just wouldn't listen. He went ahead anyway.*

In summary, the picture of early childhood and early family life emerges as one of security, harmony, certainty and acceptance of existing rules, limits and roles. The evidence is of a strong sense of belonging to one's family and community.

As is typical of never-married women, the women in this study were relatively well educated for their generation (Spreitzer and Riley, 1974).

> *...School was a happy place for me, I liked it; I enjoyed it.*
> *I loved it. I wanted to get an education, which I did.*
> *I got through for a teacher.*

Some recalled the importance of a good education to them and to their parents. In rural areas the mother was more often mentioned as the parent who encouraged education:

> *Mother would have liked all of us to have gone to university. But dad, it didn't seem to matter to him one way or the other.*

Most had achieved the highest level of education available in Prince Edward Island at the time. The majority had initially completed high school with one year of teachers' training, a typical course followed by Island girls at this time. More than half received some post secondary education, three had BA degrees and two had Master's degrees. University education was a rare thing for girls and the only degree-granting college on the Island did not accept females. University was therefore an option only to those whose families were interested and who could afford to send them off the Island. Some of the women spoke of the rarity of anyone leaving the rural community to continue their education. They were often the only ones in their age group to do so and sometimes the only member of their family:

> *I would like to go to University, but at the time St. Dunstans didn't take girls and you'd have to go away, and the money was tight, and I couldn't.*

This woman and some others did not give up the idea of university education because of family finances, however. They continued their education during their working careers, sometimes taking time off from work, sometimes attending summer schools, until they reached their objectives.

Career options for young women, as perceived by the study participants, were very few in the early decades of the century. Some of their comments are revealing:

You did what people said in those days. There was no career counseling or anything like that in schools; you went along with what you were expected to do.

From a respondent who had lived in a rural area:

It was the only thing open to me. Teaching and housework were about the only things open to girls at that time.

Apart from the limited options open to young women of the period, perhaps the most striking aspect of early career goals and choices was the influence of the family. Goals were often set or limited by family circumstances or obligations. One woman gave in to her parents' opposition to her becoming a nurse (too difficult a job for a girl) and took a secretarial course instead; another finished university, taught school for several years and then went away to nursing school despite her parents' reservations:

My father wasn't anxious for me to go into training and I knew that neither he nor my mother would be happy about me going away from home...but I was old enough to make up my own mind, surely, by that time; so I did. And once I decided to go, they never said anything.

A strong sense of obligation to the family could result in educational and career goals being postponed for a number of years. One woman, whose family could afford to send her to university, delayed her education until she was no longer needed at home. Another had postponed her early ambition of leaving P.E.I. to teach elsewhere in Canada until both her parents had died. Family ties and obligations remained strong throughout their working lives with nearly all of the women: two returned to the Island in mid-life because their families needed them.

Although some of the study participants spoke of goals they had set early in life, most of the women really had no strong career plans which they followed consistently. Career interests and ambitions seemed to evolve as they matured and were often quite circumstantial:

I think I went along with the thing that was most evident that I had to accomplish. Jobs seemed to present themselves. And I did them as best I could and as that passed, something else came up...I really didn't plan my life.

What seemed to carry most of them along through their careers was not ambition but a desire to do well at what they were doing and to be helpful and useful to others. The theme of wanting to do something worthwhile for others appears in a lot of the comments about work:

I always enjoyed teaching and I felt that I helped somebody in my work. That was rewarding.

Their occupations included teacher, nurses, one self-employed business woman, a companion and a supervisor in a utility company. One woman stayed on the family farm all her life and another had devoted most of her career to volunteer community work.

A final observation on career goals that emerges from the interviews is that plans are likely to remain tentative and short-term as long as marriage remained a possibility. One interviewee stated that married women did not work outside the home unless it was a case of dire necessity and then it was often a blow to the husband's pride. It would appear to be quite natural, therefore, to postpone career plans until one's status as a single woman was established and accepted. Thus, as the women matured, new interests and ambitions often evolved.

However, work did become an important part of the women's lives, both as a source of income and as a means of achieving a positive self-identity. There was much evidence of a strong work commitment among the women. For one woman, teaching became "the love of my life" and she further stated, "They couldn't pry me loose with a stick." It was also important to most of these women to know that they were doing their jobs well. One participant who had been dissatisfied with the quality of professional training she had first received dedicated herself to furthering her own education and to training others for her profession. She speaks of her efforts:

I nearly killed myself with work...so many things—I want to change—I'd be thinking ahead all the time.

Another woman had worked for several years at clerical and sales jobs and then decided to take the major step of setting up her own business in which she was very successful. She spoke frequently of her life-long commitment to hard work:

Oh, I always worked...my business was working...Oh, I worked, I'll tell you, all my life...Today, I could make a fortune if I was 20 years younger and able to work. It makes me sick that I can't work.

Some of the women showed a strong interest in advancement in their jobs or professions, another indication of strong work commitment. More than half of the working women attained positions of responsibility when they were supervising others or training other professionals.

Considering that most of the study participants achieved satisfaction in their working life, it is interesting to note that many found their early work experiences very difficult and stressful. They resolved their difficulties with work in different ways: by a complete change of work, or by advancement to a higher level in their professions.

Job changes were frequent for many of the women. A sense of adventure seems to have prompted others to change careers. Two went overseas during World War II—as a nurse and as a Red Cross worker. Another, who had taught school for several years, went to Western Canada to work in the hotel business when the opportunity presented itself. It seems clear from their comments that these women were community-minded for most of their lives, usually holding executive positions in voluntary organizations.

It has been suggested that the loss of work role is more problematic for never-married persons than for married (Ward, 1979). The transition from career to retirement was a difficult one for most of these women. During this time they had experienced a deep sense of loss.

> *I really didn't feel that I should retire. I felt that I had a lot to give, and I felt that it wasn't right for me not to give it.*
>
> *Some people say, "Isn't it marvelous, I'm retired, it's lovely, I'm enjoying every minute of it." But I didn't. I thought, "What good am I? Here I am, sitting down; nobody wants me, nobody needs me; I'm not working. I'm no good to anybody." I had that awful feeling...but I got over it.*

Typically, they substituted other activities and relationships for those lost with retirement. Some became more active in volunteer work and community organizations in which they had previously participated. Others started a number of new things. By being "joiners" they not only fulfilled their need to be useful to others but also met needs for social activity and status in the community.

Three aspects of the participants' lives as single women examined in this study were: perceptions and/or recollections of why they did not marry; difficulties experienced as a single woman; feelings about on-the-job discrimination toward women.

None of the women claimed to have made a conscious decision not to marry. Nor did marriage appear to have been an important goal in any of their lives. Most had friendships with men and opportunities to marry, but seemed to have been very hesitant to relinquish their independence:

> *As a young teenager, I always believed in "women's lib"...I wouldn't take the vow to obey that used to be in the marriage ceremony...I didn't agree with that. Because, while the husbands were good to their women, yet they were the boss.*

This woman had been engaged to be married when she left the Island to work and made the difficult decision later to break it off.

Other reflections:

A lot of people just get married. But there was no point in me doing this; it would just be a burden on me to marry anyone I wasn't really in love with…I'm sort of like a plant. I want to grow in my own way…I think men in those days were looking for somebody who was docile and ready to conform.

I didn't seem to see anyone that was interesting enough…Perhaps if I'd met somebody different, I might have forgotten about everything else, like lots of people do. But I didn't, and I seemed to have this awful obsession that I had to learn how to teach.

I don't think it (marriage) was one of my goals. It was just something that I put aside for the future. And then the future came.

One woman's comment that it was pretty hard for an independent woman to make marriage work sums up the attitudes of the majority. What seems to have happened is that as time went on, the marriage question merely decreased in importance as an issue in their lives. As mid-life approached, most of them were otherwise involved, in careers and/or community work.

The question of difficulties as a single woman seemed to be almost an irrelevant one. If single life was a disadvantage, study participants were unaware of it. They were absorbed in their careers, in community activities, and enjoyed friendships with other single women. Two of the women mentioned aspects of being single and female that were minor problems that did not appear to bother them greatly:

Sometimes you would feel that it would be nice to have an escort, you know, and that sort of thing, that you miss out on some things because you weren't married, but it didn't seem to bother me that much. I guess I was just peculiar.

There are some married women who I think sort of look down on you…or they think you're different in some way. I've seen that a couple of times.

When no one found single life a difficult state, there were some regrets expressed at not having children. Five of the women said that they would like to have had children, but, again, the difficulties and confinements of marriage were considered by some to be not enough of a tradeoff for the joys of parenthood.

Most of the women interviewed had entered women's professions. This may be one reason why job discrimination was not an issue for most of them in their working careers. Their comments indicate, however, that they did not feel discrimination as women because few career options and lower pay for women were accepted as normal. Only two of the women said that they had ever been aware of receiving lower pay than men for similar work. It had not occurred to either of them to object to this.

While most of the women were not aware of discrimination against themselves as women, some had mixed feelings about the feminist movement, but were hopeful for change:

> *Eventually women can be independent and men can be independent and still admire each other. As long as there isn't rivalry for ascendancy. I think the men are having a hard time now...they've all been the big bosses. I think, to value what the other person has, to give and not to be jealous of, or threatened by it, I think it's coming...It would be a wonderful thing when we can do away with that, the rivalry between the sexes. I don't think I have experienced any rivalry. I've been too independent and I had my own ideas and if you don't like them, you can lump them. I enjoy the company of men very much...I admire men...I think women should be treated equally but I don't believe in being militant about it. It's understanding that brings people together.*

Some insight was gained into personalities of the study participants and the motivating forces that guided them in their lives. Most of the interviewees felt that they had, in their lives, let nature take its course. As one woman put it, "I went along with life." Some of the group were clearly risk-takers, making moves and job changes which must have required courage. Others were fighters: they had pulled themselves through difficult periods through sheer determination. Other women who were interviewed clearly saw themselves as "doers" who had played an active role in shaping their lives and the lives of others. The women in this group seemed to have an inner determination to do well at their jobs, to achieve, and to bring about change where they saw change was needed. This determination may have been the strong motivating force which guided their lives. For the study participants as a whole, life motivation was perceived as coming mainly from the values instilled by their parents and families or from their religious beliefs.

Some insights into the women's personalities and life-attitudes was gained from their responses when they were asked about difficult times in their lives and how they handled them. Some of them drew on inner strength and determination; others turned to religion or to friends.

And finally, one woman's philosophy on dealing with failure:

> *A failure is difficult. You have to adjust to that and you can't win every time, you know. Somebody else is going to win sometimes and you have to adjust to that. If you have a few aspects of your life that you're successful in, you're lucky.*

When asked about their hopes for the future, it is not surprising that most of the women expressed a wish that they would be able to maintain things as they are and avoid any major disability or dependence on others. This was expressed in a number of ways: to continue contributing, to keep their independence, to remain at home among familiar things, to avoid major disability or illness, to retain mental functioning and control over personal affairs, to stay out of institutions.

Again, the need to be useful and to help others came out in some of their hopes for the future. For one woman, this wish took precedence over any thoughts of disability or dependency:

I hope that I can be of some use in the world. And that I can have a little bit of influence in alleviating the terrific amount of suffering that there is in the world today. Those are the only things that really matter, to make life better for other people.

The limitations of advancing age were usually accepted realistically. Looking back with regret did not appear to be a preoccupation with these women. While some conceded they would do a few things differently if they had their lives to live over, it was not something they spent a lot of time worrying about.

While the literature suggests that most older unmarrieds rely primarily on community supports (Kivett and Learner, 1980) one important finding that emerges from the interviews and from the impressions of the interviewers is that most of the women had strong support networks of family and friends. Some had compensated for losses of age peers by making friends with younger women. The majority mentioned nieces, nephews, brothers and sisters as being important in their lives. Restrictions on physical mobility were dealt with by accepting more help from family and friends. Their strong sense of connection and belonging to the Island seemed to offer a certain kind of security in their old age.

CONCLUSIONS

Available research suggests the following: that never-marrieds of both genders have had poor family relationships (Spreitzer and Riley, 1974); their inadequacies stereotype them as losers (Stein, 1976): they constitute a special type in that they have been life-long loners and live more isolate lives (Gubrium, 1976); they have difficulty living in a world where marriage is the norm (Edwards and Hoover, 1974); and in old age they have more problematic lives and are less happy than married persons due to lack of family ties and intimate relationships (Ward, 1979). Admittedly, participants in this study represent a select group, probably accounting for high levels of reported life satisfaction. However, none of the generalizations just mentioned describes the women in this study. Michalos, in discussing subjective indicators of well-being, points out that the words "satisfaction" and "happiness" are often used interchangeably in the literature. His definition of happiness "as a relatively lasting, justified, good feeling and attitude" (1987, p. 2) can well be applied to these women. Although Michalos' MDT (Multiple Discrepancies Theory), which was developed to ascertain the causes of happiness, had been mostly applied to younger persons, several of the hypotheses of this theory hold validity for the respondents to this study. There was little discrepancy between what they had or what they wanted. Their past desires to be useful had been realized in their work and many of them were still fulfilling this need through volunteer work. At the same time, their future expectations were modest and realistic given their advanced ages. They expressed few regrets about their past lives and seemed to have resolved to their own satisfaction any that had existed. Throughout their lives they were usually able to adjust their expectations to what was available at the time and to respond to the demands and needs of others. This frequently meant forgoing more immediate plans and therefore gratification. Their aspirations, particularly regarding work, were, of course, influenced by what women of that time were allowed to do. In old age, the lack of discrepancy they exhibited between what they had and wanted was most likely influenced by a further MDT hypothesis which states that discrepancies are affected by demographics. Each woman interviewed had adequate income, positive self-esteem, relatively good health and satisfying social supports. At the same time, they reported few regrets about their past lives and seemed to have resolved to their own satisfaction any that had existed. Michalos' final hypothesis concerning "human agency as a creative and constructive force" (p. 24) seems more germane for as younger women they showed initiative and risk-taking in their work and life choices. And as they aged, these women were able to substitute available satisfactions for losses incurred and ask for help when help was needed. Likewise, this study found continuity in their reported sense of satisfaction and well being over the life cycle, bearing similarity to the findings of other social indicator researchers such as Costa and McCrea (1980), who developed a code of stability vs. the effects of passing moods on happiness.

In some of the women could be a conscious suppression of problems and a control of negative feelings. These can be considered realistic, positive and rational ways of adjusting to age-related changes (Butler and Lewis, 1982). And as future cohorts of never-married women are studied, researchers need to keep in mind the diversity that exists within this group. As Rubinstein (1987) points out, cultural traditions, family orientations, personalities and personal ambitions, sexual preferences, and even demographic factors affect all elderly persons, regardless of marital status.

One of the greatest needs that never-married women have is for more formal supports in later life. Although nearly all of the women had accepted some increasing dependence on others in their current lives, it is unlikely that family and friends could be relied upon for help in the event that more caregiving was needed in the future. As is true elsewhere, such support would not likely be forthcoming (Johnson and Catalano, 1981). Even though family traditions and ties in Prince Edward Island are considered to be strong and are still governed by such basic values as family obligation and family loyalty, these and other values are in a state of transition. More than 7% of PEI's elderly live in government manors or private nursing homes (P.E.I. Department of Health and Social Services, 1981). Most of these persons are never-married, widowed or divorced (Statistics Canada, Minister of Supply and Services, 1981). Perhaps most important are the attitudes of the women themselves. Only one woman in this study mentioned moving in with relatives as an alternative offered in the event of her becoming unable to live on her own. Her reasons for rejecting this offer reflect the feelings of many older persons—she wished to maintain the independence she valued so highly. Independent living was necessary for these women to maintain their psychological integrity. For women who have remained single, the maintenance of personal dignity and positive self-image in later years consists in retaining the kind of control over their life-decisions which they have developed and cherished over a lifetime.

With more women opting for singlehood, it is reasonable to assume that their numbers will increase. Today's never-married older women may be able to shed light on future concerns and needs. For instance, what kinds of supports, both formal and informal, can realistically abate institutionalization for these women and for those who are widowed and have no children?

At the same time, older women who never married can serve as role models for today's younger women who, regardless of marital status, are striving for autonomy and identities separate from traditional roles. Many have been in unique positions in that they have not derived their social standing from men but have found it necessary to build their own identities through personal and professional achievement. Certainly these women are examples of courage and resourcefulness. By inviting them to tell their stories we can also glean something about resisting the mania to remain young with the knowledge that a rich life can await us as we age. Never-married older women's strong sense of independence can also give some insights into what the future can look like for today's younger women in later life. And as more and more women live into their 80's and 90's, it becomes increasingly important that their experience of the aging process and old age be better understood for the sake of correcting stereotypes and setting forth models of successful aging. The lives of these women need to be made more visible.

REFERENCES

Braito, R. and D. Anderson: 1984, 'The ever-single elderly woman,' in: E. Markson (ed.), Older Women: Issues and Prospects (Lexington Press, Toronto), pp. 195–225.

Butler, R. and M. Lewis: 1982, Aging and Mental Health: Positive Psychosocial and Biomedical Approaches (C.V. Mosby, St. Louis).

Costa, P. and R. McCrea: 1980, 'Influence of extraversion and neuroticism on subjective well-being: happy and unhappy people', Journal of Personality and Social Psychology, 38, pp. 668–78.

Edwards, M. and E. Hoover: 1974, The Challenge of Being Single in Old Age (J.P. Tarcher, Los Angeles).

Gubrium, J.: 1976, 'Being single in old age,' in: J. Gubrium (ed.), Time, Roles and Self in Old Age (Human Science Press, New York).

Johnson, C. and D. Catalano: 1981, 'Childless elderly and their supports,' The Gerontologist 21, pp. 610–8.

Kivett, V. and R. Learner: 1980, 'Perspectives on the childless rural elderly: a comparative analysis,' The Gerontologist 20, pp. 708–16.

Michalos, A. C.: 1987, 'What makes people happy?' Levekarsforskning Konferanserapport (Proceedings of the Seminar on Welfare Research), Norwegian Research Council for Science and the Humanities, Olso, Norway.

Towards Meeting the Needs of Senior Citizens in P.E.I.: 1981, P.E.I. Department of Social Services. Charlottetown.

Rubinstein, R.: 1987, 'Never married as social type: re-evaluating some images', The Gerontologist 27, pp. 108–13.

Spreitzer, E. and L. Riley: 1974, 'Factors Associated with Singlehood,' Journal of Marriage and the Family 36, pp. 533–42.

Statistics Canada: 1981 Census of Canada, 'Age, Sex and Marital Status.'

Statistics Canada (1981 Census): April 1984, The Elderly in Canada (Minister of Supply and Services, Ottawa).

Stein, P.: 1976, Single. (Prentice Hall, Englewood Cliffs, N.J.)

Verbrugge, L.: 'Sex differentials in morbidity and mortality in the United States', Social Biology 23, pp. 276–96.

Ward, R.: 1979, 'Never married in later life,' Journal of Gerontology 34.

Living in the Margins
LESBIAN AGING

Jeanette A. Auger

As a feminist, a lesbian and a gerontologist I have a personal, political and educational interest in the process of growing old within a predominantly heterosexist, mysogynist and ageist culture. Unlike some of my sisters I have been provided with a structured feminist analysis of patriarchal control of my sexuality. As well, as a (recently) tenured academic I can feel fairly secure in my current employment. Many older lesbians are not as fortunate. For some, the women's movement and feminists are seen as just one more set of gatekeepers making judgments on their lives. For others, being "found out" meant (and still means) the loss of jobs, ostracization by co-workers, family and friends. This is especially problematic for women who live in small, rural communities.

The material for this paper is informed by field note experiences, literature and research interviews conducted from 1982 to the present with care providers and older lesbians in institutions and community-based workshops. In it, I describe and analyze the experiences of older lesbians as they speak of their isolation within lesbian and heterosexual culture. They also speak of the many pleasures and benefits of growing old without the societal expectations and pressures placed on heterosexual women.

INTRODUCTION

In Canadian culture old lesbians are thought not to exist, not only by the media but often by the lesbian community itself. In the feminist academic press there is little or no mention of lesbian elders and the gerontological world seems oblivious to the sexuality of older persons in general, let alone that of older lesbians [Two notable exceptions are Adelman (1986) and Ashfield and Shamai (1987)]. When articles on sexuality do appear in noted journals they are about heterosexual practices or, and these are rare occurrences,

Reproduced with permission from *Canadian Woman Studies* 12(2): 80–84 (1992).

they deal with homosexual men. [See for example, Lee (1987), Berger (1982), Kelly (1977) and Weeks (1983)]. Lesbians who are old are thus in triple jeopardy as they represent at least three oppressed groups in North American culture: they are not young, they do not enjoy the privilege of patriarchal masculinity and they do not receive the social rewards for heterosexuality. In these ways they are placed within the margins of work on aging and on women. Those who are not white suffer yet another stigma, as do those defined as disabled.

Looking at aging demographics, according to the 1986 census there were 1,564,240 women aged sixty-five or more living in Canada. If we apply the Masters and Johnson (1966) and the Kinsey (1948) reports on sexuality, we can conservatively assume that at least one in ten of these women are lesbian. Theoretically we are speaking of some 156,000 women aged over sixty-five. In the census, however, there is no category "lesbian" under the marital status section. Presumably many will fall under the "single" category while others are subsumed under the categories of "married," "widowed" or "divorced." Many lesbians say they "come out" after age fifty, often from heterosexual marriages of long duration, or in later life after they have been widowed. Lesbian women are thus hidden within the official demographics of Canadian culture.

Lesbians who are old are also hidden or invisible because there is a lack of research on them. It is often difficult to identify older "lesbians" in the first place. For example, in working with and for seniors, I have heard about "possible" older lesbians mostly by accident.

I conducted interviews with women who were never married. The following is from a discussion with a seventy-four year old woman living in Vancouver:

> *Me: When you lived for twenty-three years with your friend did you ever speak of yourselves as lesbians?*
>
> *J: Oh we were not lesbians truly. We were intimate in every sense of the word but we were certainly not lesbians.*
>
> *Me: I assumed that when you said that you were gay that you meant that you were lesbians.*
>
> *J: No I said that we were gay, happy and gay. Lesbians dress like men; they do men's work and act like men. We were just women who loved each other and were happy with that. Now you'd call us lesbians maybe, but we never would then—it was a bad word.*

The co-ordinator of a support network for women who are divorced or widowed in Vancouver reminded me of the following telephone conversation which she had with an eighty year old woman:

> *Caller: I want to know where I can get a nice clean girl to replace my P. who has died.*

> *Friend: Have you tried some of the lesbian resources in the community? Or perhaps the feminist bookstore would know who you could contact about meeting other lesbian women?*
>
> *Caller: I don't want nothing to do with them libbers or lesbian types. I just want a nice clean girl to replace my P. None of these club types or "feminists" who say we should all act like women as if we didn't know that we was women. We just like to have short hair and wear men's clothes.*

Research, as well as everyday life, suggests that some older lesbians, believing in rigid sex roles (the so-called "butch" and "femme"), identify more with heterosexual men than with feminist lesbians. Some older lesbians feel themselves judged by their feminist sisters on this issue. In the last cited examples the women did not identify themselves as lesbian for different reasons. The first women objected to those lesbians who "look and act like men"; the second objected to those who *did not* look and act like men.

I conducted research in care facilities in British Columbia. On one visit to an eighty-four year old friend, we were in the dining room of a multi-level care facility. The seniors sat at tables for four, while newer residents sat alone until a regular group was formed for them by the staff. The following conversation occurred:

> *G: See that woman over there, she's one of "them," you know.*
>
> *J: One of what?*
>
> *G: You know them queers. People who like bread on bread with the same filling in the middle.*
>
> *J: Do you mean that she is a lesbian? How do you know that?*
>
> *G: Yeah, that's right. The orderly told me who cleans up the rooms. She said she lived with another one for a real long time. The other one up and dies and now she's in here.*
>
> *J: It must be terrible to lose someone you are so close to after so long.*
>
> *G: Well I don't think that sort should be allowed to live in places like this. It's one thing to lose a husband, that's—proper—but that sort of thing is not.*

I later talked with the orderly who had passed on the information about the resident. She informed me that "Nowadays two women don't live together that long unless they are up to something." She said that she had told some of the other residents to "be careful" around this woman because you "never know about them queers." When I pointed out that lesbian women are as selective about who they want to be involved with as anyone else, the orderly still felt it her "duty" to let people know "what was going on" (even though she clearly did not know!).

These illustrations make visible some of the experiences of women who are reluctant to identify themselves as lesbians because of the myths and assumptions of others about whom they think lesbians might be.

THE ISSUES

When dealing with a topic as complex as lesbianism, it is important to recognize that there is no such thing as a "typical lesbian." Lesbianism is not merely a set of behaviors based on the preference of one sex over another, whether one acts on this preference or not. For many, lesbianism is also a political and emotional stance in the world, which creates an ideological base by allowing lesbians to define ourselves and each other, regardless of age. By identifying some of the issues involved with lesbians and aging, we can recognize the diversity in lesbian experience.

Fear of Aging

We are all growing older, and have been since the day we were born. Aging affects every one of us whether twenty-five or sixty-five. In our culture old age is seen as a negative experience, as something to be dreaded. The media bombard us with images of women who look to be at most forty, yet they "hide wrinkles" with Oil of Olay, remove "age spots" on their hands with Porcelana and hide "that ugly grey" with Lady Grecian formula. Old age is not presented as something to celebrate or to look forward to. A thirty year old lesbian at a workshop on aging remarked:

> *It's neat that you sort of sell this old age thing as good but I don't want to get old. I would hate to have wrinkles and withered skin. I couldn't bear the thought of being with an old woman. She would feel so flabby to me.*

Not only do some older lesbians fear their own aging, but they receive little support from their community in seeing old age as a positive experience. In her article "Friends or Foes: Gerontological and Feminist Theory" (1989) Reinharz tries to present what she calls "conceptual linkages" (p. 223) between the lives of older women and feminist women. She fails to recognize, however, that many older women *are* feminist women, and that even feminists suffer from age denial. Although Reinharz is to be commended on the attempts to bridge the gerontological/feminist gap, she too ignores the reality of lesbian lives.

The experiences of women who are old today are probably different than they will be for teenagers, or those approaching middle-age. At a lesbian workshop on aging in Nova Scotia the group members were asked when they first thought of themselves as "old." Others related a sense of growing old based on particular life experiences, such as this fifty-eight year old:

> *My lover and I split up and suddenly I realized that no one in the world knew about us. I was alone on the farm and I had really bad arthritis and probably couldn't manage without her. Then I realized, Shit, I'm old.*

It becomes apparent that old age is relative—a state of mind that is seldom invoked unless life happenings cause us to take stock of ourselves.

Coming Out or Staying In

Lesbians who are "out of the closet" experience aging differently from those who are still "in." The informant last quoted stated that her rural community did not know about her sexuality. Therefore neighbors, family and friends could not be relied upon for support. This experience was shared by many older lesbians I spoke with. They were concerned not only with coming out to friends, family, colleagues and medical and service providers, but also to their children and grandchildren, and sometimes to spouses.

Related to this is the issue of when one recognizes one's own lesbianism and what that individual chooses to do with the knowledge. Many reject their feelings for other women because of the negative stereotypes associated with being gay; others because of the social stigma attached to those who choose to be open about their sexual preference. Some women are already in heterosexual marriages when they recognize their sexuality, and do not want to lose the rewards that heterosexual privilege provides, or risk losing their children if their husband is not supportive of their sexuality. Some older women have been lesbians as long as they can remember, while others came out in later life. Some, such as Gwen, the mother of a fifty year old daughter, came out in her late seventies:

> *I kept going to these A.A. meetings and there were some wonderful women there. When Louise [her daughter] told me that she was gay I thought about it quite a lot. I have also loved women, liked them better than men. Now I just wish that there was someone I could meet so that I could have a lesbian relationship. I have given it a lot of thought and I am ready for that thrill. No one cares about little old ladies of seventy anyway so I should be able to get away with it until I die.*

Many of the older lesbians I spoke with came out when there was no gay liberation, no political lesbian literature or movies to speak of, and no women's movement to raise awareness of sexual issues. Some of them talked about how hard it was to come out to family members, especially to children and grandchildren, as well as to their own parents, without any support systems in place. Often many reported having very few kinship networks left, because family members just could not accept their sexuality. Older lesbians said that they had never heard the word "lesbian," and believed that they were the only women in the world who love women.

There are obvious reasons, then, why some older women prefer not to identify with younger lesbians. Why would they want to, when being old or lesbian is seen only in negative terms? In this sense they choose to remain in the margins of social life.

Geography and Support Systems

Rural and urban settings also affect the lives of older lesbians. In most urban settings in Canada there are lesbian networks where women can socialize and get together for meals, dances, conferences, and so on. In addition to networks for emotional support, urban environments usually offer some services geared especially to lesbian women. In large metropolitan areas we are more likely to be able to find lesbian or lesbian positive doctors, lawyers, and dentists. As a seventy-three year old lesbian noted:

> When I found out that I had cancer I made sure to phone my friend who is a nurse at the cancer clinic. I asked her to put me in touch with a lesbian doctor so that I could be honest about my lifestyle. She was just great. My lover was allowed to be in my room anytime and the doctor discussed everything with her. It wasn't like when we lived in that village in Quebec—there was nowhere to turn if you were sick and the neighbors would have died if they knew we were gay.

Regarding institutionalization, older lesbians from small rural areas have very little choice about where they may spend the rest of their lives. Likely, they will be relocated to another town or village which has an appropriate care facility. Even when one exists locally, staff members are unlikely to be sympathetic or knowledgeable about lesbian lifestyles. When a woman has lived for most of her life in the same community, this relocation can be traumatic and severe. If she has a partner, separation can place an additional burden on both women.

Several lesbian groups across Canada have discussed the idea of setting up either lesbian homes for the aged, or communities where lesbians can grow old in a co-operative project where women of all ages live together— some with their children of both sexes, others without children or with daughters only. In this vision, articulated forcefully by a group of older lesbian women at the "Coming Together" conference in Halifax, Nova Scotia, lesbian doctors, nurses and other caregivers would also live in, or be available to these communities so that they would be fairly self-sufficient in terms of providing health care for the older group members. To my knowledge no such community yet exists.

Relationships

Older lesbians are concerned about being in or out of relationships, and how that is different as one grows older. Those who have been in long-term relationships which suddenly come to an end often say that the feeling of loss is far greater than what they experienced in their younger years. A sixty-two year old said:

> *When D. said she wanted out of the relationship, to be with a younger woman, I was really devastated. I knew that things hadn't been going all that well for a while but I really thought that after twenty-two years we would stay together forever. When I was younger I thought I was pretty cute and other women liked me a lot. I can't imagine who would want me now or where the hell I would ever meet anyone in this place. Everyone I know has been the lover of someone else. That's the trouble with living in a small community.*

Women are thought to be asexual as they grow older. The double standard dictates that men are sexy and more mature in old age. Their facial lines are said to express attractiveness and experience; ours are "wrinkles" we are supposed to hide with cosmetics. Therefore old women are sexless and ugly. This stereotype flows into the lesbian community—we are all socialized by the same system to be female regardless of our sexuality. Reboin (1986) reiterates this idea in the following way: "our culture defines lesbians as sexual beings, which implies youth and activity" (p. 178). And yet she also speaks of her "four decades of messages from the outside world that old women and lesbian women are not desirable, normal, interesting, active and acceptable human beings..." (p. 182).

Monogamy is also invoked frequently by older lesbians who seem to prefer this over open relationships, whether they are currently in a relationship, or attempting to find a partner. A fifty-eight year old lesbian succinctly stated the most frequently provided reason:

> *We went to one of those feminist do's and this psychologist who was a lesbian was saying that open relationships were the new trend among gay women she sees. F. and I have been together eighteen years now and we like each other better than anyone else we know. We don't want or need to be with anyone else. When you get older you need more stability in your life. I've had my flings—I know what it is like to love other women but I want to be settled down and get on with what's left of our lives together, so that when either one of us is gone the other will have wonderful memories to look back on without the worry of whether or not we need to have an open relationship.*

Menopause

Lesbians who become sexually dissatisfied or bored with their partners, especially those in long-term monogamous relationships, sometimes used menopause as an "excuse" for not wanting to have sex anymore. The older women in a workshop on lesbian issues explained the situation as follows:

> *When I started menopause it was somewhat of a relief because then I could say that was why I didn't want to have sex anymore. I guess we just got too used to each other or something. We are still together and are very intimate. Maybe sex just isn't as important when you are older.*

Another explained:

> *Sex never really was a big deal for us. I didn't like it all that much in the beginning but M. did. With menopause I had some pain. I was sort of itchy all the time and so that seemed like a good time to stop having sex. Other than that our relationship is perfect for me although I do think that M. would still like to have sex more often.*

This rationale has also been cited by many heterosexual women in various studies on menopause. Lesbian and heterosexual women alike are vulnerable to the myth that after menopause they are no longer sexual or attractive. There is no bio-medical evidence to support the idea that hormonal changes which occur during menopause affect sexual desire, attractiveness or sexual capacity. Women can be as sexually active, or not, during and after menopause as they were before. Another myth is that we need to be sexual to remain in relationships, but this is clearly not so. There are many other ways to be close and intimate with others.

The demographics of aging are based primarily on chronology. Medical research and common sense experiences tell us that certain physiological and social changes do occur as we grow older. What matters is how we deal with these changes. Many in our society view menopause as the end of female desire, attractiveness and sexual activity. Biologically, it is simply the end of childbearing possibilities.

The assumption is sometimes made that lesbian women are less affected by menopause than heterosexual women, due to the notion that the latter are not interested in reproduction. This assumption ignores the reality that many lesbians are mothers, and that many wanted to conceive but could not for medical, economic, political or logistical reasons.

Another assumption about lesbians is that due to their "deviant" lifestyle and thus experiences of discrimination, we are more reflective, thoughtful, open, sensitive and aware. Because of these positive attributes, we are not expected to have the same problems with retirement and menopause as heterosexual women. However we are socialized first to be women—not lesbians, so we carry around much of the same cultural self-expectations and values about what we are "supposed to do."

Many women identify as heterosexual prior to becoming lesbians. The notion of women reaching their fullest potential only through childbirth and childbearing may still be subtly at work. Choosing to relate to other women sexually does not necessarily preclude the desire to bear a child. Just as for heterosexual women, menopause may mark the regretted end of that possibility.

THE AGING EXPERIENCE PERSONALIZED

We age all of our lives, not just on our sixty-fifth birthday when we are magically eligible for government assistance based on chronology. How we experience our aging and how we learn to deal with our issues throughout the life cycle affects how we cope with aging. If we have unfinished business, unresolved conflicts, unspoken fears, resentments and angers while young, and do not deal with them, we will carry them on to our old age. It is helpful if we can resolve them while young, through therapy, dreams, fantasy, journals, or—if possible—in real life. Who we are now can be who we will become as older selves. One of the saddest thoughts I am often left with by older lesbians is the notion of unfinished business or unresolved issues— what I call the "if only's."

On the other hand, if we do not, when we are old, focus on what might have been, we could have the same attitude as an informant who was celebrating her seventieth birthday. She marvelled at how lucky she was to be in good health, in a relationship in which she could grow and flourish, and among lesbian friends whom she loved and admired. Someone asked her what it was like to be an aging lesbian, and whether or not she experienced it as a triple problem. She replied:

> *Never, I am as happy now as I ever was in my life. This is a tremendous thrill. To love and be loved by women is well worth living for. I just wish that all lesbians could learn from their loving as I have done.*

ACKNOWLEDGMENT

Thanks to Sharon D. Stone at York University for editing the original manuscript from which this article is taken.

REFERENCES

Adelman, Marcy. *Long Time Passing*. Boston: Alyson, 1986.

Alvig, C. *The Invisible Minority: Aging and Lesbianism*. New York: Utica College Institute of Gerontology, 1983.

Ashfield, Maureen and Sarah Shamai. *Lesbians and Aging: An Exploration of the Issues*. Unpublished paper, Simon Fraser University, Burnaby, B.C., 1987.

Berger, R.M. "The Unseen Minority: Older Gays and Lesbians," *Social Work,* May, 1982, 236–241.

Berger, Raymond. *Gay and Gray.* Chicago: University of Illinois Press, 1982.

Blackwood, Evelyn. *The Many Faces of Homosexuality.* New York: Harrington Park Press, 1986.

Kehoe, Monika. "Lesbians Over 65: A Triple Invisible Minority," *Journal of Homosexuality,* 12, 2–4, May 1986, 193–98.

Kelly, J. "The Aging Male Homosexual: Myth and Reality," *The Gerontologist,* 1977, 17(4), 328–332.

Kinsey, A.C., Pomeroy, W.B., and Martin, C.E. *Sexual Behaviour in the Human Male.* Philadelphia: Saunders, 1948.

Lee, John Allan. "The Invisible Lives of Canada's Gray Gays," *Aging in Canada,* Victor Marshall (ed.). Toronto: Fitzhenry and Whiteside, 1987, 138–155.

Lockard, Denyse. "The Lesbian Community: An Anthropological Approach," *The Many Faces of Homosexuality,* Evelyn Blackwood (ed.). New York: Harrington Park Press, 1986, 83–95.

Masters, W.H. and Johnson, V.E. *Human Sexual Response.* Boston: Little Brown, 1966.

Reboin, Faith. "Lesbian Grandmother," in *Long Time Passing* (March 1986), 177–83.

Reinharz, Shulamit. "Friends or Foes: Gerontological and Feminist Theory," *Radical Voices,* Renate D. Klein and Deborah Lynn Steinberg (eds.). Toronto: Pergamon, 1989, 222–244.

Weeks, Jeffrey. "The Problem of Older Homosexuals," *The Theory and Practice of Homosexuality,* John Hart and Diane Richardson (eds.), London: Routledge & Kegan Paul, 1983, 177–185.

39

A Guide to the Diagnosis and Treatment of Elder Abuse

Christopher Patterson and Elizabeth Podnieks

DEFINITION OF ELDER ABUSE

The simplest definition of elder abuse is: "Any act of commission or omission that results in harm to an elderly person" (National Clearinghouse on Family Violence, 1983).

The Department of National Health and Welfare has developed the following definition of elder abuse and neglect (National Clearinghouse on Family Violence, 1990):

Physical Abuse

Involves assault, rough handling, or the withholding of physical necessities such as food, personal care, hygienic care or medical care.

Sexual Abuse

Any form of sexual intimacy between two people without consent or by force or threat of force.

Psychological Abuse

Involves verbal assault, social isolation, lack of affection, or denying the person the chance to participate in decisions in respect to his or her own life.

Financial Abuse

Involves the misuse of money or property. This can include fraud or using funds for purposes contrary to the needs and interests (or desires) of the older person.

This article first appeared in the January 1993 issue of the *Ontario Medical Review* and is reprinted with the permission of the Ontario Medical Association.

Neglect

Can lead to any of these three types of abuse. It can be *passive* neglect if the caregiver does not intend to injure the dependent senior; or *active* when the caregiver consciously fails to meet the needs of the senior.

PREVALENCE

There have been three rigorous studies of community prevalence of elder abuse, and many estimates based upon other surveys and reviews. Gioglio and Blakemore (1983) found that one per cent of 342 people over age 65 were victims of some form of abuse. Pillemer and Finkelhor (1988) reported that 3.2 per cent of 2,025 older people residing in the Boston metropolitan area were victims of abuse. The most common form was physical violence.

Podnieks and colleagues conducted a cross-Canada telephone survey of 2,000 randomly chosen elderly persons living in private houses. Four per cent of this population had experienced some form of maltreatment since they passed their 65th birthday. Two and one-half per cent suffered material abuse (financial or property exploitation); chronic verbal abuse was reported by 1.4 per cent; 0.5 per cent experienced physical violence; and 0.4 per cent suffered from neglect (Podnieks et al., 1989). Four per cent of all seniors living in private dwellings translates into 98,000 Canadians. Many cases of abuse are chronic or repetitive. In one study, previous incidents of abuse had occurred in 58 per cent (Block, Sinnott, 1979). Repetitive abuse was noted by O'Malley in 70 per cent of cases (O'Malley et al., 1979).

Prevalence in Institutions

The true prevalence of abuse in institutions is unknown, although it is frequently reported, and is regarded as an iatrogenic complication of institutional care. In the only rigorous study carried out in nursing homes, a random sample of staff from 31 nursing homes in New Hampshire were interviewed (577 nurses and nursing aids). Physical abuse had been witnessed by 36 per cent of staff in the preceding year. Excessive use of restraints was particularly common at 21 per cent; pushing, grabbing, shoving or pinching occurred in 17 per cent; and slapping or hitting in 15 per cent. Psychological abuse was observed by 81 per cent of staff (yelling at patient in anger—70 per cent; insulting or swearing at patient—50 per cent; isolating patient inappropriately—23 per cent) (Pillemer, Moore, 1989).

An analysis of complaints brought to an advocacy group, Concerned Friends of Ontario Citizens in Care Facilities, revealed that nearly half of 56 detailed complaints revealed sufficient grounds for laying criminal charges of theft, assault or failure to provide adequate medical attention (Jorgensen, 1986). Many nursing homes and other facilities are understaffed, and in some cases the staff are inadequately trained.

RISK FACTORS: THE VICTIM

Risk factors for abuse have been compiled from a variety of sources. These include patients seeking medical attention and found to be victims of abuse; cases of suspected abuse investigated by social agencies; and cases where neglect has been evident. In the older literature, identification of risk centred upon the victim, whereas the recent literature has paid more attention to factors in the environment and characteristics of the perpetrator (Wolf, 1988). Some factors that may lead to elder abuse include the following (Council on Scientific Affairs, 1987):

Dependency

As dependency on others to provide services increases, vulnerability to abuse and neglect is enhanced.

Lack of close family ties: A dependent elderly parent can precipitate stress and frustration without the love and friendship necessary to counteract the additional responsibilities placed on adult children.

Family Violence

For some families, violence may be viewed as a normal reaction to stress; for others, caretakers may resort to violent behavior when faced with the elderly person's seemingly insatiable demands. In some cases, a history of child abuse, then spousal abuse is perpetuated as elder abuse.

Lack of Financial Resources

When pressures mount on financial resources, the elderly parent may be viewed as an economic burden, resulting in increased incidence and prevalence of elder abuse.

Psychopathology of the Abuser

Flawed psychological development of the caretaker, beset with problems of his or her own, may result in acts of abuse. Drug and alcohol abuse are commonly present.

Lack of Community Support

Lack of facilities and resources in the community to provide additional care for the elderly may contribute to frustration in the caretaker and may enhance the potential for elder abuse.

Institutional Factors

Factors such as low pay, poor working conditions and long hours may contribute to pessimistic attitudes of caretakers, resulting in neglect of the elderly.

Results of recent studies, particularly the Canadian National Survey, indicate that the profile of the victim is different depending upon the type of abuse.

RISK FACTORS: THE PERPETRATOR

Increasing attention is being paid to the characteristics of the perpetrator. Most often the abuser is a relative, approximately equally distributed between children or grandchildren and spouses. Abusers usually live with the victim (75 per cent), and have often cared for the victim for a long time (mean 9.5 years) (Taler, 1985). The abuser often has a psychological disturbance such as being the least socially integrated of the children, with alcohol or drug problems. External stresses such as employment loss, divorce, illness and death of others have been implicated. Many of the abusers have themselves been victims of abuse. The caregiver will often express frustration in dealing with the situation, and show signs of stress.

NATURAL HISTORY

The natural history of elder abuse is not one of spontaneous resolution. In the same way that spousal abuse in adult life tends to escalate, so it does in later life. Generally, the abuse will continue unless a major change occurs in the milieu. Part of the reason for this is that in many cases, victims or families refuse help. The end result may be serious illness, crisis situation or institutional admission.

■■■

DEALING WITH THE ABUSE SITUATION

The principles of dealing with the abuse situation include:

1. Recognition of the problem.
2. Provision of information.
3. Assessment of decision-making capacity of the victim:

    (a) Where the victim is competent, facilitate choices;

    (b) Where the victim is not competent to make decisions, protective action must be taken.

Having recognized a situation where abuse has occurred or is highly likely, the victim should be apprised of available options. These will include invoking the help of other professionals such as social workers, and consideration of arranging more personal help. Relocation is a further option. When there is clear-cut evidence of physical abuse or malnutrition from neglect, a short-term admission to hospital or other facility may be necessary to "defuse" the situation while appropriate help is arranged for victim and caregiver. Where competency of the victim to make decisions is in question, it may be necessary to obtain a psychiatric opinion and consider public trusteeship. Impending changes to Ontario law include the provision of advocates for people in abusive or potentially abusive situations.

In dealing with the abusive situation, the needs of the perpetrator as well as the victim should be recognized (Zarit, 1979). The following have been suggested as guidelines for managing the perpetrator:

- Provide information about the disorder.
- Give the caregiver permission to meet his or her own needs.
- Encourage the caregiver to attend support groups.
- Respond to the major behavioral problems of the impaired person.
- Arrange for respite or alternative care if the caregiver's burden becomes too great.
- Help the caregiver maximize the elderly individual's abilities.

Management of the abusive situation requires skill, diplomacy, and knowledge of a complicated health-care and legal system. Expertise is available from a variety of health professionals, and a team approach is often helpful. Geriatric services, where available, are able to review the entire situation, perform the necessary assessments, and arrange for additional services.

PREVENTION

The recognition and approach to elder abuse has lagged many years behind child abuse. As public awareness of this problem becomes greater, physicians at all levels must appreciate the extent of the problem, its recognition and approaches to management. Education in the area of elder abuse must be part of undergraduate curriculum, postgraduate and post-professional education. Particularly important is the ability to recognize warning signs in a stressed caregiver, and to anticipate those situations where abuse may subsequently occur. In this way, appropriate identification of the potentially abusive situation, timely introduction of services and, where necessary, counseling, may help to reduce what is increasingly being recognized as a major public health problem in North America....

REFERENCES

Block MR, Sinnot JD (eds.). *The battered elder syndrome: an exploratory study.* College Park Md. Centre on Aging, University of Maryland, 1979.

Council on Scientific Affairs: elder abuse and neglect. *JAMA* 1987;257(7):966–971.

Gioglio GR, Blakemore P. Elder abuse in New Jersey: the knowledge and experience of abuse among older New Jerseyans. Unpublished manuscript, Department of Human Services, Trenton, NJ, 1983.

Jorgensen B. *Crimes against the elderly in institutional care.* Toronto, Concerned Friends of Ontario Citizens in Care Facilities Inc., 1986.

National Clearinghouse on Family Violence. Frail and vulnerable: elder abuse in Canada. *Vis-a-Vis* 1983;1(2):1–2.

National Clearinghouse on Family Violence. *Elder abuse.* Ottawa, Department of National Health and Welfare, 1990.

O'Malley H, Segel H, Perez R, et al. *Elder abuse in Massachusetts: a survey of professionals and paraprofessionals.* Boston, Legal Research and Services for the Elderly, 1979.

Pillemer K, Finkelhor D. The prevalence of elder abuse: a random sample survey. *Gerontologist* 1988;28:51–57.

Pillemer K, Moore DW. Abuse of patients in nursing homes: findings from a survey of staff. *Gerontologist* 1989;29:314–320.

Podnieks E, Pillemer K, Nicholson J, Shillington J, Frizzell A. National survey on abuse of the elderly in Canada. Preliminary findings. Toronto, Office of Research and Innovation, Ryerson Polytechnical Institute, 1989.

Taler G, Ansello EF. Elder abuse. *Am Fam Phys* 1985;32:107–114.

Wolf RS, Elder abuse: ten years later. *J Am Geriatri Soc* 1988;36:758–762.

Zarit SH. The organic brain syndrome and family relationships: in Ragan E. ed. *Aging Parents.* Los Angeles, University of Southern California Press, 1979.

SECTION EIGHT

Discussion Questions

1. *Why is it a myth to say that families abandon their older members today? Give evidence from recent Canadian data to support your view.*

2. *Caregiving can make great demands on a caregiver but can also bring deep satisfaction to the caregiver. Discuss.*

3. *What can employers do to help caregivers cope with the demands of caregiving? What do the stakeholders—employees, dependants, and employers—each gain from supportive work arrangements?*

4. *What does Rosenthal mean when she says that comforters hold a "position" in the family? What type of person most often occupies this position? How is the position maintained from generation to generation?*

5. *How did the social conditions in the past influence never-married women in their career choices and relationships? What problems does the lack of a spouse pose for these women as they age? How do these women maintain their positive self-image in later life?*

6. *How does Canadian culture treat older lesbians? What unique issues do aging lesbians face? In particular, how does aging affect lesbians' relationships as they age?*

7. *Describe the types of elder abuse and neglect that exist. How prevalent is each type? What leads to abuse? How can we prevent elder abuse?*

Suggested Readings

Connidis, I.A. (1989). *Family Ties and Aging.* Toronto: Butterworths.

Lee, J.A. (1987). "What Can Homosexual Aging Studies Contribute to Theories of Aging?" *Journal of Homosexuality* 13: 43–71.

Laurence, M. (1964). *The Stone Angel.* Toronto: McClelland and Stewart.

Leroux, T.G., and M. Petrunik (1990). "The Construction of Elder Abuse as a Social Problem: A Canadian Perspective." *International Journal of Health Services* 20(4): 651–63.

McDonald, P.L., et al. (1991). *Elder Abuse and Neglect in Canada.* Toronto: Butterworths.

Podnieks, E., K. Pillemer, J.P. Nicholson, T. Shillington, and A. Frizzel (1990). *National Survey on Abuse of the Elderly in Canada.* Toronto: Ryerson Polytechnic Institute.

Rosenthal, C.J., and P. Dawson (1989). "Is Parent Care Normative? The Experiences of a Sample of Middle-Aged Women." *Research on Aging* 11(2): 244–60.

Death and Dying

Old people can expect to live longer today than at any time in the past. Extended-care units in hospitals, improved quality of care in nursing homes, and new drugs account in part for this change. Modern medicine has begun to fulfil the ancient promise of science. It gives us longer life.

But, like so many gifts of the modern age, this one raises questions about individual rights and social responsibilities. Who should decide whether to continue treatment when a person is in a coma? Can a doctor legally follow the written wishes of a confused patient? Should a doctor deny older people the use of scarce resources such as kidney dialysis machines? These questions raise issues of morality, professional ethics, and social policy.

These questions come up every day for health-care workers and others who deal with older people. And professionals give answers to these questions every day. Physicians decide who will or will not receive kidney dialysis. Nurses decide whether to continue feeding a patient who refuses food. People in the clergy counsel parishioners with terminal illnesses who feel suicidal. Few formal guidelines exist for dealing with these issues.

Bolton addresses the issue of a person's right to die. She compares American and Canadian legal precedents and concludes that Canada has only begun to look at this issue. In an epilogue written for this book, Bolton reports that case law now gives clear precedent for people to refuse treatment. Also, recent legislation in Manitoba allows a person to make an advance directive of their wishes and/or appoint a proxy to make decisions for them. Bolton's article shows the evolution of Canadian legal and ethical thinking on this subject.

The article by Saint-Arnaud places these issues in the context of the doctor–patient relationship. She encourages dialogue between doctors and patients around issues of consent to treatment. This solution gets complicated when the patient lacks the competence to make decisions. Saint-Arnaud then considers the use of advance directives and power-of-attorney as methods of giving instructions prior to incompetence. Finally, Saint-Arnaud looks at cases of competent persons who refuse treatment.

Moore takes up this last issue in her article on rational suicide. Should a health-care professional help a clear-thinking older person, with or without a terminal illness, commit suicide? What about when death would relieve pain and suffering? How should a professional respond to rational suicide?

Moore reviews the arguments for and against rational suicide. She concludes with a thoughtful personal review of her own experience as a nurse. She links the desire for death in later life to the lack of roles for older people in society today. Moore asks us to look at the social world as well as at the individual who wants to leave it. She calls for a change in social conditions so that rational suicide would be a less attractive choice for older people.

Health-care costs rise each year in Canada and the U.S. Some writers say that, to control costs, society should set limits on health-care use by the elderly. Beyond a certain age, the health-care system would keep a person from suffering, but would not provide expensive treatments. Glass presents a critical review of this position. She asks whether age provides a basis for rationing health care. She reviews a number of arguments that might support rationing by age, including social worth, merit, or the amount of effort a person puts into society. She concludes that rationing based on age amounts to discrimination.

Instead, she proposes that we learn to accept the limits of medical science and that we learn to accept death. Excessive treatment, she says, often arises from lack of communication between doctor and patient. Like Saint-Arnaud and Moore, she says that open discussion of the patient's wishes for a good life and a good death leads to appropriate treatment.

Several of the articles in this section have placed the discussion of death and dying in the context of life's meaning. Frankl makes this theme the focus of his article. Meaninglessness, he says, not death, threatens life. Life gains meaning when a person's life transcends itself. This happens when a person grows spiritually or contributes socially. Society can offer this opportunity. But a person must also see this as a personal task. The discovery of meaning goes beyond usefulness to society. It expresses the dignity of the person. And this can take place at any age, at any time, even in the face of a terminal illness.

The articles in this section put ethical issues related to death and dying in a social context. They show that death becomes less frightening if people can talk about it. These authors call for greater dialogue between physicians and patients. And they call for a society that can accept old age and death as parts of life.

40

Who Can Let You Die?

M. Anne Bolton

INTRODUCTION

Canadian Courts have not yet considered in any depth issues dealing with the right to die with dignity. In particular, there have been no cases dealing with whether incompetent persons doomed to persist in vegetative states have the right, exercised through a guardian, to refuse continued medical treatment. The American experience should be instructive to persons interested in this field, as recent jurisprudence has provided thoughtful and objective decisions in this area.

These issues deserve careful consideration by professionals in this field of aging. Developed policy and ethical positions are necessary prerequisites to advocacy, to hearings, and to the establishment of legal rights.

This article will consider an American case example, some policy and ethical considerations, and the Canadian and American jurisprudence in this area.

A CASE EXAMPLE[1]

Until the night of March 22, 1983, Paul E. Brophy was a healthy, robust man, employed as a fireman and an emergency technician in Easton, Massachusetts. At midnight on that day, he complained to his wife of a severe headache. He became unconscious and his wife took him to hospital. An angiogram conducted soon after revealed an aneurysm which surgery failed to correct. Although Mr. Brophy was not rendered technically brain dead by this accident, he did suffer serious and irreversible damage to his brain. He existed in an unconscious vegetative state, completely dependent on external care and unable to commence any voluntary activity including chewing or swallowing. All organs except his brain functioned well and he could breathe without the aid of a respirator. Some nine months after his brain

---

Reprinted with permission of *Canadian Journal on Aging*, Vol. 8: 3 (1989).

accident, a G-tube was inserted through a stoma in the abdominal wall into his stomach in order to provide him with nutrition and hydration.

Mr. Brophy was not a terminally ill man, and he appeared to be comfortable most of the time. Unlike his care-givers and loved ones, he appeared undisturbed by his "life sentence" of nothingness.

Prior to his brain accident, Mr. Brophy had on several occasions commented on the fate of people in similar states in the following manner:

> *About 10 years ago, discussing Karen Ann Quinlan, Mr. Brophy stated to his wife "I don't ever want to be on a life support system. No way do I want to live like that, that is not living." He had a favourite saying: "When your ticket is punched, it is punched." Approximately 5 or 6 years earlier, he had helped to rescue from a burning truck a man who received extensive burns and who died a few months later. He tossed the commendation for bravery in the trash and said "I should have been five minutes later, it would have been all over for him." He also said to his brother regarding the incident "If I'm ever like that, just shoot me, pull the plug."[2]*

In light of these remarks, Mr. Brophy's lack of reaction to his own situation was highly significant. Was Paul Brophy really still alive?

A DEFINITION FOR LIFE

To some, the foregoing query will appear absurd. Yet its consideration, I suggest, is a prerequisite for formulating practical policy resolutions for this issue.

To medical vitalists, Mr. Brophy was alive. This approach insists that where there is human life, be it unconscious life, or life housed in a body mutilated by pain or deformities, the sanctity of life principle forbids its taking. Life is life and no life, however debilitated, is unworthy of respect and defence. This position draws support from two flanking arguments:

(1) The "slippery slope" argument admonishes the careless that the endorsement of any kind of killing will lead to wrongs of increasing magnitude. We have the historical examples of several autocracies including Nazi Germany to give compelling illustrations of the "slippery slope".[3]

(2) No person is qualified to play God and take life.

The vitalist position is persuasive if one stays within the rigid parameters it constructs. This theory draws upon religious doctrine which holds that man's life is not his own, but a gift given and then taken by the Creator. However, the weakness inherent in the vitalists' argument is that the admonition "Don't play God" is a doubled edged sword.

Those who propose that life in a vegetative state is not life may argue with equal conviction that God's position has been usurped not by those seeking to end lives of nothingness, but by those who seek to maintain them with manmade creations such as respirators, G-tubes and intravenous tubes. Modern medical research has toyed with the age old boundaries of life and death. The concepts require new definition.

It is submitted that human life is constituted of two fundamental factors other than biological existence, and those are:

(1) A capacity for consciousness of self; and,

(2) A capacity to experience something other than pain and suffering.

Using this augmented definition of life, Mr. Brophy would not be considered to be alive.

The ethical and philosophical implications of this issue warrant expansion that cannot be fulfilled here. The preceding discussion is intended to briefly illustrate a societal dilemma, reflected in the divergence of opinion on the question of whether Mr. Brophy is alive or not alive.

AMERICAN AND CANADIAN LAW

Law attempts to reflect society's values and create a structure in which they can be enforced. In light of the above discussion, it is no surprise that a review of the Canadian and American jurisprudence reveals great differences in content and development of the law on this subject.

1. American Law

Mr. Brophy was fortunate in one sense that he lived in the State of Massachusetts. After months of reflection and prayer, his wife and guardian exercised her right of substituted judgment and requested the doctors and the Mount Sinai Hospital to remove her husband's G-tube. They refused, indicating that such an act would willfully cause Mr. Brophy's death. Mrs. Brophy brought suit against the physicians and the hospital.

The Court, in justifying its Order to authorize Mrs. Brophy to remove her husband from the Mount Sinai Hospital to the care of physicians who would remove the G-tube, made findings of law which can be summarized as follows:

(1) A competent patient has the right to refuse treatment, which right arises from the common law and from the unwritten and penumbral constitutional right to privacy.

(2) This right must extend to incompetent persons through the doctrine of substituted judgment, as those persons must be afforded the same dignity and worth, and have the same panoply of rights and choices, as competent persons.

(3) The right of the patient to self-determination must always be weighed against countervailing state interests which are:

(a) The preservation of life;
(b) The protection of interests of innocent third parties;
(c) The prevention of suicide;
(d) The maintenance of the ethical integrity of the medical profession.

(4) The state's interest in the preservation of life was implicated in this matter as Mr. Brophy was not terminally ill.

(5) The distinction between extraordinary and ordinary care as outlined in the case of *In the Matter of Karen Quinlan, An Alleged Incompetent*[4] was found to be meaningless, as was the distinction between withdrawing and withholding care, and, therefore, there was no sense in trying to classify Mr. Brophy's treatment in these heretofore established categories.

(6) The primary focus for the Court should be the patient's desires and the experience of pain and enjoyment, not the type of treatment involved.

(7) In the circumstances, the state's interest in the preservation of life was overruled by what the Court found Mr. Brophy's desires would have been, i.e., the termination of his life.

Mr. Brophy, through his guardian, sought and obtained a legal remedy for his problem. The judgment reflects the recognition by American society that in some cases the burden of maintaining the corporeal existence degrades the very humanity it was intended to serve. The Court recognized the individual's right to preserve his humanity, even if the preservation of his humanity meant allowing the natural processes of disease or affliction to bring about his death with dignity.[5]

This decision reflects recent developments in the law on this subject in the United States.[6] One area of divergence existent in the American jurisprudence is worthy of mention. This concerns the necessity of judicial review in these types of cases. The Supreme Court of New Jersey in the *Quinlan*[7] case directed that decisions regarding withdrawal or refusal of treatment should be made by the patient's guardian in consultation with a hospital ethics committee.[8] The Supreme Court of Massachusetts in the noted case of *Superintendent of Belchertown State School v Saikewicz,*[9] and cases following, has clearly stated the need for judicial review of decisions by guardian or family in this area. The merits and disadvantages of both will be discussed in the conclusion.

2. Canadian Law

In Canada there is no legal precedent which would assure Mr. Brophy or others like him a legal remedy to preserve this aspect of his right to self-determination. There exist no reported cases dealing with similar facts. The closest comment on the right to refuse treatment as exercised by a guardian deals with a parent and child situation, in which the child suffered an incurable condition, but was not doomed to a vegetative state, and the case is, therefore, distinguishable on its facts.[10]

In Canada there is no penumbral right of personal privacy recognized in law. Section 7 of *The Canadian Charter of Rights and Freedoms*[11] guarantees an individual the right to life, liberty and security of the person. Does security of the person include a right to refuse unwanted medical treatment? On two occasions Courts have found that an individual's security of the person would be infringed by the administration of medical treatment, but these cases concerned children suffering from cancer, not elderly people doomed to chronic vegetative states.[12] The recognition that Section 7 of *The Charter* may guarantee a person's protection from unwanted medical treatment is encouraging. This line of argument may be extended in the future to deal with problems concerning the aging population.

Canada has no legislation specifically authorizing guardians to refuse medical treatment on behalf of individuals. However, Canadian Courts of equity do have *parens patriae* jurisdiction which could conceivably be exercised to make a decision to refuse treatment on behalf of an incompetent person. This jurisdiction is in theory unlimited, and gives Courts power to protect persons who, by reason of legal incapacity, cannot exercise any judgment in order to serve their own best interests.[13]

Notwithstanding the hopes for the future development of precedent relying on Section 7 of *The Charter* or *parens patriae,* there exists a void of Canadian legal precedent in this area. The practical effect of such a void is that in Canada, decisions to continue or terminate treatment to persons who are terminally or chronically ill are, in practice, made by doctors. This is inappropriate. There is an inherent conflict of interest for doctors who attempt to fulfill the dual functions of treating patients on the one hand, and consenting to or refusing the administration of treatment on the other. The present scheme is antithetical to a system which reputedly enshrines individual autonomy and requires the delivery of informed consent to physicians prior to treatment.[14] Until Canadians use the Courts to challenge the present allocation of power to doctors and seek to return it to individuals or their guardians, this situation will remain static.

CONCLUSION

It is hoped that the void of legal precedent in Canada will be corrected by case challenges which entreat the Canadian Courts of equity to invoke their *parens patriae* jurisdiction to exercise substituted judgment in a way similar to precedents developed in the United States. With respect, it is submitted that the line of decisions in the United States which favours judicial review should be followed, for the following reasons:

(1) Only through judicial review can a person's substituted judgment be exercised in a completely impartial and objective manner.

(2) Judicial decision-making based on precedent is ideally principled, as cases will be decided with reasoned judgments based on established principles.

(3) The judicial process is a public one, and Judges' actions are subject to scrutiny.

Opponents of judicial review argue that the process is expensive and time consuming. However, it is submitted that concerns of time and money should pale in light of the importance of the decision to be made. In most Canadian provinces, major decisions made by the committee of an incompetent person's estate require reference to the Court. Do not matters of life and death require the same quality of attention?

Canadian law has not yet grappled with the issue of whether terminally or chronically ill persons should be allowed to die with dignity. When it does, it is hoped that the established precedent in the State of Massachusetts will give our Courts direction.

EPILOGUE (1994)

Happily, there have been some developments to the concept of according Canadians a right to death with dignity since this article was written in 1987.

Case Law

There is now clear precedent demonstrating the right of mentally competent patients to refuse consent to medical treatment, or to demand that treatment, once commenced, be withdrawn or discontinued, even if the withdrawal from or refusal of treatment may result in death.[15]

In England, the House of Lords addressed the matter of withdrawal of treatment on behalf of an incompetent patient. In the case of *Airedale NHS. v Bland*,[16] the court authorized the withdrawal of artificial feeding from a seventeen year old boy who was in a persistent vegetative state as a result of injuries suffered in soccer riots. The application was made with the consent of his parents. In that case, it was held that the principle of the sanctity of life, which was not absolute, was not violated by ceasing to give medical treatment and care involving invasive manipulation of the patient's body, to which he had not consented, and which conferred no benefit upon him.

In 1990, a court in Saskatchewan refused to find a child in need of protection when its parents refused to give consent for a liver transplant for the child who was suffering from a several terminal disease of the liver. While transplant was the only hope for survival, the chances for long term survival without severe complications were minimal. The court in this case carefully considered the submissions of experts, and the evidence of the parents in determining the realities of this child's chance of achieving a quality of life that would justify the radical medical and surgical treatment proposed by the Minister of Social Services.[17]

Recently, in the much publicized case of *Rodriguez v British Columbia (Attorney-General, et al)*,[18] the Supreme Court of Canada considered the question of whether or not a terminally ill person whose condition has become unbearable is entitled to physician assisted suicide. The majority of the court (five judges) said no. The court stated that the right to life, liberty and security of the person given to citizens by s. 7 of the *Canadian Charter of Rights and Freedoms*[19] cannot encompass a right to take action that will end one's life. The court decided that absolute prohibition of physician assisted suicide did not constitute cruel and unusual treatment under s. 12 of the *Charter*.

It must be noted that there was a strong dissenting voice in the *Rodriguez* case (four judges). In this writer's opinion, the most interesting judgment was written by McLachlin, J., who stated that the denial to Sue Rodriguez of a choice available to others (i.e. to commit suicide) cannot be justified. Such a denial deprived Sue Rodriguez of her security of the person (the right to make decisions concerning her own body which affect only her own body) in a way that offended the principles of fundamental justice.

While proponents of physical self-determination may well have wished for the majority and minority decisions in the *Rodriguez* case[20] to be reversed, the reasons of the four judges who dissented may well open the doors in future for further development.

Legislation

In the Province of Manitoba, citizens may execute in advance a health care directive which expresses the maker's health care decisions and/or appoints a proxy to make decisions on his or her behalf. The directive takes effect when the maker becomes mentally incompetent.[21] This legislation encourages citizens to take charge of their own futures, while they are still able to do so.

Therefore, in order to answer the question posed by the title of this article, I would summarize by saying:

1. if competent, you may do it yourself at any time;

2. if incompetent, the chances that a court might do it for you are much better than they were in 1987, given the *Airedale* case;[22]

3. in some provinces you may do it yourself with the help of an advanced health care directive.

NOTES

1. See *Brophy v New England Sinai Hospital Inc.* 497 N.E. (2d) 626 (Mass. 1986).

2. *Ibid.*, p. 632.

3. For an excellent discussion of these issues see "Sanctity of Life and Quality of Life", Law Reform Commission of Canada, Protection of Life series, 1979, Edward N. Keyserlingk.

4. 355 A.2d 647.

5. *Supra,* note 1, at p. 635.

6. For recent developments in the State of New Jersey, see *In Re Nancy Ellen Jobes* 529 A.2d 434 (S.C.N.J.).

7. Mass., 370 N.E, 2d 417.

8. Even less formal modes of decision making have been endorsed. See *In The Matter of Guardianship of Joseph Hamlin, An Incompetent Person* 689 P.2d 1372 (Wash. 1984) where the court held that family, if they are all in agreement with the treating physician regarding the patient's prognosis, may assert the personal right of an incompetent person to refuse life-sustaining treatment without seeking prior appointment of a guardian.

9. Mass., 370 N.E. 2d417.

10. See *Re S.D.* 34 R.F.L. (2d) 34 (B.C.S.C.).

11. "Constitution Act" 1982, s. 7.

12. See *Montreal Childrens Hospital v J.* Q.A.C. 209 (Q.C.A.); *Re L.D.K.; Childrens Aid Society of Metropolitan Toronto v K and K* 48 R.F.L. (2d) 164.

13. For a discussion of *parens patriae,* see *"Eve", by her Guardian Ad Litem, Milton B. Fitzpatrick, Official Trustee v Mrs. "E" and The Canadian Association for the Mentally Retarded and The Public Trustee of Manitoba, and the Attorney-General of Canada* (1986) 2 S.C.R. 388.

14. See *Reibl v Hughes* (1982) S.C.R. 880.

15. See *Nancy B v Hôtel-Dieu de Québec* (1992), 86 D.L.R./(4th) 385 (Que. S.C.).

16. (1993) 2 WLR 316 (H.L.).

17. *Minister of Social Services v Paulette and Paulette,* unreported, Provincial Court of Saskatchewan, April 20, 1990.

18. (1993) 158 N.R. (S.C.C.).

19. *Supra,* Note 11.

20. *Supra,* Note 18.

21. *The Health Care Directives Act* S.M. 1992c. 33 Cap. H27. The provinces of Quebec and Nova Scotia have legislation which allows for the appointment of proxies. The provinces of British Columbia and Ontario are in the process of developing legislation dealing with these issues.

22. *Supra,* note 16.

Autonomy, Self-Determination and the Decision-Making Process Concerning End-of-Life Treatment

Jocelyne Saint-Arnaud

INTRODUCTION

From the first declarations of rights formulated in the XVIIth century to the development of present-day charters, personal autonomy has gradually become the core value of industrial and post-industrial societies. The principle of personal autonomy, from which the legal principle of self-determination is derived, is based on the rational nature of human beings and on the ability of each individual to make choices and set goals for oneself. In the area of health, recognition of personal autonomy is a recent American phenomenon, which is becoming widespread in Canada.

To explain the various facets of this phenomenon, we will begin with a brief comparison between the traditional and the modern doctor-patient relationship. Then, we will define the content of the term free and informed consent and specify what means are available to citizens to make their wishes known with regards to end-of-life treatment: refusal of treatment, living wills, advance directives and the mandate or power-of-attorney. Then, we will indicate the role relatives can play in promoting personal autonomy and in respecting the wishes of a non-competent person. Finally, we will indicate the limits on respecting a person's wishes, especially with respect to euthanasia and aiding suicide.

Reproduced with the consent of the National Advisory Council on Aging (NACA) and with the permission of the Minister of Supply and Services Canada, 1993.

1. THE DECISION-MAKING PROCESS FOR A COMPETENT INDIVIDUAL

1.1 Definition of Competency

A person is competent to decide on a treatment if he/she can understand information relevant to the decision to be taken, weigh the pros and cons in terms of his/her goals and values, and is capable of communicating decisions. Such competency must be distinguished from legal capacity, which anyone has who is over the age of majority and is not under a protective regime. Legal capacity refers to the exercise of rights by all citizens.

1.2 The Doctor-Patient Relationship

Traditionally, those who consult doctors rely on them to make decisions concerning the choice of treatment based on their diagnosis and prognosis. Seen in this light, doctors are competent and experienced professionals who know the best way to treat the medical problem in question and who act in the best interests of their patients. Often, they are afraid of adversely affecting their patients' physical and psychological health by disclosing a fatal diagnosis and a forbidding prognosis. This explains why doctors tend to speak to relatives rather than to their patients, to protect them from the depressing effect of learning about their forthcoming death. In this perspective, illness and death are taboo. Everyone, including the patient, knows what is happening, but they all keep quiet. The sick person is isolated, unable to talk about the essential issues concerning the end of his/her life, harbouring a secret hope that this is only a bad dream.

Nowadays, the progress of medical science and technology offers new therapeutic alternatives creating medical and ethical choices that did not exist before. Thanks to techniques of resuscitation and intensive care, transplants, radiotherapy and chemotherapy, parenteral nutrition and antibiotics, medicine now has the means to prolong life in a person whose faculties are drastically reduced. By creating conditions in which traditional medical goals are no longer clearly attained, medical science is experiencing its limits and facing choices that are often more ethical than medical. To the extent that healing or even palliative treatment does not bring the expected medical benefits, the values of everyone involved, health caregivers and patients alike, come into play.

Under the influence of American case-law and the new conditions created by the progress of medical science and technology, some of whose consequences we have just described, the traditional relationship between doctors and patients has changed.

In Canada, the position adopted stands between the situation in the United States — where personal autonomy is the primary value — and that of some European countries such as France — where the patient's welfare, as defined by the doctor, is the supreme value. Thus, the doctor-patient relationship as currently experienced in Canada is more like a consensual agreement. Doctors are increasingly informing their patients of their diagnosis and prognosis, are more likely to explain the various treatment alternatives and try, at the very least, to obtain the consent of their patients regarding the treatment they recommend. This attitude is close to what legal experts are proposing as "free and informed consent".

1.3 Free and Informed Consent

Ideally, doctors should inform the patient clearly of their diagnosis and prognosis, of the various treatments available and of the medical benefits and risks associated with each option. Then, they should indicate which treatment they favour and the reasons for their decision, leaving patients free to choose the one that best meets their expectations. Doctors contribute their knowledge and expertise and the patients bring their own view of things based on their values, beliefs and perceptions concerning their present and future life.

In the normal course of events, there are rarely discrepancies between the medical views and that of the patient concerning treatment. However, in the borderline cases mentioned above, the chances of conflicting views are greater. It is the patients themselves who know if a treatment is too difficult for them, whether they are prepared to accept resuscitation or chemotherapy that might lead to a longer, but qualitatively diminished life, whether they could accept a life in a coma, on intravenous feeding or on a respirator for the rest of their life as a quadriplegic.

"Free and informed consent" means, first, that an individual must feel free to make the decision that he/she believes is best, given his/her own values. Nobody should be subjected to undue pressure from family or doctors to agree to a treatment that they prefer for professional, economic or other reasons. The person should not feel abandoned by them if they do not agree with his/her choice. The decision must be an informed one; the person must have received all the information needed to make a well-thought-out decision, based on the benefits and disadvantages of a treatment and accepting the foreseeable consequences. Some will not want to make the choice and will prefer to rely on their doctor following the traditional model; their decision must be respected. Those who wish to take an active role in the decision-making process, however, should receive all the information they need to make a decision.

It should be noted that consent to treatment is not given once and for all. A person may change his/her mind during the treatment and should tell the doctor about the decision. Similarly, doctors should inform patients of any new developments concerning their condition and ensure that their patients agree to continue or discontinue a treatment or begin another.

This description corresponds to the current ideal of relations between the health care team and the patient. However, there are exceptions to giving the patient full information. Doctors may have medical reasons for avoiding this. For example, if a heart patient's condition might deteriorate if he learned of the extent and seriousness of the illness, the doctor would be justified in communicating only the essentials of the diagnosis. It is up to the doctor, in conjunction with the health care team, to decide whether the diagnosis and prognosis should be disclosed and the best time for doing so. Doctors may also have ethical reasons for not providing their patients with all possible information where the patients have clearly indicated that they do not wish to know the diagnosis and prognosis. In that case, doctors are respecting their patients' wishes.

Apart from these exceptions, those who give their consent to a treatment or refuse it should be able to do so in a free and informed manner. The respect for personal autonomy in treatment means recognizing that competent persons may take an active role in making their own decisions concerning their treatment. This also means respecting the choice of the person who does not wish to be informed and the choice of the person who, having been informed, prefers to rely fully on the medical decision.

1.4 Refusal of Treatment

The principle of respect for personal autonomy is the moral basis for the legal doctrine of free and informed consent. In everyday life, personal autonomy and the resulting self-determination are asserted by the right to refuse treatment. This right is always recognized even if documents evidencing consent have been signed. Except in an emergency situation, medical treatment cannot be carried out with the free and informed consent of the person who is competent to make decisions.

1.4.1 The Legal Point of View

Quebec and Canadian law do not object to refusal of treatment by legally competent persons and the case-law unequivocally recognizes their right to refuse treatment.

The Quebec Civil Code has legalized the right to refuse treatment. Paragraph 1 of article 19.1 reads as follows:

> *No person may be made to undergo care of any nature, whether for examination, specimen taking, removal of tissue, treatment or any other act, except with his consent.*

Common law recognizes the principles of self-determination for a legally competent person and the *Criminal Code of Canada* criminalizes illegal attacks against the life and safety of others, although it does not specifically recognize the right to refuse treatment. For the Law Reform Commission of Canada, however, the wishes of a legally competent patient are supreme if he/she decides to discontinue or not undertake treatment. That is why it recommends that nothing in the new Criminal Code *should be interpreted as requiring a physician:*

(a) to continue to administer or to undertake medical treatment against the clearly expressed wishes of the person for whom such treatment is intended.

The Canadian and Québec charters protect the right to life, liberty and security of the person; the Québec Charter adds the right of the inviolability of the person. These rights may be invoked in support of the right to refuse treatment.

The right to refuse treatment is recognized in the case-law, even if death should result. In Malette v. Schulman,[1] the Ontario courts recognized a Jehovah's Witness's right to refuse blood transfusions. He had signed a form to this effect. In Nancy B. v. Hôtel-Dieu de Québec,[2] the judge decided in favour of withdrawing an irreversibly paralysed young woman from her respirator at her request. Finally, in Manoir de la Pointe bleue v. Corbeil,[3] the judge recognized the respondent's right to refuse food. The last two cases involved paraplegics whose intellectual faculties were intact. These are only a few typical examples of a new orientation of the case-law towards respecting the wishes of a person who is legally competent to agree to or refuse treatment.

Respect for a person's wishes has not yet been interpreted to mean acquiescing in the wishes of a person who desires a medically inappropriate treatment. A patient could not, legally, demand a treatment considered therapeutically harmful.

1.4.2 The Religious Point of View

In general, religions do not condemn refusal of treatments that serve only to prolong life (life-sustaining treatments). The Catholic Church has spoken out clearly on this matter. A person for whom a given course of treatment is too difficult physically and psychologically has the moral right to refuse it even if that refusal accelerates the dying process. Refusal of treatment in this case is not equivalent to suicide. The Anglican Church endorses the views of the Catholic Church. Other denominations and religions, even the most orthodox, for whom God alone is master of life and death, apparently would not agree to an artificial prolongation of life any more than they would agree to shortening it by euthanasia or suicide.

2. THE DECISION-MAKING PROCESS FOR AN INCOMPETENT INDIVIDUAL

Decisions concerning end-of-life treatment are ethically and legally easier to make when the person involved can take part in the decision-making process. Under the personal autonomy principle, rational individuals are capable of judging where their best interest lies when they have received the information they need to make a decision.

2.1 The Definition of Incompetency

An individual is not competent to decide on a treatment if unable to understand information that is relevant to the decision to be made, if unable to judge the appropriateness of a treatment in the light of his/her values and goals and, finally, if incapable of communicating decisions. Incompetency arises from a physical or mental disability which renders exercise of the decision-making capacity impossible. It should be distinguished from legal incapacity which means that the incompetent person has lost the exercise of his/her civil rights and is under a protective regime: mandate, wardship or tutorship. Under Canadian law, if the person is legally incompetent and has a legal representative (guardian, tutor, or mandatory (attorney)), it is the latter who is involved in making decisions and who answers for the incompetent person on the question of treatment. If the person is incompetent, but has no legal representative, relatives will be consulted. In Québec, such consultation is now legally recognized.

How can third parties (legal representatives and relatives) make decisions for end-of-life treatments for incompetent individuals when the treatments may include, among other things, resuscitation, use of a respirator, intubation, parenteral nutrition, use of antibiotics and pain relievers?

They will first ask themselves if the person, at a time when still able to do so, expressed wishes on the subject, either orally or in writing.

2.2 Oral Directives Prior to the Incompetency

Before becoming incompetent, the patient may have expressed preferences regarding treatment to relatives, the doctor or other members of the health care team. Conversations with the health care staff may be noted in the patient's file later for consultation. Conversations with close relatives concerning the person's wishes will be taken into consideration. However, if they are challenged by the health care team and there is no document evidencing them, it is very unlikely that they will prevail.

2.3 Written Directives Prior to the Incompetency

Before becoming incompetent, the patient may have been able to put his/her wishes in writing in a living will, advance directives or a mandate in Québec or a power-of-attorney in other provinces.

2.3.1 The Living Will

There are different forms of living wills. We will not discuss the form that requests active euthanasia, since this is an unlawful act in which no health professional should engage.

The most common form of living will is based on authenticated American forms. This is a document dated and signed by a person in full possession of his/her faculties and two witnesses. It has wording about refusing to have one's life prolonged by artificial or disproportionate means and requesting adequate relief of pain even if death is thereby accelerated. Refusal of certain specific treatments, such as resuscitation, intubation, and so on may be included. The signatory asks the witnesses to communicate the wishes regarding end-of-life treatments, but discharges them from all responsibility for the choices indicated in the document.

Contrary to the American experience, where a number of states have legalized this form of will by a *Natural Death Act,* a living will has no legal status in Canada. Most legal experts are opposed to its legalization, arguing the lack of precision in its terms, the possibility that those who have not signed such a document will be subjected to aggressive therapies and, finally, the fact that it applies only to patients at the terminal stage.

The role of a living will is actually more ethical than legal. Its purpose is to let the health caregivers and close relatives know the wishes of the person who has become incompetent with respect to end-of-life treatments. It is respected by the health caregivers and the therapists who value the person's wishes with respect to treatment. The Law Reform Commission of Canada, in *Euthanasia, aiding suicide and cessation of treatment,* recognizes the living will indicating a person's wishes. Such a document will be taken into consideration by the courts if there is litigation between the health care team and the legal representative or next of kin.

2.3.2 The Advance Directives

To compensate for certain weaknesses in the living will, in particular the fact that it is limited to the terminal phase of an illness, some groups, especially in Ontario, have suggested that competent individuals should complete an advance directives form. On this form, the competent person would give indications about preferred treatment should incompetence occur. This document applies not only to terminal illnesses but to any serious illness. Unlike the living will, it is designed to give precise directives regarding the treatments and care desired. However, it leaves less latitude to doctors who are the most qualified to gauge the medical appropriateness of a treatment and it forces the person to choose a type of treatment in advance without necessarily knowing the nature of the potential illness and the various treatments that will be available for it. From this point of view, the advance directives form, like the living will which may refer to specific treatments, proposes alternatives that do not meet the ethical criteria for free and informed consent.

2.3.3 The Mandate (Power-of-Attorney) or Substituted Consent

Contrary to the preceding forms that have limited legal pretensions, a mandate or a power-of-attorney is a document recognized in law, namely in Nova

Scotia, Québec, Manitoba and Ontario (1992). The mandate or power-of-attorney is defined by the various provincial jurisdictions and applies in the area of mental health and consent to treatment, subject to existing laws, in particular provincial laws. Its purpose is to appoint one or more legal representatives or mandataries where a person has become incompetent to make decisions concerning health care. In Québec, a mandatary is also authorized to manage the property of the incompetent person.

The mandate or power-of-attorney may include instructions concerning health care, but, generally speaking, it does not replace the forms studied above. The living will and the advance directives form indicate the person's wishes as formulated prior to incompetency, while the mandate or substituted consent are legal tools which compensate for the incompetency by appointing persons authorized to make decisions on behalf of the incompetent person. The two types of documents are complementary. The first plays an important ethical role in evidencing the person's wishes, but has no legal value and no one can be legally bound by it just because it exists. The second mainly has a legal role. It is up to the mandatory's conscience whether to take account of the wishes of the incompetent person in making decisions on his/her behalf.

2.4 The Role of Third Parties

The role of third parties in end-of-life treatments is to act in the best interests of the incompetent person. If the latter has expressed wishes orally or in writing, the relatives or legal representatives will endeavour to have the person's wishes respected.

If the incompetent person has not expressed wishes either orally or in writing, the third parties should set aside their personal interests in participating in the decision-making process. This interest is not defined only in financial terms. Some relatives who cannot accept the prospective death of the person in question ask the health care staff to employ every means possible to prolong a life whose capacities are reduced to a minimum; others demand active euthanasia because they cannot emotionally bear the physical and mental deterioration often preceding death.

From an ethical point of view, to act in the person's best interests is to choose what the person would have chosen in terms of his/her own values. If it is impossible to make such a judgment, for lack of information about the personal values of the incompetent person, the choice should be the same as that of any reasonable person in the same circumstances. To do this, an assessment of the benefits and harms that could be caused by each alternative should be made. Then, the decision that is made must be the one that brings the most benefit and the least harm possible in view of the physical and mental well-being of that person.

The ethics committees of some hospitals have established guidelines for non-resuscitation and cessation of treatment. These protocols indicate the main parameters of the decision-making process that should be used in decisions concerning these borderline cases. Independently of legal status, the person in question must participate in the decision-making process to the extent of his/her capacity. When the person is incompetent, the protocols favour consensual decisions between the health care team and the relatives. If there is no conflict between the medical team and the relatives, the decision is made, noted in the file together with the conversations that led to this decision. If not, consultations are requested from persons who are not directly involved in the case. For example, consultation with experts or the hospital ethics committee may help resolve the conflict. If disagreement persists, the last recourse is the courts.

3. THE LIMITS ON RESPECTING THE WISHES OF THE IN COMPETENT PERSON

Just as respect for a person's wishes does not mean acquiescing in medically inappropriate treatment or care, it also does not extend to acts prohibited by law, such as euthanasia or aiding suicide. The recommendations of the Law Reform Commission of Canada are very clear on this: there is no question at present of amending the *Criminal Code* in order to legalize such acts.

To support this position with respect to euthanasia, five kinds of arguments are raised: the possibility of medical errors in diagnosis and prognosis, the discovery of new medication that could reverse the dying process, the fear that acceptance of voluntary euthanasia might lead to acceptance of involuntary euthanasia, instituting a new form of eugenics, bureaucratic delays in assessing competency in those requesting euthanasia and, finally, the absence of signs that there is a real need that would justify recourse to such an act. The Law Reform Commission of Canada concludes that the advantages of legalizing euthanasia could not make up for the harm resulting from such a practice.

As for decriminalizing assisted suicide, the Commission points out the risk of abuse, i.e. that the murder of persons at a terminal stage could be disguised as aiding suicide. It should, however, be noted that most of the reasons invoked for not decriminalizing euthanasia apply also to aiding suicide.

It is important to specify that, in law, the term "euthanasia" designates the positive act of causing the death of a person for humanitarian reasons. There is currently a medical, legal, ethical and religious consensus to consider the following practices as not involving euthanasia: relieving pain and discontinuing or not initiating life-sustaining treatment at the request of the person or on the basis of a consensus between the health care team and the representatives of the incompetent person. Without dwelling on the ethical distinctions between euthanasia and the cessation or non-initiation of treatment, that is, between "active euthanasia" and "passive euthanasia", it should be noted that a gradual increase in doses of morphine to relieve pain is not considered euthanasia, no more than is the non-recourse to treatment or techniques that have the sole purpose to sustain the life of a person whose capacities are irreversibly reduced to their minimum.

The experience of Dutch and American attempts to legalize euthanasia raise the question of the appropriateness of legalizing such a practice. In following this trend, will we be led to recognize the ethical and legal legitimacy of certain acts of euthanasia responding to conditions determined by consensus and expressed in protocols or in guidelines? Some will say that acquiescence or moral and legal consensus for what was considered by some theologians and practitioners as passive euthanasia is a significant step towards acceptance of the legalization of euthanasia. The importance of this argument should not be denied since it is the avowed strategy of the societies promoting death with dignity. However, the moral and legal aspects of the issue must always be distinguished. In this sense, even if certain acts of euthanasia were morally acceptable, it would not follow that euthanasia should be legalized. In this regard, the objections of the Law Reform Commission of Canada continue to be relevant.

CONCLUSION

In conclusion, the person who is able to make a decision may take an active role in the decision-making process regarding choice of a treatment. That person may issue instructions for end-of-life treatments that she would accept or refuse. These instructions will serve as guides for the health care team and third parties who will have to make decisions in the person's best interests if he/she becomes incompetent. These instructions should, however, be limited to what is medically and legally permissible.

NOTES

1.   (1990) 72 O.R. 417.

2.   (1992) R.J.Q. 361.

3.   (1992) R.J.Q. 712.

REFERENCES

Baudouin, J.-L. and M.-H. Parizeau. "Réflections juridiques et éthiques sur le consentement au traitement médical." *Médecine/Science*, 3, 1, 1987: 8–12.

Caucanas-Pisier, P. "The right-to-die societies of the world." *The Euthanasia Review*, 1, 4, Winter 1986: 213–220.

Doucet, H. *Mourir: approches bioéthiques*. Ottawa: Novalis, 1988. 152 p.

Hastings Center. *Guidelines on the termination of life-sustaining treatment and the care of the dying.* Indianapolis: Indiana University Press, 1987. 159 p.

Jonsen, A.R. et al. *Clinical ethics: A practical approach to ethical decisions in clinical medicine.* New York: MacMillan Publishing Co., 1986. 202 p.

Kelly, J.L. et al. *Let me decide.* Hamilton, Ontario: Hamilton Civic Hospitals. November 14, 1989. 29 p.

Law Reform Commission of Canada. *Euthanasia, aiding suicide and cessation of treatment.* Working paper No. 28. Ottawa: Supply and Services Canada, 1982. 79 p.

Law Reform Commission of Canada. *Euthanasia, aiding suicide and cessation of treatment.* Report No. 20. Ottawa: Supply and Services Canada, 1983. 35 p.

Lesage-Jarjoura, P. *La cessation de traitement: au carrefour du droit et de la médecine.* Cowansville: Éditions Yvon Blais Inc., 1990. 246 p.

Moody, H.R. *Ethics in an aging society.* Baltimore: The John Hopkins University Press, 1992. 288 p.

Mullins, G. et al. "Le testament biologique accompagné ou non d'un mandat." *Le médecin du Québec,* 26, 4, April 1991: 67–77 and 26, 5, May 1991: 81–89.

Rozovsky, L.E. and F.A. Rozovsky. *The Canadian law of consent to treatment.* Vancouver: Butterworths, 1990.

Saint-Arnaud J. and G. Durand. *La réanimation cardio-respiratoire au Québec: statistiques, protocoles et repères éthiques.* Montréal: Fides, 1990. 189 p.

Saint-Arnaud J. "L'euthanasie: enjeux éthiques et politiques." *Philosopher,* 13, 1992: 93–105.

Sneiderman, B. et al. *Canadian medical law: An introduction for physicians and other health care professionals.* Toronto: Carswell, 1989. 389 p.

Toulat, J. *Faut-il tuer par amour? L'euthanasie en question.* Paris: Éditions Pygmalion, 1976. 252 p.

Verspieren, P. [Textes du Magistère catholique réunis et présentés par] *Biologie, médecine et éthique.* Paris: Le Centurion, 1987. 500 p.

Working Group on Legal Issues. "Legal issues in the care of mentally impaired elderly persons: Competence, surrogate management, and protection of rights." *Canada's Mental Health,* 35, 2, June 1987: 6–11.

Whytehead, L. and P. Chidwick. *L'acte de la mort: réflexions sur le passage de la vie à la mort.* Montréal: Bellarmin, 1983. 116 p.

42

Rational Suicide Among Older Adults: A Cause for Concern?

Sharon L. Moore

According to Baumgart (1988, p. 35), "Advances in medical technology have changed the moral landscape of society." "Who would have thought that hope-full, life-giving technology would lead to such an unconscionable prolongation of death that people would react by preferring to kill themselves?" (Curtain, 1990, p. 7). News bulletins in recent months contained headlines such as "Elderly Suicides on a Puzzling Upswing"; "A How-to-Book on Suicide Surges to the Top of Best-Seller List in Week"; "Suicide Doctor Aids in Two More Deaths"; "At Crossroads, US Ponders Ethics of Helping Others Die"; "Washington State to Vote on Euthanasia" (reported in Robinson, 1991, p. 24).

Moody (1992, p. 1) said that "the recent spread of more tolerant attitudes toward euthanasia and death with dignity makes it imperative that we think carefully about the ethics of rational suicide on grounds of age."

DEFINITIONS

Discussions about rational suicide warrant a look at related definitions. The concept of rational suicide is an extension of the right to die concept (Kjervik, 1984; Weber, 1988a). According to Weber (1988b), *right to die* has two meanings: one meaning refers to a right to refuse life-sustaining treatment and the other signifies an "affirmative right to obtain death—a right to suicide" (p. 182). Suicide is the intentional killing of oneself. "It is rationally justified to kill oneself when a "reasonable appraisal of the situation reveals that one is really better off dead" (Graber, 1981, p. 60). For purposes of this article, the latter two definitions will be used.

Reproduced with permission from *Archives of Psychiatric Nursing* 12(2): 106–10 and from the author, Sharon L. Moore.

HISTORICAL AND CURRENT INFLUENCES

Medical and technological advances have resulted in adding years to life and thus we have seen such trends as the "graying of America." Robinson (1991, p. 24) stated that we are living in an era in which society is increasingly preoccupied with individuals who want to end their lives at a time when the "human lifespan is being extended to unprecedented lengths."

Over the past decade, suicide among older adults in the United States has increased more rapidly than for any other age group, even though as a group they gained in health, longevity, and financial security (Moody, 1992; Leenaars, 1992; McIntosh, 1992). We have witnessed an increasing tolerance to suicide and, in some instances, rational suicide has been actively encouraged as a solution to problems faced by older persons (Portwood, 1983; Wickett, 1989; Humphrey, 1992).

In late 1991, Washington State's Initiative 119 (I–119), "Death with Dignity," failed after receiving 46% of the 1.5 million votes cast (Carson, 1992). Supporters of this initiative felt certain even into the final week before the vote that it would pass, making Washington one of the first places in the world to legalize voluntary euthanasia for the terminally ill. While voluntary euthanasia cannot be directly equated with rational suicide, the option it provides, that is, aid-in-dying, could very well alleviate some of the ethical and moral conflicts that some older individuals experience should they decide to end their life. Both sides in the I–119 debate fervently argued their case based on the principle of autonomy and the good of humanity. This again reflects the dilemma that nurses, other members of the health care system, and society as a whole often experience when it comes to these issues.

The I–119 campaign was closely linked in the public's mind with the Hemlock Society and coincided with the release (in late 1991) of a "How To" instruction manual on committing suicide. *Final Exit* was authored by Derek Humphrey, then executive director of the Hemlock Society. While publicity was at its peak about his manual, Humphrey, who was recently divorced from his second wife, was accused in a suicide note left by his ex-wife of killing (smothering) his first wife who had been terminally ill. "Regardless of the truth or reliability of this charge, this accusation may have served only to add to the questions in the minds of people trying to decide what is at the very least the most difficult of issues" (Robinson, 1991, p. 30).

ANALYSIS OF SUPPORTIVE ARGUMENT

There are several who argue in favor of rational suicide as a sane, honorable choice in old age or, for that matter, in other circumstances as well (Battin & Mayo, 1980; Battin, 1991; Brandt, 1980; Portwood, 1983; Prado, 1990; Humphrey, 1992; Kjervik, 1984; Moody, 1992; Pieper, 1985). The strongest arguments for rational suicide claim an individual's right to self-determination and the "evil of needless suffering" (Mayo, 1983, p. 328). Battin (1991) accuses mental health professionals of not providing adequate guidance to older persons who wish to follow this course of action and suggests 17 specific considerations a mental health professional can use to assist older persons to explore whether suicide would be rational or irrational.

Another argument that has been portrayed as supporting the view of rational suicide is the "balance sheet." As one ages, they accumulate negative points that fill up the negative side of the balance sheet with an impossibility of attaining what once was. If the negative side of the sheet fills up and outweighs the positive side, a "planned departure that serves oneself, one's family and also the state is surely worthy of decent consideration" (Portwood, 1983, p. 46). Dr. Wallace Proctor, a 75-year-old dermatologist, said in his suicide note "some of you may look upon suicide with uneasiness or disfavor, but it may also represent a logical, considerate, and effective means to satisfy one's responsibility to the world" (Rauscher 1981, p. 93).

■■■

ANALYSIS OF OPPOSING ARGUMENT

Analysis of two opposing arguments is presented in a discussion about ageism and the slippery slope argument. There are several who oppose the notion of rational suicide and question whether it can ever be a rational decision (Donnelly, 1990; Mayo, 1983; Richman, 1988, 1992; Weber, 1988b; Wrobleski, 1983). Ageism, a prejudice against older persons, is rampant in our society today (Hall, 1984; Jecker, 1991; Moody, 1992; Zarit, 1980) and, in many instances, supporters of rational suicide build their arguments based on an ageist bias. Death is offered as a solution where improving the conditions of those in need may have alleviated the desire for rational suicide. Ageism is reflected in comments such as "my grandmother had become a burden, a barely tolerated inconvenience" (Wickett, 1989, p. 4).

As Richman (1988, p. 288) points out, "self sacrifice to relieve others of being burdened is not a genuine choice." At a time when health care costs are escalating and the elderly are seen as using more than their fair share, encouraging rational suicide may become a viable intervention. Several authors have expressed concern that it might be "all too easy for societal values to shift from the recognition of an individual's right to die to a climate enforcing a social, obligatory duty to die" (Weisbard & Siegler, 1986, p. 114; Spring & Larson, 1988). This very idea was proposed by Governor Richard Lamb in his 1984 address to the Colorado Lawyers' Health Association when he said: "Elderly people who are terminally ill have a duty to die and get out of the way" (Spring & Larson, 1988, p. 48). The slippery slope argument would say that might even lead to making older persons feel guilty if they decided not to commit suicide. In fact, Weber (1988b) proposes that the "border between the current absence of a legal right to commit suicide and the proposed declaration of such a right is not a slippery slope. It is a cliff" (p. 196). The slippery slope is reflective of a deteriorating respect for the value of human life.

AUTHOR'S PERSONAL THESIS

In my clinical practice as a nurse and a psychologist with older adults, I began in favor of rational suicide in some situations; however, the more I worked with older adults who were contemplating suicide, the more I began to question the whole idea. What I have seen is that while many older adults have difficulties in the later years, there are many, despite similar problems, who have chosen the life path, rather than the rational suicide path. Berman, Leenaars, McIntosh & Richman (1992) suggest that it is individual life histories, not aging, that are critical to our understanding of suicide in the later years. They point to a number of issues related to psychic pain that "are fodder for the therapeutic mill, not causes for rational suicide" (p. 149). All too often I have seen older persons identified as "not good candidates for mental health therapy because they are 'too old and set in their ways'; 'not really worthy or not able to benefit from therapy'."

Several gerontologists point out that the majority of older persons (at least 70%) who make a choice to commit rational suicide are in fact depressed. This is based on discussions with older persons who have survived the attempt, and on a review of suicide notes (Osgood, 1991; Zarit, 1980; Leenaars, 1992; Moore & Tanney, 1991). Pohlmeier (1985) questions whether the other 30% really consisted of voluntary death by suicide performed as a result of evaluating one's life and suggests that this remains an open question. I have seen several older persons following therapy express gratitude for having another lease on life after intervention. The question that always comes into my mind is "if older adults see no alternatives other than suicide, can their decision to end life really be considered rational?"

As I have struggled to try and articulate my position on this issue of rational suicide, my first inclination was to say "I do not have one." However, I realized that was absurd and discovered that, in fact, my position is reflected in the following quotation by Richman (1992, p. 138), who expressed my own sentiments when he said: "The wish to die or to commit suicide is the communication of a problem that is perceived as insoluble except through death of the suffering person ... When someone is suicidal I try to make contact rather than obsess over whether they have a right to live or die."

NEW PERSPECTIVES, SYNTHESIS, AND IMPLICATIONS FOR NURSING

Many who have performed extensive work with older persons believe suicide can be prevented if it is understood (Leenaars, 1992; Moore & Tanney, 1991;

Osgood, 1985; Richman, 1992). However, many of the studies that have been performed have looked at this issue from the outside. There is much to be learned by trying to understand what the "suicidal experience" is like from the view of those older adults who are experiencing it. Through his study of suicide notes of older adults, Leenaars (1992) identified relationships as one of the most important themes. He speculated that the need for attachment is the "most critical unconscious process in suicide" and that lack of attachment might be the driving force behind many suicides. Older persons need to have roles that are satisfying and meaningful. Hall (1984) and Osgood (1985) believe that elders need to be linked to social relationships and meaningful roles. For many elders, their later years can be rich and fulfilling—often times, more so than their younger years, although the opposite can be true also. Old age in our society needs to be viewed once again as a valued status, rather than a cursed disease or a burden....

CONCLUSION

Well-known philosopher M.P. Battin and physician-ethicist E. Cassel propose that the issue of whether individuals have the right to control circumstances around their own death is the issue of the next 20 years. Important questions that nurses and other health care professionals will need to address are many. "Can we respect a person's election of suicide as the most viable option? How can we behave toward a person who, overtly or covertly, suggests that suicide is their choice? Are we ourselves threatened by such a choice by another? Can we accept, rather than resolve, the final dilemma—whose life is it anyway?" (Saul & Saul, 1991, p. 21). In the final analysis, we will have to address these important questions. We will have to decide if suicide can ever be rational and, if so, in what circumstances and for whom?

It is clear that there are no easy answers to these difficult questions. "Rationality may contribute to a final decision to end one's life. But rationality may also be a very misleading concept for a proper explanation of suicidal behavior. The discussion of rationality of suicide in late life deserves good and thorough research" (Kerkhof, 1991, p. 82). In closing, this author is in agreement with Richman (1992) for a rational approach to the affirmation of life, rather than its rejection, even to the very end.

REFERENCES

Battin, M.P., & Mayo, D.J. (1980). *Suicide: The philosophical issues.* New York, NY: St. Martin's.

Battin, M.P. (1988). Letter to the editor: Why the slippery slope isn't slippery: A reply to Walter M. Weber on the right to die. *Suicide and Life Threatening Behavior, 18*(2), 189–194.

Battin, M.P. (1991). Rational suicide: How can we respond to a request for help? *Crisis, 12*(2), 73–80.

Baumgart, A.J. (1988). Evolution of the Canadian health care system. In A.J. Baumgart & J. Larsen, *Canadian Nursing Faces the Future: Development and Change*, pp. 19–37, St. Louis, MO: C.V. Mosby.

Berman, A.L., Leenars, A.A., McIntosh, J., & Richman, J. (1992). Case consultation: Mary Catherine. *Suicide and Life Threatening Behavior, 22*(1), 142–149.

Brandt, R.B. (1980). The rationality of suicide. In M.P. Battin & D.J. Mayo (Eds.), *Suicide: The philosophical issues* (pp. 117–132). New York, NY: St. Martin's.

Carson, R. (1992). Washington's I–119. *Hastings Center Report, 22*(2), 7–9.

Curtain, L. (1990). Editorial opinion: A social atrocity. *Nursing Management, 21*(8), 7–8.

Donnelly, J. (Ed.). (1990). *Suicide: Right or wrong? Contemporary issues in philosophy.* New York, NY: Prometheus Books.

Graber, G.C. (1981). The rationality of suicide. In S.E. Wallace & A. Eser (Eds.), *Suicide and euthanasia: The rights of personhood* (pp. 51–65). Knoxville, TN: University of Tennessee.

Hall, B.A. (Ed.). (1984). *Mental health and the elderly.* San Francisco, CA: Grune & Stratton.

Humphrey, D. (1992). Rational suicide among the elderly. *Suicide and Life Threatening Behavior, 22*(1), 125–129.

Jecker, N.S. (Ed.). (1991). *Aging and ethics: Philosophical problems in gerontology.* Clifton, NJ: Humana.

Kerkhof, A. (1991). Suicide in the elderly: A frightful awareness. *Crisis, 12*(2), 81–87.

Kjervik, D.K. (1984). The psychotherapist's duty to act reasonably to prevent suicide: A proposal to allow rational suicide. *Behavioural Sciences and the Law, 2*(2), 207–218.

Leenaars, A.A. (1992). Suicide notes of the older adult. *Suicide and Life Threatening Behavior, 22*(1), 62–79.

Mayo, D.J. (1983). Contemporary philosophical literature on suicide: A review. *Suicide and Life Threatening Behaviour, 13*(4), 313–345.

Mayo, D.J. (1980). Irrational suicide. In M.P. Battin & D.J. Mayo (Eds.), *Suicide: The philosophical issues* (pp. 133–143). New York, NY: St. Martin's.

McIntosh, J.L. (1992). Epidemiology of suicide in the elderly. *Suicide and Life Threatening Behavior, 22*(1), 15–35.

Moody, H.R. (1992). *Ethics in an aging society.* Baltimore, MD: Johns Hopkins University.

Moore, S.L., & Tanney, B.L. (1991). *Suicide among older adults: Selected readings.* Calgary, Alberta: Suicide Information and Education Center.

Osgood, N.J. (1985). *Suicide in the elderly: A practitioner's guide to diagnosis and mental health intervention.* Rockville, MD: Aspen.

Osgood, N.J. (1991). Prevention of suicide in the elderly. *Journal of Geriatric Psychiatry*, 293–306.

Pieper, A. (1985). The right to one's own death. In Jacques Pohier &Dietmar Mieth (Eds.), *Suicide and the right to die* (pp. 39–49). Edinburgh, UK: T&T Clark.

Pohlmeier, H. (1985). Suicide and euthanasia: Special types of partner relationships. *Suicide and Life Threatening Behavior, 15*(2), 117–123.

Portwood, D. (1983). *Common sense suicide: The final right.* New York, NY: Grove.

Prado, C.G. (1990). *The last choice: Preemptive suicide in advanced age.* Westport, CT: Greenwood.

Rauscher, W.V. (1981). *The case against suicide.* New York, NY: St. Martin's.

Richman, J. (1988). The case against rational suicide. *Suicide and Life Threatening Behavior, 18*(3), 285–289.

Richman, J. (1991). Suicide and the elderly. In A. Leenars (Ed.), *Lifespan perspectives of suicide* (pp. 153–167). New York, NY: Plenum.

Richman, J. (1992). A rational approach to rational suicide. *Suicide and Life Threatening Behavior, 22*(10), 130–141.

Robinson, B. (1991, December). Contemplating suicide: New questions, no answers. *Ageing International,* 24–34.

Saul, S.R., & Saul, S. (1991). Old people talk about suicide: A discussion about suicide in a long-term care facility for frail and elderly people. In S.L. Moore & B.L. Tanney (Eds.), *Suicide among older adults: Selected readings.* Calgary, Alberta: Suicide Information and Education Center.

Spring, B., & Larson, E. (1988). *Euthanasia: Spiritual, medical and legal issues in terminal care.* Portland, OR: Multnomah.

Weber, W.M. (1988a). Letter to the editor. What right to die? *Suicide and Life Threatening Behavior, 18*(2), 181–187.

Weber, W.M. (1988b). Letter to the editor: A cliff not a slope: A response to Margaret P. Battin. *Suicide and Life Threatening Behavior, 18*(2), 194–196.

Weisbard, A.J., & Siegler, M. (1986). On killing patients with kindness: An appeal for caution. In J. Lynne (Ed.), *By no extraordinary means: The choice to forgo life-sustaining food and water.* Bloomington, IN: Indiana University.

Wickett, A. (1989). *Double exit: When aging couples die together.* Eugene, OR: Hemlock Society.

Wrobleski, A. (1983) *Rational suicide: A contradiction in terms.* Paper presented at the First Unitarian Society, Minneapolis, MN.

Zarit, S.H. (1980). *Aging and mental disorders: Psychological approaches to assessment and treatment.* New York, NY: Free Press.

43

Ethical Principles and Age-Based Rationing of Health Care

Kathleen Cranley Glass

INTRODUCTION

The starting point in any discussion concerning ethics and decisions affecting seniors is the principle, widely accepted in contemporary society, of respect for persons. The application of this principle results in the recognition of a number of rights and duties. The principle of respect for persons acknowledges the moral worth of individuals and grants them the liberty to be self-determining. Respect for persons forms the basis for the right of competent persons to have their autonomy respected. The right to respect for autonomy includes the freedom, within certain societally accepted limits, to make one's own choices. Also flowing from this principle is the duty of beneficence, which includes both the obligation to avoid inflicting harm on others (sometimes referred to as "nonmaleficence") and the duty to benefit or help other persons, particularly those who are vulnerable.

Another principle, equally prized in democratic societies, is that of justice. The principle of justice is concerned with achieving a fair distribution of benefits and of burdens.

Many rights and duties that are based upon ethical principles are embodied in our laws and social policies. Yet, even when they form the foundation for law or social policy, ethical principles cannot always be absolute in their application. One individual's right to autonomy is limited by another's right to be protected from harm. Thus, while it is presumed that laws and policies should reflect ethical principles, society is justified in placing some restrictions on the actions of its citizens in an effort to protect the well-being of others. Some of these limits are easily defined. For example, I may not cause physical damage to other persons or to their property. Other lines are more difficult to draw, particularly when individual choices affect society as a whole.

Reproduced with the consent of the National Advisory Council on Aging (NACA) and with the permission of the Minister of Supply and Services Canada, 1993.

When choices place individual self-determination in potential confrontation with the well-being of the entire community, the goals of social policies are multiple and sometimes conflicting. These goals include, often simultaneously, the maximization of the individual's right to self-determination, the protection of vulnerable persons who are unable to protect themselves, and the optimization of societal well-being.

1. RESOURCE ALLOCATION AND DISTRIBUTIVE JUSTICE

When issues of liberty and self-determination are discussed in the context of how society's resources are to be distributed, the moral ideal of liberty or autonomy must be balanced with another moral ideal, that of equality. Achieving social justice involves balancing these two ideals, which may at times conflict. With respect to health care, most developed countries, including Canada, have determined that an individual's equal right to basic health care must take priority over the rights of medical practitioners to have complete autonomy over how they exercise their professions.

Even when health care is recognized as a right, health is only one social good among many. When the supply of goods or services to be distributed is (or is perceived to be) limited, questions of distributive justice, or the fair distribution of benefits, arise. Although there is societal consensus in principle on the ideals of liberty, equality and a fair distribution of burdens and benefits, resolving competing claims for limited resources is a difficult exercise. There are no accepted principles of justice that would entitle any individual person to every potentially beneficial treatment or service.

There are several theoretical approaches to distributing benefits and burdens within society. Following each of them in any one situation would produce significantly different results. Yet all public policies based upon distributive justice derive ultimately from the acceptance or rejection of one or more of these theories and from the development of procedures for applying the chosen approach or approaches. Some theoretical bases which have been suggested[1] for distributing societal resources are:

- distribution according to contribution to society
- allocation according to ability, merit or achievement
- division based upon effort
- division into equal shares
- distribution based on need.

A society may use more than one approach to distribute its resources, with each considered as legitimate in one or another context. For example, jobs or promotions may be distributed on the basis of merit while the distribution of social service benefits may be based upon need. Nevertheless, there can and will be conflicts between these principles in certain instances.

2. AGE DIFFERENCES AS THE BASIS FOR DISTRIBUTION

2.1 Age and Rationing: Defining the Issue

Interest in establishing principles for the distribution of resources intensifies when there is a need, either perceived or real, to ration these resources because they are scarce. Within this context, discussions of "rationing" available health care resources have been in the forefront, as opposed to re-orienting national expenditures to cover the rising costs of health care. Using the word "rationing" has opened up a discussion of the social and ethical values implicit in determining whether limits should be placed on certain health care treatments or services. Escalating health care costs, demographic changes resulting in the aging of the North American population and technological advances in medical care have all made questions concerning allocation of resources an important issue of public debate. In the United States and more recently in Canada, there is evidence of a growing belief that health care requirements of the elderly are limitless and likely to grow as the proportion of seniors requiring greater care increases.[2] Because the senior population is growing both in numbers and in proportion, health care costs are sometimes depicted as "an unsustainable burden".[3] This has led to a suggestion that age be used as the justification for limiting access to certain health care goods and services.[4] The question arises: Can differences in age be considered an acceptable basis for distributing scarce goods or services? Does age reasonably fit into one of the distributional approaches noted above, and if so, can this be justified ethically?

In analyzing the suitability of each of the suggested approaches to resource allocation, especially with regard to people of different ages, it is important to keep certain facts in mind concerning older adult persons and their health care needs.

2.2 Heterogeneity of the Senior Population

Individuals over a certain age are often considered as a group for the purpose of assessing health care needs. Yet some commentators insist that seniors are so heterogeneous, even more than other age cohorts,[5] that it is impossible to consider seniors as a distinct group[6] and warn against stereotyping such a diverse segment of the population.[7] Other analysts, however, criticize this view, claiming instead that characteristics such as physical or psychological vulnerability or dependency require special attention in seniors as a whole.[8]

While it may be legitimate to consider seniors as a group for some purposes, without subjecting them to potentially harmful stereotyping, age alone is not a good predictor of any individual's health care needs. Neither does it accurately predict the utility of most health care interventions for older individuals.[9] Consequently, unless distinguishing older persons for the purpose of limiting their access to health care can be legitimated on some other distributional criteria (such as a claim that seniors contribute less, or are less meritorious), a number of important ethical considerations are distorted. These include respect for a person's self-determined choices, the obligation not to harm others and to help those who are vulnerable, as well as the just distribution of society's benefits and burdens.

3. APPLYING DISTRIBUTIONAL APPROACHES TO THE ALLOCATION OF HEALTH CARE

Applying any of the first three approaches for allocation, that is, distribution according to contribution to society, apportionment according to ability, merit or achievement, and division based on effort all pose problems when attempts are made to use them to ration health care.

3.1 Distribution According to Contribution to Society

Contribution to society, or "social worth," gives primacy to notions such as public interest or social productivity. It has been used in the past as a criterion for distribution of scarce health care resources, specifically for access to dialysis. Initially, dialysis machines were in short supply, with those needing the treatment far out-numbering its availability. A hospital in Seattle, Washington, appointed a committee to select from those who would medically benefit from dialysis. To narrow the number of patients, the committee relied upon very conventional standards, such as rewarding public service, giving preference to community volunteers and churchgoers—in effect, measuring a patient's "contribution to society". When publicized, the narrow, middle-class standards used to ration dialysis were met with a great deal of criticism.[10] While the rewarding of public service with appropriate recognition or bestowing medals or prizes is worthwhile, the imposition of one group's values as a control over life-saving therapy was generally viewed with repugnance.

In the case of elderly individuals, applying a standard of contribution to society places them at a distinct disadvantage if current, and not past, contributions are the basis for allocation; individuals with physical or cognitive impairments and persons who are mentally ill are especially at risk of exclusion. The criterion of social worth values the individual only as an instrument of society and not as a person deserving of respect simply because he or she is a human being.

3.2 Apportionment Based on Ability, Merit or Achievement

When distributing resources based upon ability, merit or achievement, particular conduct that distinguished one individual from another is being judged. Actual performance and productive contributions are assessed. It can be argued that certain jobs should be distributed on such a basis because society as a whole will benefit from having positions filled by those most capable of performing the required task. Academic and athletic prizes are awarded in this manner as well. Yet notions of merit are not well suited to determining policies for meeting basic human needs in general, nor to distributing scarce health care resources in particular. Health care should respond to need, whether for prevention or for treatment, not to merit. Inequality of need and inequality of merit are two completely different concepts.

Individuals are equal in being randomly susceptible to most health care crises. In those cases where need for health care results from behaviour, such as illness related to abuse of alcohol, drugs or tobacco, distinguishing those who are responsible for their illness from those who are not is subject to the personal values of the person assessing the behaviour (that is, what behaviours are reprehensible to whom). Distinguishing those who "merit" their condition of poor health (and therefore who are "less deserving" of health care resources) from those who are not invites discrimination of the most malicious sort.

3.3 Distribution Based on Effort

Distributing health care resources based on effort creates other difficulties. Income is frequently thought to be tied to effort, with persons of lower income, or welfare recipients, viewed as less industrious than those with higher income. In health care systems based upon free market economies, effort, to a certain extent, is the rationale for inequalities of resource allocation.

There are two difficulties associated with this rationale. First, inequalities of income are not necessarily the result of inequality of effort. Second, and more importantly, inequality of effort bears no relationship to inequality of need for health care. If the proper basis for the distribution of medical care is ill health or its prevention, then health needs must be the ground of distribution.

3.4 Need as a Distributional Criterion

In the context of allocating societal resources, "needs" are generally considered to be those which are basic and recurrent and, as such, are distinguishable from subjectively felt needs or wants. Basic needs are typically assumed to be given and not acquired.[11] Whether one is in good or ill health is most frequently the result of chance—anyone can suffer ill health. On the whole, older persons have greater health needs than younger individuals[12] and the illnesses associated with aging account for a great deal of necessary medical attention.

However, when resources are insufficient to meet all needs, need alone cannot provide a complete basis for rationing those resources unless some needs are perceived to be more important than others. Consequently, even if need is accepted as the correct basis for distributing medical goods and services, need may have to be defined narrowly in order to accommodate the resource limitation, or the criterion of need may have to be coupled with other considerations, such as that of equality.

3.5 Equality as the Basis for Distribution of Scarce Resources

A minimal principle of formal justice framed by Aristotle states that equals must be treated equally and unequals treated unequally. Applied to health care, this principle implies that no person should be treated unequally, despite all the differences with other persons, unless it can be shown that there is a difference between them relevant to the treatment at stake.[13] In general, rules, laws or policies are considered to be unjust when they make distinctions between classes of people that are actually similar in relevant respects, or when they fail to make distinctions between classes that are actually different in relevant respects.[14] An argument using a concept of justice based on fairness maintains that differences between persons are relevant distributional rules only if those persons are responsible for and deserve these differences, or if using the rules would benefit everyone.[15] In the context of medical care, both individual needs and available treatments differ. Consequently, a distributional principle based upon the equality of all individuals does not translate into a right for equal or identical treatment: rather, it requires equal consideration for treatment.

Using a principle of equal consideration, therefore, rules out rationing based on social worth, merit or effort. It also eliminates the possibility of discrimination based upon race, religion, handicap, gender or age, unless these characteristics are relevant to the medical treatment itself. Using any of these characteristics to ration needed health care is to say that persons who are, for instance, white, Buddhist, paraplegic, female or old, are not equal to those who do not have these traits. Thus, rationing of health care resources based on age alone is to say that older persons are not persons in the same sense as, or are not equal to, younger persons and, consequently, that the claims they may make for health care goods and services will not be treated equally. The principle of equal consideration rules out rationing health care on the basis of age.

4. AGE-BASED RATIONING AS UNETHICAL DISCRIMINATION

A policy that rations health care goods and services based upon age alone cannot be said to conform with the ethical principle of respect for persons. It is particularly distasteful because it would frequently discriminate against some of the most vulnerable members of society. Rationing schemes that place individuals or groups which are already disadvantaged at an even greater risk fail to distribute society's resources in an equitable manner.[16] Because many private resources are already distributed on the basis of public contribution, ability, merit or effort, the rationing of public resources in a manner that discriminates against older persons implies that older persons are somehow not contributing, have less ability, are less meritorious, give no effort to society in general and, consequently, are to be valued less by society. Depriving seniors of the medical care they need reveals what ethicist Joseph Fletcher has called "an inordinate scheme of values, a value system gone awry, a distorted pondering of what we prize and value."[17]

5. ALTERNATIVES TO RATIONING

Every society must contend with a natural tension surrounding both the allocation of scarce resources and attempts to adequately balance the rights of liberty and autonomy to make free and self-determined choices with the obligation to treat equals equally. Beyond a basic elimination of wasteful use, which is an important goal in any health care system, there are important steps to be taken that could insure a more judicious use of health care resources, thereby reducing or eliminating the need for rationing. These include a concern to apply treatment efforts that are appropriate as well as effective and a consideration for patients' wishes for medical intervention.

A primary step is the recognition that when a case by case analysis is undertaken, the overriding aim of medicine to cure cannot always be met. The preservation of all life as long as it is medically and technically feasible is not a reasonable end in itself. Medical interventions must have goals; they are appropriate when there is reasonable hope that they will result in some benefit to the patient. The enormous progress made in medicine over the past 50 years has led us to put great faith in its healing powers. Yet the increasing use of both diagnostic and treatment technologies may have given the false impression that for every illness there is "something" that can be done. This intense preoccupation with the preservation of physical life may at times be based on a failure to recognize that death is natural. It views any delay in death by medical means as "a triumph of human achievement over the limitations of nature."[18] This failure to view death as a natural event in the appropriate circumstances too frequently results in "overmedicalizing" care for many seniors, at great expense, and without worthwhile medical or social goals.

There is an increasing acknowledgement that life at any price is not a desirable goal. Many seniors fear they will be kept alive in severe states of mental and physical incapacity. The growing popularity of advance directives, giving instructions concerning medical care after one is no longer able to make competent decisions, and of powers of attorney for health care that allow the designation of trusted persons to make decisions on one's behalf is due, at least in part, to an appreciation that all medical care is not necessarily in a person's best interest. These mechanisms are usually regarded as a means of limiting treatment, of telling one's caregivers when it is appropriate to withdraw treatment because one has had "enough". They embody an important societal realization: medical care and services should not be used because they are available, they should be used to preserve or extend life when this is in the person's best interest, or to provide comfort and an improved quality of life.

Age alone will never be a telling characteristic with regard to the person's best interest or quality of life. Rather, all persons, including seniors, must be evaluated on an individual basis to determine when medical interventions will best serve their interest or their wishes *as they have defined them.* Care must be taken that treatment refusals, particularly when made by vulnerable persons, are exercised freely and without coercion, especially when resources are limited.

In the event that there are still insufficient resources, even after the adoption of clinically relevant criteria and the consideration of individual wishes, the criterion of need may have to be more narrowly defined. However, such redefinition must be done within the framework of respect for persons, independent of age. In other words, the most basic of needs should be met first, with equal consideration for access of all persons with those needs. There will always be needs that are easily and clearly defined as "basic" and others that are not. Between these two, however, there will be many needs upon which there is no consensus. These needs must be discussed openly, with an attempt to reach an equitable social agreement on the level of care that may be expected by all, rather than leaving such decisions to be made on an *ad hoc* and potentially discriminatory basis.

CONCLUSION

The principle of respect for persons acknowledges the moral worth of individuals, no matter what their age, and accords them the liberty to be self-determining and to have their autonomy respected. When scarce resources must be allocated, equals must be treated equally. In the case of medical goods and services, need is the only equitable basis for allocation. This requires recognition that respect for persons compels a fair determination of a need based upon sound medical goals, a determination of a patient's best interests and a societal consensus upon the definition of needs that must be met. It further requires a respect for the autonomous choices of persons to accept or refuse treatment offered within that fair determination, whether those choices are expressed at the time or have been given by advance directive.

REFERENCES

1. Mappes, T.A. and J.S. Zembaty. *Social ethics: Morality and social policy* (3rd ed.). New York: McGraw-Hill, 1987: 329.

Beauchamp, T.L. and J.F. Childress. *Principles of biomedical ethics* (3rd ed.). New York: Oxford University Press, 1989: 261.

Exchange of resources via the free market, an approach to distribution favoured by many, is not discussed here.

2. In the United States in 1988, health care expenditures for persons 65+ accounted for one-third of the nation's annual health care expenditures.

   U.S. House of Representatives, Select Committee on Aging. *Health care costs for America's elderly, 1977–88.* Washington, D.C.: U.S. Government Printing Office, 1989.

3. Binstock, R.H. and S.G. Post. "Old age and the rationing of health care." In R.H. Binstock and S.G. Post (eds.). *Too old for health care?* Baltimore: Johns Hopkins University Press, 1991: 4.

4. Callaghan, D. *Setting limits: Medical goals in an aging society.* New York: Simon and Shuster, 1987.

5. Kapp, M. "Law and aging." *Law, Medicine and Health Care,* 18, 3, 1990: 181–182.

6. Ostfeld, A. "Older research subjects: Not homogeneous, not especially vulnerable." *IRB: A Review of Human Subjects Research,* 2, 1980: 7–8.

   Weintraub, R. "Ethical concerns and guidelines in research in geriatric pharmacology and therapeutics: Individualization, not codification." *Journal of the American Geriatrics Society,* 32, 1, 1984: 44–48.

   Sachs, G.A. and C.K. Cassel. "Biomedical research involving older human subjects". *Law, Medicine and Health Care,* 18, 3, 1990: 234–243.

7. Neugarten, B. "Time, age and the life cycle." *American Journal of Psychiatry,* 136, 1979: 887–894.

8. Vestal R. "Physical vulnerability." *IRB: A Review of Human Subjects Research,* 2, 1980: 56.

   Ratzan, R. "Being old makes you different: The ethics of research with elderly subjects." *Hastings Center Report,* 10, 1980: 32.

   Lawton, P. "Psychological vulnerability." *IRB: A Review of Human Subjects Research,* 2, 1980: 5–6.

9. Evans, R.W. "Advanced medical technology and elderly people." In Binstock and Post, *op. cit.,* p. 44–74.

10. Fox, R.C. and J.P. Swazey. *The courage to fail.* Chicago: University of Chicago Press, 1974.

11. Outka, G. "Social justice and access to health care." In R. Munson (ed.). *Intervention and reflection: Basic issues in medical ethics* (4th ed.). Belmont, CA: Wadsworth, 1992.

12. Sachs and Cassel, *op. cit.*

    Neugarten, *op. cit.*

13. Beauchamp and Childress, *op. cit.,* p. 259.

14. Ibid., p. 263.

15. Ibid., p. 270.

16. Rawls, J. *A theory of justice.* Cambridge, MA: Harvard University Press, 1971.

17. Fletcher, J. "Setting medical limits." In P. Homer and M. Holstein (eds.). A *good old age?* New York: Simon and Shuster, 1990: 63–69.

18. Landau, R.L. and J.M. Gustafson. "Death is not the enemy." *Journal of the American Medical Association,* 252, 17, November 2, 1984: 2458.

44

Facing the Transitoriness of Human Existence

Viktor Frankl

How can we face and cope with our life's transitoriness; in other words, how is it possible to say yes to life in spite of death? We do an injustice to death by believing that it deprives and robs life of meaning. Actually, it doesn't take the meaning away from, but rather gives meaning to life. Imagine what would happen if our lives were not finite, if we were immortal. Wouldn't we be justified in postponing everything—nothing would have to be done today, for we could do it as well tomorrow, next week, next month, or next year—postponing in *in infinitum*. Only under the threat and pressure of death does it make sense to do what we can and should, right now. That is, to make proper use of the moment's offer of a meaning to fulfill—be it a deed to do, or work to create, anything to enjoy, or a period of inescapable suffering to go through with courage and dignity. If we are beings in search of meaning, meaning—as we now can see—is in no way done away with by death. But the fact that death is in wait for us does enhance our sense of responsibleness, of our being responsible beings.

At this point allow me to intersperse a personal reminiscence: Forty-five years ago, I stood on the ramp of a railway station of a place called Auschwitz. At that time, the probability that I would survive was 1 to 29, as can be statistically evidenced. Now you may understand that, if such an individual actually survives, he will ask himself day by day whether he has also been *worthy* of survival—that is to say, whether he has made proper use of each and every day. And he will have to confess: only partially, if at all. Psychiatrists, particularly in your country, have come up with the concept of survivor guilt. I don't think that this concept is a legitimate one; I rather think that what the majority of the survivors of concentration camps have been experiencing may be called "survivor responsibility." What they feel is a deep sense of being responsible, of having to carefully listen to what the prompter called

---

Reproduced with permission from *Generations* 15, 7-10 (Fall 1990) and by permission of the author.

"conscience" is whispering into their ears regarding the question of how to make the best of each single opportunity that life may offer them.

You may now understand why I arrived later on—so to speak, in the post-Auschwitz period of my life—at the formulation of a maxim that reads as follows: "Live as if you were living for the second time—and as if you had acted the first time as wrongly as you are about to act now." Once an individual really puts himself into this imagined situation, he will instantaneously become conscious of the full gravity of the responsibility that every person bears throughout every moment of his life—the responsibility for what he will make of the next hour, for how we will shape the next day.

What I have said brings to mind the famous saying by Hillel, starting with the words "if I'm not doing it, who will do it? And if I don't do it right now, when shall I do it?" This refers to the preciousness of the irrepeatable moment and to the irreversibility of human existence—that irreversibility that heuristically is bracketed by the maxim "Live as if you were living for the second time..." so that the temporality of life seems to be suspended.

But now let us come back to what has been said regarding the possibilities that alone are affected by the transitoriness of human existence. As soon as we have used an opportunity and have actualized a meaning potential, we have done so *once and for all.*

We have converted a possibility into a reality, and as such we have rescued it into the past. For in the past, nothing is irrecoverably lost, but everything is irrevocably stored. We have safely delivered and deposited it in the past because nothing and nobody can ever deprive us or rob us of what we have treasured in the past. What we have done cannot be undone! To be sure, all the more we should be aware of our responsibleness, our being responsible for what to do, whom to love, and how to suffer.

People usually tend to see only the stubble fields of transitoriness but overlook and forget the full granaries of the past into which they have brought, and saved, the harvest of their lives. Let's not forget that "having been" is still a mode of being—perhaps even the safest mode. In the phrase "being past," the emphasis is to be placed on "being." In fact, when Martin Heidegger came to Vienna and honored me by visiting me at my home, we discussed this matter among others. To express his agreement with my view on the past, he autographed his picture as follows: *"Das Vergangene geht; Das Gewesene kommt."* Or, in my own English translation: "What has passed, has gone; what *is* past, will come."

In this context, let me emphasize that whatever we have rescued into the past remains therein, irrespective of whether anyone remembers it; just as something exists, and continues to exist, irrespective of whether we look at it and even continues to exist regardless of our own existence.

What about a life of short duration—say, the life that ends too early? I think that we are not justified to draw conclusions from the duration of anyone's life about its meaningfulness. Or do we judge a biography by its length? Do we judge by the number of pages that a biographical book comprises? Do we not judge it, rather, by the richness of the respective life? Do we not know examples of people who died young and, yet, their existence had incomparably more meaning than the existence of some long-lived dull-ard? Finally, are not some of the so-called "unfinished" symphonies among the most beautiful ones?

But in this context we have also to consider those counseling situations wherein we are confronted with a patient whose life turns out to be of longer duration than that of his or her partner. There is no such case whose story could be told so briefly as the often-quoted case of a colleague of mine, the story of an old general practitioner who consulted me because of his depression after his wife had died two years before. Using a Socratic dialogue, I restricted my comment to asking him what would have happened if not his wife, but he himself had died first. "How terrible this would have been for her—how much she would have suffered," was his answer. Whereupon I reacted by asking him another question: "Well, Doctor, this suffering has been spared her. But now, you have to pay for it—by surviving and mourning her." At the same moment, he began to see his own suffering in a new light, he could see a meaning in his suffering, the meaning of a sacrifice he owed to his wife. He still was mourning her, but he no longer was desperate because, as I am used to couching it in an equation, $D = S - M$, which means that despair is suffering without meaning.

But it is not only partners who die and leave us alone—it is also children who become the victims of the transitoriness of human existence while their parents live on and thus have to survive them.

Often, people are in despair not because of having to survive their children but rather because there are no children of their own who would survive their parents. However, what underlies this type of despair is the assumption that a life with no children is ultimately meaningless, and this is a fundamental mistake because either life has a meaning—then it retains this meaning whether it is long or short, whether or not it reproduces itself—or life has no meaning, in which case it remains meaningless, no matter how long it lasts or can go on reproducing itself. If the life of a childless woman were really meaningless solely because she had no children, then humanity lives only for its children, and the whole meaning of existence is to be found in the next generation. But that is only a postponement of the problem. For every generation then hands on the problem unsolved to the next generation. The only meaning in the life of one generation would consist of raising the next. But if something is meaningless, it does not acquire meaning by being immortalized. To sum up: The assumption that procreation is the only meaning of life contradicts and defeats itself; for if life is meaningless of itself, it can never be made meaningful merely by its perpetuation.

From all of which, we see once again that life can never be an end in itself, and that its reproduction can never be its meaning; rather, it acquires meaning from other, non-biological frames of reference, from sources that necessarily lie beyond itself. To be bestowed with meaning, life must transcend itself, but it must do so not in "length"—in the sense of living on in one's children—but in "height"—in the sense of spirtually growing beyond oneself—or in "breadth"—in the sense of social engagement. As to spiritual growth, however, it was Elisabeth Kübler-Ross who coined, for the title of one of her books, a phrase that epitomizes the last and greatest chance any human being may be given: "Death, the Final Stage of Growth."

To take the chance certainly presupposes heroism. But heroism is something that, as I see it, can be expected, or demanded, of only one person, oneself. One should, therefore, always avoid approaching aging, suffering, or dying people—if I may say so—with a moralistically raised finger instead of a pointing finger—pointing to an example of someone who shows us how to die. And, as you know, in the history of philosophy someone has defined philosophy as knowing how to die.

When Sigmund Freud once complained in a letter to Lou Salome how hard, after more than 30 surgical operations, it was to come to terms with his chronic illness, she replied that there is a need to set an example. To be sure, during "the final stage," his doctor gave him a shot that spared the patient absolutely unnecessary and, in this sense, meaningless pain *in ultimis*. Preceding this stage, however, Freud had devoted himself to the completion of his writings and had refused taking pain-killers.

Of course, work itself may be considered at least a mild pain-killer, relieving suffering at least to some degree. Cushing, one of the greatest brain surgeons of all time, as an old man said to his friend and colleague, Dandy: "The only way to endure life is always to have a task to complete." I need only mention the classical example of Goethe, who as an old man had been working for no less than seven years on his "Faust" drama's part 2—seven years! And only two months after the completion of his opus magnum, he died.

It is not only work that keeps one alive and helps one "endure life," as Cushing put it; also, enriching oneself through experiences may be helpful. Let me, in this context, quote from a letter I once received from a lady. She wrote: "I am 87 years of age, but to me, each day is a gift, and mustn't we be grateful? Look: I can watch, from my window, the wonderful park; I can talk to the trees; I am deaf, but I hear my innermost self talking to me! I cannot walk, but I can think, and this is something for which I am most grateful."

All of this, of course, not only points out how important it is to keep oneself busy—by transcending oneself toward "a task to complete"—but it also should serve as an admonition not to stop being dedicated to something outside oneself. In no way does this mean overrating an individual's capacity to continue working, but on the other hand we must not underrate an individual's capacity to mobilize coping mechanisms in the sense of compensating for some deficiencies, at least to some amount. I well remember my rock-climbing guide, who, while watching me during a common tour through a steep mountain wall, commented on my rock-climbing style: "Listen, Doctor, while I observe your climbing—please, don't become angry—but as I see, you possess virtually no strength any more. But the way in which you *compensate* this lack of rude strength—compensating it through refined rock-climbing technique—I must confess that from you, one can learn rock climbing!" Whereupon I nearly exploded from self-esteem. After all, the man who had said this to me had been leading a group on a tour to the Himalayas. Encouraged by him, I continued rock climbing until five years ago, when I was close to 80.

The reader should not think that I have based my gerontological convictions merely on case material, which, at that, I have presented in a more or less anecdotal manner. There is also an increasing body of empirical studies confirming and corroborating my assumptions. Gary T. Reker (1988) of Trent University presented a paper on sources of personal meaning among young, middle-aged, and older adults. Using the Personal Meaning Index he developed, he found out that "sources of meaning that go beyond hedonistic or self-serving needs, optimally contribute to a global sense of meaning in life, supporting Frankl's view that a deeper sense of meaning can only be discovered when an individual moves toward a self-transcend state." Using the Purpose in Life Test developed by Crumbaugh and Maholick, and using supportive logotherapy in the treatment of terminally ill patients, Zuehlke and Watkins (1975; 1977) reported that "the patients experienced a significant increase in the sense of purpose and meaning in their lives as measured by the Purpose in Life Test. But even without logotherapeutic treatment, it could be evidenced by Thomas and Weiner (1974) that "patients who were critically ill had higher PIL scores than had patients with a minor ailment or non-patients."

From all this you may see that not only suffering but also dying offers a meaning potential. Since even death may be bestowed with meaning, life turns out to be potentially meaningful under each and every condition, that is to say, the meaning of life is unconditional. This too could be evidenced in strictly empirical terms—I refer to research by many scholars who have evidenced by tests and statistics that in fact meaning is available to each and every person—regardless of sex or age, IQ or educational background, environment or character structure, and—last but not least—regardless of whether or not one is religious and, if one is, regardless of the denomination to which one may belong.

Furthermore, this unconditional quality of meaning is paralleled by an equally unconditional value of each and every human being—that unconditional value that usually is called dignity. And why is dignity something unconditional? It is unconditional because it must not be confounded with mere usefulness in terms of functioning for the benefit of today's society—a society that is characterized by achievement orientation and consequently adores people who are successful and happy, and in particular adores the young. The decisive difference, then, between being valuable in the sense of dignity and being valuable in the sense of usefulness is blurred. If, however, you are not cognizant of this difference but believe that an individual's value depends on present usefulness, you owe it only to personal inconsistency if you don't go ahead and plead for euthanasia in the strictest sense of Hitler's program. Euthanasia, we may say, then, is "mercy" killing of all those who have lost their usefulness, be it because of old age, incurable illness, mental deterioration, or whatever handicap they may suffer. I possess some experience with regard to euthanasia under the Nazi regime because, together with my former boss, the head of the Psychiatric University Hospital of Vienna, Professor Otto Potzl, I was involved in illegally but successfully sabotaging euthanasia. (I used false certificates wherein I diagnosed fever delirium instead of endogenous depression, and aphasia instead of schizophrenia.)

Usefulness, at any rate, may have left a person, but dignity will stay with him or her. Those who still cannot but have contempt for old people should take heed not to fall prey to self-contempt once they have grown old themselves and then are immersed in the nagging feeling of being inferior.

There is no need to pity old people. For what reason should we pity them? Because they have no longer any opportunities in store for them, any possibilities in the future? They have more than that: Instead of possibilities in the future, they have their realities in the past—the deeds done, the loved ones loved, and, last but not least, the sufferings they have gone through with courage and dignity. In a word, they have already brought in the harvest of their lives and now may, as it has been said in the Book of Job, come to their graves, "like a shock of corn cometh in his season."

In concluding, let me share with you a transcript of an interview I had with an 80-year-old patient of mine in front of an audience. She was suffering a terminal cancer, and she knew that she was. Now the following dialogue developed:

> **Frankl:** *What do you think when you look back on your life? Has life been worth living?*
>
> **Patient:** *Well, Doctor, I must say that I had a good life. Life was nice, indeed. And I must thank the Lord for what it held for me: I went to theaters, I attended concerts, and so forth. You see, Doctor, I went there with the family in whose house I served for many decades as a maid; in Prague at first, and later, in Vienna. And for the grace of all those wonderful experiences, I am grateful to the Lord.*

(I nevertheless felt that she also was doubtful about the ultimate meaning of her life, and I wanted to steer her through her doubts, so I asked her to question the meaning of her life on the conscious level rather than repressing her doubts.)

> **Frankl:** *You are speaking of some wonderful experiences, but all of this will have an end now, won't it?*

Patient *(thoughtfully)*: Yes, everything ends....

Frankl: Well, do you think that all of the wonderful things of your life might be annihilated?

Patient: *(still more thoughtfully)*: All those wonderful things....

Frankl: But tell me, do you think that anyone can undo the happiness that you have experienced? Can anyone blot it out?

Patient: No, Doctor, nobody can blot it out!

Frankl: Or can anyone blot out the goodness that you have met in your life?

Patient: *(becoming increasingly emotionally involved)*: Nobody can blot it out!

Frankl: What you have achieved and accomplished....

Patient: Nobody can blot it out!

Frankl: Or what you have bravely and honestly suffered; can anyone remove it from the world—remove it from the past where you have stored it?

Patient *(now moved to tears)*: No one can remove it. It is true, I have had a great deal to suffer; but I also tried to be courageous and steadfast in enduring what I must. You see, Doctor, I regard my suffering as a punishment. I believe in God.

Frankl *(trying to put himself in the place of the patient)*: But cannot suffering also sometimes be a challenge? Is it not conceivable that God wanted to see how Anastasia Kotek would bear it? And perhaps He had to admit, "Yes, she did so very bravely." And now tell me, can anyone remove such an achievement and accomplishment from the world, Frau Kotek?

Patient: Certainly, no one can do it!

Frankl: This remains, doesn't it?

Patient: It does!

Frankl: By the way, you had no children, had you?

Patient: I had none.

Frankl: Well, do you think that life is meaningful only if one has children?

Patient: If they had good children, why shouldn't it be a blessing?

Frankl: Right, but you should not forget that, for instance, the greatest philosopher of all times, Immanuel Kant, had no children, but would anyone venture to doubt the extraordinary meaningfulness of his life?

If children were the only meaning of life, life would become meaningless because to procreate something which in itself is meaningless would certainly be the most meaningless thing. What matters in life is to achieve something. And this is precisely what you have done. You have made the best of your suffering. You have become an example for our patients because of the way you take your suffering upon yourself. I congratulate the other patients who have the opportunity to witness such an example. (The audience burst into spontaneous applause.) This applause is for you, Frau Kotek. (She is weeping now.) It concerns your life, which has been a great achievement. You may be proud of it, Frau Kotek. And how few people may be proud of their lives. I should say, your life is a monument. And no one can remove it from the world.

Patient *(regaining her self-control): What you have said, Professor Frankl, is a consolation. It comforts me. Indeed, I never had an opportunity to hear any thing like this. (Slowly and quietly she leaves the lecture hall.)*

A week later the woman died. During the last week of her life, she was no longer depressed, but, on the contrary, full of faith and pride. Prior to this, she had felt agonized, ridden by the anxiety that she was useless. Our interview had made her aware that her life was meaningful and that even her suffering was not in vain. Her last words were: "My life is a monument. So Professor Frankl said to the whole audience, to all of the students in the lecture hall. My life was not in vain."

REFERENCES

Reker, G.T., 1988. "Sources of Personal Meaning Among Young, Middle-Aged, and Older Adults." Paper presented at the Annual Meeting of the Gerontological Society of America, San Francisco, Calif.

Thomas, J. and Weiner, E., 1974. "Psychological Differences Among Groups of Critically Ill Hospitalized Patients, Non-Critically Ill Hospitalized Patients, and Well Controls." *Journal of Consulting and Clinical Psychology* 42:274–79.

Zuehlke, T.E. and Watkins, J.T., 1975. "The Use of Psychotherapy with Dying Patients," *Journal of Clinical Psychology* 31:729–32.

Zuehlke, T.E. and Watkins, J.T., 1977. "Psychotherapy with Terminally Ill Patients," *Psychotherapy: Theory, Research and Practice* 14:403–10.

SECTION NINE

Discussion Questions

1. *Describe two changes in the past few years in the Canadian legal view of the right to die.*

2. *What is an advance directive and what does it do? What potential effects do advance directives have on decision-making and the quality of life in old age?*

3. *Give the arguments in favour of and against rational suicide in old age. What position does Moore take on this issue? Why does she hold this view?*

4. *Should medical science keep people alive as long as possible? Or should the medical system set limits on the use of health services by older adults? How would society benefit from setting limits?*

5. *How, according to Frankl, can a person endure suffering, pain, and death in old age? How can the sense of meaning redeem even sickness and suffering? What role can the past play in creating a meaningful and good old age?*

Suggested Readings

Callwood, J. (1986). *Twelve Weeks in Spring*. Toronto: Lester & Orpen Dennys.

National Advisory Council on Aging (1993). *Ethics and Aging*. Cat. No. H71–3/16-1993E. Ottawa: Minister of Supply and Services Canada.

Thornton, J.E. and E.R. Winkler, eds. *Ethics and Aging: The Right to Live, the Right to Die*. Vancouver: University of British Columbia Press.

Politics and Policies

Population aging has led to changes in health-care, pension, and housing policies. The future will bring more changes to social institutions and new social policies.

Burke projects a near-doubling of social spending on older people in the future. Pension costs may go up more than 200 percent. Canada's ability to afford these costs will depend on economic conditions, unemployment, and other large-scale social trends. Even with increased economic growth, Canada may have to increase its tax rates in order to maintain benefits for older people. This could give rise to social tensions in the future.

Gee and McDaniel discuss the way that population aging frames debate over many policy issues in Canada. The early part of this article could serve as a critique of Burke's article on population aging. Gee and McDaniel want to move debate beyond the view that population aging will drive social policy. They review a number of policies that can help Canadians respond to an older population. These include increased fertility, child care, and caregiver support. These policies balance the demands of an aging society with programs that can help meet these demands.

Gifford discusses the use of seniors' political power to achieve social change. Seniors have rarely engaged in power politics in the past. They have generally not voted as a bloc. Nor have they formed a strong lobby group. Gifford calls for a seniors' coalition made up of the seniors' organizations that would serve all seniors' interests. He says that senior power depends on organization. And this organization would involve many seniors who today take little part in Canadian political life. The seniors' movement, as Gifford defines it, will shape Canadian social policy in the next century.

Canada has a broad web of policies—from health care to housing to pensions—related to seniors' issues. These policies have responded to an aging population by adjusting benefits, creating new programs, and serving new groups of older people. Together these policies have created a good old age for the majority of Canada's older people. But the system works less well for minority groups like immigrants, very old women, Native people, and homemakers. A good old age in the future will depend on policies that respond to the needs of seniors and that give fair treatment to all older people in Canada.

45

Implications of an Aging Society

Mary Anne Burke

Canada, forty years hence, will be very different demographically from what it is today. The elderly population (arbitrarily defined as those aged 65 and over) is projected to increase dramatically as the people born during the baby boom begin to reach old age around 2010. By the year 2030, for the first time in Canada's history, people aged 65 and over are projected to out-number dependants under age 15, according to projections from the Organization for Economic Cooperation and Development (OECD). As well, the proportion of people potentially economically dependent on the population aged 15–64 will reach levels not experienced since the height of the baby boom in the mid-1960s.

An aging society has implications for the costs associated with social programs and for the ability of the working population to finance social expenditure. Overall, social spending can be expected to increase, with elderly people consuming a greater share of the resources because of increased pension expenditure and higher health care costs. Demographic changes will also affect the size of the labour force, and in turn, the capacity to finance social programs.

MOST SPENDING ON THE ELDERLY

According to projections from the OECD, within the next fifty years, half of all social spending in Canada will be on the elderly, if current spending levels continue and demographic projections are realized. This compares with just 26% in 1980. Over the same period, relative spending on the rest of the population is expected to decline. The share of expenditure devoted to the

Statistics Canada, *Canadian Social Trends*, Catalogue 11–008 (Spring 1991): 6–8. Reproduced by authority of the Minister of Industry, 1994.

Readers wishing further information on data provided through the cooperation of Statistics Canada may obtain copies of related publications by mail from: Publications Sales, Statistics Canada, Ottawa, Ontario, K1A 0T6, by calling 1-613-951-7277, or toll free 1-800-267-6677. Readers may also facsimile their order by dialing 1-613-951-1584.

young is projected to drop to 15% from 24%, and for people aged 15–64, to 35% from 50%.

HIGHER PER CAPITA SOCIAL OUTLAY ON THE ELDERLY

While the bulge of people entering old age in the next century will be partially offset by declining numbers of young dependants, the OECD expects the demand for social program support to increase substantially. In large part, this is because per capita spending for elderly people in Canada far exceeds that for the young. Overall per capita expenditure in 1980, for example, was $6,500 for the elderly, 2.7 times greater than the $2,500 spent on the young, and just $1,800 for those aged 15–64.

PENSION EXPENDITURE HIGHEST

Pensions (which include publicly financed old age, survivors' and permanent sickness pensions) are expected to account for the largest proportion of social expenditure. With the dramatic increase in the number of elderly people after 2010, overall pension expenditure in Canada is expected to increase 204% over the projection period—more than for any other social program. As a result, by 2040, pensions are projected to account for 38% of social spending, up from just 24% in 1980.

Spending on health care is expected to account for the next largest proportion of the social program budget. Following a projected 118% increase in total health care spending, such expenditure is projected to account for 33% of all spending, up from 29% in 1980. This is largely because health care of the elderly is much more costly than for the rest of the population.

For example, in 1974, health care spending on people aged 65 and over was 4.5 times greater than for those under age 65. Health care of those aged 75 and over was even more costly, 6.7 times greater than for those under age 65. As the elderly and very elderly increase dramatically in number early in the next century, the impact of these numbers will be felt on the public purse, unless there are significant changes in health care expenditure patterns.

Expenditure on other programs is expected to drop as a percentage of all social spending. The proportion spent on education is projected to drop to 18% from 32% in 1980, with unemployment insurance declining to 9% from 12% in 1980, and family benefits, to 2% from 3%.

In large part, the reduction in proportions spent on education, unemployment, and family benefits will occur because growth in spending on these programs will be slower than that for pensions and health care. For example, over the projection period, unemployment insurance expediture is expected to increase 29%, family benefits, 10%, and education, just 3%.

GROWTH OF SOCIAL EXPENDITURE

One result of these trends is that social expenditure in Canada would substantially increase over the projection period. Overall social spending in Canada is projected to increase 87% by 2040. By comparison, social spending in the United States and Japan is projected to increase 65% and 40%, respectively, while in many European countries it is expected to increase only slightly or even decrease. Since the study assumed constant per capita expenditure on the various social programs, differences in projected social expenditure growth rates of the various countries are related entirely to differing total population trends and growth rates of the elderly population.

FINANCING GROWING SOCIAL EXPENDITURES

Social programs in Canada are financed largely through tax and social security contributions of the labour force. Future capacity to finance social expenditure will be affected by the rate of real growth in the economy, the number of employed people and their real earnings, and the rate of increase in the level of real social benefits.

Changes in the demographic structure of the Canadian population are expected to lead to substantial increases in social expenditure between 2005 and 2040. According to OECD projections, social expenditure is projected to increase 43% from 2005 to 2040, following a dramatic growth of almost 50% in the number aged 65 and over, and an increase of just 2% in the size of the working age population.

To finance this increase in social expenditure, the OECD projects that average real earnings of workers would have to increase 40% or 1.7% per annum from 2005 to 2040, assuming that labour force participation and unemployment remain at 1980 levels. Changes in these assumptions would affect the outcome of the projection.[1]

According to the OECD, a gap between the living standards of the working population and the levels of social benefits provided by the social programs would likely develop if increases in productivity were used to finance growing social expenditure. Given past social spending trends, however, the OECD expects that benefit levels cannot be held constant over a long period of time. For example, government expenditure on health, education and pensions had an average annual cost increase of 4.4% between 1961 and 1985, close to double the economic growth rate during the same period.

If the level of social benefits increases, as it has in the past, the OECD projects that Canada will be faced with sharp increases in tax burdens during the 2005 to 2040 period. Canadians will most likely have to choose between increasing tax rates and social security contributions or lower levels of social benefits.

NOTE

1. In fact, the labour force participation rate increased to 67% in 1989 from 64% in 1980. On the other hand, the unemployment rate in 1989 was at the same level as in 1980 (7.5%), following a peak of 11.8% during the recession of the early 1980s.

46

Social Policy for an Aging Society

Ellen M. Gee and Susan A. McDaniel

...

SOCIAL POLICY ISSUES IN AN AGING SOCIETY

Social policy is grounded in the distribution and redistribution of social resources. Given the bases of social resources in income, housing, health, etc., it is not possible to examine social policy in a vacuum; the economic and political context in which social policy issues and debates occur matters greatly in a discussion of the broader societal dimensions of aging and social policy. Issues of aging are not limited to the aged, but affect virtually all groups in society.

Intergenerational Equity/Economics of Aging

The contemporary model of distribution/redistribution of societal resources is one of competition amongst stakeholders, with political forces determining the allocation of resources (allowing that some consideration be given to the aim of distributive justice). Broadly, intergenerational equity encompasses the idea that the young and the old should have similar access to opportunities, including social policy benefits. A core aspect is that the young have been deprived of their fair share of opportunities/benefits due to excessive allocation to the old.[1]

While intergenerational/equity conflict has received considerable public attention in the United States, it has not yet emerged as an issue in Canada. However, its underlying basis—pessimism about the economic implications of population aging—is present.[2] As a result, attention in Canada focuses upon *how* (significantly, not *whether*) social policy is influenced by population aging. The aging population has become, in many ways, the paradigm by which social policy is driven.[3] If welfare, health and/or public pension costs are increasing, population aging is seen as the culprit. These arguments continue to be made, despite strong evidence to the contrary;

Reproduced with permission from *Journal of Canadian Studies*, Vol. 28, No. 1 (Spring 1993).

moreover, "solutions" such as increasing immigration and fertility rates are proposed. That these solutions to a problem (that may not be a problem after all) may entail their own set of problems is seldom considered.

Supported by the language of deficits and public purse burdens, the image is created of a society that cannot afford to provide social benefits to its older members who worked hard (whether at the work-place, in the home, or on the farm) to provide societal benefit and a good start for their children and grandchildren. The old are viewed as a "burden" carried by the young who, as the argument goes, can little afford it.

Issues of generational allocation are largely issues in other realms, redefined as generational. What are these other issues? For the most part, they involve the relationship between economic and social policy. As Neysmith points out, there is increasingly a conceptual amalgamation of economic and social policy which has led to the subordination of social policy to economic policy.[5] With economic policy aims such as deficit reduction, reduced government intervention in the marketplace, and investor encouragement taking precedence, there are not many options for social policy. The overriding focus on economic policy—witnessed by such actions as cutbacks to Established Programs Financing, the free trade agreement with the United States, and the current discussions of tri-lateral free trade—makes the two-way relationship between economic policy and social policy less visible. While it is easy to see that economic productivity and growth are necessary for social policies (i.e. to pay for them), it is perhaps less obvious that social policies, by contributing to the well-being of the population, enhance the economy. For example, the end of Medicare (which is a possibility given current trends in federal transfers to the provinces) would have many indirect economic and social costs. The emphasis on economic policy also fosters absurdities such as the view that public pensions are a burden whereas "private" pensions and RRSPs—although they are heavily state-subsidized—are not a drain on the public purse.[6]

This is not to say that economic policy is unimportant. Indeed, it is estimated that the Canadian Gross Domestic Product (GDP) will have to grow by one percent (low projection) to 2.3 percent (high projection) per annum over the next 50 years in order to maintain current levels of expenditures in the areas of health, education and pensions. To put this in context, the real growth in GDP over the past 30 years has averaged 2.1 percent per annum.[7] However, the point is that social policies can contribute to economic growth. For example, the work-place policies discussed earlier can facilitate a longer working life, even as they can ease the unemployment burden of older people.

A policy challenge ahead is to foster a recognition of the complex relationships between economic and social policy and the means to translate that knowledge into measures that will benefit all Canadians. We need to move beyond a view of population aging as the inexorable force behind social policy. Research is needed to counter the rhetoric and myths about what population aging means in terms of social policy.

Demographic Policies

In order to "stem the tide" of population decline and population aging, the federal governmment has turned to immigration policy—increasing the number of immigrants allowed into Canada in recent years to 220,000 per annum. Such a level, if maintained and assuming no significant levels of out-migration, may be high enough to prevent the Canadian population from declining; it is estimated that the number of immigrants needed annually to prevent declining size ranges, depending upon fertility assumptions, from 200,000 to 310,000.[8] But what about population aging? In order for the age structure to be significantly affected, the number of immigrants needed per year would exceed 600,000! It is doubtful that Canadian society could absorb this number of immigrants per year, especially given that immigrants now come from much more diverse backgrounds in terms of country of origin, religion, language and race.

Even if changes were made in the ages of immigrants allowed into Canada (from the current situation in which 23 percent are under 15 years of age to 30 or even to 50 percent), no long-term effects on the overall population age structure would result.[9] This point seems to be lost on policy-makers. In late 1991, the Minister of Employment and Immigration announced that the age of dependent children of immigrants allowed into Canada would be lowered from 21 to 19, presumably to make for a younger age distribution of immigrants.

Immigration is not a viable mechanism to "solve" population aging. Given that immigration is desirable for other reasons, immigration policy should focus less on demographic manipulation attempts and more on providing services and support to new Canadians. Immigrant programs are being cut back, in cost-saving measures, while immigration remains relatively high.

If we want to reverse the trend of population aging, the key lies in increasing fertility levels. However, a major increase would be required—from current (total) fertility rates of approximately 1.6 to rates about 3.1; that is, to a level approaching that of the baby boom years in Canada.[10] The virtual impossibility of such a task may be a factor in why Canadian policy has generally not focused upon trying to increase fertility levels, but rather on increasing immigration levels.

However, in Quebec, the Bourassa government has launched a pro-natalist policy which is driven by many forces. The policy pays parents bonuses based on the number of children they have, with the third and fourth child worth more than the first or second. One aspect of this policy is to increase the pool of future labour force participants to counter population aging. Fertility levels have increased somewhat in the province, but it remains for researchers to ascertain whether this is due to the policy, other factors such as the baby-boom cohort reaching the end of its child-bearing years, or a growing sense of nationhood.

Child Care Policy

At first glance, it might seem that child care is unrelated to population aging. However, population aging is the direct result of decreased fertility, which is in turn related, among other factors, to the increased labour force participation of women. Thus, an aging population is one with a high proportion of young mothers (and fathers) who are working and have child-care needs. In 1988, 67 percent of Canadian mothers with at least one child under the age of 16 were in the paid labour force; for mothers with at least one child under the age of three, the figure approaches 59 percent.[11] Access to high-quality day-care at reasonable costs is a critical issue for many families with children. Most children with parents in the labour force (or full-time students) are not cared for in licensed child-care settings, despite parental preference for this type of care.[12]

Although a national child-care policy was promised by the federal government in 1987, it was officially abandoned in early 1992. The lack of a child-care policy may be viewed as one factor that increases the opportunity cost of children, and keeps fertility lower than it might otherwise be.[13] The social, personal, and economic costs of continuing to ignore child-care policy must be considered as well.

Informal Care-Giving to the Elderly

Many middle-aged women (daughters and daughters-in-law, in particular) are engaged in care-giving to elderly family members.[14] A "care-giving crisis" is upon us, not because of the increased numbers of older persons who are living longer, but rather because of a shortage in the traditional "supply" of care-givers as more and more women enter the paid labour force. This will be exacerbated in the future as the number of younger-generation women declines.[15]

Canadian policies for elder care have taken this family support for granted. However, as the pool of children dwindles, policies that are supportive of children, rather than dependent upon them, will be needed. These policies need not be based on the assumption that the family bears the primary responsibility for aged members; indeed, Alan Walker states that "perhaps the main principle that policy-makers and society in general must recognize is that not all families should be expected to care" and Susan McDaniel argues that one of the policy challenges facing us regarding elder care is dismantling the ideology of familism.[16]

The above notwithstanding, there is a need for policies that assist middle-aged women with elder care. What kind of policies are required? One approach is to provide assistance, in the forms of respite care and adult day-care, to children giving hands-on care to aged parents.[17] Another approach is pension policy reform, most probably in the C/QPP, which would allow for a drop-out provision to allow children to leave the labour force for a period of time to attend to elder care-giving without forfeiting pension credits. Tax deductions or family allowances for elder care are other possibilities. Finally, the gender-based division of labour of care-giving needs to be challenged. Policies that encourage men to be more involved in care-giving seem appropriate.[18] Piecemeal policies will help only minimally, as entrenched values, behaviours, and attitudes as well as wider social and economic factors structure the gender inequalities of care-giving. Perhaps the most we can hope for now are policies that do not reinforce gender inequalities in elder care-giving.[19]

CONCLUSION

Population aging does not create a crisis in social policy; rather, population aging is, in fact, the *result* of successful social policies that have made it possible for people to live long lives and to control their fertility. Nevertheless, an aging Canada faces a number of policy challenges; changing demographics call for creative ways to deal with individual and social welfare.

Policy aspects of population aging involve complex issues for society as a whole. Policies concerning the aged and other age groups in society are not unrelated. In this paper, the division of the issues into two parts is put forward for analytical purposes only. In reality, the policy issues of the aged and of aging are closely intertwined. For example, work-place policies and service delivery issues are related to care-giving by the middle-aged; demographic policies, designed to counter population aging, have an indirect effect on other social policies aimed at the aged; pension policy influences the economics of aging and informal care-giving.

Ideological tensions in Canada, past and current, play a key role in defining problems and policy solutions. The economic underpinnings of social policy are particularly salient in the 1990s, given the emphasis on economic policy to the neglect of social policy. Ironically, the down-playing of social policy, based on financial consideration, may stall initiatives and innovations important in promoting economic development.

The last point emphasized here is that gender will figure more prominently in social policy as the population ages. Any failings of policies for the elderly are felt more acutely by women, partly given women's greater life expectancy and partly because gender-based injustices accumulate with age. Many social policies (e.g. on child care, informal care-giving, and certain work-place policies such as pay equity and pensions) are of more concern to the daily lives of women. Women (of all ages) are, of course, a heterogeneous group and "there is no guarantee that women will become the agent of change that will reverse emergent trends."[20] Nevertheless, as the social power of women increases, policy issues central to the lives of women, including aged women and the middle-aged women who care for them, will gain more visibility and legitimacy.

NOTES

1. Samuel H. Preston, "Children and the Elderly: Divergent Paths for America's Dependents." *Demography* 21, 4 (1984), 435–57.

2. Alan Walker, "The Economic 'Burden' of Ageing and the Prospect of Intergenerational Conflict," *Ageing and Society* 10 (1990), 377–96.

3. Susan A. McDaniel, "Demographic Aging as a Paradigm in Canada's Welfare State," *Canadian Public Policy* 13, 1 (1987), 330–36.

4. See, for example, Ivan P. Fellegi, "Can We Afford an Aging Population?" *Canadian Economic Observer* (October 1988), 4.1–4.34; Brian B. Murphy and Michael C. Wolfson, "When the Baby Boom Grows Old: Impact on Canada's Public Sector," *Statistical Journal of the United Nations* 8 (1991), 25–43; Michael C. Wolfson, "International Perspectives on the Economics of Aging," *Canadian Economic Observer* (August 1991), 1–16.

5. Neysmith, "Social Policy Implications of an Aging Society," 594.

6. Gee and McDaniel, "Pension Politics and Pension Challenges"; Walker, "The Economic 'Burden' of Ageing and the Prospect of Intergenerational Conflict."

7. Fellegi, "Can We Afford an Aging Society?" 4.17.

8. *Ibid.,* 4.4–4.5.

9. Health and Welfare Canada, *Charting Canada's Future: A Report of the Demographic Review* (Ottawa: Minister of Supply and Services, 1989), 24.

10. *Ibid.*

11. Statistics Canada, *Labour Force Annual Averages, 1981–1988* (Ottawa: Minister of Supply and Services, 1989).

12. Status of Women Canada, *Report of the Task Force on Child Care* (Ottawa: Minister of Supply and Services, 1986).

13. Douglas E. Hyatt and William J. Milne, "Countercyclical Fertility in Canada: Some Empirical Results," *Canadian Studies in Population* 18, 1 (1991), 1–16.

14. Elderly persons provide much care-giving, particularly aged wives. However, we wish here to emphasize the care-giving that is provided by a different age group—the middle-aged.

15. John Myles, "Editorial: Women, the Welfare State and Care-giving," *Canadian Journal on Aging* 10, 2 (1991), 82–85. Gee, "Demographic Change and Intergenerational Relations in Canadian Families."

16. Alan Walker, "The Relationship between the Family and the State in the Care of Older People," *Canadian Journal on Aging* 10, 2 (1991), 94–112. Susan A. McDaniel, "Challenges to Family Policy in an Aging Canada," paper presented at the annual meeting of the Canadian Association on Gerontology, Ottawa, 1989.

17. Such support is needed more by spouse care-givers, given that most adult children do not reside with frail elderly parents; however, among those who do, the need is critical.

18. Gee, "Demographic Change and Intergenerational Relations in Canadian Families"; Walker, "The Relationship Between the Family and the State in the Care of Older People."

19. Walker, *ibid.*

20. Myles and Quadagno, "Explaining the Difference," 37.

47

Canada's Fighting Seniors

C.G. Gifford

AN AGENDA FOR THE 1990S

"The clubs are fantastic. I say they are great. What I'm critical of is that they haven't made this move into looking ahead and thinking with vision."

Chuck Bayley, Vancouver, 1984.

■ ■ ■

Political Power

Some say that the seniors' movement can only persuade and appeal to the sense of justice, but seniors have real power far greater than that.

First, is political power—the power that elects seniors to town councils. It can pressure a government into changing policy. It can block setting up an advisory council on aging in which seniors would be outnumbered by civil servants. It can embarrass a government into fulfilling an election promise, as it did in 1985.

With the loosening of party affiliations, block voting also has become a possibility. It is implied by actions like FADOQ's [Fédération de l'âge d'Or du Québec] statement that ending universality through the "clawback" means that the Mulroney government does not deserve seniors' support, and by the 1988 election guides prepared by OCSCO [Ontario Coalition of Senior Citizens' Organizations] and One Voice. The resolutions passed by the NPSCF [National Pensioners' and Senior Citizens' Federation] and the provincial federations also imply it. Such resolutions have little weight, unless grassroots federation members are willing to use them in their voting decisions.

Many election races are close in Canada, and in these, a block of seniors could work for the candidate of their choice and make the difference between winning and losing. If seniors have a clear statement of their

Reproduced with permission from James Lorimer and Company, Toronto (1990).

common expectations for an election, part way through the campaign they can announce their support for the party or candidate closest to the policies they approve, or their rejection of the party they believe is most in conflict with seniors' interests. This technique is widely used in individual election races in the United States, where politicians' performance is not so tightly bound to parties as in Canada.

Although seniors have clear common interests, the movement is not yet at the stage of Canada-wide united action among its organizations, except in a crisis. An important challenge is to establish a long-term seniors' agenda to serve as a rallying point over the life of several governments, and a long-term way of organizing a truly united impact on politicians. To put it bluntly, the forces trying to reduce the corporate share of taxes and therefore to decrease services never sleep. What is needed is a permanent counterweight of mobilized senior power, which puts all politicians on notice that only a tax system in which those with ability to pay pay their fair share is acceptable.

Consumer Power

Widows Helping Others showed consumer power on a town-sized scale by letting garage owners know that 150 people would hear about good or bad service to one person. The Manitoba Society of Seniors experimented with consumer power, to influence both businesses and government, with its planned boycott of products subject to the Goods and Services Tax in January, 1990. The Quebec coalition is reported ready to join such a boycott.[1] It is seniors' consumer power which causes so many stores and restaurants to offer seniors' discounts.

With a good national communication network to make possible joint action by hundreds or thousands of seniors' groups, consumer power will become a significant national force. It could be used to convince drugstores to stock less expensive generic drugs in place of brand names, oil companies to change their neglect of the environment, supermarket chains to stop stocking the aerosol cans and styrofoam products which do so much damage to the ozone layer. It would require some study, but there are retired scientists, pharmacists, and other experts who would help. It's a matter of organizing it.

Investment Power

The enormous concentrations of capital which pension funds make belong to those who paid in. Corporations and other institutions are recognizing this now, by accepting employee representation on the committees which decide on how such funds are invested. Seniors' ranks include retired accountants, economists, and other experts who can knowledgeably represent pensioners' interests in the direction of such funds.

Are pensioners concerned only to see that their pension funds generate as much interest as possible, or are they also concerned whether the money goes to build low-rental dwellings rather than high-priced condominiums, or to encourage cooperative housing rather than components of nuclear weapons? One of the great assets of the retired population is that it includes lawyers and researchers, businessmen like Fred Grayston and Lloyd Shaw, and every kind of expert, who can assess and simplify the required information, to enable the rest to present informed proposals to pension fund managers.

Partner Power

The fourth source of power is those who have a vested interest in the path the seniors' organizations are clearing. Our children, our grandchildren, and all the people to whom retirement has become a conscious prospect, have an interest in the movement's success in breaking ground for the future.

The fact-finding which CPC [Canadian Pensioners Concerned], AQDR [Association Québécoise de défense des droits des retraité-e-s et préretraité-e-s], VANA [Veterans Against Nuclear Arms] and other organizations have emphasized is a vital tool for all these forms of power, and can be expanded. This is not a dry library search for statistics, but an exploration of the human condition of seniors. Seniors who can afford it love to learn and travel. Could not this include fact-finding on behalf of the whole movement, to find out, for example, why France and Germany are willing to devote a far higher proportion of national income to the well-being of retired people, and to explore how the same approach could be built in to Canadian life?

Common Interests

Jack Lerette became a pensioner in 1958, more than thirty years ago. Sixty-five-year-olds ending their employed life today, who live as long as Mr. Lerette, will see the time when one in every five Canadians is retired. In fact it will be more than that, because more and more people are retiring younger and younger. Their work is not needed in the job market.

What present retirees do with their "extra years" will influence what kind of life those survivors will have when the year 2020 comes around. It will also affect the lives of our grandchildren long past that time. It will condition our own lives in the year 2000, because most of us will still be here.

"Never before in AARP's [American Association of Retired Persons] history have we faced the kind of challenges and opportunities that the 1990s will bring. That is because many of the most dramatic changes facing America will be inextricably linked to the aging of our society," said Horace Deets, executive director of AARP. This statement applies to Europe and Canada as much as to the U.S. Eurolink Age seeks to make 1993 a European Year for Seniors. It is working to add to the Council of Europe's "European Social Charter" a "Charter on Ageing." It is time for a Canadian Seniors' Movement Agenda for the 1990s and beyond.

As FADOQ has said, we must "look beyond our noses" to formulate a seniors' agenda in Canada, which includes the hopes and wishes of all seniors.

One common interest is to defend hard-won financial and medical security from inflation and from political erosion. When this common interest is threatened, voices arise all over the country, to protect the present level of pensions and indexation, and to raise their level so that the submerged 50 percent rise above poverty;[2] to protect medicare as a tax-supported universal system, including universally available prescription drugs; and to achieve a minimum standard of safe, comfortable, and healthy housing for all seniors.

Consultation by governments with seniors' organizations at the beginning of exploring new policies rather than later in the process, is another shared interest of seniors' organizations.

Beyond this minimum, deciding what is in the seniors' best interests will require study, debate, and finding consensus. In the long run, would an adequate guaranteed income for all citizens, replacing the many kinds of government pensions and allowances, be better than the present arrangement? Saskatchewan Seniors Action Now proposed this as fairer, more dignified, and easier to administer than the present system.

Would pensioners prefer to have enough income to pay their way, instead of seniors' discounts such as reduced transportation fares, free admission to provincial parks, etc.?

Chuck Bayley said of medical care that "money is not the issue. The issue is having the right kind of care." Establishing guidelines to "the right kind of care" is a challenge which must be met in order to urge politicians and the health professions to change.

A long-term agenda will need a seniors' approach to taxation, since taxation policy will determine whether resources are available for other parts of the agenda. This means a political struggle with the corporate sector for a fair sharing of the tax burden. Since so much of Canadian business is owned by U.S. interests, this could involve joint action with U.S. seniors' organizations. It will probably mean restoring an inheritance tax above a certain level of property, and removing tax shelters which benefit people who have enough income to save for their old age. It could include a net wealth tax such as some countries have, since wealth is even more unevenly distributed than income.

In 1984, while the richest 20 percent of Canadians received 43 percent of all income, the top 20 percent owned 69 percent of the wealth. The top 10 percent owned more than half of all wealth.[3]

Another approach would be a gross revenue tax (GRT), applied to three percent of all business income. This would bring in as much revenue as the GST, and it would be easier to administer. Both a GRT and the net wealth tax ideas are fairer and more realistic than the GST.

And what about broader issues? The NPSCF, One Voice and OCSCO all spoke out against the free trade deal in 1988. They believed that it risks cutting down Canada's social security system, and that this will hurt seniors. Did the grassroots groups agree that this affects seniors' vital interests? In a closely fought election, like that of 1988, a united view by seniors of where their interests lay could have determined the outcome.

Concern about the environment is becoming very widespread. This comes close to home, touching on the gasoline we use, the cups we drink out of at meetings, how we dispose of our garbage—almost everything we do. The globe's population has doubled in our lifetime, and another billion will be added by the year 2000. We are part of the 25 percent of the global population that lives in the "developed" nations and that consumes 60 percent of the world's resources and creates most of the pollution that is suffocating the planet.[4] Can we afford to say, "That's too modern for us"? In our own interest, and even more, in the interest of our grandchildren, should not *this* be on the seniors' long-term agenda?

To assist such pursuits, the "single issue" restrictions should be removed from New Horizons' grant criteria. These constitute political discrimination in the use of these tax-based funds. It is a form of political interference to refuse access to these funds to seniors who want to work for peace, environmental healing, native rights, or other topics at the heart of democratic societies.

Setting priorities about what should or should not be included will be a challenge in itself. We live in times of risk and opportunity in the world. Seniors make their individual choices about whether to be part of that or not, and many, through volunteer work, through their churches, through working for various causes like Amnesty International, make their contribution. But we multiply our strength through groups. The Third International Assembly of AIFA, the Association internationale francophone des aînés, in Reims, France, in September, 1989, defined the role of the elderly as builders of progress, including leadership in defence of the environment.[5] The Canadian seniors' movement could become a strong influence in such matters.

A Seniors' Coalition for the 1990s

The three-and-a-half million retired people in Canada fall into five overlapping categories.

There is the seniors' movement, the dynamic complex of groups and organizations that seniors have created for themselves, and that thrive also in the seniors' centres that others have created for them. More than one-third of the retired population belongs to some part of this movement.

There are the many seniors who participate actively in community life apart from the movement, as part of the army of senior volunteers in myriad service activities, or in employment on their own time. There are the many among low-income seniors whose lack of resources prevents active participation in community life. There are the uninvolved, because of personal inclination, lack of confidence, or a choice of some wealthy seniors to live a leisured social life in high-priced retirement communities. And there are those, especially among the very old, whom frailty or illness prevent from active engagement.

The focus throughout this book has been on the first category, the seniors' movement, the active ingredient in this mosaic.

Creating a united voice to represent all interests is a challenge for the movement in the 1990s. There is not yet any ongoing universal coalition in Canada, like the Leadership Council of Aging Organizations in the U.S. The NPSCF brings together the provincial federations of clubs, a few of the employment-based organizations, and one or two of the advocacy groups. It has the largest base, but has yet to turn that into concerted action at the grassroots level. One Voice reaches a few of the same provincial federations, some of the advocacy groups, and the Canadian Legion, and it reaches across the language divide more than NPSCF, but it misses the largest organizations and it too has no clear plan for involving the grassroots groups.

Some of the French-speaking organizations both in and outside of Quebec are only weakly or not at all involved with either aspiring national coalition.

And yet, the movement has enormous potential for influence. This lies in its numbers, in its volume as a proportion of the population, the talent in its ranks, and its presence in literally every community.[6] As Yvette Brunet of AQDR said, "Gray power does not grow automatically by the increase of the proportion of retired people in the population."[7] Gray power comes from organization. The basis for a comprehensive, Canada-wide coalition is there. What remains is for it to be developed out of the components which are in existence.

What forms could such a Canada-wide universal coalition take? Should it follow the common example of bodies like the Canadian Manufacturers Association and the Canadian Labour Congress, with a strong central national organization representing the whole? Should it be a loose coalition like the Leadership Council of Aging Organizations in the United States?

Should it be a periodic assembly of seniors' organizations with leadership rotating among the organizations between times?

Whatever the form, it will succeed only if it involves the grassroots groups, and if it fits our language differences, our geography, and the wide diversity of Canadian seniors' groups.

To bring united action to anything as large as the Canadian seniors' movement requires professional staff. From YMCAs and churches, to labour unions and Chambers of Commerce, there are many examples of successful voluntary organizations that have enhanced their work through the engagement of staff. The challenges ahead require a common front, and organizing it requires the employment of some full-time people. The issue is not whether to have staff or not, but how clearly their tasks and those of the elected leaders who hire and evaluate them are set out, and how well trained they are to perform them.

Some parts of the movement have already met for national communication—the seniors' press representatives twice, self-education organizations once—but many organizations have no ongoing means of developing a shared national strategy. Choosing priorities, seeking allies, creating a strategy, are needed if the seniors' movement is to have full impact.

There are many local and provincial newspapers for seniors, but none Canada-wide. There are several local television programs aimed at seniors. The only national one, CBC's "Best Years," is at noon on Sunday, when some seniors are in church. This scheduling may reflect a low programming priority for this significant segment of the population. A first-rate program at the right time of the week could have an audience of hundreds of thousands. "Morningside" is widely listened to by seniors—could it include a weekly seniors' news hour?

Modern means of communication exist—the ham radio operators, the computer networks which home computer operators can use, the fax machines which send messages from one office to another instantaneously—which can provide the kind of national scale communication which "telephone trees"[8] provide locally. It costs some money, but not enormous amounts. It will be a rare community which does not have a senior or other resident who is a ham radio operator or uses a home computer, who would be willing to be a link in a seniors' communication network. A first step towards a national communication network was described by Bernard Richard, but it is a long way from that step to linking up the grassroots groups.

Enabling a seniors' movement agenda to emerge and influence political life may seem ambitious. Yet, the resources to work on it are present, both in seniors' own pockets, and in Canada's New Horizons and Seniors' Independence programs. The latter between them make more than 30 million dollars a year available to seniors' organizations. The 1981 U.S. White House Conference on Aging was financed with $6 million over three years, and it involved 10,000 local and regional seniors' consultative meetings. A comprehensive national seniors' coalition could find financing to take the movement the next step in its development.

Towards a Movement Without Barriers

When Bill Corns felt that the chairman of a Canadian Pensioners' Concerned meeting insulted him, some years ago, perceptions of class difference were there on both sides. At that time, it prevented Mr. Corns from joining forces with CPC. Whether the feelings remain or not, the newer coalitions clearly bring together both working-class and middle-class seniors for their common defence. As the retired Swiss parliamentarian, Nancy Ericson, said, "When you retire, your interests change, and you find you have more in common with people from whom you felt separated before."

Language is a more difficult problem, but here, too, shared concerns can cause bridges to be built, as in the Coalition des aînés du Québec.

There is also a hint of barrier between the "game-players" who are organized primarily for leisure pleasure, whether of the weekly bridge and bingo variety or the more expensive delights of world travel and culture, on the one hand, and the self-educators and advocates on the other. In Britain, Pensioners for Peace had a friendly hearing in the "game-players'" clubs. In France, the Clubs ruraux successfully brought together leisure and contributing simply to Third World development. Distances between game-players and self-educators and advocates in Canada can be bridged so they strengthen each other for the challenges ahead.

The advocates reflect in the seniors' movement the ancient concern for social justice, for full inclusion in the human family of those who have been neglected and deprived. The book includes some people for whom this has been a lifetime concern—Claire McAllister, Doris Marshall, Claude deMestral—but others for whom either it had been a discovery of their senior years—Fred Grayston, Corabel Penfold—or for whom retirement has been a special opportunity for action—Bill Corns, Stan Sugarbroad.

This is in the religious-moral tradition which led to the abolition of slavery and of child labour, the fight to eliminate war, the kindly concern for the poor. Can that kindly concern colour the whole of the seniors' movement, so it is, as AIFA expressed it, a "builder of progress" in this world, which is so in need of human warmth to soften its harshness?

A seniors' movement where all are genuinely accepted, no matter what their educational level, economic status, or other differences, helps communication and enriches individual lives. A difficult problem is the self-limiting effect of belittling one's own capacities.

This was evident in Fred Wildsmith's comment, "We're not modern enough for that," in a well-spoken Cape Bretoner's statement that he had not joined a seniors' group because "I only have fourth grade"; and the feeling of Mr. Gravel's Northern Ontario working-class friends that because their children are better educated than they are, they themselves have nothing to say. Such self-denial means a loss to the movement of talented people, and a loss to the individuals of satisfaction from considering horizons new to them. If only such self-doubters could be persuaded of the truth that they can think, they can contribute, they can vote, they can make a difference.

Every senior's action is needed to help protect what has been gained, to help extend real security to the submerged 50 percent, and to play a part in helping our planet out of its troubles. The challenge facing us is to build the knowledge that this is so into all the varied parts of the seniors' movement.

Voting is practised by most of us once every two to four years. Active citizenship, in the sense of participating directly in a political party, or in a cause like the environmental movement or the peace movement or the movement for Third World development, normally involves only a small part of the population—no more than five or six per cent. The last three are now part of the planet's survival. How many seniors will join the survival army? We don't know, but our organizations can encourage the idea.

These problems look huge and complex, but they have connections to our daily lives. How life will be for us and our grandchildren in ten years depends on what happens on these issues. It is possible to take hold of one part of a world problem, see how it connects with one's own daily life, and take some action about it. Doris Marshall and her friends found that, working away persistently at their own pace, they were able to produce something of real community value, and it was exciting and satisfying. Amnesty International has shown that individuals writing letters once a month can save the lives of brave quiet people in distant countries, arrested for speaking up for human rights. Much can be done in a quiet way, by people who are willing to set aside a few minutes a week. The Canadian seniors' movement could be a seed bed for such activity.

The movement is a massive, dynamic, many-sided enterprise. Its members participate in thousands of groups, share vital common interests, and pursue an almost limitless variety of activities.

Until the 1920s it did not exist, and until the late 1960s it was hardly visible. Now it is built right into the fabric of Canadian society.

The movement has work to do and satisfaction to gain in defending its own interests and those of generations of seniors to follow. In the multiple changes facing our country as one century prepares to turn into the next, it has its own vital contribution to make, for humane responses to the challenges, great and small.

NOTES

1. *Globe and Mail,* January 24, 1990, A9.

2. In 1987, 49 percent of Canadians 65 and over received the Guaranteed Income Supplement. If the same percentage applied in 1989, the single pensioners, usually women, had total incomes below $9,720. Couples where both partners were 65 or over had total incomes below $12,672. *Income Security Programs, 1987.* National Health and Welfare Canada, Ottawa January 1988.

3. "Taxation justice for all? Base it on personal worth," op. ed. article, *Globe and Mail,* February 6, 1989. "How about a brand new tax?" op ed. article *Globe and Mail,* May 1, 1990.

4. "Mother Earth choked, trampled by human mass," *Globe and Mail,* March 10, 1990.

5. *Info-Seniors,* Fédération de l'âge d'or du Québec, Montreal, November, 1989.

6. Even in brand new communities seniors are an important presence. Thompson, Manitoba, was built out of the wilderness in the late 1950s. When the Manitoba Department of Community Services started a seniors' program in 1974, the community nurses thought there might be about 20 elders in the town. But when the word got around and a New Horizons grant came through, "Lo and behold 250 seniors came out of the woodwork. They had just not been visible until that time." They were people who were strangers to each other, having moved in to

live with their children. Interview with Eric Lubosch, Manitoba Department of Community Services, 1981.

7. *La Force de l'Âge,* Vol. 3, No. 2, 6.

8. Many groups have "telephone trees," whereby one person phones several others with a message, which each of them in turn passes on to several others, and so on, until the whole group is covered.

SECTION TEN

Discussion Questions

1. What impact will societal aging have on public spending in Canada? How can Canadian society respond to the impact of population aging?

2. What policy challenges does population aging raise in Canada? What changes in policy has Canada made in response to population aging? What future policies will Canada need to put in place as the population ages?

3. What types of power does the seniors' movement have in Canada, according to Gifford? What steps does this movement need to take to make it a force for change in Canada in the years ahead? What challenge does the movement have to overcome for it to play this role in national and regional politics?

4. Discuss the policy challenges and opportunities that lie ahead as the Canadian population ages. How will health-care, housing, income, and retirement policies change as the population ages? Will these changes lead to a better quality of life in old age in the future?

Suggested Readings

Clark, P.G. (1991). "Ethical Dimensions of Quality of Life in Aging: Autonomy vs Collectivism in the United States and Canada." *The Gerontologist* 31 (5): 631–39.

Fellegi, I. (1988). "Can We Afford an Aging Society?" *Canadian Economic Observer*, October: 4.1–4.32.

McDaniel S.A., and E.M. Gee (1991). *Aging and Social Policy in Canada*. Toronto: Butterworths.

McDaniel, S.A., and E.M. Gee (1993). "Social Policies Regarding Caregiving to Elders: Canadian Contradictions." *Journal of Aging & Social Policy* 5(1/2): 57–72.

Marshall, V.W., F.L. Cook, and J.G. Marshall (1993). "Conflict over Intergenerational Equity: Rhetoric and Reality in a Comparative Context." In *The changing contract across generations*, ed. V.L. Bengtson and W.A. Achenbaum. New York: Aldine De Gruyter.

Yelaja, S.A. (1989). "Gray Power: Agenda for Future Research." *Canadian Journal on Aging* 8: 118–27.

About the Author

Mark Novak is Associate Dean (Academic) in the Continuing Education Division at the University of Manitoba. He has taught courses to the field staff of the Department of Veterans Affairs and has designed professional education programs for pharmacists and housing managers.

Dr. Novak has published articles on aging in scholarly journals, including the *International Journal of Aging and Human Development* (USA), *Age and Aging* (Britain), and *The Gerontologist* (USA). In 1985 he published *Successful Aging: The Myths, Realities and Future of Aging in Canada* (Penguin). He has also written the most widely used gerontology textbook for Canadian students, *Aging and Society: A Canadian Perspective*, 2nd ed. (Nelson Canada, 1993).

Dr. Novak has won several scholarly awards, which include a major Social Sciences and Humanities Research Council (SSHRC) award, two SSHRC leave fellowships, and the Secretary of State of Canada, Canadian Studies Writing Award, for 1986. He is currently studying caregivers of confused and disoriented older people.

He has attended the Management of Lifelong Education program (MLE) at Harvard University and has served on the National University Continuing Education Association (NUCEA) professional development committee for the past three years. Dr. Novak lives in Winnipeg with his wife and four children.